THE NEW
MASTERS

To Goblet
A dear friend and good companion for more than 14 years, who left his
many friends just as this book was completed.

THE NEW MASTERS

CAN THE WEST MATCH JAPAN?

PHILLIP OPPENHEIM

BUSINESS BOOKS LIMITED

First published in Great Britain in 1991 by
Business Books Limited
An imprint of Random Century Limited
20 Vauxhall Bridge Road, London SW1V 2SA

Random Century Australia (Pty) Limited
20 Alfred Street, Milsons Point, Sydney
New South Wales 2061, Australia

Random Century New Zealand Limited
9–11 Rothwell Avenue, Albany
Glenfield, Auckland 10, New Zealand

Century Hutchinson South Africa (Pty) Limited
PO Box 337, Bergvlei 2012, South Africa

Set in Linotron Garamond by CentraCet, Cambridge
Printed and bound in Great Britain by
Butler and Tanner Ltd, Frome, Somerset

British Library Cataloguing in Publication Data
Oppenheim, Phillip
The new masters: can the West match Japan?
industrial development of Japan   2. Japan. Industrial
development compared with industrial development of
Western world.
I. Title
338.0952

ISBN 0-09-174693-0
ISBN 0-7126-4190-4 pbk

Contents

CONTENTS

Acknowledgements

IT WOULD HAVE been very pleasant to have been able to have closeted myself somewhere quiet for a year or so to write this book, but the demands of Westminster and my constituency had to come first. If this book succeeds, therefore, it is significantly due to the assistance given me by a large number of people.

I am particularly grateful to the journalist, Claudia Cragg, for her great knowledge of Japan and editorial help. Likewise, Cynthia Mack, who has lived in Japan with her grandmother, provided valuable insights into the Japanese way of life. Other people with great experience of Japan whose assistance was much appreciated include Richard Greer of Baring Securities' Tokyo office, David Mathew and Anthony Garner. Needless to say, any opinions expressed or errors in this book are my own and should in no way reflect on those who helped.

I am also indebted to the late Ian Gow MP for his prodigious knowledge of economic matters – he is irreplaceable and his cruel murder represents an enormous loss to his many friends; the late Jock Bruce-Gardyne whose advice and encouragement was invaluable; Quentin Davies MP who contributed his wide experience of financial affairs; Tim Wood MP for his help on the computer industry; and Robin Maxwell-Hyslop MP for his knowledge of naval and military history.

Chris Norall of Forrester & Norall was immensely generous in providing me with help and information on the European Community's trade policy, as was Neville Williams, formerly of the Department of Trade and Industry. Michael Perry of Unilever, Jim Salmon of Crosfield, Peter Bartlett of Bonar & Flotex, Peter Heaps of Thorntons, Ivor Ditchfield of Codnor Light Fabrications, Philip Bouverat of Intersolar and Michael Rose and his staff at Butterley Brick also contributed greatly to the section on selling in Japan. I would like particularly to thank Richard Boyd, a fellow of the School of Oriental and African Studies of the University of London, for providing me with invaluable information on MITI and Japanese industrial policy.

ACKNOWLEDGEMENTS

Warm thanks are also due to David Kirk for his help and encouragement at the commencement of this project and his continued support and advice; to Douglas Slater for reading parts of the book and for advising me on cultural matters; to my sister, Carolyn, who helped with the editing; to Fred Smith for his help and support; and to Masahiro, Kikuno and Hiromi Takada for their kindness and hospitality during a visit to Japan.

My gratitude is also due to those who helped with research, particularly Paul Gerrard, Tim Mitchell, Ruth Thomas, Catherine Owst, Paul Gibney, John Cunningham and Evie Kohnstam. Above all, I would like sincerely to thank David Menhennet, Head of the House of Commons Library, together with his staff for their unfailing good humour and for the speed and efficiency with which they invariably responded to requests for books, journals and information.

The teams at the New York and London offices of *What to Buy for Business*, the consumer report for businesses, also provided enormous assistance with research and background material for the information technology chapters, as well as computer printing facilities which were extremely useful. I am particularly grateful to my former partner and co-editor at *What to Buy*, John Derrick, for his help and advice, as well as to *What to Buy*'s managing director, Julian Lloyd. I should also mention my indebtedness to Nina Knox-Pebbles for inputting most of the early chapters into the computer with great efficiency and good humour; as well as Kate Bull, Sarah Frater, Corinne de Palma, Tracey Baines and Carrie Cappucino for help and advice on the office equipment and computer industries. Thanks, too, to Rebecca Rollings for her patient assistance in printing out the text in its various stages.

I am also grateful to my agent, David Grossman, to Joe de Courcy, Anthony Cheetham of publishers Random Century, as well as Lucy Shankleman and Martin Liu of Hutchinson Business Books for their help.

Above all, I owe the greatest possible debt to Sarah Harding, for her suggestions, invaluable editing and stylistic assistance, research work and for tirelessly and patiently typing the bulk of the book into the computer. Without her help, I doubt if this book would have been possible.

The author is indebted to a large number of books, magazines and newspapers from which he has quoted. He has always endeavoured to acknowledge the sources of quotations or information and is particularly grateful to those publications and publishers who gave permission to quote where permission was necessary.

Particularly valuable was the *Financial Times* whose coverage of trade and industry issues was of enormous help, and special thanks are due to Martin Wolf for his advice on the Multi Fibre Arrangement. Also of great assistance were: *The Wall Street Journal, The Economist, Business Week, Fortune, US News and World Report, Time, Newsweek*, the *Daily Telegraph, The Independent, The Times*, the *Observer* and *Car* magazine. Thanks are also due to Dataquest for permission to use and quote from their reports on the information technology industry.

Note on currency conversions: for the sake of consistency, the yen has been converted to sterling at the rate of ¥250 to the pound – the rate prevailing early in 1990 – throughout this book.

'Free Trade! What is it? Why, breaking down the barriers that separate nations; those barriers behind which nestle the feelings of pride, revenge, hatred and jealousy, which every now and then burst their bounds and deluge whole countries with blood; those feelings which nourish the poison of war and conquest, which assert that without conquest we can have no trade, which foster that lust for conquest and dominion.'
Richard Cobden (1804–65), speech on free trade, London, 1843.

新大国

INTRODUCTION

'After centuries of the closest intercourse with our Continental neighbours, how many of the latter have succeeded in describing us so as to our derision and indignation. We have been long enough en evidence to furnish ample materials for analysis. Our literature is an open book; our domestic habits are well known; our institutions, our social customs, in short, all phases of our public and private lives are, or ought to be, familiar. Yet we are perpetually and grossly misjudged. Is it not reasonable to suppose that Western estimates of Japanese character err at least as flagrantly?'
Sir Henry Norman, Nineteenth-Century British traveller to Japan.[1]

WHEN, IN THE 1950s, unscrupulous Japanese manufacturers were caught out for having marked their export goods 'Made in the USA', they used innocently to explain that the merchandise came from the small town of Usa in Kyushu, Japan's main southern island. Even Sony's founder, Akio Morita, admitted to printing 'Made in Japan' on his products as small as possible in the early post-War years.[2] At that time, 'Made in Japan' implied unsophisticated, cheap and shoddy goods.

Thirty years later, Stanley Kalms, who runs one of the largest electrical goods chains in the world with more than 1,300 shops in Britain and the United States, deliberately chose a Japanese-sounding name, Matsui, for his in-house brand, advertising it under the slogan: 'Japanese technology made perfect'. Unfortunately it transpired that the Matsui televisions, video recorders, microwave ovens, freezers and refrigerators came not from Japan, but from Britain, Italy, Yugoslavia, Singapore, Taiwan and Korea. The company was fined £4,000 for misrepresentation.

Other Western purveyors of consumer durables have increasingly felt it expedient to sell under Japanese-sounding names, like the Scottish company which brands its range of electrical household products Hinari, although

1

they come from all over the world. The cheekiest attempt to pass off a product as Japanese which I have spotted was a low-budget portable radio-cassette marketed under the name Crown–Japan, although it was actually made in China. Even America's proud Chrysler Corporation, which originally used to hide the origins of the cars it imported from Japan under its own all-American 'Dodge' brand name, now makes a virtue of its Japanese provenance by using Kanji characters in its advertisements, for now Japanese products enjoy a reputation second to none, while 'Made in the USA' is no longer a selling point.

Japan's rising power and influence and the relative decline of the United States is evident in other areas. Whereas, in 1917, the growing power of America was displayed when she bought the Danish Virgin Islands, now it is Japanese interests that are negotiating to purchase the Danish Faeroe Islands for nearly £1 billion. Moreover, just as London Bridge was bought and transported to Texas by an American multi-millionaire in the 1960s, so a wealthy Japanese purchased a Scottish castle in 1987 and sent the 3,200 tons of stonework 9,500 kilometres by train across Siberia to his homeland.

But the most galling parallel for the Americans must have been the news in 1989 that one of their most popular presidents had been hired to star in a Japanese public relations extravaganza. Former President Reagan, barely nine months out of the Oval Office, received $2 million for his nine-day trip to Japan during which he was used as promotional material by a local PR firm. In the early 1970s, it had been $2 million of American money which 'bought' the then Japanese Prime Minister, Tanaka, in the infamous Lockheed bribery scandal.

Not surprisingly, ex-President Reagan's trip struck a particularly raw nerve with increasingly sensitive Americans, prompting one cartoonist to portray a Commerce Department official bearing a TV showing the former President, telling his chief: 'Sir, we finally found an American product the Japanese want to buy . . .'3

Behind such increasingly obvious manifestations of Japanese power lies Japan's huge economic success. Bombed into near oblivion in 1945, Japan's per capita GNP had overtaken that of the United States by 1986 and, by the year 2000, her overall output is expected to exceed America's total. In spite of her almost total lack of natural resources, Japan not only supplies the world with manufactured goods, but also lends it the money to pay for her products. For the Japanese are also now the world's creditors, with net external assets of close to $600 billion and dollar reserves of more than $1,000 billion.

Compare that with the United States' amazing turnaround. In 1979–80, the United States had a trade surplus of $17 billion, an accumulated federal debt of only about $650 billion, a budget deficit which was barely two per cent of GNP, and she was still the world's largest creditor nation. By 1986, however, the trade surplus had turned into a deficit of $136 billion, the debt had tripled to around $2,000 billion, the budget deficit had risen to nearly five per cent of GNP and the United States had, in six years, switched from being the largest creditor in history to being the biggest borrower, with debts dwarfing those of the Third World. Some people even claim that the Japanese now call the shots in American politics: Japanese monetary policy, it is said, was geared towards propping up the dollar in the late 1980s to help secure the election of George Bush over the more protectionist Democrat, Dukakis.

This astonishingly rapid reversal of roles has given rise to confusion and not a little paradox in American attitudes to Japan. One might have thought that the fact that the Japanese have worked diligently to produce high-quality products which would otherwise have been available only to the wealthy should not be a cause of resentment. But life is seldom so simple.

While, on the one hand, Americans buy Japanese products in vast quantities and consider Japanese-sounding brand names to be more appealing than Western ones, on the other, a *Washington Post/ABC News* poll early in 1989 found that nearly half of those questioned felt that Japan was more of a threat to America than was the Soviet Union. Two-thirds also favoured restrictions on Japanese imports, although nearly as many again said that Americans should not be forced to buy domestic products if foreign ones are superior. The poll also revealed that despite the fact that two-thirds of respondents agreed that Japanese companies were better managed, its workers more diligent and its technology superior, the same proportion thought that Japan's success was due to unfair trade barriers and a cheaper labour force.

It is this widespread and muddled assumption that Japanese economic success must be due to cheating or some unfair advantage that is giving anti-Japanese sentiment a special bitterness – a bitterness which is increasingly being reciprocated in Japan herself as the Japanese grow ever-more resentful of finger-wagging American politicians and their apparent inability to sort out their own problems.

新　大　国

My own interest in Japan really began in the early 1980s when I was working in Britain and the United States as co-editor of *What To Buy For Business*, a consumer report for business which covers in detail information technology products such as facsimile machines, personal computers, typewriters and photocopiers. Whereas European and American companies at that time seemed almost totally incapable of producing proficient office copiers, I was fascinated by the ease with which a whole raft of Japanese companies – mostly ones not normally associated with office technology – were producing a stream of highly-competent products.

Camera makers like Canon, Ricoh and Minolta had, by the early 1980s, virtually wiped the effective founder of the modern photocopier industry, Xerox, out of large areas of the market. Brother and Juki, primarily sewing-machine manufacturers, eased into the typewriter market once dominated by experienced producers such as IBM and Olivetti. And by the mid-1980s, when no fewer than 20 Japanese companies were producing facsimile machines, only one Western manufacturer remained in the business – and it only survived on a life-support system of government subsidies and a protected home market. By then, too, the Japanese were making deep inroads into the still relatively new personal computer market up until then dominated by American companies.

How did they do it? Like many Westerners, I began with certain inbred assumptions, such as that the Japanese could only have beaten our manufacturers by underhand means. But as I looked further, I realized that it was not as simple as that. For one thing, they were undeniably making superior products that people wanted to buy and marketing them effectively, which was more than could be said for many of their Western competitors.

Yet despite a general acceptance of the quality of Japanese products, impressions of unfairness are widespread and deeply ingrained. And almost invariably, if you talk to Western businesspeople or politicians about trade matters, they will quickly tell you all about unfair competition from the Japanese, citing intervention and subsidies by Japan's Ministry of International Trade and Industry (MITI), together with barriers to imports of whisky, skis and cars.

But if you tell those same people that the suits they are wearing are subject to barriers against low-cost imports through the Multi Fibre Arrangement, which all industrialized Western nations accede to; that the cars they will drive are also subject to trade restrictions which limit Japanese imports to a certain percentage of the market; and that the video recorders, TVs or CD players which will entertain them at home are, in many Western countries, subject to import tariffs and quotas against the Japanese, they will look at you in blank astonishment.

Quite simply, although Western journalists, politicians and businesspeople are more than well aware of the supposed unfair trade practices of the Japanese, they are almost wholly ignorant of similar practices in the West. For if Japan has not always played by the rules of free and fair trade, then neither has virtually every Western industrialized country. The United States and European countries have subsidized their industries and protected home markets at least as much as the Japanese have. But very few people are aware of this and most still assume that only the Japanese are guilty of these practices.

Western perceptions of Japan are not always helped by media coverage. For example, when, in 1987, a popular British newspaper ran a major four-part series on Japan, written by a top journalist, the sensational introduction to one of the reports included the statement that: 'Genuine Scotch is taxed at seven times the rate of local Japanese brands. Even Western-made skis are refused entry to ski-ing mad Japan – on the grounds that Japanese snow is different from Western snow' along with the question: 'Why do the Japanese refuse to "fight fair" in the world's market places? Is it just that "fighting dirty" is the easiest way to win?'[4]

Not only does such journalism give a very selective view of Japan, it also gives a misleading and exaggerated impression of Japan's trade practices. Scotch is not taxed at seven times the rate of local brands and Western-made skis were not refused entry into Japan. Nor, to take another well-publicized trade dispute, have the Japanese unfairly excluded British and American telecommunications companies – in fact, the Japanese telecommunications market is more open than most European ones.

Lop-sided and sensationalist reporting is, unfortunately, nothing new. The spectre of the 'yellow peril' was the subject of a *Fortune* article way back in 1936, when French and Italian newspapers were bursting with attacks on the Japanese silk industry which was undercutting their own. This type of coverage has, over the years, produced a series of distorted and often contradictory stereotypes of the Japanese in the Western mind, veering from *Madame Butterfly* daydreams of a miniature country full of gentle *geisha* and obliging gentlemen, to the opposite extreme of fanatical conquering hordes and, more recently, devious economic predators.

In fact, many of these representations of Japan are false clichés. The nation of presumed super-exporters, for example, actually sells abroad a smaller percentage of its GDP than most other industrialized countries. Japanese industry, underpinned in the Western consciousness by the loyal company worker who dutifully performs group exercises as he chants banal company songs, was not very long ago racked by bitter and violent industrial disputes. On the other hand, the common image of a crime-free Japan where old ladies can safely walk the street, has an underworld of colourful but vicious gangsters who dominate Japan's thriving vice industry and have deeply insinuated themselves into the world of business and politics.

Misleading stereotypes have for a long time been partly responsible first for the West's underestimation of Japan, and later for a misunderstanding of the real reasons for Japanese success. Tsar Nicholas II, who hated the Japanese and habitually referred to them as 'monkeys', found his attitude costly when the Japanese destroyed his fleet in 1905. Canadian officers, arriving to reinforce the British garrison in Hong Kong in November 1941, were told during a lecture by a British officer that Japanese troops were ill-equipped, inept at night-fighting, their aircraft mostly obsolete and their pilots myoptic.[5] The colony fell a few weeks later. It took the Japanese only a little longer to sweep up most of the other American, British, French and Dutch possessions in East Asia. The arrogant ease with which Japan took the 'impregnable' British stronghold of Singapore on 15 February 1942 shocked the West and signalled the beginning of the end of the White man's domination of Asia.

And after the Second World War, engineers working for large American and European manufacturers were accustomed to looking down their noses at Japanese goods, not even doing them the courtesy of scrutinizing their wares. Now those same companies often make their living either by re-labelling and selling Japanese products, by assembling goods from Japanese kits or, at best, building their manufactures with a high proportion of Japanese parts.

Inadequate coverage has also meant that, too often, Japanese success has been explained away with simple, easily digestible characterizations which neatly fit a given set of prejudices and preconceptions. Low wages, group cohesion, poor living conditions, Confucian harmony, 'dumping', protectionism and state direction of industry have all been singled out as reasons, or excuses, for Japan's economic preponderance. More recently, commentators have fixed on the supposed under-valuation of the yen, following which the low cost of capital became the fashionable explanation for Japan's success.

This book seeks to show that such 'special' factors are either not as significant as they have been made out to be, or are illusory or are at least not unique to Japan. Take trade barriers and that most common explanation for Japanese economic success – government aid for industry. I have read book after book on Japan which contain endless detailed pages about how the Japanese have restricted market access or how MITI has subsidized Japanese industry. Likewise, Western newspapers report any example of Japanese trade barriers at length. But there is virtually no mention of such practices in the West, which may be why so many people have come to the conclusion that the Japanese are fundamentally different and do not play by the same rules. The purpose of this book is not to deny that the Japanese have both subsidized their industries and maintained trade barriers, but to place such methods in the context of similar Western practices in a way which clearly demonstrates that they are not central to Japan's economic achievements.

For the inescapable fact is that the very Western countries which whine loudest about such practices are themselves far from guiltless. Businesspeople, attempting to cover up their own failures by muttering darkly about some Japanese industrial and governmental plot against which they stand no chance, often themselves have their noses deeply embedded in the trough of government subsidies, quotas, voluntary restraint agreements and non-tariff barriers. Unfortunately, the myth is perpetuated by Western politicians, equally anxious to ensure that any blame for industrial failure is not seen to rest with them. This is, however, a false and ultimately dangerous trail.

The truth is that Japan's economic achievements are not the result of malpractice, nor is there any single overriding cause of Japanese success, no Holy Grail for the West to find and imitate. Rather, Japan's attainments are the result of a complex of factors – historical, educational and governmental – which this book attempts to uncover.

Finally, one has to come to the all-important question: Can the West recover to the point where she can turn the tables on Japan?

So far, the soft option of erecting yet more protectionist barriers has too often been seen as the easy political solution to meeting the Japanese challenge. There is rarely even much coherence in this policy. On the one hand, sly constraints are constructed against the flow of Japanese goods, creating artificially high-priced markets at the consumer's expense. On the other hand, Western governments bid against one another to offer the largest bribe to persuade the Japanese to jump the barriers and assemble the offending products in their country or region.*

But the West will only succeed in recapturing its lost lead if it abandons the comforting excuse that Japanese superiority is due to underhand trade practices or inimitable cultural differences. Instead, we need to look both at the real causes of Japanese success and the underlying reasons for the West's relative failure – from this point of view, this book is as much about the West as it is about Japan, examining questions such as the extent to which

---

* Toyota's Kentucky plant, for example, benefited from $112 million worth of new roads, 1,500 acres of free land and low-cost loans.

we should accept Japanese investment and whether we can rely on the Japanese to give us access to technologies in which they are taking a widening lead. But on one issue I am certain: in a changing world the West must drop the arrogant assumption that it has nothing to learn from others and be prepared, where possible, to imitate parts of the Japanese system.

There is, unfortunately, little evidence yet that this is happening. Widespread misassessments of Japan are leading to the wrong conclusions and false remedies. Americans, in particular, stung by the speed with which they have been overhauled by Japan, are retreating into a self-righteous cocoon of moral indignation over what they see as Japanese malpractices. Europeans find comfort in increasing internal integration coupled with growing barriers to unsettling competition from the East. In Japan, meanwhile, frequently hypocritical criticism is beginning to provoke an angry and hurt backlash – none of which has any positive impact on the underlying problems of the American and Western economies in general.

新　　大　　国

In the Soviet Union, there is a highly influential ministry called Gosplan, which simply means 'Stateplan'. It was created in 1921 and has existed ever since as the body responsible for harmonizing the work of all the Soviet economic ministries within the framework of a general state plan for industry. Although Gosplan began with a staff of only 44 officials in 1934, it is now one of the USSR's largest ministries, employing so many tens of thousands of bureaucrats throughout the Soviet Union that no one really knows the true figure.[6]

As is well known, the disastrous state of the Soviet economy has prompted second thoughts about the nature of its economic system. Yet at the very time that the Soviets and other communist and ex-communist states are actively reducing the power of the state over their economies, some Western countries, and particularly the United States, are doing just the opposite. For today, Trotsky's words justifying Gosplan, 'If we condemn heavy industry to the free play of the market, it would run on the rocks', find curious echoes in the statements of leading American businesspeople and politicians like Senator Kennedy who believes that 'the basis for the restoration of the United States economy is the development of an industrial policy'.[7]

The reason is that they have convinced themselves that Japan's success is grounded on state planning, the interventionist role of the Japanese government in industry and fundamental cultural differences, a view which has been strongly propounded by an influential school of writing on Japan. This genre promotes the view that Japan's economic success is based on little less than a sinister government–industry conspiracy to dominate world markets and defeat the West; that the Japanese are really so different that they can never really be fair competitors; and that the only solution lies in the West adopting 'industrial strategies' and erecting trade barriers against the Japanese.

The more that Westerners are deluded by such alluring theses, the more likely they are to draw false conclusions regarding which policies should be adopted in the West. So my main purpose in writing this book is not to deny that the Japanese have been protectionist, nor that the Japanese bureaucracy is relatively powerful, nor that there are some cultural differences, nor that there has been a good deal of state intervention in Japan's industry. Rather, I aim to demonstrate that much comment on Japan has exaggerated these factors – often for self-serving reasons; that similar features in the West are often played down; and that, therefore, these policies are not central to Japan's economic success, nor the answer to the West's difficulties.

Finally, I realize that in defending the Japanese government and industry from widespread charges of underhand trade practices, this book might be seen as pro-Japanese, and even anti-American. It is not intended as such. On the contrary, my aim in writing is to strengthen industry in the West by contributing to the understanding of the real causes of Japanese success, and by examining ways in which the West can match the competition from Japan. For it is only if we discard prejudices, however deeply held, and really understand Japan, that we in the West will be able to reform and meet the challenge.

Prologue

新
大
国

'NOT NECESSARILY TO OUR ADVANTAGE...'

'Terrible as was what the world did to me, what I did to myself was far more terrible still.'
Oscar Wilde in *De Profondis*, left by the bedside of pre-War Japanese Prime Minister, Konoe, before his suicide in 1945.

PRIVATE FIRST CLASS Ikenatusu was working 400 feet up on the face of Mount Inasa, overlooking Nagasaki harbour, where he was helping with the installation of anti-submarine guns on the morning of 9 August 1945. The day had begun clear, but by 11.00am it was hot, overcast and hazy. Ikenatusu stopped work a little early to head for the mess hall where he had heard that his unit was to have a treat for lunch – pork with rice and vegetables. As he neared the mess he noticed a solitary plane high above in the sky, popping in and out of the clouds as it circled the city at about 30,000 feet. An ex-aerial artillery gunner, he knew it to be a B-29 Superfortress, but assumed that it was on some kind of reconnaissance run.

Suddenly he saw a parachute blossom far up in the sky with something dangling from it. The plane was banking sharply, making nearly a full turn. A moment later the sky exploded into a blazing glare. Ikenatusu shielded his eyes with his arm, but as he lowered it he saw a silver line ripple soundlessly towards him through the air and all at once he was thrown on his back as the mess hall disintegrated.[1]

Three weeks earlier, on 17 July, Winston Churchill had been in the midst of talks with President Truman in Berlin when Henry Stimson, the United States Secretary for War, called at his abode and handed him a sheet of paper on which was written: 'Baby satisfactorily born'. An atomic bomb had been successfully exploded at the top of a pylon in the New Mexico desert. No one had been sure whether the device would have any military value or even work, but it had absolutely devastated a circle a mile in width.

'Here was a speedy end to the Second World War,' Churchill wrote, 'and perhaps to much else besides.'[2]

In fact, the cathedral city of Nagasaki, centre of Christianity in Japan, did not feature on the original list of four possible targets for the second atomic bomb; it was added only after the elimination of Kyoto when it was realized that this ancient city was packed with historic temples. Even then, Nagasaki was not the first choice target of Major Charles Sweeney of the United States Army Airforce as he lumbered his heavily laden B-29, called 'Bock's Car', down the dark runway of the small Pacific island of Tinian at 2.56am on the morning of 9 August. When the wheels finally lifted and the propellers bit the night air, the scientists and technicians on the ground let out a sigh of relief – for the five-ton bomb carried by the B-29, which was much larger than the one already cast on Hiroshima and hence dubbed 'Fat Boy', was already armed.

From the start, the mission did not go smoothly. First, the plane developed a fuel problem. Then, when it reached the first target, the city of Kokura on the northern coast of Kyushu just before 10.00am, heavy and persistent flak began and it was too cloudy to sight the target. Visibility was further impaired by smoke from the burning Yawata steelworks which had been bombed two days earlier.

So Bock's Car turned towards Nagasaki, a coastal town built in two valleys on a deep natural harbour which, despite its relatively small size, had a huge Mitsubishi shipyard as well as Mitsubishi steel and armament plants. Weather planes had reported Nagasaki clear, but by the time the plane reached its position six miles above the city, winds from the China Sea had blown the weather back over the city and cloud cover was 70 per cent. The outline of the harbour was only just visible to the bombardier, but not the target aiming point: the Mitsubishi shipyard. As the clouds parted for a brief instant, however, the pilot managed to sight the Mitsubishi arms plant, a secondary target, and set the automatic bombsight mechanism. Seconds later the bomb wires snapped and the plane lurched upwards, freed of the great weight.

The parachute spotted by Private Ikenatusu was not the bomb itself, but almost certainly an instrument canister which was dropped from the accompanying plane. 'Fat Boy' itself free fell to 1,540 feet where its volatile plutonium atoms were rent apart under the pressure of triggering conventional explosives in the surrounding case. Instantaneously, a fantastic amount of energy was released in the form of heat, light, pressure and gamma radiation. For some 1,000 yards from the epicentre all unprotected living organisms instantly perished. Wood burst into flames. Steel girders and galvanized roofs bubbled and melted. Stones crumbled and the air burned.

After the heat came the blast, a hundred times greater than the strongest typhoon, travelling outward at a speed of 9,000 miles an hour, echoing off the valley walls and blowing the tiles off houses three miles away. Hard on the heels of the heat and the blast came the silent killer – radiation: beta, gamma, alpha, and X rays. Strontium 90 and Cesium 137, the products of fission – the ash of death – were scattered everywhere.

As Sweeney's plane streaked away from the mushroom cloud which hung over Nagasaki to crash land almost out of fuel in Okinawa 90 minutes later, pilot Cadet Komatsu listened to news of the explosion as it was flashed through to cadet corps HQ at Sasebo. He had heard of the bomb which had devastated Hiroshima two days earlier and had discussed it with fellow cadets. Eager to study the weapon's effects at first hand, Komatsu didn't wait for orders but snatched his helmet and hurried out to a seaplane with two comrades following close behind. As they neared Nagasaki, flying at 10,000 feet, the cadets emerged from the clouds to find the way blocked by an enormous, churning, black pillar of smoke spreading across the sky.

Unable to see the ground, Komatsu approached the cloud. Immediately the cabin became unbearably hot. Opening the window he stretched out his gloved hand and quickly pulled it back in: it was as though he had plunged it into live steam. Pulling the window shut, Komatsu noticed a sticky dew on his glove. Then the plane cut into the great cloud and in an instant they were in total darkness. A strange odour hit them and the other men in the plane began retching.

Eight minutes later they emerged from the cloud, descended to 1,000 feet and saw Nagasaki blanketed in red flames. Komatsu circled, landed in the harbour and jumped into the water to swim to the shore only to find the water shallow enough to wade in. As the shocked airmen walked up from the harbour, some two miles from the explosion's centre, they were at first surprised to find the damage so slight. What they saw next, however, quickly changed this impression: flattened trees and telegraph poles, blackened and blinded people, some with strips of flesh hanging from them, one man with an eyeball out of its socket, a child crying for mother. The stunned men turned back to their seaplane and returned to base.[3]

About 40,000 people died that day in Nagasaki. Perhaps as many again perished from the after-effects in subsequent years. At Hiroshima, around another 100,000 were killed. But even these totals were lower than the 200,000 people killed in the raid of 9 March 1945 when wave after wave of Superfortresses dumped 700,000 bombs on Tokyo – ten times the weight of the explosives dropped by the *Luftwaffe* on London in the whole of September 1940.

新　大　国

Nearly a century of prodigious effort since Japan had been opened to the West in the mid-Nineteenth Century lay in ruins. To a significant extent, this was the result of a sad history of misunderstanding and misjudgement in which the West was as much to blame as Japan herself. Initially, condescension had typified Western attitudes towards the Japanese, who were frequently regarded with indifference and scorn. At best, romantic images of an exotic Oriental fantasy land of diminutive, quaint and sometimes ridiculous people prevailed, one result of which was a craze for Japanese *objets d'art* which became known as 'Japonaiserie'.

So Japan's stunning victories, first over China in 1895 and then over

Russia in 1905, came as a shock to many. According to a London *Times* leader of 11 February 1904:

> The trouble [was] the past inability of the West to take Japan seriously
> . . . due to the superficial study of Japan which has characterized Western
> contact with it . . . they were still pleased to look upon the Japanese
> through the eyes of the aesthetic penman and thought of the nation as a
> people of pretty dolls dressed in flowered silks and dwelling in paper
> houses.

Japanese perceptions of Westerners had, by contrast, been largely positive during the early formative period and Westerners were generally regarded with respect. But some of this admiration was dissipated towards the end of the century as many Japanese became increasingly disillusioned by the racism and prejudice which they encountered in the West, as well as by the developed nations' double standards over trade and colonies. The 'unequal treaties', imposed on Japan in the middle of the Nineteenth Century down the barrel of American and European guns, had also aroused bitter resentment and weakened the position of Japanese liberals, especially when efforts to negotiate their revocation broke down in 1887, leading to an upsurge in nationalist societies dedicated to combatting Westernization and the loss of Japanese values. This was aggravated by the loss of face over the Triple Intervention by Western powers which prevented Japan from keeping her gains following her defeat of China, despite the fact that the United States seized the Philippines with impunity three years later. All of this further exacerbated the militarists complex of resentments and intensified the desire for revenge.

It is true that there was a brief period when it seemed as though Japan might be able to play the role of trusty acolyte of the Western Powers, rather than dangerous new upstart. In 1900, when the Western legations in Peking came under attack from a group of nationalist fanatics with tacit support from the Chinese government, it was the Japanese who played the leading part in the combined rescue mission, earning themselves the admiration of the British press who portrayed 'the gallant little Jap' as Britain's new, junior ally in the East.

The British alliance, the defeat of Russia and gains during the First World War seemed finally to confirm Japan's position as one of the world powers, but the other powers refused her request at Versailles after the Great War for legal equality among nations without 'discrimination . . . on account of race'. And although the renewal of the British alliance, due in 1921, was expected to be a formality, especially as Crown Prince Hirohito had completed a highly successful visit to England that year, the Americans were becoming increasingly wary of Japan and succeeded in persuading the British not to renew the pact. Japan was further insulted when, later that year, a United States Supreme Court decision declared the Japanese as ineligible for naturalization as American citizens, the culmination of a long dispute caused by Japanese emigration to the United States. This failure to secure Western respect was a major factor in Japan's rejection of liberal values and subsequent espousal of militarism. For these cumulative snubs represented a tremendous loss of face for a nation still insecure in her new role.

By the 1930s, trade tensions were adding to this volatile blend of mistrust and indignation. As Japanese goods made inroads into traditional Western markets at a time of high unemployment, tariffs were erected against Japanese goods at an accelerating rate, causing one Japanese official to note wryly:

> Eighty years ago, Japan was compelled to open her door to Europe and America. Small-scale industries of Japan could not stand the competition of Western goods which were produced with superior machinery. Consequently they all ceased to exist. That is history. Japan was then told that free trade was a means whereby the common welfare of mankind was promoted. By discarding industries which did not suit her, and by concentrating on those best suited to her, she has now attained that stage where some of her industries are superior to those of the old industrial countries. As soon as she begins competing with them, she is condemned in the name of humanity.[4]

So when for many the economic situation became difficult, when high tariffs restricted Japanese exports, when the slights and stinging rebuffs of the West injured the pride of a nation still insecure in its progress, they naturally turned to the increasingly successful Army as a rock of stability and tradition in an uncertain and unpredictable world.

While the immigration controversy had been largely responsible for the growth of antagonism between Japan and the United States, it was, by the 1920s, being overshadowed by a worse dispute concerning Japanese policy in China, a country for which the Americans felt a special responsibility and affection. Japan's invasion of China's northern province of Manchuria in 1931 further heightened tension, and in July 1939, the United States gave six months notice of the abrogation of its commercial treaty with Japan. Two months later, the United States effectively embargoed exports of scrap metal to Japan and when, shortly after the fall of France in June 1940, the Japanese occupied northern French Indo-China, the United States embargoed all oil exports to Japan.

From the Japanese point of view, more than merely atavistic aggression against the weaker Asian neighbours had impelled their drive into Asia. After all, this was the high noon of imperialism, and Japan was not the only country with Asian colonies. To the Japanese, the White races were hogging far too much of the world – Australia, New Zealand and North America had long since been grabbed by the White man, the Indian Ocean was still a British lake and most of South-East Asia was under Dutch, French, American, Portuguese or British control. Only Siam enjoyed any measure of independence. The Japanese felt encircled by the Powers and some also considered that they had a mission to free the Asian races from White domination.

Imperial theory or altruism were not, however, the main motives behind Japanese expansion – it was economic necessity which provided the driving force. For Japan was not just dependent on the United States for 80 per cent of her oil, and Western colonies for her remaining oil and rubber, but much of her food, too, had to be imported. So Japan was impelled, like the other 'have not' powers of Italy and Germany, by a need for *lebensraum* (*living space*) during an era when colonialism was considered perfectly acceptable. After all, it was little more than a century since the Russians had taken control of most of their Asian territories and Britain, together with the other European powers, had necklaced China with a series of foreign enclaves. The French had snatched Indo-China and America seized the Philippines even more recently, so why not the Japanese? Did not they, like the Western Powers, need to ensure supplies of raw materials as well as to secure captive markes for their manufactures?

With oil and raw materials beginning to run out late in 1941 the Japanese had to make a move. They initially attempted negotiations. Although some members of the Japanese government, realizing that war with America would be a disaster, were prepared to make concessions, the American Secretary of State, Cordell Hull, insisted on a complete withdrawal by Japanese troops from their new Asian possessions. At that stage Japan had two options. First, she could back down and accede to all of the American demands: that is, relinquish her Asian empire, cede control of her raw material supplies to the Western Powers with their Asian colonies and accept the permanent status of a second-class power. Or she could fight, in which case the onset of the monsoon season by the end of December would make landings in South-East Asia hazardous. This factor, combined with the desperate oil situation and the knowledge that the Western Powers were steadily reinforcing their positions in Asia, militated for the rapid and ultimately disastrous strike on Pearl Harbour, initiating the chain of events which led to the unleashing of atom bombs on Hiroshima and Nagasaki and the almost total destruction of the Japanese economy.

新　大　国

Never before had Japan felt the tread of a foreign conqueror. The nearest she had come was in the Twelfth Century when the Mongol hordes of Kubla Khan, grandson of Ghengis Khan, swept across the vast plains of northern China, breaching the Great Wall and demanding allegiance from the Japanese. When this was refused, Kubla Khan attacked in 1281 with a fleet of 4,400 ships and 140,000 Mongol, Chinese and Korean warriors. By contrast, the *Spanish Armada*, launched three centuries later by Europe's then most powerful nation, numbered a mere 130 ships with 27,500 men. A huge land and sea battle raged for 53 days. But as the Emperor sought the aid of the spirits at Shinto shrines, a 48-hour long typhoon blew up and wrecked the Mongol fleet, stranding their armies which were slaughtered without mercy. The Japanese called the storm 'kamikaze', which means 'divine wind', and Japan remained free of invaders for nearly seven centuries.

This time, no divine wind came to the rescue. Six days after the bomb fell on Nagasaki, on a stiflingly hot August day, people stood to attention all over Japan. Everyone knew that something exceptional was about to happen. Rumours of the atomic explosions had already penetrated most areas, and early that morning, the Japan National Broadcasting Company requested people to listen to the Emperor's broadcast. Few places by then had regular power supplies, but the electricity had been switched on everywhere specially for the broadcast. In streets, parks, factories and homes throughout Japan a frail voice, never before heard by the vast majority of the Japanese, addressed the people over loudspeakers and radios:

> We declared war on America and Britain out of our sincere desire to secure Japan's self-preservation and the stabilization of East Asia, it being far from our thoughts either to infringe upon the sovereignty of other nations or to embark upon territorial aggrandizement .... But now ... the war situation has not developed necessarily to our advantage

the disembodied voice went on, mouthing one of the greatest euphemisms of all time. 'Moreover,' the Emperor continued,

> the enemy has begun to employ a new and most cruel bomb, the power of which to do damage is incalculable. Should we continue to fight, it would ... result not only in an ultimate collapse and obliteration of the Japanese nation, but also to the extinction of human civilization .... We cannot but express the deepest sense of regret to our allied nations of East Asia who have consistently co-operated with the new Empire to secure the emancipation of East Asia .... We have resolved to pave the way for a grand peace for all the generations to come by ending the unendurable and suffering what is insufferable.

The throngs in the squares wept, incredulous, humiliated – and wearily relieved.

Part I

After the War – Reconstruction

JAPAN. A POOR, barren, inhospitable group of islands, with no natural resources, perched uneasily on the north-eastern edge of the Asian mainland. Rocky and largely infertile, swept by chill Siberian winds in winter and sweltering in sub-tropical heat by summer, frequently racked by typhoons, volcanic eruptions, earthquakes and, finally, by the most savage destruction the world had then seen.

Japan's remarkable resilience and regeneration in the face of national humiliation and seemingly insuperable disasters is, perhaps, the greatest achievement of the post-War world. Yet at one point, it seemed as though Japan would lapse into anarchy and become an industrial backwater. That she did not was due in part to the legacy of the country's rapid development in the 70 years up to the outbreak of the Pacific War; to a far-sighted military occupation administration; and to government policies geared, above all, to industrial growth.

新大国

1

RENEWAL

'Japan will be defeated, of that I am sure. But she will be born again and become a greater nation than ever before', a Japanese officer in a suicide-torpedo unit told a young volunteer in the dying days of the Second World War, before explaining that a nation had to suffer and be purified every few generations so that it could become stronger by having its impurities removed. *'Our land is now being bathed in fire,'* he said, *'and she will emerge all the better because of it.'*[1]

THAT JAPAN WAS reborn and emerged stronger than at any other time in her history was, to a large extent, due to possibly the most benevolent and far-sighted military occupation in history. It was led by the victor of the Pacific War, General Douglas MacArthur, who came from a family experienced in dealing with the Japanese. His father, General Arthur MacArthur, had been one of the American military observers posted with the Japanese army during its 1904–5 war with Russia. The young Mac-Arthur had also been in and out of Japan when his father had been in charge of pacifying the Philippines, seized by the United States during the Spanish–American War.

Although he retired from the United States Army in 1937, MacArthur was recalled to active service in July 1941 by his close personal friend, Franklin Roosevelt, to defend the Philippines. He subsequently commanded the American army in the Pacific and led the heroic but ultimately unsuccessful struggle against the rampant Japanese at Bataan, for which he won the Congressional Medal of Honour. The General gained his revenge on the Japanese when he led the invasion of Luzon in January 1945, driving them out and marching into the liberated capital of Manila as the conquering hero. This was a victory not without great bloodshed, however. The Philippines capital was three-quarters destroyed and in the carnage 100,000

19

Filipinos, 16,000 Japanese and 1,000 Americans perished due, some historians have argued, to MacArthur's miscalculation of the strength of Japanese resistance.[2]

Whether or not MacArthur's heroism and competence as a military commander was exaggerated by Roosevelt's PR machine – which undoubtedly needed a war hero – his five years of almost absolute rule in Japan were a tremendous success, largely because he managed to disregard almost all the suggestions proposed by the other Allied governments, but also because he was given a virtually free hand by President Truman. Seldom since the days of the Roman Empire had a proconsul had so much power over a conquered people and never had one been as popular as MacArthur was to become with the Japanese people.

The occupation began well. Despite the fears of many Japanese people, the American soldiers behaved almost impeccably. By 31 August 1945, when there were almost 50,000 occupation troops in the Yokohama area, the police had reported only 216 complaints against them, 167 of which had been lodged by the police themselves over matters of jurisdiction. Most of the remaining 49 cases were alleged thefts, and by September, the GI crime rate had fallen to an average of only two offences a day.

By the end of 1945, the process of reforming Japan was well underway. MacArthur and the occupation administration – which became known as Supreme Command Allied Pacific (SCAP) – approved the Emperor and his cabinet's decision to appoint Baron Kijuro Shidehara, a 73-year-old diplomat and former Foreign Minister, as Prime Minister in October. Shidehara complied with MacArthur's demand to dissolve the secret police and release political prisoners. He also enfranchised women and lowered the voting age from 25 to 20, dissolved the Japanese General Staff and demobilized the Japanese Army and Navy.

In the election of the following spring, 38 women were elected to the Diet. By this time, the majority of the occupation forces were no longer combat veterans, hardened by years of bitter jungle warfare, but fresh recruits from the United States, and the occupation had effectively ceased to be a military operation and instead had become a social experiment. Both MacArthur and Japan were fortunate during this vital period of reform in having a former diplomat and Anglophile, Shigero Yoshida, as Prime Minister following the 1946 election. Yoshida was 67 when he replaced Shidehara and he held on to his position with tenacity for nearly nine years, seeing the new system through from its inception to maturity.

The advantage of MacArthur's new constitution for Japan, which came into effect in 1946, lay in the fact that it was not the result of a compromise between different parties, but rather a combination of the best aspects of the American constitution and British parliamentary practice, steering a skilful course between the executive and the legislature. Supreme political power was assigned to the lower house, the Diet, to which cabinets were made responsible by having the Prime Minister elected by the lower house. The old House of Peers was replaced by an elected upper House of Councillors and the Emperor publicly denied his divinity, although he retained a symbolic role.

An American-style Supreme Court with an independent judiciary further underwrote individual rights and civil liberties. Other SCAP laws created free trades unions and a free press and replaced the education system with one patterned on that of the United States. Nearly five million tenant farmers also benefited from a highly-effective land reform programme which gave them freehold tenure, so raising the proportion of owner-farmed land from less than half to over 90 per cent. The overall result was the creation of a firm base for a strong, property-owning democracy which almost certainly made the occupation of Japan the greatest achievement of American overseas policy in the post-War period. In the process, it also helped to create a powerful competitor for the future.

Matters might not have turned out as well as they did, however, if it had not been for a dramatic shift in SCAP policies. Up until the summer of 1947, the plan had been simply to sign a peace treaty with Japan and evacuate the troops, even though the country was disarmed, had no central police system and faced a semi-circle of hostility from the Soviet-controlled islands to the north, round to communist North Korea.

Before this plan could be put into operation, however, Mao's communists defeated Chiang's nationalists in China, causing the Americans to have second thoughts. Japan was no longer seen as being a potential enemy, but rather as a strategically important future ally. So the policy was reversed and the emphasis shifted from punishment and neutralism to economic expansion and the integration of Japan into the Western system. SCAP directed the Japanese government to organize a Police Reserve Force which later became the Self-Defence Agency, while a new Maritime Safety Agency was sent to Korean waters to sweep mines during the Korean War which began in 1950. SCAP also connived in the July 1950 'Red Purge', when communists were expelled from many public sector, education and media jobs. So by the time the Peace and Security Treaties restored full sovereignty to the Japanese government in 1952, the situation was very different from that which had been envisaged at the end of the Second World War.

A protracted miracle

Although it is common to talk in terms of Japan's 'post-War economic miracle', the lineage of her industrial triumph stretches back way before the Second World War to the 1860s when incursions by the Western colonial powers led a group of young *samurai* reformers to overturn two and a half centuries of military rule by the Tokugawa shoguns, during which time the emperor had been little more than a symbol. The reformers set up a constitutional monarchy with a new Emperor, Meiji, in what is generally known as the Meiji Restoration.

No other country responded as quickly or as successfully to the challenge posed by superior Western economic and military technology. Japan's rapid modernization in the last three decades of the Nineteenth Century was aided by the homogeneity of her people, her strong sense of self-identity, an awareness of the need to learn from abroad, the existence of relatively sophisticated political institutions and an already well-educated population. Furthermore, Japan benefited enormously by starting her modernization process early, for the technological gap separating Japan from the West was not then as great as it was to become for developing nations in the Twentieth Century. The lack of any precedent also allowed the Japanese some freedom from unrealistic expectations of overnight industrialization or instantaneous democracy which have hindered subsequent attempts at rapid modernization.

Industrialization at first took place under the close tutelage of the state. Steamship lines were inaugurated, shipyards taken over and developed, cotton mills opened and machinery imported to be sold to entrepreneurs on an instalment plan. Initially, however, only a fragile and delicate structure emerged from this frenetic early development. The balance of trade was deeply in the red for most of the 1870s and foreign merchants and banks dominated the new trade. The main imports were cloth and machinery. Exports consisted mainly of tea, raw silk and silkworm eggs – the latter assuming an increasing importance as, fortuitously for Japan, European silk farming was hit by recurrent silkworm disease during the 1870s.

But modernization was an expensive process and the government was forced to run up large budget deficits. Combined with a shaky banking sector and increased demand for raw materials, this led to growing inflation by the late 1870s. The result was a huge sell-off of state assets at give-away prices. The large merchant traders, Mitsui, Ono and Shimada, formed under the Tokugawa regime, were the main beneficiaries along with Sumitomo, which traced its origins back to copper mining and rice trading in the Sixteenth Century, and Yasuda, a money lending house. But newer groups also gained from the sell-offs which helped to finance their expansion. The origin of the Mitsubishi group lay with a *samurai*, Yataro Iwasaki, who won contracts for transporting troops and leased Nagasaki docks to begin building ships. He also bought government land near the Imperial Palace in Tokyo in 1890 which was developed into the Marunouchi business district. Kawasaki, too, was founded by a sharp, upwardly mobile *samurai* on the make who rented state land and bought out the government Hyolo shipyard in 1886. These organiz- ations played a pivotal role in the early industrialization of Japan and became known as the *zaibatsu*, which literally means 'money groups'.

Apart from government support and the impact of Western finance and technology, ample supplies of female labour were also a vital factor in the industry's development. Peasant families contracted with employers and agents for their daughters' labour and the girls were housed, fed and even entertained under the terms of their employment. Western-style industrial- ization was, from the beginning, sometimes modified by the existence of the local social environment and did not so often give rise to the grim conditions and subsequent bitterness found in many Western countries.

Textiles were in the van of early industrialization. As an industry with relatively low capital, skill and technical requirements, textiles were ideally suited to the initial stages of industrial development and remained the basis of Japan's industry until the First World War, by which time well over half of all factory employees worked in textiles.

The lack of large supplies of indigenous ore and coking coal impeded the more capital- and technology-intensive metal industries. So the government acted by opening the Yawata iron works in 1901; by 1913, mainly state- owned mills accounted for about half of the nation's iron and a third of its steel needs. Japan's first steel ship was built in 1895, although the Imperial Navy was initially largely dependent on British-built warships. However, subsidies were introduced for large ships and marine engines in 1896, and by 1913 the keels of the first locally-built warships had been laid.

As with ship building and the metal industries, general engineering lagged well behind textiles. By 1913, however, almost 90,000 people were employed in these advanced industries and many of the subsequent giants of Japanese business had been founded. Some, like Kawasaki and Mitsubishi, were helped by state subsidies to diversify vertically, from operating steamship lines into shipbuilding and then into marine engines and railway rolling stock. Other advanced industries sprung up with relatively little government encouragement. Tokyo Electric Company (TEC) and Oki Electric Company were both founded in the last decade of the century to fulfill the growing demand for electrical products. Foreign capital and know-how supplemented state encouragement and the entrepreneurial flair of the Japanese. The General Electric Company of the United States, for example, bought a stake in TEC in 1905, allowing the young Japanese manufacturer to produce its Mazda electric light bulbs.

But although the pace was set by the large *zaibatsu*, there was a great deal of diversity and small manufacturers sprang up, many specializing in making relatively long runs of a small number of components. Former gun makers at Sakai, for example, turned first to making parts for imported bicycles and then went into full assembly from standardized components.

Complementing the growth of the production industries was a rapidly-swelling infrastructure. Seven thousand miles of railway were operational by 1913 and shipping was also expanding. As late as 1893 only 14 per cent of ships entering Japan's ports were Japanese, but by 1913 this had risen to around 50 per cent.

Slowly Japan was levering herself into the ranks of the industrialized nations. At the time of the Restoration, 80 per cent of the working population was in agriculture, forestry or fishing. By the outbreak of the First World War, this proportion was down to 60 per cent. Over the half century from the Meiji Restoration, the Japanese economy had developed from one which was highly dependent on government support and basic products such as silk, rice and tea, to one which was largely self-sustaining and primarily based on low-level manufactures such as textiles, while more advanced industries such as steel, engineering and shipbuilding were gaining a foothold.

The First World War was a godsend to the embryonic Japanese industry in that it was able to meet demand unable to be fulfilled by the distracted Europeans. Exports trebled, Japan replaced Britain as the world's major spinner of yarn and her trade balance moved into surplus. Industry also began to upgrade its production performance. Mitsubishi's Nagasaki yards launched two destroyers in 1914 within 14 weeks of laying their keels, while Kawasaki claimed records for the rapid construction of merchant ships. In 1918, its Kobe yard launched and trialed the 5,800-ton steamer, *Raifuku Maru*, in a mere 29 days. For the first time, too, significant amounts of Japanese capital were exported in the form of purchases of Allied government securities and loans to China and the Tsar.

Despite political instability, the great Tokyo earthquake of 1923 and inflationary problems in the 1920s, Japanese industry generally prospered and advanced. Whereas the bulk of cotton exports in 1913 had been simple yarn, by 1929 the majority were higher added-value finished cotton goods. Over the same period, steel output and electrical power capacity increased eight fold and 70 per cent of the nation's steel needs were now furnished from home.

Nonetheless, Japan was still only a semi-developed industrial country. Although no longer dependent on raw materials or unfinished goods for her exports, she was still very reliant on imports for more sophisticated goods, such as machine tools and industrial feedstocks. Japan's industry was by then, however, becoming largely self-sustaining. Only about three per cent of government spending in the late 1920s went to industry, of which nearly half was spent on agriculture. Tariffs and protection were also no greater than in the West. Non-financial assistance was at least as important to Japanese industry as subsidies. Compulsory government quality-inspections were, for example, introduced for many types of goods, and in 1925, exporters' guilds were set up to inspect products.

It was during these unstable inter-War years that many of today's industrial household names took their first, tentative steps. For example, Matsushita, the consumer electronics company, better known today by its international brand names of Panasonic, National, Technics and Quasar, was founded by Konosuke Matsushita, whose father had lost his money in rice speculation in the 1890s. Fascinated by the new electric tram cars which had just been installed in Osaka, Matsushita's break came with the introduction of electricity into urban homes in the 1920s. Most homes had just one electrical socket so he invented a two-way adaptor. This was followed by a bicycle light, a household electric lamp and an electric heater. During the subsequent Depression, Matsushita refused to fire any of his workforce, instead putting them on half time while still paying them a full wage. His motto being 'the purpose of production is to serve the needs of society and improve the quality of life', Matsushita assiduously exploited his knowledge of the latest in Western technology, producing his first radios in 1931. Today, Matsushita is the largest manufacturer of domestic electrical goods in the world.

The early 1930s were marked by a shift in industry from lower added-value, basic-technology textiles to metals, engineering and chemical products. By 1936, Japan's finished-steel production fully replaced imports; ship tonnage soared and by 1937, the Japanese merchant fleet was the third largest in the world. Export volumes also rose by two-thirds between 1929 and 1936 and the proportion of finished manufactures in exports rose from 44 to 59 per cent. Progress in the higher technology products was also steady. By 1937, having rapidly overhauled Britain, Japan was the largest producer of the new artificial fibre, rayon. She was by then also capable of making large turbines and quite proficient aircraft.

The Depression also had some beneficial side-effects by concentrating Japanese industry into largely more efficient enterprises. The *zaibatsu*, in particular, profited and reached the zenith of their power and influence during the early 1930s. As well as having their corporate fingers in almost every industrial pie as a result of their close association with the leading politicians, they had also developed their own banking and financial interests. The underdeveloped nature of the capital markets made it difficult for companies to raise funds by public issue, so expanding industries had to sell securities to the banks. As the *zaibatsu* dominated banking, so they gained a huge influence even over industries in which they were not directly involved.

But the concentration of *zaibatsu* power caused great resentment, especially after the hardships of the Depression. To many, the large industrial and financial conglomerates epitomized the evils of unbridled Western-style capitalism and were the negation of the harmonious ethos of old Japan, and anti-*zaibatsu* sentiment was oxygen to the fire which was being fanned by the military extremists and ideologues.

The Army's antipathy towards the *zaibatsu* led to the establishment of army-backed conglomerates – called the *shinko zaibatsu*, or the 'new money groups', one of the largest being Nippon Sangyo Kaisha, usually shortened to Nissan – originally founded to facilitate the colonization and exploitation of the new empire in Asia. It was hoped that the new groups would supplant the old *zaibatsu*, but the Army soon realized that it needed them and links were rapidly established between the old and the new enterprises. Many *zaibatsu* chiefs soon reappeared in new guises. The former head of Mitsui Bank, for example, was made governor of the Bank of Japan.

Despite the instability and huge military spending which already accounted for half of the state budget by 1934, Japan's economy again responded well and grew steadily in the latter years of the decade. Indeed, throughout the troubled 1930s, Japan's trade expanded by nearly three-quarters at a time when world trade was stagnant. Overall, between 1900 and the outbreak of the European war in 1939, Japan's economy had grown faster than that of any other major economy. It was a magnificent achievement and, although it was not to be enough to sustain the nation in a major war against the Western powers, it did provide a considerable base for the post-War 'economic miracle'.

Government for industry

Although from the viewpoint of the 1990s, Japan's subsequent economic rise seems almost inevitable, matters were far less certain from the perspective of the late 1940s. Japan in 1945 was effectively in the same position she had been in 1868. She was stripped of all her gains from the Sino–Japanese War of 1894–5, the Russo–Japanese War of 1904–5, the First World War and the Chinese War which had begun in 1937. In addition, Russia had seized the Kurile, Ryuku and Senkaku islands to the north of Hokkaido, an act which clouds Japanese–Soviet relations to this day.

With the disappearance of her colonies in Formosa, Korea and Manchuria went the markets for two-thirds of Japanese exports and the source of most of her raw material imports. Japan's major towns were in ruins, most of her merchant marine fleet had been sunk and her foreign assets had been seized. On the plus side, although badly damaged and cut off from her traditional markets and suppliers, Japan still possessed some industrial infrastructure which could be repaired and a well-educated and socially cohesive population whose determination to improve themselves could now be channelled into peacetime pursuits.

Few observers at the time gave the Japanese economy much chance of success, however. Although money was poured into industry from the American and Japanese governments via the Reconstruction Finance Bank, runaway inflation meant that by 1949 prices had risen to 13 times the 1945 figure, while output still remained below 1937 levels. Japanese industry was to some extent saved by 'special procurement' orders for the United States forces, which stimulated export-oriented industries: Toyota, for example, was on the verge of bankruptcy when the first United States Army orders for its trucks came to the rescue.

So by the time the Japanese government regained full control of the country in 1952, the situation had at least stabilized both economically and politically. Prime Minister Yoshida was head of a coalition of revived versions of the two pre-War right-of-centre parties, which merged to form the Liberal Democratic Party (LDP) in 1955 in the face of a rising leftist vote. Henceforth the parties of the left, the Communists and Socialists, which also had pre-War antecedents, went into a steady decline which was exacerbated by the splitting-off of the moderate Democratic Socialists from the very left-wing Socialist Party. Apart from that, the only really new major post-War party was the Komeito, loosely translated as the 'Clean Government Party', which originated in the 1960s as the political arm of a new Buddhist-oriented religious movement, the Soka Gakkai.

Yoshida's government and its successors spent the next four decades pursuing a consistent series of policies geared towards one primary, overriding objective: economic growth. Moderate taxation and low government spending – which by 1974 was still only just under a quarter of GNP, compared to well over 40 per cent for most developed Western countries – together with balanced budgets between 1949 and 1965, minimized the state's demands on productive industry. Expenditure on welfare in particular was kept extremely low, at less than 15 per cent of state spending in the late 1950s and early 1960s – less than half the level of the main European economies, while defence spending was also tightly controlled, at about one per cent of GNP (compared to three to seven per cent in the West).

High rates of personal savings and low consumer spending were also encouraged through tax breaks on savings and credit restrictions. Part of these savings was channelled into industry through the banking system, leading to a very high percentage of fixed capital formation, primarily in productive investments, facilitating a rapid replacement of industrial plant. Foreign technology licensing was also encouraged, and the educational system was expanded and closely geared to commercial needs to provide a pool of well-educated and skilled people for industry.

As well as restricting state and private consumption and gearing resources towards industry, the LDP government's policies also kept inflation down – a major plank of Japanese government policy and one which has been a significant factor in Japanese industry's ability to plan and invest for the long term. By 1969, export prices were no higher than they had been in 1950, while between 1963 and 1972, wholesale prices rose by only 12 per cent in Japan, compared to 16 per cent in West Germany, 26 per cent in the United States, 32 per cent in France and 40 per cent in the UK. Economic conservatism of this type did come to an end as government spending rose significantly to boost the flagging economy during the oil crises of the 1970s, leading to higher levels of inflation and a large public debt; but by the early 1980s Japanese public finances were back on a balanced footing and inflation was once again under control.

TVs, steel, ships and cars

Although it took a full decade for Japan's per capita production to creep back to the levels of the mid-1930s, when growth came it was dramatic. Between 1950 and 1973, Japan's GDP grew at a staggering average of 10.5 per cent a year – nearly twice the rate of any other major industrialized nation in the post-War period. Even after the oil crisis of 1973–4, Japan's growth rates remained nearly twice as large as those of her major competitors. Her products soon challenged and overtook the Swiss watch industry, devastated American TV makers, all but destroyed the British and American motor-cycle producers and virtually wiped out the German camera manufacturers.

By the early 1960s, Japan's shipyards were building more than half the world's tonnage, while a decade later, her steel works were producing as much as the American industry and almost as much as the entire European Community. Between 1960 and 1984, Japan's car output rose one hundred fold, taking nearly a quarter of the world market as Japanese cars were exported in their millions all over the world. As a result, whereas when the SCAP occupation ended in 1952 Japan's GNP had been little more than a third that of either France or the United Kingdom, by the late 1970s Japanese output was as large as Britain's and France's combined.

Japan's economy also underwent a series of fundamental changes during the post-War decades. Before the Second World War, Japan had mainly traded with the United States and East Asia. To the United States she had exported silk, canned fish, tea, pottery and textiles; importing cotton, oil, wheat, scrap metal and engineering goods. To East Asia Japan sold textiles and machinery; buying in return cotton, rubber, oil, ores, metals, rice, sugar and soya.

After the War, the privileged trade with the East Asian 'yen bloc' ended, synthetics such as nylon hit the silk trade and Asia developed its own textile industries. As a result, Japanese industry switched away from relatively labour-intensive, lower added-value goods to more sophisticated products. Textile exports as a share of total exports fell from 52 per cent in 1936 to 30 per cent in 1960 and to a mere five per cent by 1978. Engineering goods, instruments, cameras, binoculars, clocks, ships and vehicles took their place. Sony launched the first pocket-sized transistor radio in 1957, and by 1959 exports of such products had grown by 1,000 per cent. By 1978, machinery, vehicles and ships represented two-thirds of the value of Japan's exports, by which time she was the world's largest shipbuilder and dominated world trade in TVs and radios. And from this immensely strong base of medium-technology goods, Japanese industry began to forge into the most advanced areas of industry, rapidly developing powerful semiconductor, computer, telecommunications and information technology industries in the late 1970s and 1980s.

The River of Seven Colours

Japan was not, however, without its labour problems during this period. Thousands of leftists had been released from jail in 1945 and there were no fewer than 34,000 trades unions by 1949. Despite the later reversal of the SCAP policy of encouraging trade-unionism, the late 1940s and early 1950s witnessed a great deal of industrial unrest and many strikes. Even as late as 1960, an intensely bitter and violent strike broke out at Mitsui's Miike mine in Kyushu as a result of the government's policy of reducing domestic output of expensive coal and gearing its energy policy towards cheap imported oil.

The Miike strike was, however, the swan song of militant trade-unionism in Japan. The key factor in the increasing moderation of Japanese labour was the fact that Japanese wage rates rose faster than those of any other major industrial country, while overall, Japanese workers also enjoyed the highest degree of job security and the lowest unemployment. On top of this, by the 1970s, Japan had achieved a greater equality of income distribution than any other industrialized economy. As a result, whereas in 1949 56 per cent of Japan's industrial workers had been unionized, by 1978 the figure had slumped to only 32 per cent.

The common image of modern Japan as a peaceful, cohesive and united society was, however, still occasionally belied by further vicious outbursts of public protest and violence. But after 1960, when Prime Minister Hoyato Ikeda told the country that the national income would double in ten years, labour problems abated as economic progress brought prosperity unparalleled in Japanese history, and the new wealth helped to ease internal frictions, taking much of the fire out of political debate. The great annual May Day demonstrations by the Left, which had once threatened Japan's shaky post-War stability, became more akin to a good-natured folk festival. Strikes and serious labour unrest were rare and were largely limited to the state-run and heavily-subsidized Japan National Railway system.

But prosperity brought with it new problems and challenges. By the 1960s, the Omuta River, which flows through the city of Omuta, was known as the 'River of Seven Colours', not because it refracted the sun's rays, but rather due to the fact that it changed colour seven times a day depending on the discharge from the city's chemical works. The terrible pollution and environmental problems which assailed Japan by the beginning of the 1970s as a result of her breakneck growth and concentrated industrial production were becoming increasingly apparent.

In the spring of 1970, 18 contributors – mostly economists – wrote a series of articles in the *Asahi Shimbun* daily newspaper on the theme 'Kutabare GNP!' ('To hell with GNP!'). The Japanese were beginning to realize that they may have built quality into their products, but there was no real quality in their living conditions. For the first time, the price of industry's breakneck growth was being seriously questioned. But the issue only really grabbed the nation's attention when in July 1971 a group of school children suddenly collapsed, blue in the face and gasping for air while doing exercises. They had been stricken with a photochemical smog. At about the same time, cats which had fed on mercury-laden fish began to have spasms and jump into the sea in Minamata. Not long after, it became clear that humans were also being affected, some dying of exhaustion after spasms caused by their injured nervous systems.

Fortunately, the economic growth which had caused the problem also brought the prosperity to help deal with it, and from the early 1970s Japan began to devote more of her resources on improving her quality of life. Among the measures were vehicle emission standards stricter than those in force in the United States, together with smoke emission limits from newly-opened plants that remain the most rigid in the world. A 1975 OECD report estimated that Japan was spending around three per cent of its GNP on anti-pollution programmes – several times more than any other member country – and concluded that by then the air in the main Japanese cities was as clean as that in the large American, French, British or German cities.

The success of the Tokyo Olympic Games in 1964 allowed Japan to show off her achievements to foreigners with some pride and the Japanese were able to bask in a sense of self-satisfaction which they had not felt for years. It was a self-esteem, however, very different to that which afflicted sections of Japanese society in the 1920s and 1930s. The respect for the military as unselfish patriots and pure servants of the Emperor had long since turned to contempt. Although defeat had initially confused, disillusioned and demoralized the Japanese, to many the success of the United States proved the superiority of the liberal democratic system and they looked to their conqueror as the guiding example for the future.

Nikson Shokku

At a few minutes past 10.00am Tokyo time on Monday 16 August 1971, a month after he had stated his decision to visit China, President Nixon announced a series of 'temporary' measures designed to ease the domestic economic problems which had been largely caused by high spending as a result of the Vietnam War. The measures announced in the 18-minute speech included the devaluation of the dollar and an import duty of ten per cent, the intention being to make American exports more competitive and reduce imports. As each new policy was announced, billions of dollars were wiped off the value of Japanese stocks as increasingly hysterical sell orders flashed from the brokers' head offices to the trading floors in Tokyo, Osaka, Nagoya and the other main centres.

Nixon's statement became known to the Japanese as the *Nikson Shokku*. As with the earlier decision to visit China, the Japanese had received little warning from their ally: in this case, Prime Minister Sato had been given a mere ten minutes advance notice of the announcement. Overall, the main Tokyo stocks were marked down by between 25 and 50 per cent, while comments by American analysts, such as Edwin Dale of the *New York Times*, twisted the knife deeper. Dale's opinion, which was reprinted in Japan, was that 'the United States, in a single dramatic stroke has shown the world exactly how powerful it still is . . . the US has shown who is Gulliver and who are the Lilliputians' – among which he included Japan.[3]

For several months, the Japanese remained in shock – not merely over stock-market losses, but also because they had been under the impression that the Americans harboured friendly feelings towards them. By the end of the year, however, the stock market had recovered and even surpassed its pre-shock levels by April the following year: the distinction between Gulliver and the Lilliputians was becoming increasingly blurred.

The Nixon Shock was but a mild taste of what was to come. Because of its highly-priced domestic coal, the Japanese government had made the decision in the late 1950s and early 1960s to import most of its energy. Coal imports rose from eight million tons in 1960 to 50 million tons in 1970, while oil imports increased nearly 1,000 per cent between 1960 and 1973, by which time Japan was dependent on the OPEC countries for three-quarters of her requirements. So when the November 1973 oil crisis struck, Japan was uniquely vulnerable. As oil prices rose from $3.29 a barrel in late 1973 to $12.53 in 1976, Japanese industry suffered and production fell sharply, only recovering to the pre-crisis level by 1978. After a long period of surpluses, the Japanese trade balance moved into a small deficit in 1973, which increased to $6.6 billion in 1974.

Although Japanese industry began to move into a new gear and the trade surplus was at $18.4 billion again by 1978, the second oil crisis in 1979 found Japan still the most oil-dependent of the major industralized nations. Oil then accounted for three-quarters of Japan's energy needs, compared to 52 per cent in West Germany, 48 per cent in the United States and 43 per cent in the UK. Again, Japan suffered two years of large trade deficits, but again made a second decisive move back into surplus in 1981.

With its disproportionate dependence on manufactured exports and imported energy, Japan should have suffered more deeply from the decade of Nixon and oil shocks than any other industrialized nation. Instead, she emerged by the early 1980s as undoubtedly the most resilient economy in the world – and by a significant margin. For, less than a generation after the most thoroughgoing destruction wrought on any nation, so strong and flexible had her economy and society become that not only was Japan able to weather a series of shocks and crises which would have tipped lesser nations into headlong decline, but she also emerged more powerful than ever before in her history.

Part II

People – Japan's Natural Resource

JAPAN'S ONLY SIGNIFICANT natural resource is the most important kind – her people. With just 0.1 per cent of the earth's inhabitable land and 2.6 per cent of its total population, she nonetheless produces a tenth of the world's GNP. How do so few people manage to achieve so much? Some people attribute the Japanese capacity for production to government policies, but however wise these may be, they would be ineffective without the skill, diligence and assiduity of the Japanese people.

So what does drive the Japanese? A very large part of the answer lies in their attitudes and education. For although Japan is very wealthy, many Japanese still believe themselves to be the poor inhabitants of an isolated, rocky and largely infertile set of islands. This conditions their outlook and motivates them from their school days to retirement. It also lies at the heart of the enormous effort put into education in Japan, which in turn has produced the best-educated and most highly-skilled workforce in the world.

Other aspects of Japanese life are not so well reported in the West as their propensity for hard work. Although the Japanese may be industrious they are hardworking hedonists too, enjoying their pleasures and taking them in full measure, with little of the moral condemnation that such activities elicit in the West. Further, despite her image as a cohesive, law-abiding, crime-free society, Japan is not without severe divisions. And the country has a vicious criminal class so interwoven with legitimate enterprises and activities that it makes many Western countries' organized criminals look amateur by comparison. These are just some of the many aspects of this least understood of advanced societies which have largely escaped the attention of the West.

新大国 2

POOR LITTLE RICH COUNTRY

'If, in the revolution of time and events a country should be found (which is probable) whose cottons and woollens shall be cheaper than those of England and the rest of the world, then to that spot – even should it, by supposition, be buried in the remotest nook of the globe – will all the traders of the earth flock; and no human power, no fleets or armies, will prevent Manchester or Liverpool, and Leeds, from sharing the fate of their once proud predecessors in Holland, Italy, and Phoenicia.'
Richard Cobden (1804–65).[1]

STANDING ON THE edge of the high, coiling, mountain-hugging coastal road which leads from Nagasaki to Shimbara, you receive a good impression of the bleak environment of much of Japan – chilled by a blasting winter wind which sweeps in from Siberia, across the wide Manchurian plain to numb the west coast of Kyushu. Below lies a thin, green, coastal strip, dotted with villages and small farms surrounded by glasshouses. Beyond are the cold, grey Tsushima straits, speckled with craggy islets. Behind and above rise rugged granite mountains, their lower reaches covered with spruce and cypress.

'Look,' said Murasawa Kazuyoshi, a slight, mustachioed graduate of around 25 years who was our guide in Kyushu, Japan's main southern island, 'you see how poor Japan really is. We have nothing, no resources, little fertile land to farm, only rocks and mountains. We have to work hard. There is no choice for us. We compete just to survive.'

The view from the new, non-stop flights from London to Tokyo presents a loftier perspective of Japan's precarious position, perched as it is in an arc around 500 miles off the north-eastern coast of the Asian land mass. After the cold, white vacuousness of Siberia, you pass over the chilly, drab depths of the Sea of Japan to the Japanese archipelago, four-fifths of which is

33

largely incapable of serving any useful purpose. It is a precipitous, intricate country, haphazardly divided by excited, silver trails of rivers and streams. Yet the useful one-fifth of the land is busy, inhabited, cultivated and industrialized with an almost frenzied intensity.

As you descend, you see neither the neat agricultural grid of America nor the patchwork daintiness of Europe, but rather a landscape consisting of a tumble of paddies which squeeze and spill into every conceivable crevice, mingling bright green with the darker mass of the mountains, villages, towns and cities where most of the Japanese live.

Japan's 4,000 island chain, strung out along more than 2,000 miles from the subtropics to the subarctic, rises sharply from some of the Pacific's deepest, coldest waters to summits of more than 12,000 feet. The four main islands of Honshu (the 'mainland'), Shikoku and Kyushu to the south and Hokkaido to the north, together with the long chain of Ryuku islands extending south-west from Kyushu, inhabit the same latitudes as Florida in the south and Montreal in the north – or from central France to the southern part of Algeria.

But Japan's situation in relation to the great land mass of Asia places it firmly under the influence of the cold, dry, winter air stream which issues from that great continent. As a result, Japan suffers freezing, desiccated winters, followed by dripping wet summers caused by the Asiabound indraught of warm, moist Pacific air. So Hokkaido, on a parallel latitude with the south of France, endures winter months with a mean temperature of below freezing point, while the south is affected by vicious typhoons at the end of its sultry, dripping summer. The few exceptions to the general rule of numbing winters and humid summers are the small southern islands, which enjoy a year-round, subtropical climate, together with the western half of Hokkaido where the Siberian winter winds pick up sea moisture *en route* and set it down in the form of ample, powdery snow.

All of Japan is also subject to periodic seismic shocks, of which one of the worst destroyed most of Tokyo and killed more than 100,000 people in 1923. Such climatic conditions may help to explain why the Japanese, in common with the Eastern Asiatic peoples, have become renowned for their hard work and tireless energy. Paucity of resources has probably been a major factor in producing a people with what seems to be the most deeply ingrained work ethic in the world, while to survive the colder months, hard work has traditionally been necessary to build up food stocks for the winter.

Smaller in area than California and only marginally larger than the British Isles, Japan's population of 122 million is more than four times that of the United States' largest state and more than twice as large as Britain's. But Japan's topography squeezes the mass of her people into narrow coastal strips, river valleys and the occasional plain. For reasons of economics, the Japanese are further concentrated into the relatively broad, 120-mile long Kanto Plain on the southern side of Honshu island. Here, clustered around Tokyo, 40 per cent of the population live on a mere 1.5 per cent of the total land, the remainder of Honshu supporting a further 40 per cent of the people.

As a result, from the top of a sleek Tokyo skyscraper you can, on a rare clear day, see a horizon which encompasses close to half of Japan's GNP – around five per cent of the world's output. For no less than one in three Japanese lives within 100 miles of the Imperial Palace. On the other hand, no part of Japan is more than 70 miles from the sea, and mountains are within view almost everywhere. With abundant rainfall in all seasons except winter, the country is also luxuriantly green and wooded.

The crowded nature of Japan's living space – there are 125 people per square mile compared with only ten in America – elicited the comment by a prominent Western politician in the mid-1980s that the Japanese lived in 'rabbit hutches'. This epitomizes the commonly-held view that the Japanese have paid a high price for their economic success in their living standards and conditions. The comment, however, also caused great resentment and consternation in Japan. For although the Japanese do live in undoubtedly cramped conditions in the larger cities – indeed their social environment inspired the concept of minimalism now so admired in the West – Western perceptions are generally exaggerated. As has been pointed out by the *Economist* writer, Bill Emmott, in the mid-1980s the average Japanese dwelling had a floor space of 870.8 square feet – below spacious America's average of around 1,450 square feet, but not so much less than France's 920 square feet or West Germany's 1,010 square feet.[2]

Another of the comforting myths about Japan is that it is still terribly polluted. In November 1987, for example, *The Times* printed a large photograph of customers at a Tokyo store inhaling oxygen at its 'Oxygen Bar'. Yet Japanese cities, which once were awful, have long since been cleaned up to levels which are no worse – and in some cases rather better – than Western cities. Japanese cities may also lack the splendid centres of many of their European and some of their American rivals owing to earthquakes and bombing, but apart from this they are now not much worse from the point of view of aesthetics than most Western cities. Can anyone who has experienced the Bronx, the outskirts of Paris and Milan or parts of London really complain that Japanese cities are worse than Western ones?

What is certainly true is that the pace of Japanese life does induce a high degree of stress, as evidenced by the boom in stress parlours which offer treatments including vibration chairs and the fact that CBS–Sony sold 200,000 albums of stress-relief music in less than a year. But all of this has not prevented the Japanese from becoming the longest lived nation in the world. According to the *British Medical Journal*, a Japanese boy born in 1990 can expect to live for 75.2 years and a girl until she is 80.9 – three years longer than their British, American, French or German equivalents.[3]

A god of money

Visit a Japanese school and you may be surprised to see mothers sitting in classes avidly taking notes. They are, in fact, standing in for their absent children, ensuring that they are not disadvantaged through missed lessons. For the Japanese have an intense desire to get on in life and to be successful – something which itself is closely linked to the traditional insecurity of life in Japan where there has never been any opportunity to catch the British disease of living off past economic achievements. Indeed, the aspiration to be *Ichiban* (*Number One*) is deeply ingrained in the Japanese consciousness in a way in which it is not in parts of the West, where such yearnings are sometimes frowned upon or even despised and where anti-enterprise attitudes are still deeply ingrained in sections of the Establishment.

Such aspirations, together with the recognized need for a strong economy in view of Japan's lack of indigenous resources, have resulted in generalized feelings of respect towards business, commerce and profit. Certainly, the average Japanese person is better informed on economic affairs than the average Westerner. Japanese economic journalism is of a high standard and interest in economic affairs is widespread: a four-volume economics manual in pictures called *A Cartoon Introduction to the Japanese Economy* sold no less than 1.8 million copies. Japanese newspapers regularly run opinion polls to find the most popular businessmen: significantly, it is generally the most entrepreneurial self-made people who come top. Around 22 million Japanese adults also own shares – a higher proportion than in most Western countries. Their average portfolios are ¥5 million (£20,000) in size, and Japan's stock-market punters are serviced by no fewer than 80,000 salespeople who hawk share offers from door to door. When Nippon Telegraph and Telephone (NTT) was partially privatized in 1987, 10.7 million people signed up for the special lottery to allocate the 1.95 million shares which each cost a hefty ¥1.2 million (£5,300).

This respect and even enthusiasm for the world of trade, still so often considered grubby in the West where success is frequently equated with greed or crude materialism, is no post-War phenomenon, but part of a tradition going back at least to the late Tokugawa times of the Eighteenth and Nineteenth Centuries. Although entrepreneurship is not a characteristic of feudal societies, the concentration of *samurai* in the capital of the shogun and the lords' castle towns largely freed the villages and countryside from feudal control, while the early unification of the country into a single economic unit gave wide scope to commercial activities. Indeed, the very fact that merchants and peasants were largely denied the possibility of feudal political power made economic achievement the only real outlet for their energies. Merchants and peasants, barred from participation in politics, also developed their own philosophy which viewed economic success – like the political and military endeavours of the *samurai* class – as a service to society.

Nor do the Japanese suffer from any residual religious objections to money-making. There is no distinction in Japan's indigenous religion, Shinto, between gods and Mammon and no trace of the Christian belief in the sanctity of poverty. Indeed, one common word for 'market' – 'ichi' – originally meant 'coming of god'. There is even a Shinto shrine to the god Ebisu in Osaka, the city of merchants, where businessmen come to pray for the deity's liberal favours. Tsue Takao, the chief priest at the shrine, who dresses like a banker in a dark suit and silver tie, justifies his vocation by saying: 'Because wealth and property is a gift from God, you have to develop it to do God's will. In Japanese Shinto, we think highly of this approach.'

Ebisu was, in fact, formerly the god of fishing, but the advent of industrialization transformed the deity into a god of money. In January of each year a strange festival is enacted at the Ebisu shrine, attended by more than a million people. The worshippers crowd into the shrine grounds, walking shoulder to shoulder in a long procession, carrying bamboo sticks hung with paper symbols of wealth, such as wallets, accounting books, gold coins and banknotes. When they near the shrine buildings, they throw money into a giant net or discreetly pass envelopes full of banknotes to the priests before praying intently, punctuating their worship by clapping their hands to attract the god's attention. In 1988, the offerings totalled ¥213 million (nearly £1 million).

The generally pro-business attitude of the Japanese also manifests itself in the almost invariably excellent service in shops, restaurants and other outlets. Businessmen and shopkeepers together with their employees take real pride in the speed and efficiency of their service and rarely accept tips. To serve is considered a privilege – or at least a normal part of the job, not requiring any special remuneration. Stop at a Japanese petrol station, for example, and immediately attendants literally run across the forecourt: one fills your tank, one cleans the windscreen, and another empties ashtrays. A further attendant takes your money, while yet another guides you on to the road. On the famous *shinkansen* (*bullet train*), food vendors bow and greet passengers as they enter each compartment, bowing again and thanking passengers as they leave.

Are such attitudes merely artful and commercially inspired? It is certainly true that competition is fierce within Japan and good service builds customer loyalty. On the other hand, there is an innate and traditional service ethos in Japan and I believe that the Japanese genuinely enjoy offering a good service – in marked contrast to the frequently resentful attitude encountered in parts of Europe. Perhaps this is because most Japanese feel part of 'the system'. Opinion polls regularly report around 85 per cent of Japanese regarding themselves as middle class and there is little of the confusion between service and servility so prevalent in the West, nor the feeling of alienation also sometimes apparent in Western countries.

Contributing to the almost universal sense of middle classness in Japan is the extremely even distribution of wealth. In the early 1980s, when the national average index of non-farm households' income stood at 100, blue-collar workers' incomes averaged 82.5, white collar workers were on 109, government workers on 116.2 and executives made 205.5.[4] This relatively even income spread is approximately similar to that of the United States in the middle brackets, but differs markedly from it at the two ends. For in Japan there is a much smaller low-paid group at the bottom, and much less great wealth at the top. One recent study ranked Japan together with Australia and Sweden as the three developed democracies with the smallest income gap between the rich and the poor.[5]

Harmony among men

In 1980, Prime Minister Suzuki quoted Mencius in a statement to the Diet: 'A good castle and favourable terrain are not equal to harmony among men.'

Harmony is particularly valued by the Japanese and a high degree of social cohesion undoubtedly characterizes Japanese society. A feeling of belonging to the system has certainly been an important factor since the Second World War. In part, too, Japan's relative unity has been due to racial homogeneity and the unifying task of rebuilding the nation from the ruins of the War. This is reinforced by the country's relative isolation, together with a long tradition of political centralization and a typically East Asian emphasis on the state as the embodiment and guarantor of civilization. Others have seen it as primarily a legacy of the long Confucian tradition.

Japanese Confucianism stressed a rational natural order of which man was one element of a harmonious whole. Society was based on strict ethical rules, focusing on a centralized state ruled by men of superior moral wisdom. Stress was laid on loyalty to the ruler, filial piety and strict observance of proper social ritual and etiquette. Although Confucianism barely survived the great reforms of the late Nineteenth Century, when its inherently conservative aspects were abandoned in the face of the Western challenge, fundamental Confucian ethical values continued to permeate Japanese thinking and some traits persist to this day, particularly the belief in the moral basis of government, the emphasis on good social relations and loyalty. Confucianism's greatest legacy in Japan, however, is perhaps its emphasis on education and diligence.

Related to Japan's cohesion is the long tradition of group, rather than personalized, leadership. This was marked in Tokugawa times by the sharing of power between councils of 'Elders' and of 'Junior Elders' which were the two highest decision-making bodies. The same general pattern was followed by the Meiji reformers during the 1860s. No single dictatorial leader ever achieved, or even seriously sought to gain, supreme power. Instead, the leaders, who informally came to be known derogatorily as the 'Genro' ('Elder Statesmen'), formed a group, taking turns at various tasks, including the role of prime minister after the creation of the post in 1885.

Even when, on the eve of the attack on the United States late in 1941, more power was concentrated in the hands of General Tojo than any individual had enjoyed for many years, his authority was still largely that of a group leader rather than a dictator. When, in 1944, the War began to turn sour, Tojo meekly left office, making way for another member of the team. This aversion to dictatorial power or charismatic leadership, together with a strong tendency towards group co-operation were, and are still, pronounced features of Japan's body politic.

Neither is the group ethos in Japan only confined to the leadership: it is spread throughout the community. There are as many theories of the Japanese group as there are commentators. Some say that certain elements of the old feudal society have persisted owing to Japan's rapid conversion from an agrarian to an industrial state. Life in the medieval Japanese village and work in the paddy fields demanded the total involvement of all members of the community. Going it alone was not an option.

Commentators also assert that the way in which small Japanese children are treated has contributed to their sense of respect for authority and resultant social concord. Japanese infants are in almost constant contact with their mothers, nursed for a relatively long period, fed almost at will and are frequently carried on the backs of their mothers when they go out. Further, they frequently sleep with their parents until quite a late age. Japanese children are, therefore, indulged and babied, rather than treated as small adults.

The result is a degree of dependence considered unusual in the West. First the child, and then the adult, is accustomed to basking in the affection of others. And what begins with dependence on the mother for gratification, so the argument goes, grows into a dependence for fulfilment on the security and approval of the group. On the one hand the child develops an expectation of tolerant indulgence from the mother, but on the other also implicitly accepts her authority which eventually develops into an acceptance of the authority of society and a need for and dependence on social approval.

It should be remembered, however, that although Japanese society may generally be more unified and consensual than most Western societies, and although the group ethos may be stronger, this image has to be balanced by the often bitter and violent disputes and internecine strife which has characterized Japanese history as much as that of any other nation. The inter-War years were particularly disastrous with the military hardliners pitched against the constitutionalists, a situation further complicated by severe factional strife which even existed within each party. Bitter 'rice riots' broke out after the First World War, while the 1920s and 1930s saw school and industrial strikes, peasant revolts against landlords, large-scale demonstrations and frequent bloody assassinations, culminating in an army mutiny in 1936.

Since the Second World War, of course, many of the sources of internal conflict have disappeared. Few Japanese people now have military or imperial aspirations; land reform has taken the heat out of the rural problems; and general prosperity has blunted the edge of protest. Even so, Japan's relatively pacific recent history has still been punctuated by regular incidents of violence and protest, such as the massive school walk-out by half a million teachers in 1954 in protest at legislation preventing organizations which encouraged teachers to engage in political activity; the violent Miike coal miners' strike in 1960; and vicious riots against treaties with the United States, also in 1960, when Eisenhower's press secretary had to be rescued by United States marines from a howling mob on his way into Tokyo, while Prime Minister Kishi was forced to resign.

The late 1960s and early 1970s were marred by bitter street protests by masked and steel-helmeted students who overturned cars, stoned police and set fire to Tokyo University. In 1969 alone, at the peak of the riots, police arrested 20,000 people. In 1974, commuters smashed up Tokyo stations in frustration at a railwaymen's go-slow, while riots over Narita Airport delayed its opening by seven years. Just before the official opening in 1978, radicals penetrated the control tower via the sewage system and smashed the equipment. Even now, Narita is heavily guarded and ringed with electrified fencing. Nor has the Diet always been a shining example of group ethos and consensus politics. Five hundred policemen had to guard the chamber in May 1954 to prevent fist fights between members, causing the Diet's stenographers to demand a pledge from the members that they would not walk over their tables or grab their notes during fights. Six years later, the speaker was manhandled by left wing members trying to prevent him from taking the chair.

Nor do Confucian concepts of respect and loyalty necessarily prevent the Japanese public from sometimes complaining bitterly if they feel they are getting a poor service. At the annual meeting of Nippon Telephone and Telegraph (NTT) in 1989, the beleaguered board were overwhelmed by angry protests, including one from a Ms Tori who asked if the case of an NTT repair man who assaulted a restaurateur with a knife following a complaint about a faulty phone was typical of NTT's attitude to customer complaints.[6]

Even in industry, where the group ethos and consensus decision-making has been considered by many as central to its success, appearances can be deceptive. According to Akio Morita, one of the founders of Sony:

The concept of consensus is natural to the Japanese, but it does not necessarily mean that every decision comes out of a spontaneous group impulse. Gaining consensus in a Japanese company often means spending time preparing the groundwork for it, and very often the consensus is formed from the top down.[7]

Another of Japanese industry's elder statesmen, Isamu Yamashita, put it thus:

Consensus management is frequently misunderstood abroad. Daily business is conducted from the bottom up, but long-term planning is top-down. Basic policy does not originate at lower levels.[8]

So intrinsic Japanese harmony may have been exaggerated by outside observers. Inevitably, too, the relatively high degree of social cohesion and the work ethic among the Japanese people is steadily changing under the influence of the country's increasing prosperity. For once the fundamental imperative of economic rebuilding had passed, the horizon of the average Japanese began to extend beyond the daily grind. As far back as 1975, the Research Institute for Broadcasting and Public Opinion reported that health, home life and happiness had replaced an earlier emphasis on material success and wealth as the priorities of most Japanese people.

This is particularly marked among the young where a new class of 'shin jin rui' ('soft young') are more interested in leisure than work. Casual crime, an example of the breakdown in social cohesion, is also on the increase. For example, in 1988, the Tokyo City Council banned motorbikes after 8.00pm in downtown Tokyo for fear of ibosozoku bike gangs. Inevitably, too, Japan's new affluence, and especially the huge fortunes made out of the rise in land values, has led to a certain amount of resentment among those who have done less well. Late in 1990, for example, police in Osaka battled for days against thousands of day-labourers protesting about police corruption and bribe-taking from gangsters who exploit the temporary workers by controlling labour on building sites. The fact that the firebomb-throwing protestors, who looted shops, cars and vending machines, were joined by company workers is indicative of the way in which the new wealth is leading to steady changes in Japan's society, shifts which will later be examined in greater detail.

3

新
大
国

A HUNDRED
HARVESTS

'If you plan for a year, plant a seed.
If for ten years, plant a tree.
If for a hundred years, teach the people.
If you plant a seed once, you will reap one harvest.
If you plant a tree, you will reap ten harvests.
If you teach the people, you will reap a hundred harvests.'
Kuan-tzu, Chinese philosopher, Sixth Century BC.

WE DROVE INTO the small, peaceful Kyushu town of Shimbara late on
Sunday morning having spent the night at a nearby hot spring resort, the
scene of many cruelties to the early Japanese Christian communities.
Kyushu, being closest to the Asian mainland and on the shipping routes,
was always more open to outside influences than the rest of Japan and
had a 300,000-strong Christian community by the early Seventeenth
Century. Shimbara's present tranquillity, however, belies its history, for
fearing the subversive nature of the religion and resentful of meddling
Jesuit and Franciscan missionaries, the Tokugawa regime decided to
enforce its many edicts against Christianity in 1612 and persecutions began
in earnest.

Nowadays, Shimbara's quiet main street could almost be small-town
USA. Apart from the fact that it is a little narrower than most American
streets, it has the same array of shops, restaurants and car showrooms as its
American counterparts – low, nondescript structures set back off the road,
strung together with hazardous-looking electricity and telephone wires
slung precariously from wooden poles. We opted for lunch in the Ringer
Hut, a fast food establishment built in the whiteboard 'New England junk
food' idiom. Once inside, however, the immaculately turned out girls
behind the counter substituted bows for 'Have a nice day', and beautifully

decorated porcelain bowls of noodles and oriental delicacies supplanted fried chicken and hamburgers.

Settling down to eat, I suddenly noticed that all of the children in the Ringer Hut were in uniform, the boys smart in dark, Nineteenth Century-style high-collared cadet livery, and the girls demure in immaculate blue sailor suits and bonnets. Our guide, Murasawa, explained that Japanese children not only have to wear uniform in school, but are often also required to wear it out of school, even on Sundays. He went on: 'Uniforms are seen as the outer manifestation of the discipline needed to succeed against the odds, and a badly dressed child would dishonour its parents. Japanese children are taught in primary school that they will become citizens of a poor country with no natural resources. Teachers really drum into them that our only hope is in our people. This is reinforced by most parents who are generally very ambitious for their children and push them, making sure they work hard.'

This beleaguered attitude certainly does seem to produce results. The first of four major comparative studies of international educational standards was carried out in the mid-1960s and tested mathematics among 13- and 18-year-olds in the main developed countries. Japan came top in both groups. In the early 1970s, ten- and 14-year-olds from 17 developed and developing countries were assessed in general science. Japanese children again did the best. Another major study took place in the early 1980s and covered mathematics attainment among 13- and 18-year-olds – Japanese children won once more.[1] The last of the major studies reported on science achievement in 17 countries, ranking Japanese ten-year-olds first and 14-year-olds second. The study also found that standards in Japanese schools were more consistent than in the other surveyed countries.[2] In addition to these major studies, further comparisons have been made between Japanese and American youngsters which show Japanese children to be well ahead of their American counterparts at the age of six, the advantage steadily growing until they reach 18.[3]

Language alone subjects Japanese schoolchildren to a rigorous discipline. The Chinese-derived *Kanji* pictographic alphabet, which still closely resembles Chinese, has around 4,000 characters in regular use and Japanese children have to learn 1,800 of these at school. On top of that is the albeit fairly simple 46-character *Hiragana* alphabet used for phonetics, together with 46 more *Katakana* phonetic characters used mainly for imported words, such as technical terms or 'Japlish', the strange amalgams which the Japanese have derived largely from English, such as the contraction of 'telly' and 'TV' into *'terebi'*. Several thousand of these mongrel words are in general currency, ranging from *esukareta* for escalator to *depato* for department store.

Finally, Japanese children all learn the Latin alphabet at school, and virtually everyone can at least read English, though most cannot understand more than a few key words. Their trials do not end there, however. Japanese is an intensely status-conscious language and there are no fewer than nine different terms for the simple word 'I', each appropriate to the differing relative status of speaker and listener.

Compulsory education in Japan begins when children are aged six, although about 85 per cent of pre-school children attend voluntary kinder-garten from the ages of three or four. (In Britain and the United States, only around 40 per cent of four-year-olds receive pre-school education, though primary school generally begins at the age of five.) About three-quarters of the kindergartens in Japan are private, receiving two-thirds of their revenue from fees, about five per cent from the state and the remainder from private sources such as endowments. The remaining quarter of the kindergartens are state-run and charge modest fees which contribute about eight per cent to their revenue, the remainder of their costs being met by local authorities. Japanese kindergartens are not simply play schools: they include a formal academic curriculum covering the first stages of reading and arithmetic and children are expected to be able to read and do simple sums by the time they leave. Japanese education, however, really begins before kindergarten, in the home, where ambitious mothers push their children from a tender age. 'It is as if mothers had their own built-in curriculum,' says Shigefumi Nagano, a director of the National Institute for Educational Research.[4]

From the ages of six to 15, education is compulsory in Japan. Approxi-mately 98 per cent of children attend state-run schools for six- to 11-year-olds and junior high schools for 12- to 15-year-olds. The remainder go to elite academic private schools, many of which are affiliated to universities.

Attached to the state provision chosen by the vast majority, however, is the curious phenomenon of private supplementary schools which many Japanese children attend in addition to their principal schools. Known as *juku*, these additional schools cater for children of all ages and include special *juku* specializing in the entrance examinations for the top high schools and universities. Originating in the 1920s, the early *juku* were modest establishments consisting typically of retired or moonlighting schoolteachers taking a few pupils for extra coaching. Now, however, most *juku* are large-scale enterprises, operated by national chains and accommo-dated in purpose-built buildings.

Japanese adolescents spend an appreciable part of their time at their *juku*, typically attending two or three evenings a week and on Saturday after-noons. Further, in the school holidays, attendance at the *juku* becomes full-time. The *juku* receive no government subsidies and are purely commercial enterprises paid for by parents, but Japanese Ministry of Education surveys show that more than half of the 12- to 14-year-old age group are enrolled in *juku* in Tokyo, Osaka and other large cities, and over a third in Japan as a whole.

After junior high, the majority of Japanese adolescents go on to senior high schools, about a third of which are private institutions operating on broadly similar principles to the private American universities. These private institutions receive subsidies from the government which cover about 40 per cent of their costs. The remainder of the senior high schools are state institutions which also charge small fees amounting to around ¥80,000–¥108,000 (£300–£400) a year.

American sociologists who have studied the Japanese high school system estimate that they turn out graduates at the age of 18 who are at about the same academic level as the average 22-year-old American college graduate.[5] Virtually all children leaving the Japanese education system have a solid grounding in the basic academic skills, with the result that Japan does not have the problem endemic to the West of large numbers of illiterate and innumerate adolescents.

Schooling the nation

Among the reasons for the system's success is that it provides schoolchildren with examination-based incentives for academic work which are far more powerful than those in many Western countries. Though the strong examination orientation of the system does produce genuine strains known as *shiken jigoku* (*examination hell*), it also inculcates both discipline and concentration and has been an important factor in producing a better-educated and more literate society than is the case in most Western countries.

The first real test occurs at the age of 14, when Japanese children take entrance examinations to the senior high schools which are ranked in a hierarchy of public esteem in each locality. Being at a prestigious senior high school confers both status and the benefits of good teaching, so places are keenly competed for. Once placed in these schools, Japanese teenagers are confronted with a fresh set of incentives in the form of university entrance examinations.

The prestige associated with the best universities motivates students, especially as leading Japanese corporations and the civil service often recruit their high-grade trainees virtually exclusively from the top dozen universities. Most eminent is the University of Tokyo, which has a standing in Japan analogous to Harvard and Yale in the United States, Oxford and Cambridge in Britain or the *école polytechnique* in France. Only slightly less illustrious than Tokyo is the University of Kyoto, after which are ranked a dozen or so other universities in the major provincial cities such as Nagoya, Osaka and Yokohama. Also counted among the elite is Hitotsubashi Technical University, resembling the Massachusetts Institute of Technology in technological excellence and public standing. Below the top dozen universities stand around 40 provincial colleges enjoying sound reputations and, finally, several hundred small, localized universities and colleges. Japanese students are far more able to take life easy once they have reached university, for Japan's universities are difficult to enter, but very easy to graduate from. Once in, it is almost impossible to fail to gain a degree and in marked contrast to the earlier years of their education, students are able to relax and enjoy life a little. The courses generally last four years, during which grants for students are minimal, although interest-free loans are available and repayment is waived for graduates entering the teaching profession.

One of the most significant aspects of the Japanese educational system is the fact that, unlike the United States and Britain (until the implementation of the recent reforms), the Japanese Ministry of Education specifies a detailed core curriculum which schools are required to teach children. This covers the Japanese Language, Japanese Literature, English, History, Geography, Social Studies, Music, Maths and Science. Government inspectors regularly visit schools to ensure that this responsibility is properly discharged.

There are a number of other factors which differentiate Japanese education from that in the West. First, the system contains a stronger market element than most Western educational systems owing to the presence of the kindergarten and *juku*, which have to compete for parents' money. Second, Japanese schoolchildren may be no smarter than those elsewhere, but they undoubtedly work much harder. After a regular six hours of schooling during normal week days, many also toil for three to four hours at the *juku*, follow that with four to five hours of serious study supervised by solicitous mothers at home, as well as attending compulsory Saturday morning lessons. Overall, excluding *juku* sessions, Japanese schoolchildren work for 240 days of the year, compared to only 180 in England and the United States.[6]

Third, Japanese education is considered to be an integral part of the economic system. Unlike in parts of the West where emphasis has been placed on goals such as 'personal growth' and 'the development of the individual', or where the ideal of egalitarianism has been pursued at the expense of excellence, the Japanese system is unashamedly based on the overriding premise that the main priority of schooling must be to enable a living to be earned. As a result, Japanese education is heavily geared towards studies likely to be of use in a future working life.

This more practical vein in Japanese education dates back at least to the Meiji era. When, in 1886, the country's first national university, the Imperial University, later to become Tokyo University, was founded, it included departments in vocational fields such as engineering and agriculture. At that time, such subjects were only really taught in technical schools in Europe. More recently, the utilitarian bias in Japan's education has been reinforced by the 1962 educational reform, which committed the system to more work-oriented studies which were seen as vital to the success of the economy. As a result, Japanese ten-year-olds spend an average of 336 hours a year on science instruction, compared to 252 hours in the United States and 135 in England. By the age of 14, the Japanese child is studying science for 870 hours a year, as opposed to 720 hours in the United States, 648 hours in England and 553 hours in France.[7]

This bias towards science continues up through the system. By 1978, 40 per cent of university students were studying science, technology and mathematics and particular stress was placed on engineering with about 21 per cent of undergraduates and 33 per cent of postgraduates specializing in this field, compared to 15 per cent and 13 per cent respectively in Britain. Furthermore, engineering is especially strong at the best universities such as Kyoto and Osaka, where engineers account for 40 per cent of all undergraduates. The core curriculum also leans strongly towards science, maths and languages, which constitute 90 per cent of the elementary and 80 per cent of the secondary curricula.

Consequently, with just over twice the population of Britain, Japan, in 1983, produced three times as many mechanical engineering graduates, five times as many graduates in chemical engineering and no fewer than nine times as many production engineers. There is, however, a lower concentration on the less vocational natural sciences in Japan: these disciplines are studied by fewer than five per cent of Japanese undergraduates, compared to almost a quarter in the UK.

Reinforcing the practical bias of Japanese education, business and industry are also more closely involved with, and supportive of, education than in some Western countries. Mitsui, for example, for many years supported the Tokyo University of Commerce and recruited from it, as they have done since the Second World War when the university's name was changed to Hitotsubashi.

Many people are misled into thinking that the high quality of Japanese education must be very costly. Far from it. Class sizes typically consist of around 30 to 40 children, compared to between 20 and 30 in the United States and Europe, while per capita expenditure on school children is about half that in the United States and approximately a quarter less than in the UK or West Germany. Japan only spends around six per cent of her GNP on education, which is far less than in America and many European countries,[8] with higher education particularly poorly funded as some 80 per cent of students attend private universities.

This leads to another very significant aspect of the Japanese system: the fact that such a high proportion of Japanese parents, including blue-collar workers, are willing or feel it essential to top up free state education with additional and sometimes costly private provision. At an early stage in the Japanese education, for example, a very large number of Japanese parents – about 70 per cent – voluntarily pay quite appreciable fees to give their children a good start in kindergarten – yet Japanese parents do not have greater disposable incomes than their European or American counterparts.

Later, many also dig deep into their pockets to pay for supplementary *juku* lessons and to help fund their children's progress through university. The fact, too, that Japanese mothers frequently attend school to take notes for sick children – something unheard of in the West – is symptomatic of the attitude of typical Japanese parents who are extremely ambitious for their children.

All of which helps to explain why, although compulsory education ends at 15 years of age, 94 per cent of Japanese children continue their education in upper secondary schools while 40 per cent go on from there to colleges and universities – a far higher proportion, in both cases, than in most Western countries. In Britain, for example, only around a third of pupils continue school after the age of 16 and only a fifth go on to higher education. Incidentally, if you want a clue as to why Japanese cities tend to be much cleaner than their Western counterparts, it may be because there are no professional cleaners in Japanese schools – the children themselves clean the school every day after lessons.

A long tradition

Those who search for the key to Japan's astonishing post-War economic success could do a great deal worse than settle on her educational system. The fundamental basis of Japan's modern educational system dates back to the Meiji Restoration, although today's educational standards are under-pinned by a strong tradition of inquisitiveness and learning that goes back far further than the mid-Nineteenth Century.

By the time of the Meiji Restoration in 1868, 40 to 50 per cent of boys and ten to 15 per cent of girls were already receiving some kind of formal education – a far higher proportion than in some Western countries. The Meiji reformers were well aware of the importance of education in modern-izing Japan and strengthening her economy. In 1872, their Education Law modelled the new system on the French Educational Code, making primary education compulsory for all regardless of class or sex – a mere seven years after the abolition of slavery in the United States and two years after the implementation of Britain's Education Act.

The Meiji system was centred on a powerful education department called *Mombusho* and largely funded by local government which devoted as much as a third of its expenditure to schools. Teachers were mainly drawn from the abolished *samurai* class. While the new system built upon the relatively high educational standards of the pre-Meiji era, at the same time, it made a clean break in ensuring that Japan was not encumbered with the aristocratic or religious education which epitomized much of the earlier Japanese system and those of Western nations. Instead, Japanese education became both secular and relatively egalitarian. Furthermore, the emphasis was initially and firmly laid on elementary education which was to provide a strong foundation for later advances into secondary and higher education. Many recently modernizing countries, by contrast, have placed the stress on higher education, which tends to produce graduates whose accomplishments are of little use in a society where prevailing educational standards are low.

So successful were the Meiji educational reforms, and so fertile was the seedbed of educational tradition in Japan at the time of the Restoration, that by 1900 close to 98 per cent of all Japanese children went to primary school for at least four years, which was extended to six years in 1908. By then, the system of middle schools and high schools had also been instituted along with five new imperial universities. Vocational technological colleges were also established as well as business schools such as that founded by Viscount Mori, the Minister of Education, which later became Hitotsubashi University.

In addition, by 1921, Japan also had eleven commercial colleges modelled on the German Handel Shoch Schulen, each with 500 to 600 students and, by the 1920s, 800,000 students also attended middle-grade technical schools. By then, most Japanese businessmen and managers received at least some vocational education relevant to their jobs. Already, practical education in Japan had to a large extent surpassed that available in Britain, where Nineteenth Century reformers such as Cardinal Newman and Matthew Arnold, swept up in the new religious fervour of that time, had helped to institute a system of education that was more geared to the romantic ideal of producing the Christian gentleman of high moral purpose than a system which would produce a person whose scientific knowledge would benefit industry and help to create wealth.

The contrast between British and Japanese attitudes to education in the

Nineteenth Century is sharp and there can be little doubt that the non-utilitarian bias in the British educational system, propounded at a time of huge scientific progress, ultimately contributed greatly to Britain's industrial decline. For while Japan was churning out engineers and technicians, Britain was advancing a curriculum that was of more benefit to a man with ideas of going into the Church or to university, with the result that the job of managing British industry was increasingly being carried out by inspired amateurs rather than trained professionals.[9]

The tradition of respect for education in Japan largely stems from Confucianism which laid a great deal of emphasis on the importance of learning. The great lords of pre-Meiji Japan, *daimyo*, employed many Confucian scholars (*jusha*) as advisors and tutors to their families, while the official domain schools were for the most part Confucian institutions. By 1865, 73 per cent of the *daimyo* had such schools in their domains, many of which also published Confucian texts. These colleges were supplemented by smaller private institutions, often run by a single Confucian scholar; by 1870, there were some 1,400 such schools in Japan. Even the largely Buddhist-run *terakoya* (*temple schools*) often emphasized Confucian ethics, particularly filial piety, in their teaching.

Although the domain schools were largely refounded as Western-style institutions after the Meiji Restoration, Confucianism was by then so well established that it remained an important element, even if only in fragmented forms. Some of the fundamental precepts of Confucianism also gradually re-emerged in the discipline and loyalty inculcated by the Imperial Rescript on Education of 1890. This fused a smattering of Shinto tradition relating to the supremacy of the imperial dynasty with a Confucian view of the duties of subjects and a Western orientation towards the nation state. Thus Confucian ethics, reinterpreted in the service of national objectives, became a fundamental part of the elementary school curriculum. This helps to explain why, in contrast to China, Confucianism in Japan, freed from much of the deep cultural conservatism of the tradition as a whole, became a positive force in the modernization process in so far as the Confucian precepts of discipline, loyalty and education promoted harmony, national solidarity and progress.

Although after their defeat in the Second World War the Japanese once more turned their backs on their Confucian heritage, the Confucian classics continued to be published and widely quoted in graduation day speeches. Exposure to Confucianism over more than a millennium and a half had by then left a complex legacy which it is hard to assess precisely. But almost certainly the most important and lasting influence remains in the field of education, where the value Confucian thought placed on rationality and on learning still indirectly contributes to Japan's present high standards.

It would be wrong, however, to think of Japan's present education system as being the result of an unbroken and harmonious series of developments. As the 1920s and 1930s wore on, *Mombusho* increasingly became the instrument of nationalists. After the War, there were conflicts between *Mombusho* supporters on the one hand and radical supporters of the left-wing Japan Teachers Union (JTU) on the other. When the 1956 School Board Act changed the elected school boards to appointed ones beholden to *Mombusho*, violent JTU-inspired demonstrations resulted, though the influence of the union gradually decreased as its members fell from nearly 90 per cent of Japanese teachers to less than half by the end of the 1970s. Trouble also flared in the 1960s, which, as elsewhere, manifested itself in violence and demonstrations in the universities. Parts of Tokyo University were virtually non-operational in 1968–9 when the situation became so bad that no new freshman class was taken in.

Suicides and rewriting history

Many who accept the importance of the Japanese educational system in the country's rapid economic development nonetheless criticize it on other grounds. Severe though Japanese education undoubtedly is, it is a shame that so few people involved in education in the West are aware of its achievements, concentrating instead on criticizing its weaknesses. Some critics, for example, assert that its pounding, science-based curriculum, demanding long hours and high academic success at an early age, produces a 'worker ant' mentality and high suicide rates. Many also consider that Japanese children are taught to learn by rote – a not unjustifiable criticism.

Besides this, the 1982 controversy over the 'rewriting' of Japanese history books has led many outside observers to regard Japan's educational system as nationalistic to the point of deceitfulness. Such diversions serve to obscure not only the practical achievements of the Japanese system, but also the fact that it has produced a cultured, highly literate nation as well as great economic achievement.

I remember visiting a school in the British Midlands where, after a tour of the facilities, I sat down with a group of teachers to discuss educational issues. When I raised the academic attainments and discipline of typical Japanese schoolchildren, the immediate response from one of the more vociferous teachers at the meeting was: 'Oh, but Japanese school children are under such pressure that they have an appalling suicide rate.' The implication was clear: while the British system produces broadly educated human beings, the Japanese churn out drones who are driven to suicide by the insistence on success.

Taken aback, I took the trouble to check comparative suicide rates for the main industrialized countries and was rather surprised to learn that in 1985 suicide rates among Japanese children aged from five to 14 were, in fact, rather lower than in most Western countries at five per million children. This compares with eight suicides per million children in the United States and nine per million in West Germany (the figure for England is statistically insignificant). In the 15- to 24-year-old age group, the figures are 95 suicides per million Japanese, compared to 129 per million in the United States, 127 per million in West Germany and 52 per million in Britain. Nor does the pressure of life in Japan cause her to have a significantly higher overall suicide rate than other developed countries. The 1985 figures are 194 per million of the population, compared to 227 in France, 207 in West Germany, 182 in Sweden, 123 in the United States and 89 in England.[10]

The teachers at a Midlands school may have been misled by an article in a popular British newspaper, headlined 'The hell of being a Japanese schoolchild', which read:

> What British mother would be so 'shamed' by her child's exam failure that she'd murder the child and then kill herself? What British pupil would decide that the only way to purge the 'shame' of poor marks is to commit suicide? Yet such 'shame'-inspired deaths are all too common in Japan.

The piece went on to claim that each year there were 400 cases of mother–child suicide pacts 'resulting in the deaths of almost 1,000 children'.[11] But when I checked with the journalist who had written the article, she was unable to quote her source either for the story or the figures.

Possibly one of the reasons why the suicide rate is lower than might be expected is the fact that, although Japanese schoolchildren work hard, the atmosphere in the classroom is often warm and nurturing. High academic standards are stressed, but emphasis is also placed on teamwork: children are taught to be part of a group so they can be good citizens as well as good students.

It has also been fashionable to sneer at the Japanese system for supposedly producing bleak automatons, mere economic animals without culture. Take, for example, the words of the Dutch journalist, Karel van Wolferen, who wrote in his influential book, *The Enigma of Japanese Power*:

> The aims of Japanese schools could hardly be further removed from the original sense of the English word 'education': to bring forth and develop the powers of the mind, rather than merely imparting factual information.[12]

Yet the French writer, Robert Guillain, who spent much of his life in Japan and became the Japanese correspondent of *Le Monde*, observed in the late 1960s that the ten bestsellers in the leading Tokyo bookshop, Kunokuniya, included Plato's *Apology* (at number one), Thomas More's *Utopia*, Simone de Beauvoir's *The Second Sex* and works by Engels, Goethe and Jean-Jacques Rousseau. According to Guillain:

> One has to have lived in Japan fully to appreciate the way culture 'goes deep', penetrating all social levels right down to the humblest with a greater intensity than it does even in our most cultivated Western countries. Of course, there are exceptions and gaps, and it would be possible to quote plenty of examples of Japanese coarseness or uncouth behaviour. But when one lives side by side with the Japanese, one finds on the whole that they possess not only a delicacy in feeling and action that is not often to be seen among our ordinary people, but also artistic, literary and intellectual taste and knowledge – in short, a cultivation, an openness of mind, and an interest in the outer world that is rarely to be found in the West among what are conventionally termed 'the common people'.[13]

Moreover, one American observer who had carried out a thorough study of Japanese and American elementary music education, commented:

> By the sixth grade, [Japanese] music students are able to switch readily between at least three different instruments. The first time I saw this level of achievement, I could not believe my ears. But after the fifth primary school, I had to recognize that it was widespread. While the members of the orchestras and bands in American primary schools achieve this level, most of the remaining students are musically illiterate.[14]

An uncultured nation with its eye permanently fixed on the economic game would not have flocked to the Covent Garden opera tour of three Japanese cities which sold out in 1986. Nor would they have justified a visit by the Bayreuth Festival's *Tannhauser*, complete with 300 imported personnel, nor the International Opera Festival's *Aida* which played to tens of thousands in the Tokyo Dome, usually the home of the champion baseball team, the Giants.

Traditional Japanese architecture, sculpture, painting, literature, drama and the applied arts, dating back to the Seventh and Eighth Centuries, are also keenly followed by a large number of people, and an extraordinarily high percentage of Japan's population finds self-expression in poetry – indeed, three million copies of a book of poems called *Salad Anniversary* by Miss Machi Tawara were sold in 1987. In all, Tokyo supports no less than six full professional symphony orchestras, while Japanese films have achieved international renown. More of the world's classical literature, furthermore, is available in translation in Japanese than in any other language in the world, including English.

In addition, the extraordinarily high literacy rate produced by the education system has resulted in the highest per capita newspaper circulation of all the large developed countries. Japan's three main national papers, the *Asahi*, *Mainichi* and *Yomiuri*, sell between four and seven million of their morning editions, as well as more than half that number in the evening – and none of them are examples of what is known in the West as the 'gutter press'. Two other national papers, the conservative *Sankei* and the financial daily, *Nihon Keizai* (comparable to the *Financial Times* or *Wall Street Journal*), have circulations in the millions, while four regional papers have a combined circulation of close to four million.

Of course, Japanese newspapers could be criticized for their uniformity in coverage and treatment, but they do tend to report issues more seriously than does the bulk of the Western press. The common Japanese habit of perusing salacious and often violent comic books – *manga* – and the low quality of some of their television could be cited as evidence of educational failure, but similar criticisms could be levelled against most other developed countries. It would, therefore, be a very arrogant or ill-informed Westerner who was to assume that the Japanese are merely a race of uncultured workaholics.

Unfortunately, though, it is often the less sympathetic and more sensational aspects of Japan's educational system, rather than its successes, which tend to occupy Western observers. The 'rewriting of history' episode of 1982 was just one such occasion. In July of that year, the Japanese press reported that the Ministry of Education had forced a publisher to revise the term 'aggression' to 'advance' in a reference to the Japanese army's activities in Northern China during the 1930s. South Korea and China wasted no time in making vigorous protests against the Japanese government and the story was rapidly picked up by the Western press. In fact, an examination of the textbook shows that there had been no such change. A television reporter had mistakenly told colleagues of the 'revision' and they ran the story. Despite corrections, it has been difficult ever since to eradicate the common view that the Japanese government systematically allows history to be rewritten to cover up past wrongdoings.

Ironically, the extent to which Japanese school history books are revised is often the result of early post-War editions written by left-wing authors, strongly backed by the JTU, whose members taught students to boycott the national flag and anthem. These go almost too far the other way in excluding any comment on opposition to the militarists within pre-War Japan. Many textbook writers also presented the Western democracies in the harshest light, while being uncritically adulatory of communist ones such as that of North Korea.

What is certainly true is that, in general, controversy is avoided in Japanese textbooks. Where there are genuine differences of opinion, or where claims are difficult to verify, more than one view is presented. This in itself can lead to problems. In one case, for example, a textbook written by a famous historian, Ienaga Saburo, was judged to be too one-sided. Ienaga was asked to include alternative propositions but refused, so the book was not approved, a decision which was upheld in a subsequent court case. At least one survey by an American, William Cummings, concluded that as a result of this process, although some cases were debatable, on the whole textbooks 'presented a remarkably open-minded, even a progressive picture'.[15]

The West's preoccupation with the 'rewriting' episode is, moreover, somewhat one-sided. Few complaints, for example, are heard about the often partial history textbooks in other countries. Do, for example, Chinese school books mention the tens of millions of Chinese killed over the past 60 years by their fellow countrymen? Yet China is one of the main critics of Japanese history books.

新　大　国

Numerous studies have shown the vital connection between sound education and economic growth. In 1964, for example, Edward F Denison, who worked on the United States National Council on Economic Development, wrote a doctoral thesis analysing modern factors in productivity, concluding that the role of education was central. Shortly after, a study by the Department of Statistics of the US Bureau of Census found that education had been the single most important factor in economic growth in the middle years of the Twentieth Century – and that its importance was accelerating.

Many informed observers, moreover, have remarked on the close link between Japan's educational system and the country's economic success. In the 1960s, a French mission of inquiry observed that the average intellectual level of technical staff in Japanese factories was higher than in their French equivalents. The inquiry found that the Japanese foreman was the equivalent of the French assistant engineer and the Japanese assistant engineer up to the standard of a French full engineer.[16] At about the same time, *The Economist's* Norman Macrae wrote:

> The British visitor always feels a shock when he realizes what the greatest advantage of the Japanese is: it is that the level of education in the Japanese community is now higher than it is in Great Britain.

One of the great American authorities on Japan, the former American Ambassador, Professor Edwin Reischauer, noticed it, too:

> It is probable that there is no country in which the people have a greater longing for education .... The importance given to education and the successes that have been gained in this field seem to be taken for granted in Japan, so much so that some Japanese do not realize what great part they have played in the modernization of the country.[17]

But perhaps Japan's business rivals feel the gap most keenly. In 1989, a British parliamentary committee was told by an industrialist that 'the Japanese education system produced production line workers whom he would be happy to see in his development laboratories in Britian'.[18] And when Nissan set up its plant in Sunderland in Britain's north-east, it recruited some of the British motor industry's best production and engineering management, all of whom were 'amazed at the strength of their Japanese counterparts'.[19]

It is a shame, therefore, that analyses of Japan's breakneck post-War economic progress have tended to concentrate on supposed factors such as government intervention in industry, trade barriers and cheap labour. For no country can successfully develop economically without a skilled, educated and engaged workforce. The fact that Japan has such employees in abundance is, perhaps, the greatest factor in her economic achievement. And for that Japan owes much to both her current educational system and to her long tradition of curiosity and respect for learning.

4

GLIMPSES OF
UNFAMILIAR JAPAN

*'The people are tractable, civill, wittie, courteous, without deceit, in vertue
and honest conversation exceeding all other nations lately discovered, but so
much standing upon their reputation, that their chiefe Idole may be thought
honour. The contempt thereof causeth among them much discord and debate,
manslaughter and murther . . . . They live chiefly by fish, hearbes and fruites,
so healthfully that they die very old . . . . They feede moderately, but they
drink largely.'*
R Willes (c.1565), in Richard Hakluyt, *Principal Navigations of the English
Nation.*

ABOVE THE LOW-RISE, concrete mediocrity which typifies the fringes
of Japan's cities loom exalted cathedrals to two of the country's great leisure
passions: golf and sex. Vast domes of netting allow those Japanese who
cannot afford massive golf club fees to practise their shots safely, driving
one above the other off tiered structures which are often several storeys
high, allowing hundreds of players to use the range at the same time. Then
there are the conspicuously garish 'love hotels'. Always the very last word
in bad taste, these are often designed as pink pseudo-fairytale castles,
liberally adorned with purple neon hearts. Here Japanese men can take their
girlfriends, mistresses, prostitutes or wives for an hour, a night or a day of
fantasy away from their claustrophobic homes. Rooms decorated as medieval dungeons, nunneries, harems or *fin-de-siècle* bordellos offer the illusion
of their fancy and an escape from the drabness of the factory or office. For
in Japan – clean, pure, traditionalist Japan – sex for sale is considered very
much part of everyday life: unexceptional, ubiquitous and stacked high like
hi-fi equipment in an Akihabara electronics store.

You might be forgiven for thinking that a 'soapland' was a type of public
bath, and in a way you would be right. But Japan's many soaplands are

designed to satisfy a deeper need than outward cleanliness. Originally known as *tokuru*, Japlish for 'Turkish Bath', the possibly apocryphal story goes that after years of complaints from the Turkish Embassy, the Japanese government finally decreed that these seedy establishments could no longer sell their services using a name which was so demeaning to the Turkish nation. Not wholly coincidentally, several Japanese-led consortia were, at that time, bidding for large Turkish construction projects. When the alternative name 'soapland' was chosen, legions of civil servants issued forth, scuttling all over Japan's towns and cities to ensure that all *tokuru* signs were obliterated. Even so, it is said that provincials visiting Tokyo still sometimes call at the Turkish Embassy thinking it to be a place of pleasure – much to the irritation of the ambassador and his staff.

Activities such as these do not attract the same knee-jerk moral condemnation in Japan that is so common in the West. For despite their disciplined upbringing, the Japanese have less of a sense of sin and a more flexible demarcation between right and wrong than do Westerners. There are no Ten Commandments or lists of what you must or must not do. Moderation rather than interdiction is the key concept. To the Japanese, sex has always seemed to be a natural phenomenon, like eating or drinking, which is there to be enjoyed. Even drunkenness, so apparent in Japanese entertainment areas late at night, is looked upon indulgently as long as it does not get out of hand. Words spoken under the influence of alcohol are rarely taken into account and drunks are forgiven almost anything except drunken driving – but though hard drinking is very much part of the Japanese male social ethos, alcoholism and hard drug-taking have never been serious problems.

The lack of a clear moral sense extends into politics, where corruption has been endemic since the Meiji Restoration. It is a significant indication of Japanese attitudes that despite all of the fuss over the Recruit scandal in 1988–9 (which is dealt with in more detail later), when it came to the February 1990 election, most of the politicians involved in the bribery scandal were re-elected, even though the hapless architect of a new and unpopular sales tax, Sadanori Yamanaka, was thrown out despite 13 terms as a faithful and hard-working representative of the electors of Kagoshima in the deep south of Kyushu.

In part, this relaxed attitude to what many Japanese consider to be harmless or inevitable sin has its origin in religion – or rather the lack of it – for Japan has a long history both of secularism and relative religious tolerance. The Nineteenth-Century traveller, Isabella Bird, noted in her book, *Unbeaten Tracks in Japan*, that: 'The Japanese are the most irreligious people that I have ever seen – their pilgrimages are picnics, and their religious festivals fairs.'

More recently, the co-founder of Sony, Akio Morita, joked: 'We are Buddhists, Confucianists, Shintoists, and Christians, but we are also very pragmatic. We often joke that most Japanese are born Shinto, live a Confucian life, get married Christian-style, and have a Buddhist funeral.'[1] Although around 80 per cent of Japanese consider themselves to be Buddhist, the various sects of the creed co-exist harmoniously with what is still virtually the state religion of Shinto – 'the way of the gods,' an indigenous religion which emerged at the dawn of Japan's history. One reason for this mutual respect lies in the fact that when Buddhism first came to Japan from China in the Seventh Century, temples were often built in or adjacent to Shinto shrines. Though shrines and monasteries still dot the Japanese landscape, Shinto and Buddhism are for most people now a matter of custom rather than deeply held belief. This secularism results both from the virtual destruction of the politically powerful Buddhist institutions by the unifiers in the late Sixteenth Century who paved the way for two and a half centuries of centralized Tokugawa rule, as well as from the relentless attack by the Nineteenth-Century Meiji government which saw Buddhism as an element of the discredited past, standing in the way of the new political system.

Instead the Meiji reformers developed Shinto into a prop of the new order, supporting the historic Shinto shrines and building new ones, while at the same time changing the creed from something which was at least akin to a religion to an essentially synthetic creation deriving more from modern nationalism than from Shinto tradition – a transmutation which ultimately evolved into the frenzied 'State Shinto' of the 1930s and early 1940s. After the War, the occupying forces attacked Shinto which they regarded as a dangerous manifestation of xenophobia, following which it further declined during the post-War reaction against the militarism with which it had become closely associated. Shinto survives today mainly in the annual shrine festivals which retain some religious meaning in rural Japan, but which, in the cities, have now taken on the characteristics of somewhat self-conscious historical pageants.

This really only leaves Christianity to uphold the banner of moral rectitude. After promising beginnings following its introduction by Saint Francis Xavier in 1549, Christianity spread rapidly, attracting close to half a million converts by the turn of the century. The early Tokugawa shoguns, however, began to view the new creed with suspicion, especially when rivalry between the Jesuits and Franciscans began to threaten the nascent political unity they were trying to impose. Ruthless persecution created a large number of martyrs, but virtually wiped the religion out by 1638.

Although the prohibition was dropped in 1873 and religious toleration became a feature of the new Meiji state, Christianity spread only slowly: today its adherents number about two per cent of the population. Nonetheless, its influence is greater than mere numbers would suggest because Christians are strongly represented among the best-educated and leading elements in society. Christians also played a major role in education during the Meiji period and today a large percentage of private secondary schools and private universities are Christian foundations. Even so, Christian morals have to jostle with a smattering of Confucian ethics, Shinto tradition and Buddhist ideals, and have never approached the kind of underlying intellectual dominance which they still maintain in many Western countries.

A bumpy flight

Thai International's daily Flight 620 from Bangkok to Osaka via Manila was cruising at just under 30,000 feet as it entered Japanese airspace on 9

October 1986. The three-and-a-half-hour Manila–Osaka leg was on schedule and had been typically uneventful. Dusk was drawing in as, in preparation for the descent into Osaka, the stewardesses started clearing the last drinks and meals from the 247 passengers on board the brand new Airbus 300–600 series, standing aside as a squat, middle-aged Japanese gentleman, who had been drinking heavily throughout the flight, made his way unsteadily to the rear toilets.

A few moments later the aircraft was rocked by a shattering blast. As the cabin lost pressure and air rushed in, the yellow oxygen masks automatically dropped into place. Chaos ensued as the plane plunged to a few thousand feet and passengers who were not strapped in were hurled around the cabin, some falling into the cargo bay through a gaping hole which had opened up in the floor.

For ten, terrifying minutes Captain Amphole Hoymeekha struggled to regain control of his lurching plane. It was a miracle that he succeeded, landing his stricken jet at Osaka and allowing most passengers to escape with no worse than severe bruising. Their lives had been saved by a three-foot-square inspection hatch, designed to enable engineers to check the internal mechanism below the tailplane. It had blown out as the plane depressurized and had acted as a valve for the escaping air, so preventing the plane from breaking up and plunging into the sea.

Japanese Transport Ministry officials who investigated the near disaster were baffled. Mr Hiroshu Fujiwara, leading the team, reported that the wall of one of the rear toilets was riddled with small holes which had sheared the umbrella-shaped bulkhead separating the passenger cabin from the unpressurized tail section. Of the plane's three independent hydraulic control systems, two had ruptured; the Airbus landed on the undamaged third.

Metal fatigue was quickly ruled out as the plane had only completed a handful of flights. Next it was feared that a design error had been incorporated into the 600 series, a newly introduced stretched version of the long-serving and immensely reliable Airbus 300. When this theory was eliminated, the investigators turned to the possibility that the explosion had been caused by a faulty gas cylinder. Forensic tests soon showed, however, that a grenade was the culprit. Suspicion fell upon Mr Seiki Nakagawa, the gentleman occupying the toilet at the time of the explosion, who had been retrieved from an air vent into which he had been sucked when the plane depressurized.

Following interrogations with Mr Nakagawa, it transpired that he had been so drunk when he went to answer the call of nature that he had accidentally pulled the pin out of a grenade he was carrying, presumably mistaking it for his zip. Panic-stricken, the hapless Nakagawa tried to flush the grenade down the toilet bowl where it exploded. Nakagawa was later charged with attempted murder, a crime which he denied on the grounds that he was *non compos mentis* at the time of the incident.

In fact, the offending grenade was part of a consignment being smuggled into Japan by Nakagawa on a route commonly used by Japan's own special brand of mobster: the *yakuza*. Nakagawa's gang, the Suzuhide-gumi, an affiliate of the Yamaguchi-gumi, had hoped to use the weapons in a vicious gang war it was waging with a rival.

Ask a Japanese person whether their country has a crime problem and they will, with just a hint of smugness, reply in the negative. For unless pressed, they will not mention the close to 100,000 gangsters organized into powerful syndicates – the largest being the Yamaguchi-gumi with more than 20,000 members – which operate in large sections of the construction and entertainment industries, including the ubiquitous *pachinko* parlours where the Japanese play a type of vertical pinball, as well as many areas of legitimate business life. A sub-group of the *yakuza*, the *sokaiya*, for example, specializes in offering its services to companies wanting awkward questions suppressed at their annual general meetings.

Yakuza refers to the lowest numbers in a popular card game, and in the Edo period in the Eighteenth Century was the generic term used for gamblers, petty crooks and wasters. Under the Tokugawa, control of the expanding towns was maintained by a network of neighbourhood chiefs, usually local macho-men such as builders or firemen, called *machi-yakko*, who defended the town from marauding *samurai*. It is from these groups that the *yakuza* gangs originated. However, like most Robin Hood types throughout history, the *yakuza* owe their reputation less to deed than to legend: they were commonly portrayed as heroes in Eighteenth-Century plays, out of which arose the myth of the noble outlaw, tied to a code of honour vaguely related to the military *bushido*.

Yakuza flourished after the Meiji Restoration and, through leaders like Toyama, became closely associated with the militarists and nationalist idealogues who used their services. Toyama's career had begun at the time of the Restoration as a cunning 13-year-old yam peddler in Fukuoka, in the southern island of Kyushu. By guile and the judicious use of violence, he rose to become a leader of the labour bosses in the new industrial cities, employing as his henchmen masterless ex-*samurai* who had gravitated to the city slums and who were attracted by his leadership and prowess as a wrestler and swordsman.

A mere gangster to Western observers, Toyama appeared a patriot to many Japanese, who viewed his most shady and savage acts in terms of loyal deeds in the service of the Throne. Brazenly standing on street corners, Toyama would pass packets of bank notes to his devoted cut-throats and frequently stride into a rival's office with a scroll of signatures advising him to commit *hari-kiri*. On one occasion, a newspaper reporter, having finally been granted an interview with Toyama, was shown in to find the gangster on top of one of his mistresses and was forced to conduct his interview as the gangster continued his erotic manoeuvres. Toyama became Japan's premier 'arranger' and his services were sold to the highest bidder. When he died in his 90s, the *Tokyo Times* published a special supplement in his honour. The *yakuza* were also adept at moving with the times, however, and after the Second World War, when President Eisenhower visited Japan, Kodama, the main *yakuza* leader at that time, recruited an army of 28,000 *yakuza* and rightists to protect him.

Like American mobsters, current *yakuza* syndicates control the vice industry: prostitution, pornography, drugs and gambling. Half of the sizeable income of the *yakuza* – $9.3 billion annually by one estimate –

comes from drug dealing, particularly amphetamines which, known in Japan as the 'awakening drug', were popular both with kamikaze pilots and, in the aftermath of the Second World War, with people who took it to revive their drooping spirits in defeated Japan. The beginnings of *yakuza* control of the world of prostitution also occurred at the end of the War, when many women were sold by their families to service the United States military and when, soon after, prostitution was made illegal, facilitating its control by criminals.

Traditionally, Japanese politicians and police have proved remarkably indifferent to the *yakuza*, who brazenly wear lapel pins for identification, publish newspapers which feature legal advice and poetry and prominently display gang emblems over their offices. Some even see the *yakuza* as a necessary evil, requiring containment rather than eradication, although there have been instances of anti-*yakuza* movements in some areas.

Returning Japanese tourists and businessmen, when relating to friends and relatives their experiences overseas, are prone to shake their heads at the endemic violence of large Western cities. By contrast, Japanese crime figures are low and their streets are extremely safe. But in their midst, largely unrecorded in crime statistics and at an unknown cost, is an institution which belies the country's reputation as a tranquil haven free of crime and violence.

Japan's untouchables

Look carefully at the people on a Japanese street, and once you have got past the fact that virtually all Japanese have black hair and brown eyes, you begin to see as much variety as you would in New York, Paris or London. There are dark, round-faced, squat Japanese, akin to the southern Chinese or some Polynesians; taller, thin-faced Japanese with sallow skins, closer to the northern Chinese or Siberian peoples; and everything in-between. Descended as they are from ancestors of Siberian, Mongol, south-east Asian, Aboriginal and some Korean stock, this is not too surprising.

So perhaps the widespread, but not generally openly expressed, belief that Japan is, and always should be, racially homogenous, springs in part from inner doubts. For though the Japanese are undoubtedly the most culturally unified and homogenous large bloc of people in the world today, they are, in reality, a mongrel race. Like most other peoples, they are the product of long and largely unrecorded mixtures, with the major difference being that owing to Japan's relative isolation, this process largely ended some 2,000 years ago. None of which stops most Japanese clinging on to the myth of their own racial uniqueness, an attitude which manifests itself in the poor treatment often meted out to Koreans, whose country, ironically, acted as the medium for much of the culture which the Japanese received second-hand from China.

The Japanese see themselves as being a highly homogenous nation, a kind of vast extended family. They take pride and comfort in the notion of their purity and many have difficulty comprehending the Western concept of ethnic diversity. This attitude found rare public expression when in 1986 Japan's former Prime Minister, Yasuhiro Nakasone, made a speech in which he stated that Japan, as a monoracial society, was more intelligent than the multiracial United States and that the number of Blacks, Puerto Ricans and Mexicans in America lowered the average intelligence score – a statement which was predictably poorly received in the United States itself. Despite his subsequent 'heartfelt' apology, the Prime Minister's comment confirmed the worst suspicions of many people about Japanese attitudes and upped the paranoia meter by several points. In fact, attitudes of this type, although common, are rarely shown to Westerners, tending only to be discussed in the relative privacy of the home, club or work-place. Such sensitivity does not, however, extend to the 667,000 Koreans resident in Japan.

When Japan humbled the Russians in 1905, finally taking effective control of Korea, which she annexed in 1910, ending the 519-year reign of the Yi dynasty, many of Korea's mandarin class were uprooted and forcibly re-settled in Japan. More Koreans were imported after war with China broke out in 1937, when Japan experienced a severe manpower shortage. Koreans proved particularly useful in menial and dangerous jobs, such as in munitions factories, and were also used to help the military, rivalling their Japanese masters in brutality as prison-camp guards.

After the end of the Second World War, most of the Koreans had no family left in their native land or had homes stranded in the North, and so remained in Japan. Under current Japanese law, however, neither they nor their children can become Japanese citizens unless they marry a native. As many Japanese still despise the Koreans, such intermarriages are rare. In fact, prior to 1952, most resettled Koreans were able to attain Japanese citizenship, but in 1951 a committee of the Supreme Commander for Allied Powers had the Japanese government introduce an immigration control law as a measure against communist infiltration. When the law was enacted in 1952, people from the former colonies, including Korea, were stripped of their Japanese nationality.

As a result, pre-1952 Korean immigrants now have to carry an alien identification card at all times and renew it at three-yearly intervals. Their children are also rigidly screened to prove that they have a good reason to stay in Japan, even though they have no other homeland. They are the relatively privileged ones, however, for post-1952 arrivals have to renew their card annually. All such 'stateless' Koreans may only make two trips abroad during their lifetime if they wish to remain residents of Japan. Furthermore, Koreans have to give fingerprints when applying for passports – the Japanese do not.

Koreans can, nonetheless, prosper in Japan. Take the world's sixth richest man, Shin Kyuk Ho, who established his wealth by making 'Cowboy' chewing gum after the Second World War and staging promotional chew-off contests. He now owns the Lotte hotel and confectionery empire. But the nearly 700,000 people of Korean descent who live in Japan, many of whom were born there, live in the country only as second-class citizens.

Shabby treatment is not restricted to the Koreans, however. The largest minority in Japan is not an ethnic one: it consists of the invisible three million *eta*, who are as racially Japanese as the man on the Shinjuku subway. These *polluted ones* exist in Japan as untouchables, an underclass which is still to a substantial extent segregated from the rest of the nation. Also known by the euphemism '*burakumin*', literally '*hamlet dwellers*', the origins of the *eta* lie in the class of people which dealt with dead animals in pre-Meiji times.

Although many of those who could afford to did eat meat, and while *samurai* happily wore a light, tough armour made of wood or steel held together with leather thongs, Buddhist doctrine taught that eating meat was barbaric. So the curse of the *eta* fell on those who handled the dead – slaughterers, grave tenders, cobblers, tanners, leather workers, musical-instrument makers who used animal gut strings, and even candle-makers who used tallow.

During Tokugawa times the *eta* became a hereditary caste – even such outcasts who moved to 'clean' occupations still retained their *eta* stigma. The untouchables were subject to harsh discrimination, not allowed to wear shoes and confined to their ghettos and villages from sunset to sunrise. When they conducted business with others, they were made to fall to their knees before speaking. *Eta* people who entered Shinto shrines were often beaten and sometimes killed. After one such incident in 1859, the local magistrate said that the life of one *eta* was worth one-seventh of the life of a townsman. Unless seven *eta* were murdered, he could not punish a single townsman.

With the installation in 1868 of the Emperor Meiji, the ban on the eating of meat was officially ended and a government decree issued to terminate the legal restrictions on the *eta*. Few, however, recognized the new status and killings and anti-*eta* riots continued. Though the *eta* are physically indistinguishable from their fellow Japanese, they are even now subject to intolerance despite periodic government campaigns to eradicate discrimination.

About 17,000 *eta* still reside in ancestral *buraku* near Kyoto, while the rest mainly live in large city ghettos. I was informed by one young Japanese man that many people still avoid even speaking of the *eta*. 'They consider the mere mention of the name to be rude. Instead they splay the four fingers of the hand towards the ground to represent the four legs of an animal. Most people of my generation are unconcerned by the *eta* issue, but prejudice remains very much alive in the minds of the older generation. If I wanted to marry a girl of *eta* ancestry, my parents would probably disown me.'

It has become the hallmark of the 'Japanese conspiracy' school of writing to take the problems of the Koreans and *eta* in Japan as illustrations of the dangerous racism and ultra-nationalism which, it is maintained, typify the Japanese. But in truth, an unsympathetic or sensationalist author could make out similar cases for most Western countries, few of which are immune to racial or regional problems. Further, although the unpleasantness of some common Japanese attitudes should not be denied, they should also be put into the context of Japanese history and her relative isolation until the mid-Nineteenth Century. So it would be unwise to assume smugly that the Japanese have an especially bad problem. On the contrary, bearing in mind the hospitality and consideration with which foreigners are usually treated in the out-of-the-way parts of Japan, it can be shaming to see how poorly that welcome is sometimes reciprocated in the West.

Part III

Trade – Don't Do As I Do . . .

ASK ANY WESTERN politician or industrialist for examples of underhand Japanese trade practices, and telecommunications, Scotch whisky or cars are almost inevitably cited. For, deeply ingrained in Western perceptions of Japan is the belief that the Japanese have prospered by protecting their industries from foreign competition, using the security of their home base to attack Western markets.

In fact, contrary to received wisdom, the Japanese are neither particularly prolific exporters, nor especially protective of their domestic industries. Indeed, many of the most celebrated cases of supposed Japanese protectionism have been based on misunderstandings and sloppy reporting, while the West's own underhand trade practices are rarely covered in the media.

Nonetheless, the view of Japan as a predatory trader gives comfort to injured Western pride and provides ammunition for European and American industrialists who find it less taxing to lobby their governments for subsidies, protection and support than to tackle their own deficiencies. Indeed, one of the great ironies of the debate about Japan's business practices is that it is those very Western businesspeople who have been most cosseted by their own governments who complain loudest about Japanese wrongdoings. As so often in its dealings with Japan, the West's attitude seems to be: 'Don't do as I do, do as I say'.

5

新大国

CROSSED LINES

'I refer to the tendencies in men to blame their own misfortunes and those of their cultures on others: to exercise judgement they need for themselves on the lives of others; to search for a villain to explain everything that goes wrong in their private and collective courses. It is easy to be high-minded about the lives of others and afterwards to feel one has been high-minded in one's own.'
Laurens Van Der Post, *The Night of the New Moon.*

TRADE AND INDUSTRY question time in the oak-panelled, neo-gothic splendour of the British House of Commons is a monthly ritual when ministers from the government department can be queried for an hour by back-bench Members of Parliament. Question time on the afternoon of 25 March 1987 had not been especially eventful. MPs lounged in their accustomed style on the green leather benches of the half-empty chamber of the Commons, listening fitfully to inquiries ranging from regional grants to company law. Some talked distractedly among themselves, others read correspondence, some even dozed, until just before the allotted time was up, Alan Clark, the languid Minister for Trade, gave sudden vent to a fierce attack on the Japanese government's attitude to the attempt of a British company called Cable & Wireless to break into the Japanese telecommunications market.

The experience of Cable & Wireless, he said, in response to a question about Britain's trade balance, 'encapsulates the Japanese attitude and the difficulty of breaking into a most important sector'. The Minister continued by pointing out that 'a large number of British goods that would otherwise be competitive ... are excluded by government or quasi-governmental devices'. MPs started to perk up and, in a rare display of cross-party unity, members from both sides of the House rose to express their indignation at

Japanese deceit. One MP, probably epitomizing the mood of the Commons, even asserted that 'MITI and Japan are planning world domination through trade'. Asked if there was any evidence of improved access to the Japanese market, Mr Clark simply answered 'None'. An assenting clamour of 'hear, hear' rose from both sides of the chamber.

Speaking on the same subject in the House of Commons the next day, the Chancellor of the Exchequer, Nigel Lawson, stated that the 'shutting out of Cable & Wireless from an important contract in Japan is unacceptable'. The Prime Minister herself, Margaret Thatcher, later added: 'We see this as a test case of Japanese willingness to trade in a fair and balanced manner'. Media comment over subsequent days was predictably shrill in its condemnation of Japanese trade policies.

Behind the dispute, which had dragged on for more than a year, stood the enormous changes then underway in international telecommunications. Until the early 1980s, most transcontinental telephone connections were carried along broad cables of copper wires stretched along the sea bed, or by expensive satellites which bounced signals from one country to another. Both were almost invariably owned and operated by giant, monopolistic, state-owned telephone companies.

By the middle of the decade, however, things were beginning to change on both the technical and political levels. First, relatively low-cost optical-fibre cables made of hair-thin strands of glass-fibre, each of which could carry 100,000 simultaneous conversations in the form of pulses of light, were finally coming into their own after a decade of intensive development. Second, some governments were cautiously beginning to edge away from single, monopolistic telecommunications authorities to allow private operators to run the more diverse services being demanded by increasingly sophisticated consumers. Allied to this was the fact that satellite technology itself was falling in cost, enabling private operators such as Cable & Wireless – itself only just sold into the private sector by the British government – to build international digital highways which complement, as well as compete against, existing national and international networks.

Cable & Wireless' ambitious plan was to build what they called a 'Global Digital Highway', capable of yoking the world's three main financial markets: North America, Western Europe and the Far East. The company had already begun to develop the international alliances needed for such a project. In a joint venture with the New York and New England telephone operator, Nynex, it had agreed to share a cable across the Atlantic, which would continue on in a coast-to-coast connection over the American mainland, running along the tracks of the Missouri–Texas railroad before linking in with a Pacific leg at Seattle and Anchorage.

In April 1985, at about the same time as Cable & Wireless' far-reaching plan was beginning to take shape, the Japanese government decided to begin liberalizing its own telecommunications system by licensing a competitor for Kokusai Denshin Denwa (KDD), the Japanese monopoly operator for international calls. Ten per cent of KDD was owned by the state, ten per cent by Nippon Telegraph and Telephone (NTT) and the rest lay in private shareholders' hands. KDD complemented NTT, the monopoly internal telecommunications company which, at that time, was in the process of being privatized.

Spotting the chance to break into the Japanese international telephone market, forecast by KDD to be worth ¥560 billion (about £2 billion) by 1992, Cable & Wireless swiftly assembled a consortium called International Digital Communications (IDC). This included the powerful Japanese trading house of C Itoh which held 20 per cent of the equity, as did Cable & Wireless; Pacific Telesis International, the overseas arm of the American West Coast telephone operator was a major partner, as well as Merrill Lynch, Toyota, Hitachi and Fujitsu. However, just when it looked as if Cable & Wireless' agility had paid off, a second, purely Japanese group called International Telecom Japan (ITJ) sprung up, headed by the three powerful combines of Mitsui, Mitsubishi and Sumitomo. Soon after, the Japanese Ministry of Posts and Telecommunications (MPT) suggested that the two consortia merge, substantially diluting the stakes of Cable & Wireless and Pacific Telesis to around three per cent each. Hence the row, which involved Mrs Thatcher penning a plaintive letter to the then Japanese Prime Minister, Yasuhiro Nakasone, warning that a failure to compromise would bring retaliation against Japanese electronics exports as well as a cancellation of banking licences recently issued to allow Japanese organizations to operate in the City of London.

Many people in the City feared that not only would any withdrawal of banking licences for Japanese firms damage the City more than it would the Japanese, but also believed that the political reaction in Britain and the United States was seriously over the top and would actually damage Cable & Wireless' chances. They were wrong. The Japanese government reacted swiftly, making changes at the top of MPT which rapidly issued a licence to IDC allowing the consortium everything it had originally applied for. The only change was a slight reduction in the share of the two main participants from 20 per cent to 16.83 per cent each, with Pacific Telesis' equity being set at ten per cent.

Almost certainly behind the emergence of the all-Japanese ITJ consortium was the conservative and traditionalist Japanese MPT. Initially fiercely opposed to the deregulation and liberalization of Japan's telecommunications market, MPT had consistently intervened to ensure 'orderly deregulation'. Previously, for example, the ministry had argued that two competing car-phone consortia should merge, and it had subsequently forced a reduction in five proposed pocket-pager operators on the grounds that too many companies would lead to over-supply and bankruptcies. Sony's attempts to break into satellite communications had been disallowed on similar grounds. So bureaucratic conservatism and the fear of a 'free-for-all', rather than just protectionist sentiments, lay behind the MPT attitude.

Ranged against MPT in this incident, however, was the Japanese Ministry of Trade and Industry (MITI) and the Prime Minister, both concerned about increasing anti-Japanese feeling in the West. The powerful duo proved too much for the bureaucratic traditionalists, which is why the MPT political chiefs were replaced. One of the incoming politicians at the chastised MPT was Vice-Minister Katsuhiro Shirakawa, an ex-lawyer who represents one of the Osaka constituencies for the ruling Liberal Democratic

Party (LDP). He typifies the new breed of more outward-looking Japanese. A short, genial, powerful man, looking less than his 45 years, he prefers smart Western suits and a Burberry to the dowdy, poorly cut suits which were the common uniform of Japanese businessmen and politicians until recently.

In his panelled office in the relatively new and smart MPT building in Tokyo's Kumafasaui government quarter, which lies between the Imperial Palace and the Diet close to Hibiya Park, a tranquil oasis of cafés and trees where office workers and pigeons lunch and old men talk over past times, Shirakawa gave me a hint of the in-fighting which had resulted in the MPT climbdown. Over the statutory cups of green tea he told me:

> Our ministry had felt that the market was too small for two operators in addition to KDD. It considered that only five per cent of the international business would be available to the secondary networks, and hence at least one of them would have gone out of business. But whatever the reasoning behind the proposed merger, we have to face facts – things are changing and Japan has to be more international in outlook.

Despite the climbdown, on the face of it this stormy little affair seems to offer yet another example of devious, albeit unsuccessful on this occasion, Japanese attempts to exclude Western companies from her market. In fact the Cable & Wireless case illustrates just the opposite. By even allowing a foreign company to take a tiny share in her telecommunications market, Japan was opening her market further than most other developed nations, for the telecommunications networks in the majority of the industrialized West are still run by state-owned monopolies which jealously guard their own territories. These monopolies are nurtured and cosseted by ministries of posts and telecommunications (usually referred to simply as PTTs) every bit as conservative and protectionist as Japan's MPT.

There is, for example, simply no question in France, West Germany, Italy, Belgium, Holland, Spain, Sweden or Switzerland of a second telecommunications operator being allowed to supplement the main PTT, let alone one with a significant foreign shareholding. In Britain, alone of the major European nations, Mercury Communications, owned by Cable & Wireless, has been licensed to operate a second domestic and international network. But both Mercury and British Telecom (the main operator, which was privatized in 1984) have severe limitations on foreign participation or shareholdings.

Only the United States' telecommunications system is significantly more liberal than the new regime introduced by the Japanese government. Even there, the Federal Communications Commission retains powers to licence operators in a way that can still be restrictive of competition – each American city is at present served by only two cellular licences, for example – and the stakes of foreign companies in the national and international network operators are very small. So in fact, by allowing foreign participation of up to a third in their secondary international network franchisee, Japan's position is relatively liberal.

Cable & Wireless would certainly have stood no chance of any serious participation in the telecommunications system of any significant European country outside of the United Kingdom. In fact, so illiberal and protectionist are the European Community (EC – formerly known as the EEC, European Economic Community, sometimes also referred to as the Common Market) members in their attitude to telecommunications, which they habitually consider to be an indivisible part of their national sovereignty and prestige, that in 1988 the EC Commission, the Community's effective ruling body, had to publish a timetable for its member states' own telecommunications markets to be opened up to one another.

A subsidiary and associated complaint about the Japanese during the Cable & Wireless dispute concerned the fact that while Japan had, by the early 1980s, become a major exporter of telecommunications equipment, her market remained largely closed to imports of such products. The reason for this was the position of NTT and KDD as the monopoly operators until the mid-1980s. Ministers of Posts and Telecommunications and senior civil servants could expect lucrative posts with Japanese equipment suppliers after 'retirement', and hence were encouraged to place orders with local companies who accounted for the vast bulk of sales.

But Japan was in this respect little different to most other industrialized countries. In West Germany, for example, the giant Siemens electrical group virtually automatically wins the lion's share of orders for exchanges – the central switching systems which are the core of any telecommunications system. In France, Alcatel is in the same position; in Britain, until recently, a cosy cartel consisting of GEC, STC and Plessey worked in league with British Telecom to maintain control of the supply of exchange equipment; while in Canada, the largest telecommunications service provider, Bell Canada, has long maintained a preferred supplier relationship with Canada's main telecommunications manufacturer, Northern Telecom.

In the United States, prior to liberalization in the late 1970s, AT&T not only operated the telecommunications system but also produced almost all of the equipment, effectively freezing out foreign suppliers. Since the breakup of Ma Bell's near monopoly in the early 1980s, purchasing policy in America has been liberalized. Nonetheless, the vast majority of exchanges purchased by the AT&T regional operating companies in the 1980s have been of North American origin. When it comes to terminal equipment – telephone handsets, office exchanges, fax machines, etc – while both the United States and Britain now have a very liberal market, most of the Western European nations still maintain tight controls over sales of such equipment and to a large extent exclude Japanese suppliers from these fields.

The Japanese, by contrast, have at least taken steps to open their market up to imports of telecommunications equipment of all types over the past few years. Unfortunately for Western suppliers, the Japanese market is extremely competitive, with no fewer than three major suppliers of central exchanges vying bitterly with one another for orders, while the terminal equipment market is even more hotly contested. This, rather than significant remaining protectionism, accounts for the fact that imports of telecommunications equipment into Japan continue to be relatively small. Moreover, when in 1988 NTT published details of about 150 proposed procurements in the European Community's official journal, only seven applications to supply the equipment came from EC countries. Despite the political furore over the Cable & Wireless affair, the indisputable fact is that Japan is, and has for some time now, been far more open and less protectionist in her telecommunications market than the majority of her industrial competitors.

An expensive tipple

If you had walked into any of the small, proprietor-run grocery stores on the Ginza, one of Tokyo's premier shopping streets, early in 1988, you would have found neat piles of bitter Japanese *mikan* oranges alongside the delicious but expensive green musk melons which are commonly bought as wedding gifts. Towards the back of the store you would have seen shelves laden with liquor, including bottles of Ballantine's 12-year-old Scotch whisky on sale at ¥3,000 (£14) – about the same price as in Europe – and Japanese blended Suntory Special Reserve Scotch on offer at a similar cost.

Yet ask a British industrialist or politician for an example of Japanese protectionism and he or she will unhesitatingly quote Scotch whisky. James Moorhouse, a British Conservative Member of the European Parliament, for example, states in his pamphlet, *Righting the Balance – A New Agenda for Euro-Japanese Trade*, that 'a standard bottle [of Scotch] will normally be marketed at around $100, deluxe variants at much more', claiming that Japanese duty discriminates against Scotch and prices it out of the market.

How does this statement square with prices in the Ginza? The answer is that it does not, nor would it have done even before the appreciation of the yen in 1985–6 helped to bring down the price of imported Scotch. It is just an example of the type of hearsay so beloved by those who are convinced that the Japanese have triumphed only through a protectionist conspiracy.

It was at least true to say that the duty levied on Scotch whisky in Japan was, until recently, higher than on some other locally produced spirits, and this was what lay behind a widely misreported dispute between the Scotch whisky industry and the Japanese government. Germane to the argument is a basic cultural attitude. Most Western countries tax alcoholic drinks according to their strength – a legacy of the insistence on taxing an 'evil' product. The Japanese, however, take a more relaxed view, and have traditionally, and arguably more logically, imposed duty on alcohol according to price and quality rather than strength, on the progressive principle that if you can afford a more expensive drink, you can also manage to make a larger contribution to the nation's coffers. Thus a poor man's drink, such as crude *sake*, or the even rougher *shochu* (a type of vodka made from barley and potatoes), was taxed less heavily than the rich man's premium-grade Scotch – or, indeed, higher quality *sake* or locally produced whisky. Import duty is also imposed on imported whisky, but at around a mere 50 pence a bottle it is hardly significant.

There is, perhaps, the grain of an argument in the assertion that this tax system constituted an import barrier, designed to protect the many small Japanese *shochu* producers. Yet nothing prevented Scotch importers from selling rougher grades of their products at prices closer to that of *shochu*. But although bulk Scotch producers happily sold their cheaper spirit to Japanese companies for blending, the main Scotch distillers took the commercial decision to avoid selling very downmarket Scotch in the Japanese market in order to protect their prestige image. This largely dated back to the period after the Second World War when whisky was genuinely subject to high duties and quotas and gained a great deal of cachet and social status as a result.

So the price premium of Scotch over lower grade tipples, far from representing a problem, has been a significant advantage to the whisky producers. This is illustrated by the fact that as import restrictions were phased out after the Second World War and prices fell, Scotch sales failed to rise. Why? Because in Japan, the more expensively you drink, the higher the class to which you belong. When, for example, the lower-priced Johnnie Walker Red appeared alongside the premium Black brand (*Johnnie-kuro*), it failed to inspire the Japanese drinker. This was because to be seen drinking Red was an obvious signal that one was not of the status to be drinking Black.[1]

When in 1979, moreover, import procedures which had prevented unofficial importers from bringing in products in competition with exclusive agents were liberalized, so allowing 'parallel importers' to bring in products and undercut accredited shippers, and the main agents reduced prices to meet the new competition, Scotch whisky sales actually fell because the price reduction had effectively lowered its value as a gift.

In fact, this remains a problem for the main Scotch importers even now. A brand manager at Jardine Matheson Wines and Spirits, Japan's leading whisky importer, admitted to me that the main obstacle he now faced was not high prices, but low ones, due to the undercutting of the parallel importers. He gave me the example of one of his leading brands, White Horse Fine Old Scotch, which he wholesales for the recommended retail price of ¥4,150 (£18), but which the parallel importers can get into the shops for as little as ¥2,500 (£11).

The clear implications of this are first, that the Scotch importers could have cut their prices long ago; and second, the result of any changes in the tax structure to bring it in line with Western tax practice would not be lower Scotch prices in the shops, but rather higher profits for Scotch whisky importers who would see no advantage in cutting prices and would simply increase their margins – all of which rather undermines the argument that the Japanese were taxing Scotch out of the market.

In the event, the Japanese did reduce the tax on high-grade spirits. After a complaint on behalf of the Scotch distillers from the EC Commission, the General Agreement on Tariffs and Trade (GATT) surprisingly ruled in 1988 that the Japanese tax system was in fact unfair. GATT, which was founded in 1948, is a club of trading nations which aims to promote freer trade worldwide. Based in a sombre, grey headquarters overlooking Lake Geneva, GATT in fact has no official existence and was only created as a provisional body after the United States Congress refused to ratify proposals to create a more powerful body called the International Trade Organization. As its name indicates, GATT is an agreement and not an institution, with all the limitations that implies. It has 'contracting parties' rather than members and is the least powerful of the trio of economic bureaucracies created after the Second World War, the others being the International Monetary Fund and the World Bank. Although a positive force, GATT is not infallible and does rely to a large extent on trade-offs to placate its sponsors. In this instance, its ruling that the Japanese tax system did constitute an import barrier had to be a marginal one, although the Japanese government acceded to the verdict and agreed to equalize spirit duties.

If the tax system really had significantly forced up Scotch prices and had been an impediment to sales, the GATT-induced tax changes introduced early in 1989 should have resulted in price reductions. In fact, despite a ¥688 (£3) tax cut on a 750ml bottle of Bell's, the importers maintained the retail price at ¥3,200 (£14). So ironically, the result of years of hard lobbying looked like being no price reduction at all on some brands – at least until Japan's National Tax Administration Agency, presumably hardly able to contain their glee, told the importers to cut their prices by the amount of the tax reduction. In fairness, one main agent did decide for competitive reasons to cut the price of Johnnie Walker Black Label by a full ¥2,000 to ¥6,000 (£24), despite the fact that the tax break was only ¥607 (£2.50),[2] but this was largely because many outlets were already making a nonsense of the list price by heavily discounting it – which simply illustrates the fat margins the importers had enjoyed and the dubious nature of their complaints against the tax system.

The conclusions should be obvious. First, Japan's idiosyncratic system of taxing spirits actually made very little difference to Scotch prices. Rather, the main reason for high Scotch prices was the margins maintained by the accredited agents, as evidenced both by the low prices charged by parallel importers and the large reduction which the Johnnie Walker agents were able to make when they had to. Moreover, high prices were probably an advantage in the status-conscious Japanese market. Indeed, the position of Scotch is probably far more threatened by downward price pressure caused by the tax cuts and pirate importers than by any import barriers, supposed or otherwise – which may be why a new 15-year-old blend of Johnnie Walker called Gold Label is now being launched, selling for ¥10,000 (£40) a bottle and available only from retail outlets in Japan.

In fact, as an example of Japanese protectionism Scotch whisky has to be a particularly bad one, despite all the media attention it has received in the West. Indeed, some of Britain's EC partners have discriminated far more against Scotch than the Japanese. Until recently France, for example, subdivided spirits into those produced from wine and those derived from grain. Taxation on the latter, the vast majority of which were imported, was far higher than the duty levied on grape-based spirits, with one exception – 'Geneva' (a spirit distilled from grain flavoured with juniper berries), which, it just so happened, was produced in France.

Furthermore, the French Code on the Retailing of Beverages and Measures against Alcoholism divided alcoholic drinks into five groups. Group Five consists primarily of aniseed-based aperitifs, which are included for the harmful presence of acethol, together with mainly imported products, including whisky, which does not contain acethol. Products in the fifth group were only allowed to be advertised under very strict conditions.

Italy also maintained discriminative tax arrangements which favoured liquors distilled from wine and grape waste, and against spirits obtained from cereals and sugar cane, most of which are imported. Furthermore, the value-added-tax (VAT) rate levied on grape-based brandy was 20 per cent, compared to 38 per cent on mainly imported gin and whisky. Italy also imposed a special frontier surcharge on spirits distilled from grain. West Germany prevented the import of French *crème de cassis* on the grounds that it was too alcoholic to be classified as a wine, but not strong enough to be a liqueur. Bonn even, for a time, blocked imports of still mineral water on the grounds that bubbles were needed to kill micro-organisms.

Only after the EC Commission took France, Germany and Italy to the European Court did these countries end such blatantly prejudiced treatment of foreign spirits, which largely discriminated against fellow members of the Common Market. And such barriers are not restricted to Europe, for only after a GATT ruling did Canada agree to end the system whereby provincial liquor boards had a monopoly on the import of foreign alcoholic drinks. They refused to stock many items and, where they did, charged far higher mark-ups on foreign brands than they did on domestic products – a practice which particularly hit imports of American beer, despite Canada's huge trade surplus with its mighty neighbour. Yet you rarely, if ever, hear complaints about French, Italian, German or Canadian barriers to liquor imports.

Japanese snow

In August 1986, the Japanese Consumer Product Safety Association suddenly announced that standards for ski equipment would be changed with immediate effect. A special voluntary quality label, called the 'SG-mark', would henceforth be reserved for products that met the specific requirements of Japanese conditions. The move rapidly took on a ridiculous dimension when a spokesman somewhat absurdly stated that the new standard was needed because of the distinctly different properties of Japanese snow.

Needless to say the hapless official's comments were gleefully seized upon by Western reporters while European and American ski companies were outraged. Although there was no question of a ban on foreign skis, Western manufacturers felt that the new mark would be a selling point and meeting the new conditions, they said, would entail either interfering with their production lines or cutting down on exports in a market where foreign firms accounted for about half of the $500-million ski equipment sales. One correspondent to the *Financial Times* urged retaliation in the form of curbing Japanese imports, suggesting that if special Japanese skis needed to be developed for use on Japanese snow, so 'we must assume that . . . they would be totally unsuitable for use in Europe and America and should be banned from sale on those continents'. Western governments were urged by the ski-makers to make representations to GATT and, after much-publicized discussions, Japan reluctantly agreed to withdraw the new standards with effect from late 1987.

On the face of it, this is a blatant, if bizarre, example of Japanese protectionism. But there is more to this story than that reported in the Western media, since little mention was made of a dispute which had arisen between the two main Western standards bodies, ISO and DIN, on ski quality. The Japanese, rather than wait for this to be resolved, had simply decided to introduce their own standard. Of course, foreign manufacturers were welcome to accede to it, in the same way that Japanese manufacturers would be expected to comply with Western standards if they wanted to sell to Europe or North America.

It might be asked how, in a reverse situation, the Germans or French would have reacted if the Japanese had insisted that they use a Japanese standard on their home market. For, in effect, the Western ski-makers were asking the Japanese to use a European or American standard in their domestic market. In the context of Japan's export surpluses and growing trade tensions, of course, the decision to promote a Japanese ski mark was, at worst, a foolish one, but probably no more than that. Unfortunately, the ski saga has now entered the realms of mythology, and is periodically trotted out by journalists and politicians as yet another example of devious Japanese trade practices.

新　大　国

One-sided media comment on trade conflicts with Japan may help to provide a convenient scapegoat on which Western business leaders and politicians can vent frustration for their failures. Such reporting also provides useful ammunition for the powerful industrial lobbies seeking protection from Japanese competition and yet more subsidies. But each new dispute enters the national consciousness, and even after the squabble has died down, public opinion on the Japanese never quite returns to normal, merely helping to set a scene of animosity and distrust for the next round and encouraging some journalists in their quest for yet more examples of oriental deceit.

In his book *Second to None – American Companies in Japan,*[3] the former senior editor of *Time* magazine, Robert Christopher, quotes Kneale Ashworth, the head of Johnson & Johnson's Japanese operation:

Not long ago, a reporter for the *New York Times* came to see me, sat himself down . . . and said: 'Tell me about non-tariff barriers that Johnson & Johnson face here in Japan'. When I told him we didn't face any, he said: 'I beg your pardon'. So I said again: 'We don't face any non-tariff barriers. We've got lots of problems, but that isn't one of them.' With that, he shut his notebook and got up to leave. I was a bit surprised and asked him: 'Don't you want to hear the good news?' He said: 'No, I just want to hear about non-tariff barriers' – and away he went.

新大国 6

TRADE WARS

'Defeated soldiers in their own defence have to protest that their adversary was something out of the ordinary, that he had all the advantages of preparation, equipment, and terrain, and that they themselves suffered from every corresponding hardship. The harder they have run away, the more they must exaggerate the unfair superiority of the enemy.'
Field-Marshal Slim, Allied Commander in Burma 1942–5.[1]

ONE OF THE most widely held beliefs about the Japanese is that they are super-exporters who protect their home market to give themselves a secure base from which to launch withering assaults on Western industries. Apart from formal trade barriers, so the received wisdom goes, the Japanese are adept at using informal 'administrative guidance' to hinder imports, on top of which their labyrinthine distribution system acts as a disincentive to importers. Further, the Japanese people themselves have a deep cultural bias against foreign goods.

How do these assumptions stack up? Despite their reputation for being highly successful exporters, the Japanese in fact fare pretty badly by international comparison. At the peak of trade tensions in 1988, figures produced by the Organization for Economic Co-operation and Development (OECD), the research and advisory grouping of 23 westernized industrial nations, showed that Japan managed to beat only the United States in terms of the percentage of her gross domestic product (GDP) taken up by exports. Moreover, at 9.3 per cent of GDP, Japan's figure was less than half that of Canada, West Germany, Sweden, Switzerland, Denmark, Iceland, New Zealand, Austria, Finland, Norway and Portugal. It was also far lower than the figure for Britain, even excluding oil exports, and only a fifth of the totals for Belgium and Ireland, both of which exported more than half of their GDP.

The objection could, of course, be made that as Japan's GDP is so large, it is irrelevant that she exports only a low proportion of it. In that case, exports per head of population would be a fairer guide. But even there, Japan ranked only seventeenth out of the 23 OECD nations, beating Turkey, Portugal, Spain, Greece, Australia and New Zealand, and outsold by countries as diverse as Switzerland, Britain and Ireland. Canadians, Austrians, Germans, Swedes, Finns and Danes, in fact, exported about twice as much per head as the Japanese, while the Swiss, Dutch and Belgians each sold three times as much abroad.[2]

Nor, taking into account the large size of her population, is Japan even substantially responsible for the huge trade deficits run by the United States since the early 1980s. In 1984, for example, Japan, with a population of just over 120 million, ran a bilateral surplus with the United States of $36.795 billion, while Canada, with only 25 million people, exported no less than $20.387 billion more to the United States than it imported. Tiny Hong Kong, with a population of 5.5 million, did even better relative to its size, running a surplus of $5.837 billion.

Further, in terms of overall sales, Japan is soundly beaten in export markets by the United States, which sent $364 billion worth of goods overseas in 1989 compared to Japan's $275 billion. West Germany also outsells Japan, managing $341 billion worth of overseas sales despite having a population only half the size of Japan's.[3] Yet few politicians or commentators complain about German surpluses. It is also worth pointing out one largely ignored fact: namely that Japan runs a large deficit on its services – areas such as shipping, transport, travel and insurance. This deficit was a massive $24 billion in 1987 according to GATT figures.

Some people argue that, although Japan's exports may not be as high as they are sometimes made out to be, her imports are very low: indeed, Japan comes eighteenth in the OECD imports per capita table and bottom on the basis of imports as a percentage of GDP. The reasons for this are complex. Trade barriers do play a part, but so do other factors. First, Japan has a relatively large and rich domestic market – as a rule, the larger the home market, the lower the imports in relation to GNP become. This is because bigger economies tend to supply more goods internally whereas smaller ones, such as Holland and Belgium, cannot do so as easily and so both import and export more as a proportion of their overall production.

Moreover, Japan's relatively isolated geographic position tends to inhibit imports – especially of manufactures. In this respect Japan is in a similar position to Australia and New Zealand which also demonstrate low levels of manufactured imports. Then there is the competitiveness of Japan's industry and economy which undoubtedly makes life difficult for Western goods (in this last regard, Japan's low propensity to import is not so very different from that of the United States in the 1950s).

It is also often argued that low Japanese domestic demand has inhibited imports. Although there is an undoubted element of truth in this, by the same token many Western countries, and particularly the United States, have consumed too much and hence sucked in imports. At least in recent years the Japanese have taken steps to increase their domestic demand, while

America appears to have done little to address the problems of a society living beyond its means.

Japan has also been criticized for the fact that she has traditionally imported more commodities than manufactured goods: oil alone accounts for about a fifth of her total import bill and she is the world's largest importer of fuel and food. In 1985, the Japanese imported only $347 of manufactures per head, compared to $1,078 in the United States – in fact, Japan's total imports of manufactured goods that year were lower than in the Netherlands – while her exports were predominantly in the manufactured sector.

This, however, is no more than might be expected of a country with few natural resources apart from her inhabitants. Japan has little to export except what she makes and has to import virtually all of her essential raw materials. There is not an ounce of cotton in Japanese textiles, not a scrap of metal in her cars, railcars or bridges which Japan does not have to buy in from distant countries. She also imports 99 per cent of her oil, all of her nickel, tin, phosphates and bauxite, half of her food and a high proportion of her coal, coke, lead and potash. As overall imports grow, however, the situation is changing rapidly and purchases of foreign manufactured goods are rising fast. By 1988, 50 per cent of Japan's imports were of manufactured goods, compared with only 20 per cent in 1980, while sales of imported manufactured goods rose by 80 per cent between 1985 and 1989 (car imports, for example, surged by 35 per cent to 182,000 units in 1989).

Targeting

Many commentators have regarded the preponderance of certain products in Japan's exports as part of a concerted policy by Japanese companies – guided by government policies – to 'target' Western industries. It is certainly true that Japan's exports are concentrated disproportionately in sensitive areas. In the early 1970s they consisted of ships, steel, radios, TVs, tape recorders, synthetic cloth, toys and cameras. Now it is vehicles (25 per cent of Japan's exports), office information and telecommunications products (20 per cent), electronic components, machine tools and consumer electronics.

But the important point about Japan's export industries is that they did not necessarily start out selling overseas. In 1966, only 14 per cent of cars and colour TVs, 27 per cent of steel and 40 per cent of Japanese motor cycles were exported.[4] Such industries arose from rapid growth in Japan's large and intensely competitive domestic market for consumer and industrial goods which led to economies of scale, cost reductions and high-quality products. This, in turn, has militated for successful exporting which has tended to begin during periods when domestic demand has been saturated.

It is easy for Westerners to grow purple in the face about the success Japan has achieved in export markets for some products and to impute their 'targeting' of certain industries to all kinds of evil motives. But all the Japanese have done in export markets is sensibly to concentrate on those areas where their comparative advantage over Western producers is greatest. Put simply, the Japanese have sold what has been easiest for them to sell.

The OECD's 1988-9 *Economic Survey on Japan*, for example, pointed out that the country's strong export performance in certain industries had been underpinned by 'strong price competitiveness, high quality and an outstanding ability to adapt to change in world demand'. The same survey, incidentally, also examined the issue of Japan's relatively low level of imports and found that 'there is little evidence in general to support the contention that import impediments (either formal or informal) imposed by the government are a decisive factor' in the country's trade surpluses.

One common refrain is that Japan must be protectionist because her surpluses are so large. A little history should cure that. For most of the 1950s and the first half of the 1960s the United States actually ran a significant trading surplus with the Japanese. Does this mean therefore that Japan was then open and the United States protectionist? Far from it. In those days, the Japanese were far more protectionist than they are now. Yet as the Japanese opened their markets more and more in the 1970s and 1980s and the Americans began erecting trade barriers at an accelerating rate, the American trade deficit with Japan grew and grew. A country which maintains a trade surplus is not necessarily protectionist.

In fact, American exports to Japan actually expanded very rapidly from $843.8 million in 1958 to $4,652 million in 1970 – a fivefold increase. This could not have happened if Japan was as protectionist as many people have made out. The problem for the United States was that Japan's sales to America grew tenfold during the same period. More recently, in 1989, Japan imported far more from the United States than did West Germany, Italy and France combined, even though the combined GNP and population of these countries is larger than that of Japan. Again the difficulty was that America imported even more from Japan – all of which should indicate that the real problem is not trade barriers, but a relative decline in American competitiveness. Matters are seldom as simple as they at first appear.

It is also worth noting the enormous help given to Japanese exporters by Western companies which have often made the conscious decision to concede the superiority of Japanese manufactures. Japanese photocopiers, cars, personal computers, electronic typewriters, pickup trucks, printers, fax machines, televisions, music centres and machine tools have all been distributed in vast quantities bearing well-known American and European brand names such as Xerox, IBM, Chevrolet, RCA, Olivetti, Gestetner, Ford, Philips and Siemens, to name but a few. Indeed, in 1985, about one-third of the total Japanese sales to the United States were of products branded with American names. It is these factors, rather than deep conspiracies, which lie behind Japan's export success in certain industries.

A hungry attitude

The Clean Air Act, passed by the United States Government in the early 1970s, had severe implications for car manufacturers, especially foreign ones, for it meant they would have to specially adapt their cars for the American market. At the time, the Toyota chairman, Eiji Toyoda, on being asked by the chairman of Renault of France what he thought of the new legislation, replied that it was a 'disaster'. The Renault boss responded by saying: 'I refuse to pay any attention to a country that does such idiotic things. Renault is going to stop exports to the United States.' And it did. The French car maker simply gave up selling Renaults in America until the late 1970s, when it resumed sales with only limited success. Toyota, on the other hand, fitted its cars with catalytic converters and managed to carve out a huge and profitable market in America.[5]

Toyota's export effort in the United States was assisted by the lethargy of its Western rivals. Except for Volkswagen, none of the volume European manufacturers was prepared to make the heavy investment in marketing and distribution necessary for the huge American market, while Detroit failed to develop a really competitive subcompact car and even Volkswagen was slow in replacing the Beetle in the early 1970s. Japanese manufacturers had no such inhibitions and were able to capture a large part of the booming American small-car market.

So, when considering Japan's export success in certain key areas, you also have to look closely at the attitudes of both Japanese and Western industry and compare the willingness of the Japanese to tackle export markets aggressively and flexibly. In the early 1980s, for example, Honda and Britain's then state-owned motor group, British Leyland, agreed jointly to develop an executive car code-named the XX. Honda launched its version – the Legend – in 1985 and immediately began marketing it in the United States. By 1988, the Japanese company had achieved American sales of close to 100,000. By contrast, the British company did not get into production until 1986 and only began exporting its version – the Sterling – to America a year later. With sales of just over 10,000 in 1989, the Sterling never did emulate the success of its Japanese sibling.

Consider, too, the fact that in 1989 *Car and Driver* magazine recognized nine out of the ten best cars sold in America to be Japanese, while in the same year a Japanese model was the bestseller on the American market. As the Sony founder, Akio Morita, once asked his American host who had been complaining about Japan being 'unfair', but whose house was full of Japanese products: 'Are you asking us to buy something you won't buy yourself?'

A less hungry attitude to exports has, of course, also affected sales of Western companies' products in Japan itself. When Akio Morita set up a company to sell American products in Japan, Whirlpool was one of the American companies to come forward with its refrigerators. Unfortunately, the Whirlpool products ran on the American voltage system, but it took the company five long years to begin replacing the standard American motor with one usable in Japan. Until they did so, Morita's company had to install a voltage converter in each unit shipped.[6]

Contrast, too, the differing attitudes of various Western countries towards selling in Japan. While, in the 1970s, American car manufacturers sold about 20,000 cars a year in the Japanese market, by 1984 sales had plummeted to a mere 2,000. But over the same period sales of European cars soared: by 1990, they were rising at an annual rate of around 60 per cent. By then, the combined imports of the Big Three American car makers in Japan had been overtaken by those of Britain's Rover group alone. If trade barriers prevented American car makers from selling in Japan, why did they not also stop BMW, Rover, Mercedes, Jaguar and Volkswagen? Perhaps part of the answer lies in the fact that these companies took the trouble to build up sales and service organizations and actually supplied right-hand drive cars, which GM, Ford and Chrysler never bothered to do. This also helps to explain why America's trade deficit with Japan has been worse than other countries and why, between 1985 and 1989, America's share of the rapidly growing Japanese import market slipped from 35 to 26 per cent.

Whose fault?

Of course, the question remains as to whether Japan would import even more if it were not for trade barriers – visible or otherwise. Japan did maintain a protectionist policy in the 1950s and 1960s when she was rebuilding her war-shattered economy. But even then, Japan was rather less protectionist than most developing countries and not very much more so than some developed ones at that time. By the mid-1970s, however, only imports of food and some minor manufactures were still limited by quota, while duties were generally in line with those prevailing in Europe.

Despite these substantial market-opening measures, Japan is still a difficult market in which to sell. But this is largely on account of its competitiveness and quality-oriented nature, which many people persist in erroneously confusing with protectionism. In fact, by 1981 Japan retained only five import quotas in the mining and manufacturing sector, compared to 27 in France, six in the United States and five in Italy. A decade earlier, Japan had maintained 35 such quotas, making her joint equal top of the developed countries with France.[7]

Moreover, as a result of trade frictions caused by the increase in Japan's trade surpluses in the 1980s, the Japanese government actually took significant steps – at least on the surface – towards encouraging imports, something which few other countries have done. In January 1982, for example, as part of a package of market-opening measures, the Japanese government set up an Office of the Trade Ombudsman (OTO) to adjudicate in individual trade disputes. Moreover, the Japan External Trade Organization (JETRO), which was originally created to promote Japanese goods abroad, has now largely reversed its role and concentrates primarily on helping foreign firms to do business in Japan.

Perhaps the best arbiter of whether or not Japanese trade restrictions have been the real cause of American trade deficits is the United States Federal Trade Commission (FTC) itself. In June 1987, it released a study on protectionism, which included an admission that the United States trade deficit had been largely caused not by unfair foreign trade barriers, but by internal American factors such as the high dollar and rapid growth within the United States. The FTC report went on to argue against the erection of trade barriers by the United States.

It is also worth noting the point made by the Washington-based Institute for International Economics. In a study published in mid-1985, the Institute estimated that the United States might sell an additional $5 billion to $8 billion worth of goods a year to the Japanese market if Japan were to dismantle 'all overt and intangible barriers against American products'. The

American deficit with Japan that year was close to $60 billion. But the report went on to point out that the United States itself excluded about $4.3 billion worth of Japanese goods each year through a variety of protectionist mechanisms. This may explain why former United States Trade Representative, William Brock, confessed to having a 'nightmare' in which 'the Japanese do all the things we ask them to do – and nothing changes', a point which was later stressed when Brock conceded that in his judgement two-thirds to three-quarters of the United States trade deficit with Japan 'is our own fault'.[8]

Rolling a ball downhill?

There is a tendency toward self-righteousness in much Western comment on Japan's trading performance. Take, for example, this comment in the best-selling book, *Trading Places*: 'The problem is that Japan's prosperity rests on the United States-sponsored free-trade system.'[9] Or the assertion by James Fallows in *The Atlantic*:

> The difference [between the US and Japan] is the natural tendency of the system. The United States, putting the consumer's interest first, naturally buys up whatever offers the best value . . . . Selling to America is like rolling a ball downhill.

How do these remarks stack up? The Washington Institute for International Economics study offers a clue. Many writers on Japan seem to ignore just how guilty almost all Western countries – yes, including, or maybe especially the Land of the Free – are when it comes to discriminating against imports. So the main purpose of this chapter is not to deny that the Japanese have been protectionist – particularly in the past – but rather to point out first, that the extent of Japanese import restrictions has been exaggerated for self-serving reasons by politicians and industrialists, abetted by misleading reporting; and second, that the West itself is and has been protectionist to an extent that is seldom realized and rarely mentioned in the media.

Few people realize, for example, that in recent years citizens of most EC countries have paid substantially more for their cars, video recorders, microcomputers, telephones, televisions, compact disc players and clothes, among other items, as a result of national or EC-wide import controls, quotas or high tariffs. Indeed, in 1987, EC Commission officials admitted that a variety of internal barriers between the supposedly mutually open national markets of EC countries alone was costing no less than £83 billion a year. Americans have also paid over the odds for a wide range of products including clothes, cars and electronic goods, as a result of their import restrictions.

Of course, on the face of it, the need to maintain a liberal, free-trading, international economy to preclude a return to the dark days of the 1930s has been the stated policy of most Western – and particularly American – leaders since the Second World War. With bipartisan regularity, American Presidents since Roosevelt have proclaimed the virtues of free trade.

Unfortunately, although they have inaugurated bold international pro-grammes to reduce tariff and non-tariff barriers, most Presidents have, in the same breath, accepted special measures to protect problem American industries.

In the post-Second World War era, for example, Presidents Eisenhower and Kennedy launched America into a new sphere of protectionism, first with 'voluntary' restraints on Japanese exports of cotton textiles in the 1950s which later developed into the Short-Term and Long-Term Cotton Textile Arrangements, and then with mandatory controls on all textile imports. Following on from that, President Johnson ushered in the appara-tus for restricting meat imports; steel imports were restrained under President Nixon and tightened still further by President Ford; textile and footwear imports were further limited under President Carter; while, during his first term, President Reagan responded to further pressure from the textile and steel industries and added automobiles to the long list of foreign products which were denied free access to the American market. Indeed, whatever its rhetoric, the Reagan Administration was the most protectionist since President Hoover.

This contradiction between word and deed has been largely the result of tensions caused by the division of power between a constituent-minded Congress and a globally-inclined President. For while the President has tended to come out against trade restrictions wherever possible, it has been Congress – particularly in recent years – which has triumphed on trade issues.

Pressure for protection in the United States has usually been initiated from below, its greatest advocate being the large industrial labour unions which, throughout the 1980s, have devoted considerable efforts to retaking control of the Senate for the Democratic Party. Very simply, this has meant that a great many new Democratic Senators owe a strong allegiance and loyalty to organized labour. So when a union like the Teamsters, the biggest in the United States, runs million dollar advertising campaigns urging people to 'Buy American', it can be imagined what they will be saying to every Democratic Senator whose election they supported.

That is not all, for anti-Japanese, pro-protectionist sentiment has been used by Congressional and Senatorial candidates to prove their strong sense of patriotism to their electors: this was how Senators Danforth and Packwood became household names. The issue has been particularly exploited by candidates running in states with high unemployment, especially where large numbers of people drive Japanese cars. In August 1985, for example, a Texan Democrat used the imports issue to triumph in a very tight race for a Congressional seat. Nor do Democrats have a monopoly on guilt in this respect. Republicans are not immune to political pressures and the need to be elected. During the 1968 Presidential contest, for example, Richard Nixon promised relief from imports to Southern textile manufacturers if he was elected.

These are the types of pressure which have provided much of the impetus for growing import restrictions in the United States and the West in general. For industrial lobbies have almost always been more powerful and vociferous than those of the more diffuse and shapeless consumer groups which have been harmed by trade restraints; furthermore, those consumers have often themselves been infected by anti-Japanese sentiment. Almost invariably, therefore, it has been the protectionist lobby which has won hands down.

Bikes, cars, trains and steel ...

Examples of such protectionism in the United States and in the West in general, rarely more in reality than a soft-option response to Japanese competition, are so legion that a whole book could be devoted to them – perhaps a good title would be *The Western Conspiracy*. Let just some random examples of recent Western import restrictions – mostly against Japan – suffice:

- America was motor-bike mad in the mid-1970s, which should have been good news for Harley–Davidson, the last American motor-cycle maker whose products were an institution, their raw power a macho-symbol to the legions of fanatically devoted owners. But despite trebling production to 75,000 by the late 1970s, quality deteriorated and more than half the cycles came off the line missing parts. The boast that Harley's roar made other bikes sound like effete sewing machines rang increasingly hollow as bikers found that those despised Japanese machines offered smoother power and greater reliability for less money than the all-American product.

   Harley should really have gone out of business, but on 1 September 1982, the Harley–Davidson Motor Company filed a petition to the United States International Trade Commission (USITC) asking for a restriction on motor-cycle imports. The Commission recommended an increase in duties for a five-year period, beginning at 45 per cent in the first year of protection and falling to ten per cent in the fifth year. President Reagan accepted the USITC recommendation and announced the implementation of increased duties and imposition of tariff-rate quotas (TRQ) by which imports above a certain level were subject to high tariffs. These applied to all motor cycles with a capacity of 700cc and over, despite the fact that Harley–Davidson sold few motor cycles smaller than 1000cc.

   The way in which the TRQs were allocated discriminated against Japanese imports in favour of those from European manufacturers. The TRQ for West Germany, which accounted for only 0.4 per cent of American motor cycle imports in 1981, started at 5,000 units in 1983 and increased to 10,000 units by 1988. For Japan, which in 1981 accounted for 93 per cent of motor cycle imports, the TRQ was a mere 1,000 units higher than West Germany's. In the event, the tariffs and quotas were removed a year early in 1987 after Harley–Davidson announced that it no longer needed relief.

- On 12 June 1980, the United Auto Workers (UAW) filed a petition with USITC claiming that the domestic motor industry was being seriously injured by foreign imports. Before long, the Ford Motor

Company joined the union as a co-petitioner for import relief, while President Carter also requested the Commission to accelerate its investigation. The petitioners specifically sought to have Canadian imports excluded from the investigation, arguing that such imports were produced almost exclusively by subsidiaries of United States companies. However, on 10 November 1980, the USITC determined that automobiles and light trucks were *not* being imported into the United States in such a way as to be a substantial cause of injury to the domestic industry and found that the failure of American manufacturers to adjust sufficiently to increased demand for smaller, more fuel-efficient vehicles was a major cause of the problem.

Despite the decision, the auto industry appealed to President Carter for trade restrictions. Although this pressure was initially resisted, by early 1981 legislation to restrict Japanese imports was gaining broad support in Congress. In April 1981, following meetings with American trade officials, the Japanese trade industry, MITI, agreed to proposals for 'voluntary' restraints of auto exports to the United States to allow its industry time to become competitive. The next month, an agreement was reached restraining Japanese imports to 1.68 million units for the subsequent year. A later agreement also restricted imports of four-wheel drives to 82,500 units.

At the end of the first year of restriction, and under severe pressure, Japan agreed to renew the Voluntary Restraint Agreement (VRA) for a further year (which was repeated again in 1983 and 1984). In October of that year, Ford, Chrysler, American Motors and the UAW urged the Reagan administration to extend the VRA for a fifth year; only General Motors and the American International Automobile Dealers Association of the American interests opposed continuation of the restraints. MITI also protested, citing record profits by the large American auto makers and the sharp reduction in unemployment in the American auto industry. Nonetheless, the Japanese agreed to hold auto exports for 1985 to 2.3 million units – up 24 per cent from 1984. At that time a Department of Commerce report estimated that a lifting of the restraints would have allowed Japan to export more than three million cars to the United States. The VRA, in fact, remained in force until 1988 and pickup trucks are still protected by a massive 25 per cent tariff.

• Each year, officers and staff of the British Society of Motor Manufacturers and Traders (SMMT) meet their Japanese counterparts from the Automobile Manufacturers Association (JAMA) in either Britain or Japan. When in Britain, they usually stay for a pleasant couple of days' golf at Gleneagles and discuss the so-called 'Gentlemen's Agreement', a VRA dating from 1977, by which the Japanese motor manufacturers agreed to limit exports of cars and light commercial vehicles to Britain to no more than 11 per cent of the market.

Sales of Japanese cars in many unrestricted European countries such as Denmark, Finland, Ireland, Holland and Belgium account for 20 to 40 per cent of the market, indicating that the agreement limits the Japanese to less than half the sales which they might achieve in a free market. The same agreement also includes an 'industry to industry understanding' which prohibits shipments of heavy commercial vehicles. As a result, when in the early 1980s attempts were made to sell Japanese Hino trucks, which were assembled in the Republic of Ireland, into the British market, they had to be withdrawn – although the Hino assembler did later succeed in selling some trucks in Britain. The Japanese originally accepted these restraints under the threat of more formal restrictions from the then Labour government, which was concerned about the poor state of the British motor industry. Governments since then have refused to act against this restrictive agreement. In addition, France allows the Japanese a mere three per cent of her market, Italy only permits 17,500 Japanese cars to be sold annually, while Spain confines Japan's car makers to 1,200 sales a year.

• As part of a programme for modernizing Spain's ageing train system, which involved a new network of 190mph high speed trains, a $1 billion contract for the new rolling stock was put out to tender in 1987. When the bids were opened on 14 June 1988, that of Japan's Mitsubishi was discovered to be 30 per cent lower than either the French or West German bids. Although Mitsubishi had already supplied the Spanish with more than 300 locomotives since 1967, the Spanish felt that the political prestige involved in the contract dictated that it should go to an EC partner: both the French and Germans were asked to resubmit their bids. Despite the fact that the Mitsubishi trains were said by many experts to be technically superior to the European products, as well as being less costly, the contract eventually went to the French.

• A few years ago, a popular cartoon in the American press depicted a steel worker impaled on a steel beam. Written on the side of the beam were the words: 'Greetings from Japan'. At the time, the large American steel companies, sometimes nicknamed 'Big Steel', were fighting a long battle against what they called 'unfair competition' from imported steel. In 1984, they finally convinced the President to sign a voluntary restraint programme that would give them a five-year respite from soaring steel imports in order to restructure. This, however, was only the latest in a long series of import restrictions dating back to 1969.

In 1960, the United States and the nine EC countries produced 78 per cent of the free world's steel output. But during the early 1960s, a rapidly growing home market encouraged Japanese producers to invest in large-scale integrated plants. Located on coastal sites, they benefited from reductions in transport costs for raw materials as well as for shipping the finished product and, by the mid-1970s, more than two-thirds of Japanese steel was made in works with a capacity exceeding eight million tonnes: no American plant has yet achieved this size. These new works, which benefited from automated process control, incorporated cost-saving, quality-enhancing technology such as low energy iron-making, basic oxygen steel-making and continuous casting.

American steel-makers, meanwhile, had either failed to invest or had spent their money on obsolete technology, like the giant Bethlehem Steel which installed $200 million worth of open-hearth technology at Sparrows Point in 1956, just as improved basic oxygen furnace techniques were becoming available. By 1958, United States imports of steel exceeded exports for the first time since America's industrial revolution. A year later, the United States became the world's largest steel importer. The result of this intensifying competition was a series of VRAs, import quotas and 'Trigger Price Mechanisms' to ensure that the Japanese and other suppliers would not sell at below prevailing American market prices.

The 1984 programme restricted imports further by effectively limiting foreign steel to around 20 per cent of the 100 million-ton United States steel market for five years. The euphemistically termed 'global arrangements on steel specifying export quotas' covered various categories of steel product from Argentina, Australia, Austria, Brazil, Bulgaria, Czechoslovakia, the EC countries, East Germany, Finland, Hungary, Japan, South Korea, Mexico, Poland, Portugal, Romania, South Africa, Spain, Taiwan, Venezuela and Yugoslavia.[10] At the end of the five-year period, the steel companies again began lobbying for a renewal of the ostensibly temporary VRAs and found support from President Bush during his 1988 election campaign. In 1989, true to his word, the President extended them for a further two-and-a-half-year term. Under this last programme, Japan's import quota was actually cut, while those of ultra-protectionist Brazil and Mexico were increased.

• Until 1988, the EC maintained internal national steel quotas for its various constituent countries, supposedly to allow for the orderly capacity reductions to restructure the market. Despite the dismantling of internal quotas, a series of limitations on imports of non-EC steel, originally imposed in the 1970s, remains in force. They ensure that importers do not bring steel in below a certain price, and are euphemistically referred to as 'Consulting Arrangements', 'Price Monitoring Systems' and 'Basic Price Systems'. The countries so limited include South Korea, Austria, Brazil, Bulgaria, Czechoslovakia, Finland, Hungary, Norway, Poland, Romania, Venezuela and, of course, Japan.

...and the rest

A row broke out late in 1989 when Denmark awarded a contract to build a giant £250-million, 6.6-kilometre road and rail bridge from Sjaelland to the Jutland peninsula to a consortium which had agreed to use largely Danish labour, equipment and materials. The European Community threatened to take the Danes to court over what was seen as an illicit barrier to free trade within the Community. Unfortunately, the case was only too typical. Fewer than five per cent of all non-defence government procurement in the EC goes to foreign bidders and many contracts are still awarded on a non-competitive, single tender basis. According to EC figures, in 1984 this cost member governments an extra £9.8 billion. Although the EC is trying to get its member states to open up their public procurement to one another, it still intends to allow all public utilities to impose a 50 per cent 'buy national' or local content requirement to exclude non-EC suppliers.

Nor is the United States whiter than white when it comes to public procurement. At federal, state and local government levels, the Buy America Act is used to limit foreign participation. Generally, if American companies are no more than six per cent more expensive than foreign ones, they get the contract; but in the mass transit sector, the rate increases to 25 per cent, meaning that, all other things being equal, a foreign bus or locomotive manufacturer can be up to a quarter cheaper than an American company and still not make the sale. The Department of Defence is also prohibited from purchasing certain products from foreign sources and must give preference to American manufacturers. Affected products include: machine tools, coal and coke, carbon fibres, textiles, stainless steel, valves, anchor chains, vehicles and bearings.

In addition to such protectionist government procurement policies, a wide range of other foreign products have been or are discriminated against by Western countries:

• In 1986, the United States established a 'Superfund' tax on petroleum to pay for environmental clean-ups – but the tax was only levied on imports. So now imported petroleum products are taxed at 11.7 cents per barrel, compared with 8.2 cents per barrel for domestic products. Imported chemical derivatives of oil are also taxed at a higher rate dependent on their oil content; and if the importer cannot provide sufficient information, the tax is levied at five per cent of value.

• In 1988, the EC Commission allowed Spain to bar imported Japanese and South Korean video recorders which were being channelled through other EC states. In justifying its decision, the Commission said the imports were aggravating the problems of Spain's domestic industry which had seen its market share fall to 15.7 per cent the previous year. Overall, individual member states of the EC maintained more than 150 import quotas on Japanese goods in 1989.

• A European Community report shows that the United States has recently increased a number of tariff rates which now stand at very high levels. They include clothing (20–30 per cent), ceramic tiles (20 per cent), tableware (26–35 per cent), glassware (20–38 per cent) and some types of footwear (37.5–48 per cent).[11]

• In a Parliamentary reply on 26 April 1988, Mr Alan Clark, the Minister for Trade, admitted that Britain had maintained VRAs on imports of black and white TVs from Singapore, South Korea, Taiwan and Thailand; on colour TVs from Japan, Singapore, South Korea and Taiwan; on music centres from Japan, South Korea and Taiwan; on pottery from Japan and Taiwan; on stainless steel cutlery from Japan and South Korea; and on footwear from Taiwan. Most of the VRAs had been running since the 1970s, though some dated back to the mid-1960s. All were enforced until 1985.

- The EC has maintained a series of special tariffs and quotas aimed primarily at limiting imports of especially competitive Japanese goods. Japanese-made video recorders and colour televisions are limited to a maximum of 14 per cent of the EC market, while a special 19 per cent 'pre-emptive' tariff on compact disc players was imposed in 1983.

- In 1986, following Congressional pressure, the United States government concluded VRAs with Japan and Taiwan limiting imports of machine tools up to 1991. A similar deal was sought with West Germany but, following the refusal of the Germans to co-operate, the United States unilaterally declared maximum market-share levels for certain types of German machine tools. Other EC countries remain under threat of 'remedial action' if they increase their market share in the United States.

- Apart from the many restrictions mentioned above, GATT's six-monthly report on world trade in mid-1988 listed 135 export restraint arrangements of various types in operation during the period under review. Sixty-nine of these protected the market of the EC or its individual member states, 48 protected the American market and seven restrained imports into the Canadian market. These mostly affected exports from Japan (25 arrangements), closely followed by those from South Korea (24 arrangements).

Having perused this long, bleak list, it is unlikely that any objective observer could seek to maintain that Japan is uniquely hostile to imports. Yet many do. In part this is due to the fact that nearly every pronouncement made by American and European officials and politicians on the subject is critical of Japan. Further, these condemnations are slavishly reported in much of the Western media which lacks in trade matters some of that well-known searching scepticism to which government pronouncements are usually treated.

There may also be another factor. According to Victor Harris, the president of Max Factor's Japanese subsidiary in the 1980s: 'When I talk to groups in the States, I always tell them it's impossible to get into the Japanese market. I'm not going to help people compete with me – and I think there's a lot of that.'[12] To this you have to add the natural hostility to the top dog, resentment at Japan's success in overtaking the West, the need for a scapegoat for the West's relative economic failure and, perhaps, just a hint of racism – after all, the Japanese are devious and unscrupulous orientals, aren't they?

Costly barriers

It is perhaps surprising that so many Western observers should have laid such emphasis on protectionism as one of the keys to Japan's economic success. A 1989 British parliamentary report on Japan, for example, stated that: 'One factor in Japan's economic strength has been the past protection from foreign competition.'[13] Yet virtually all of the developing countries, in addition to the Eastern Bloc nations, are infinitely more restrictive of free trade than Japan, but few are models of industrial prowess. For despite the skills of industrialists and trades unions in cloaking their sectional interests in the supposed public good, the fact is that protectionism is generally a very damaging industrial policy, tending to exacerbate rather than ameliorate deep-seated industrial problems.

The reasons for this are manifold. First, trade restraints, although raising the profits of domestic producers, almost invariably also increase costs to both private and industrial consumers, so distorting the economy and diverting resources from efficient to inefficient industries. The London-based Institute of Economic Affairs estimated that in 1983 the annual cost to consumers of the SMMT's 'Gentlemen's Agreement' was close to £180 million in increased prices.[14] A 1988 estimate in *What to Buy for Business* magazine put the cost rather higher at £2 billion, on the basis that ex-tax car prices in Britain were around five per cent higher than in Switzerland's free car market. Similar restraints on imports of Japanese automobiles into the United States were estimated to be costing American car buyers $400 extra per car: an average total annual cost of $3.9 billion over the 1981–4 period.[15] An OECD study put the additional cost of import quotas even higher at six to 15 per cent in the United States, Canada, Britain and France.

Similarly, limits on the imports of Japanese video tape recorders meant higher prices for UK consumers. Between March 1983 and March 1984, the cost of video recorders in Japan fell by 8.87 per cent. Over the same period, VCR prices in Britain rose by 15.41 per cent – a relative price change of around a quarter.[16] It has also been calculated that import restrictions and tariffs on textiles and clothing in the United States have cost consumers a massive $27 billion a year,[17] while in Britain the Department of Trade and Industry's 1989 Silberston Report placed the cost at £980 million a year. An assessment of the cost of import restraints on footwear to British consumers was put at £117 million a year.[18]

Many trade-limited goods do not in fact cater for end-consumers, but rather consist of industrial feedstocks. Those industries which have to pay more for such products owing to protectionist measures lose competitiveness and so are themselves less likely to be able to export their own products to other markets. United States downstream steel-processors, for example, pay prices 25 per cent higher than those in Japan and 20 per cent more than West Germany. They claim they would have saved at least $38 billion between 1981 and 1985 if they had been able to obtain steel at Japanese prices. For despite the fact that the costs of steel production fell in the late 1980s, American steel users had to endure price rises averaging 15 per cent in 1987 and 1988. So instead of importing steel in large volumes for processing into finished goods, America is buying in more manufactured products containing foreign steel, with the result that for every job preserved in the steel industry, others are lost elsewhere in the economy.

The same effect can be seen in Japan where, in response to pressure, the government halved duties on imported chocolate to ten per cent, while retaining high tariffs on chocolate ingredients – sugar, dairy products and cocoa – to appease domestic vested interests. The effect has simply been to allow foreign companies to undercut Japanese chocolate makers. Sales of imported chocolate rose fourfold between 1986 and 1989 and M&M/Mars, Hershey, Jacobs–Suchard and Lindt are willingly reaping the profits.

In general, however, Japan's lack of natural resources has been turned to her advantage in this respect. For whereas Western countries such as the United States, Great Britain and West Germany have imposed handicaps on their domestic industry by protecting high-cost domestic sources of supply for some raw materials, the Japanese have been forced to search the world for the lowest-cost supplies. Moreover, innovations in mill siting and bulk carriers enabled the Japanese in the early 1970s to cut the cost of transporting iron ore from Australia and Brazil to Japan to half the cost of shipping Upper Minnesota iron ore to Pittsburgh.

Import quotas and trade restraints also limit choice and create shortages. Here again, American steel import restraints have severely disadvantaged American steel processors. Several rerolling companies in the United States – those that roll semi-finished slabs into strips – complain bitterly about shortfalls in their supply of raw materials. West Coast-based California Steel reported in 1987 that it had to turn away orders because of a lack of sufficient steel slabs. 'We have to stop our mill for a week or so every month, because we just cannot get enough raw material,' said one official. Such mills complain of having to face bureaucratic applications to the Commerce Department to gain exemptions to import steel above the legal limits. An official at Lone Star Steel in Texas described its four short-supply applications as a 'frustrating' experience. It took several months for the Department even to review the applications, with no guarantee of success.

Consumers also suffer because Japanese companies with overseas operations within protected markets can more readily get away with selling effectively obsolete products, simply because the protected market is that much less competitive. For example, the Bluebird car assembled by Nissan in the north-east of England in 1988–9 was a model that had already been replaced in the Japanese market and elsewhere. Similarly, the Rover group assembled the Honda Civic saloon for Honda until 1989 for sale in the UK market, two years after Honda itself had replaced that same Civic model with a new one which it was selling in most other markets.

The per job costs of protectionism are therefore generally extremely high. According to the World Bank's 1987 *World Development Report* survey, jobs preserved in the British car industry as a result of quotas cost the equivalent of the wages of four British industrial workers. The cost in the United States of preserving a steel or car worker's job was estimated at $100,000.

Nor do the protected industries gain much real benefit. Where, as a result of restraints increased profits are made by domestic producers, these are often dissipated in higher wages and costs because competitive pressures are relaxed as a result of the import controls. This is exactly what happened to the American auto industry. In September 1984, General Motors and the United Auto Workers Union signed a three-year contract which raised wages and benefits from $22.80 to $27.80 an hour, so further widening the production cost disadvantage *vis-à-vis* Japan from about $1,500 to around $2,000 a car. And who can blame the auto-workers for demanding more when the Big Three car makers were making enormous profits from a protected market and bosses like Chrysler's Lee Iacocca and GM's Roger Smith were receiving more than a million dollars each in bonuses? Employee compensation in the protected United States steel industry also rose more rapidly than average manufacturing earnings in the decade to 1979, despite the fact that productivity growth in the industry was slower than that of its main competitors.[19]

Moreover, much of the increased profitability in the protected market accrues to the importers who are able to sell their goods, which are in short supply as a result of restraints, at premium prices. This effect is especially apparent with Japanese cars in restricted markets where, taking available discounts into account, they invariably sell at a premium to Japanese prices or equivalent Western makes. For example, the top version of Toyota's best-selling MR2 mid-engined sports car cost ¥2,000,000 (£8,000) ex-tax in Tokyo in 1990; the same car was priced at close to £11,000 before tax in Britain. The high prices paid by consumers of import-restricted products therefore frequently go straight into the pockets of foreign industry.

So far from creaming their own domestic market to dump at low prices abroad, Japanese industry, if anything, effectively does the opposite. For the truth is that protection in the West has allowed the Japanese to make huge profits at the expense of Western consumers. Japanese steel prices are around a quarter lower than those in the United States, while with many types of machinery, ranging from bulldozers to cars, Japanese consumers enjoy lower prices than the West. I remember, for example, buying a small Sony short-wave radio in Tokyo in 1985 for £16 which I later saw on sale in London for £40 and in the Zurich airport 'duty-free' shop for £50.

Trade barriers have also indirectly advantaged Japanese producers in that quantitative limitations in the form of quotas have often forced the Japanese producers to move upmarket, to compensate for reduced numbers with higher value and more profit per unit. This has been a major factor in the shift made by Japanese car manufacturers towards executive and luxury models. Before American and British import quotas, Japanese producers had virtually no presence in this area: now they are mounting a strong challenge to the likes of BMW and Mercedes.

Another reason why domestic industries are generally helped very little by trade protection is that imports from countries restricted by VRAs or quotas are often simply replaced by imports from other countries. After the imposition of the 'Gentlemen's Agreement' in Britain in 1975, for example, sales of domestically-produced cars, far from increasing, fell substantially as European manufacturers rushed in to fill the gap left by the Japanese. As a result, sales of British-made cars fell to around 45 per cent of the market by the mid-1980s, and many of those 'UK-produced' models were, in reality, only assembled from imported main components.

Furthermore, far from trying to match their rivals, both the British and American car industries have become increasingly dependent on Japanese technology. Most of the American producers now rely totally on Japanese or South Korean designs or products for their subcompact models. In Britain, the Rover group, which the 'Gentlemen's Agreement' was supposed to protect, has become very dependent on Honda technology. By 1989, two of its four model ranges, the 200 and 800 series, were based predominantly on Japanese designs and extensively used Honda drivetrains.

French and Italian motor manufacturers, even more protected than their

British counterparts, have become disproportionately dependent on their home markets and have met with little success outside of Europe. Fiat of Italy and Renault of France both make more than three-quarters of their total sales in the most protected markets of France, Italy and Spain. French Peugeot generates 80 per cent of its European sales in the five protected markets (France, Italy, Spain, Portugal and Britain), managing only 6.44 market share in the free European markets. Nor have the Italian motor cycle manufacturers, also insulated from Japanese competition, made much headway in foreign markets. The most successful European car manufacturers in selling outside of Europe are those of West Germany and Sweden, which enjoy no protection from Japanese products in their home markets, while the sole successful European motor-cycle manufacturer is similarly unprotected BMW.

Overall, reduced competitive pressures as a result of import restraints almost invariably merely compound the inefficiencies and weaknesses of protected industries, create industrial oligopolies, cartelize markets, and make it far less likely that the protected industries will be able to compete in overseas markets where they have to meet the Japanese on an equal footing. Exposure to full international competition, on the other hand, frequently has the effect of sweeping away complacency.

Import restraints in the United States merely allowed Chrysler, General Motors and Ford to raise prices, rebuild profits and pay huge bonuses to their bosses without regaining market share or rebuilding exports. In the American steel industry, import restraints were presented as a temporary measure to give the industry a breathing space to restructure and improve its competitiveness. With one or two notable exceptions, firms used the substantial benefits which they received in the form of higher prices largely to get out of steel-making – into shopping malls, among other things. In the period from 1979 to 1983 alone, American steel-making capacity was cut by nearly 20 million tonnes and 200,000 steel-workers lost their jobs. Indeed, trade barriers have proved particularly unsuccessful in protecting jobs. A study of employment in steel, textiles and shipbuilding in the industrialized countries showed that the number of jobs in Japan in these sectors generally fell by less between 1974 and 1984 than in the more protected Western countries. For example, by 1984, employment in Japan's steel industry had only fallen by 20 per cent, compared to 48 per cent in France and 69 per cent in Britain.[20]

新　大　国

It is often claimed that trade barriers do at least encourage Japanese manufacturers to set up production facilities within the protected countries. For while PR men speaking for Japanese companies will generally claim that they wish to set up in a particular country because of the highly skilled, native work force, excellent communications, etc, often the strongest motive is the need to circumvent trade barriers. Where this is the case, the Japanese benefit from the higher prices, and hence higher profits, prevailing in protected markets; but the number of jobs created by these factories tends to be relatively few as main components are usually sourced from Japan. Pressure applied to buy more components may improve the jobs situation, but often at the cost of higher prices and lower quality – an issue which will be discussed in more detail later. The net result is effectively to make transfers from local consumers to Japanese businesses and distort the overall efficiency of the economy. In the case of video recorders, the extra costs on European consumers resulting from import restraints meant that every new job created through inward investment cost between £106,000 and £300,000 – a very expensive method of boosting employment.[21]

Moreover, by indirectly encouraging Japanese companies to boost their manufacturing presence in foreign markets, trade barriers may well be weakening domestic manufacturers whose ability to compete with the Japanese can be reduced if they are close at hand. When, for example, in May 1987 the United States levied 100 per cent tariffs on many types of personal computer as a punishment for the Japanese breaking a 1986 agreement on semi conductor sales, Toshiba, NEC, Sharp and Mitsubishi promptly shifted manufacturing to the United States to avoid the levy. As a result, product specifications are increasingly set in the United States and the Japanese producers have become more attuned to the American market. One benefit for NEC was that it launched a personal computer using the advanced Intel 80486 processor chip at the same time as top American producers, resulting in booming sales for the Japanese company.

These disadvantages for Western industry which arise from protectionism go some way towards explaining the sometimes ambivalent Japanese response to such moves in the West. Genuine concern about possible exclusion from vital export markets is tempered by the realization that the more protectionist Western countries are effectively cutting their own throats. Furthermore, quotas often freeze the existing market shares of importing manufacturers and are therefore used as a competitive weapon by Japanese companies against their rivals. Thus Nissan, whose high market share in Britain in the mid-1970s gave the company the lion's share of the 'Gentlemen's Agreement' quota, is more favourably disposed towards it than Toyota which leads Nissan in other major markets, but is effectively excluded from doing so in Britain.

All of which may leave the reader wondering why, if the disadvantages are so great, is protectionism so rife? One reason is that trade-limiting measures provide large benefits to small numbers of people in protected industries and slight losses to large numbers of consumers – and consumer lobbies tend to be diffuse and neither as vocal nor politically powerful as industrial and trade union lobbies. I have myself seen this effect many times when groups of MPs, backed up by labour unions and management, lobby ministers for import quotas on whatever domestically-made product is under threat. If the government does nothing, it can be blamed for factory closures and job losses. And if the MPs in question are on the government side, their constituency position is more than difficult if they cannot persuade their own government to act.

Then there is the fact that it is always easy to blame your problems on devious foreigners. That way, both politicians and industrialists absolve themselves from any responsibility for their troubles. And in blaming foreigners, these governments, industrialists and labour leaders are more often than not wholeheartedly supported by the very public most harmed by trade barriers. As the great Nineteenth-Century Whig historian, Thomas Babington Macaulay, once said: 'Free trade, one of the greatest blessings which a government can confer on a people, is in almost every country unpopular.'[22]

7

STRUCTURAL IMPEDIMENTS

新大国

'*A wise man blames himself – a fool blames others.*'
Confucius.

WALK DOWN ALMOST any street in a Japanese town or city and one of the first things to strike you will be the multitude of small 'mom and pop' stores, usually run by elderly and retired people who are willing to accept both long hours and low incomes. Japan does have plenty of sizeable department stores, or *departo*, which are often linked to one of the major trading groups and trace their origins back as far as the Eighteenth Century, but the number of supermarkets is still small by comparison with many Western countries. They only account for around 15 per cent of retail sales, while small stores account for well over half. Remarkably, the country with the world's most productive manufacturing industry maintains one of the least efficient retailing and distribution systems. Japan, with half of America's population, actually has more stores and twice the proportion of wholesalers as the United States.[1]

One of the reasons for the complex and fragmented nature of Japanese retailing is the Japanese love for fresh fish and vegetables. Watch a Japanese housewife shop, and you will see her pick up and examine several small bunches of vegetables before selecting the one she wants. She will also often leave the store with only enough shopping for one day, for with the emphasis being on freshness and variety, it is the custom to make almost daily purchases of small quantities of foodstuffs. The Japanese housewife thus contributes to maintaining a diversified network of neighbourhood fishmongers, greengrocers and foodstores which are also aided by local governments, which are legally obliged to maintain wholesale markets for perishables.

Yet this labyrinthine and often picturesque distribution system has been described by The Confederation of British Industry (CBI) as 'the strongest barrier to the mass marketing of European products in Japan'.[2] The Dutch author, Karel van Wolferen, went one better, claiming: 'The distribution system is not complicated. It is rigged.'[3] Opinions like this explain why Japan's retailers are now at the centre of trade disputes with Western countries. For many people who are prepared to admit that most of Japan's formal trade barriers have now been dismantled, nonetheless maintain that the Japanese retain a series of more subtle import restrictions. Referring to these as 'non-tariff barriers', they cite Japan's retailing system, together with semi-official 'administrative guidances' which make life difficult for importers, problems with setting up Japanese operations and the apparent unwillingness of the Japanese to buy Western goods as the main obstacles to foreign sales. So much importance is now attached to these problems that they have spawned a series of US–Japanese talks under the so-called 'Structural Impediments Initiative'.

Tough for everyone

It is certainly true that importers into Britain and the United States in particular have their paths eased by an extremely concentrated retail sector (which means that they only have to secure distribution deals with a few large chains). Selling in Japan, meanwhile, almost invariably involves acting through a trading house and often several layers of middlemen and wholesalers before the goods reach the stores. The system emanates from a social policy designed to protect small shopkeepers, bolstered by the desire for fresh, high-quality food. Under Japanese law, permission for all new openings or expansions has to be sought from MITI which refers applications to an advisory council which in turn consults regional councils, on which local Chambers of Commerce and Industry are well represented. Invariably, the interests of existing retailers are noted and these come out against large stores.

But the Japanese distribution system is not primarily intended as a protectionist mechanism: it operates against all new entrants to the market, not just foreign ones. In the early 1980s, Michael Perry was in charge of Nippon Lever, the Japanese arm of the giant Anglo–Dutch detergent and personal products company, Unilever. Talking of the intricate Japanese distribution and retail system, Perry adamantly states:

> At no time in our experience was there a shred of evidence to support the view that the Japanese distribution system was used to discriminate against foreign manufacturers. Sure, it is complex, multi-layered and inefficient. It made life tough for us – but that was true for everybody else as well.

Although many Western producers have found the Japanese system cumbersome, to many it has not been an impediment to success. For example, the American razor blade producer, Schick, began selling its razor blades in Japan through the local distributor Hattori in the 1960s. Although Hattori deals with no fewer than 800 wholesalers, who cover up to 300,000 retailers, this has not prevented Schick from becoming the market leader in Japan.

Moreover, some Western companies have actually found they can turn the system to their advantage. The San Francisco-based Shacklee pharmaceutical company benefited from the fact that vitamin pills were not legally classified as drugs by the Japanese government and did not therefore have to be sold in drug stores. So while Japanese pharmaceutical companies were selling their vitamin pills through the same drug stores as their prescription drugs, Shacklee decided to peddle its vitamins direct to customers by means of door-to-door salespeople. The Japanese pharmaceutical companies hesitated to follow Shacklee's example for fear of alienating the distributors on which they relied for their prescription drugs. As a result, within a decade, Shacklee found itself accounting for a significant share of the vitamin market, with total sales amounting to more than $100 million a year.[4]

Another company which successfully bypassed the distribution system was Coca Cola, which was warned in the early 1960s that its normal sales methods would prove unworkable in Japan. Undeterred, it ignored local distributors and set up its own network of bottlers. Today, Coca Cola's distribution system is among the most efficient in Japan and more profitable than its American one. Amway – the direct seller of household goods which achieved the fastest sales and profits growth of any foreign company in Japan during the 1980s, and whose 1989 profits were second in the health and household products sector only to the market leader, Kao – also achieved success by using its own network of 700,000 mainly part-time agents who sell Amway's largely American-manufactured range to friends and neighbours through catalogues.

It would, anyway, be misleading to think of Japan's restrictions on large retail outlets, whether protectionist in effect or not, as unique. It is true that the United States, as befits a spacious and relatively sparsely populated country, has the most liberal planning laws when it comes to setting up large stores. But even in fairly deregulated Britain, local authorities have a large degree of control over applications for new supermarkets and shopping centres. Indeed, it is incumbent on local councils, as the planning authorities, to take note of the interests of existing retailers when deciding upon an application. Such applications are frequently rejected on the grounds that there are already sufficient retail outlets in the area, or out of a desire to protect small town-centre shops.

The continental European countries take an even less relaxed view, with the result that their retailing and distribution systems, although not as intricate and fragmented as Japan's, are nonetheless still dominated by independent stores or small chains. West Germany, for example, uses its *Baunutzungs Verordhung* law to virtually prohibit any new retail outlets above 10,000 square metres in size. As with Japan, these policies are social, or perhaps political, in origin, but can also have the effect of making life harder for importers.

Further, a retail structure which puts massive purchasing power into the hands of large chains of stores is no guarantor of success for it can make access to shelf-space harder, as evidenced by frequent complaints from manufacturers about the overwhelming power of Britain's large supermarket groups. As it is, a combination of pressure from the large store groups and consumers in Japan is already resulting in a slow but steady erosion of her small-store sector. According to MITI figures, the number of retail establishments in Japan is decreasing by around two per cent a year as small supermarkets and convenience stores steadily encroach on their territory. Whereas getting planning permission for big new stores once took up to ten years, it now normally takes just over 12 months.

In addition, many small shopkeepers have taken an 'if you can't beat them, join them' line and have rushed to get franchises for Lawsons, Family Mart and Seven–Eleven convenience stores, operated by the three largest supermarket groups, Daiei, Itoh–Yokaido and Seyu, which themselves are also expanding their own directly-managed supermarket operations. A new entrant, Shuwa, founded by the flamboyant Shigeru Kobayashi, is also building a fourth major supermarket chain by mounting takeover bids for smaller groups. As if this were not enough for Japan's hard-pressed, small storekeepers, sales at a new breed of discount store like I World and Mr Max, already estimated at close to $5 billion a year, are growing at more than twice the rate of ordinary department stores.

This helps to explain why the silver-haired proprietors of Japan's old style 'mom and pop' stores, for whom buying a small shop has been the favourite retirement choice for decades, are increasingly unable to persuade their sons and daughters to take over the business; an estimated 100,000 stores pull down their shutters for the last time each year. Perhaps, though, Western politicians and businesspeople should pause for thought before trying to impose a more efficient retail system upon the Japanese. The result may not be quite as beneficial as many Westerners, accustomed to using Japan's retailers as an excuse for their own shortcomings, might expect. An improved distribution system would substantially boost the overall efficiency of the Japanese economy, so allowing yet more resources to be diverted into the already formidable Japanese manufacturing sector. Retail reform in Japan may lead to lower prices: but it will not necessarily raise imports.

Cedrics, Sweat and Mustangs

Some years ago, when I was on my way to Tokyo via the United States on business, I mentioned to an American friend of mine that I was going to Japan and he insisted on arranging for an old friend, Masahiro Takada, to look after me. Masahiro and his wife, Hiromi, met me at the airport and took me to their small flat in the quiet, residential Meguro district. I had just made my first social *faux pas* by not changing into specially provided slippers before visiting the lavatory when the final dinner guest arrived, a formidable but cheerful lady, dressed in high Western fashion and clutching a Harrods shopping bag. Masahiro introduced me to Kikuno Takada, his mother and his 'boss'. Assuming this latter title was made in jest, I laughed politely. It turned out, however, that Mrs Takada really was the boss. For Mrs Takada runs and owns a substantial cosmetics company, Kikuno Cosmetics, which she herself founded.

Whenever henceforth I met Mrs Takada she was always carrying her Harrods bag. That this lady, as a citizen of a land which manufactures some of the best products in the world and sells them through stores where the service is impeccable, should seem to be so attached to her Harrods shopping bag seemed a little odd to me. She was carrying it the morning after the dinner in her son's flat when she took me to the station to catch the early Kyoto bullet train; and she was gripping it two days later when she came to meet me on my return to Tokyo.

In fact, Mrs Takada greatly valued her Harrods bag because of its associations with upmarket Western style and quality. For despite the common view that the Japanese will not buy Western goods, they are in fact suckers for impressive Western brand names: Chanel 19 is Japan's best-selling scent, Tokyo's fashionable ladies wrap themselves in Hermes scarves and YSL logos adorn the shirts and belts of middle-managers. Even relatively downmarket, but quintessentially Western products like McDonalds and Pizza Hut do very well in Japan.

Advertising hoardings also frequently use English slogans, many of which make little sense or would invite mockery in the English speaking world, but which, in Japan, impart a spurious air of Western sophistication and general well-being. Kanebo, a large pharmaceuticals and cosmetics firm, has the bizarre English slogan 'For beautiful human life' on its hoardings, while European and American models can make a good living in Japan posing in advertisements for upmarket local goods. English names are also commonly used for Japanese products, such as the Nissan Cedric, while it never fails to amuse visitors to Japan that one best-selling soft drink is called 'Sweat'. Ironically, Mitsubishi only sells its four-wheel drive vehicle under the Shogun name abroad, marketing the vehicle in Japan under a Western name.

'How', one friend familiar with Japan asked me, 'can anyone say that the Japanese won't buy foreign goods – haven't they seen the queues outside the Hermès and Luis Vuitton shops?' But matters are not quite so straightforward. For there is a strange ambivalence in the Japanese attitude to buying Western goods which gives some justification to those who persist in thinking that the Japanese are not open to Western goods or influence and are actively hostile to foreigners. Part of the blame, it has to be said, lies with the foreign products themselves: too often Western manufacturers have sold unsuitable or shoddy goods in Japan, and horror stories abound.

But sometimes, it is true, the Japanese are simply nationalistic in their purchasing. To an extent this is due to the fact that the Japanese still perceive themselves as being a poor country and many feel an obligation to buy locally-made goods; but it is also in part due to a complex of resentments at the snubs which many Japanese feel they have received at the hands of Westerners over the past century or so, and also a certain cultural arrogance which stems from Japan's geographical position and history.

Although much of Japan's early culture came second-hand from China, via the Korean peninsula, her geographical isolation allowed her both to impose her own modifications on these newly-imported ideas and to preserve a large measure of her self-identity. She thus developed the means to learn and adapt foreign ideas without losing her own cultural singularity; resulting in a tenacious pride in her own forms and methods, allied with an extraordinary openness to outside influences – a unique combination.

But the fact that Japan has imported so much of her civilization from China and the West has also given rise to a confidence problem. For centuries Japan felt inferior to China and later to the West. And even now, despite their recent manifest achievements, the Japanese often still lack self-assurance, and hence are sometimes embarrassed to deal with or talk to foreigners lest they should make fools of themselves. Hostility to foreigners, or an aggressive assertion of nationality, can offer compensation for this insecurity.

The net result of this complex of factors, with a little generalization and perhaps over-simplification, is that although on the one hand the Japanese are very open to and respectful of good-quality Western goods and influences and are eager to learn, there is also a very strong attachment to local products and traditions, born of a combination of genuine pride as well as the need to buy Japanese in order that the nation might survive. Affecting both attitudes in contrary ways is the confidence problem which sometimes makes the Japanese over-respectful to things Western, while occasionally provoking overt, defensive hostility.

It is commonly assumed that the citizens of most Western countries have, by contrast, a very open attitude to imports. This is more true, perhaps, of Americans than of, say, the French. Indeed, Americans can be over-influenced in their quality judgments by the fact that a product is advertised as imported. But even their cultural attitudes are not invariably well-disposed towards foreign goods.

The Ford Mustang, when launched in the 1960s, was one of the great symbols of the prowess of the American motor industry. Based on standard saloon car components, the two-door Mustang gave its owners sports car feel and performance for the cost of an average family motor. It spawned a whole host of imitators and became one of the great American automotive legends. But the Mustang has also come to symbolize the decline of that industry, for though the first Mustangs have become sought-after collectors' items, subsequent models bearing the proud name have become progressively flabbier and more mundane. The last model was, in fact, so ordinary and uninspiring that Ford decided to buy in the coupé version of the Japanese Mazda 626 as its replacement and badge it with the Mustang name.

When word of this leaked out to automobile *aficionados*, however, a huge outcry ensued. For despite the fact that the Mustang-badged 626s were to be assembled in the United States, and although the impressive high-tech Japanese car was a huge advance on the previous American model, many Americans felt Ford's move to be a grave insult to their national pride and self-esteem. Such was the protest, in fact, that Ford rapidly dropped the idea in favour of continuing its production of the old model, selling the American-assembled Mazdas under a more anonymous and less emotive model designation.

And while it may surprise no one to learn that in France a car dealer was expelled from his Rotary Club for taking on a Japanese franchise, it may be a revelation to some that Detroit for a time came out in a rash of 'No Japanese' signs in car parks and it was not uncommon for Japanese cars to be damaged.

So whatever truth there is in the common assertion that the Japanese have a cultural bias against imported goods, it should be balanced by an awareness of often similar attitudes in Western countries. Furthermore, the Japanese government is now making a unique effort to encourage imports. Although some question the sincerity of this campaign, at least Japan is the only country to actively honour importers. MITI even went so far as to propose tax incentives for the purchase of imported manufactured goods. The Japanese Deputy Prime Minister is chauffeured in a British Bentley; while government ministry car parks in Tokyo all now sport a handful of Volvos, Saabs, Oldsmobiles and even Jaguars. What would the reaction be in Britain, France or the United States if senior politicians were seen to be riding around in government-provided Nissans or Toyotas?

Making a commitment

Another oft-quoted impediment to doing business in the Japanese market is the supposed difficulty of setting up foreign-owned companies. It is certainly true that during the 1950s and early 1960s, when Japan was essentially a siege economy, flows of goods, capital and technology were subject to specific government approvals. In fact, this did not prevent companies from setting up in Japan, but only from repatriating profits until the yen became convertible – a similar policy to that employed by many developing countries besides Japan.

Coca Cola and General Foods were, in the 1950s and 1960s, among the first foreign companies to set up in post-War Japan – and because Coca Cola could not repatriate the large profits which it made in Japan, it aggressively reinvested in distribution and promotion instead, which in turn helped sales. Another success was AMP, which has survived competition from NEC in the electrical connector business and remains the market leader.

From 1964, when the yen became convertible, until 1973, all direct investment required specific government screening and approval, while foreign equity participation was limited to no more than 50 per cent. Even with these restrictions, the sufficiently determined and powerful were able to succeed. When Texas Instruments (TI), for example, threatened to with-hold its essential patents from Japanese companies, MITI called upon Sony President, Akio Morita, to serve as ambassador. He came up with a compromise whereby TI set up a joint venture with Sony, with an agreement that at the end of three years the Japanese company would sell its shares back to TI at cost. In return, TI agreed to license its patents to Japanese firms. By using its advanced technology, TI managed to force its way into establishing a wholly-owned subsidiary in a vital sector of the Japanese economy.

General liberalization of foreign investment began in 1967 and within six years Japan was as open to capital investment as other OECD members. But, far from resulting in a flood of foreign direct investment, this only increased at about the same rate as the growth of the economy in general. Too many Western companies, including many already established in Japan, simply decided that the Japanese market was not worth the time or effort and so did not take opportunities or reinvest profits. Among the Western companies which failed to capitalize on the possibilities was tyre maker Dunlop, which sold a majority of its long-established Japanese company to the Sumitomo group, eventually disposing of its worldwide tyre operations to the Japanese company; and American tyre maker, Goodrich, which withdrew from its interest in Yokohama Rubber.

ITT, which owned 45 per cent of NEC in the 1950s, gradually sold its stake in subsequent years. General Electric also owned a substantial holding in Toshiba, but largely relinquished this by failing to take up rights issues, selling its shares and repatriating dividends. Otis was the Japanese market leader in elevators in the 1950s, but it too preferred largely to ship its profits back to the United States and is now only a minor player in the Japanese market.[5]

Neither Ford not General Motors made any substantial effort to rebuild their considerable pre-War positions inside Japan in the 1950s. Although, together with Chrysler, they did later acquire stakes in local vehicle manufacturers – Mazda, Isuzu, Suzuki and Mitsubishi Motor – in 1990 General Motors reduced its shareholding in Isuzu, while Chrysler nearly halved its holding in Mitsubishi to 12.1 per cent.

Those companies which did set up in Japan were experiencing few government-induced barriers by the 1980s. When, in 1983, for example, the Study Group on Direct Foreign Investment in Japan asked 285 overseas affiliates there to rank their five biggest problems, government regulation and interference came fourth on the list, barely ahead of the problem of communication with their parent company's head office.[6] And if the Japanese have sometimes impeded foreign companies in the past, they are not alone – Western countries have not always been as open to foreign investment as might be supposed. France, for example, has on many occasions discouraged inward investment in order to preserve indigenous capacity. In the 1950s and 1960s, this policy was mainly aimed at the United States. In order to help the French car manufacturers, for example, General Motors was prevented from setting up a car plant in Strasbourg and Ford was discouraged from establishing a factory in Thionville. Phillips Petroleum was also dissuaded from building a refinery in Bordeaux lest it should prove too much competition for the state-owned petroleum group, Elf–Aquitaine.

But the real point is that the many companies which did decide to make the commitment necessary to succeed in post-War Japan disprove those who claim that Western companies have been severely impeded. It is true that TI and IBM were forced to license some of their technology to local firms, but, again, this was no more than was demanded by other developing countries at that time. Far more significant than government constraints has been the failure of many foreign investors to make the commitment and effort necessary for success in Japan.

Enterprise groups

'Kyohokai' is a grouping of 300 car-component manufacturers, most of which do almost all of their business with Toyota. Moreover, the automobile giant itself owns stakes in many of the Kyohokai suppliers and buys the bulk of its parts from them. Similar groups are run by other major companies. This 'enterprise group' system, as it is known, has been developed as a compromise between the low costs and management time-saving benefits of contracting out component manufacture, and the close supervision and quality control which can be maintained by in-house manufacture. It attains some of the efficiency benefits resulting from competitive pressure compared with in-house production, while eliminating the costs of frequent contract negotiation and permitting tighter inventory control.

The enterprise group strategy almost certainly makes good business sense: indeed, many Western manufacturers are now considering emulating it. Yet these networks of tied suppliers are often cited as a structural impediment by Western components manufacturers who claim that they prevent the sale of foreign parts to Japanese car manufacturers. In fact, Western car manufacturers source a far greater proportion of their components in-house or through wholly-owned subsidiaries than do the Japanese. General Motors, for example, buys a very large part of its components from AC Delco, while GM's Saginaw subsidiary, which manufactures steering systems, makes 80 per cent of its sales to GM, yet this has never been cited as an impediment to selling parts to GM.

The successful British retailer, Marks & Spencer, which also has outlets in continental Europe, North America and the Far East, itself has a tradition of maintaining very close, almost paternalistic relations with its suppliers, awarding them long-term contracts, just as Toyota does. In return for such a commitment, Marks & Spencer's suppliers are able to invest heavily in producing to the quality and specification which the retailer desires. This policy has also enabled Marks & Spencer to retain a very high proportion of British suppliers – a point the group makes much of in its advertising. But no one has ever quoted Marks & Spencer as an example of a British structural impediment.

Level playing fields

One businesswoman, familiar with Japan, complains regularly to me that the Japanese discourage imports by insisting that customs documents should be filled out in Japanese. An American journalist, working in Tokyo for a leading financial newspaper, told me of 'non-tariff barriers' restricting imports in Japan, citing the fact that Japan did not allow intense rear fog lights for cars of the type that are mandatory in Europe. While the president of BMW Japan recently quoted Japanese inspection and type-approval procedures, insurance costs for BMWs and higher sales tax on large cars as obstacles to selling foreign cars in Japan.[7]

Since virtually every other country insists on customs documents being completed in the native language, that complaint seems a little unreasonable to me. As for the American journalist's charge, this requirement seems no more a barrier to Western car imports than the condition that Japanese cars going to Europe should have fog lights is a barrier to them. The president of BMW Japan failed to mention that Japanese inspection and type-approval procedures are hardly different from those prevailing in the United States or Europe. In 1977, the Japanese government even went so far as to allow a three-year grace period for European car makers to meet new exhaust emission regulations. Insurance cover for BMWs, moreover, is frequently more costly than for other makes of car largely due to the fact that BMW spare parts and servicing tend to be expensive – costs obviously reflected in insurance rates, and not only in Japan.

It is true that up until 1990 the Japanese sales tax on sub two-litre cars was 18.5 per cent, as compared to 23 to 30 per cent on larger capacity models – which represented the bulk of BMW's sales – while road tax ranged from ¥20,000 to ¥80,000 (about £80 to £320) a year depending on car size. Yet high taxes on large cars are not an exclusively Japanese phenomenon. A British car purchaser, for example, pays about 25 per cent of the value of the car in VAT and Special Car Tax, meaning that the purchaser of a typical small car would pay around £2,000 in taxes, while the buyer of a large BMW 7 Series would pay more like £10,000. Likewise, in West Germany, a buyer would pay far more in VAT on a large car than he would a small one; while in France, annual road tax is based on a car's power. Even the United States administration proposed an additional ten per cent tax on expensive cars late in 1990. All of these imposts discriminate against larger cars, but are never cited as non-tariff barriers.

With its crowded and cramped cities, Japan does, in fact, have good reason to restrict larger cars, but the important point is that it taxes imported cars and locally produced cars at the same rate. It has, of course, been open to Western manufacturers to sell smaller vehicles in Japan, so attracting lower tax rates, but smaller American and European models have rarely been of a low enough cost or of a sufficient quality to tempt fastidious Japanese buyers. Japan's narrow, crowded streets are not barriers to trade which need to be altered to suit the dimensions of BMWs or larger American cars. Rather, Western manufacturers should market products in Japan that are suited to local conditions and needs.

Many, however, would agree with such complaints and consider these examples as evidence of more subtle forms of protectionism which, they assert, persist even where formal trade restrictions have been abandoned.

There has, it is fair to say, been some truth in such allegations, especially in the past. But making life difficult for importers is not an exclusively Japanese pastime. Perhaps the most celebrated recent case in the West was when the French government ordered that all Japanese video recorders should be cleared through a tiny customs office in Poitiers which is nowhere near a port. Possibly, too, they insisted on the documents being filled out in French.

France, however, has a reputation for hostility to imports second only to Japan's. But it may come as something of a surprise to learn that the self-styled champion of free trade, the United States, is itself not above the occasional devious or underhand trade practice. In 1988, for example, the United States introduced a customs user fee, the only major country to levy such a charge. The fee, which was charged at 0.22 per cent of the value of the goods imported, raised $536 million in the first ten months of operation. Only when GATT ruled that the levy was not commensurate with the real cost of processing imports and was being applied for protectionist reasons, did the United States agree to withdraw it, subject to the relevant legislation being passed in Congress.

In other respects, the United States often resorts to underhand practices to damage the chances of its foreign competitors. Although by no means the worst in this respect, American examples deserve highlighting because of the finger-wagging to which United States leaders frequently subject the Japanese. In 1987, for example, the University of Rochester's business school succumbed to pressure from the main local employer, Kodak, and barred an employee of its arch rival, Fuji Photo Film. He was eventually found a place at the Massachusetts Institute of Technology (MIT). But MIT, in turn, ruled out buying a supercomputer made by Japan's NEC following a United States Commerce Department official's warning that it might attract anti-dumping charges if the price were too low.[8]

None of which quite squares with the statement in *Trading Places – How We Allowed Japan to Take the Lead*, a book by former American trade negotiator, Clyde Prestowitz, in which he claims that: 'The United States has been relatively easy to penetrate. Its open society makes for an open market that has welcomed foreign goods.'[9] For when it comes to niggling import restrictions, America deals out more than its fair share. United States customs, for example, follow a sampling and inspection procedure which fails to distinguish between perishable and non-perishable products. Perishable products thus stand in line waiting to be tested behind long queues of goods such as steel, and are often spoiled in the process. As a result, shipments of Spanish citrus fruit have had to be dumped, with no compensation to the producers.

Seemingly reasonable regulations have also, on occasions, been used as non-tariff barriers to imports. Plants entering the United States are governed by quarantine regulations designed to protect American agriculture against the importation of foreign diseases and pests. The process is, however, often a very laborious one which the American government has failed to improve, allegedly due to inadequate manpower. In fact, pressure from American growers against amending the regulations in order to impede imports is suspected to be a major factor in American procrastination.

The United States also prohibits imports of firearms and munitions unless the importer can demonstrate that the imports are for specific uses and obtains a licence from the United States Treasury – something which American manufacturers do not have to do; while the United States Merchant Marine Act of 1920 requires that only registered vessels be used in American territorial waters for activities such as dredging, towing and salvaging. Unfortunately, only American-built vessels are eligible for American registration for these purposes, effectively prohibiting the purchase of foreign-constructed vessels for such work. American law also requires that vessels registered in the United States for coastal commerce should be built in the United States. The same applies to American flagged vessels fishing in American waters. The total market from which foreign-built vessels are thus effectively excluded is worth about $1.3 billion a year. Furthermore, the United States applies a hefty 50 per cent tariff on most repairs of United States ships abroad on the grounds that the ship repair industry must be protected for defence purposes.

Similarly, the fact that some individual American states assess corporate income tax for foreign-owned companies on the basis of an arbitrarily calculated proportion of the company's total worldwide turnover is another bone of contention. As a result, companies frequently find that they have to pay tax on income arising outside the state, giving rise to double taxation. In addition to this so-called 'unitary taxation', companies may also face the heavy compliance costs of furnishing details of worldwide operations. Despite repeated representations, states such as California have only marginally amended such tax regimes which continue to discriminate against foreign-owned companies.[10]

This may be why one survey of non-tariff barriers found that on a 1981 index of 100, by 1986 Japan's figure had fallen to 98.6, while that of the United States had risen to 123 and the European Community figure was up to 118.3.[11] Another estimate, by the World Bank, of the extent of non-tariff barriers in 1983 showed that in Japan they covered nine per cent of all goods and 5.4 per cent of manufactures, while in America they affected 34.3 per cent of all products and 12.3 per cent of manufactured goods. France was even worse, with non-tariff barriers covering 44.2 per cent of all products and even the Netherlands came in with a figure of 21.4 per cent. Overall, Japan's totals were the third lowest of the sixteen countries in the survey.[12] For the truth is that when it comes to crafty import restrictions, there is little that the West can learn from Japan. The whole nature of unofficial, or semi-official, voluntary restraint agreements is about as devious as it is possible to be, especially in view of the fact that such pacts often directly contravene the monopolies and anti-trust legislation of the governments which connive in them.

Many of the industrialists whose salaries are partly paid from the illicit profits gleaned from exploiting protected home markets are not even staunch enough to admit that such agreements exist. For example, the chairman of Britain's Society of Motor Manufacturers and Traders (SMMT), which negotiates the 'Gentlemen's Agreement' restricting Japanese vehicle imports to 11 per cent of the UK market, absolutely refused to admit to me that any such agreement existed.

This was particularly surprising since he also runs a major UK car-assembly operation, which itself benefits greatly from reduced Japanese competition. Graham Day, former chairman of Britain's last remaining indigenous volume motor manufacturer, the Rover group, was less coy. Not only did he openly admit both that the agreement existed and that he himself had taken part in the annual negotiations, but he also acknowledged that, without the agreement, the British motor industry would be almost totally wiped out, a view echoed by the chairman of the French Peugeot group, Jacques Calvet, who admitted frankly: 'If we completely opened our frontiers in the present circumstances, we would be eliminated.'[13]

新　大　国

Of course, nothing is more natural than to blame foreigners for one's own failures. British industrialists, for example, love to tell politicians that they would be able to compete in Japanese or other markets 'if only there were level playing fields'. Others suggest that, while the British are 'playing cricket', the Japanese are playing harder games by different rules. The implication is that it is always the foreigner – usually the Japanese – who is not playing by the rules, while the poor old British lose out.

Ironically, far from being a gentle and mellow game, cricket can be a hard and tough sport – which is appropriate because the game these industrialists are playing is indeed a rough one. In maintaining that the Japanese do not trade fairly, such people are not only making excuses for their own failures – such as poor industrial management – but, more often than not, they are also lobbying the government for subsidies or protection for themselves.

Politicians play the same kind of game. One very easy way to help secure re-election in the United States has been to 'bash' the Japanese for running huge trade surpluses with America – a ploy which is particularly effective in those states which produce cars or other items in direct competition with Japanese goods. Making whipping boys of the Japanese also has the comforting effect of absolving the American political and industrial establishments from their own responsibility for trade deficits.

But the fact is that the West itself must bear the bulk of the responsibility. The poor external trade performance of much of the EC and the United States has been largely governed by generally inflationary and consumption-oriented government policies. A country which consumes far more than it saves is always likely to have a trading deficit with nations which insist on saving more.

Governmental errors have also been compounded by the often inadequate performance of many Western companies in approaching the Japanese market – a fact recognized by most objective observers. For example, when asked in a magazine interview whether he was interested in the Japanese market, Raymond Levy, the boss of the French car company, Renault, replied, 'It's not really an important market . . . France and northern Europe are our priorities'.[14] Even in 1978, when Japan was more protectionist than she currently is, a study prepared by the Boston Consulting Group for the United States Treasury showed that the main reason for the then trade imbalance was inferior United States competitiveness and a lack of interest in exporting to Japan.[15]

The harsh fact is that foreign firms have too often simply made insufficient efforts to sell into the Japanese market. In 1981, for example, Western firms had only one-eighth as many offices in Japan as Japanese firms had overseas, and only one-twentieth as many people stationed in Japan.[16] For many Western exporters have found it more convenient and profitable to export into geographically and culturally closer markets in Europe and North America, as well as into their old colonies. The Japanese, on the other hand, have been forced to sell into the large Western market, it being the only alternative to their own intensely competitive market which, although large in national terms, is much smaller than the totality of Western markets.

The failure by the West to admit its shortcomings in this respect may have some unfortunate consequences, particularly as so much of Western policy and thought now seems geared towards spuriously attractive short-term remedies, such as managed trade. For it would be a strange and sad irony if the deep fear in the United States of Japan's economic success, and its implied threat to American leadership, should push her towards exactly the type of economic ideals which the former Eastern Bloc is finally in the process of renouncing; or result in the same type of protectionist devices which failed so dismally in the 1930s.

新大国 8

HONOURABLE RICE

'It is often supposed that agricultural subsidies are different, and that, unlike other forms of protection, they preserve employment in the long run. They don't. They only do so at the expense of other sectors of the economy, reducing efficiency and incomes overall.'
Sir Geoffrey Howe, then British Foreign Secretary, May 1987.

RICE HAS FOR a long time maintained a disproportionate influence on Japanese life. Ever since wet-field rice cultivation was introduced from China around the second century AD, transforming much of Japan's agricultural landscape into small dyke-surrounded, water-filled plots of land fed by intricate man-made systems of tiny waterways, rice has been the staple of the Japanese diet. The high yields attainable from intensive rice paddy cultivation and double-cropping have also played a crucial part in allowing Japan, like much of the rest of East Asia, to support heavier concentrations of population than the drier or colder lands of Western Asia and Europe.

So highly regarded is rice that the three main meals in Japan are still described in terms of *gohan* – literally *honourable rice*. Breakfast is called *asa gohan* (*morning rice*); lunch is *hiru gohan* (*midday rice*) and *ban gohan* is the term for dinner (*evening rice*). Even today, around 40 per cent of Japan's agricultural land is devoted to rice production and the crop represents close to a third of her gross farm output.[1] Yet this inoffensive but essential food has, together with other agricultural produce, been for some time at the epicentre of perhaps the bitterest trade dispute between Japan and the United States.

For years the United States has been attempting, with only limited success, to gain the right to sell her food surfeit to Japan's masses in the

teeth of fierce resistance from Japanese politicians who are disproportionately influenced by Japan's vociferous farmers' lobby. Underlying this
conflict is the fundamental insecurity which the Japanese feel about their
food supply, an insecurity which issues both from the knowledge that their
own agricultural yields are insufficient to feed the whole population, and
the memory of food shortages before, during and after the Second World
War.

The reason for Japan's low food output is the fact that only around 15
per cent of Japan's surface is viable for agriculture, the remainder being
taken up by mountains, forests and towns. So the Japanese have to squeeze
as much production as possible out of their 5,410 million hectares of
farmland, which compares to West Germany's 12,080 million hectares,
31,570 million hectares in France and the United States' 414,480 million
hectares.

Agriculture is unlike most industries. In manufacturing, output can be
cranked up simply by adding capacity in the form of factories and plant,
and the more you produce, the lower the cost tends to be. Increase
production on a hectare of land, however, and, although you produce more,
that production also becomes far more expensive because of the extra inputs
such as fertilizer. In order to maintain a reasonable degree of self-sufficiency
from limited land, Japanese farm output has to be maximized. But this
means maintaining high food prices in order to give farmers the incentive to
produce more, bearing in mind the increased cost of high yields. It also
means import barriers to prevent low-cost foreign food from driving Japan's
farmers out of business. Thus the Japanese farmer has become the most
efficient in the world when measured by his high output per hectare, but
among the most inefficient when the cost of that production is taken into
account. Costs have also been increased by the tiny average size of Japanese
farms – less than two hectares, compared to an average size of 200 hectares
in the United States.

So in order to sustain high levels of output from her small farm area to
guarantee at least a reasonable proportion of home food production, the
Japanese government has maintained a network of controls, subsidies, price
supports and import restrictions which cover produce from wheat to
oranges – but it is rice which receives the most support. Guaranteed prices,
allied to tough import quotas, have also meant high prices being paid by
Japanese consumers. One informed estimate calculates that, up until 1986,
the Japanese had paid a total of ¥3 trillion (£130 billion) more than world
market prices for their rice.[2] As a result, although they eat less than most
developed nations, around a quarter of the income of the average Japanese
family is spent on food, compared to only about 13 per cent in America.

Food-exporting countries – often those which purchase considerable
quantities of Japanese manufactures – bitterly resent what they see as the
unfair exclusion of their competitive produce from the Japanese market.
Japan's problem is that allowing low-cost food exporting countries totally
free access to her market would almost certainly bankrupt the majority of
her farmers, leaving her almost totally dependent on world markets for her
survival.

As it is, Japan's relatively small cultivable area means that she already imports half of her food needs – up from only 15 per cent in 1967 – making her now the world's largest net importer of agricultural products, buying close to $27 billion worth of foreign food a year. The leading exporter is, in fact, none other than Japan's greatest critic, the United States, which sells around $6 billion worth of food to Japan annually, closely followed by China and Australia which each sell nearly $2 billion worth every year.

Surprisingly, perhaps, Japanese consumers, who do undoubtedly pay over the odds for much of their food, have nonetheless traditionally supported the high-priced, protectionist system. A public opinion poll carried out by the Prime Minister's office in September 1984 showed that 65.3 per cent of the Japanese felt that Japan's food self-sufficiency rate was too low, while 75 per cent considered that the country should supply what it was capable of producing, with only 14.1 per cent feeling that cheaper foreign products should be imported in place of more expensive home-produced food.

In part, this attitude stems from a strong sense of sympathy for the Japanese farming community, which arises from the fact that many Japanese town-dwellers have come to the cities much more recently than their Western cousins, and many still have relatives involved in agriculture. There is also a strong sense of historical debt to the farming community, which largely bore the brunt of the cost of reconstructing Japan after the Meiji Restoration.

Furthermore, the sheer weight in numbers of Japanese farmers reinforces political support for the system. Japan's 4.5 million farmers represent in all about 15 per cent of the working population – a far higher proportion than in Britain or the United States where less than three per cent of the working population are on the land, and even more than France where around eight per cent of the active population are involved in farming. Even Tokyo has no fewer than 125,000 registered 'farmers', each tending tiny, protected urban farms. And in parts of Europe, many people with well-paid jobs elsewhere in the economy still maintain an involvement in farming.

This force of numbers has given Japanese farmers a political clout greater than is the case in most Western countries. Almost half of the 450 or so Liberal Democrat Party (LDP) MPs have significant agricultural interests in their constituencies, and 11 out of 46 prefectures have more than 30 per cent of their households classified as agricultural. The LDP has traditionally been able to rely on the votes of Japanese farmers and in turn has rewarded them with generous protection and subsidies. This mutuality of interests has resulted in the LDP conspiring to maintain an electoral system which is weighted towards the rural vote. For example, the Fifth District of Hyogo prefecture, a farming region, elects a Diet member for every 80,000 voters, while it takes 286,000 voters to elect one in the Fourth District of Chiba prefecture, a crowded urban area.[3]

The rural rich

Visit a small Japanese agricultural town and several things may surprise you. First, you may well be able to travel all the way on the super-fast *shinkansen* (*bullet train*) because the LDP has rewarded the loyalty of the farmers with good road and rail links, which have the added bonus of allowing many farmers to retire as wealthy men from selling their land at inflated prices to the railways. You may also notice the number of smart shops in the town and a preponderance of late model cars and pick-ups.

Drive out into the countryside and you will find generally well-paved roads and spacious houses with adjoining glasshouses, nestled among the neatly tended tea and *mikan* groves and lush paddy. Rural Japan has prospered greatly both from the political deal it has struck with the LDP, and from the nation's need for some degree of food security.

Things may be changing, however. As a result of a steady decline in the number of farmers, gradually changing public attitudes, the ageing of the rural community and relentless pressure from the major food-producing countries (particularly the United States) for Japan to open up her market, the Japanese government is reviewing its farm policy.

In 1960, there were six million farm households in Japan; this number declined to 4.5 million by the mid-1980s and is still falling. At the same time, part-time farm households with only low agricultural incomes have continued to increase and now exceed 70 per cent of all farm households. This part-time farm life is called *san chan nogyo* by the Japanese, and usually comprises of a home in which a middle-aged couple live together with a grandparent or two and their daughter-in-law. Only just over 600,000 of Japan's farm households are now full-time, and about a third of these have no males aged between 16 and 64. Indeed, by 1995, 43 per cent of the rural population will be over 65, compared with 14 per cent of the population as a whole. Moreover, Japan's farmers now only account for 2.7 per cent of net domestic product, down from 26 per cent in 1965.

The corollary has been a recent reduction in public support for the high-priced food policy, as evidenced by an opinion poll early in 1990 which showed two-thirds of Japanese people favour opening the rice market, as well as an erosion of the albeit still powerful influence which Japan's farmers and the 4,000 *nokyo* – agricultural co-operatives with a total of eight million members – hold over their politicians. Commenting on the fact that most farmers now draw the bulk of their income from non-agricultural occupations, a LDP Diet member from the Hokuirku district pointed out that 'to get their votes, you should ask their employers. They do the job far more effectively than the *nokyo*'.

As a result, former Prime Minister Takeshita and his successors have been anxious to shift the emphasis of their party away from the farming lobby and towards the urban consumers. To win more support in the cities, the LDP is promoting the de-control of farm products, which would lead to lower prices. Newspaper comment is also increasingly outspoken in its criticism of the agricultural system and late in 1987, during one of Japan's periodic agricultural trade disputes with the United States, the influential *Yomiuri Shimbum*'s leader column pronounced:

> The system is in a state of disintegration . . . changes in the government's policy are being provoked by a realization that the market mechanism can no longer be ignored. Yet the more the government tries to shore up the faltering system, the more distorted it becomes.

The overall result has been a steady liberalization of the food market and the tentative beginnings of the dismantlement of the extensive regulatory system. But there appears to be a sharp sting in the tail of the Japanese farming lobby which is far from giving up and is fighting a strong rearguard action. Their opposition to market liberalization moves was one factor in the LDP's loss of its upper-house majority in the 1989 elections and each market-opening measure is met with fierce and sometimes violent demonstrations.

Cheeseburger and fries

Perhaps nothing so symbolizes the United States as the land of plenty as the ubiquitous cheeseburger and fries. It is ironic, therefore, that what has become virtually the national dish of a country which takes pride in its self-reliant, free-enterprise culture, is also among the most heavily subsidized and controlled food products in the world.

With its broad grasslands and lush pastures, you would not, perhaps, have thought that America's aggressively independent and often very wealthy ranchers needed much state support. But the cost of the meat in America's burgers has been pushed up by import restrictions dating back to August 1964, when a Senate Committee on Finance investigation into meat imports concluded that 'imported meat has played an important part in creating the distressed market conditions' in the domestic industry and Congress enacted the Meat Import Act which limited shipments of most types of meat.[4]

Along with the meat, the cheese in the all-American burger also costs more than it needs to because the United States government maintains a series of VRAs, as well as official quotas under a special GATT waiver, which severely restricts the quantity of dairy products allowed into the country from Australia, New Zealand, the EC, Finland, Austria, Switzerland and even Canada. American cheese and other dairy products also benefit from price support in the form of government buying programmes which absorb surpluses and keep prices artificially high. As a result, in 1987, United States government subsidies amounted to no less than $835 per dairy cow, and overall, American farmers receive around three times the world price for milk and butter.

Nor do those United States prairie farmers growing the wheat for the burger bun miss out on the handouts, benefiting from a policy called the 'deficiency-payment' system, whereby the United States government makes up any difference between prevailing market prices and higher government target prices for grains – including rice. Payments are also made for grain storage to keep surpluses off the market to maintain prices.

Even the humble fries have not been exempt for long: the United States maintained strict quotas on imports of Canadian potatoes until 1988. Nor is the innocent milkshake: if you were to have a strawberry shake with your meal, and in the unlikely event of it containing real fruit, the chances are that it will have been grown in California with the benefit of heavily subsidized irrigation.

Restrictions, controls and subsidies do not end with burgers, however.

No self-respecting American would consider breakfast complete without a glass of orange juice. But, as the world's largest consumers of orange juice sip their morning glassful, they probably do not realize that their often huge and wealthy juice producers are protected by a 35 cents per gallon duty on imports of concentrated orange juice – a tariff established originally in 1930, but which now discriminates against imports from much poorer Brazil and other less well-off countries. Even requests from Peru, Bolivia, Ecuador and Columbia for the elimination of tariffs on frozen orange juice to allow them to develop agricultural industries to replace the growing of coca leaves, the raw material for cocaine, have been successfully fought by the US citrus industry and their congressional supporters.

You might also have expected that, with almost ideal growing conditions, the staunch peanut farmers of the Deep South would neither need nor want protection from imports. But in addition to an extensive programme of price support, a strict import quota has been in force since 1953 to prevent foreign peanuts from undermining prices: China, for example, is limited to only 777 tonnes of sales a year.

All of this may come as a surprise – even to those who are well aware of the EC's far better known system of farm support and subsidies, the Common Agricultural Policy (CAP). Behind long-standing government support for farmers in Europe, with its many small farms, lie motives not dissimilar to those found in Japan. Long before the Second World War, continental European nations supported their farmers both to guarantee themselves a supply of food and to ensure a steady provision of tough peasant recruits for their armies. But for the first recorded state intervention in the free market for food you have to go back to Old Testament times when Joseph persuaded the Pharaoh to withhold grain from the market and store it for seven years of plenty, in preparation for the lean years to come.

Even in Britain, the first Corn Laws governing the import and export of grain were imposed in the Twelfth Century and were not finally repealed until 1846. Between then and the Second World War, Britain alone of the major European economies enjoyed a relatively free agricultural market, importing low-cost food primarily from the United States, Australia, New Zealand and Canada. The War, however, highlighted the vital importance of home food production, resulting in the introduction of a complex system of subsidies and price supports to maximize production.

After the Second World War, the main continental European countries continued their national agricultural support policies for political and social reasons, considering a strong rural community to be an essential bulwark against communism; and, in 1957, when the Common Market (now called the EC) was formed, it took over this policy on a supra-national basis. Britain became subject to the EC regime when she joined the organization in 1973, as did Greece in 1981 and Spain and Portugal in 1986.

Despite some attempts to de-control the system and provide lower prices for consumers, the EC's farm support system, with its strict import controls and labyrinthine series of market intervention measures to maintain prices, has simply grown and grown. By the mid-1980s, when Japan's agricultural budget was running at just over $11 billion, France, with less than half Japan's population, was spending close to $12 billion (from a combination of EC and national agricultural subsidies). By 1987, total EC expenditure on agriculture was nearly $60 billion – a far higher figure than Japan's expenditure, even taking into account the EC's larger population. In that year, the EC subsidy from consumers and tax payers to dairy farmers was some $410 per cow – greater than the personal income of half the people in the world.[5] Bearing this in mind, the EC has, perhaps wisely, been fairly muted in its criticism of Japan's farm import restrictions. Not so the United States – despite the fact that it was America herself who, in 1955, first sought a GATT waiver for agricultural trade, with the result that food import barriers are not covered by GATT agreements.

There are some who accept the basic principles of the CAP as a social policy, designed to protect the small, inefficient continental European farmers and guarantee food supplies. But American farmers probably need support far less than most others. The huge North American landmass has endowed her with a plentiful agricultural acreage, some 70 times as large as Japan's. This allows American farmers, with much larger farms on average than their European or Japanese counterparts, to produce food more 'extensively'. Using lower inputs of fertilizers and chemicals, they produce less food per acre than under more intensive systems, but at a far lower price.

Yet American farmers are treated in many ways even more indulgently by their avowedly free-market government than their Japanese rivals. In fact, with a population around twice that of Japan, the United States spent nearly five times as much on its farmers in the mid-1980s, at $53 billion a year. Each American farm household also received, on average, nine times as much state support in comparison with Japan. In fact, the American farm support system is every bit as extensive and restrictive as Japan's, though it is geared in such a way that food prices are lower.

Even where the United States has apparently reduced its agricultural import quotas and tariffs in some areas, these improvements have been matched by stricter controls on other products. The most significant recent changes came, ironically perhaps, during the Tokyo Round of GATT negotiations in 1979 when the United States agreed to enlarge quotas on cheese imports. At the same time, however, she applied quota restrictions to some cheeses not previously covered, as a result of which about 85 per cent of all cheese imports now enter the United States under quota, the main exception being specialist and soft cheeses made from goat's and sheep's milk.

It is not wholly surprising, therefore, that the Japanese increasingly view American attempts to prize open Japan's food markets as inconsistent and hypocritical, which gives rise to bitterness not only among the Japanese farming lobby, but also among those in Japan who are unsympathetic to the farm support system but who see American pressure as an attack upon their national sovereignty. This resentment is only increased by the special treatment meted out to Japan. For example, despite the 1988 United States–Canada Free Trade Agreement, America's northern neighbour introduced a fresh series of import restrictions that same year which required import permits for ice-cream, yoghurt, skimmed milk, buttermilk and most other dairy products. Moreover, under the Free Trade Agreement American farmers had their quotas of the Canadian chicken market fixed at 7.5 per cent of the previous year's domestic production, along with three per cent for turkeys and a mere 1.647 per cent for eggs. Yet Canada rarely figures in attacks by angry congressmen.

The zero option

The inconsistency of United States farm policy has been neatly summarized by the agricultural economist and professor at the University of Minnesota, Leonard Weiss, who remarked:

> The export subsidy and import restriction programmes have been embarrassing to the State Department. We have attempted to lead the world in encouraging trade and to raise incomes in many countries of the world by direct economic assistance. Yet our agricultural policy has required trade restrictions and export subsidies of the very sort we object to abroad and it often tends to undermine foreign producers' incomes.[6]

The classic example of this is sugar – heavily price supported and protected both in the EC and the United States. The United States first imposed tariffs on imported sugar in 1914 and quotas were established in 1934. Several changes followed, including the institution of a price support programme for domestic producers in 1977. When inroads into sugar usage were made by corn sweeteners, it was the sugar import quota which was sharply reduced in 1985 to compensate American producers. In 1985 President Reagan extended quotas to imports of sweetened products, such as cocoa and pancake mixes, immediately creating enormous problems for importers of such products which often contained only minimal amounts of sugar, but which were nonetheless excluded as they had no quota allocation.

The overall effect of these policies, and especially of the sale of artificially cheap sugar onto world markets, has been devastating for sugar-producing countries in the Third World which are largely excluded from the American market, while subsidized exports of United States sugar destroy their chance of selling elsewhere. Further, despite the tremendous support given to European and American farmers, their agricultural economies are nonetheless running into severe difficulties. This has partly been because larger, more efficient farmers have generally reaped most of the benefits from higher prices. In addition, high prices have tended to discourage sales and produce surpluses which have had to be sold overseas at a loss – something which in other contexts both the United States and EC have termed 'dumping'. This has depressed overall world prices for the various agricultural commodities and caused severe damage to many of the poorer, underdeveloped countries which are particularly dependent on agricultural exports. At least the Japanese farm support system is less irresponsible than that of the EC or the United States in that it does not wreck the economies of poor, single-commodity producers around the world by dumping agricultural surpluses at a fraction of the prices paid to their own producers.

In fairness, the Americans are fully aware of the competitive advantages which their natural land resources and climate would give them in a totally free world food-market. So now, official American policy is based on the so-called 'zero option', involving the abolition by the developed nations of all duties, levies, export subsidies and import restrictions on basic commodities by the year 2000. But while this would mean the end of farm trade barriers, the United States does not propose to relinquish most of its hefty farm subsidies, so allowing it to continue to give American farmers unfair advantages over rivals.* The 'zero option' is backed by the Cairns Group of southern hemisphere food producers, which is led by the Australians and consists of low-cost food producers who see the advantages of a free market in food, although they tend to be among the most protectionist countries when it comes to manufactured goods and services.

The Japanese not unreasonably argue that to abolish export subsidies without doing away with internal subsidies is fairly meaningless. If a true 'zero option' were to be realized, involving the abolition of all farm support, a period of rationalization would follow causing production to concentrate in the most viable areas around the world. Consumers would undoubtedly benefit and the efficiency gains to the world economy would almost certainly ensure the redeployment of displaced farmers in other industries. But, particularly in Japan, the 'zero option' would above all result in the virtual elimination of the small farmer with major social and political consequences for the nation as a whole. In addition, in such a situation, Japan would be forced to buy virtually all her rice, with all this food's historical and cultural implications, from overseas. The precedents are not encouraging from Japan's point of view.

Soyabeans are another food of great importance in the Japanese diet, but when, in the summer of 1973, the United States feared a domestic shortage, they suddenly imposed an embargo on soyabean exports – an event which is well remembered in Japan and which has only served to reinforce nervousness about its food supply.

So when the United States and other food-exporting nations criticize Japan's food policy, they should both be aware of their own deficiencies in this area and also of Japan's very special situation. For Japan already imports half of her food, and few developed nations would accept a position in which they were dependent on the vagaries of world markets for the bulk of their food supplies.

Despite, therefore, the massive political pressure being applied to Japan in order to prize open her food market, the liberalization process will most probably only be a limited one and the prosperous small Japanese farmer is likely to be tending his patch of emerald-green 'honourable rice' for many years to come.

* The United States changed her position to include some cuts in internal farm subsidies towards the end of the GATT negotiations in 1990.

Part IV

Government – Structure of Success

MANY ASSERT THAT Japan's tremendous economic success has been overwhelmingly due to the cohesive relationship between her industry and the bureaucracy, which has wisely nurtured, protected and guided her enterprises towards near world domination in a process sometimes referred to as 'state-sponsored capitalism', or even 'competitive communism'. Japan's Confucian tradition and her disciplined attitudes are also often seen as essential elements in a tight state–industry embrace which has spawned the monolithic and impenetrable 'Japan Inc'.

At the very centre of this relationship is MITI, Japan's supposedly far-seeing and all-powerful trade and industry ministry whose positive influence in Japan's industrial development is also considered to have a darker side that condones and encourages unfair trading practices.

That, anyway, is the commonly held view. It is often conveniently forgotten, however, that Western countries have been at least as guilty in the game of state-intervention in industry as Japan. The role of MITI and the Japanese government in the country's economic achievement has also been consistently exaggerated – not least by writers for whom conspiracy theories sell books, or businesspeople and politicians for whom they offer comforting excuses. But although its successes are widely reported, MITI has also been responsible for a number of failures. Moreover, Japan's industrial accomplishments are attributable to far wider causes than MITI – not least among which is the fact that her post-War governments have consistently geared their more general policies to economic growth and enterprise. 'Industrial strategies' and the subtle controls of shadowy bureaucrats, may be simple and soothing concepts for Westerners bewildered by Japan's rapid advance, but her government's influence on Japan's economy has been far more complex than that.

9

新
大
国

AN OVER-ANXIOUS
MOTHER

'Industrial policy as it has been practised in Japan is neither an unholy alliance of big business and big government, nor a curtailment of business's legitimate freedom. Business and government leaders in Japan do not have an adversary relationship. Rather, the government is continually researching and investigating economic, technological and business trends so that the country will be prepared to meet problems before they become crippling. But a strength of the system is that business not only has access to government advice but also has the freedom to reject it.'
Mark Zimmerman, former Japan-based pharmaceuticals executive.[1]

CLOSE TO THE bright green splash of Hibiya Park, the verdant richness of which relieves the grey density of Central Tokyo, rises a gaunt, modern, 17-storey block made of grimy white stone, situated in the heart of the Kumagasaki government office district, a sprawl of monotonous buildings stretching around the moats which guard Emperor Akahito's Sixteenth-Century palace. This is the headquarters of MITI, Japan's Ministry of International Trade and Industry, whose very name sets pulses racing in the minds of foreign businesspeople and politicians, conjuring up images of sinister conspiracies to dominate world industry hatched over cups of green tea in secluded rooms which foreigners are unlikely ever to penetrate.

So emotive has the name of MITI become to many Westerners, that it has been variously described as the 'puppet master with invisible strings' and 'a spiderless web'. Epitomizing the near paranoia often evoked by MITI is the following description from a best-selling book on Japan:

> Behind their [the Japanese] massive penetration of foreign markets is a
> system of business activity which can best be described as 'economic

totalitarianism', a government-directed enterprise in which all the energies of Japan have been mobilized to overwhelm world competition. It is a national conspiracy directed from a central command post, a squat building in Central Tokyo, the headquarters of MITI.[2]

Enter the portals of this supposed nerve centre of the Japanese conspiracy for world domination and, striding down the dimly lit, linoleum-floored corridors, you catch glimpses of harassed bureaucrats sitting at utilitarian, steel desks, toiling among mountains of papers and files. Every now and then you are passed by a functionary, staggering beneath a heap of files. Is this really the place where the West's economic defeat was planned and directed?

The origins of MITI date from the early years of the Meiji era. In 1881, the government established the Ministry of Agriculture and Commerce, which was divided in 1925 into two separate ministries, one covering agriculture and forestry and the other commerce and industry, MITI's predecessor. It was this latter ministry which helped to organize Japan's industrial colonization of Manchuria and the War economy. Less than two weeks after Japanese wartime leaders signed the surrender document on the decks of the *US Missouri*, the entire Ministry changed its name to the Ministry of Commerce and Industry and returned to work largely intact.

In 1949, it became MITI, organized into 12 bureaux, one for each major industry and each headed by a bureau chief under the overall control of the Minister, by law a political appointee and member of the Diet. At the peak of the pyramid of 12,600 civil servants who now make up MITI's staff is the Vice Minister who reports directly to the Minister. Political control over the Ministry, however, is relatively weak, not least because of the long-standing custom by which the Vice Minister appoints his own successor.

There is no doubt that MITI's widespread reputation for being a powerful and competent bureaucratic force is to a large extent justified. The chief reasons for its effectiveness, and that of the Japanese bureaucracy as a whole, lie in the quality of the people it employs and its tightly cohesive structure. Japan's leading bureaucrats have invariably attended the top universities – and, in contrast to many Western countries where the best candidates go to the foreign affairs ministry, MITI's officials are among the brightest and the best.

Each year more than 32,000 university graduates take the exam which could gain them entry into the top civil service jobs in Japan. On average, fewer than 2,000 pass. Of these, around 600 apply to MITI and fewer than 50 are selected. Around three-quarters of these will have come from the Tokyo University's Law Faculty which provides a broad-based training in politics, law and public administration. The rest will almost certainly have been top students at other prestigious universities like Hitotsubashi and Kyoto, at private universities like Keio and Waseda, or at the Economics Faculty of Tokyo University.[3] The selection procedure ensures that top bureaucrats are not only extremely able but that they also gain an aura of respect, comparable perhaps only to the elite bureaucrats of France.

By the time Ministry officials reach their 30s, those who are likely to fill the top posts in the next two decades are generally identifiable. Around the age of 50, the top handful are promoted to become chiefs of the most important divisions. A few years later, a Vice Minister from that age group is chosen partly through a system of consensus, but with the approval of the outgoing Vice Minister. It is then the custom for all remaining peers to retire. Some of these men walk into top positions in commerce and industry in a process known as *amakudari (descent from heaven)*. Others are allotted safe constituencies to become LDP stalwarts in the Diet.

In 1977, 27 per cent of the Diet and 35 per cent of the Upper House were ex-bureaucrats,[4] and since the mid 1950s, only four Prime Ministers, Miki, Tanaka, Takeshita and Kaifu, have not been former bureaucrats. Just as significant, most have also been graduates of Tokyo University, while about a quarter of all parliamentarians and more than a third of LDP members also studied at Tokyo University. The same seat of learning also supplies a high proportion of the top executives and managers of Japan's leading corporations. Also worthy of note is the fact that former bureaucrats from the Ministry of Home Affairs occupy about a third of Japan's prefectural governorships as well as high positions in municipal governments.[5]

This combination of competence and interdependence between the bureaucracy and the worlds of business and politics has helped to ensure a degree of cohesion rarely found in the West. As a result, a consensus decision-making process involving wide consultation has evolved. Known as *nemawashi (rootbinding)*, after a gardening term which describes the careful untangling and binding of the roots of a tree before it is moved, the 'roots' of all parties relevant to a decision are considered to be bound when, having been closely informed of all that is going on, they reach a full understanding of the ensuing decisions. Deliberative councils consisting of former bureaucrats and businessmen, together with press clubs of relevant journalists which are closely linked to the ministries, widen the process further. If a group's interests are not in line with the emerging decision, they are less able to impede the effective implementation of the decision since their 'roots' are bound – although it is generally made clear that they will be given special consideration in the future.

In implementing its policies, MITI has a variety of means at its disposal. Particularly important in the early post-War years was finance. Investment in strategic industries was encouraged by tax incentives and loans from the Japanese Development Bank (JDB). Between 1952 and 1955, Japanese industry drew no less than 13 per cent of its external financing from the JDB and a further 15 per cent from another MITI-controlled fund, the Fiscal Investment and Loan Programme (FILP), which channelled postal savings accounts and public pension reserve funds into trust funds for the promotion of public policy. Four key selected industries – electric power, shipping, coal and steel – were the main beneficiaries, receiving 37 per cent of their external financing from a combination of JDB and FILP, although between 1971 and 1975, the figures for industrial finance stemming from the JDB and FLIP declined to four per cent and ten per cent respectively.[6]

Perhaps one of the greatest success stories of MITI guidance was the Japanese steel industry, which was extremely backward in the late 1940s. MITI drew up a master plan for large, new, integrated steel works sited at deep-water ports to facilitate the cheap import of ore and coal. Generous depreciation and tax allowances were allowed on the new plant, while imports of capital equipment were exempted from duty. This was backed by loans from both official and commercial banks with special credit dispensations from the Central Bank.

Investment was also made in overseas finishing plants, including Brazil, as well as in marketing outlets. As a result, by the late 1970s, Japan had no fewer than 25 two-million-ton blast furnaces, compared to only seven in the European Common Market and none at all in the United States. Japanese steel output rose from less than five million tons in 1951 to 22 million tons in 1960. By 1970, output was up to 93 million tons and 112 million tons in 1979, by which time Japan had leapt ahead of the United States, West Germany, Britain and France to become the free world's leading steel producer.

Shipbuilding was likewise successfully encouraged by very low interest loans, which were backed by an official programme of orders for Japanese shipbuilders which lasted up until 1962. Car production was also protected by high tariffs and quotas in the early 1950s and helped by MITI-inspired 'Buy Japanese' campaigns among the taxicab companies. MITI also contributed to the import of foreign automotive technology, particularly from Britain and France, by promulgating guidelines for car-assembly licensing agreements in 1952.

But in practical terms, MITI, with a budget of ¥650 billion (around £3 billion), less than two per cent of overall government spending, now ensures that most of its methods are relatively inexpensive. They include the regular two-way flow of information between industry and the ministry; the provision of tax and financial incentives; advice on special financing facilities provided by government institutions such as The Japan Development Bank, the Export–Import Bank and the Small Business Finance Corporation; the drawing up of regulations covering areas such as environmental safety and anti-trust legislation; the arrangement of advisory committees, involving academics, journalists, trades unionists and industrialists to help develop long-range strategies; and the provision of a certain amount of research and development and funding.

MITI's role in research and development operates mainly through its Agency of Industrial Science and Technology (AIST). This formulates policies relating to industrial technology and takes the initiative in R&D through 16 research institutes. With an annual budget of around $770 million, AIST is a catalyst for private-sector research efforts and is currently prioritizing research on biotechnology, electronics, alternative energy sources and new industrial materials. Among its successes was a water desalination process that was later commercialized and sold in the Middle East. Its current major ventures include a $50 million-a-year project of research into superconductivity, including a project involving a superconductor-based power generator, as well as research into advanced electronic devices such as the Josephson Junction, considered to be one of the key technologies in developing super-fast semiconductors.

Forecasting is another weapon that MITI and other agencies use to nudge Japanese industry in the appropriate direction. Dr Hisao Kanamori is a good example of one of Japan's far-sighted mandarins. Having spent five years with MITI in the early 1950s, Dr Kanamori then moved to the Economic Planning Agency as well as spending a spell overseas studying at Oxford. Later, he became the chief economist at Japan's Economic Research Centre. In papers entitled *Japan's Economic Future* and *The Outlook for Japan's Trillion Dollar Economy* in the early 1970s, he predicted that the country would have the largest per capita GNP in the world by 1985 and an average annual after-tax salary level of $23,700 – both pretty good predictions. Japan would achieve these levels, Dr Kanamori wrote, by upgrading its industry with more investment and research. This educative role regarding the prospects and direction of the economy is one of MITI's most important functions. It provides industry with visions, rather than directed plans, of where it should be going, and this has been an important factor in the widespread acceptance in Japan that industries decline as well as grow – an understanding which is of crucial importance to Japan's economic development.

For perhaps MITI's most significant role has been in sponsoring 'recession cartels' which have controlled prices or production to ease the transition of older industries in structural decline or during times of recession or crisis. Under the 1953 Amendment of the Anti-Monopoly Act, MITI has assisted with the rationalization of the bearings and car components industries, helped to reduce capacity in the aluminium sector, allocated production to help both the chemical and steel industries during recessions and imposed export price-floors on textiles, steel and other sectors during trade crises.

A toothless old dog

MITI's undoubted successes have given rise to an image of effortless command, of a monolithic Japan Inc where a compliant business community sways to the whims of a wise and far-sighted bureaucracy. In fact, MITI is very far from being all-powerful and all-seeing, and as the Japanese economy has developed in complexity, so MITI has become relatively less effective. It is now sometimes even referred to as *kyoyku mama* (*an over-anxious mother*) or even 'a faithful but toothless old dog'.

Even in its heyday, MITI's attempts to reorganize and encourage Japanese industry frequently met with fierce opposition and failure. In 1955, for example, when MITI attempted to create a mass car market within Japan by nurturing a small, low-cost 'people's car' along Volkswagen lines, the scheme was leaked to Japan's aggressive press and created such a storm of protest from existing and would-be car makers that it had to be abandoned.

Shortly after, in 1957, when Toyota began marketing a new diesel truck, MITI called in Eiji Toyoda, now the company's chairman, and told him to stop the project on the grounds that Isuzu was already in that market. Toyoda refused and set up a separate franchise network to distribute his diesel trucks which were ultimately very successful.[7] In the mid-1960s, MITI again attempted to rationalize Japan's burgeoning car manufacturers, but was barely successful. Toyota and Nissan, the two largest, did absorb a handful of the weaker auto makers, but Isuzu, Toyo Kogyo (Mazda), Honda and Mitsubishi remained and were soon joined by yet more new entrants in the form of Fuji Heavy Industries (Subaru), Suzuki and Daihatsu. The car industry again caused MITI problems when, soon after, Mitsubishi decided to join with Chrysler of the United States in the formation of a new car company – a decision taken without reference to MITI and at a time when the ministry believed it had sewn up a Mitsubishi–Isuzu merger.[8]

Later, in 1989, the motor industry again thwarted MITI when the Ministry warned the industry against expanding domestic capacity and so aggravating trade frictions. Toyota and Nissan quietly ignored the caution, but Yoshihiro Wada, the Mazda vice president, openly defied MITI saying that the industry had been short of capacity for years. He was joined by Honda's Tadashi Kume who claimed that his plants were already operating at full capacity.

MITI's attempts in the 1960s to encourage mergers among steel and chemical companies failed after a great deal of opposition and, to the embarrassment of the Ministry, the relevant bill had to be withdrawn from the Diet. Again, in 1965, when MITI tried to persuade steel companies to restrict their production in order to increase prices, the plan failed owing to the opposition of just one firm, Sumitomo. Similar attempts to restructure the aluminium industry were also unsuccessful, as were efforts to consolidate the computer industry in the 1970s. Sharp also led the calculator manufacturers in opposition to MITI's bid to shut off semiconductor imports, a move aimed at helping the infant Japanese microchip industry but which would have greatly harmed the calculator manufacturers.

Nor did MITI always get its predictions of up and coming industries right. It was only after a decade of successful private sector endeavour in robotics that the first MITI development programme was initiated. On other occasions, the bureaucrats simply misjudged situations, as when Sony had to postpone efforts to import transistor technology for two years because MITI officials thought that the company would be unable to make good use of the technology.

It is also worth remembering that other ministries have been at least as influential as MITI in shaping Japan's economic direction. This is particularly true of the prestigious Ministry of Finance which also draws more than 80 per cent of its recruits from Tokyo University. The Ministry of Finance's powers rested both on its role in setting MITI's annual budgets and on its control of foreign exchange, the banking system and its influence over the Central Bank on which Japan's large corporations were very dependent in the post-War period owing to a scarcity of capital and their high levels of debt. As a result, the Ministry of Finance was able to exert a great deal of influence over the economy and industry through its effective control of credit. As with MITI, however, the Ministry of Finance's power has declined steadily. As cash became more abundant in the 1980s, it became less necessary for the Ministry to channel capital into industry and in an increasingly liberalized market, companies have been better able to shop around internationally for the best deal.

Another aspect of the Japanese bureaucracy's power which has been exaggerated is its control over exchange rates, the theory being that the Japanese have kept theirs artificially low in order to boost exports and make imports more expensive. This was a common accusation before the appreciation of the yen in 1985 – for example in the *Washington Post* in 1984, Henry Kissinger accused the Japanese government of 'manipulating the exchange rate for the yen to favour Japanese exports'. Unfortunately, only a few months earlier the United States General Accounting Office had investigated this very charge and had declared that there was no evidence to support it.[9] What may be true is that as a country with poor resources, Japan's currency was unlikely to be strong in the oil-obsessed 1970s. Moreover, Japanese governments have tended to avoid public sector spending deficits and discouraged domestic consumption, hence helping to keep interest rates low and so reducing the attractiveness of the yen for investors. By contrast United States government deficits in the early 1980s were a major factor in that country's high interest rates and hence the strength of the dollar. To that extent, the problem was more one of dollar strength than yen weakness.

On some occasions, different arms of the bureaucracy have found themselves in conflict, as when, in 1951, many bureaucrats advised the Bank of Japan to refuse a loan to create the first modern post-War steel plant – a MITI-inspired project – on the grounds that Japan could not hope to compete against America's steel industry. Problems over the Narita International Airport in the 1970s which, owing to public resistance, had stood idle for a decade, were further compounded by jurisdictional disputes between ministries.[10] More recently, the Ministry of Finance and the Bank of Japan indulged in very public squabbling over whether or not to raise Japan's interest rates in order to support the yen – a row which was one factor in the destabilization of Japan's stock market early in 1990.

MITI's plans have not invariably met with success even when they have enjoyed strong political support. The Ministry lost one battle in 1963 when it promoted a law to empower itself to set up cartels in certain industries. Despite backing from Prime Minister Ikeda, the measure failed in the Diet owing to opposition from business and the Ministry of Finance.

There have been times too, when MITI has found itself embroiled in general domestic controversy, as in the infamous *Yami Karuteru (Black Cartel)* case in the 1970s. Japan's 12 leading oil companies, together with 17 senior executives, were indicted by the Japanese Fair Trade Commission (JFTC) for operating an illegal cartel, which involved price fixing and withholding products from the market in order to drive up prices. This was not the only time that the JFTC and MITI were on opposing sides. In 1974, the JFTC attempted to pass an anti-monopoly law which would have increased its powers to break up cartels. MITI fought the law tooth and nail, with the result that when it was eventually passed by the Diet in June 1977, it was considerably weaker than the original version, although still not to MITI's liking.

'Pinching money from a blind man's tin . . .'

On 3 April 1989, banner headlines all over Europe proudly proclaimed the fact that Airbus Industrie, the European aircraft manufacturing consortium, had won yet another huge order for 20 of its new A-330 long-range jetliners from the Hong Kong airline, Cathay Pacific. It seemed almost like a fairytale success story for the European aerospace industry which for so long had played second fiddle to the United States. Most galling to Airbus' main rival, Boeing, must have been the fact that one of America's top flag-carrying airlines, TWA, had also just ordered 40 of the aircraft, all on top of a substantial sale of the smaller, mid-range A-320 to America's Northwest Airlines just a year earlier.

Behind the headlines, however, lay a two-decade long government-sponsored endeavour, led primarily by the French, to make a mark in the commercial jet-liner market, which the individual aerospace industries of the main European nations had manifestly failed to penetrate on their own. Thus arose the Airbus consortium which, by the mid-1980s, consisted of France's Aerospatiale (37.9 per cent), West German Messerschmitt-Bolkow-Blohm (MBB) (37.9 per cent), British Aerospace (20 per cent) and Casa of Spain (4.2 per cent).

Despite its increasing sales success, however, Airbus has never sold an aircraft at a profit and has swallowed up a massive $13.9 billion* in unpaid loans and guarantees without ever having produced any proper accounts. For Airbus is primarily financed by the national governments of the consortium companies, which cover the losses sustained in the manu-facture of the various parts of Airbus aircraft. For example, the British government provided British Aerospace with £250 million in launch aid for the A-320 and a further £450 million for the longer-range A-330/340 programme. West German support for Airbus since 1967 has totalled $5.6 billion, including $1.65 billion for the A-330/340 announced in 1987. France has injected a total of $2.7 billion into Airbus, including $975 million in 1987, while Spain's contribution has amounted to $500 million since 1972.[11]

Moreover, the efficiency of the project is compromised by the fact that the Airbus member aerospace companies not only own the consortium, but are also prime contractors for the parts of the aircraft for which they are responsible, so are effectively acting as both producer and customer. In addition, national and political interests rather than industrial efficiency tend to dictate where different parts of the aircraft are made. So wings are produced in Britain and other major sub-assemblies all over Europe, which have to be expensively transported to Toulouse in France for final assembly – all in all, hardly a recipe for cost control.

This helps to explain why, early in 1989, the Bonn government had to offer guarantees of up to DM1.7 billion (£620million) to cover possible exchange-rate related losses on sales of Airbus aircraft, on top of earlier obligations for the development and production of Airbus models. This guarantee was part of a successful government attempt to persuade the giant motor and electricals conglomerate, Daimler–Benz, to take a controlling stake in MBB which was majority-owned by the public sector – in spite of

---

* In fact, because Airbus does not maintain proper accounts, the precise figure is unknown. This estimate is based on a report by the accountancy firm Coopers & Lybrand.

opposition from the Federal Cartel Office which was against the concentration of too much industrial power in the hands of Daimler–Benz.

新　大　国

A common theme among writers on the Japanese economic miracle is to claim that Japan is somehow unique or different from the West in that the Japanese government – primarily through MITI – has closely supported and subsidized Japan's industry in a way which allows it to compete unfairly with the West. The American political scientist Chalmers Johnson has even coined a special term – the 'capitalist developmental state' – for industrial nations which are fundamentally capitalist, but where bureaucrats and industrialists cling together in a close embrace. And Karel van Wolferen, in his influential book *The Enigma of Japanese Power*, put it thus: 'Somewhat belatedly it began to dawn on a few anxious United States and European observers that Japan, far from "beating the West at its own game", it might not be playing the Western "game" at all'; and asks 'whether international free trade as a system can survive as long as the countries without a trade strategy are locked in a struggle to accommodate these formidable capitalist developmental states'.[12]

I believe that the problem with such interpretations is that many writers simply do not realize the extent to which almost all Western industrialized nations have indulged in the same practices of trying to pick strategically important industries and promoting, protecting and subsidizing them. Aerospace has been one of these privileged industries. Indeed, in 1967, Britain's Minister of Technology, Anthony Wedgwood-Benn, recounted at a dinner how Ministers of Aviation had been ' . . . the most hated and feared ministers in the government. While their colleagues were grateful for anything they could wring from the Chancellor of the Exchequer, Ministers of Aviation ran off with sums of money that made the great train robbers look like schoolboys pinching money from a blind man's tin.'[13]

In Britain and France, the main aerospace manufacturers have consistently won lucrative contracts for military aircraft and engines which have helped to subsidize their commercial operations. Even so, not one of the many post-War British or French commercial airliners, ranging from the Caravelle to the Trident, would have flown without substantial government aid, including the purchase of such aircraft by state-owned airlines. Between 1945 and 1974, total British government contributions to a swarm of exotically named aircraft, ranging from the Brabazon to the Hermes and the Comet to the Brittania, totalled £741.2 million at 1974 prices, from which investment the state received a return of only £54.5 million. The losses on the joint Anglo-French supersonic aircraft, Concorde, are alone believed to have reached £1 billion (at 1970 prices).

The British government has also been a keen promoter of the nation's aerospace products overseas. In 1986, for example, a fleet of Westland helicopters was purchased by the Indian government after the personal intervention of Mrs Thatcher, despite having earlier been rejected by the Indian Ministry of Civil Aviation. This type of support led Akio Morita to comment:

> Japan Inc, as many Americans and Europeans call our government–business relationship, is second-rate compared to the French government–business relationship, or the English one for that matter. For one thing, I have never heard a Japanese head of state or head of government try to sell in that way.[14]

This state intervention in favour of the domestic industry has, on occasions, left governments with substantial quantities of egg on their faces. When, in 1977, the British Ministry of Defence wanted to buy American-made early-warning AWAC aircraft, lobbying by interested trade unions and the giant British electronics and engineering company, GEC, led to the contract being awarded to GEC's Marconi division. The British Nimrod AWACs never met specifications, however, and by the time the project was eventually abandoned in 1986 in favour of bought-in Boeing AWACs, more than £1 billion had been lost.

These examples should not be allowed to create the impression that Britain has cosseted her plane-makers any more than have France or West Germany. If anything, in recent years British aerospace subsidies have been reduced. And many of the smaller European nations have been just as guilty. The Swedish government, for example, granted Saab-Scania a $187.5 million loan for the development of the Saab 2000 airliner in 1989; the Italian government has given huge subsidies to its state-owned aerospace companies, Aeritalia and Agusta, while the Dutch government was closely involved in bailing out Fokker in 1988.

Yet ask a Western industrialist about their Japanese competition, and there is a good chance that they will tell you, with a perfectly straight face, that the contest is unfair because of an interventionist conspiracy to direct Japan's industry to world domination. What they will rarely mention is the massive government intervention in industry in Europe, which amounted to £517 per employed person (£65 billion in total) in the EC in 1986, according to a report by Sir Leon Brittan, the EC Commissioner in charge of competition. 'The amounts are so high', said Mr Brittan, who himself is an ex-British Secretary of State for Trade and Industry, 'that . . . the effects on competition [are] pronounced.'

Aerospace is only the most popular and high-profile field of government intervention in Europe. According to the Brittan report, the manufacturing sector as a whole receives no less than £1,200 per employee in state aid. Steel and shipbuilding are the most favoured industries, getting £4 billion and £900 million respectively, but the report goes on to show that even excluding these two most subsidized areas, each EC manufacturing worker is supported to the tune of £1,050. Britain and Denmark offend least in this respect, subsidizing their manufacturing employees by only £448 and £360 respectively while, at the other end of the scale, Italian workers are state-supported to the tune of £3,523 per person. The Brittan report's highlighting of Italian subsidies was confirmed by a survey by Italy's independent accounting watchdog, the Corte dei Conti, which alleged that in 1988 Italy's pampered companies had pocketed £20 billion of the state's money.

'This intervention', reported Mr Brittan, 'is usually concentrated in loss-making industrial enterprises which might otherwise disappear from the market . . . they prevent the market mechanism bringing about normal rationalization . . . and are grossly unfair.' He went on to say, however, that 'certain Member States apply an interventionist industrial policy in what they consider key sectors. Such aids are often deliberately designed to promote and protect national champions – well-known large companies'.[15]

In addition to straight protectionism, most European countries have included a mixture of subsidies, tax breaks, export credits, research and development assistance, loan guarantees and soft loans, equity participation and state procurement policies geared to aid key industries in their recipe for economic success. For example, over the course of its 70-year history, Britain's state-backed export credits body, the ECGD, has lent some £250 billion to help cover the risks involved in exporting, losing a cumulative £693 million in the process. Even little Switzerland has its Export Risk Guarantee programme, which lost nearly £100 million in both 1987 and 1988 and has built up an accumulated debt to the Swiss government of SFr1.6 billion (£650 million).

Most Western governments also spend far more on industrial research and development than Japan. Only around two per cent of Japan's total non-defence R&D is accounted for by government spending, a level that is extremely low by comparison with most developed countries. In West Germany, for example, even after excluding defence-related spending, 17.8 per cent of R&D was state-funded in 1985.

Examples of state aid to industry in Europe are legion and go back a long way: in Britain, the Macmillan government set up the National Economic Development Council to provide a guiding hand and subsidies to industry, while attempts by successive Labour governments to control the commanding heights of the economy, particularly steel, also resulted in certain industries receiving massive governmental support. In the 1960s and 1970s, the instruments of this policy were economic planning boards such as the Industrial Reorganization Corporation and the National Enterprise Board, which subsidized and nurtured strategic, high-technology industries and encouraged industrial reorganization. Britain's nationalized industries were particularly heavily subsidized – support reached £3 billion a year by the late 1970s, although it has since been cut to about £500 million a year as a result of privatization and restructuring.[16] In Italy, too, the post-War Istitutio per la Ricostruzione Industriale (IRI) liaised with state-owned banks to establish a modern heavy and light engineering sector.

France's industrial policy has been characterized by a series of nationalistic economic plans which have included encouraging inward investment and heavy subsidies to key industries. Jean-François Saglio, France's current Directeur Général de l'Industrie, the top civil servant in the French industry ministry, has admitted that before 1985 the government, directly or indirectly, pumped FFr30 to FFr40 billion (£3 to £4 billion) a year into industry. This included aid to shipbuilding of between FFr5 to FFr7 billion (£500 to £700 million) a year, between FFr7 and FFr15 billion (£700 million to £1.5 billion) a year to the steel industry and around FFr 1.5 billion (£150 million) to the computer industry. The country's state-controlled companies, which account for a third of France's industrial production, are the main recipients – businesses like Renault (cars), Groupe Bull (computers) and Pechiney (aluminium) have debts of well over 100 per cent of shareholders' funds, even after receiving huge state loan write-offs, and would almost certainly be insolvent if it were not for French Government guarantees. The 1989 French budget included FFr4 billion (£400 million) for straight capital contributions to state companies and the 1990 figure was even higher to account for investment in new technologies, including FFr1 billion (£100 million) for Groupe Bull and FFr2 billion (£200 million) for the Thomson electronics group.

The vehicle industry is among the strategic industries targeted for intervention by most Western European governments. Here the French again have been the main culprits. Apart from being substantially protected from Japanese imports, state-owned Renault has absorbed a huge sum of government money, believed to be close to FFr100 million (£10 billion), since 1970. Renault used the money both to cover losses and to expand into automobile-related areas such as robotics for car factories and Formula One racing. One ill-starred venture even involved them entering the coffee market in a countertrade deal with Columbia, involving the exchange of cars for coffee. Renault bought two brand new instant coffee plants which utilized a new process from a Belgian conman, only to discover that the technology didn't work – by which time the coffee had gone off.

Britain's car industry has also been subject to extensive intervention – and not always with good results. In 1968, the Labour government, through its Industrial Reorganization Corporation, encouraged the two main indigenous car manufacturers, Leyland and BMC, to merge in a market-rationalization move. But the group had to be taken into state-ownership in 1976 after running into difficulties and, apart from being protected from Japanese imports, was given subsidies amounting to £2 billion before being sold back into the private sector in 1988. Similar, ill thought-out state intervention in the British motor-cycle industry encouraged the merger of Norton and Triumph, hastening the demise of both companies, despite subsidies. Even West Germany intervened in its auto industry by bailing out Volkswagen in the early 1970s.

Land of the free

When, during his State of the Union address in 1986, President Reagan talked of a plane which would be 'a new Orient Express that could, by the end of the next decade, take off from Dulles Airport and accelerate up to 25 times the speed of sound, attaining low Earth orbit or flying to Tokyo within two hours', his audience broke into a spontaneous ripple of applause. President Reagan was outlining plans for a state-promoted hypersonic plane now known as the 'National Aerospace Plane' or 'NASP' for short.

Lest any American reader should at this point be getting self-righteous about how much European countries promote and aid their industries, it is worth dwelling a little on the fact that America is hardly Mr Clean in this respect. Since President Reagan's far-sighted address, for example, Congress has provided nearly $1 billion[17] in funding for the NASP project which involves developing the X-30 ('X' for experimental) – a space plane about the size of a Boeing 727 airliner which will take off from an ordinary runway, before accelerating and leaping into orbit at Mach 25, 25 times the speed of sound. The craft would be a major departure from current space vehicles in that it would be powered by air-breathing engines for its flight through the atmosphere before moving on to conventional rocket motors. The ultimate goal is to develop two different types of craft, one for passenger transport and the other for carrying satellites and cargo into space.

It may well be that the X-30 will never make its dramatic leap into orbit or transport well-heeled travellers from Washington to Tokyo in a mere two hours, for many in President Bush's administration are getting cold feet about the project's ultimate viability. But NASP is, nonetheless, a very good example of the type of support given to American industry by its government. For not only do United States aircraft manufacturers such as Lockheed and McDonnell–Douglas gain lucrative contracts from such projects, they also stand to benefit from any NASP technology which might be developed.

In fact, NASP is untypical of American industrial support in that it is fairly overtly aimed at the civilian commercial market. More generally, United States support for industry has tended to be disguised in the garb of military spending. Although, for example, the Pentagon's Defence Advanced Projects Agency (Darpa) is a military research body with a budget of more than $1 billion in 1990, it funds a variety of primarily commercial research projects, including super-fast computers and light-weight satellites.

Moreover, the United States has for a long time run expensive R&D development programmes operated by the Department of Defence as well as by the National Aeronautics and Space Administration (NASA) which, though primarily defence-oriented, have led to significant commercial benefits for American manufacturers. These have included the $5 billion C-5A Galaxy Airforce Transport plane programme in the 1960s which spawned both the Boeing 747 jumbo jet and the DC-10, as well as helping General Electric and Pratt & Whitney to major advances in engine technology. The Pentagon has also strongly supported the United States machine tool industry which it considers to be of vital strategic importance. For example, the Manufacturing Technology programme, which began in 1949, involved Air Force funding of research leading to the development of computer-controlled machine tools, technology which was transferred to American manufacturers through licences and large orders. Programmes of this type have resulted in some of America's largest corporations being primarily dependent on government contracts. In 1988, three American companies, General Dynamics, Lockheed and McDonnell–Douglas each benefited from more than $8 billion in government defence purchases.[18] (In the case of Lockheed, government orders accounted for 85 per cent of its revenues.)

The United States has also used military aid to ensure orders for American industry: one recent example was the financing in 1990 of the acquisition by Portugal of 20 General Dynamics F-16 fighters, worth about $450 million, through United States Foreign Military Sales credits. In fact, economic and military assistance to less developed countries has frequently come tied to the procurement of the American goods: United States foreign assistance and military credit sales amounted to $15.5 billion in 1982, about 4.5 per cent of total United States exports of goods and services in that year.

It is sometimes asserted that military-based intervention in industry is not as effective as the more directly commercially oriented support which predominates in Japan or Europe. Leaving aside the fact that some 'defence' funding relates directly to commercial products, there is some truth in this, for support directed primarily toward military objectives tends to involve batch production of relatively small runs of expensive, highly-specified products. There are other disadvantages to the economy as a whole in having high-tech companies too geared to military production, an issue examined in more detail later (in Chapter 17). But although military-oriented intervention may be an inefficient way of supporting industry, it still offers immensely valuable spin-offs from military contracts and research and does give advantages to certain specific civilian industries such as aerospace. Indeed, time and time again American politicians have made this very point in justifying expenditure on expensive, technology-intensive space and military programmes.

Nor has all of the United States' support for her industry been even indirectly related to military needs. NASA has aided General Electric in the development of its new 90,000lb thrust GE90 big fan engine, with a diameter as large as that of a Boeing 737, which is aimed at the next generation of twin-engined long-range aircraft. One of the largest federal-sponsored research programmes, the super-conductor collider project, is funded to the tune of $8 million. Overall American state funding for R&D in 1987 was $60 billion, of which $41 billion was estimated to be defence-related.[19] In fact, the proportion of United States civil R&D which is government-financed is far higher than Japan's at 33.9 per cent; moreover, in 1985, 76.2 per cent of the United States aerospace industry's R&D was supplied by the state, compared to only 9.3 per cent in Japan; while 40.3 per cent of American electrical industry research was government funded, as opposed to only one per cent in Japan.[20]

One major, but generally unreported, way in which America has subsidized its industry is through specially targeted tax breaks geared to helping exporters. In 1972, the United States adopted Domestic International Sales Corporation (DISC) legislation under which United States firms were allowed to defer payment of corporation tax on export earnings. This was effectively an export subsidy, illegal under GATT which ruled against the law in 1976. But it was not until 1984 that the United States finally did away with DISC, and in doing so she merely changed the system into the Foreign Sales Corporation which converted the tax deferment into a tax remission. One estimate puts the effective subsidy afforded by DISC at about $10 to 12 billion: Boeing alone benefited by $397 million according to its 1985 annual report.[21] An OECD survey puts overall American tax concessions and grants for industry in 1988 at $66.3 billion.

In addition, apart from the import restrictions, geared to helping the United States auto industry, outlined earlier, the American government intervened in 1980 to rescue the virtually bankrupt car maker, Chrysler Corporation, with $1.5 million in loan guarantees. Lee Iacocca, Chrysler's Chief Executive Officer, who at the time became an instant American folk hero for his part in the Chrysler rescue, claims to be an ardent free-marketeer and writes: 'Ideologically, I've always been a free-enterpriser, a believer in survival of the fittest.' He is also bitterly critical of interventionism in Japan:

> The field where this game is being played is not level. Instead, it's strongly tilted in favour of Japan. As a result we are playing with one hand tied behind our back . . . to begin with, Japanese industry is not playing by itself. It's backed to the hilt in its close relationship to the Japanese government in the form of MITI . . . its overall impact on Japanese industry has been incredible.[22]

Yet not only has Chrysler itself been the recipient of massive United States government aid designed to prevent a prestigious company from becoming bankrupt, but it has also long been among the largest importers of Japanese cars into the United States, bringing Mitsubishi models to sell under its Dodge and Plymouth names – often in direct competition with its own American-produced cars and trucks.

10

新
大
国

PREVENTING GREAT HARM

'The principal role of the government of Japan at the operating, business level of industrial change and growth has been to facilitate and accelerate the workings of the market, to speed the process of reduction of declining sectors, and to work to clear the way for market forces to have full play in emerging growth sectors.'
James Abegglen, consultant and Japanese industry expert.[1]

MITI's CHIEF TRADE negotiator is Makoto Kuroda, the Vice Minister for International Affairs. He is not known for his reticence, having a reputation for being blunt, even to the point of arrogance, and has crossed swords on occasions with the Western press – notably the *Washington Post* in 1988 over comments he was alleged to have made on trade barriers. Fluent in English, Kuroda loves travel and has a habit of playing bridge deep into the night. During the period in which he has occupied his current office, 58-year-old Kuroda has seen Japan's image change from being an industrial success story to that of an economic bogey man. He strongly rejects charges of unfair trading, however, saying that Japan does not cheat, and that she does not differ from the West in having elements of state planning in her economy. The difference, he says, is that Japan has simply implemented her industrial strategy better than most of her trading partners.

When questioned as to whether MITI's primary role is in support of industry, he replies that 'MITI nurtures industry, helping to guide it away from a crisis in the first place rather than helping to dig it out later'. By contrast, he says, 'even Washington's attitude towards business is basically adversarial. Government is considered to be necessary because of the need to control industry's abuses. In Japan, government is here to foster industry.'

Though MITI is often held up as an example of the kind of control seen in planned economies, Kuroda asserts that its real strength lies in the fact that it has always been based on free-market principles. One example, he says, is that Japan, unlike the United States, allowed the full 1970s oil price rises to be passed straight on to consumers:

> We had no other way but to absorb all the price hike in the market. The result, I think, is very clear: our way of conducting the economy is much better because the economy has adapted fairly flexibly to these changes. And that has built confidence amongst government officials as well as businessmen to rely on the force of the markets.[2]

As examples quoted earlier show, Western countries have intervened in almost every area of their economies. They have used a variety of instruments ranging from overt or covert import protection, to subsidies, the provision of credit and public procurement. So all in all, it is very difficult to sustain the thesis that the Japanese have been significantly more interventionist than the Europeans or Americans. What may, however, be true is that where they have intervened, the Japanese do appear to have been more successful – or perhaps to have done less harm.

There is one major, and a number of subsidiary, reasons for this. Above all, as Kuroda asserts, the extent to which intervention has succeeded and been of significance in the development of the Japanese economy has been almost entirely due to the fact that, unlike European intervention, the Japanese variety has been primarily geared to run with the grain of market forces, rather than against it.

Put simply, MITI, and Japanese bureaucrats and politicians in general, have well understood that the nature of economic development is for countries to move from labour-intensive, low technology, low added-value products (the so-called 'soft technologies', such as textiles), on to less labour-intensive, medium technology, higher added-value products (the 'hard technologies' such as steel, heavy engineering and shipbuilding) before moving on to sophisticated, capital and technology-intensive products, such as computers and software – often called the 'knowledge industries'.

In that way, not only does productivity steadily increase, but the economy continually stays ahead of advancing rivals. So as the Japanese have seen newer or developing economies like South Korea and Taiwan steadily gaining ground on their older industries, MITI has cushioned their abandonment while encouraging business to move on to areas of higher development. This helps to explain why there was little for the Japanese to worry about when Japan's steel production fell between 1980 and 1988, while South Korea's doubled. Nor was there much concern over the slippage in Japanese ship production over the same period, at a time when South Korea's expanded sixfold to almost equal Japan's output.

For the Japanese have generally recognized the interdependence of developing and developed economies. By allowing up and coming countries to move into industries which she had largely vacated, Japan has ensured that such economies have been better able to afford to buy her more advanced products, which often include major components and assemblies at the higher technology end of those industries which she had largely relinquished. One example is marine engines. Although South Korea almost caught up with Japanese ship production in the late 1980s, most of the engines going into South Korean-built vessels, together with many of the more complex assemblies and equipment, are still either Japanese or assembled under licence to Japanese companies.

So as the share of Japan's exports taken by textiles slipped from 15 per cent to five per cent between 1965 and 1985, and as over the same period shipbuilding's share fell from ten per cent to five per cent and iron and steel declined from a peak of 20 per cent in the mid-1970s to six per cent a decade later, other industries have risen to take their place – like vehicles, which only accounted for five per cent of exports in 1965, but had grown to 20 per cent by the mid-1980s.

MITI's role, therefore, has been one of keeping a step ahead of market forces, by setting high standards for new plants and concentrating resources in areas where it thinks Japan might be internationally competitive. As wages rose to Western levels in the late 1960s, for example, MITI encouraged industry to redeploy its resources into capital-intensive rather than labour-intensive industries. Again, after the 1973 oil shock, they pushed through plans to move Japan into service and knowledge-intensive industries and away from energy-intensive ones.

As a result, unlike its counterparts in Europe, MITI has not been preoccupied with bailing out ailing public-sector industries. Rather, it has concerned itself with positive changes in the industrial structure of the economy. Declining industries, or those operating in fields in which MITI officials considered that Japan could not be competitive, were either assisted in diversification, encouraged to merge or even to go out of business. Thus, far from being an example of state socialism, as some have alleged, the Japanese government has accepted the ultimate value and inevitability of market forces, largely limiting its role to hastening industrial adjustment to the trends.

In recent years, therefore, MITI has, on the one hand, helped new industries with a variety of high technology projects, while on the other, the Ministry has run a series of programmes for steadily running down depressed Japanese industries. Firms which produce two-thirds of the output of a declining industry can petition the government for a restructuring plan, agreeing to capacity reductions in return for loan guarantees and tax benefits. In mid-1984, there were 22 such officially designated industries, of which five (paper, ethylene, fertilizer, polyolefins and PVC resin) were allowed to form legal cartels to restrict output and price competition.

Under such sponsorship, the output of the older industries was, by the 1980s, cut down to a third of its pre-1973 level. Indeed, the Japanese government has had no sentimental attachment to declining industries and has consistently allowed them to run down. The percentage of GNP accounted for by textiles, for example, fell from 18.5 per cent in 1954 to 8.2 per cent in 1977, while the share of GNP accounted for by machinery rose from 13.6 per cent to 23 per cent. In the process, the 600,000 textile workers of 1950 had, by 1970, fallen to 150,000.

According to industry expert James Abegglen, this managing of declining sectors, rather than the promotion of sunrise industries, may well be MITI's greatest contribution to the Japanese economy. As he says:

> It may be the case that it is in the power of governments to prevent great harm but not to do great good. In contrast to the governments of the Western economies, it is the Japanese government's policy towards declining industries that is most impressive. The government is capable of a real recognition of the need for and desirability of industrial structural change. Money is not spent in efforts to shore up declining industries. Tariffs are not raised to defend declining industries. Instead, assistance is given to the prompt and effective closing down of capacity.[3]

Cushioning decline

Shipbuilding is one industry which MITI has helped to a genteel decline. Large tankers are really a combination of steel and labour with little advanced technology. Hence this is just the type of industry which should migrate to lower-wage economies, particularly those with efficient steel industries. This was precisely what happened in the 1970s. As South Korea expanded its shipbuilding, the major Japanese yards agreed capacity reductions with government support for the scrapping of facilities and a short-term cartel to put a floor under prices. The result was that between 1976 and 1978, Japan's shipbuilding capacity was reduced by 40 per cent. In the process, Japan's heavy industrial companies have reduced their dependence on shipbuilding and diversified into other areas of engineering in a way unmatched by their Western counterparts. By the early 1980s, shipbuilding and repair only accounted for a quarter of their sales, a proportion which had fallen to only 13 per cent by 1988. Instead, companies like Mitsubishi Heavy Industries and Ishikawajima-Harima Heavy Industries have moved aggressively into more sophisticated areas such as aerospace, rolling stock and construction equipment.

Western interventionism, by contrast, has often been out of line with market forces. For while it is true that much state support has gone to higher-tech industries, such aerospace, mentioned earlier, together with computers and semiconductors (the subject of Chapter 18), the more complex political imperatives of Western economies, with their massive traditional industrial sectors employing vast numbers of workers represented by powerful political lobbies, has ensured that a great deal of state aid has been targeted on keeping alive the very industries which the Japanese have vacated.

This difference in approach is expounded by Katsuo Seiki, MITI's Director for Western Europe, Africa and the Middle East in the Ministry's International Trade Policy Bureau. Twenty-two years a MITI man, Katsuo Seiki, a squat, plump but well-dressed man in his mid-40s, is no stranger to the West, having spent three years in Paris and two in the United States. I met him in his fifteenth-floor office, which was dominated by an incongruous and rather ancient Air France map of the world.

Oozing confidence and fluent in English, Seiki told me that Western countries were wrong to attribute too much of Japan's success to state intervention in industry, pointing out that:

> In Japan we rarely intervene to subsidize and keep alive old industries. Rather, we would like to cushion their decline and allow newer, developing economies to move into those industries which can no longer afford to pay for the standard of living which we want for our people.
>
> By keeping such industries alive, not only is the West dooming itself to a retarded economic development, but it is also forfeiting the right of underdeveloped countries to advance their economies as quickly as they might, while at the same time making them less able to buy goods from the developed world.

Perhaps the classic example of this difference in approach lies in the textile and clothing industry, an essential sector in a developing economy, but, owing to its relatively labour-intensive and low added-value nature, not one which should form a large component of an advanced economy. Nonetheless, textiles has long been subject to both protection and subsidies in the West. In the 1920s and 1930s, most Western countries imposed higher tariffs on textile imports than they did on other manufactures and this system continued after the Second World War, with even the United States insisting on restrictions on cotton textile exports from Japan in 1955. This was followed by a more formal 'voluntary export restraint programme', beginning with the 1956 Agricultural Act, which empowered the President to negotiate restraints with low-cost textile-producing countries.

1961 and 1962 saw the Short- and Long-Term Arrangements on cotton textiles which further limited imports; and by 1963, the United States had set up import restrictions against 17 countries and territories. Most of the main Western European economies maintained similar restraints, and these were all consolidated into the international Multi-Fibre Arrangement (MFA) of 1974. Originally considered a temporary measure to give Western textile industries a four-year 'breathing space' to restructure and meet low-cost competition from developing countries, the MFA has nonetheless been renewed every four years following shrill and effective lobbying from the textile manufacturers and unions, which is, perhaps, understandable bearing in mind that much textile production tends to be concentrated in areas of high unemployment.

Many industrialized countries also now conclude additional bilateral import restrictions on top of the MFA. China and the United States, for example, signed an agreement in February 1988 limiting the growth of Chinese textile exports to a mere three per cent annually for the next four years, reducing a growth rate of 19 per cent which was allowed under a previous agreement. The new agreement was signed by United States Trade Representative Clayton Yeutter – one of the fiercest critics of Japanese trade practices – and covered all major categories of textiles, including products not previously subject to restraint such as silk, ramie and other natural fibres.

Japan's textile industry was, of course, a major component in her early industrial development. Japan had already become a major exporter of synthetics in the 1930s, and textiles formed the basis of her post-War recovery. Cotton textile manufacturers like Toyobo were for a long time the largest companies in Japan. But although subject to import restraints abroad, Japan has offered her own textile manufacturers only limited protection from imports from developing countries. As a result, between 1980 and 1987, textile production fell by seven per cent, import penetration more than doubled to 37 per cent and Japan's share of world textile exports fell to only 3.8 per cent, slipping below South Korea's seven per cent and Italy's 10.1 per cent.[4] Moreover, by 1985, Japan was running a deficit in her textile trade. Toyobo had by then long since lost its pre-eminent position as Japan's largest company first to shipbuilder Mitsubishi Heavy Industries in the 1960s, which itself was succeeded by steel-maker Nippon Steel in the 1970s. It, in turn, was supplanted by Toyota in 1983.

The Japanese textile companies have in recent years lobbied more actively for the protection which is available under the MFA, the provisions of which Japan, alone among the developed countries, has never implemented, although she maintained some import quotas. But they have been vigorously resisted by MITI for the very reason that it has particularly wanted to see Japan move out of the lower-value end of the textile market and into other areas. (In fact, Japan has been well in advance of the West in calling for the rapid abolition of the MFA during the Uruguay Round of GATT trade talks.) Instead, MITI has organized a series of schemes to cut capacity in the textile industry. These, together with the pressure applied to Japanese textile manufacturers by the relative absence of protection, have not only improved their competitiveness but also tended to push them into the upper end of the textile market. Kanebo, for example, is now earning big profits from new products such as its line of scented fabrics, used in a brand of underwear called 'Casablanca' which is supposed to exude a romantic aroma!

Moreover, Japanese textile companies have also been forced into diversifying out of textiles and clothing. In the 1970s, for example, many of Japan's major textile firms moved into chemicals, construction and car components. As a result, by 1978, 35.7 per cent of the sales of the six leading synthetics producers were non-textile, compared to only 11.8 per cent in 1968. Teijin, the company that pioneered the production of man-made fibres in Japan in 1918, now dominates the global market for magnetic tape together with another venerable Japanese textile company, Toray, which has also moved into advanced materials (its Torayca product, used in carbon-fibre reinforced plastic, has been employed in the tail sections of Airbus aircraft and is certified by Boeing).

Meanwhile, in the West, job losses in the textile industry have continued unabated, despite the protection afforded by the MFA. Many Western textile and clothing firms are still producing goods in the lower sector of the market where profits are slim and where they even find it difficult, in many instances, to find employees prepared to work for the low wages on offer in what is inevitably a relatively unproductive industry. Should all protection disappear, on the most extreme assumption around 2.5 million jobs might be lost over a decade (one per cent of total employment in the developed countries).[5] To put this into perspective, the decline in employment in agriculture alone in France, West Germany and Italy between 1959 and 1974 was 5.2 million. Against that, many commentators claim there would be the widespread economic gains of lower textile prices which would benefit the economy as a whole and help to create jobs in other industrial sectors.

Above all, trade experts claim that the end of the MFA would greatly assist the developing countries, with substantial knock-on benefits for the industrialized world. For whereas textiles only accounts for some 14 per cent of manufacturing employment and seven per cent of output in the developed world, in developing countries those figures are 28 per cent and 15 per cent respectively.[6] Restricting textile exports from such countries reduces their potential to expand their industrial base, diminishing the possibility of their treading the same path to industrialization that Japan, Hong Kong, South Korea and Taiwan have taken and raising their miserable living standards – something which makes the almost fanatical support for the MFA by socialists appear somewhat strange. The MFA also makes it far less likely that such poor countries will be able to afford to increase their imports of higher technology products from the developed world.

Textiles, however, is not the only declining industry which has been supported through state intervention. OECD figures for 1981–6 show how disproportionately European countries have concentrated industrial subsidies on declining sectors of the economy. Over this period, support for France's steel industry equalled 58.3 per cent of its output, while 56.6 per cent of her shipbuilding industry's production was accounted for by subsidies, compared to only 3.6 per cent for other manufacturing industries. The comparable figures for Italy were 71.4 per cent, 34.2 per cent and 15.8 per cent; for Belgium they were 40.4 per cent, 27.7 per cent and 4.5 per cent; and for the United Kingdom 57.6 per cent, 21.6 per cent and 2.9 per cent.[7]

And while Japan largely abandoned her high-cost coal industry in the 1960s and 1970s, most of the main European countries have clung onto theirs. The British state-owned electricity generating corporation for a long time operated a system whereby it guaranteed to buy 95 per cent of its coal needs from the state-owned coal industry (this changed under the 1989 Electricity Privatization Act). The resultant higher power prices cost electricity consumers in excess of £1 billion a year – on top of a direct government subsidy to the coal industry of close to £2 billion a year.

West Germany has also protected its 155,000 coal miners to the tune of more than DM10 billion (£4 billion) a year. Under the *Jahrhundertvertrag* (*century contract*), the power utilities are committed to buying at least 45 million tonnes of domestic coal a year until 1995. To cover the difference between the price of home-produced coal and cheaper imports, the government allows utilities to levy an extra 7.25 per cent on electricity bills – known as the *Kohlepfennig* (*coal penny*), while steel producers are compensated through the *Huttenvertrag* (*steel works contract*).

National champions

Even where state intervention in the West has been geared towards the encouragement of the industries of the future, such efforts have often been hamstrung by confused objectives, political meddling and conflicting imperatives, not to mention the unsuitability of some advanced industries to economies incapable of sustaining them. Take Britain's nuclear power industry, for example. Britain's engineers and scientists led the world during the 1950s in harnessing the power of the atom to produce electricity: indeed, Britain was the first country to build a civil nuclear power station. The problems began with political in-fighting between technocrats at the national Atomic Energy Authority and the state-run generating company, the Central Electricity Generating Board (CEGB). They could not agree between several competing reactor designs with the result that Britain decided in 1965 to go ahead with home-grown advanced gas-cooled (AGR) reactor technology, despite offers of cheaper boiling-water and pressurized-water reactors (PWR) from General Electric and Westinghouse of the United States.

The decision to go for AGR technology was shrouded in secrecy: no record of the discussions was made. But the outcome, involving a relatively small and weak British consortium being chosen to build a reactor hugely more complex than those on offer from the United States, must indicate that the decision was taken as part of a nationalistic industrial strategy to build up an advanced British nuclear power generating capacity. In fact, AGR technology never worked properly: by the early 1970s, all five of the new AGR stations were in deep trouble. Indeed, after nearly two decades, the first AGR reactor at Dungeness is still only producing a fraction of its planned output.

The CEGB chairman, Arthur Hawkins, called the programme in 1974 'a catastrophe which we cannot repeat', arguing that the country should now go with American-designed PWRs. But he reckoned without good old nationalism, as epitomized by the MP who asked in the House of Commons for an assurance that 'any [power] gap in the 1980s will not in any circumstances be met by the introduction of American light-water reactors'. So the decision was made in 1974 to go ahead with yet another British design, the heavy-water SGHWR, with eight reactors commissioned. Three years later, the new design was abandoned on cost and safety grounds and two more AGRs were ordered instead.

When a new government was elected in 1979 it ordered an immediate review of nuclear generating capacity, leading finally to a decision to build American-designed PWRs, by which time the overall economics of nuclear power generation was coming under increasing doubt. And so the dreams of scientists, technocrats and politicians resulted in 40 years of gigantic waste of talent and resources which ended with Britain finally going with American technology after all, having first lumbered herself with a hugely expensive nuclear generating capacity with running costs which added billions of pounds to the nation's electricity bills.[8]

There have also been other errors in Western industrial strategies, such as the tendency to promote 'national champion' companies with protected, near monopolies of the home market and guaranteed government contracts. The idea has been to give them a secure base from which to attack world markets, but too often the policy has led to unnecessary duplication. These industrial standard-bearers have also tended to prefer the cosy security and fat profits of their home markets over venturing into the leaner, meaner world of exports. By contrast, MITI has generally tried to maintain several competitors in play so as to keep them sharp, such as in telecommunications, where three major Japanese public switch manufacturers – NEC, Fujitsu and Hitachi – all compete vigorously against one another to sell largely compatible systems.

In comparison, France has for a long time allowed its main manufacturer of public telephone switching equipment, Alcatel, a virtual monopoly of the domestic market, while Siemens has enjoyed a similar position in West Germany. In Britain, the three main manufacturers in the 1970s – GEC, Plessey and STC – were encouraged by the Labour government at the time to co-operate in a cosy, non-competitive manner to develop the System X public switch which the then monopoly state-owned telephone company, the General Post Office, was forced to buy. Smaller European countries trod similar paths.

This, incidentally, puts into context assertions that Japanese intervention has been different from that in the West because it is geared to producing 'risk-reducing' consortia such as that between NTT and the fibre-optics producers. In fact, in that Japanese support for advanced industries has tended to be only for pre-competitive research, it is far less 'risk-reducing' than the strategies pursued by many Western countries. Indeed, after the completion of basic research in projects such as the Very Large Scale Integration semiconductor programme, each participant embarks on a headlong and intensely competitive rush to be the winner in commercializing, producing and marketing the technology.

By contrast, Western countries – and America is not guiltless in this respect – have tended to pick their national champions and cosset them right through from subsidized R&D, to generous state-procurement policies and huge capital injections to facilitate production and marketing. These national champions have, however, according to a report by the Industrial Bank of Japan, become one of the major structural weaknesses in the European economy and have led to 'monopolistic market structures, killing market forces in individual countries while leading to an overcrowding of companies in the Community'.[9] The result in the telecommunications market is that Europeans have invested more than £7 billion in the development of sophisticated digital exchanges and ended up with nine different systems, whereas if there had been freer, cross-border competition, they would have ended up with fewer, probably better, systems at a lower cost.

Often, too, intervention in the West has been driven by social or political, rather than commercial motives, as with the creation of huge over-capacity in the British electricity-generating and steel industries in the 1960s and 1970s, with politicians directing steel producers to build uneconomically small plants at unsuitable inland sites, while state-sponsored mergers too often contained little industrial logic and actually created more problems than they solved. When the British Industrial Reorganization Corporation encouraged the merger of Britain's two major car manufacturers, BMC and Leyland, in 1968, the new group became so absorbed with the tremendous difficulty of integrating the two companies' model ranges that basic indus-trial problems were left unattended. As a result, potentially profitable and successful parts of the group were steadily dragged down by less prosperous parts.

At the time of the merger, Leyland was the world's largest truck manufacturer, with companies like Mercedes beating a path to its door suggesting co-operative deals in the manufacture of major components; while Land Rover's four-wheel drive vehicles were rivalled only by those of Jeep in overseas markets. By 1976, however, the new group was in desperate trouble because the formerly successful parts of the business had been forced to cross-subsidize loss-making parts of the group. By the time the once mighty truck division was sold off to the Dutch DAF group in 1987, it had shrunk to being a tiny player in the European market, while Land Rover had been overtaken in world markets by no fewer than seven Japanese producers of four-wheel drive vehicles. The introduction of new Land Rover models had been delayed for so long that, by the end of the 1980s, most Land Rovers were still powered by engines largely based on early post-Second World War designs.

Sir John Egan, the chairman of Jaguar – the luxury car-making arm of the group which was privatized separately in 1984 – said in 1988 that one of his major post-privatization problems was the need to make up for the omissions of the past, when investments in new capital equipment and models had been continually delayed. He maintains that at the time of privatization the average age of Jaguar's machine tools was 25 years, while an audit found a lathe still working from 1895, with a refurbishment slip dated 1936.

Industrial strategies: for and against

Richard Greer knows more about Japanese industry than most Westerners. A slim and cultured-looking man in his mid-30s, Greer is far from the stereotype high-flyer of the financial world and would not look out of place on a university campus. But Greer has spent much of his working life in the frenetic bustle of the Tokyo financial markets where he is one of the directors of Baring Securities and manager of the Tokyo office of one of Britain's oldest merchant banks, which is among the most successful of Tokyo's foreign financial houses and now employs 800 people. He told me:

> The basic problem in evaluating the efficacy of industrial policy is that one has no information as to how growth might have proceeded in the absence of such policy. So merely noting that targeted industries grew is not a compelling argument. Moreover, the list of industries in Japan which grew without the benefit of any specific policy is extensive and includes sewing machines, cameras, bicycles, motor bikes, transistor radios, colour televisions, tape recorders, magnetic tape, audio equip-ment, watches, calculators, textile equipment, farm machinery, robots and photocopiers.

Even if one assumes that industrial policy was successful in the past, there is no evidence that success can continue in the future. It is relatively easy to identify potential high-growth industries in the early stages of economic development. However, it is not at all clear that winners can be picked once there are no patterns to imitate.

This is a view echoed by John Sumeolo, the project leader of a one-year study on the Japanese government's targeting of industries, undertaken by the United States International Trade Commission. 'Japanese companies are much less affected by MITI than they used to be,' says Sumeolo. 'MITI isn't the reason any more.'[10] For as the Japanese economy has developed in size and complexity, so MITI's influence has waned.

So how important is industrial intervention, and has it been of significant benefit to Japan's economy? The author and journalist Karel van Wolferen encapsulated what he considered to be the advantages of an interventionist industrial policy in Japan in his book, *The Enigma of Japanese Power*:[11]

> The economy prospers, because areas of industry that show promise are stimulated by fiscal policies favouring investment. Industries considered of strategic importance are carefully nursed and protected against genuine foreign competition. Those that are in trouble are temporarily protected to give the firms concerned an opportunity to diversify, while those that appear to have reached a dead end are more easily abandoned by policies forcing reorganization. In other words, this is a partnership sealed by a shared industrial policy and trade strategy.

There may well be a case for saying that a *dirigiste* industrial policy is relatively more effective and justified during the early stages of economic development. It is certainly more likely to work if carried out by a well-educated, cohesive bureaucracy with close business links and, above all, as long as the general policy is in line with market forces. However, the very concept of state intervention in business contains within it the inherent assumption that bureaucrats and politicians know better than the industrialists themselves and can second guess the market. This is a very risky assumption – all the more so when in practice the politicians often tend to make their decisions on political rather than commercial criteria.

Even in Japan, to many the very model of successful interventionism, major mistakes have been made. MITI's industrial policies in the 1950s, for example, were geared towards preventing the domination of the aluminium, PVC and caustic soda industries by large competitors. So the Ministry insisted that all of the main companies should expand their capacity at about the same rate, with the result that companies were saddled with high-cost, small-scale facilities which have continued to stunt the development of these industries to this day. It would also be legitimate to ask by how much was Sony's development impaired by the difficulty it experienced in obtaining permission to buy transistor technology from the United States? Or to what extent was Toyo Kogyo, the maker of Mazda cars, harmed by MITI's refusal to allow it to import radiator technology in 1968 because the company had opposed the Ministry's consolidation plans? And what could the resources directed into certain favoured industries have achieved elsewhere if it had been left to market forces? For whatever help MITI has given one industry has been at the expense of others.

Even the impact of MITI on those industries which it has encouraged and which have been successful is open to some doubt. In the 1960s, European missions went to Japan to investigate the miracle of progress in her shipbuilding industry and concluded that complaints that Japan's advantage was partly based on state support and concealed subsidies had no real substance. Indeed, an *Economist* survey in March 1968 determined that state aid for Japanese shipbuilders was considerably less than that given in England, Italy or France. Likewise, a thorough OECD inquiry concluded that indirect subsidies to Japanese shipbuilders did not exceed ten per cent, which was far less than their overall cost-advantage and a lower level than in many Western countries.[12] MITI's involvement in semiconductors and computers has also been seen to have been crucial. Yet its programme in the early 1970s to support the development of large-scale integrated circuitry involved only $100 million over seven years, divided among a number of companies – a minuscule amount by the standards of electronics industry R&D, or compared to subsidies provided by other governments.

It should above all be borne in mind that on top of the central planning of industry operated (but now in the process of abandonment) by the former Eastern Bloc nations and many developing countries, virtually every industrialized nation has intervened heavily in industry since the Second World War, through a combination of subsidies, protection and the nurturing of key industries. Indeed, an OECD survey for 1988 placed Japan only twentieth out of 24 industrialized countries when it came to subsidies. Japan's support for its industries totalled under one per cent of GDP, which was less than the OECD average of 1.5 per cent and well under the levels for the Netherlands (4.3 per cent), West Germany (2.3 per cent), France (2.5 per cent) or Italy (three per cent). The same survey also shows that even back in 1970 Japan's level was below that of most of its main competitors at 1.1 per cent, which placed her eighteenth out of the 24 countries.[13]

True, intervention has been more overt in some countries and less open in nations like the United States. But it has, nonetheless, been a common denominator among both successful and unsuccessful economies and cannot in any way be taken as a key factor in industrial success. Indeed, some of the least successful economies in the world are subject to the largest measure of state control. Apart from the obvious failure of interventionist policies in the communist countries, they have more than their share of conspicuous failures in the free world: India and Brazil are, perhaps, the classic example of misguided industrial policies, though there is a long and wretched catalogue of illustrations.

So critics who assert that Japan is different from the West in that she does not practise pure, free-market economic policies simply ignore the fact that virtually every Western economy – including the United States – has also pursued policies which more or less deviate from the free-market line. In fact, in that Japan's industrial intervention has been more closely geared to working with the grain of market forces, striving to spot and fully exploit them, the Japanese have in many ways been more market-oriented than their European and American counterparts. The Japanese bureaucracy, with its close links with the business world, has also established a non-adversarial relationship with industry with the result that they work well together, unlike the situation in many other countries where bureaucrats and politicians like to try to exert a more controlling influence.

Perhaps, therefore, it is less a matter of by how much Japanese industrial intervention has benefited her economy, than how little relative damage Japan has sustained as a result of MITI's actions. At the very most, MITI and its industrial policies have been only one of many factors in Japan's economic success. Japan's educational system, the vigour and skill of her workforce, sound and sustainable economic and fiscal policies, pro-business attitudes and a solidly productive social and economic cultural base have all been at least as significant.

Nonetheless, conspiracy theories based primarily on interventionist policies are always seductive, and MITI has been the ideal repository of such theories which have been largely propagated by commentators, pundits, journalists and writers who have found it easier to sell articles and books on the basis of simple intrigues and plots, rather than discovering the more intricate realities of the situation.

Interventionism is, moreover, also always popular with politicians and bureaucrats because it increases their power and, when attributed to others, excuses relative economic failures at home. It is, further, often favoured by businesspeople, for it both explains away their own lack of success while holding out the prospect of subsidies, protected markets and an easy life at home. Industrial strategies are also liked by the public because they provide simple answers to complex problems – and these simple solutions appeal both to would-be imitators and detractors of Japan's economic performance.

So it should, perhaps, come as no surprise to learn that the attributing of economic dominance primarily to such uncomplicated, easily digested factors is nothing new. In 1967, the United States was, perhaps, at the zenith of its economic, political and military power. With six per cent of the world's population, America's industries produced twice as much as the whole of Europe combined and accounted for a third of the world's output. American companies then produced 70 per cent of the world's machinery, 73 per cent of its oil, 68 per cent of its electronics and 62 per cent of its chemicals. Two out of every five trucks on the roads were American-built, while it took the combined profits of the ten largest companies in each of the United Kingdom, Japan, West Germany and France to equal those of General Motors alone.

Commentators at that time searched for easy, saleable explanations for America's success, as they do now with Japan's, while politicians groped for plausible policies to counter it. One of the most successful books on the subject was *The American Challenge* by the French publisher and radical politician, Jean-Jacques Servan-Schreiber, which became a European bestseller when it was published in 1967. 'A highly organized economic system, based on enormously large units, nourished by an industrial–academic–governmental complex and stimulated, financed and guided by the national government' was how the foreword to Servan-Schreiber's book then described not Japan, but the United States, concluding that a major factor in America's economic dominance was the close relationship between its industry and government.[14] Among his evidence, Servan-Schreiber cited the fact that the American electronics industry did 63 per cent of its business with the government, compared to only 12 per cent in Europe. He also pointed out that the United States government accounted for 85 per cent of total national research and development.

All of which illustrates two things: first, that Western countries have been as interventionist as Oriental ones; and second, the strong propensity of commentators to ascribe economic success to such a policy. Faith in the productive power of the 'command economy' even caused many after the Second World War to assume that the Soviet Union would overtake the United States: instead, the planners preside with dwindling mastery over a crumbling ruin of an economy.

Then, as now, uncomplicated, easily digestible theories of government intervention as one of the primary causes of economic success were appealing to politicians, businessmen and the public, all seeking absolution from responsibility for their relative failure, together with quick-fix solutions for deep-seated problems. Then, as now, the cause was wrongly diagnosed and the remedy falsely prescribed.

11

新大国

GOVERNMENT FOR GROWTH

'For forms of government let fools contest;
whate'er is best administer'd is best.'
Alexander Pope, *An Essay on Man*, 1733.

TO DOWNPLAY THE overrated influence of MITI on Japan's industrial success is not to deny the vital role played by her governments since the Second World War. For apart from the state's influence over the country's educational system – an essential element in Japan's economic achievements – wise government policies in general have also been of key importance.

Japan is, of course, a democracy, but not in quite the same way as the term is applied in the West. One party, the Liberal Democratic Party (LDP), has governed uninterruptedly for 35 years – a record for the democratic, developed world. The LDP has held a majority in the Diet since it was created in 1955 from the merger of the Liberal and Democratic parties – an amalgamation prompted by the reunification of the Japan Socialist Party, which represented the interests of the country's independent trades unions.

Since then, the LDP's power base has consisted of a tight coalition of business interests, farmers and the bureaucracy. Together, they have formed to date an unbeatable combination, not least because the party has brought Japan unparalleled economic prosperity, but also partly because of the ineptitude of the Socialists who have consistently failed to take any lasting advantage from a series of corruption scandals involving the ruling party. In 1967, for example, the Socialists lost an election which they themselves had forced as a result of a scandal, because of their openly expressed sympathies with the Cultural Revolution in China then at the height of its excesses which were being luridly reported by the Japanese press. Similarly, the Socialists lost the 1990 election, when again the LDP was tainted by the

150

whiff of corruption, in part because they obstinately refused to break their links with Kim Il Sung's monolithic North Korean regime.

The LDP is not a political party in the Western sense, however; rather it is a loose coalition of mini-parties called *habatsu*, grouped around individual leaders who maintain their power by mobilizing political funds and dispensing patronage in the form of government offices and benefits to members' constituencies. *Habatsu* members are also bonded by ties which include personal obligation and, frequently, marriage: nearly every post-War Prime Minister, for example, has had a son or son-in-law in politics. Control of the LDP passes back and forth between the leaders of the largest political cliques, with success being measured by the number of official posts meted out to faction members and the pork-barrel largesse heaped on faction members' constituencies. The system is one of which an Eighteenth-Century English politician would have been proud.

This helps to explain why the top LDP posts are considered to be more powerful than all but the major cabinet portfolios. Michio Watanabe, for example, himself a former Finance Minister, rejected even the Foreign Minister's job in the Takeshita cabinet in order to take the chairmanship of the LDP's main policy committee which would prove to be a better springboard for his political aspirations. Lesser ministerial offices are shared around the factions like toys among children, and since the Second World War, the average ministerial term of office has been less than a year.

The dispersal of power throughout the factions has made it difficult for the LDP to push unpopular or very controversial legislation through the Diet, which has given rise, by default, to a sometimes superficial appearance of harmonious consensus. It has also meant that large, vested interests – the farmers in particular – have, until very recently, seldom been threatened with reform or a cut in their subsidies. Nonetheless, the system has, on the whole, worked well: indeed the very stability of the government, allied to its close ties with big business, has been a major factor in Japan's economic success. On the few occasions when change has been forced on Japan – usually as a result of external influences – this prosperity and continuity has made the transitions easier.

Noboru Takeshita perhaps best epitomizes the system. The son of a wealthy rural *sake* brewer, he succeeded Kakuei Nakasone to the prime ministership in 1987 before being forced to resign two years later. Takeshita is a prodigious raiser and dispenser of political funds, with close connections in the construction industry. He is also a consummate backroom politician. Like the disgraced Tanaka before him, his capacity to persuade was reinforced by his powerful patronage. Despite also resigning under a cloud, Takeshita still heads the LDP's largest faction, which happens to be the grouping once directed by Tanaka.

Patronage and deliberate policy can, of course, go hand in hand. Takeshita called his strategy of spreading wealth and economic development around the regions, *'furosato'* (*'hometown policy'*). Tanaka before him called his version 'a regional restructuring policy for the Japanese Archipelago'. But it comes as no surprise to hear that when Tanaka was Prime Minister, his Niigata constituency received more government grants per head of the population than did any other prefecture in Japan. Takeshita's Shimane prefecture in turn topped the pork-barrel league table during his leadership. When asked by a journalist what expectations he had of Takeshita's Prime Ministership, a local businessman in Shimane's capital, Matsue, just held out his cupped hands and grinned broadly.

The chief patronage merchants do not always hold the highest offices even within the LDP. The backroom nature of the system is typified by Shin Kanemaru. Although little known outside Japan, 75-year-old Mr Kanemaru is probably more powerful than Japan's Prime Minister, yet he has shown virtually no interest in international issues and is hardly bothered with ideology. Kanemaru first came to prominence in 1971 when he was appointed Minister of Construction in the Tanaka cabinet. In order to relieve congestion in Tokyo, Kanemaru conceived the idea of moving the entire government out to a new capital city, and he still chairs a LDP committee which is looking into the project, estimated to cost a massive ¥20,000 billion (£90 billion). Kanemaru later increased his power with stints as Minister responsible for the Defence Agency and the National Land Agency in the mid-1970s. His son married Takeshita's eldest daughter and Kanemaru went on to play an instrumental part in Mr Takeshita's rise to the prime ministership in 1987.

Kanemaru's power has also been used, in true Japanese fashion, to benefit his constituents. He managed to win, for example, the prestigious ¥200 billion (£900 million) test track for linear motors for his Yamanashi constituency west of Tokyo, in 1989, despite the fact that it was expected to go to one of the depressed regions in Hokkaido or Kyushu. He is also an outstanding fund-raiser: as part of his campaign to make Noboru Takeshita Prime Minister, he helped raise ¥2 billion (£8 million) at a single political rally – a record sum.

Fund-raising for electioneering purposes is an important part of the Japanese political system – particularly as politicians have expensive obligations. A Diet member is expected to turn up to constituents' weddings bearing reasonably expensive gifts and to make donations to worthy constituency causes, which can go as high as ¥500,000 (£2,000) for a local sports team competing in a national tournament, while the huge size of Japanese constituencies necessitates the employment of armies of secretaries to keep on top of the correspondence. As a result, a Diet member's annual expenses can be well in excess of ¥100 million (£440,000) a year, only a small fraction of which is covered by allowances.

But this well-oiled system of money politics, which the Japanese call 'kin-kenseiji', also verges on straightforward corruption. In 1989, much to the embarrassment of the Japanese, the attention of the world was drawn to this unsavoury aspect of Japanese politics by the Recruit bribery scandal. Prime Minister Noboru Takeshita, among other leading politicians, was forced to resign for allegedly granting political favours to Recruit, an aggressive publishing, real estate and employment agency group, in return for campaign contributions, stocks and secret loans totalling $1 million.

Takeshita may just have been unlucky, for at least 11 of the 21 post-War Japanese Prime Ministers have been investigated for corruption at some stage in their careers. Most spectacular was Kakuei Tanaka who was forced to resign the premiership in 1974 after magazine articles had exposed some of his shady financial dealings. In 1976, he was also indicted and briefly jailed for taking $2 million in bribes from American plane-maker Lockheed. Despite this conviction and his subsequent resignation from the LDP, Tanaka still held his seat in the Diet as an independent, kept control of his faction until it was taken over by Takeshita, and nominated three Prime Ministers.

Where exactly the dividing line between corruption and legitimate patronage occurs is always a matter of opinion. Despite the resignations of Tanaka and Takeshita, the Japanese take a very much more relaxed view of the boundary than is the case in the West. The same is true in other fields of Japanese life. Practices such as insider trading, for example, are still common in the Japanese stock market, long after they were outlawed in most Western markets. On the other hand, Japanese money politics differs from other systems mainly in degree. After all, American politicians take huge campaign contributions from corporations, organized labour and interest groups, while European politicians are frequently 'retained' by companies to perform special services for them.

Perhaps the extent to which Japanese money politics is so overt owes something to the fact that Japan has had a far shorter experience of parliamentary democracy than either Britain or the United States. Japanese parliamentary politics is arguably at roughly the same stage as the British or American system in the early part of the century, when a series of scandals – some not dissimilar to the Recruit case – forced changes to be made. In the same way, the 1989 Recruit scandal may well be the catalyst for changes in Japan – indeed, early in 1990, a young LDP Diet member, Asahiko Mihara, together with 15 of his colleagues, formed the oddly named Utopian Political Research Group to press for just such political reforms.

Creating wealth

The talent and cohesion of Japan's bureaucracy, the LDP's lack of interest in political doctrine and the patronage basis of the *habatsu* system has led many commentators to conclude that Japan's political system is fundamentally different from Western ones. Among the theses advanced is that Japan has no clear centre of political power and control is widely spread among a number of influential groups which include sections of the bureaucracy, industrialists, interest groups such as the *nokyo* and even the *yakuza*.

There may well be a great deal of truth in this. But the strength of national leaders in the West also tends to be exaggerated. For while it is true that Japanese Prime Ministers play less powerful roles than do their foreign counterparts, all democracies are subject to forceful lobbies and a certain amount of bureaucratic control. West German Chancellors, American Presidents and British Prime Ministers may 'take responsibility' or be 'held accountable', but in reality their decisions are tempered by advice and pressure from bureaucrats, other politicians, interest groups, the media, supranational bodies such as the European Community, industrialists, allies and, of course, considerations as to what is politically possible. They do not have a free rein and have to carry a wide range of interests with them – whatever their image. So the real difference between Japan's political system and those of its developed Western counterparts may lie more in the extent to which power is diffused than in any fundamental dissimilarity.

Another related criticism is that close links between government and industry make Japan a 'producer-dominated' society, where the interests of state and business merge and bureaucrats collude with industrialists to form cartels at the expense of consumers and living standards in general. Van Wolferen, in his book, *The Enigma of Japanese Power*,[1] states: 'One can understand the Japanese wanting to make money, but their conquest of ever greater foreign market shares does not translate into noticeably more rewarding or more comfortable lives.' He cites the weakness of consumer pressure groups, while pointing out that producer lobbies have enormous influence in Japan. For example, van Wolferen asserts that the Japan Medical Association, the doctors' representative body, together with Japanese pharmaceutical companies have used their power over the government to ensure lucrative over-prescribing of medicines.

Anyone who has observed the periodic battles in Britain between the British Medical Association and the government over the use of unnecessarily expensive drugs will not find this so exceptional. No British Secretary of State for Health can make any move without considering carefully reactions from numerous pressure groups. For the fact is that producer lobbies are every bit as powerful in the West as they are in Japan, as should be apparent from the extensive list of import barriers and subsidies mentioned earlier.

Nor are producer cartels unique to Japan. Early in 1990, the newly set-up French Competition Council fined 80 construction firms and 43 electrical groups, including some of France's top companies such as Bouygues and Schneider, for fixing prices and conspiring to carve up major public contracts. Often, cartels in the West flourish under the protective blanket afforded by trade barriers, such as those found to be operating in 1988 in at least two industries covered by European Community anti-dumping duties, PVC and polythene. Thirty cartels have been acted on by the EC since 1980, with a further unidentified number where the EC has received undertakings which precluded further action. In some instances, the Community itself sanctions cartels, like the one set up to cover the steel industry in the late 1970s.

So while it may be true that links between the LDP and industry are strong (the organization of big business, the *Keidanren*, played a major part in the formation of the LDP in 1955 and provided more than 90 per cent of the party's officially-reported income in the 1960s and 1970s) Japanese consumers, who enjoy some of the highest-quality products and some of the best safety standards in the world, and whose living standards have risen to levels undreamt of in 1945, might be surprised to learn that a supposedly producer-dominated political system has uniquely lowered their living standards.

The real problem with the producer-domination thesis is that it confuses two different things: being in the thrall of special interest groups, be they industries, trades unions or any other body, is one thing; running a government in such a way that economic growth is given priority is quite another. For what really differentiates Japanese post-War government from its Western rivals is the consistent way in which Japanese policy has been geared to sustainable economic growth. This was reinforced by a realization after the Second World War of Japan's desperate position which helped to free Japanese government from some of the constraints under which many Western countries laboured.

Japanese government has also been free of imperial or post-imperial distractions, making it far better able to pursue the primary objective of securing economic growth. So the Japanese system has been less the frequently portrayed, close conspiratorial public–private sector embrace, than government which has understood that industry and commerce, rather than politicians and bureaucrats, are the true engines of progress and wealth creation.

That does not mean that Japanese governments have always been slavishly pro-business. It is not often realized, for example, that Japan's corporate tax regime has not been very helpful to entrepreneurial business. While American venture capitalists can get through difficult early years by writing off losses by carrying them forward, this is not the case in Japan. Whereas if you lose money on an investment in the United States you can deduct it from tax, in Japan you forfeit the lot.

Eiji Toyoda, the chairman of Toyota, tells how anti-industry attitudes also came to the fore when Japan was debating the introduction of automobile emission controls in 1970, after they had been introduced in the United States. At that time, many of Japan's cities were wreathed in a petrochemical smog and lead pollution was an increasing problem. The contribution of one of Toyota's executives was to suggest the placing of giant extractor fans at the worst urban intersections, a proposal that was deservedly ridiculed in the press. When the Environment Agency came up with new emission-control laws, the car industry was very hostile, but feeling in the country and the Diet was strong. Toyoda himself was hauled before Diet hearings in an atmosphere he described as being like a 'witch hunt' and the new laws were duly passed.[2]

However it is true to say that by generally putting economic growth first, Japan's managerial governments have helped their industry, and industry in turn has created a great deal of wealth for the Japanese people. There is certainly little of the hostility between state and business that is so familiar in the West. As the industry guru and joint-founder of the Hudson Institute, Herman Kahn, eloquently wrote in his book, *The Emerging Japanese Superstate*,[3] back in 1970:

> The situation in Japan is very different from that in the United States. Probably more than 50 per cent of all Japanese government officials devote their time to improving the prospects of business. However, one would conjecture that in the United States more than 50 per cent of all government officials devote their time to almost the opposite task – many of them to sponsoring groups with grudges against the business system and the establishment, or groups that are anti-business, anti-economic growth, anti-capitalist, and even anti-rationalist, at least from the economic point of view.

Growth first

Where American and many European administrations' high spending and deficit financing has tended to boost inflation and penalize the productive sides of their economies, Japan has more often than not favoured production and industry over consumption and state spending. The result in the mid-1980s was that Japan's gross fixed-capital formation (a measure of productive investment) was the highest in the world at $3,000 per head, compared to $2,200 per head across the OECD countries.[4]

Japan has aided business and economic growth and achieved this level of investment in a number of ways. First and foremost, Japanese state spending has been relatively very low as a proportion of GNP, allowing more resources to be channelled into industry. In 1967, during the period when it was becoming increasingly apparent that Japan was beginning to outpace many of her Western rivals, the government was only spending 20.6 per cent of the nation's GNP, compared to 31.4 per cent in the United States and 39 per cent in the United Kingdom, the latter being roughly in line with the rest of Western Europe. At that time, only eight per cent of Japan's workforce was in the public sector, compared to 22 per cent in Britain. By 1988, Japan's state spending had risen to 32.6 per cent of her GDP, but that was still comfortably the lowest of the OECD countries and well below the OECD average of 39.9 per cent. Likewise, only 6.4 per cent of Japan's workforce was in the public sector in 1986 – again the lowest of the OECD countries and well below the United States' 15.8 per cent as well as the European OECD countries' average of 18.1 per cent.[5]

The corollary of the low public-spending policy has been relatively modest taxation. Japan's base rate of taxation is extremely low at ten per cent, compared to 15 to 30 per cent for most Western countries. In addition, with some exceptions, the Japanese pay no capital gains tax. Although local taxation is typically around ten per cent, which is higher than in many Western countries, as is company tax, the overall ratio of all taxes to GNP is low at around 20 per cent. Figures for the early 1980s show that the total marginal tax rate* on a Japanese single-earner married couple with two children on the average industrial wage was the lowest of 21 industrialized countries at 39.9 per cent, well below the average of 55 per cent.[6]

This does not mean that Japan has always eschewed public sector deficits. Although a balanced budget or public sector surplus has been achieved for much of the post-War period, during economic crises the Japanese government has plunged spectacularly into debt to boost the economy. In the last half of the 1970s, for example, governments used heavy deficit financing to spend their way out of the oil crisis-induced recession. By 1982, the budget deficit of $70 billion represented 6.4 per cent of GNP, although spending was subsequently cut in real terms to bring the budget back into balance.

When the Japanese government does spend, it lavishes its resources – to a far greater extent than its competitors – on public works and infrastructure-improvement projects rather than on outright consumption. The famed

---

* Including payroll tax, employer's contribution, employee's contribution, personal income tax and indirect tax.

shinkansen (bullet train) costs a staggering $60 million per mile, and one station in the obscure mountain town of Urasa – population 15,000 – cost $100 million to build.[7] Similarly huge amounts have been paid out for other projects, such as the 53.9 kilometre Seikan rail tunnel, linking the northern island of Hokkaido with central Honshu, opened in 1988, which took 23 years and ¥690 billion (£2.9 billion) to build.

This type of spending is partly the result of the patronage system – needless to say the LDP is very popular in Urasa – and partly the result of a policy to spend on projects which will benefit the economy and aid growth. In addition, profligate though some of the schemes have been, the effect on public finances has not been further exacerbated by massive spending on subsidizing state-owned industries – with the significant exception of Japan National Railways, which lost $7 billion a year at one point and has accumulated $100 billion in losses overall.

Japanese spending on health, pensions and social security is also comparatively modest. Japan does have a National Health Insurance scheme which was introduced in 1961 and to which most Japanese belong, but social expenditure as a proportion of GDP has long lagged behind that of Western industrial rivals. In 1960, social expenditure as a proportion of GDP was only 7.6 per cent, compared to 9.9 per cent in the United States, 12.4 per cent in the UK and 17.1 per cent in West Germany. This demonstrates Japan's post-War strategy of concentrating first on industrial growth, then on wages and finally on state welfare. Even though spending in this area has risen faster than GNP growth in recent years, it remains significantly lower than in the West. By 1985, when Japanese social security spending had risen to 16.2 per cent of GDP, it still lagged behind the United States, which spent 18.2 per cent of GDP, the UK 20.9 per cent, and Germany at 25.8 per cent. Japan was also well under the OECD average of 24.6 per cent. In fact, the only major Western country to spend less than Japan was Spain, at 15.2 per cent.[8]

There are a number of other reasons why Japanese social spending remains relatively modest. Among these is the fact that Japan has low unemployment, a high proportion of young people and a tradition of family provision: in 1985, 15 per cent of households still had three generations living together and approximately 70 per cent of older Japanese people share their homes with their offspring. These factors help to explain why, despite relatively low spending on health and social services, Japan nonetheless had achieved the lowest infant mortality rate in the world by the mid-1970s, and had surpassed Sweden's life expectancy to become the longest-lived nation.

There is also the Japanese propensity to save to cover for retirement and health emergencies. Overall, the Japanese save close to a fifth of their income – about three times the level in the United States. Gross savings as a percentage of overall GDP in Japan are 31.7 per cent – way ahead of the United States at 16.5 per cent or Britain at 19.2 per cent – and the typical Japanese family has more than $60,000 hoarded away, nearly twice the average annual salary. Cause and effect are obviously related, however, for it is the low level of state provision which necessitates savings, and high private savings in turn permit lower levels of health and social spending.

A tradition of thrift and the need to provide for old age or ill health has been reinforced by government encouragement to save. Indeed, boosting savings levels has been a major plank of government policy which dates back to the late Nineteenth Century when Count Matsukata set up the Treasury Deposits Bureau to channel savings into investment via the official banks. Since the Second World War, savings in the Post Office Savings Bureau have been encouraged through small accounts called 'maruyu' which were, until recently, exempt from taxation on the interest on the first ¥3 million (£14,000) deposited in each account, along with up to ¥11 million (£48,000) in government bonds. On top of this, a further ¥3 million (£14,000) both in bank accounts and bonds, plus up to ¥5 million (£23,000) in company schemes, were tax exempt until 1988. As tax officials were not given access to Post Office records, people could have several tax-exempt savings accounts simply by giving false names, with the result that the Post Office came to have more accounts than the total Japanese population. The Bureau's 23,000 branches are now the most popular place for savings and its approximately $1,000 billion in deposits makes it the world's largest savings institution.

Credit restrictions have reinforced the savings policy. Although liberalization of credit in the 1960s allowed the growth of a commercial bond market, it was only in 1978 that five large American finance companies were permitted to operate in Japan. Up until then, consumer credit had been largely restricted to loans via sarakin lending houses, which offered short-term advances with very high interest rates. On top of this, the strong Japanese savings ethic has been bolstered by the almost total absence of the tax credits for interest payments on loans so common in the West. In this way Japanese policy has been the mirror image of most Western systems, exempting savings from tax to encourage thrift, but giving no tax benefits to consumption. By contrast, many Western governments penalize savers with high taxes and subsidize consumption with tax breaks.

Japanese savings have been further boosted by the common practice of paying bonuses to employees, amounting to around 20 per cent of total annual renumeration, twice yearly, a windfall which has tended to go straight into savings accounts. In addition, since Japan currently has a smaller proportion of its population aged 65 and over compared with its main industrial competitors, so it has a higher proportion of net savers than net spenders compared to other countries – although this factor is steadily changing as the Japanese population ages. Moreover, partly in response to Western criticisms that they spend too little, and hence do not import enough, the Japanese government has been steadily reducing the incentives to save. In 1988, the tax breaks on maruyu were ended and, except for some exempt groups, interest is now taxed at 20 per cent. But to date, Japan's high levels of savings have been an important factor in her economic success, obviating high welfare spending and providing a pool of finance which has helped to boost productive investment in the economy as a whole. Japan's savers have also helped to restrain inflation and keep interest rates low, which in turn has contributed towards preventing the yen from being overvalued.

A sincere attachment to Article 9

Ask people which country they think spends the most on defence after the United States and the Soviet Union, and few would come up with 'Japan'. Yet, by the end of the 1980s, despite being prevented from maintaining armed forces by her post-War constitution and spending one of the lowest proportions of GNP on defence, Japan had indeed become the third highest defence spender in the world.

Article 9 of Japan's post-War constitution, largely written by the American occupation administration, states: 'The Japanese people forever renounce war as a sovereign right of the nation . . . . Land, sea and air forces, as well as other war potential, will never be maintained. The right of belligerency of the state will not be recognized.' But when, in 1950, during the Korean War, most of the American troops stationed in Japan were rapidly despatched to Korea to stem the communist advance, American policy changed and MacArthur ordered the Japanese government to create the National Police Reserve which later became the Defence Force.

Even these relatively slight moves towards rearmament were resisted. In a meeting in January 1951 that must have been heavy with irony, John Foster Dulles, the American Secretary of State, who was pessimistic about the outcome of the Korean fighting which was then at its height, thumped the table and repeatedly told premier Yoshida: 'You must rearm!', while old man Yoshida, with an ironic look from behind his spectacles, politely reiterated the Japanese people's sincere attachment to Article 9. What he was in fact reiterating was opposition to the expense of rebuilding Japan's defence capacity and subsequent governments limited themselves to spending no more than one per cent of their GNP on the armed forces.

Japan has been relieved of the need to spend heavily on defence by the presence of American forces in the North Pacific. As a result, in 1983, when the United States spent $1,023 per head of population on defence and Britain laid out $439, defence cost each Japanese citizen a mere $98. Now, whereas the United States spends close to $300 billion on defence, which is almost $1,300 per head and nearly seven per cent of her GNP, Japanese spending is still less than $30 billion, only $250 per head and around one per cent of her GNP.* So although Japan's population size and huge GNP make her total spending considerable in world terms, in proportion to her economy the amount is extremely small.

Memories of a disastrous imperialist war, together with the vast improvement in the quality of life brought about by the peaceful pursuit of making cars and TV sets, have caused the Japanese to feel a certain resistance towards increased defence spending. Although a vociferous radical right-wing fringe has for some time argued that Japan should throw off its mantle of Second World War guilt and become an independent military power again, public opinion polls show that well over half the Japanese population favours the present level of spending while only about ten per cent want higher expenditure.

---

* Unlike most Western countries, Japan excludes military pensions from her total defence expenditure figure which, if included, would boost spending closer to 1.5 per cent of GNP.

Nonetheless, Japan has in recent years come under a great deal of pressure from the United States to increase her defence burden. Not long ago, Gary Hart, the former American presidential hopeful who is not known for his hawkish views on defence policy, told the Tokyo press that, while the United States 'has allocated too much of its national treasure into military hardware', Japan should 'over time and, given its relative prosperity, increase its investment and defensive capability'. Hart was asking Japan to 'help the United States to put its house in order'. This was echoed by the United States Congress 1988 Defence Burdensharing Panel report which asked:

> Why do the Japanese – whose drive and ingenuity led them from total devastation to economic superpower status in a mere 40 years – appear unwilling to assume free-world burdens at a level more commensurate with their ability to pay than they currently assume?

American pressure such as this lies behind increases in Japan's defence capability in recent years and her plans to expand further. Already Japan watches over 1,000 nautical miles – her fleet of 60 destroyers now surpasses Britain's capability – and she is also contributing more towards the cost of keeping American forces in Japan by paying the Americans $2.2 billion (£1.3 billion) a year or $45,000 (£28,000) per American serviceman stationed in Japan. Even so, Japan's defence spending will remain small relative to her economic size for the foreseeable future. Most importantly, it was minuscule during the period when it was crucial that Japan's resources should be concentrated on boosting her economy. For although high defence spending obviously benefits certain sectors of industry and does produce spin-offs, there is little doubt that it also absorbs financial resources and valuable skills which could be used more effectively elsewhere in the economy.

This is not to make a judgment on whether the United States and others were wrong to spend massively on defence – particularly given the world situation until recently – nor on whether the United States was mistaken in discouraging Japanese spending in this field immediately after the Second World War. Neither is it to assert that low defence spending has been more than one cause among many for Japan's economic success. But there is no doubt that Japan has greatly benefited from the free ride it has enjoyed courtesy of the American defence umbrella, and the Americans are surely justified in demanding some increase in the Japanese effort.

Few distractions

Should you visit Pyongyang, capital of North Korea and one of the most conservative of the remaining diehard communist regimes under its old-guard ruler, Kim Il Sung, you might expect the streets to be filled with Russian Lada and Volga cars, and the hotels to use Soviet equipment. Instead, apart from a few battered old four-wheel drives used by the military, and some crumbling Soviet-built taxis, most of the cars in Pyongyang's largely empty thoroughfares are Toyotas, Nissans and Hondas. Even the North Korean Tourist Authority uses Toyota minibuses.

In the capital's brand new 20-storey showpiece hotel you would be whisked to your floor in Mitsubishi lifts and cooled with Hitachi air conditioning, while the visiting Soviet advisers and technicians who throng the foreign currency shop near the diplomatic quarter ignore the local handicrafts and stuffed animals to queue instead to buy Sapporo beer and Sony TVs and hi-fis.

North Korea, which fought against predominantly American UN forces in an intensely bitter War in the early 1950s, is still regarded by most Western governments as a pariah state. Few maintain diplomatic relations and trade with the free world is minuscule – with the single exception of the Japanese who, ironically, next to the South Koreans, probably had most to lose had not the North Koreans been checked by the UN forces.

This typifies the attitudes of successive Japanese governments towards trade and commerce: they have simply never allowed themselves the luxury of refusing to trade with regimes of which they disapproved. So, in 1953, when Mussadeq tried to nationalize the Anglo–Iranian Oil Company, it was the Japanese who took advantage, buying oil cheaply from the Iranians. Nor was the war in Vietnam enough to interrupt trade between Japan and both South and North Vietnam. The American bombing of Haiphong only slightly slowed shipments of Japanese textiles, chemicals, fertilizers, steel and machinery. Again, during the 444-day Iranian–American hostage crisis in 1979–80, the Japanese tried to break President Carter's embargo on oil purchases from Iran by offering to buy the United States' allocation. Earlier, during the 1973–4 oil crisis which followed the Yom Kippur War, Japan quickly adopted a pro-Arab stance, was reclassified as a 'friendly country' by the Arabs and soon received all the oil she wanted. And when Arab countries ask Japanese companies not to trade with Israel, they generally comply. Although Japan claims that she does not observe the Arab economic boycott of Israel, Toyota has never sold a car in Israel.

Closer to home, Japan's eagerness to maintain trading links with China has sometimes taken on a ridiculous aspect. In the 1960s, at the height of the Cultural Revolution, one condition of trade was that a quasi-official Japanese delegation should annually sign a communiqué condemning in highly coloured language the 'rise of Japanese militarism' and 'American imperialism' in a ritual analogous to the old *kowtow* ceremony. Prime Minister Tanaka also swallowed his pride and in 1972 apologized abjectly to China for Japan's wartime atrocities, so easing the way for trade between the two countries to begin in earnest. By 1973, trade had shot up by 62 per cent to $871.5 million.

In June 1989, while Western countries tried to outdo each other in the virulence of their condemnation of the Peking massacre, the Japanese reaction was muted. Prime Minister Sosuke Uno bit his lip as he gave the ingenious excuse that it would be inappropriate for Japan to comment on China's internal affairs, bearing in mind Japan's own record in China. Only after growing Western criticism of her stance did Japan budge a little and suspend a $5.5 billion soft-loan package; even so, it was Japanese business-men who were the first to scramble back into China after the fuss had died down. Again, Japan had to be cajoled into supporting the United States' position over the Iraqi invasion of Kuwait. Many Japanese took the view that this was not their quarrel, they have no historic links with the region and, anyway, whoever was in control would have to sell oil, so Japan had no economic interest in getting involved.

In short, trade always takes precedence over politics – or almost always, for there has been one exception to this rule: the Japanese bear a particularly bitter grudge against the Soviet Union for the breach of her non-aggression treaties with Japan in the dying days of the Second World War, when Stalin took advantage of Japanese helplessness and marched into four islands in the southern Kurile chain to the north of Hokkaido. The Japanese have consistently refused to recognize Soviet sovereignty of these islands, never signed a peace treaty with the Soviet Union and largely turn a cold shoulder to Russian offers of better relations. Despite Soviet eagerness to gain access to Japanese technology, and fears by Japanese businessmen that they are being beaten to opportunities in the Soviet Union by their Western competitors, Japan has rejected potentially profitable joint venture proposals, which include the exploitation of rich Siberian natural resources and the setting up of a special economic zone around the port of Nakhodka close to Vladivostock. Although Japan's trade with the USSR has increased since the early days of *perestroika*, trade with the Soviet Union accounted for only 1.2 per cent of total Japanese trade in 1989.

This stance, however, is very much the exception to the rule, and most of what the Japanese government does is geared unashamedly towards its economic advantage. Such an attitude should cause no surprise. The Japanese, devoid of natural resources, feel that they are a poor nation and that economic survival comes before all else. Further, unburdened by empire and with her military might broken after the Second World War, Japan had no choice but to make her way quietly in the world and concentrate her energies on economic recovery. Unlike Britain, who was successively preoccupied with the Malayan Emergency, Korea, the MauMau in Kenya, Cyprus, Aden and Borneo; or the French with Vietnam and Algeria; or America with her many involvements worldwide, Japan was fortunate enough to run in the race of international competition carrying as little weight as possible and with few distractions to divert her from the task of making steel, ships, cars and TVs better than anyone else.

Neither could Japan bask in the type of complacency that afflicted her conquerors, nor afford to be inspired by the romantic delusions of grandeur that led some of them to attempt to build a 'New Jerusalem' in the form of a welfare state long before they could afford it.[9] Instead, while others dabbled, dreamed and erected the costly scaffolding of new Utopias, Japan's managerial post-War governments primarily contributed to the country's economic success by concentrating almost single-mindedly on the mundane and unromantic objective of building a first-class economy.

Part V

Industry – The Bicycle Economy

IN ONLY 50 years Japanese industry has moved from poverty and economic insignificance to the highest levels of income and leadership; from dependence on foreign technology and capital to being major exporters of both.

Cars are perhaps the most potent symbol of Japan's industrial success. In the 1950s, Toyota and other Japanese car-makers relied largely on licensed designs and foreign technology (even the old Austin A40 was still in production in Japan until the mid-1960s). At that time, Japanese cars were more the butt of jokes than feared competitors. Then, Britain exported ten times as many cars as Japan and the United States 15 times as many. But by 1981, they made 11 million vehicles, overtaking the United States to become the largest car manufacturer.

Now it comes as little surprise to hear that the New York subway system buys carriages from Kawasaki Heavy Industries; that the 400-tonne boring machine called 'Virginie' being used to drill a section of the Channel Tunnel to link Britain and France was built by Mitsubishi Heavy Engineering; or that 16 of the world's top 50 industrial groupings – including four out of the first five – are Japanese.

Yet the progress of Japan's industry was for a time uncertain. Racked by bitter labour unrest and renowned for her slipshod goods, Japan in the 1950s was few people's bet for economic superpower status. Even after her success began to become apparent in the 1960s and 1970s, it was for a long time under-rated, and her achievements are still sometimes explained away in terms of either reckless price-cutting, copying or the inter-relationships between groups of companies and banks.

Perhaps the most significant feature of Japanese economic success is the extraordinary ability of Japanese industry to produce very long runs of high-quality products at low prices. Why this is the case is the subject of the following chapters, which examine Japanese business attitudes, management techniques and labour relations, as well as at the vexed question: Are the Japanese merely a nation of 'copiers'; or is their open-minded willingness to look at other peoples' ideas one of their fundamental strengths?

12

新大国

COMPETITIVE CONDITIONING

'The glory and the nemesis of Japanese business, the life's blood of our industrial engine, is good old-fashioned competition.'
Akio Morita, joint-founder of Sony.[1]

NOT MANY PEOPLE remember Tohatsu now. Yet in the early 1950s, with a 22 per cent market share, this company led the Japanese motor-cycle industry. With the rest of the market shared by more than 50 other participants, and demand growing at over 40 per cent a year, Tohatsu's future seemed assured.

Tohatsu's major rival at that time was a company called Honda, though Honda's debt situation and Tohatsu's profitability then placed the former a clear second. Five short years later, however, Honda was to emerge the undisputed market leader with a 44 per cent market share, while Tohatsu's sales had plummeted to less than four per cent of total demand. In 1964, its funds exhausted, its bills unpaid and a restructuring attempt by Fuji Electric ending in failure, Tohatsu filed for bankruptcy. It was not the only casualty of the intensively competitive Japanese motor-cycle market. The 50 manu-facturers of the early 1950s had shrunk to 30 by 1960 and to only eight in 1965. By 1969 they were a mere four.

Borrowing heavily, Honda had triumphed by concentrating on expanding its market share, pushing sales up by close to 66 per cent a year. As sales grew, so its increasing profits and volume allowed the company to reduce costs thus further boosting sales. Complacent Tohatsu, on the other hand, chose the conservative course, which proved fatal in a rapidly growing market.

With growth in the motor-cycle market slowing by the mid-1960s,

Honda decided to maintain its corporate momentum by diversifying into cars – despite the fact that the Japanese auto industry was in the process of a major shake-up. By 1975, the company's revenue from automobiles exceeded that of motorcycles. It was while Honda's management was preoccupied with the auto-making venture that rival Yamaha decided to pounce. Like Honda before, it had invested heavily in production capacity and by 1982 Yamaha had almost closed the gap on the market leader. But spurred by Yamaha President Koike's aggressive statements to his share-holders' meeting in January 1982, Honda President Kawashima issued the battle cry, 'Yamaha wo tsubusu!', roughly translated as 'We will slaughter Yamaha!'.

Honda did just that. Over the next year and a half its share of production increased from 40 per cent to 47 per cent, while Yamaha's slumped from 35 per cent to 27 per cent. This was achieved by a very simple combination of massive price cuts, increased marketing and high dealer stock levels to ensure a ready availability of models. When competition between Honda and Yamaha reached its peak, retail prices for popular motor bikes fell by more than a third. At one point, in the summer of 1982, it was possible to buy a 50cc motorbike for less than the cost of a ten-speed bicycle.

Product variety was also high on the agenda of Honda's counter-attack: in one year the company introduced 81 new motor-cycle models in Japan, while Yamaha could only bring 34 new machines to the market. To the consumer, Honda's models increasingly represented state-of-the-art tech-nology, leaving Yamaha's appearing obsolescent by comparison. As a result, Yamaha's sales plummeted by more than 50 per cent, pushing the company into heavy losses. By January 1983, President Koike of Yamaha admitted that he could not match Honda's product development and sales strength and accepted his company's position as Number Two. In April of the same year, having announced a huge loss, Yamaha cut its production plans by 18 per cent and removed 700 employees from the motor-cycle payroll. Honda's victory was complete.[2]

Western writers have often claimed that collusion, rather than relentless competition, is what typifies Japan's industry. Large Japanese firms, the argument goes, take very few risks. 'They are ensconced', says van Wolferen in *The Enigma of Japanese Power*,[3] 'in a protective environment that not only shields them from foreign competitors but also fosters forms of mutual protection. It is this basis that permits them to move simultaneously into foreign markets with rock-bottom prices.' Another writer, Clyde Prestow-itz, asserted in his book, *Trading Places*,[4] that in Japan, 'reduction of risk by the government is the key to the whole game'.

Disregard any illusion that the Japanese market is cosily carved up among Japanese big businesses in league with MITI bureaucrats. What characterizes Japan's market above all is its intensely competitive nature, which is typified by the enormous numbers of entrants into any new field which opens up. This is in sharp contrast to some Western countries where government policy has often been simply to foster one 'national champion' company in each major industry.

There were 36 Japanese camera manufacturers in 1950 and 40 companies producing electronic calculators in 1960. The competitive process has honed these down to seven and four respectively – and those survivors have been sharpened by the pressure of relentless competition and hardened in the world's most difficult market. Further evidence of the burning pace of Japan's domestic market lies in the high level of bankruptcies. Between 1980 and 1986, there averaged more than 15,000 bankruptcies each year of companies with debts of more than Y10m (about £4.5 million) each. These figures are around 12.5 per cent higher than those for the United States, even though Japan's corporate population is only 40 per cent that of America's. Nor are all of the failed companies small ones: one of the most spectacular in recent years was the $5 billion collapse of Sanko Steamship – the world's largest bankruptcy. The Japanese call this the 'bicycle economy'. To stay on, riders have to pedal forward; if they slow down, they topple and fall.

The winners' competitive cycle

Some people talk of Japan's businessmen as possessing a unique *samurai* spirit, which is reinforced by the single-minded fanaticism of the Japanese worker. Together, these 'economic animals' are, so the theory goes, absolutely ruthless in their willingness to sacrifice all for their own economic gain. The Japanese may display some cultural continuities and they have certainly been more responsive than most to changing conditions, but contemporary Japanese people are no more latter-day *samurai* than are the Italians conditioned by the fighting prowess of their Roman ancestors. *Samurai* traditions are of far less significance than the conditioning demanded of them by the intense Darwinian struggle in their home market.

For it is the very challenge of surviving in business in Japan that has given her businessmen an overriding sense of vulnerability and rivalry. Each Japanese company fights for market share with all the desperation of a beleaguered garrison, an attitude epitomized by the number of managers sent to training schools which resemble a cross between Marine boot camps and Zen monasteries. At one such training school at the foot of Mount Fuji, 5,000 trainees are annually put through a 13-day course combining severe physical ordeals with assertiveness training. Nissan, NEC, Matsushita, Toyota and NTT are among those companies which pay more than $1,000 a head for their rising stars to go on forced marches, sing morale-building songs at the top of their voices, undergo martial arts training and participate in a number of other, often humiliating, activities.[5]

The experience of Japan's major companies within their own market has led them to a series of fundamental conclusions: that market share is vital; investment in productive capacity must at least keep pace with – and preferably exceed – the market's growth; the principal weapon with which to gain and hold market share is price, which must decline steadily along with costs; and new products must be constantly introduced to continue the cycle of investment, cost reduction and market share gain.

Xerox strategist Lyndon Haddon put it like this: 'The Europeans would be very happy with a three times mark up. Americans would try to figure out a way to make it four times. And the Japanese would cut the price in half and sell four times as much.'[6] This was certainly true of perhaps the archetypal ultra-competitive Japanese industry – electronic calculators. From the mid-1960s to the mid-1970s, calculator production more than doubled each year; as the original three Japanese producers (Sharp, Canon and Oki) rapidly expanded to around 40, prices fell first by about a quarter each year in the 1960s, and then by around a half every year in the 1970s.

Sharp had been the leading manufacturer in the early years, controlling about a third of production. But relatively unknown Casio, a small company run by two brothers, forged ahead by sharply increasing its production capacity to lower unit costs, while simultaneously expanding model variety and slashing prices to appeal to consumers. So while Sharp grew at 100 per cent each year, Casio expanded at double that rate, achieving the leading position in Japan by 1973 with a 35 per cent share of production. Sharp's share, meanwhile, had slipped to only 17 per cent. At the same time, the number of participants in the industry fell to four. Well-known companies such as Sony, Ricoh and Hitachi withdrew gracefully, while lesser-known companies like Vizicon and Sigma went out of business altogether.

So the strong inclination towards growth in successful Japanese companies is closely linked to their desire to survive. They have witnessed the fate of too many companies that failed to grow faster than their competitors and they have themselves been constructed in an environment of rapid growth. All of which has led to what James Abegglen, the management expert and founder of the Tokyo office of the Boston Consulting Group, has called the 'winners' competitive cycle'.[7]

Kamikaze tactics

When domestic demand slows, growth-oriented Japanese companies tend also to seek quick additional overseas sales volumes to offset maturing domestic markets. By the time Japanese corporations have reached this stage, they will generally have built up a large capacity for low-cost, high-quality production which ensures their success. The reactions of Western businesspeople to these low-priced, quality products can at times be quite paranoid. Charges of 'predatory pricing', 'targeting markets until competitors have been bankrupted', 'kamikaze tactics' and, needless to say, 'dumping' are common.

Such interpretations of Japanese efficiency are nothing new. Well before the Second World War, Japanese traders shipped goods to depressed markets at irresistibly low prices by cutting costs to the minimum. At that time, their merchandise was often shoddy, but they later devised ways of producing standard-quality goods at prices that confounded their competitors. By replacing old weaving machinery with the latest Toyoda automatic looms, for example, Japanese mills overtook the British in 1932 to make Japan the world's largest cotton goods exporter. Cheap Japanese textiles drove Britain's producers out of her own colonies and even found willing buyers in the weaving towns of Britain herself.

Even after importing logs from North America, Japanese plywood makers were able to sell their product to the American East Coast at half the price of American producers. Japanese 150-power microscopes could be bought at $1.95 retail when comparable American-made products were wholesaling at $7.50 and Woolworths sold Japanese imitations of American toothbrushes for only ten cents – the American originals cost 39 cents.[8] At that time, discomforted Western competitors complained of cheap Japanese labour and 'sweatshop conditions', but labour costs in fact constituted a very small fraction of production costs – it was more a question of efficiency. 'The Italian government, while its press screamed Yellow Peril and Social Dumping and Wake Up Europe,' wrote *Fortune* magazine in 1936, 'admitted that one reason why Japanese silks were selling in silk-making Italy might be that Japanese machinery and Japanese organization were better.'

Present-day commentators also often fall into the same trap of attributing Japanese industry's high-volume, low-cost products to unfair tactics. One writer recently cited the fact that Japan's seven video-recorder manufacturers quadrupled output between 1979 and 1981 to 9.5 million units, and then pushed production up further to 33.8 million VCRs in 1986 – five-sixths of which were exported – as an example of over-investment and dumping which drove RCA and Zenith out of the market and severely threatened Philips and Grundig who were then only producing 700,000 units annually.[9] This begs a number of questions. If the Japanese exported five-sixths of their production, how could they use profits made in a supposedly protected home market to subsidize such a high volume of exports? And why did Grundig and Philips – the latter a very substantial and well-financed company – only produce 700,000 VCRs a year? Surely the truth is that Japanese industry did what the Americans and Europeans (who did in fact have a protected home market) were not prepared to do – namely, they invested, geared up and took the risk of raising production, so lowering prices to the great benefit of consumers.

Volume plus quality, variety and design

Because Japanese companies excel at making long runs of high volume goods, standards which make products in a particular field compatible – such as those covering fax machines and personal computers – are important in helping to increase the size of the market. Standards have also facilitated the use of more, low-cost standardized components which, again, play a part in reducing costs.

To some extent, Japanese companies have traditionally also achieved high volumes of production by focusing their efforts on restricted product lines. Toyota followed this strategy against Western forklift-truck manufacturers when, in the early 1970s, it manufactured a relatively limited line of six forklift-truck families in its Nagoya factory. Although Toyota was smaller than its main European competitor, the reduced complexity at the Nagoya plant enabled the Japanese company to drive down costs and beat its Western competitors on price.

Flexible manufacturing systems have, however, altered production economics in recent years. Construction equipment maker Komatsu originally followed the narrow-line policy, but its recent huge investment in flexible manufacturing systems and quick changeover tooling has helped it to become a producer of a broad line of products, allowing Komatsu to gain the edge on its main rival, Caterpillar, in terms of product variety.

But while many Japanese manufacturers have grasped the opportunity of gaining a competitive advantage by using new manufacturing technology to offer increased model variety at a low cost, many Western companies, by contrast, are one step behind. Under pressure from Japanese manufacturers, they often reduce model variety to cut costs at the very time when changing production technology makes that less necessary.

Flexible manufacturing has facilitated a further greatly significant change in the emphasis of Japan's manufacturing industry. Originally, Japanese industry's rapid growth and increasing volumes were largely based on low-end products. But as increased volumes have led to reduced costs, Japanese companies have been more and more able to fund an upgrading of their technology and products which has steadily diminished the distinction between top-end Western products and their leading Japanese rivals.

So although the competitive strength of Japanese companies has, since the Second World War, been largely founded first on price and later on quality, product innovation and state-of-the-art features have lately provided the basis for their competitive capabilities. Canon began the process in its camera line back in 1960. Originally operated by gearwheel mechanisms, the product was redesigned into an assembly of electronic devices and a major upgrade in the form of the electronic eye was introduced in 1960. Large lenses, range finders, low-speed and high-speed shutters, focal-plane shutters, single lens reflex systems and flashes were all steadily fitted to ordinary, low-priced cameras, and in 1980 Canon developed an automatic focusing camera which was an immediate hit.

This process has been more recent in Japan's car industry. Not so long ago, most Japanese cars resembled awful, European-sized versions of American models – unkindly dubbed 'the mid-Atlantic look' by one motor magazine. Acres of tacky plastic mock-leather stitching adorned their interiors and the vehicles had little design integrity. No one bought a Japanese car for its looks: they sold strictly on price and reliability.

Yet, more recently, Japanese products have often become the design leaders in their fields. The success of their consumer electronics industry is well known, but now Japanese cars, too, have increasingly taken on an attractive, non-derivative design-coherence of their own, as epitomized by Toyota's stylish 1988-model-year Corolla range, while the latest sports cars from Honda, Toyota and Nissan are every bit as attractive and enjoyable as their European competitors.

Indeed, *Car* magazine raved about the 'scorching performance and brilliant handling' of Nissan's new 300ZX sports coupé in its March 1990 edition, likening it to 'a Porsche 944 Turbo and 928S4 rolled into one' and concluding that 'Porsche now has a serious rival that it cannot begin to match on price'. Japanese industry, after years of producing boring, reliable products, has now moved into a new league.

There has been a tendency to see the stark simplicity and beauty of some of the better examples of Japanese design as being the product of some kind of deeply inbred Zen minimalism. But the fact that Japanese products have by no means always been paragons of good design should indicate that this is, at best, a minor factor. In part, the Japanese design sense is conditioned by the country's space problem which has precluded her manufacturers from filling the streets with sloppilly-built Cadillacs, or congesting people's homes with oversized televisions and massive refrigerators. But what really lies behind the recent massive improvement is the great effort that Japanese companies are now putting into design as they upgrade their products and move into the more sophisticated areas of the market.

Increasingly, Japanese consumer product companies see design as a major strategic weapon and their design departments are given equal status to other departments. At Ricoh and Canon, for example, design now has its own special business unit, while Sony and Sharp have design chiefs on the board. In many Western companies, by contrast, design is still often an afterthought, rather than something that is engineered into the product.

According to research by design professionals, Arnold Wasserman and Bill Moggridge,[10] Japanese companies typically now spend in excess of four per cent of their total R&D budget on design, which has become an integral part of their policy of innovation. By comparison, no major American company spends as much as two per cent of their R&D on design, and, in marked contrast to recent sharp increases in Japanese in-house design staff, many American companies have reduced theirs.

Where next?

All of which should offer clues as to which Western industries will next succumb to the well-oiled industrial might of Japan. It is, however, worth bearing in mind that there are still large industries in which Japan does not reign supreme. She tends not to do well, for example, in large-scale process industries such as chemicals, one of the biggest international manufacturing sectors with annual sales of about $1,000 billion, where her largest operator, Mitsubishi Chemical Industries, is less than a third the size of the main American and European companies.

In addition, the areas in which Japan's industry has been most successful have also varied as the nation's comparative competitive advantage has altered at different stages in her economic development. After the last War, Japan's primary source of competitive advantage lay in her low wage costs. As wage levels increased and Japanese industry moved on to more sophisticated, higher added-value products, the source of comparative advantage shifted to high-volume, large-scale facilities producing standardized products. In such industries, Japan could exploit to the maximum her advantage in organizational effectiveness.

Today, the emerging source of Japan's competitive advantage appears to be in developing organizational efficiency to allow for more manufacturing flexibility, while stepping up the research and design effort to produce ever more advanced and marketable products. As a result, Japanese industry now excels at making items which require complex, multi-stage production processes, such as consumer electronics, vehicles and information technology products.

Recently, aerospace, software and pharmaceuticals have been the pundits' favourites for Japan's next success stories. On the basis that Japan's industry must constantly move upwards to ever more sophisticated products, they say, Japan's next attack will come in these knowledge-based industries. In fact, a great deal of effort has already gone into developing industries such as aerospace, named by MITI as a future pillar of the economy back in the 1960s. Japanese companies have had a presence in the aircraft market since the 1920s and produced a turbo prop passenger plane in the 1950s. Now, about 30 Japanese suppliers, some of them former ship builders, make jet-engine components and structural parts for Boeing, Rolls Royce and other leading Western companies – and Japanese companies are actively courted by Western manufacturers who increasingly need partners to share massive development costs. Japan already does about $1 billion a year worth of airframe subcontracting for United States manufacturers alone. Fifteen per cent of Boeing's 767 aeroplane is produced by Fuji Heavy Industries, Mitsubishi and Kawasaki who are also being considered as risk-sharing partners, rather than just subcontractors, in the development of the new, upsized Boeing 777.

Japanese manufacturers are now discussing the feasibility of collaborating to produce all-Japanese 75- and 150-seat medium-sized airliners for the rapidly growing Asian feeder routes. But Japan's ambitions do not end there. For some time Japan has had a little-publicized space programme which began in 1966 with a very small team of researchers under a young Tokyo University professor working with a shoestring budget in a meagerly equipped laboratory. The result was a series of tiny rockets, so thin they were called 'pencils', launched from a stretch of waste ground that was their Cape Kennedy. The Agency for Space Development is now responsible for the latest development, the H-2, a satellite-launch rocket which is likely to become a direct competitor to the European Ariane and American launchers. This space effort cost Japan ¥140 billion (£560 million) in 1988, largely spent on the development of the launch vehicle together with communications and observation satellites.

Compared to aerospace, Japan's pharmaceutical sector is still relatively puny – especially when it comes to exporting. While European companies typically earn 75 per cent of their revenues in export markets, and the large American drugs companies earn 30 per cent of their sales overseas, the export ratio of Japan's companies is a paltry six per cent. Only one Japanese company, Takeda, is rated among the top 15 drugs groups worldwide, while Japanese-developed medicines account for a trifling two per cent of the Western European and American pharmaceutical market. Nonetheless, some significant progress has been made by the Japanese industry over the past decade. For, by 1987, more totally new drugs were coming from Japan than from any other country.

It therefore comes as no surprise to learn that Japan's drug makers are now aiming to grab a larger slice of the world's $130-billion-a-year pharmaceutical market. However, large Western drug companies employ networks of thousands of salespeople who establish relationships with the medical community and convince doctors to prescribe their products. The setting up of this kind of salesforce – euphemistically called 'detail staff' – is a long and painstaking business and remains a weak point for the Japanese.

The answer is to buy up Western drug companies, so the Japanese are now jostling to buy up medium-sized producers to gain access to their distribution networks. And the deals have been getting steadily bigger.

They include Yamanouchi's acquisition of the American vitamin and healthcare company, Shacklee, followed by the largest buy-out to date when Fujisawa Pharmaceutical, one of Japan's top drugs companies, spent $1 billion on LyphoMed, an Illinois-based pharmaceutical producer.

Software is the weakest of the three areas tipped to be future Japanese success stories, for Japan's growing expertise in the computer market is somewhat offset by her weakness in computer programs. By most estimates, United States producers still hold about 70 per cent of the $55-billion world software market and, to date, MITI-orchestrated efforts to improve the situation have not been notably successful. Their first project, in 1976, was a flop. The latest effort to date, the ten-year, $357-million, Fifth Generation Project, set up in 1982 to research artificial intelligence, has succeeded in producing a 'parallel' computer which uses 64 simultaneously working microprocessors programmed to translate text from one language to another, but it has not yet found any commercial application.

Despite such intensive efforts in these three fields, there must be some doubt as to whether the next Japanese industrial success story really will be in software, drugs or aerospace, since none of these industries is ideally matched to Japan's chief strengths – that is, volume production of sophisticated, complex products. Software cannot yet be produced in capital-intensive factories geared to high volumes and flexibility, while pharmaceuticals, as a research-based process industry, is also far from being an ideal candidate despite Japan's burgeoning R&D effort. Aerospace may well be a better bet, especially bearing in mind the inefficiencies inherent in Airbus construction, strikes at European plants and Boeing's problems with quality, delivery and labour. But scope for Japanese producers to exploit their traditional strengths in high-volume production and automation appear relatively limited, while Japan is still very weak when it comes to the all-important area of international servicing, a vital factor in the aircraft and engine market.

Nonetheless, to write Japan out of any field would, bearing in mind her recent industrial history, be foolish. Much depends on the responses of Western companies, who at least cannot complain that they have not had ample warning to adjust their operations and investments to counter any Japanese threat. For if action is taken before the Japanese develop a position strong enough to erode the home market strengths of their Western competitors, they may well be held at bay.

Whatever the future of these advanced industries, one of the most striking features of Japan's economic performance in the second half of the 1980s was that, far from moving into reverse, Japan's more traditional manufacturing sector has advanced strongly and looks set to expand further. Powering this ongoing success has been a dramatic expansion in capital investment. By the end of 1989, the backlog of orders among Japan's main machine-tool builders was well in excess of £2 billion – the largest in the industry's history. Far from beginning a slow retreat, Japan's industry is about to embark on another round of low-cost, high-quality manufacturing. Further, as Japan's industry becomes more sophisticated, the type of machine tools being ordered are more complex. Three-quarters of the late 1989 machine-tool backlog was for computerized equipment, rather than the simpler standard machines which make up half of the sales in West Germany.

One of the front-runners in the new wave of capital investment is Japan's vehicle industry – now the world's biggest – where overall capital expenditure for year-end March 1989 was up by nearly 20 per cent. In fact, Japan's vehicle industry offers two important indicators of where her manufacturing is going. First, there is a great deal of evidence that Japan's corporations will significantly increase their lead in areas like vehicles and electronics, where they are currently already strong. Second, huge capital investment, together with efficient and flexible industrial organization, will increasingly allow the Japanese to make product innovation and differentiation their competitive hallmark in the 1990s.

Already the Japanese are some five years ahead of their American rivals and about three years in advance of the Europeans in volume car-production technology. But they are also way ahead in many other areas of automotive technology, such as multi-valve and ceramic engines and four-wheel steering. In addition, Japanese automobile manufacturers are best placed to take advantage of the growth in automotive electronics – and according to General Motors, the market for computerized engine and suspension management systems and other electronic components is set to more than double to $35 billion by the mid-1990s.

So as the 1990s wear on, Western vehicle makers, who not so long ago sneered at low-tech Japanese tin-boxes, may find themselves taking a back seat as the Japanese get into gear to exploit their technological lead and manufacturing flexibility in order to shower the market with models designed to appeal to every segment, including the executive and luxury sectors, currently dominated by European manufacturers. The biggest casualty so far has been General Motors, which once dominated the North American market with a near 50 per cent share, a figure that had slid to 35 per cent by the end of the 1980s, pushing GM's United States automotive business into losses in the second half of 1989.

The 1990s will also see Japan's consumer electronics industry take an even larger share of this giant, $120-billion market. For, in response to challenges from South Korea and other East Asian rivals, the Japanese are ready to launch an arsenal of high-tech products of the type that do not yet even feature in their main Western rivals' plans. While European producers struggle to match the Japanese at building products like video recorders and CD players, the Japanese are already two steps ahead. Innovative products in the pipeline include filmless cameras, using a Sony-pioneered technology to digitally record images; flat TV screens you hang on your wall; translation telephones – initially with simple vocabularies – that handle multi-lingual conversations; tiny, but fully functional, personal computers, a fraction the size of even the latest generation 'pocketbook' models; high-definition TV; and tape recorders the size of a matchbox.

Into services

Japan's service economy has been growing rapidly, too, in recent years – and Japanese companies have also been pushing into overseas service markets. In the year to March 1987, services accounted for more than three-quarters of Japan's new direct overseas investment. The most dramatic and visible moves came two yeas later when Sony bought both CBS Records and Columbia Pictures in a single year; shortly afterwards, JVC, 50 per cent-owned by Matsushita, signed a $100 million-plus deal with a prominent American producer to form a new film company. This was on top of the 41 overseas resorts, ranging from Hawaii to Spain's Costa del Sol, which were being developed by Japanese investors in 1988. Such frenetic activity has helped to lever Japan's five biggest construction companies – Kajima, Taisei, Takenaka, Ohbayashi and Shimizu (which, in 1987, overtook a French company to become the world's biggest builder with orders in excess of $12 billion) – into the world's top ten construction firms by revenue.

But Japan's most dramatic advance in the international service sector has come in a totally different area. For while the success of Japan's consumer electronics and automobile giants is obvious to all, and while Japanese purchases of prime American real-estate has aroused well-documented concerns, few outside the world of finance have yet appreciated the extent or significance of Japan's less visible, but growing dominance in the high ground of international banking and finance.

Not many people, for example, realize that nine of the top ten international banks in terms of assets are Japanese. The largest is Dai-Ichi Kangyo, closely followed by the new Mitsui Taiyo Kobe bank, Sumitomo and Mitsubishi – which itself is two-thirds larger than America's biggest bank, Citicorp. And at year-end March 1989, the Japanese long-term credit banks' hidden reserves totalled $340 billion – more than the capital of all the rest of the world's banks put together.

Further, the most profitable financial institution in the world is Nomura Securities. At the beginning of 1990, it had assets of $384 billion – $110 billion more than the assets of the world's biggest bank – and made pre-tax profits of $999 billion in 1989. An estimated 1,000 of its 15,000 worldwide employees are dollar millionaires and in many months it is the biggest single buyer at the US Treasury bond auctions. Nomura was also, by 1988, the top Eurobond underwriter, with Daiwa Securities second and Nikko and Yamaichi not far behind.

This should come as no surprise. Japanese-owned banks and financial institutions are virtually forced to recycle finance overseas for lack of scope for investing their vast sums even in Japan's huge market. As a result, they now hold 25 per cent of California's and about ten per cent of America's total banking assets. And Japanese financial institutions are unlikely to be satisfied with merely dominating the world of banking. In 1989, JCB, Japan's credit and charge card company, began a major drive to boost its non-Japanese cardholders from a mere 30,000 to more than one million, with the ultimate aim of establishing JCB alongside the main international card payments systems, Visa, Master Card and American Express.

So in the 1990s, Japan's car and electronics industries will stamp their increasing dominance on world markets, while more and more Japanese banks will call the shots in global finance. But the problems of making predictions have been shown many times in the past. Even one of the most perceptive observers of post-War Japan, the French journalist, Robert

Guillain, wrote from the vantage point of the late 1960s that the outlook for the Japanese car industry might not be too good because of the large number of manufacturers, an excessive number of models and 'a superfluity of cars that are all very like one another, all competing in the same class'.[11] But that should not be of any comfort to companies in those areas where the West retains its greatest strengths – aerospace, software and pharmaceuticals. They have been warned.

13

新
大
国

THE COST OF MONEY

'You must spend money, if you wish to make money.'
Plautus (254–184 BC).

WHEN THE NIPPON Kokan Company's (NKK) 16-million-ton steel plant at Fukuyama, the largest in the world, was nearing completion in 1968, their older Keihan plant near Tokyo was obsolescent and suffering from pollution-control problems. Although NKK's president was satisfied with the extent of his company's investment in the Fukuyama plant, the company's Director of Corporate Planning strongly urged him immediately to replace the aged, uncompetitive Keihan plant with a parallel version of the new Fukuyama plant. The president hesitated, fearing that another massive investment would worsen his company's financial ratio (at that stage equity capital only accounted for only 14 per cent of the company's requirements and NKK was heavily in debt).

Next day, however, he visited the president of Fuji Bank who wholeheartedly recommended the new investment and promised the bank would make every effort to support the new construction. Work at the new $4 billion Keihan plant began that year, and from reclaimed land there arose a superbly organized, computerized and automated complex which became one of the most efficient steel plants in the world.[1] At one end, huge ore ships discharged their cargo by means of the most modern equipment, capable of unloading 62,000 tons every 24 hours, while at the far end, a mile or so away, other ships sailed off with the finished products to the tune of ten million tons a year – all produced by a labour force of only 5,000.

Cameras used to be assembled by hand until successful Japanese manufacturers invested capital in mass-production systems. Canon introduced its first really automated camera production line in 1960 to make the Canonette, which it sold for $30 – equivalent cameras at the time cost $100 – and went on to complete a new factory at Toride in 1961 which produced 30,000 cameras a month, so further adding to the downward cost spiral.

Some years later, when a visiting American Congressional Delegation was taken to Nissan's new automated manufacturing plant at Zama near Tokyo, observers recorded the shock that registered on their faces: the only jobs for people in the factory were checking readings and occasionally giving instructions to the computer.

Capital investment, one of Japanese industry's most powerful competitive weapons, has made all of this possible. By almost every measure, the Japanese have beaten the West hands down in productive capacity. Overall, fixed capital investment in Japan, excluding housing, rose from 12 per cent of GNP in 1965 to 23 per cent by 1989. Over the same period, investment in the United States only increased from 11 per cent of GNP to 12 per cent. In 1980, General Motors only employed 30 per cent of the net fixed assets per employee compared to Toyota, while British Leyland employed a mere 15 per cent. Between 1981 and 1988 the number of robots at work in Japanese factories grew from 21,000 to 176,000, while in the United States the figure climbed from 6,000 to just 32,600, in West Germany from 2,300 to 17,700 and in the UK from 713 to 5,034.*

The result of such capital investment has been huge increases in efficiency and productivity. Between 1955 and 1972, when the foundations of her current economic success were laid, Japan's export prices fell by a fifth compared with her main competitors. During the same period, productivity gains far outstripped wage rises. Overall, labour productivity in Japan's manufacturing sector rose from a base index of a 100 in 1975 to 160 in 1985, while during the same period the UK, West Germany and the United States could only engineer their respective worker productivity index levels to between 130 and 140.

Long-termism

The ability of Japanese industry to invest huge sums in improvements to their factories and production equipment in the hope of gaining long-term market share has been contrasted with the pursuit of short-term profits which is said to typify many Western corporations. It is frequently asserted that the financial structure of Japanese companies facilitates such 'long-termism'. Since equity stock accounts for only 30 per cent of the average Japanese company's capital needs, the argument runs, they are therefore under less pressure to show a profit and a return to shareholders each year and are also in less danger of takeover by predators. The banks which account for the ownership or debt which make up most of Japanese industry's capital requirements are, it is said, more prone to take risks and more interested in the company's long-range growth. This is in contrast to the situation in the United States and Britain in particular where stockholders, especially financial institutions and pension funds, account for around half of the average large corporation's capital and are always ready to sell out to the highest bidder.

---

* It is worth noting that the Japanese figure is slightly inflated owing to their broader definition of what constitutes a robot, which includes relatively simple devices such as one-arm pick-and-place machines.

As with most widely held received wisdoms, there is some truth and a fair proportion of exaggeration in this scenario. There is certainly evidence to support the belief that the Japanese banks, with their close relations with industry, and the Japanese financial system in general, have played a major part in Japan's economic success.

It is undeniable that Japanese companies like NKK have used debt aggressively in order to finance their breakneck growth. In the late 1970s and early 1980s, the financial policies of the average Japanese company made it possible for them to sustain a growth rate nearly 25 per cent higher than their American counterpart, despite their lower profitability. For while the average debt:equity ratio – the proportion of cash from loans to money raised from selling shares in the company – for an American manufacturer was 0.6:1, it was 1.6:1 for the Japanese manufacturer. Put more simply, American companies use debt far less than the sale of shares to raise money, while Japanese companies do the opposite and use debt capital to finance more rapid growth.

Similarly, the relative lack of shareholder power in Japan seems to make it possible for Japanese companies to pay less of their profits in dividends: an average of 3.5 per cent after tax, compared to 6.5 per cent in the United States. Toyota's dividends in the mid-1980s, for example, were only around 1.3 per cent of its share price, compared to 7.1 per cent for General Motors. The combined effect of these differences, according to industry expert James Abegglen, is that the average Japanese manufacturer can grow at around ten per cent a year, while the average American producer can only grow at eight per cent a year.

That, however, is only part of the story for although Japanese shareholders seem unprotestingly to accept low profits and meagre dividends, James Abegglen points out that if you include the growth performance of Japanese stocks, the picture changes drastically. When the performance of the stocks of 21 industry leaders in Japan and the United States were compared, Japanese shareholders in fact fared better than their American counterparts in 16 of the cases, on average out-scoring the Americans by no less than 175 per cent to 39 per cent in pre-tax appreciation of the aggregated share price together with cumulative dividends.

While dividends would have accounted for 85 per cent of the American investors' profit, they would have been only 11 per cent of the Japanese shareholders' gain because the Japanese shares rose faster than the American dividends. To an extent, this imbalance has been determined by the Japanese tax system, which taxes dividends as ordinary income but levies no taxes on capital gains. This makes Japanese shareholders far less interested in profits passed on as dividends than in growth paid out in increased share prices. But the fact remains that, on a pre-tax basis, Japanese shareholders would have fared more than four times better than their American counterparts.

On top of this, the view that Japanese banks are more willing to take on risky industrial ventures has to be balanced by the fact that the debt and risk exposure of the Japanese financial institutions is often exaggerated. For one thing, loans to corporations in Japan are usually backed up by collateral corporate assets. These are often underestimated due to the conservatism of

Japanese accounting which habitually books assets such as land at their original costs, even though they may have considerably appreciated.

Take Hitachi of Japan and America's General Electric (GE), for example. They are very similar companies in terms of products. Both are diversified manufacturers of electronic and electromechanical equipment, but their financial structures appear very different. Hitachi is much more leveraged than GE – its debt:equity ratio is more than 1:1, compared to GE's 0.25:1 – and its return on sales is also lower. Yet the financial risk of Hitachi is greatly overstated owing to four major differences in the two companies' balance sheets.

First, Hitachi consolidates into its overall figures the accounts of its long-term financing and credit company subsidiary which provides loans to its customers. This increases Hitachi's apparent exposure to bad debts, while GE, like many other American companies, keeps its high-debt credit operations off its main balance sheet. Second, Hitachi's balance sheet includes housing loans to employees – a common practice among major Japanese companies, but not among American ones. Third, Hitachi's accounts understate its holdings of marketable securities which appear on its balance sheet at cost, while GE constantly revalues its portfolio. Fourth, and perhaps most significantly, Hitachi's land holdings are greatly under-stated on its balance sheet. This is a common trait with Japanese companies. The Mitsubishi Estate Company, for example, is the main landowner in the Marunouchi banking district in Tokyo, which the firm's predecessor acquired for the equivalent of $6,400 in 1882. Although the land today is estimated to be worth several billion dollars, it is still carried on the books at the original acquisition cost.

Japanese accounting practices also minimize their companies' profitabil-ity. Western businesspeople tend to use return on sales as the bench-mark of profitability. On this basis, Japanese companies are far less profitable than American companies with after-tax returns averaging one to two per cent in the 1980s, compared to five–six per cent for American corporations. If, however, you measure profitability by after-tax return on shareholders' investment, the position is reversed. The average Japanese manufacturer has achieved an after-tax return on equity of around 20 per cent, while the position in the United States has been in a ten to 15 per cent range. In addition, OECD studies report consistently higher real rates of return on investments in Japan compared to the major industrialized Western economies.[2]

So, taking into account the fact that Japanese shareholders benefit more from the growth in their companies' shares than from their dividends, that the exposure of Japanese banks and financial institutions is not nearly as great as might appear from a superficial reading of balance sheets, and that by some measures Japanese companies' profitability has exceeded that in the West, the picture begins to look somewhat different. Certainly, Japanese manufacturers have used debt aggressively to finance growth. But Japanese banks have not in reality been significantly more adventurous than their Western counterparts in financing that growth: indeed, Japanese banks' loan losses are lower than for most other countries' banks. Nor have Japanese shareholders quiescently accepted low returns from their investments.

Cheap money?

What about the argument that the tendency for Japanese companies to raise money less through tradable equity finance than through debt finance has helped to both lower the cost of their finance and to guard them from the unwanted attentions of hostile bidders? Again, there is some truth in this assertion, especially as even those Japanese companies which have sold equity have often guarded their positions by selling chunks of their shares to friendly corporations, which often reciprocate to form interlocking 'cross-holdings'. Such takeover defences have often been cited among the impediments to doing business in Japan, while the relative ease with which American and British companies can be bought and sold has been said to put intolerable pressure on managers to go for short-term profits at the expense of long-term growth.

Why, then, have Western companies not gone down the same route and borrowed or sold restricted equity? It has, in fact, generally been open to Western companies to ease shareholder pressure and restrict takeover opportunities as the Japanese have done. There are two main reasons why many have not done so.

First, selling freely-tradable equity, with full voting rights, on the open market is a cheaper way to raise capital than limiting equity sales to a small number of other companies, or issuing stock with restricted voting rights to safeguard against takeovers. Second, while it is true that in theory debt finance is less costly than equity, this is not invariably the case, especially as the capital has to be repaid at some point. Industrialists who raise finance through share offerings must realize that they are steadily relinquishing total control over their companies, but obviously feel that it is worth trading some freedom of manoeuvre for the benefits of raising equity capital – benefits which include the fact that while equity capital does not allow for as fast growth as loan finance, it is far less risky. So while Japanese companies' higher exposure to loans helps them to sustain rapid growth during good times, it also creates problems during downturns, as evidenced by Japan's very high bankruptcy rate.

Third, one of the major reasons why share flotations have been so popular among the Western business community is that going public is one of the fastest routes to personal wealth. Directors and managers who own part of the company make huge gains – and those gains are all the greater if they offer attractive shares with as few limitations as possible. Directors of companies where these choices have been made can hardly complain if, as a result of freely selling chunks of their business, it becomes a takeover target.

These are among the reasons why debt finance or restricted equity options have been eschewed by many – although by no means all – Western companies. But a further argument deployed by those who feel that Japanese industry benefits from unfair advantages is that it has gained from artificially low interest rates on its debt: in other words, the cost of capital is lower in Japan. It is certainly true that the monetary policy pursued for most of the post-War period by successive Japanese governments has been geared to keeping both inflation and interest rates at low levels, a policy reinforced by the limits placed on domestic consumption and incentives for savings. It has been open, of course, for Western governments to pursue similar policies, but for the most part they have been subject to different political imperatives which have led to greater priority being given to increasing domestic consumption or channelling funds into housing to keep voters happy; in many cases, governments have also been led for ideological reasons into a policy of penalizing savers through taxation which has led to a shortage of available capital and hence higher interest rates.

It is also fair to say that Japanese Ministry of Finance policy has been strongly geared towards encouraging the banks to lend to industry. But this state of affairs has been changing steadily as capital markets have been liberalized, allowing companies to shop around for finance. It is worth noting, moreover, that the cost of debt for Japanese industry has been higher than is at first apparent because for a long time Japanese banks insisted that firms 'offset' a portion of loans by depositing some of the money back with the bank, effectively raising the actual cost of the loan. In addition, a great deal of Japanese industry's capital in the 1960s was actually loaned by American banks, which certainly did not subsidize their rates. In 1968, American loans to Japan amounted to $3 billion and most of the money was very short-term and so extremely expensive.

Oriental sharks

Takami Takahashi started out in a shack, making bearings in the 1950s. His company, Minebea, has baulked the norms of Japanese business by pursuing almost predatory acquisition tactics which have taken it into fasteners, measuring instruments, furniture distribution, hand-guns, hi-fi speakers (bought from Sony) and vehicle wheel manufacture. More recently, Minebea has set up its own successful subsidiaries manufacturing computer keyboards and semiconductors, and the next project is a large-scale pig farming operation in Thailand.

Although Takahashi's career puts paid to the commonly-held view that Japan's business community is a cohesive whole in which takeovers are impossible, it has to be accepted that on top of the difficulty of buying companies primarily financed by debt rather than equity, company acquisition is not viewed in quite the same way as it is in the West. Under Japanese law, mergers or acquisitions are only possible with the unanimous consent of all the company's directors. The sale of a company implies both a failure and a sense of buying and selling people, with implications of social irresponsibility. In addition, scope for rationalization as a result of merger is limited where promotion by seniority and lifetime employment prevails.

It should, however, be acknowledged that there have been some successful mergers and takeovers in Japanese industry and Takahashi is not merely an exception to the rule. In pre-War days, Hitachi and Mitsubishi acquired a number of companies, and, more recently, ceramics and electronic components maker, Kyocera, bought up the troubled camera maker, Yashica. Japan now even has its own successful 'greenmailer': predatory takeover specialist, Kitaro Watanabe, who has been dubbed the T Boone Pickens of Tokyo because of his successful corporate raids. Fifty-seven-year-old Watanabe has built up a personal fortune – estimated at more than $1 billion

– through his practice of buying up stakes in undervalued companies and then selling them back at a higher price to a management eager to avoid a takeover. Watanabe began his career when he came to Tokyo in the early 1950s, a penniless orphan after losing his parents and five brothers in a wartime air raid. He began his climb into *Fortune* magazine's list of the world's richest men by selling second-hand cars and then real estate. Today he is a major property owner in Tokyo and has two luxury hotels in Hawaii in his portfolio. Watanabe's success, which is based on money borrowed from the ultra-traditional Mitsui Trust Bank, together with similar successes by other investment groups, indicates that things are beginning to change in Japanese industry.

This is borne out by the statistics. In the period from the end of the Second World War to the beginning of the Korean War, there was only an average of about 330 mergers and complete acquisitions in Japan each year. In the period from the Korean War to 1970, the figure rose to a little over 500, while in the subsequent ten years it climbed again to an average of more than 1,000 a year.[3] Western companies, too, have increasingly featured in takeovers, the acquisition of control of joint-ventures or the purchase of large stakes in Japanese companies. These include the acquisition by the British industrial gases group, BOC, of a 43 per cent stake in Osaka Oxygen in 1982, followed in 1983 by the American pharmaceutical group, Merck, buying a majority in Banyu – the first takeover of a top Tokyo Stock Exchange quoted company by a foreign firm.

Moreover, the number of staff involved in mergers and acquisitions (M&A) at the Long-Term Credit Bank of Japan rose from five in 1988 to 15 in 1990. Other Japanese institutions with growing M&A departments include Sanwa Bank and Sumitomo Bank, while Nomura Wasserstein Perella, the joint venture between Nomura Securities and the Wall Street M&A specialist, had 35 full-time M&A staff in Japan by 1990.

The theory that Japan's industry has benefited uniquely from its financial system and impediments to hostile bids is, anyway, weakened by the fact that similar bank–industry relationships and takeover barriers exist in other countries. West Germany is probably the best example, where the Deutsche Bank owns substantial stakes in major German companies, including a 28.24 per cent holding in Daimler–Benz. In Germany, as in Japan, the banks played a crucial role in the development of industry in the late Nineteenth Century and after the Second World War in the absence of a well-developed financial system of the type possessed by Great Britain and the United States. This has brought certain advantages, but in both cases the system is changing steadily and perhaps moving more towards the Anglo–Saxon pattern. It is worth noting, moreover, that the system is not universally popular in West Germany. The Federal Cartel Office, for example, is pushing for bank representatives to be barred from sitting on the supervisory boards of companies which compete with one another.

Furthermore, impediments to takeovers, legitimate or otherwise, are prevalent in other Western countries. In continental Europe in particular, numerous companies have issued non-voting shares or relied heavily on debt financing to protect themselves. In Italy, by one estimate, only seven out of over 200 leading listed companies have the majority of their shares in public hands.[4] No hostile takeover has yet succeeded in the Netherlands owing to a network of restrictions including limited voting rights for shareholders, priority shares and special powers enjoyed by sitting management. According to a cheeky study in 1990 by Japanese stockbroker, Yamaichi, even in Britain 14 of the 100 leading stocks are largely protected from takeovers by family or trust holdings, nine by controlling 'golden shares' which prevent hostile bids, and seven by restrictions on bank takeovers.

State intervention to block hostile overseas bids is also far from uncommon in the West. In the late 1960s, when Britain's biggest bearings company, Ransome Marles, was about to be taken over by Sweden's SKF, the government decided that such a takeover would be bad for British industry and engineered a rival deal which brought the three main British bearings manufacturers together to form Ransome Hoffman Pollard. When, in 1988, Ford looked likely to take over ailing Italian sports saloon manufacturer, Alfa Romeo, the Italian government stepped in and ensured that their national champion car maker, Fiat, pipped the American multinational to clinch the deal. France's government blocked the acquisition of a leading car-component maker by British parts maker, Lucas, in 1977; in fact, as much as 20 per cent of the equity of France's larger publicly-quoted companies is owned by state-run shareholders, particularly the nationalized banks, which would undoubtedly use their stock-holdings to impede unwelcome foreign bidders. In 1984, the West German government was partly responsible for preventing British electronics company, GEC, from taking over the ailing German company, AEG Telefunken, helping to orchestrate a more politically acceptable buyer in the form of Daimler–Benz.

In Britain, nationalistic sentiment in Parliament and the country as a whole in 1986 forced even the free-market Conservative government to turn down good bids from Ford for the state-run Rover group's car business, and from General Motors for Rover's four-wheel drive and commercial vehicle operations. Ironically, such jingoism did not get the British industry very far and indirectly resulted in substantial benefits for the Japanese, for Rover's car side, which was eventually sold to British Aerospace, is now largely dependent on Japanese Honda technology; while GM, exasperated at the British attitude, effectively pulled out of its existing UK commercial vehicle operation, leaving it to Japanese Isuzu to run.

Nor has the United States been innocent of such tactics. When, in 1987, Fujitsu wanted to take over semiconductor pioneer, Fairchild Semiconductor, it was prevented from doing so by the Pentagon, which claimed the California-based chip-maker was of vital strategic importance – even though it had been owned by the French oil exploration company, Schlumberger, since 1979.

The shareholder as whipping boy

Is there, anyway, really much to stop well-run Western companies from announcing that they will pay low dividends and aim for long-term growth rather than short-term profits? The few that have done so – and they include minicomputer leader, Digital Equipment Corporation (DEC) – have generally found financial institutions and shareholders understanding. In the case of DEC, these investors have, on the whole, been amply rewarded for their confidence by increases in the share price.

Moreover, what evidence there is on the attitudes of financial institutions to companies which sacrifice short term profits for long-term growth in Britain and the United States does not wholly support those who complain about the inhibiting effect of institutional shareholders. According to a study by the United States Securities and Exchange Commission (SEC),[5] the R&D:sales ratio in a sample of 324 companies grew on average regardless of whether institutional shareholding increased, refuting the claim that greater institutional share ownership causes managers to focus on the short-term. Moreover, the SEC report also showed that R&D spending in 57 companies subject to takeover was less than half the average for their industry group in the year preceding the takeover offer, indicating that, if anything, lower research commitments rather than higher ones lead to takeovers. Finally, the SEC study found that far from public announcements of long-term investment projects leading to a fall in stock prices, they actually led to a significant rise above general share price movements, which rebuts the argument that the market penalizes companies that invest for the long term.

Lord Hunt, chairman of Prudential, Britain's largest institutional investor, pointed out that in 1989 his organization accepted only five per cent of the offers out of a total of 54 bids for companies in which Prudential held shares. Between 1984 and 1989, moreover, Prudential failed to support the management in only 25 out of 490 bids.[6] All of which goes some way towards refuting the theory resounding throughout the boardrooms of Britain and the United States that institutional ownership of shares is in part responsible for the poor performance of industry. Simple explanations such as this are always appealing, but perhaps the inhabitants of those boardrooms should look more to their own shortcomings.

There is one further point. A well-managed company which optimizes its business opportunities should be a very difficult target for predators. They, after all, are going to find it tough to pay the interest on the loan raised to purchase the company if they cannot enhance that company's performance. Who would ever dream of launching a hostile bid for IBM or Boeing, for example?

Indeed, despite the bad press often accorded to acquisitive companies like the Anglo–American giant, Hanson Industries, the fact is that they often do industry as a whole a great service by restructuring badly managed companies and getting the best out of them. And if, in the process, they make money by off-loading some businesses which they bought at a discount, does not at least some of the responsibility lie with the old management that allowed itself to get into that position? The very threat of buy-outs and takeovers should, therefore, be an excellent source of motivation for management to become more efficient.

So for all of their disadvantages, hostile takeovers remain an important link in the chain of managerial accountability and some of the prime targets for hostile bids have been companies whose own management and performance have left something to be desired. The $25-billion takeover battle for

RJR Nabisco in 1988 was, for example, unmatched in its scale and aggression as well as the hostility it aroused. But for all its qualities, one of the shortcomings that made the biscuit and snack giant vulnerable to predators was the feeling that it was run more for the benefit of its management than its shareholders. Most potent among the symbols of corporate excess was the so-called RJR Air Force, a fleet of executive jets housed at Atlanta's Charlie Brown airport, furnished with marble and mahogany passenger suites and on which directors could call at will.

To argue the same case from another angle, the Dutch electronics giant, Philips, has been sheltered from the consequences of its poor performance and hostile takeovers by a variety of elaborate devices, including a two-tier board. As a result, the company has been largely immune to short-term pressures and interference from its shareholders whom it has been able to treat with lordly disdain. But by almost every measure, the £18 billion-a-year turnover company has performed far worse than its main Japanese rivals. Its sales per employee in 1989, for example, were one-seventh those of Matsushita and its pre-tax profit margin stood at only just over two per cent, compared to the Japanese company's ten per cent, shortcomings which slashed operating profits and led to an urgent boardroom reshuffle in the spring of 1990, prompting one aggrieved shareholder at an extraordinary general meeting to ask: 'Do you hate your shareholders?' Yet might not the stolid Dutch company have performed better if its management had been placed under more pressure?

The inflexibility caused by the relative lack of takeovers has also been a two-edged sword in Japan and has resulted in severe disadvantages for some Japanese industries. It would make good economic sense, for example, if several of the fertilizer companies within the Mitsubishi group were to merge. But despite difficult trading conditions in that sector, they have been unable to do so.

The Japanese system is, anyway, beginning to change. As Japan's financial markets began to be liberalized in the early 1980s, industrial firms increasingly began to shop around for cheaper finance, which they generally found in the Euromarkets. As a result, Japanese companies became less concerned about preserving long-term relationships with their banks. Once it was in their interest to break the ties, they did so, and now Japanese companies raise most of their capital through overseas bond issues.[7]

Indeed, Toyota provided an ironic twist to the theory that Japanese companies have unfairly benefited from low interest rates, when the car giant found that it could make a profit by selling convertible bonds* on international markets and investing the proceeds in deposit accounts in Japan where the return was higher. Toyota was both taking advantage of the cheaper capital available overseas, as well as using the equity element of its convertible bonds to lower the cost of raising funds from foreigners, and

---

* These can be traded in for equity at a later date and so offer lower interest rates – known as the 'coupon'. Warrant bonds, which include an option to buy equity in the bond issuing company, have also been popular. But with $120 billion of these bonds redeemable by corporate Japan between 1991 and 1995, and with the sharp fall in the Japanese stock market in 1990, it is extremely unlikely that warrant holders will exercise their options which, some experts argue, will lead to severe liquidity problems for Japanese industry in the 90s.

then using the higher interest rates prevailing in the Japanese market to make easy money. In fact, in 1987, Toyota made more than $1 billion playing such money games, which became known as *'zaiteku'* (*'financial engineering'*).

So you have to look beyond just the banking system, debt finance or even high capital investment in itself for the reasons behind Japan's business success. It may be true that wise government policies in Japan, geared towards curbing domestic over-consumption and boosting savings, have often led to lower interest rates and a bigger pool of investment capital for industry. But many large Western corporations have nonetheless had huge sums at their disposal and it certainly has not invariably been the case that primarily equity-financed Western companies have been short of capital (General Motors spent a massive $70 billion under its president, Roger B Smith, from 1982–90).

Often, however, Western companies have preferred to use their money to fund acquisitions rather than organic growth. The United States car industry, for example, spent many billions of dollars acquiring aerospace and computer companies in the 1980s. Even where capital has been invested in internal growth it has not always been carried out wisely. When, for example, GM decided to put $3 billion into a new, state-of-the-art plant for its import-busting Saturn subcompact, the American vehicle giant found that much of the technology it had hoped to use was unworkable. Moreover, while Honda, Nissan, Toyota and Mazda take less than a year to move from a basic clay model to a working prototype, and only another two years before the first production model rolls off the line, the Saturn was only finally launched after eight long years of development. All of which illustrates that pumping huge amounts of money into capital investment is not, of itself, enough to guarantee success.

Education is one factor. The American earthmoving and construction equipment giant, Caterpillar, embarked on a $2-billion factory moderniza-tion programme in the late 1980s. But according to Bernie Sorel, the company's vice president responsible for manufacturing, one of the greatest problems he faced in implementing the programme was that whereas 'in Japan people running even small manufacturing systems are professional engineers', by contrast, 'here in the United States we sometimes start with people with very little education'.[8]

Gavin Laird, the Scottish leader of one of Britain's largest trades unions, the Amalgamated Engineering Union, offers another important clue as to why many Western companies have not succeeded, despite high capital investment. Laird retains both his deep Scots accent and the practical, no-nonsense attitude of someone who spent 30 years working on the shop floor. This has helped him in dealing with the wave of incoming Japanese companies with which he has been highly successful in making pragmatic, single-union deals to represent their workforces in return for agreed working practices and disputes procedures. As a result, Laird has visited many plants in Japan. He told me that he was initially surprised that some of the most successful Japanese companies had old plants without the latest equipment. 'But they still do well,' he said. 'The key is in the way they organize themselves – if you don't get that right, you can forget all of your fancy equipment.'

The fact is that the Japanese make their capital work harder. It is not low-cost capital but capital expenditure plus effective organization and management which have made much of Japan's industry so awesomely efficient. Their car industry, for example, designs quality into the products, rather than just relying on quality control when the car comes off the line. They co-operate more closely with their suppliers, involving them at an earlier stage and encouraging them to share in the development work. Within the company, multi-functional development teams work cohesively with the production engineers, with the result that model development takes half the man hours required in the West. And they are more flexible. While the Big Three American car makers have the luxury of 62 plants, most of which cannot build more than 250,000 cars a year and only one of which can build more than two models on the same line, Honda requires only two factories to churn out more than a million cars – and it can assemble up to eight models on the same line.[9] So rather than making shareholders the whipping boys for their own mismanagement, Western industrialists might find it more profitable to look at ways in which they can spend their money more effectively.

14

新大国

TAKING TROUBLE

'We were being wiped out by the Japanese because they were better managers. It wasn't robotics, or culture, or morning calisthenics and company songs – it was professional managers who understood their business and paid attention to detail.'
Vaughan Beals, Chairman of Harley–Davidson Motor Co.[1]

IN JULY 1950, a little-known American statistician called Dr W Edwards Demming was invited as a guest of the Occupation Forces to speak on the use of statistics in quality control at the Industry Club of Japan. At that time Japanese products were not noted for their superiority and it seemed unlikely that Dr Demming, whose views were largely ignored in his home country, would make much difference.

Now, each year Japanese industry honours Dr Demming by competing fiercely for the annual Demming Award, which goes to the company considered to have made the greatest improvement in quality. Virtually all major Japanese companies have long since implemented Dr Demming's method of using statistical analysis to monitor quality control and Japanese products are renowned the world over for their excellence. Other Japanese management practices, such as going for high-volume production and adding features to products, have also been anticipated by advanced Western thinkers, such as GM's pre-War chief, Alfred Sloan.

Even that most Japanese of industrial institutions, the company song, was foreshadowed by American corporations. IBM, for example, had a company song book before the Second World War, which included a corporate anthem with inspiring choruses such as:

EVER ONWARD – EVER ONWARD!
That's the spirit that has brought us fame!

We're big, but bigger we will be.
We can't fail for all can see
That to serve humanity has been our aim!
Our products are known in every zone.
Our reputation sparkles like a gem!
We've fought our way through – and new
Fields we're sure to conquer too
For the EVER ONWARD IBM.

Yet the misconception that Japan's management success is based on a unique, non-transferable cultural background is still common. In fact, most of the characteristics of Japanese management style were formed after the Second World War and were to a large extent the result of picking the best business practices and theories from the United States or Europe – including many which were ignored or which had fallen into abeyance in the West. As a foreign visitor to a Japanese business was once told: 'There was no new fish, but the method of cooking was better.'

Much Western attention has been focused on Japanese quality in recent years, particularly the concept of 'Quality Circles' (QCs). These are self-managed, small groups of workers who initiate improvements within their own work area. Usually consisting of five to ten people with a group leader, the emphasis is on individual worker responsibility for the quality of the goods together with production and safety problems. Often the improvements are small, but incrementally and over large volumes they add up to a great deal. A Canon copier plant QC consisting of women who drive in 8,000 screws a day, for example, suggested boosting efficiency by rearranging the assembly line so screws went in vertically, not horizontally, while a Ricoh QC reduced the amount of tape needed to package copier paper.[2]

Each circle meets once or twice a month – sometimes during, and sometimes after, work – and they are regularly evaluated by management and awarded prizes for successful work. There are now more than 100,000 quality circles in Japan, which only work because they are part of an overall philosophy of putting quality first, to which everyone at all levels is committed. As a result, Japanese plants rarely employ small armies of quality inspectors, as is the norm in many Western factories, as this just helps to inculcate the attitude that 'If I don't get it right, someone else will pick it up'. Rather, production staff in Japan are expected to assure the quality of their own work – the slogan 'Right First Time' means just that.

There is a further point. According to Takeomi Nagafuchi, the general manager in charge of quality control at Ricoh, '70 per cent of quality control is determined at the product design stage. So naturally the biggest effort is made at that stage.'[3] Japanese manufacturers design quality and ease of production into their products to ensure quality on the production line. And far from costing extra, built-in quality actually helps to reduce Japanese industry's costs. In a comparative study of American and Japanese air-conditioner manufacturers in 1983, Harvard Business School Professor David Garvin found that the highest-quality American manufacturer spent three times as much money on warranty claims as the average Japanese manufacturer; and the lowest-quality American supplier spent almost nine times as much. The extra money which the Japanese spent on building higher quality into their production came to only half what the Americans spent on repairing defective units.[4]

A more recent Japanese management development is *Kanban*, or *Just In Time* (JIT), which was really started in the 1950s by Toyota, although foreshadowed by some of Henry Ford's early methods. The idea is to reduce the volume of stock and materials flowing through the factory both to save on space and to reduce finance costs. Buffer stocks of components are reduced or replaced with small, frequent deliveries geared to production. *Kanban* is now widespread in Japanese industry and has resulted in huge gains from inventory reductions and increased efficiency in plant utilization.

'Tell us what you want'

Concealed among the paddy fields near Shibetsu, on Japan's northern island of Hokkaido, there is a Toyota proving ground which they call 'Little Europe'. Covering more than 1,000 acres and costing well over £100 million, it contains exact replicas of every type of road on which Toyota cars are driven, including American-style freeways, *autobahns* and poorly-paved minor roads – all painstakingly reproduced by photographing, measuring and analysing the surface materials of the originals. Even the roadside signs for the *autobahn* section have been imported from West Germany.

It was here that Toyota managed to make its new, four-litre V8 Lexus luxury saloon handle so uncannily like a European thoroughbred car. When noises were tracked down during the six-year, $500-million development programme, rather than merely stifling them with sound-deadening materials, Toyota designed them out. Toyota also hired anthropologists to observe their own dealerships and those of rivals in three American cities, while a Toyota design team spent three months in the affluent Laguna Beach area of Southern California studying the market and its needs.

Moreover, to ensure quality is of an even higher standard than Mercedes–Benz, Jaguar or BMW, white-gloved inspectors feel every Lexus car all over for the smallest imperfection as it rolls off the assembly track at the Tahara factory, near Nagoya. It is then put on a rig to test for the slightest rattle, while another device spins the wheels up to high speeds and electronic sensors search for balancing faults too slight for most human testers to detect. Every Lexus 32-valve V8 engine is also run on a test bench while a robot microphone scans the unit, locating and analysing every source of noise to ensure each one is as perfect as possible.

Nissan followed its Japanese rival's example by billeting its chief engineer for the new Infiniti luxury car line with an American family to learn how they think and feel about their cars. Honda went one better. Its R&D engineers attended Hells Angels bike rallies and found that American riders were adding fairings and saddle bags to their machines and using them as long-distance tourers rather than as street 'superbikes'. So Honda's engineers redesigned their powerful Gold Wing model into a luxury touring machine.[5] This obsessive attention to detail, increasingly seen in the design of Japanese consumer and business electronics products such as Toshiba laptop computers, is one of Japanese industry's greatest but least quantifiable skills. It extends also to packaging which is often of a very high standard: the Sapporo brewery even managed to improve on the humble beer can with a barrel shaped can which won accolades.

Some time ago, in a Tokyo suburb, two large stores, one specializing in home appliances and the other in more general merchandise, were locked in a bitter rivalry. When the home appliance store began marketing a small, electric fan, the second store ran a leaflet campaign to homes in the area offering virtually identical fans for ¥1,000 less.

When the management of the first store found this out, they went to great lengths to seek out 28 out of the 30 original buyers. Each one received an apology for having been sold the fan at the higher price, and a ¥1,000 refund. Most of the buyers had been unaware of the lower offer, but they nonetheless appreciated the *makoto* (*sincerity*) of the store management and, as word went around, sales subsequently shot up.

These stories are indicative of the way Japanese management takes trouble to stay close to its customers. When the founder of Matsushita, Konosuke Matsushita, was recalled from retirement in the early 1960s, after the company had been hit by a sales slump, one of his first moves was to assemble a meeting of the company's dealers: 'Tell us what you want and we will give it to you,' he is reported to have said. Matsushita is now the world's largest manufacturer of consumer electronics products.

Japanese car makers have likewise assiduously responded to consumer requirements, and have often helped to foster demand for a product through competitive pricing, high levels of specification and strong marketing. Early Japanese sports models offered more car for less money, like the Honda N360 which caused a sensation during the 1967 Paris and London automobile shows, provoking what one English magazine called 'an anxious rage' in the hearts of European manufacturers. Two years later, the Datsun Fairlady Z must have caused further anxious rages when it was launched, offering Porsche performance for the price of an MGB.

During the 1970s, when virtually all of the major European volume car manufacturers were withdrawing from sports car and coupé production, arguing that it was too small a market to bother with, Japanese manufacturers eagerly seized on this niche. As a result, Toyota's mid-engined MR2 has given enthusiasts a sophisticated, low-cost sports car of the kind that the Western volume manufacturers have not made for years. Mazda's $13,000 Miata small sports car was such a runaway success that American dealers were able to charge premiums of up to $5,000 per car. And now, when Chrysler wants its own sports car, it has to go to Mitsubishi who will be responsible for most of the design and development and all of the production of the new joint-venture Stealth model.[6] Not only have the Japanese succeeded in selling far more sports cars and coupés than the Europeans have ever done, but by producing desirable cars they have also managed to improve their perceived status.

Japanese auto makers also offer consumers more up-to-date models by changing their ranges on four-year cycles, compared to the eight-year-plus change-overs common with Western manufacturers. By the time Ford's top selling Escort model, launched in 1980, was replaced in 1990, Toyota's similarly sized Corolla and Honda's Civic had been through no fewer than three model changes.

Microvans are purpose-built, small, manoeuvrable, economic commercial vehicles with a load capacity of around half a ton, which are ideally suited to European towns and cities. Yet most European manufacturers have traditionally only produced half-ton vans derived from their family-car ranges. These vehicles are something of a compromise, with larger overall dimensions but a smaller load area than the purpose-built microvans. Japanese manufacturers began selling microvans, originally developed for their domestic market, in Europe in the mid-1970s, since when these versatile products have taken a substantial proportion of small van sales. So far, no European manufacturer has responded with an indigenous product, although GM assembles a Suzuki microvan in Britain. Time and time again, Japanese manufacturers have proved to be more closely attuned to the requirements of Western consumers than Western industry itself. So who can blame those consumers for so often choosing Japanese products?

A potent symbol

The storyline was dramatic: the Japanese Arctic sled team are battling through the dense blizzard when, all of a sudden, they come face to face with something that shocks them. Almost invisible beneath its thick coating of snow stands the unmistakable outline of a vehicle. The team leader rushes to the spot, tears off his goggles and wipes the snow from the front of the vehicle. A look of shock breaks across his frozen face as he sees the revealed badge – it is a Land Rover.

Thus ran the immensely popular advertisement for the launch of the new Land Rover Discovery four-wheel-drive vehicle, which found its way into the hearts of the British public because it suggested that the Japanese feared the new competition represented by the Discovery. This was somewhat ironic because four-wheel-drive vehicles (4x4s), those most potent symbols of male machismo, offer perhaps the best example of the different approaches of Japanese and Western industry.

Traditionally, 4x4s have come in two types: the first include the basic, rugged, utilitarian vehicles like the American Jeep, four-wheel-drive pick-up trucks from the major American car makers, and the famous British Land Rover, which had the advantage of being built like a tank but the drawback of also driving like one; and the second type, luxury 4x4s like Land Rover's Range Rover model and upmarket derivations of American vehicles, which rarely see a muddy field and are mainly bought as a status symbol.

Land Rover, Jeep, Ford, General Motors and Chrysler dominated world 4x4 markets in the early 1970s. But then, American products became over-large, uneconomical and too geared to domestic needs to be competitive on export markets which were subsequently largely ignored. Land Rover and Range Rover models, by contrast, were in great worldwide demand in the mid-1970s. But rather than sharply stepping up production levels to reduce costs and satisfy their customers, Land Rover only marginally increased volumes with the result that their models were only available after a 12-month wait – or for a premium. In Iran in the 1970s, for example, Range Rovers were selling for up to twice their list-price.

This, of course, provided precisely the opening which the Japanese wanted. Delighted, they swooped in on the neglected customers, satisfying those Americans who did not want huge, thirsty 4x4s, Europeans who did not care to wait for high-priced British vehicles and Third World buyers who could not afford them. More than that, they discovered new markets for four-wheel drive which the Western manufacturers never thought existed. Subaru led the way by adding four-wheel drive to ordinary family cars, producing a vehicle which is as much at home in the supermarket car park as churning through axle-deep mud. Daihatsu and Suzuki successfully mass-marketed very small, low-cost, utility four-wheel drives which are favoured both by the growing band of sports enthusiasts who buy 4x4s, as well as by farmers who use them for personal transport rather than as load carriers: Suzuki sold more than 50,000 of its Samurai light 4x4 in the United States in 1988.

But above all, Japanese manufacturers have, since the 1970s, produced four-wheel-drive utility vehicles which are largely based on standardized car or small pick-up truck components and so have managed to undercut the traditional Western four-wheel-drive manufacturers by a substantial margin. Neither quite as tough or as durable as Land Rover or Jeep workhorse-type vehicles on the one hand, nor quite as luxurious or good on the road as Range Rovers, 4x4s like the Toyota Land Cruiser and Mitsubishi Shogun (called the Pajero in some markets and the Montero in the United States) have nonetheless opened a whole new leisure 4x4 market which in Europe grew from 25,000 in 1983 to 100,000 by 1988, and is forecast to reach 200,000 by 1993. Further, these lower-cost intermediate Japanese 4x4s have proved very popular in cost-conscious developing countries, with the result that 'Land Cruiser' has largely replaced 'Jeep' or 'Land Rover' as the generic name for 4x4s in many parts of the world.

By 1980, virtually every Japanese manufacturer was in the 4x4 market. The only serious new Western entrant, by contrast, was Daimler–Benz of West Germany which went into production (in co-operation with Steyr-Puch of Austria) with a very highly engineered 4x4 called the Gelendawagen in 1978. But this was only produced in tiny volumes of around 10,000 a year which made it far too costly for most buyers. Moreover, until 1989 no European manufacturer competed in the intermediate, leisure 4x4 market. By then, Japanese producers accounted for three-quarters of the 250,000 4x4s sold annually in Europe.

It took Land Rover until the mid-1980s finally to double capacity for the Range Rover to about 25,000 units a year; it was not until 1987 that they introduced the luxury 4x4 on to the American market – 17 years after its launch; they also barely altered the basic Land Rover between its 1948 launch and 1985; and when, in 1989, Land Rover finally came up with a lower cost, intermediate 4x4 vehicle of its own – the Discovery which so stunned the Japanese sled team in the advertisement – the company actually boasted in its launch press release that this was the first all-new Land Rover model since 1970! Even then the company again made the error of introducing the Discovery at production volumes which were far too low (less than 20,000 a year), causing waiting lists and delaying export launches.

The Japanese have suffered from no such inhibitions, eagerly seizing market opportunities left to them by sleepier Western companies. In fact, virtually the only four-wheel-drive area in which Western manufacturers have been quicker off the mark than the Japanese has been in adding four-wheel drive to high performance, road-going cars to enhance their road-holding capabilities – although Japanese manufacturers quickly caught up.

新　大　国

The strong market orientation of Japanese industry, together with the fear of being beaten to it by competitors, is further demonstrated by the constant flow of new products from Japanese manufacturers. In 1987, Mitsubishi produced no fewer than 257 new consumer products, closely followed by Hitachi with 243 and Toshiba with 233. Among the delights which Japanese consumers could enjoy that year was the Dani Punch, a vacuum cleaner from Mitsubishi which not only sucked up dust and grime but also used heat from its motors to kill the ticks (*dani* in Japanese) and fleas that often infest urban appartments in Japan, prompting one Japanese customer (according to *Time* magazine) to comment: 'It makes me feel great to see all those fleas toasted dead in the vacuum cleaner.' Within a year, Mitsubishi had sold some 300,000 units, ranging from $215 to $415 apiece.

Also on offer that year was the Secher, a cylindrical appliance used to dry women's knickers. It was conceived for Mitsubishi by a team of five female market researchers who found that most young Japanese women hand-washed their underwear but were reluctant to hang them out for fear of attracting sexual perverts. The product sold 100,000 units at $105 each in its first 18 months.

But unquestionably the hottest new item that year was Matsushita's Automatic Bread Baker, of which some 666,000 were sold in a six-month period at an average price of $252. The small square machine automatically mixes and kneads the dough, and then bakes perfect loaves in less than four hours. Although Western-style bread is readily available in local bakeries, the special appeal of this product seemed to be the very fact that home bread-making was not part of the Japanese housewife's traditional repertoire.[7]

Lest, however, you are beginning to think that the Japanese are infallible marketeers, bear in mind one of the sales ploys of SORD, the personal computer manufacturer which was once Japan's fastest growing company. When it launched a new model onto Western markets in 1982, SORD issued a press release which comprised a brief history of the origins of the company. This included a story about the early, pioneering days when the company's offices had been broken into by a thief who left an idiosyncratic visiting card by defecating on the blueprints of a new machine. 'Aha,' the press release reported SORD's founder Takayoshi Shiina as saying, 'so this will bring us good fortune, for the thief has fertilized our plans.' Not ideal copy for the Western computer press – SORD went bankrupt three years later.

新大国 15

SHARED FATE

'Regard your soldiers as your children, and they will follow you into the deepest valleys; look on them as your own beloved sons, and they will stand by you even unto death.'
Sun Tzu, Fifth-Century BC Chinese military philosopher, *Art of War*.

JAPANESE WORKERS ARE actually the most dissatisfied in the world. This surprising piece of information comes from a survey carried out in 1988 covering 650 companies with 11.5 million employees in 45 countries. Only 54 per cent of Japanese took a favourable view of their work organization, compared to 82 per cent of Brazilians.[1]

Some kind of rogue survey? A report from the Japanese Prime Minister's office on job satisfaction might carry more weight: this showed that only eight per cent of young Japanese, and 15 per cent of adults, were satisfied with their workplace. The comparative figures for young workers were 32 per cent in both United States and Britain, and 49 per cent and 42 per cent respectively for older people.

This oddity can probably best be explained not by the fact that Japanese workers are badly treated, nor that they are a society of whingers, but rather that as a highly-educated and relatively egalitarian society, their workplace aspirations and expectations are far higher than anywhere else in the world. It is, perhaps, this very lack of complacency which is one of Japan's greatest strengths. But above all, surveys such as these provide a useful counterpoint to those who explain Japan's success as being the result of a semi-mystical Oriental or Confucian spirit of harmony which pervades her industry.

From strife to enterprise unions

1947, 28 January, 10.00am: 300,000 workers and trades unionists gather in a sea of red flags and placards in front of the Imperial Palace, Tokyo, where they are addressed by Japan Socialist Party chairman Kanju Kato on the subject of the national general strike planned for 1 February. It looks to many as though Japan is about to sink into an abyss of industrial conflict, until the Occupation Forces chief, General MacArthur, steps in at the last minute to outlaw the strike. The secretary general of the Joint Strike Committee weeps as he reports to his committee the news that the strike has been stopped.

After the War, the Occupation Forces administration, SCAP, sought to foster democratic ideals by attempting to encourage the trades union movement through the release of many pre-War left-wingers and union leaders. Thousands of unions sprung up, but it soon became clear to the Americans that industrial chaos was not the best way of ensuring that Japan became a bulwark against the advance of Communism in the East. The outbreak of the Korean War, the Communist takeover in China and the Soviet explosion of an atomic bomb convinced SCAP to backtrack further by withdrawing the right to strike.

Even so, Japanese industry remained beset by labour problems for many years, and for some time it looked likely that Japan would become less an economic superpower than a lame duck. In 1950, for example, assailed by high inflation and a market downturn, Toyota suffered from severe labour unrest and had to be bailed out by the banks. As part of the rescue package, the company cut its workforce by 1,600, leading to more strikes and unrest which took a considerable time to settle.

One element of the problem was the reluctance of the Toyota workforce to man more than one machine at a time. According to Taiichi Ohno, who was then leading the Toyota production technology development team, 'resistance from the production workers was naturally strong. Although there was no increase in the amount of work or working time, the skilled workers at the time were fellows with the strong temperament of craftsmen and they strongly resisted change. They did not change easily from the old system of one man, one machine to the system of one man, many machines in a sequence of different processes – being required to work as a multi-skilled operator'.[2]

The 1950s and 1960s were also racked with bitter strikes on the railways and among seamen, while the 1960 Miike coal-mine strike was as long and as violent as anything in the West, prompting huge demonstrations and the formation of more than 300 miners' defence societies nationwide. Sony, too, suffered from unrest and a strike in 1961 when their union was taken over by leftists who demanded a closed shop.

Increasing prosperity took the edge off labour's militancy as the 1960s wore on. But even as late as 1986, group leaders among the workforce of the state-run Japan National Railways who supported the government's privatization plans were viciously attacked in their homes, one being beaten to death with a steel pipe.

The most intensely bitter period of industrial chaos largely ended during the 1950s, however, when managers and employees concluded that there was little time for conflicts which neither side could win, and collaborated instead to 'enlarge the cake'. The present state of Japanese labour relations therefore evolved out of the painstaking efforts of both sides of Japanese industry to establish stable relations in order to survive the early post-War years.

In-house enterprise unions, organized along company, rather than industry, lines were set up. These had a number of advantages, including the fact that the union structure posed no barriers to the movement of workers from one job to another – unlike the situation in Britain where inter-union demarcation disputes were a major cause of industrial unrest until the early 1980s. In addition, the enterprise union system means that Japanese corporations deal with a single negotiating unit. This may provide the union with a certain leverage, but this is mitigated by the fact that the unions identify to a large extent with the company's interests. It also means that Japanese industry is free from the problems inherent in the multiple union bargaining situations which are so common in some Western countries.

Crucial to the success of the whole structure is the mobility between enterprise union personnel and company management. A 1981 survey showed that three-quarters of 313 major companies had at least one executive director who had been high up in the company's union; while at Nissan more than 50 per cent of full-time officials in the company union are also foremen.[3] Kenichi Yamamoto, president of Mazda, was actually the leader of the company union. As a result, Japanese industry in general, although not free from labour problems, has for long had an enviably low strike record and minimal absenteeism. In 1978, for example, at a time when many Western countries were undergoing a period of extended industrial unrest, Japan lost only 36 days per 1,000 head of population through strikes, compared with 125 days lost in France, 203 in West Germany, 414 in Britain, 428 in the United States and 720 in Italy.

By then, West German absenteeism was running at twice the Japanese rate, while in the United States it was nearly four times, and in Britain and France between seven and eight times higher than in Japan. The annual Japanese wage-round, the *Shunto*, is now a largely ceremonial affair, and strikes are often symbolic, timed to take place before work or during the lunch hour so as not to disrupt production schedules. When Japanese companies run into trouble, they can expect more co-operation from their unions than is often the case in the West. For example, Kyocera's company union even went so far as to suggest a wage-freeze in order to preserve the company's competitiveness during the 1979 oil crisis.

More communist than the communists

The Germans have a concept, *Gemeinshaft*, which broadly refers to a community organization, as opposed to *Gesellschaft*, which is a more contractual association. Whereas in a *Gemeinshaft*, people are combined by mutual affection and interest, as in a family, a *Gesellschaft* is a purely profit-making economic structure. In the former, people help, trust and understand one another, sharing bad times as well as good. In the latter, there is no spiritual unity and people work for a reward. Although yoked together by contract, they exist apart and in a state of tension, merely atoms of the organization.

It was in this way that Toyohiro Kono, Professor of Administration at

Tokyo's Gakushin University, described the difference between Japanese and Western companies. Although the contrast might be a touch too sharply drawn, especially bearing in mind the above surveys on worker satisfaction in Japan, the fact is that Japanese business organizations do tend to respect the welfare of their employees and give them relatively equal treatment, which in turn causes employees to devote themselves more willingly to the company. As a result, the Japanese corporation is not simply an economic institution, but a deeply social one as well – one which Shinsuke Ohkawara, President of Kentucky Fried Chicken Japan, has called 'more communist than the communist countries themselves'.[4]

Just before he left the chairman's job at UK car and truck maker, British Leyland, Sir Michael Edwardes took a group of Japanese motor-industry executives round his largest plant, the huge Longbridge complex in Birmingham. The Japanese, who included representatives from Honda, a company with which BL had just established a partnership deal, were astonished at the way in which the Longbridge workforce was divided into different social groupings. They could not understand how a major enterprise could function efficiently in such a divisive atmosphere. What particularly shocked them was the half-dozen different grades of eating establishment, which ranged from shopfloor canteens to the Board's private dining rooms.

'He will win whose army is animated by the same spirit throughout all its ranks' wrote the Fifth-Century BC Chinese military philosopher, Sun Tzu, whose book, *Art of War*, is something of a cult text among Japanese management trainees. Animating the ranks involves establishing relative equality between different levels of workers which is demonstrated by the treatment shown to blue- and white-collar workers. Plant managers in Japan wear basically the same uniform as newly-hired workers and all use the same canteen and washing facilities. Like the wage system, the method of payment and the bonus scheme are also similar, inculcating high morale and a better sense of responsibility among the workers.

There is, admittedly, another side. I have visited Japanese factories where, despite the identical basic workwear worn by everyone, rank was indicated by different cap markings, and it is not uncommon for Japanese managers to have their own reserved car-parking spaces, while even in single status canteens the managers usually sit together. Although Japan may not be class-conscious, it is still intensely status-conscious, as exemplified by the different degrees of bowing depending on rank. But generally Japanese companies manage to inculcate a sense of togetherness which is frequently lacking in Western industry. In short, Japanese companies usually treat their workforce as members of the organization, not mere employees.

Underpinning the ethos of the Japanese corporation is a relative equality of earnings. Since the Second World War, the pay levels of the lower ranks of Japanese industry have been rising much more rapidly than have the pay levels of top executives, while the pre-tax compensation at the top levels of Japanese industry is still relatively low, at around $200,000. *Fortune* magazine reported in 1984 that the salaries of Japanese chairmen and presidents ranged from $50,000 to $250,000, depending on company size.

At that time, at least 85 American chief executives earned more than $1,000,000.

新　大　国

The difference between Japanese and Western employee management systems is only to a limited extent rooted in Japanese history and culture. During the Meiji period in the late Nineteenth Century, for example, when Japan was industrializing rapidly, the shortage of skilled workers for the new industries meant that some Japanese companies had to give their employees a range of incentives, such as guaranteed lifetime employment, in order to attract and keep them. Japan also largely avoided the grim industrial conditions which bred enduring conflict in some Western countries. Even so, Japanese employers – even in large corporations – were not invariably noted for their paternalism and there is a great deal which is relatively new in the way Japanese industry treats its workers.

For a time after the Second World War, many large Japanese companies considered copying the Western pattern of flexible employment, whereby workers could be dismissed at will, and hired in mid-career – the obvious advantages being the ability to dismiss poorly performing employees and reward hard-workers. Most large Japanese companies decided, however, to adopt a system whereby they guaranteed their employees lifetime employment and promoted them on the basis of seniority. There were, nonetheless, severe doubts as to the efficacy of this system until the late 1960s, when it became increasingly clear that Japanese industry was outperforming its Western counterparts, and Japanese management theorists began to be satisfied that their system was preferable to the Western pattern.

Among the advantages of the lifetime employment system, which is operated by many major Japanese companies, is that Japanese employees who know that they will be kept on by their company, and retrained in mid-career if necessary, are less likely to resist innovation and technological change. Indeed, Japanese workers who are concerned about the future of their company will eagerly embrace it. From the employer's point of view, the system also helps to engender a sense of all being together in the same boat, while employees perceive that diligence brings them long-term benefits if they remain with the company for life. In the West, incentive systems such as stock holding and share options are designed to foster the same type of involvement with the company, but can also encourage managers to go for short-term profits instead of long-term growth – not a problem with lifetime employment.

The *sempai (seniority promotion)* system means that seniors do not fear that clever juniors will be promoted above them, so they do not discourage or restrain them. Indeed, the success and achievements of junior employees tend to be credited to the seniors. But promotion under the seniority system tends to be slow, with very few exceptional promotions of younger men and one looming and very serious problem for the seniority system is the ageing of Japan. Although Japan has enjoyed a relatively young workforce since the Second World War, by the turn of the century the Japanese population's age and distribution will be closer to that of Western countries, with more than 15 per cent of the total population aged 65 or over. This means that the average age of the labour force is rising rapidly, upping salary costs, causing promotion bottlenecks and putting pressure on the seniority system. According to Ken Moroi, Chairman of Chichi Bu Cement:

> In both the industrial and the political worlds, the pattern has been that people have to wait at least until their 50s before they hope to reach the top. Obviously this view of what is appropriate at different stages of a life cycle should be rethought. Promotion by seniority is not a system that can be sustained in an ageing society.[5]

That there is now pressure to abandon the system is evidenced by the 1988 annual report on corporate management by the Japanese Association of Corporate Executives (Keizei Doyuokai). Their survey of 1,200 major firms in Japan, the United States, Europe and the Asian Newly Industrialized Countries (NICs) recommended that Japanese firms change to a Western-style system which emphasizes individual abilities. A new corporate goal of creativity and individuality should replace the traditional features of Japanese-style management, the report urged, together with a shift from egalitarianism to individualism. Already, the disadvantages inherent in the seniority system explain why many major companies, including Nomura and Matsushita, promote on merit rather than on seniority.

Another notable facet of Japanese man-management is the bonus system. Bonuses, which often amount to as much as 20 per cent of total annual remuneration, are usually awarded twice a year to almost all employees on the basis of the company's performance. Bonus sizes are related to salary levels and increase disproportionately with seniority: in other words, the more senior the employee, the higher proportion of his remuneration is likely to come in the form of the bonus, making the incentive increasingly effective as an employee advances within the organization. It also gives a company the flexibility to reduce or withhold bonuses during difficult times, which helps to obviate the necessity of laying off employees.

The effect of the bonus system and lifelong employment on senior management can be seen by the fact that the vast majority of the boards of most of Japan's major companies are composed of people who have been with the company since leaving university. A survey by the economic journal *Diamond* shows that 80 per cent of 1,522 promotions within the major companies surveyed were from within that company, with a further 13 per cent from the parent company or a subsidiary. Only seven per cent were complete outsiders. Even in such rapidly growing companies as Canon and Honda, there is no director who has not spent his entire working life with the company, while Hitachi and Matsushita have only two or three board members who have not been with the company since they left university.

Either through policy or necessity, however, some large companies deviate from the norm. Sony has a long-standing policy of recruiting talented people from the outside, while Toray, the textiles group, had to reduce its workforce, through natural wastage and an early retirement programme, from 12,500 in 1985 to 9,600 by the end of the decade, owing to fierce overseas competition. Moreover, a 1984 survey conducted by the Japanese Prime Minister's office found that nearly half of all Japanese in their 20s preferred an 'employment changing' job to one with guaranteed lifetime employment. This may explain why employment agencies have been one of Japan's most rapidly-growing businesses in recent years – including the now infamous Recruit company which managed a turnover of ¥420 billion (£1.9 billion) in 1987, before it ran into trouble.

Of more significance is the fact that fewer than a third of Japan's workers benefit from the lifetime employment system overall. This is because Japan's large number of small- and medium-sized companies rarely offer their employees lifetime employment or wages as high as those in larger corporations – about 67 per cent of Japan's enterprises employ less than 500 people, compared to 28 per cent in the United States.[6]

The majority of Japan's small- and medium-sized companies almost invariably offer wages and benefits which are lower than those of the larger companies. They also tend to operate on a six-day week, compared to the five-and-a-half day week which is the norm for larger companies. In addition, women rarely benefit from the lifetime employment system, not least because most female manual workers leave their jobs on marriage, although many return after raising their families. This has led some commentators to criticize Japan's 'two tier economy' on the grounds that a minority of large corporation workers gain disproportionately at the expense of the less fortunate majority, who often work for subcontracting companies.

It is fair to say, however, that virtually all developed economies manifest disparities in wages and conditions between different companies. In the United States, for example, employees in large-scale, unionized industries, such as steel and automobiles, have traditionally enjoyed wages and benefits well in excess of those in small companies, many of which may well be supplying components, services and raw materials to their plants. Besides, there is also evidence that the wage disparities between large and small companies in Japan have narrowed substantially since the 1950s, although smaller companies can still rarely match large ones when it comes to fringe benefits.

What is undoubtedly true is that in intensely meritocratic Japan, while those who pass their exams and go to university can do very well, those who do poorly are almost invariably relegated to low-status jobs for life. There are virtually no second chances for those who fail their exams, and such people tend to be the very ones who end up in the lower tiers of industry or in the less important end of the service sector. Such significant class divisions take some of the shine away from the prevalent image of single-status canteens, company uniforms and lifetime employment.

新　　大　　国

Japan is fortunate in that she does not need to spend very much on training her workforce. A recent Japanese Ministry of Labour survey found that, on average, companies spent £5 per employee per month on training – rather less than they spend on sport and leisure. Training expenditure averaged a mere 0.07 per cent of companies' turnover – less than half the amount spent by British companies, according to a 1985 estimate by the Manpower Services Commission. Moreover, virtually all training in Japan is done within industry, with virtually no government assistance.

Low expenditure on training partly stems from efficiency and cost-consciousness. Much in-company training is carried out through correspondence courses which workers take in their spare time, as evidenced by the plethora of books on management techniques and quality control in Tokyo bookshops.[7] Japanese industry is also, of course, blessed with an educated and disciplined pool of potential employees, largely due to the fact that her educational system is far more geared to vocational studies and the applied sciences, such as engineering, than is the case in the major Western countries. In 1980, for example, Canon employed 424 university graduates in Japan of whom 191 came from engineering and science faculties. In the same year, Hitachi recruited 1,440 high school students and 565 university graduates, of whom 464 were from engineering and the natural sciences; while no fewer than 28 per cent of the 3,600 staff of Hitachi's Musashi semiconductor plant are university graduates.[8] Overall, about 86 per cent of top Japanese managers are university graduates, compared to only around 24 per cent in Britain.[9] According to a British Embassy report in 1979, 67 per cent of all directors of leading Japanese companies also had at least some formal training in applied science while only about ten per cent of British management has an engineering or science background.

Fostering commitment

The late Lord Bruce-Gardyne, a British Treasury minister in Mrs Thatcher's first administration, liked to tell the story of how, during a visit to Japan, he fell into conversation with a young man in a Tokyo bar who proudly introduced himself as an ardent communist, dedicated to the violent overthrow of the capitalist order. He then noticed that the young revolutionary was wearing a Mitsui company badge. When Lord Bruce-Gardyne commented on this, he was treated to a heartfelt lecture about the man's employer that would have made Mitsui's PR department glow with pride.

If you ask a Japanese what he or she does for a living, the chances are that they will tell you that they work for Komatsu, Toyota, Toshiba etc. Ask a Westerner, and he or she will usually say that they are an engineer, production worker, etc. In Japan, one of the primary allegiances is to the company rather than the job. Vertical loyalty to the corporation, group or faction is often far more important than horizontal loyalties to class or ideology. This commitment to the workplace is typified by the common practice of asking superiors to assist in marriage arrangements and inviting senior company staff to the wedding as principal guests.

Loyalty manifests itself in a variety of other ways. Although, for example, International Labour Organization figures show that the average weekly hours worked in Japanese industry are less than in many Western countries, overall annual working hours are far higher – the average Japanese worker puts in 2,125 hours each year, compared to 1,957 in Britain, 1,934 in the United States and 1,728 in West Germany. The main reason for this is that Japanese workers use only about 55 per cent of their annual leave which, at 15 days*, tends to be shorter than in most Western countries.[10] In fact, until the 1960s, the Japanese did not even really have a word for 'holiday' at all – so they borrowed *vacance* from the French and Japanified it to *vakansu*.

Another measure of the commitment and loyalty of the Japanese work-force is their eagerness to suggest improvements in the workplace. Certainly, many Western companies have suggestion schemes, but these are often viewed with a certain amount of detachment and cynicism by the workforce. In 1981 Hitachi received 4.21 million suggestions, which saved it ¥225.3 billion (around £1 billion), while suggestions at Fuji Xerox's Ebina plant near Tokyo run at 200 per employee each year. By contrast, in Britain, ten suggestions a month in the whole of one sizeable plant is considered a pretty good haul.

The word *uchi*, which means *home*, is also often used by workers to refer to their company. But this is a loyalty which has been earned. Matsushita offers its employees pay and perks which would be the envy of most European workers. These include bonuses, low-cost homes, hospital care, travel loans and wedding grants. In return, the company is accorded almost total dedication. The Matsushita employee does not strike, is flexible in the work place, accepts low pay rises in lean years, declines to take all the holiday due and is prepared to adjust working hours to fit production schedules.

In part, this loyalty is also due to the virtuous triangle of lifelong employment, the seniority system and enterprise unions. Above all, though, it is a product of the painstaking efforts of both sides of Japanese industry to establish stable relations in order to survive in an intensely competitive market. So the system may well be very Japanese in the sense that it has been conditioned by the realities of the Japanese situation, but at the same time it is also the result of a great deal of intelligent appraisal of, as well as learning from, the West.

But there was nothing inevitable about the Japanese system. It largely grew up after the Second World War, following a period of severe labour problems, when, galvanized by the shock of defeat, Japanese management began to accept that loyalty had to be worked at and earned, while employees came to the sophisticated realization that their fate and that of their companies was much the same. A survey carried out in the early 1980s by the Aspen Institute and the Public Agenda Foundation found that while the percentage of Japanese who felt that they should do their best at work regardless of pay was actually slightly smaller than the American percentage, some 98 per cent of the Japanese workers believed that they would be the

---

* The Japanese do, however, have more national holidays than many other counties – 18 per year compared to about ten in most Western countries.

primary beneficiaries of any increase in their own productivity: only nine per cent of the American workers polled felt the same way.[11]

So Japanese industry has prospered not because of any semi-mystical group loyalty inherent in the Japanese race and not transferable to the West, but because it fosters commitment by engaging workers' loyalty as well as giving them a sense of belonging and pride in what they do. This extends to outside normal working hours when managers and team leaders regularly go out on drinking bouts with those under their direct control, something which helps to engender a sense of camaraderie and group identification.

Akio Morita of Sony, one of the grand old men of Japanese industry, perhaps sums up best what he calls the 'shared fate' attitude prevalent in Japanese industry:

What we in industry learned in dealing with people, is that people do not work just for money and that if you are trying to motivate, money is not the most effective tool. To motivate people, you must bring them into the family and treat them like respected members of it. Granted, in our one-race nation this might be easier to do than elsewhere, but it is still possible if you have an educated population.[12]

16

新大国

THE IMPROVERS

'Although Japanese success in recent years has been based on adaptation of Western, mainly American, technology, and on the capacity to commercialize it more rapidly than its competitors, it would be wrong to conclude from this that the Japanese are mere imitators who, once they have attained to the world state-of-the-art in a field, will not continue to move forward the frontiers of technology. On the contrary, history suggests that imitation, followed by more and more innovative adaptation, leading eventually to pioneering, creative innovation forms is the natural sequence of economic and industrial developments . . . it may be only those who try continually to reinvent the wheel that will lose out in the innovative race. In my opinion, the United States, so long accustomed to leading the world, may have lost the art of creative imitation, and is deficient in scanning the world's science and technology for potential commercial opportunities relative to what is done by its competitors, particularly Japan.'
Professor Harvey Brooks, Harvard University, in reply to a question by the United States House of Representatives Committee on Science, Research and Technology as to whether the United States was losing the technological race.[1]

IN 1543, THREE Portuguese adventurers arrived in a Chinese ship at Tanaga, a small island to the south of Kyushu. Although they were among the very first Europeans to arrive in Japan, they were warmly welcomed by the lord of the island who was so impressed with their guns that he bought two matchlocks from them for the vast sum of 2,000 taels and passed them to his swordsmith to copy. This was more difficult than he at first imagined. Fortunately, the swordsmith was blessed with an extremely attractive daughter who was handed over to the captain of the next Portuguese ship that arrived, in return for lessons from the ship's gunsmith. Within a few years, the Japanese were making improved versions of the weapons in large quantities and to very high standards.[2]

The Japanese quickly learnt how to put the new invention to good use, and a few years later, 500 of the new matchlocks were ordered by a vain young noble of imperial stock, Oda Nobunaga, who set about raising an army of professional troops to enlarge his domain. His successful tactic was to organize his 3,000 musketeers into three, alternately firing ranks, which allowed him to maintain a continuous, withering barrage of fire – tactics which were not used by British infantry for another two centuries. Nobunaga eventually subdued almost the whole of Japan and thus paved the way for the imposition of the highly centralized Tokugawa shogunate which was to rule Japan for the next two and a half centuries.

Fearful that their rule would be challenged by enemies who might lay hands on even more advanced Western weapons, the Tokugawa regime largely closed Japan to Western trade until, on a sweltering summer's day in July 1853, Commodore Matthew Perry sailed into the small port of Uraga, in what is now outer Tokyo Bay, on a mission from the American President to prize Japan open. Hardly had they dropped anchor when the Americans were surprised to find themselves surrounded by boat-loads of quick-sketch artists sent out to record every detail of the rigging for imitation. When Perry returned on his second mission a year later, he brought with him as gifts some examples of the latest products of Western ingenuity. They included a miniature steam locomotive, the size of a donkey, which ran on a circular 18-inch track. Great crowds of spectators gathered to see the device and Japanese men, lifting their skirts, clambered astride the diminutive machine, whooping as they rode at speeds of up to 30 miles an hour. In the midst of the excitement, however, and unbeknown to the Americans, a Japanese student was taking notes. When the track was later moved to Edo Park outside the Shogun's castle, it came as a shock to the Americans that he was able to set up and operate the train unaided.

Catching up

The root of the Japanese word *manabu* (*to learn*) is *manebu* (*to imitate*). The Japanese trait of imitation, or perhaps assimilation would be a fairer word, has a long pedigree and owes much to Japan's role as a late developer. Throughout their history, the Japanese have found themselves needing to catch up and have used great skill and painstaking effort in mastering and refining imported technology.

When, for example, the old Tokugawa military regime fell as an indirect result of the Western incursions, and a new government under Emperor Meiji came to power in 1868, Japanese scholars were sent out to America and Europe to search out the best of Western practices to bring back to Japan for adaptation. Over a thousand years earlier, Japan had been a primitive, tribal society when she first came into contact with T'ang China, then the most sophisticated nation on earth. The Japanese became voracious pupils and received a large measure of their culture from China, establishing an enduring attitude towards learning from outsiders and self-improvement. The imperial capitals at Nara and Heian, for example, were laid out in the

Eighth Century as copies of the great Chinese capital Chang'an (modern Xian), and the Japanese were also introduced by the Chinese to wet-field rice agriculture and the casting of bronze and iron.

It was not long before they caught up with their mentors, however. The Two Great Buddhas of Nara and Kamakura of the Eighth and Thirteenth Centuries are still among the largest bronze figures ever cast, while by the Twelfth Century the steel of Japanese swords had become the finest in the world.

During the Seventeenth and Eighteenth Centuries, both China and Japan, fearful of rapidly advancing Western technology, largely withdrew from outside contacts, but by the middle of the Nineteenth Century, both nations had fallen so far behind the West that their leaders realized the need to modernize. As this process developed, in the last decades of the Nineteenth Century, many contemporary foreign observers expected Japan to be easily outrun by much larger China in this modernization process.

The few travellers who observed that Western warships acquired by the Chinese navy were kept in an appalling and filthy condition, whereas Japanese naval vessels were spotless and functioned well, were largely ignored. So commentators anticipated that when Japan went to war with China in 1894 over the control of Korea, she would be easily defeated. Instead, to the surprise of the world, the Japanese sunk the Chinese fleet and won the war with ease. Even after this shock, Chinese attempts to reform and adopt Western practices were largely doomed to failure, while Japan went from strength to strength before acquiring the temerity to challenge militarily the Western powers in 1941.

One of the main reasons for Japan's success and China's failure lay in the willingness of the Japanese to learn, assimilate and, yes, copy from the West – a factor which was recognized by some of the more progressive Chinese leaders such as Sun Yat-sen, a great admirer of Meiji Japan who wrote in 1894 that Japan's success was to a large extent due to her open-door policy, her positive reaction to Western culture and the spirit of adventure and curiosity with which she actively sought out and used those ideas which would benefit the nation.[3] For although there was a certain amount of opposition within Japan to imported ideas, the ambivalence in China was much greater. As of 1862, for example, only 11 Chinese could read Western books, compared to as many as 500 in Japan. The Chinese attitude was, at best, typified by Feng Gulfen, the Nineteenth-Century counsellor to Chinese governments and an advocate of reform, who advised: 'We should use the instruments of the barbarians, but not adopt the ways of the barbarians. We should use them so that we can repel them.'

This xenophobic streak and equivocalness towards foreign ideas is rooted deep in Chinese history and culture. For one thing, new ideas had often came hand in hand with military defeat, such as the Mongol and Manchu invasions. Moreover, China's long record of achievement had the effect of inducing complacency. For example, during the T'ang dynasty (AD 618–907), when Europe languished in the Dark Ages, China was already a highly advanced and sophisticated society. It was an era to which the Chinese still hark back as their golden age. The vast Chinese empire, ruled by a Confucian bureaucracy, was then criss-crossed with roads and canals, while trade and commerce flourished in her great cities. Printing, gun-powder and glassmaking were also invented in China long before they were developed in Europe.

But under the Ming dynasty (1355–1644), China became increasingly isolated and began to stagnate under emperors who saw their country as culturally superior and economically self-sufficient, with nothing to learn from other countries. The process continued under subsequent dynasties until China became a huge, torpid, inward-looking empire, oblivious to the scientific advances by then taking place in Europe. The hostility to foreign ideas and methods, together with the arrogant view that China is culturally superior and more civilized than other nations, still lingers. By contrast, although Japan's geographical isolation was responsible for her relative backwardness in the Seventh and Eighth Centuries BC before she learned so much from China, it also meant that when ideas from overseas arrived, they tended to be welcomed and assimilated as they did not imply conquest or the domination suffered by other lands with larger and less secure borders. Nor did Japan have any great indigenous tradition of scientific progress or an empire to induce smug complacency or self-satisfaction. These factors have made the Japanese extremely receptive to new ideas during most of their history, and this openness is a key factor in Japan's more recent successful assimilation of Western technology – in sharp contrast to her former teacher, China.

新　大　国

On the outskirts of the old imperial city of Kyoto stands a somewhat incongruous little group of Western-style houses. They were built in the 1920s for a team of European engineers who had come to the city to construct an artificial fibre factory. Many of the engineers were former employees of the British textile group which had pioneered the development of rayon – the man-made wonder fabric of the day. Toray Industries was then one of the rapidly growing fibre producers, but it had failed in an attempt to secure a licence for rayon and had, therefore, imported the engineers to build a replica of the British plant.

Toray today is Japan's largest textile and fibre group with interests in other fields such as chemicals and plastics, and its £2 billion annual sales dwarf most American and European producers. Toray was not the only Japanese company to eagerly grasp Western technology during this period of rapid industrialization in the early part of the century. Bell's telephone was copied by Japanese companies only two years after it had been invented, while Edison's light bulb was duplicated 11 years after. In the 1930s, the Toyoda Automatic Loom company used the proceeds of the sale of its technology to buy a licence to manufacture a British-designed car, a venture which subsequently developed into Toyota; while in the 1950s Nissan, Isuzu, Hino and Mitsubishi used technology from Austin, Rootes, Renault and Willy's respectively.

This willingness to learn from foreigners persists. In 1980, 28,000 Japanese researchers went to the United States, while only 4,300 American researchers travelled to Japan. In the same year, Japan imported ¥170 billion (£800 million) worth of technology from the United States, while America imported only ¥58 billion (£270 billion) worth of Japanese technology in return. Barely 800 American citizens currently study at Japanese universities, compared to the 13,000 Japanese who study at American colleges, while more than 300 Japanese scientists also work at the United States government-funded research centre, the National Institute of Health in Bethesda, Maryland.

In part, it is fair to say, this is due to the fact that it has been harder for Americans to study and research in Japan than the other way round, but it is also because the Americans have felt that they have less to learn from the Japanese. According to a leader in the *Mainichi Daily News* in January 1988: 'The one-sided flow of technological information in favour of Japan is to a large measure due to insufficient efforts by the United States side. Japanese scientists learn English and read theses in English. American scientists should learn Japanese to obtain needed information in Japanese.'

For the most part, the strategy of Japan's companies has been to gain access to the best Western technology through the legitimate purchase of licences: buying in technology as cheaply as possible and improving on it, rather than engaging in expensive and often fruitless research and development. For example, in the late 1980s, semiconductor manufacturer, NMB, bought the design for their main 256K D-Ram product from Britain's Inmos and put resources into manufacturing efficiency which helped them rapidly to overtake Inmos' own production. Matsushita, now the largest consumer electronics manufacturer employing 135,000 people worldwide, has purchased no fewer than 49,000 patents. This strategy explains why, although Japan might have had only three Nobel prize winners – less than half the total won by scientists at AT&T's Bell Labs alone, and way beneath Great Britain's 63 and the United States' 139 – she nonetheless has the world's strongest manufacturing industry.

In fact, Japan has for some time been by far the biggest purchaser of foreign intellectual property. In 1985, she spent a massive $2.361 billion on overseas licences, royalties, patents, trademarks and copyrights – way ahead of the $847 million spent by the United States or the $598 million by Britain, making this area one of the few in which Japan runs a very substantial deficit with the United States and Britain. Neither is it a coincidence that one of her nearest rivals in the purchase of intellectual property (spending $1.207 billion in 1985) is also one of her most vigorous trading adversaries – West Germany.

This capacity to adapt and assimilate technology is frequently dismissed as 'copying' or 'aping' Western ideas. Yet the process is, to a large extent, part of the normal progression of industrial rise and fall whereby developing economies first copy and then improve products, moving on to innovate before finally lapsing into complacency. Complaints by declining industrial powers of being imitated by ascending ones are also not without historical precedents. At the Great Exhibition of 1851, for example, the British industrialists strolling around the Crystal Palace in London were horrified at the quality of the latest American guns, and claimed that the pernicious former colonials were unfairly using a British idea – a new lathe – to produce weapons with greater precision than the British ones. The British were later to make complaints about other nations' exploitation of their inventions, including artificial fibres, radar, penicillin, jet engines, carbon fibre and much more.

When the French sociologist and politician, Alexis de Tocqueville, visited the United States in the last century, he found the Americans too preoccupied with making money to be capable of innovative and original thought. During the early period of American development, American Nobel prize winners were scarce, American universities were not noted for their original research and the United States was frequently dubbed a 'copycat' economy. Today Japan, likewise, is often called a 'copycat' which gets a 'free ride' from others' research – and wins few Nobel prizes. But Japan is simply showing the same flair for creative adaptation that the United States did in an earlier era.

There has, moreover, been a tendency for many major Western companies to dismiss developments which they themselves did not first discover or develop. Aaron Gellman, the president of a major American consulting firm, commenting on the willingness of American firms to sell licences for their technology without asking for the right in return to use any improvements, pointed out that this was indicative of a 'very arrogant' attitude, which 'implied that no one could improve on our technology'.[4]

The Japanese, by contrast, have rarely fallen victim to this 'Not Made Here' syndrome and their willingness to accept that others might have a better way of doing things is a great strength, particularly as their resources can instead be devoted to improving, producing and marketing products rather than inventing them, which can be a risky and expensive process.

Of course, imitation can sometimes go a little too far, and there have been numerous controversial cases of Japanese companies illegally imitating Western products. In a famous 'sting' in 1982, for example, executives of Hitachi offered to pay FBI agents posing as consultants more than $600,000 in an attempt to get hold of information on IBM software. As a result, Hitachi had to negotiate a settlement with IBM which cost it an estimated $300 million. And in September 1987, IBM and Fujitsu also finally settled a long-running copyright dispute that dated back to 1982, when IBM accused Fujitsu of copying software used to control its mainframe computers. After reference to the American Arbitration Association, Fujitsu agreed to pay a royalty for the software for a limited period.[5] More recently, a United States federal judge ruled that Sumitomo Electric had stolen a patent for making fibre-optic cable from Corning Glass. As a result, Sumitomo had to stop manufacturing the fibres at its North Carolina plant.

The Japanese are not alone in this, however: sometimes they have even been the victims. During the early days of Sony, for example, the company had to fight a court case against a Tokyo importer which was bringing in American-made tape recorders which used patented Japanese technology. Early in 1989, Italian police armed with search warrants raided two Italian parts distribution companies during an investigation into the sale of counterfeit parts for American Caterpillar construction machinery. Caterpillar at that time also had suits pending against companies in Brazil, Jordan and Malaysia for making fake parts and – five years earlier – had even sued an American manufacturer for making counterfeit fuel nozzles, although this case was settled out of court.

In May 1989, American software producers attacked the illicit copying of their computer programs in Italy and announced prosecutions against the state-owned Enichem Agricoltura. This followed hard on the heels of an announcement of legal action against the Italian multinational chemical producer, Montedison, following raids on its offices. According to one American report, Italy is the worst offender out of all the developed countries when it comes to theft of software-based intellectual property.[6]

But perhaps the biggest ever case of industrial copying came not from a Japanese or Italian firm, but rather from good old all-American Eastman Kodak, which lost a lawsuit in 1985 for infringing Polaroid instant photography patents. The legal wrangling over compensation ended with Kodak paying Polaroid $900 million, the most expensive patent damage award in history.

Potentially more damaging to the American self-image as a nation that would never stoop to the illicit copying of rivals' industrial designs was the ruling by a judge in Austin, Texas, early in 1990, on a long-running legal battle over semiconductor patents between Motorola and Hitachi that the American company was also guilty of infringing patents. As a result, while Hitachi had to pay damages to Motorola, the American company also had briefly to withdraw its flagship 32-bit microprocessor, the 68030, which powers the top versions of Apple's personal computer range. Motorola was, in addition, forced to pay Hitachi $500,000 in damages.

The three creativities

If Japan's industry has 'copied' from the West, it is only following a well-worn route. Imitation and the acquisition of imported techniques is an unavoidable first stage in the process of economic development, and one for which Japan's history made her particularly well suited. Anyway, according to Akio Morita, the president of consumer electronics giant Sony, industry requires not just inventiveness, but three types of creativity. The first, basic creativity, is necessary to make discoveries, but this alone is not sufficient for a strong industry. The second type of creativity involves using the new technology in an appropriate way – product planning and production. The third type of creativity is in marketing your products – without which the most advanced and best manufactured items will fail. 'In basic technology,' Morita says, 'it is true that Japan has relied on a number of foreign sources. But turning that technology into products is where Japan is number one in the world.'

The Sony president uses the transistor radio as an example. It was an American company, Regency, which made the first transistor radio with help from Texas Instruments, but Regency pulled out of the market because there seemed to be little demand for small radios when larger models offered better sound quality. Morita, however, felt that the proliferation of radio stations brought with it a market for small, portable radios which would allow each person to tune into the station he or she wanted. Using this sales concept, Sony persevered, and despite being second on to the market with its product, Sony's marketing creativity brought it success – and who has now heard of Regency?[7]

Video tape recorders (VCRs) were originally brought on to the market by Western companies, but were never turned into mass-market products until the Japanese began producing domestic models in 1975. Within a decade, 100 million had been sold worldwide, 95 per cent of which were either of Japanese manufacture or assembled from primarily Japanese components. The intense competition which prevails in the Japanese market is intertwined with this process. Initially, there were two main Japanese VCR formats: VHS, pioneered by the Japan Victor Company (controlled by the giant Matsushita) and Sony's Betamax. European manufacturers, led by Philips, had an expensive and technically-advanced standard known as V2000, but they never managed to produce high enough volumes of the product and V2000 was the first to lose out in the VCR standards war.

Matsushita initially feared that Betamax would sweep the American market, so the company took an enormous risk by contracting to supply American electricals giant, RCA, with VHS machines with a four-hour recording time capacity – even though a two-hour VCR had not then been built. Matsushita's engineers worked day and night to meet the contract deadline. They succeeded, and Betamax was soundly beaten by the mid-1980s. But having realized that its format had failed, Sony was not too proud to buy a licence for VHS technology, although it did attempt to leap-frog its rival by launching a new 8mm compact video format ideal for use with handheld 'camcorders'.

The VHS producers immediately struck back with a smaller, lighter camcorder compatible with the VHS format. And so the battle went on, with the consumer benefiting from ever better, lower-cost products. The original technology was Western, but Japanese companies took the risks, produced the volumes and thus managed to produce lower-cost, higher-quality products than their American and European competitors. In the process, they turned the VCR from a luxury product into one which has become an unremarkable part of the furniture in millions of homes.

新　大　国

In November 1987, *Time* magazine carried a full-page colour advertisement from Toyota, which read: 'Record News – Toyota leads the world's car makers in equipping an entire major model range with multi-valve engines as standard equipment'. Multi-valve engines use more than one inlet and/or outlet valve per cylinder to allow the easier flow of petrol and air in, and exhaust gases out of the cylinder. This results in a higher power output per litre than conventional engines, is more economical and produces fewer pollutants.

Multi-valve engines were not, in fact, invented by the Japanese: the technology was first used in a racing car back in 1913. But, for a long time, Western producers never really managed to master the precision-machining technology necessary for the low-cost, volume production of such complex engines. For the most part, therefore, multi-valve engines were limited to very high-priced, top-end versions of their ranges or specialist rally cars. In fact, in 1988, only two volume Western manufacturers offered complete ranges with multi-valve engines, and these were relatively low volume products: the Saab 9000 and the Rover 800/Sterling series, of which the latter anyway relied partly on Honda for its power plants. A year later, GM was the only American company making such an engine which was an option on some Oldsmobile and Pontiac models, and when Ford wanted a multi-valve engine for a performance version of its Taurus medium-sized car – one of the bestsellers on the North American market – it had to go to Yamaha for a supply of 20,000 of the advanced three-litre engines per year.

By the beginning of 1988 Toyota had already produced more than two million multi-valve engines and had even developed two types: one geared to smooth, economical running for the bulk of their ranges; and the other tuned for high performance. By the end of the same year, almost every Toyota model and the whole of the Honda range boasted multi-valve engines, while Nissan, Mazda and Mitsubishi had similarly equipped nearly half of their models. Suzuki had even produced a 1,300cc small car with a multi-valve engine, something considered virtually out of the question for Western manufacturers; and Honda have taken the concept a stage further with their V-TEC engines which have variable valve lift to suit speed and load. By 1992, few Japanese car manufacturers will be producing cars which are not equipped with these advanced engines, while at best only a small handful of Western car makers will offer them across whole ranges.

Such comparisons between Japanese and Western industries show that the Japanese are not so much a nation of copiers, but of improvers. This is an important point, for being first with a product or in the lead in the early days of an industry is not always an advantage if you do not have the production and engineering skills to capitalize on that lead. The British built the first jet airliner, the Comet, but thereafter lost the lead to the Americans. Britain, too, at one time led the way in commercializing computers: English Electric's Star computers were the first to be aimed at businesses in the 1950s; Ferranti later went on to pioneer customized semiconductors and built the fastest computers in the early 1960s, but are now out of both markets. Britain also led the world during the 1950s in harnessing the power of the atom for generating electricity, but rapidly lost the edge.

The Japanese skill at adaption, assimilation and improvement has, moreover, involved not just end products, but all stages of the production process and has in turn been crucial in allowing Japanese manufacturers to lower the cost of products originally thought up by other people. Electronic calculators were pioneered by a small British company led by Sir Clive Sinclair, as well as by Olivetti of Italy, yet it was Japanese manufacturers who managed to reduce the number of components and so produce calculators in sufficient quantities to turn them into mass-market products. Among the techniques used by the Japanese was the process of continuous improvement. Whereas Western producers aimed to redesign their models every few years, the Japanese were constantly going back to the assembly line to improve their products so that they effectively came up with a new generation machine every year. Soon, Facit of Sweden, Olympia of Germany and Olivetti of Italy were pasting their names on Japanese-made calculators. Likewise, although Motorola was the first company with a prototype solid-state television in 1966, Hitachi was the first to come out with a production model in 1969. A year later, 90 per cent of Japanese sets were solid-state, three years before the leading American firms were producing completely solid-state lines.

This process of improvement has included some important advances in electronics which somewhat belie the prevalent image of the Japanese as not being creative. Even before the Second World War, Japanese science made important contributions to the development of radar and Osaka Imperial University's physics department also invented the magnetron. Moreover, after Sony had licensed transistor technology from Western Electric of the United States in the late 1950s, it found that the device was not powerful enough to be used in its radios. So Sony experimented until it discovered that by reversing the polarity of the device it could attain a higher frequency.

An outdated notion

The view of the Japanese as a nation of copiers, or even just improvers, is anyway becoming rather outdated, for Japan's industry is racing ahead of Western rivals in technologies like new materials – ceramics for engines, for example. Ceramics have the advantage of being able to operate better than conventional engines at the very high temperatures demanded by perform-ance and turbo-charged cars, and because they can withstand tremendous temperatures they also need no cooling system. They are also lighter and offer reduced friction and wear and so are extremely economical. No Western manufacturer was anywhere near producing a ceramic engine when Isuzu began trial production of its ceramic four-cylinder petrol engine in 1989. The Japanese company is on schedule to offer a ceramic turbo diesel engine by 1992.

So while it will not come as any surprise to learn that in the immediate post-War years Japanese spending on primary R&D was modest, by the late 1970s they were beginning to catch up. Already by 1978, Japanese companies were spending 2.15 per cent of their net income on R&D, compared to 2.9 per cent in the UK, 2.46 per cent in the United States and 2.64 per cent in West Germany, and the effective Japanese R&D investment was higher than the bare figures indicate because around half of Western R&D went on defence, while Japanese companies' defence-related R&D was less than five per cent of the total.

This accelerating thrust of Japanese industry into R&D and the steady move into more innovative research is inevitable as the Japanese economy moves on to the next stage in its development. For as Japan's economy shifts to higher levels of production and income, as a result of the steady progress of productivity and product sophistication, so a stage is reached at which autonomous research and development becomes a necessity. More-over, as the Japanese have already overtaken the West in many areas, buying in licences is becoming a less viable game.

As a result, the Japanese are themselves now accounting for an increasing share of patents issued. A detailed analysis of patent applications from 1975 to 1987, for example, showed that the number of Japanese patents had risen from 8.8 per cent of all those granted in 1975 to 19.3 per cent in 1987, by which time their number exceeded the total issued to the British, French and West Germans combined.[8] In addition, by the mid-1980s, the number of patents being granted to United States nationals was only twice those granted to Japanese nationals – and the Japanese are gaining all the time.

Further evidence of the Japanese advance came in a 1989 report by the United States Congress' Office of Technology Assessment which stated that Japan was already capable of taking a lead in a wide range of technologies, ranging from car design to optical fibres. This followed a report in 1987 from the National Academy of Engineering which concluded that Japan was superior in 25 out of 34 critical technologies.[9] Moreover, OECD figures for 1985 show that Japan spent the second highest proportion of GDP on research and development out of 19 industrialized countries – up from fourth place in 1981. In addition, unlike the West, where around half of all R&D – including defence – is government-funded, in Japan only about a quarter of total research funding comes from the government.

The steady increase in Japan's R&D effort is, therefore, primarily driven by private industry, and particularly by powerful and successful corporations such as Toyota, which has one research laboratory and two technical centres employing 2,500 people in R&D – five per cent of its total workforce; while a comparison between ten major Japanese companies and their nearest American counterparts in a survey in 1983 showed that eight of the Japanese companies already spent a higher percentage of their sales on R&D.[10] For the first time since the golden age of the Chinese Empire, the West is beginning to have to share scientific leadership with another culture.

Superconductors

Superconductors were discovered in a Dutch university laboratory in 1911. They are special materials which, when cooled to ultra-low temperatures, conduct electricity with virtually no resistance. As a result, unlike ordinary conductors, such as wire, superconductors do not heat up while conducting and therefore they waste little electricity. The potential for lower-cost power transmission and electric motors is enormous. Of greater significance is the possibility for vastly more powerful computers, since one of the biggest problems with existing machines is overheating in closely-packed, integrated circuits.

Until recently, applied superconductivity was only a distant possibility. Only a small number of metals were suitable, and then only if they were cooled to four degrees above absolute zero – the temperature of highly-expensive liquid helium. Then, in 1986, two Swiss IBM scientists discovered an entirely new type of ceramic superconductor which worked at the relatively warm temperature of 30 degrees above absolute zero. Since then, scientists have scrambled to devise materials which would work at higher and higher temperatures. Much of the progress has been in Japan, especially since early in 1988, when Hiroshi Maeda of Japan's National Research

Institute for Metals managed to make a bismuth-based compound which acted as a superconductor at 120 degrees above absolute zero.

The scale and nature of Japan's superconductor effort sets it apart from other countries except for the United States. But whereas in Japan about 56 per cent of the national superconductivity budget is being funded by the private sector, only 38 per cent of the American effort is privately financed, according to United States government data. At NEC, for example, superconductivity is the biggest single project at the company's fundamental research laboratories, where about 30 researchers are working on the project – treble the number working on 64-megabyte D-ram memory chips, which are expected to come into production within about ten years.

But although such examples point to a shift in the scale and emphasis of Japan's R&D, the Japanese research effort in superconductors is not based on any love of pure science for its own sake. According to Sumitomo Electric, one of Japan's superconductor pioneers, if the technology can be commercialized, the market might be worth $36 billion by the year 2000. Superconductor technology is already being developed for energy storage, like giant batteries, to cut power transmission costs by allowing power stations to be run at a constant rate instead of fluctuating in response to changing demand patterns. Superconductor-powered ships are also planned, using superconducting magnets which exert a powerful magnetic force on sea water passing through a duct in the magnet, driving the water out of the stern and creating forward motion.

A 5.2-kilometre long underground magnetic levitation train, called 'Mag-level', which uses a superconducting linear motor has already been built in Osaka. Superconducting magnets and electric coils are positioned on the train and repel it over a metal bar running down the centre of the track. Japan's main rival in this field is West Germany, but whereas the German experimental floating train has only managed a levitation height of eight millimetres, a Japanese experimental train has been raised as high as ten centimeters, allowing it to accelerate safely to speeds of nearly 300 miles an hour.

The new Japanese research effort is not, however, limited to headline-grabbing high-tech products. One reason for the success of Japan's construction-contracting industry in international markets is that the Japanese spend about one per cent of their sales on research – far more than their American counterparts. The Big Five Japanese contractors employ an average of 400 researchers each, in well-equipped labs doing research into areas such as earthquake resistant concrete. One result is a machine that bores 30-foot wide holes for tunnels by turning the soil into slurry and piping it to the surface, while sensors relay data to a computerized control room on the surface.[11]

Full circle

Will the Japanese license their new technology to the West, or will they, as some commentators fear, hog it to reinforce their dominance? So far it looks as though these fears are unfounded. While Japanese payments for foreign technology fell between 1970 and 1985, their receipts have risen far more sharply from $373 million to $898 million over the same period, indicating both increasing R&D levels and a willingness to trade their technology. Indeed, as the Japanese research effort cranks up, so the wheel is beginning to turn full circle. In the 1950s, Matsushita was largely dependent on Philips technology and was a major Philips' licencee. By 1960, the electronics giant had built its own large R&D centre and by the mid-1970s, Matsushita's income from licence fees exceeded its pay-outs. America's sluggish steel producers are already benefiting from Japanese continuous-casting production technology, whereby metal is processed as it would be on a production line, rather than being made into ingots which then have to be rolled. Japan now earns six times as much in royalties and fees for iron and steel technology than it pays out. And Toray, so eager for Western technology in the 1920s, now licenses its advanced-materials technology to European companies.

But whether the West will benefit from Japan's new technology will, of course, depend in part on the willingness of Western industry to take advantage of what is on offer. When the American Electronics Association wrote to 17,000 of its members advertising a subscription to a newsletter on Japanese electronics, it received only 21 orders and had to close it down.[12]

On the other hand, many Western companies are beginning to realize the research potential in Japan, as evidenced by the rush of companies opening Japanese R&D facilities. These include Philips and ICI, while Glaxo is opening a £40-million, 300-scientist facility at Japan's 'Science City', Tsukuba. Motorola, one of America's most technologically advanced companies, has also made the difficult decision to use Japanese technology where it outperforms its own, swapping some of its microprocessor knowledge in return for Toshiba's memory chip designs. AT&T, one of the pioneers of the semiconductor industry, also signed deals early in 1990 involving the manufacture and marketing of a type of memory chip called 'Static RAMs' designed by Mitsubishi Electric, as well as NEC-designed gate array chips which are used for customized applications. Even IBM has decided to re-engineer its mainframes for the Japanese market to mimic Fujitsu and Hitachi machines and so allow their customers to switch to IBM without discarding their software.

One of the most significant recent Japanese technology sales, however, occurred when Hitachi agreed to sell semiconductor-manufacturing technology to the South Korean group, Goldstar, in the first technology transfer of its kind between a Japanese semiconductor maker and South Korea. Under the agreement, Hitachi is showing Gold Star how to make one-megabit D-Ram memory chips. Goldstar's intention is to use the technology to help develop its own new generation four-megabit and next generation 16 megabit D-Rams. According to MITI figures for 1987, there were no fewer than 816 cases of Japanese technology transfers to South Korea in that year. These included the sale of optical compact disc pickup technology by Mitsubishi Electric to Goldstar Electric, Sanyo's sharing of information on plain paper copiers with Samsung and the sale of robot-welding technology by Fanuc to Daewoo Heavy Industries.

There may, however, have been just the faintest whiff of *déjà vu* when, in 1989, Sony filed a suit against an American company distributing

Chinese-made children's cassette players which too closely mimicked the Japanese company's 'My Own' line.[13] Or when, in the same year, Hitachi sued the semiconductor arm of South Korean conglomerate, Samsung, for illegally using its semiconductor-manufacturing processes. It is, perhaps, not too far-fetched to imagine disgruntled Japanese businessmen in the not too distant future muttering into their Suntory Special Reserve 'Scotch' about the pernicious, upstart South Korean 'copycats'.

17

新大国

THE COMMANDING
HEIGHTS

'From Noodles to Atomic Power.'
Unofficial slogan of the Mitsubishi Group.

A VISIT TO Nippon Electric Company's (NEC) Abiko plant, the company's engineering and design centre for digital communications systems and office automation products, gives an excellent preview of the future of the top echelons of Japanese industry. I was met there by Giro Okuda, a scrupulously polite Japanese manager of the old school, and a lifelong NEC employee who has risen to the post of Vice President and Director. Okuda talked about his company's future over green tea and biscuits served on a large mahogany table, decorated with small British and Japanese flags.

NEC traces its history back to the pioneering days of Japan's industrial development. It was originally founded in 1899 to manufacture Bell's new invention, the telephone. From there, it moved into public switches (central telephone exchanges) and general telecommunications equipment and, since the Second World War, has diversified into computers, semiconductors, fax machines and consumer goods like fridges, TVs and video recorders. Avoiding products like photocopiers and typewriters, NEC has concentrated on the higher-tech information technology areas, and is Japan's market-leader in personal computers, accounting for around half the market. NEC also comes second in mainframes after Fujitsu, but ahead of IBM Japan, and claims that its latest SX2 supercomputer is the fastest in the world. Since the end of the 1970s, NEC's sales have quadrupled to more than $20 billion annually, while its workforce increased from 60,000 to more than 100,000.

NEC's Abiko plant was opened in 1983 and is about an hour's drive away from Tokyo. Bordered on its south side by the extensive Teganuma marshes, and to the north by the Tone River, Abiko is blessed with a natural environment which belies the grimy image associated with much of Japan's industry. I was shown around the plant by NEC's general manager in charge of public switching equipment, Yuichi Shimojo. A small, relaxed man who spoke good English, his crewcut matching his American accent, he could not hide an intense pride in his company and its people. Shimojo showed me NEC's tele-conferencing system, which NEC makes itself and markets around the world. Eight NEC sites – five in Japan and three in the United States – are linked by the system which cost close to £1.6 million. Using digital satellite links, executives and R&D personnel hold live conferences which save an enormous amount of time and money on travel.

I also saw research and development work on computers, and a computer-aided design facility which is linked to each of the company's Japanese factories. This allows NEC's designers to produce computer models of integrated circuits and components which can be sent straight to their other plants and, in some instances, linked in to the production machines which will make them. The undoubted favourite among NEC's workers was, however, a prototype robot messenger which trundles around the plant delivering mail and small packages. The robot's arrival was invariably greeted by delighted NEC personnel who bowed deeply in mock respect as the machine passed them in the corridor.

Diversify and grow

One of the most impressive features of NEC is the ease with which the company has managed to diversify into related product areas, as well as into the components used in those products. Canon is another Japanese company whose ability to broaden into new product areas has been matched by few, if any, Western companies. Still the world's leading manufacturer of quality, 35mm SLR cameras, in just two decades Canon has also advanced into calculators, photocopiers, electronic typewriters, personal computers, fax machines and computer printers, and now employs 40,000 people in 130 countries. Canon's technical advances have included the world's first non-xerographic plain paper copier in 1968, a computerized camera in 1976, an ultra low-cost 'personal' plain-paper copier which was launched in 1982 and used a disposable cartridge, the first really inexpensive office laser printer in 1984 and the first full-colour plain paper copier using laser technology in 1988. Canon is now working on its next generation products which include a CD-like optical disc storage system for computers which, unlike current CD-based systems will allow users to rewrite data as opposed to just accessing it. Like its fellow leading Japanese corporations, Canon has also moved into the manufacture of components to ensure rapid access to technological developments.

Contrast the progress of Canon and NEC with their Western equivalents. In the 1960s and 1970s, the West boasted a large number of diversified electronics and electrical engineering companies which, at that time, dwarfed their Japanese rivals. Most of them have long since been overtaken by their Japanese competitors, while none have managed to venture successfully into the range of product areas which Canon and NEC have penetrated.

France's Thomson Group, for example, was nationalized by the Mitter- and Government in 1982 after making substantial losses. Thomson has superficial similarities with Japanese electronics companies. It makes a variety of products, including semiconductors, consumer electronics prod- ucts like TVs, VCRs and fridges, as well as industrial and aerospace equipment such as scanners, avionics and radar. But look beneath the surface and you will find that nearly half of the group's turnover is accounted for by defence contracts. This is a common trait among Western electronics companies: defence-related sales account for nearly 40 per cent of British electronics companies' sales,[1] more than 25 per cent in the United States and close to 25 per cent in France.[2] Although the figure in West Germany is relatively low at five per cent,[3] in Japan defence products account for a mere 0.7 per cent of their electronics industry's turnover.[4] Examples of highly defence-dependent high-tech Western companies include Northrop in the United States, which makes 92 per cent of its sales to the Pentagon, together with Martin Marietta and Lockheed which derive close to three-quarters of their revenue from United States military pro- grammes. In 1988, no fewer than ten American corporations made at least $4 billion in military sales and three made sales in excess of $8 billion. Three French, two British and one West German company also made defence- related sales in excess of $2 billion.

This dependence on military contracts among many high-tech European and American companies stems, of course, from the high defence expendi- ture of most Western industrialized countries relative to Japan. There may have been strong imperatives for this. It is also true to say that some Western companies and industries have benefited greatly from spin-offs resulting from defence-related work. The problem is that as so much of many key Western companies' defence turnover consists of largely protected sales to their own governments, often on the basis of cosy cost-plus contracts in which they are guaranteed a profit on top of end costs, they have not always had enough incentive to be efficient or to diversify and seek new markets. It has been easier to bid for government contracts than to develop new products, while resources and skilled personnel have been diverted away from consumer product development.

So although Thomson does also hold a strong position in TVs, this has been more due to acquisition – funded substantially by the French govern- ment – than growth since they have in recent years bought up the TV interests of RCA in the United States, Thorn EMI (Ferguson brand TVs) in Britain and AEG Telefunken in West Germany. Thomson has failed, however, to make any significant progress into new growth areas such as personal computers and fax machines, and its consumer products other than TVs sell mainly in France.

Moreover, whereas in Japan competition has always been maintained in the home market, with or without the presence of foreign products, Thomson is largely the result of the Western European habit of nurturing single 'national champion' flag-carrying companies in key industries by giving them easy, monopolistic profits in their home markets. Far from encouraging their expansion overseas, as intended, this has merely meant that many companies stay comfortably at home, resulting in the creation of separate, monopolistic markets, overcrowded with companies which are too dependent on their domestic markets and not strong enough to be significant players on the world stage.

NEC, by contrast, has a minimal presence in the defence market and has never been allowed the luxury of complacency because it has had to compete bitterly with rivals such as Hitachi, Oki and Fujitsu in the Japanese telecommunications market. Furthermore, such competition has forced NEC to diversify into new products and exports in order to push up their production volumes and improve their position. The net result of these differences has been an explosive growth in the successful Japanese diversified electronics companies, compared with only a sluggish progression in their Western rivals. Thomson's total sales, including defence products, are, at around £8 billion a year, less than those of their main Japanese competitors: Mitsubishi Electric, Hitachi and Toshiba all achieve annual sales in the £8 to £14 billion range, almost wholly consisting of consumer and business products – and, unlike Thomson, all are very profitable.

Diversifying vertically

In 1958, Seiko engineers and company directors looked on with satisfaction and some trepidation as a huge clock the size of a freight locomotive neared completion at one of the company's plants. The world's very first working electronic crystal clock, it used huge numbers of bulky vacuum tubes and had been constructed because Seiko's top management believed that crystal technology held the key to the future of watch making.

The next year, a special project team was set up at the Suwa Seiko company, one of the group's subsidiaries, to develop a commercially-viable crystal watch. It was led by a 35-year-old engineer, Mr Nakamura, who had been with the company all his working life. His team of ten members set about studying a new crystal timing device which was to be used in the Tokyo Olympic Games in 1964, and also analysed the alternative tuning-fork technology which Bulova of the United States had decided to major in. So hard did Nakamura's team work that the company had to provide a *tatami* mat-floored room for the researchers to sleep in when they worked late; but, two years later, they had produced a crystal watch small enough to be held in the palm of the hand.

Their real target had yet to be reached, however, for in order to be a success the crystal watch had to be small enough to be used as a wrist watch. It also had to use very little electric power and include an anti-shock mechanism. Three separate technical breakthroughs were necessary for this: the development of a small motor, a tiny integrated circuit and the production of a miniscule crystal device. Working night and day, the team cracked these problems by using a special type of motor called a 'stepping motor', while, by employing the tuning-fork shape for the crystal, they both decreased its size and made it shock-proof.

By 1969, Seiko was ready proudly to announce its new crystal wristwatch to the world, which it launched on to the market for a price of around $2,000. A year later, the company's top management made the decision to go into full-scale production. But there was still one final problem to be solved: how to obtain small enough integrated circuits. Unable to buy them from outside, Seiko took the brave decision to produce the chips themselves, forming a research team to study integrated circuit technology. In 1971, 13 years after the locomotive-sized crystal clock had been produced, Seiko succeeded in mass-producing small, low-cost liquid crystal wristwatches. At that time, Japanese watch manufacturing was only one third of Swiss production, but a decade later, the Swiss had been decisively overtaken.[5]

The story of the invention and eventual production of Seiko's revolutionary wristwatch contains within it many of the most significant features of the upper levels of Japanese industry. First, the company both carefully studied outside technology, and developed its own where necessary. Second, it was prepared to invest in the necessary resources over the long term, despite the risky nature of the project and the minimal short-term return; third, above all, Seiko was prepared to diversify vertically and produce its own components where that was essential to maintain a technological edge.

This type of vertical integration – producing components in-house – is very much a feature of Japan's high-tech industries. But the manufacture of a large number of components and sub-assemblies for your own products is far from being a guaranteed recipe for success, for vertical integration runs inherently contrary to the basic economic principles of division of labour, large-scale production and free competition. Subsidiaries which know that they have a secure market for their products within the group are seldom under enough competitive pressure to perform truly efficiently.

During my visit to the Abiko plant, I asked Yuichi Shimojo about these disadvantages, as NEC manufactures most of its own major components. Shimojo replied:

> Each department within NEC is a separate profit centre. We can and do buy chips from outside the company when they beat ours on price and performance. But a company like NEC is now very much driven by technology. We are doing more and more research and development, as you can see here, and having our own facility to design chips for our products, particularly custom chips which can cut down on the total number of components used, gives us huge advantages. Not only are the chip designers close to the people involved with the end product, but it also offers us the benefit of speed which is essential in a fast moving industry like ours.

Matsushita is another company which produces a very high proportion of its components in-house: some estimates put purchases of materials and components which are catered for by Matsushita's own subsidiaries as high as 80 per cent by value. But, as with NEC, Matsushita never guarantees that it will buy parts from its subsidiaries, although it does feel it important to produce a high proportion of its core components to ensure quality and availability. For in an intensely quality conscious market such as Japan's, it is far more important to ensure product quality than to buy the cheapest available components from the outside.

It is, of course, not unusual for Western manufacturers of electrical and electronic equipment to produce key parts inside their own company. GE of the United States, GEC of Britain, Philips of the Netherlands and Thomson of France all produce many of their own components; while companies such as Motorola and Texas Instruments, which are now primarily semiconductor manufacturers, also make other products which use their own chips. Yet Japanese companies like NEC and Matsushita produce far more of their own essential and technology intensive components than do their Western counterparts, giving them an edge in ensuring a rapid response to market requirements.

Sony, for example, could never have become the undisputed leader in the camcorder market by producing the TR-55 in 1989, a product which marked a significant size breakthrough at just seven inches long, without the ability to produce key components in-house. Toshiba's success with its down-sized T1000 Dyna Book 'notebook' computer was also achieved in part due to the company's technology which allowed it to 'super-integrate' semi-customized chips, so that only one chip was required to control both the keyboard and the input – tasks carried out by separate devices in previous models.

Of course, vertical integration does contain within it the seeds of failure, and it tends to fail where there is no real logic or technological overlap to the process. It is, however, in technology intensive industries that the case for vertical integration is strongest – and it is in these very high technology areas that Japanese industry is, of course, increasingly beginning to specialize. The advantages are, first, that it makes it possible to carry out innovation promptly. Second, vertical integration can help to spread technological expertise within a company. Third, in markets where product life cycles are short, vertical integration can help to ensure that they come to the market quickly; and fourth, the quality of essential components can be assured.

In order to succeed, however, the company must be sure that it integrates primarily the key processes. Hitachi and NEC both make a high proportion of their own semiconductors, and particularly custom chips, but they largely buy in simple plastic components such as TV cabinets. Matsushita is happy to buy in less advanced products, such as steel plate and wire, but it makes many of its own semiconductors, condensers, transformers, speakers, tuners, batteries and magnetic heads.

Those Japanese electronics companies that have failed to heed these lessons have tended to perform poorly. The Standard Kogyo Company was once a successful producer of consumer electronics and, by 1970, its sales were booming – but the company purchased all of its components from outside suppliers. It was weak in new product development and increasingly became a follower of products developed by its rivals. With no strong market identity, Standard Kogyo concentrated on selling through foreign wholesalers, but soon slipped into a loss and was taken over.

Good examples of the success of vertical integration lie in the pioneering use of semiconductors in radios and TVs by Sony and Matsushita and, of course, in the development of small quartz crystal watches by Seiko which involved it producing its own integrated circuits, liquid crystal displays, small crystal forks and stepping motors. The watch industry, in fact, offers a particularly good example of the advantages of vertical integration in a technology-intensive industry. In 1960, there were in excess of 500 Swiss watch manufacturers who bought in the bulk of their parts from more than 1,000 independent component manufacturers. Even after a joint research lab was established in 1962, the Swiss largely failed to develop advanced new products.

Seiko, by contrast, although not initially strong in electronics, clearly saw the need to diversify into components, and recruited the necessary engineers. Now, not only does it make most of its own parts, but even produces the automated machines which manufacture its watches. Whereas technological innovation was a continual source of conflict among component makers in Switzerland, Seiko produced its own parts and had no problems adapting to new technology.

At this point, it is worth introducing a cautionary tale in the form of the Hong Kong watch industry which has, in recent years, massively increased its market share by producing cheap quartz watches, using bought-in electronic components and sub-assemblies – mainly imported from Japan. There is, moreover, an argument that the Hong Kong watch assemblers found it easier to introduce new technology because they did not have to develop components themselves and so could move quickly. But, on the other hand, Hong Kong's producers are probably trapped in the low end of the market and many would say that they do not have the key technologies to expand in the future. So lack of vertical integration can be an advantage in a technology-intensive industry in the short term, but it may not be enough to push companies into new, high-growth areas, or to produce the type of massively successful international companies which command the heights of the Japanese economy.

A further caveat is that there exist some important exceptions to the general rule that high-tech Japanese companies are fairly intensely vertically-integrated. Casio was one of a handful of Japanese calculator producers which survived out of the original 40 or so manufacturers. It succeeded only by waging a price war based on large scale production volumes. Unlike most of its rivals, however, Casio produces no components, purchasing all of its semiconductors from outside suppliers on long-term contracts and, by concentrating its orders, obtains massive pricing discounts. Hitachi, for example, is said to run a special production line for Casio. The company even subcontracts most of its assembly: its handful of factories are mainly used for testing large-scale production methods and for inspecting finished products. Instead, Casio concentrates its resources on research and product development at one end, and marketing at the other, and spends a huge amount on advertising.

There are other levels of vertical integration which have been successfully utilized by Japanese industry in a way which largely sets them apart from their Western competitors. Toyota, Japan's leading car manufacturer, has a very low level of direct vertical integration but operates a system of quasi-vertical integration by controlling more than 300 semi-independent components manufacturers called the 'Kyohokai' (the Toyota Co-operation Association). About 60 per cent of Toyota's expenditure on materials and parts is paid to these affiliated companies, which manufacture parts largely for the company.

Broadly speaking, Toyota's strategy is to divide its parts and sub-assemblies into three areas: basic, low-technology, standard parts, such as bolts and wheel pressings, are brought in from outside; key components and processes, such as engine assembly, body pressing and paint spraying, are for the most part done within the company, as is the case with Western auto manufacturers. But it is the components which fall between these two levels, such as crankshafts, castings, engine and body components, transmission parts, meters, radiators and filters which are largely brought in from subsidiaries or affiliated companies. And to avoid dependence, Toyota selects at least two of its parts suppliers for each component. This close co-operation also facilitates the operation of Toyota's *Kanban* (*Just In Time*) parts delivery system, which involves the delivery of parts every two hours to Toyota plants. Component companies can only really deliver such a service with detailed planning, and the affiliated companies are able to integrate closely with Toyota's schedules to ensure a synchronized delivery of parts.

The new *zaibatsu*

Some commentators see the re-emergence of the pre-War *zaibatsu* company groups in Japan's post-War conglomerates. The *zaibatsu* date from the early days of the Meiji Restoration and ran trading houses (*sogoshosha*) which dominated the export and import trade. *Zaibatsu* financial power gave them enormous influence in the 1920s and 1930s, but it also brought them into increasing conflict with the militarists, which was exacerbated when the *zaibatsu* emerged as some of the main beneficiaries of the post-Depression growth and concentration of Japanese industry in the 1930s.

Ironically, the *zaibatsu* were disbanded by the Occupation Forces administration after the War as they were considered one of the prime instigators of Japanese imperialism and militarism, although they did later manage to re-form to a large extent at the end of occupation rule. The modern Fuji Bank is, for example, effectively the old *zaibatsu*-controlled Yasuda Bank, and is now at the very centre of an industrial confederation not dissimilar to Yasuda's pre-War holding. Mitsubishi's combine also re-emerged almost intact.

But the modern descendants of the *zaibatsu* are really the wider groupings called *keiretsu*, or *zaikai*, meaning *financial circles*, in which close relationships with group companies are maintained by such means as cross shareholdings and interlocking directorships. The largest of these latter-day *zaibatsu* is one of the pre-War leaders, Mitsubishi, which includes 160 companies in its group with total annual sales of around $270 billion. Others are Sumitomo, Sanwa, Mitsui, Fuyo and Dai Ichi Kangyo. Despite their similarities with the *zaibatsu*, however, *zaikai* groupings are no longer as closely controlled by single families as the *zaibatsu* used to be, while the concentration of stock holdings in the hands of the mainstream companies of each group is much smaller, so power is distributed more broadly. As a result, whereas the pre-War *zaibatsu* tended to be distinct, exclusive organizations, the *zaikai* now co-operate more freely among themselves in forming enterprises to tackle large projects and are prepared to join forces and trade products where economic logic dictates.

The *sogoshosha* have also survived largely intact. Japan's massive trading companies have no real equal in the West, although the chartered traders and merchant houses of Britain's early commercial history bear some similarities. They are middlemen who manufacture virtually nothing, but handle a great deal. The nine largest *sogoshosha* control close to two-thirds of Japan's imports and half of her exports and have a combined turnover of close to $400 billion.

It has been written of the Mitsui Bussan *sogoshosha*, the trading arm of the Mitsui combine, that its head office transmitted to, or received from, the organization's 125 overseas branches 10,000 messages a day while the telephone bill amounted to more than $20,000 a day – and that was in 1972.[6] Mitsui, however, is only Number Two behind Mitsubishi's trading company, which racked up sales of nearly $97 billion in 1988 and has 170 offices in 88 countries. The other main *sogoshosha* are C Itoh, Chori, Itoman, Marubeni, Sumitomo, Okura and Toshoki. The power of these organizations extends well beyond the Japanese markets for they are also involved in mining and commodity activities all over the world. Six of the Japanese traders together control a fifth of the United States grain trade, worth $60 billion a year, for example. Despite the enormous sales volumes of the *sogoshosha*, they also work on tiny margins – on average, between 1.5 per cent and 2.0 per cent of pre-tax sales. That helps to explain why, in the 1960s, one of the great trading houses, Ataka, went spectacularly bankrupt.

The role of the *sogoshosha* is also beginning to change. As Japan's industrial leaders, whether involved with *zaikai* groupings or not, have gained the financial and marketing strength to handle their own overseas sales, so the *sogoshosha* have been pushed into more downmarket, low-margin products. As a result, the trading volumes of the major groups have increased only relatively slowly since the mid-1980s. They have reacted by helping small- and medium-sized companies, particularly components suppliers, to invest abroad. Marubeni, for example, assisted Sanko Plastic, an electronic consumer goods industry supplier, to set up a UK plant in which it took a 30 per cent stake. The traders have also become more involved with offshore projects, such as Sumitomo's participation in selling Soviet cars to Latin America. It has even organized chemicals trading between two Eastern Bloc countries – Romania and the USSR.

Foreign observers have tended to read a great deal into the power and importance of the *zaikai* and the interlinked *sogoshosha*. At their most extreme, commentators see a sinister significance in the way in which the *zaibatsu* managed to survive the hostility of the militarists in the 1930s and re-emerge after the War. They view these groups and their close links with the trading houses as the epitome of the Japanese conspiracy to dominate world markets. Others simply see the *zaikai* system, and the way in which group companies support each other, as one of the fundamental strengths of the Japanese economy.

But while it is certainly true that the *zaikai* still wield great power within Japan, and while there are many examples of successful, high-growth companies originating from within them – such as NEC, which is in the

Sumitomo group, and brewer, Kirin, which forms part of the Mitsubishi family – many companies within the traditional groups are in slow-moving or declining industries. This is partly due to the fact that, historically, the groups were major players in the raw-material processing and heavy industries which now have problems in Japan. It is also worth considering whether it actually helps the Japanese economy when group members bail each other out, as when Sumitomo rescued Mazda when it ran into trouble in the 1970s. Quite possibly the Japanese car industry as a whole, with its raft of medium-sized manufacturers operating not very profitably below the four main manufacturers, is weaker as a result.

Nor is being at the very epicentre of a huge group like Mitsui necessarily any guarantee of success. One of the reasons why Mitsui Bank merged with Taiyo Kobe early in 1990 is that Mitsui was in trouble: years of cultivating its traditional big-business corporate contacts had left it without a strong presence in the retail or small company market which led to a 28 per cent profits plunge in 1988–9. As a result, Mitsui will be very much the junior partner in the new venture: its chairman is Taiyo Kobe's president and the headquarters is Taiyo Kobe's main branch.

Moreover, many companies which epitomize the growth and success of Japan's post-War economy are not group members. Hitachi, Sharp, Matsushita and Sony in electronics; Fuji, Canon and Ricoh in cameras, photocopiers and office automation; Minebea in components; Seiko in watches and other consumer products; Kubota in farm equipment; and Toyota, Honda, Hino and Suzuki in vehicles are all highly independent companies with relatively recent origins which have succeeded on their own terms in the fastest growing and highest technology sectors of the market. These companies demonstrate that Japanese industry does not consist of a large conformist block, controlled either by *zaikai* or by the *Keidanren*, the business representative organization with close government links which was established in 1946, and of which it has been said: 'What's good for *Keidanren* is good for Japan'. On the contrary, there has been a great deal of room in Japanese industry for colourful, non-conformist, self-made entrepreneurs such as Konosuke Matsushita, Soichiro Honda and Minebea's Takami Takahashi.

Sixty-year-old, Jaguar-driving Takahashi is, in fact, a good example of how non-conformist Japanese business can be. He owns condominiums in Hawaii, Los Angeles, Thailand and Singapore and is one of the more flamboyant of the new breed. Nor is he afraid to criticize the management style of his fellow Japanese industrialists. 'The problem', he once said in an interview in the *Business Tokyo* magazine, 'is that there are no executives who can make decisions in Japan. During rapidly changing situations, the lack of management qualified to make decisions presents serious problems.'

Soichiro Honda is another example of industrial success outside of the *zaikai* charmed circle. Honda was born in 1905, the son of a village blacksmith. He went to Tokyo to become an apprentice mechanic and in 1928 returned to his village to set up a car-repair shop. He continued to study engineering, however, and in 1934 began manufacturing piston rings. After the Second World War, Honda bought 500 war-surplus engines which he attached to bicycles to make a basic form of motor bike. The bikes were such a success that he soon moved into large-scale manufacture and began exporting in 1957. By the late 1960s, Honda not only dominated the Japanese market, but had driven the British manufacturers out of world markets and was exporting a million motorbikes a year. From there, Honda moved into small cars and microvans, before moving steadily upmarket.

Now Honda's cars are probably the most technically advanced of any Japanese auto maker – and perhaps of any volume manufacturer in the world – and have a high perceived status in export markets. Far from being squeezed out of Japan's post-War economy by huge combines, controlled by predatory businessmen in league with grasping politicians and shadowy bureaucrats, Honda's success epitomizes the competitive and even entrepreneurial nature of Japan's post-War economic achievement.

新 大 国

Japanese industry has not succeeded because it has stuck to any particular rules. Nor is there a mystical, Oriental magic about it which cannot be transferred to America or Europe. And anyone who seeks slavishly to copy Japanese management practice will come up against some fundamental problems, not least of which is the fact that there are no hard and fast rules. Many Japanese companies offer lifetime employment, but not all do. A large number of Japan's top electronics companies are intensely vertically-integrated, but not all are. Many Japanese companies use debt aggressively, but the influence and adventurousness of Japan's banks has undoubtedly been exaggerated.

Ultimately, the factors which probably differentiate much of Japan's industry from the West's are these: an open-minded willingness to adopt the best technology and practices for a given situation; an eagerness to enter new fields and markets as a means of surviving in the face of unrelenting competition; the high quality and educational attainment at all levels of Japanese industry; and a preparedness to take pains to make employees feel part of their organization. Above all, there is the seeming infinite capacity of Japan's managers to take trouble and to ensure that the customer is their chief priority.

Part VI

Information Technology – How the Japanese Won an Industry, and the West's Sad Response

WHEN, IN THE mid-1970s, the potential of information technology (IT) first really dawned on people, few considered the Japanese as a serious threat. The story of how they have since then come to dominate vast swathes of the new industry closely parallels their achievements in other areas. As with motor cycles, cameras, consumer electronics, computer-controlled machine tools – which all fell to the Japanese strategy of standardized, volume production to secure economies of scale – so the Japanese have also succeeded in churning out millions of high-quality, low-cost photocopiers, facsimile machines, computer printers and electronic typewriters. By the mid-1980s, Japan accounted for 27 per cent of world exports of electronic products, outstripping the United States with 17 per cent and West Germany with nine per cent.

Some have seen evidence of a deep plot in the way in which the Japanese have homed in on the electronics and IT markets, a view which has been used to justify the increasing use of trade barriers to disadvantage Japanese competition. But there is nothing devious or conspiratorial in the fact that Japanese companies realized ITs potential. Indeed, almost all of the major Western electronics and computer companies also attempted to expand into this field – often with considerable state support. Yet it is a collection of until recently relatively obscure Japanese camera and watch makers which have done best. Here is how they did it.

新大国 | 18

OFFICE WARS

'American computers have become the giftboxes in which Japanese technology is delivered.'
Wilfred Corrigan, chairman of LSI Logic.[1]

1970 WAS A balmy year for the West's traditional producers of office equipment. Makers of typewriters, accounting machines, tabulating devices and adding machines from the United States and Europe dominated world markets. American manufacturers such as IBM, Litton and Remington Rand held 35.9 per cent of the international market, while Western European producers like Adler, Olivetti, Facit and Imperial accounted for a further 38.4 per cent of world sales. With their mere 6.8 per cent market share, Japanese companies were no more than a niggling inconvenience on the horizon.[2] In those days, if you wanted an office typewriter, the chances were that you would buy an IBM; and if it was a photocopier you were after, it would almost certainly have been a Xerox.

However, the industry was about to undergo two periods of fundamental change. Within a decade, the low-cost electronic calculator would sweep away the electromechanical adding machine; and small photocopiers would find their way into almost every office. Traditional suppliers of office equipment would not be the ones to take most advantage of the opportunities afforded by this first wave of change during the 1970s. Rather, it was to be a handful of more or less unknown manufacturers of cameras, sewing machines and consumer durables who would best grasp the significance and take advantage of the new openings. All of them were Japanese.

By the beginning of the 1980s, a second surge of change began to engulf the industry as the fastest growing of the new office equipment sectors – the microcomputer – made its entrance. Since the late 1970s, microcomputers have grown from insignificant beginnings to annual sales of more than

$25 billion a year. Many at first said that the Japanese would not make inroads into such a fast-moving and innovative industry. For a time, they were right. In the beginning, all-American entrepreneurial start-up companies, together with the computer world's market leader, IBM, grabbed the lion's share of the new market.

But the Japanese have steadily caught up. Whereas, in 1983, Japan's share of the United States market for personal computers was only around seven per cent, by 1989 it was close to 25 per cent and rising. Out of nearly 300 PCs available on the American market in the same year, only 20 per cent were American-made, with more than half coming from Japan and most of the rest from other East Asian countries.[3] Furthermore, if you were to peer beneath the plastic casing of a personal computer proudly bearing a well-known American brand name, such as Compaq or Zenith, the chances are that a good proportion of the key components would now be Japanese.

On top of that, the Japanese have been progressing on other fronts, such as office typewriters, where their presence was negligible in the 1970s. Whereas in 1980, only one out of the 32 office typewriters available on the UK market was Japanese, by 1987, 86 out of 158 available machines were produced by Japanese companies.[4] In 1980, most facsimile (fax) machines were American-produced. Now there are no American-made machines – virtually all come from Japan.

So by 1990, the Japanese had carved out a substantial chunk of the rapidly growing office technology market for themselves, and they look set to stay. The story of how this came to pass, how the Japanese came to command an industry once thought as American as root beer and apple-pie, has little to do with dumping or predatory trade practices, but it is a story replete with cautionary tales that the West would do well to heed.

Digits – the first wave

Up to the early 1970s, electro-mechanical products for the most part dominated industry. Most such machines worked on the 'analogue' principle, which means they were devices in which variable quantities, such as electric currents or mechanical motion, analogously represent corresponding quantities or features. In analogue telephone systems, for example, varying electrical currents represent voice tones.

The early electronic computers of the 1930s, however, used 'digital' technology, which is the key to most modern developments in electronics. Digital technology, or 'digitization', is based on the principle that all functions can be reduced to a very simple binary code, using the symbols 1 or 0 to encode the alphabet, while binary arithmetic is used to perform calculations. The great benefit of reducing things to such a simple code is that it works perfectly with electrical circuits, where on/off switches or 'gates' can be used to represent 1s or 0s.

It is not only numbers and letters that can be digitally encoded, however. It was also discovered in the 1930s that sound, and later pictures and even mechanical functions, could also be rendered into simple 1s and 0s. Voice, for example, can be digitized by allotting each of thousands of tones with a code which can be converted back into audible sounds. One of the advantages of digital encoding in this context is that the scope for line interference with the simple digits is less than on an analogue phone system with its continually varying currents. Digitization also means that complex mechanical control devices can be replaced by electronic circuits; that sound and pictures can be encoded and transmitted in digital form; and that both can easily be controlled or processed by computers. As so often, however, the practical applications of the new technology lagged behind the theoretical possibilities. At first, only expensive computers operated digitally. By the 1970s, however, microchips began making electronic products cheaper, and designers found that it was far easier to replace complicated mechanical movements with electronic components.

As a result, as the 1970s wore on and electronics advanced, it became apparent to those in the office equipment industry that widely varying types of equipment and technology would steadily merge, using digital technology. More than that, however, the new technology also changed the way things were made, ultimately lowering their costs to affordable levels and giving rise to whole new generations of products.

Above all, the new technology could be applied to a whole range of office equipment and used to expedite the dissemination of information to workers who would increasingly rely on their brains and knowledge, rather than on brute strength or machinery. The age of Information Technology (IT), the buzz term of the 1980s, was born. It spawned a thousand new companies to exploit it and a myriad government schemes for its promotion.

One of the first pieces of office equipment to be affected by digitization was the venerable typewriter itself, the founding product of the office-equipment industry. In typewriters of the 'golfball' or traditional typebar sort, the typeface was activated by a series of cogs, levers, pulleys and other physical devices, which were merely aided by electric motors in electric models. In electronic typewriters, however, instead of activating a bar when the key is depressed, an electronic, digital instruction is sent by wire to the typehead, which only then mechanically hits the paper through the ribbon.

Further, the fact that each key depression activates an electronic, digital signal means that a microprocessor – a small computer – can be interposed between the key and the typehead to allow for some automated functions, such as a memory to store formats and phrases. In short, the electronic typewriter was effectively a computer adapted to typing, fundamentally using the same technology as an increasingly wide range of other equipment and able to communicate with them with relative ease.

This process was called the 'integration' of office technology. It did not end there, however, for the same technology was used on an increasing range of equipment: compact disc (CD) audio machines, for example, are effectively just computers geared to reproducing music, while the new-generation digital cameras pioneered by Sony and also being developed by Toshiba and Fuji, are really computers with an image sensor and processor. Such devices are now designed and manufactured in much the same way as many types of formerly very different equipment, like typewriters. So while, in the 1970s, there would have been little technological or manufacturing overlap between a producer of a typewriter and a hi-fi system, by the mid-1980s, all that had changed.

Personal computers – the second wave

The product which most benefited from the new technology, however, was the computer. Already, in the 1970s, a few manufacturers had latched on to the possibilities of using lower-cost electronic components to produce inexpensive business computers, but none were produced in high volumes. The business microcomputer, now more generally called the personal computer (PC), really entered the arena at the beginning of the 1980s. Over subsequent years, the increasingly powerful and versatile PC was to steadily displace several separate and usually electro-mechanical pieces of equipment. With word-processing software, the PC could supplant the typewriter; with accounting packages, it replaced old-style accounting machines; database programs made addressing machines obsolete; and ever more sophisticated software packages meant that it could help with a range of formerly laborious tasks, such as design and financial planning.

The enormous power of microcomputers in relation to their size had been made possible by the rapid advance in semiconductor technology over the previous decade. In fact, the microchip and personal computer industries have long been locked together in a close embrace of mutual profit and advantage, for while semiconductor technology has provided PCs with ever-more advanced microprocessors – the brains of PCs – as well as low-cost, high-capacity Dynamic Random Access Memory (D-Ram) chips which store data and programs, the PC and office automation market has acted as the driving force behind the semiconductor industry, consuming two-thirds of its D-Ram output, of which around half goes into PCs.[5]

Today's massive world computer and semiconductor business really originated during the Second World War with the hugely successful British electronic code-breaking machine, Colossus, together with an American joint computer project involving Harvard and IBM, which produced a glistening, 50-foot long, stainless steel and glass-encased monster run by Navy personnel who stood to attention while operating it.

After the War, computers remained largely the preserve of the military until the advent of the most pervasive invention since the wheel – the transistor – discovered at the laboratories of Bell Telephone at Murray Hill, New York in 1947. Computers at that time generally used bulky and unreliable glass vacuum valves as 'gates' to switch and amplify electronic signals. The transistor had several clear advantages: it was one-hundredth the size of a valve; it was much faster; and it needed neither a vacuum nor a heater to make electrons flow – everything happened inside a chip of crystal which transferred an electrical signal across a resistor, which is why the device and its spin-off, the microchip, are sometimes called 'semiconductors'. The new invention was initially costly, however, and limited therefore to applications such as hearing aids.

The next step forward came in 1952, when a British defence scientist by the name of Geoffrey Dummer began to speculate on the possibility of making entire electronic circuits from semiconducting crystals. He proposed layers of insulating and conducting materials, interconnected by cutting away areas of the various layers to form several complete circuits and transistors on one device. Seven years later, a Texas Instruments (TI) scientist managed to make such a device out of silicon – the world's first silicon chip. The 'Solid Circuit', as TI called it, made its debut in New York early in 1959, but its potential was at first largely neglected by the American companies like Westinghouse Electric and Sylvania which then dominated the electronic-components business, so leaving the field open to new, more entrepreneurial companies like TI and Fairchild Semiconductor.

Throughout the 1960s, these companies vied with other, mainly Californian, laboratories, largely based in Palo Alto, a small valley in a fruit-growing area south of San Francisco, to turn the handful of transistors which had been incorporated into the first chips into thousands. More and more circuits were crammed on to a single chip until, by 1970, the first 'large-scale integrated' chip (LSI) containing over 100,000 individual transistors was produced.

A Massachusetts-based company called Digital Equipment Corporation (DEC) was the first computer firm to exploit the increasing potential of the microchip by producing minicomputers: small, relatively low-cost machines which made computing power much more accessible to businesses and laboratories which could not generally afford large, expensive mainframes. Many imitators followed, but small computers did not really come into their own until the development of the low-cost, single-chip microprocessor in 1976 by an offshoot of Fairchild Semiconductor called Intel.

Before long, a number of enthusiasts had begun to realize the potential of using relatively low-cost microprocessors to produce basic, but cheap, small computers. In 1975, the American magazine, *Popular Electronics*, featured a machine called the Altair at only $397, which was made by an Albuquerque company called MITS. They sold 2,000 of their machines that year and received a visit from the Homebrew Computer Club, among whose members was Bill Gates, who later founded the Microsoft software company, and two young computer buffs called Steve Jobs and Stephen Wozniak.

Jobs and Wozniak could not afford an Altair, so they built one themselves in Jobs' garage in Los Altos, California. The Apple I, as they called their machine, was shown in 1976. The response was so positive that Jobs sold his VW Beetle and raised $1,300 to put it into production. At that time, Jobs worked for video-games manufacturer, Atari, while Wozniak was employed by minicomputer and scientific instruments maker, Hewlett Packard, but neither company was interested in the invention. The next year the pair sold $2.5 million of their Apple II computers. By 1981, sales had soared to $355 million.

Apple entered the *Fortune* 500 a year later, making 100 of their stockholding employees millionaires. By then, the large American mainframe and minicomputer makers and the traditional office equipment manufacturers had also finally cottoned on to the possibilities. Only one succeeded – IBM – which used its name and marketing muscle to win a large chunk of the market and to set the standard for the industry after the launch of its first personal computer in 1981. But it was generally left to younger, more entrepreneurial companies, to make the running during the early days.

The key to the success of the new breed of small, entrepreneurial computer companies was the fact that, up until then, anyone wishing seriously to enter the computer market needed to invest hundreds of millions, and possibly billions, of dollars. Designing the main processing unit alone would absorb at least $100 million, while setting up a distribution and service network would cost at least as much again. The advent of the microprocessor changed all that and spawned a whole new industry based on low-cost, standardized components. The most sophisticated part of a computer – the processor – was now available 'off-the-shelf' for a few dollars and, by the end of the 1970s, so were most of the rest of the major components; while low cost networks of franchised dealers replaced expensive, in-house sales and service organizations. Almost overnight, the cost of entry into the computer market fell dramatically.

Then came the standardization of operating systems – the software that controls the computer and allows it to run application software, such as word-processing programs. So, not only did the new breed of microcomputer assemblers no longer have to design and make their own processors, but they were also released from the task of writing operating systems and programs. Instead, by buying in standard ones, their machines could run huge libraries of applications software written for the operating system.

So far, little had been heard from the Japanese. This, many thought, was one industry that the Japanese could be barred from. Perhaps, some said, the hard lessons of the car and motor-bike industries had been learned. Others asserted that the Japanese did not have the mind-set to succeed in such an innovative industry. But while they speculated, work was in progress in Tokyo and Osaka – the first shock came, however, not in the form of an onslaught of Japanese PCs, but in the components from which they were made.

Screwing up

1979 was a good time to be in Palo Alto, California's Silicon Valley. The recently founded, American-dominated microchip industry was one where heady success provided Americans with consolation for the loss of other markets to the rising competition from the East. The future, people said, is with microchips. Let the others take over the old, decaying smoke-stack industries. They can slave over hot steel furnaces and bash metal into ships, motor cycles and cars if they want. We'll concentrate on the clean technology of tomorrow.

So Silicon Valley's computer scientists, technicians and young whizzkids were the toasts of the nation. Sales were rising by nearly a quarter per year in the late 1970s, and revenues had reached $5 billion annually. Optimism and faith in American ingenuity characterized these new industries – and the 1980s seemed only to promise more. In 1978, seven of the top ten chip makers were American, with NEC, the only Japanese representative, in the Number Seven slot.

A decade later, one of the most dramatic industrial reversals of all times was complete. By 1988, NEC had grabbed the position of top semiconductor maker, displacing the former leader, TI, to Number Five, while six other Japanese chip makers had entered the top ten, giving Japanese companies nearly half of the overall world market in microchips and more like 90 per cent of global D-Rams sales. The once-proud American-led industry was largely controlled by the Japanese.

Already, by the turn of the decade, there had been warnings of what was to come. American semiconductor producers had been caught off-guard by the boom market of the late 1970s, which, in 1980, had allowed Japanese producers to take 42 per cent of the market in 16K D-Rams, the basic commodity memory chips of the time. But America's young, thrusting, semiconductor manufacturers were then busily working on the next generation of D-Rams, silicon wafers no larger than a thumb-nail which would store 64,000 bits of data, four times as powerful as the 16K chips. Product development teams at several companies were just finalizing their designs of the new high-capacity chips and beginning to ship samples of their elegant new 64K designs when a thunderbolt struck: they learnt that the Japanese were already in volume production and selling their 64K D-Rams in commercial quantities.

The Japanese product was not as sophisticated as those emanating from the American chip houses, and many in the industry called it 'a brute force product'. But six Japanese companies had begun selling their virtually identical 64K circuits, while the American chips were still under development. John A Calhoun, a senior officer at leading chip manufacturer, Intel, admitted: 'We were trying to be too elegant, and maybe too smart. And we let the market window disappear on us.' Tim Propeck, Director of Product Marketing at another of the leading American chip makers, Mostek, put it rather more graphically: 'We screwed up.'[6]

By 1981, world markets were inundated with a typhoon of Japanese 64K D-Rams, at prices far below Silicon Valley's. During that year, the market price for a 64K D-Ram fell from $30 a chip to $15, before plummeting in early 1982 to $5 a chip. By that time, Japanese companies had cleaned up three-quarters of the world market. A year later, the American industry suffered yet another blow when Fujitsu brought out samples of its new 256K chip. Any prospect of the American manufacturers being able to maintain their 64K lines long enough to make a profit faded. Over the next few years, almost all of the American D-Ram makers pulled out of the business, while TI was reduced to importing memory chips from its Japanese plants.

To add insult to injury, whereas in 1980 nine out of the top ten semiconductor equipment companies were American and three-quarters of the sophisticated equipment required for the Japanese semiconductor industry was imported from the United States, by 1982 Japanese suppliers were providing half of it. In 1987, the Japanese camera maker, Nikon, displaced Connecticut-based Perkin–Elmer as the industry's chief supplier of the machinery; two years later, the American company put its semiconductor equipment division – by then ranking only eighth in the world – up for sale and, when no American bidder materialized, six companies had hurriedly to band together to purchase the unit. By then, five of the top ten semiconductor manufacturing equipment suppliers were Japanese, including the two largest.

So desperate is the current state of the once all-powerful American industry that, in a last ditch attempt to regain its former mastery, no fewer than 30 of America's top computer and semiconductor companies – including IBM, DEC, Hewlett-Packard, Intel, National Semiconductor and Advanced Micro Devices – have got together to form a joint company called US Memories, whose aim is to better the Japanese by producing a 4-Megabit D-Ram.

There are, it should be said, areas where American producers are still predominant: one is microprocessors, the brains of computers. Intel and Motorola dominate the market for PC processors. But now the main Japanese semiconductor makers are planning a new generation of 32–bit, all-Japanese chips. The main contender is a 32–bit microprocessor being developed by Hitachi, Fujitsu and Mitsubishi based on The Realtime Operating System Nucleus (Tron) architecture, originally developed by a young University of Tokyo professor called Ken Sakumara whom a Hitachi executive had met by chance during a seminar. The first Tron-based chips are expected in 1991 and their ten million instructions per second (MIPS) to 20 MIPS speeds will surpass the world's fastest microprocessor to date, Motorola's 7 MIPS 68030 chip. Although American producers are still pre-eminent in microprocessors, and currently producing ever more powerful 32–bit chips such as the Intel 80486 series, and although Japanese personal computer makers are still largely dependent on American-designed micro-processor products, the Japanese have made a start, and few doubt that they will be a force in the microprocessor segment of the semiconductor market by the mid-1990s.

Beneath the plastic casing

The PC came at just the right time for the Japanese semiconductor industry. First, because it dramatically increased demand for semiconductors at just the time that the Japanese were really gearing up to massive production volumes. Second, because the microcomputer itself was developing rapidly into just the kind of long-production-run, standardized product which the Japanese industry excelled at.

Japanese progress in microcomputers was, however, initially slow. With the exception of one small, entrepreneurial start-up venture called SORD, the bulk of Japanese production came from established mainframe and electronics manufacturers, who at first offered fairly lacklustre machines. Steadily, however, they improved their machines' performance and, taking advantage of their financial strength and manufacturing capabilities, began to churn out IBM-compatible PCs in large numbers.

By 1989, Japanese manufacturers already controlled about a quarter of the global PC market, but although the market-leaders remain the American trio of IBM, Apple and Compaq, the predominance of Western brand names on microcomputers obscures the fact that beneath the plastic casing lurk components that are predominantly Japanese. So, even where Western manufacturers have apparently held the Japanese at bay, in truth they are becoming increasingly dependent on Japanese components and technology.

At the height of IBM's success in the PC market in the mid-1980s, for example, $625 worth of the $860 manufacturing cost of a standard IBM PC was made up by non-American, mainly Japanese components, although

IBM has latterly made strenuous attempts to develop and manufacture more parts in-house. In 1978, when the Apple II was the state of the art, everything but the screen was American-made: now, Apple sources slightly more than half of its parts from Japan, and a further 15 per cent or so from other East Asian countries. From 1984 to 1989, imports of components and peripherals into the United States jumped by 150 per cent to $7.2 billion a year.

It is the Japanese who now dominate the market for the more expensive elements of a computer – the disc drives and most of the chips on the logic board, with the exception of the microprocessor – leaving the less valuable parts to be fought over by a pack of producers from the smaller East Asian countries and the United States. Other key high-value components and sub-assemblies which are overwhelmingly supplied by Japanese companies are: flat-panel displays, used in laptop computers; colour flat-panel screens, employed in both computers and new-generation TVs; laser-printer mechanisms; and erasable optical disk-drives, which use technology similar to compact disc players and are likely to supercede magnetic drives. Long before the end of the 1980s, Japan had also become dominant in computer peripherals, such as scanners and printers. By 1989, three-quarters of the $3 billion-plus computer printer market was accounted for by Japanese producers. American manufacturers, who had predominated in the 1970s, were by then reduced to a less than ten per cent market share.

The technology food chain

Some Americans still draw hope from the fact that the United States retains its superiority in larger computers. That, however, is unlikely to last very much longer. For Japan's computer manufacturers are reinforcing their well-known engineering and production skills with increasing research muscle in order to present a real challenge to American dominance in the ultimate knowledge-based industry.

Standards are again playing a key role in the Japanese assault, since standardized products will be produced more cheaply and be easier to sell, while a wide range of manufacturers will have access to the same technology. In the late 1970s, Fujitsu and Hitachi successfully marketed mainframe computers which would run IBM software, often using well-known Western companies such as Siemens, ICL and BASF as distributors. Known as 'plug compatibles', these products offered more power and speed than the IBM product for less money. American companies also competed in the 'plug compatible' market, but it was Japanese ones which succeeded. Now, IBM is really beginning to feel the pressure. Late in 1989, the massive company, whose stock was languishing well below mid-80s levels, announced unprecedented plans to reduce its American workforce by 10,000. The other main American suppliers of larger computers are in a far worse shape. Long-time IBM rivals such as Honeywell are now all but out of computers, while once-promising minicomputer makers like Data General and Wang are in severe difficulties.

The problem is that the same low-cost semiconducturs, disc drives and standards which created the PC are increasingly finding their way into higher level minicomputers and mainframes, thereby lowering product costs and allowing users to run a wide range of software. For example, machines running on the standard Unix operating system are already eating into a market traditionally dominated by companies which once imposed their own proprietary operating systems.

And the main Japanese computer producers are now showing signs of the type of exponential growth which, in an earlier era, catapulted a group of tiny, unknown car makers into global giants. From 1984 to 1988, the worldwide computer systems revenue of the main Japanese manufacturers rose at a 45 per cent compound annual rate to reach $53 billion. Over the same period, sales by American suppliers grew by only ten per cent annually to reach $148 billion.[7] A few more years of such growth differentials will put the Japanese industry neck and neck with America's. Already, Japanese companies occupy third, fourth and sixth positions in the world league and five Japanese companies rank among the top 20 computer makers – up from only three in 1988. Having made their mark in personal computers, microcomputers and workstations, NEC, Toshiba, Fujitsu, Mitsubishi and Hitachi are currently planning to make serious inroads into the American market for larger computers. In 1988, their revenues totalled just $2 billion of the $49 billion in total American hardware sales. But these electronics giants, which already dominate the market for key computer components and peripherals such as disc drives, printers and memory chips, intend to move rapidly up what former IBM technology vice president, Sanford Kane, calls 'the technology food chain'.[8]

This chain leads from PCs to minicomputers and workstations, on to mainframes and ends with supercomputers – the ultra-fast, very expensive machines used in areas such as aerospace design, weather forecasting and defence. Up to 1989, American-based Cray Research dominated the world market, accounting for about two-thirds of the 350 or so machines installed worldwide, and seemed to have an unassailable lead. But, early in 1989, NEC unveiled its $24-million SX-3, so offering the first serious challenge to the American supercomputer supremacy, and Fujitsu are set to follow. Already the American number two supercomputer maker, Control Data, has thrown in the towel and dropped out of the business, while Cray have ominously announced that they can only afford to finance one supercomputer project at a time. Many inside the American computer industry are increasingly fearful that larger computers will go the same way as semiconductors and few now doubt that the Japanese have the capability to mount a real challenge – even to IBM.

Guile, deception and subsidies?

Jerry Sanders, the president of a leading American semiconductor manufacturer, Advanced Micro Devices (AMD), in many ways typifies the spirit which motivated the American semiconductor industry in its early days. One of a poor, Chicago family of 12 children, Sanders gained a scholarship to the University of Illinois which had been given by George Pullman, a pioneering entrepreneur of an earlier era who developed the Pullman railcar. Sanders had risen to be head of marketing at Fairchild Semiconductor, before going on to found AMD with the help of other engineers and finance from venture capitalists. Now, his company is hurting from Japanese competition. 'Clearly,' he says, 'our industry has been deprived of hundreds of millions of dollars – more like into the low numbers of billions – of profits, because of Japanese predatory pricing, resulting from their protected home market and their subsidies.'[9] Sanders' words merely echo what many in Silicon Valley genuinely believe: namely, that the Japanese have stolen their markets by guile and deception.

It is undeniable, of course, that Japan's semiconductor and mainframe-computer industries have received government support. A MITI report in 1966 on the future of Japan's then fragmented and vulnerable computer industry heralded a series of government-sponsored research programmes linking the main Japanese computer makers – Oki, Mitsubishi, NEC, Toshiba, Hitachi and Fujitsu – who at that time were largely dependent on American-licenced technology. MITI had already established a computer-leasing company called the Japanese Electronic Computer Corporation (JECC) in 1961, but the report accelerated the channelling of aid into the nascent industry. Projects included one for the prototype manufacture of super high-performance computers while, during the 1970s, the government provided half the costs for a programme to produce peripheral equipment compatible with IBM's 370 series computers – subsidies totalled nearly $200 million. A later project aimed to outperform the then dominant IBM 360 mainframe. All of the companies involved had succeeded in producing a competitor for the IBM machine by 1975, by which time the American company's share of the Japanese market had plummeted from 70 to around 40 per cent.

MITI later organized and supported semiconductor research and development programmes, particularly the Very Large Scale Integration (VLSI) project undertaken from 1976 to 1979, with government subsidies of $132 million, to establish three co-operative laboratories with the aim of developing next generation D-Rams. MITI also helped with a project to develop 'fifth generation' computers, capable of humanlike deductive thinking. Aside from direct government help, Japanese computer makers were protected, to an extent, by import duties, which were raised sharply during the early 1960s, but lowered again in 1972, and by 1987 were a relatively insigificant 4.9 per cent for mainframes.

But in this respect Japan's industry is not very different from most Western producers, which have also been strongly aided by their own governments. Western European governments, in particular, have long seen their semiconductor and computer industries as being of vital strategic importance and have helped them with subsidies, protection and government contracts.

Take, for example, Britain's main computer manufacturer, ICL, which was formed in 1968 as a result of a state-sponsored merger of smaller firms. Not only did the company get substantial R&D funding throughout the 1970s, but it also benefited from helpful government procurement policies. The Central Computer Agency, which was responsible for government purchases of computer equipment, consistently gave 90 per cent of its orders to ICL until the mid 1980s. When, in 1981, the company nonetheless went through a rocky patch, the government stepped in with a £200 million loan guarantee. Two years later, the British government committed £250 million to the Alvey programme, designed to co-ordinate research in four key new technologies, including very large-scale integration; while the Microcomputer in Schools programme, which aimed to put a computer in every school in the early 1980s, almost exclusively benefited British suppliers.

The British government also set up and fully-funded semiconductor maker, Inmos, in the late 1970s, helping it and other British chip makers with development costs through the Micro-electronics Support Programme. Inmos was sold to the private sector-company, Thorn EMI, in 1985, which subsequently passed it on to Franco–Italian SGS–Thomson, having sunk several hundred million dollars into the company without making any return. SGS–Thomson itself was formed in 1987 out of two state-controlled semiconductor companies which had both been subject to significant government subsidies over a very long period. The new joint company continued the tradition by losing £56.6 million in 1988, underwritten by the French government and an Italian state holding company.

This was in line with a long-established European practice of supporting high-tech industry. As far back as 1966, France had its Plan Calcul, designed to counter the American threat by forming a major French flagship computer company which received $250 million in state subsidies in the subsequent ten years, as well as support in the form of government procurement, protection and export subsidies. By the mid-1970s, when it had become clear that the master plan to challenge American leadership had failed, the French government encouraged its merger with American computer maker, Honeywell, pumping a further $700 million into the new enterprise. In 1982, the French government bought out Honeywell's share in the venture and nationalized the whole group, since when further large chunks of public money have gone its way. Altogether, by the mid-1980s, major French electronics and telecommunications companies were being funded to the tune of about £400 million a year by their government.

Nor is the United States whiter than white in this respect. Although United States governments have eschewed formal support programmes until relatively recently, the computer and semiconductor industries have, since the Second World War, benefited greatly from enormous government procurement and development programmes, particularly in the defence sector. More than half of the production of American semiconductor companies, for example, went to the United States military in the 1960s, and in the early 1980s, the American government spent $15 billion annually on computer hardware – far more than total Japanese production at that time – and virtually all of it went to American suppliers.

The US Defence Department has also generously funded research programmes, ostensibly for military purposes, but which have also secured substantial commercial benefits for American producers. One of the largest, the $1-billion Very High Speed Integrated Circuit (VHSIC) project, resulted in Motorola and TRW producing a 1.5-inch-square silicon 'superchip' containing four million transistors – effectively a supercomputer on a chip. According to TRW director, Dr Thomas Zimmersman, 'commercial successors of the superchip could find uses in a wide variety of applications where high speed, small size and great computing power and reliability are needed. Among these are computer-aided design, medical diagnostics, plant process control and complex imaging.'[10]

In addition, more recently, restrictions have been placed in the United States on the purchase of Japanese supercomputers by United States government agencies and by Defence Department-funded research establishments, which together account for nearly half of the American market. The American industry is also indirectly funded by the Defence Department – its Defence Advanced Research Projects Agency, for example, has partly financed an Intel subsidiary to produce a new generation supercomputer.

So if the Japanese have protected and subsidized their computer and semiconductor industries, Western European countries have been at least as guilty and the United States has not been far behind. Further, the Japanese have at least always allowed American mainframe manufacturers reasonable access to the Japanese market: IBM's Japanese operation dates from the 1950s, while Sperry Rand began manufacturing in Japan in 1963 in a joint venture with Oki. RCA, TRW, Honeywell and GE also had major involvements in Japanese computer-manufacturing ventures. Certainly, any obstacles faced by American manufacturers in Japan, and there have been some, have been no worse than nationalistic government procurement policies in Europe, which have worked against American suppliers – although such favouritism is less marked now than it was in the 1960s and 1970s.

That government support has not been a significant or special factor in the success of Japan's IT industry is also denoted by the fact that vast swathes of it have received little or no support. Manufacturers of microcomputers, fax machines, computer printers and photocopiers were not the beneficiaries of long-term government-funded research programmes, nor did they receive subsidies or have a significantly protected home market. The illusion that the Japanese industry has received unique support from its government and that this has ensured its success may be comforting, but the real reasons for Japan's progress in the IT market lie elsewhere.

Fax of life

Back in 1980, just before the fax market really took off, I visited the sales showroom of Nexos, the now defunct UK government-backed office equipment company, while conducting a survey of fax machines for *What to Buy for Business* magazine. In its eighteenth-floor showroom in London's Centre Point office tower, Nexos was selling two fax machines: one from a British company, Muirhead; and a second model from Oki of Japan. The Oki model on display was neat, well put together and fairly compact, but the Muirhead machine was hidden away in a corner of the showroom. When I asked to see it, I was shown a bulky machine that looked as though it had been put together as part of a one-off batch. What is more, it was £400 more expensive than the Japanese model.

So it came as no surprise to me to learn that, by 1983, all but two of the Western manufacturers had pulled out of the fax market. The survivors were Siemens, which was already fleshing out its range with Fujitsu machines which it sold under its own label; and the French state-owned electronics and telecommunications company, Thomson, which survived largely on account of a totally protected home market. Almost all of the other former Western manufacturers were, by that time, only selling Japanese machines under their own labels. Few industries have grown as fast as fax in the past decade, and there cannot be many major world industries so totally dominated by one country.

How did the Japanese do it? Government support was certainly not a factor. Although the Japanese computer and semiconductor industry benefited from state support, fax manufacture, and office equipment in general, received very little government help – in marked contrast to the strategy pursued by many Western countries. In Britain in the late 1970s, for example, the government's National Enterprise Board (NEB) set up state-owned Nexos with the avowed aim of taking on IBM by marketing largely British office equipment made by a series of NEB-backed satellite companies. It ended as a disaster on a grand scale, collapsing in 1982 with the loss of about £35 million.

The West German government also heavily supported electricals group, AEG Telefunken, which owns Olympia, the typewriter manufacturer and which was taken by Daimler–Benz in 1984 after a financial crisis. During the 1970s, AEG received at least $50 million in subsidies on top of more general government support for electronics R&D. In 1976, for example, the West German government put up $300 million for a six-year research project designed to aid the IT industry, and later a $1-billion programme was announced for research into the information technology, computer and robotics fields. A number of other, relatively small, nationally-based state programmes to support and develop local IT industries have been supplemented in recent years by EC-wide schemes, such as the £860-million EC Esprit programme – half-funded by the EC; and the Eureka programme, to which £320 million was committed by the EC in 1989 alone.

A Japanese failure

In the early 1980s, Western producers looked with trepidation at a company called SORD, founded by Takayoishi Shiina, a relatively rare Japanese animal in that he was a self-made entrepreneur who, at the age of 27, started the company with $2,000 and one employee – his mother. SORD's name is made up of 'SO' for 'software' and 'RD' for 'hardware' because the company designed its micro computers around its software, which allowed users to write their own programmes as well as run programmes written for other operating systems. For a time, SORD was the fastest growing Japanese company and its turnover in 1983 reached close to $85 million.

Thereafter, the company ran into trouble. Its main problem lay in its attempt to market a creative, non-standard product in a market increasingly dominated by either the IBM or Apple standard. In doing so, SORD was abandoning one of the traditional strengths of Japanese industry – namely, the production of long, low-cost runs of frequently derivative, standardized products – which was an especially unwise move bearing in mind the fact that SORD was neither as large nor as well financed as Japan's major electronics producers. In 1985, the company went bankrupt and had to be taken over by Toshiba, since when there have been no serious Japanese attempts to sell non-standard PCs or business microcomputer software in the West.

SORD's failure, however, provides an important clue as to why the Japanese office-equipment, computer and semiconductor industries have been so successful. First, to a far greater extent than in the West, Japan's efforts in these fields have been dominated by large, diversified electronics and engineering conglomerates which have been able to take a long-term view of market development. This is why companies like NEC – whose early microcomputer products, launched on to Western markets at the beginning of the 1980s, were so uncompetitive that they had to be sold off cheaply as remaindered stock – managed to sustain losses to emerge by the end of the decade as one of the major players.

Only rarely, by contrast, have the Western microcomputer specialists been able to survive major setbacks. Adam Osborne, for example, was unable to build on the success of his innovative portable computer in 1981 – lack of finance pushed him into Chapter 6 by the end of 1983. Apple is the exception, managing to pull itself back from the brink after its 1984 crisis when, following the failure of its advanced, but over-priced, Lisa model and the obsolescence of the rest of its range, it was forced to shut down two of its factories.

Unlike the large American computer makers, who tend to be specialists, Japan's main computer-makers began life either as primarily telecommunications manufacturers such as NEC, Fujitsu and Oki; or, like Hitachi, Toshiba and Mitsubishi, they originated as manufacturers of general electrical and electronics products. All of these companies now have divisions for the development and manufacture of semiconductors and they all now rank among the world's top producers.

But this is only part of the story, for even Japanese companies which were primarily associated with old industries have surprised many by successfully moving into the new world of semiconductors: Kawasaki Steel, Nippon Steel and ceramics maker, Kyocera, are examples. But perhaps the most dramatic diversification has been made by the ball-bearing manufacturer, Minebea. Its NMB Semiconductor offshoot, founded in 1984, has, in just four years, become the fifth largest supplier in the world of 256K D-Rams, churning out 40 million chips a year to achieve a near ten per cent market share. Early in 1990, the company scored its greatest *coup* when Intel, one of the founders of the semiconductor industry, agreed to purchase all of NMB's chips to resell to its customers.

One key factor is that Japanese companies have traditionally excelled at long runs of standardized goods, as opposed to more creative and individualistic products, and so have particularly benefited from steady moves towards standardization in the information technology equipment world. That is why they have done far better churning out hundreds of thousands of IBM-compatible PCs and millions of Group III fax machines than they have in the relatively entrepreneurial and innovative world of software.

But above all, the onset of digitization has blurred the boundaries between different types of office equipment, as well as telecommunications, computers and consumer electronics, making it far easier for manufacturers of one type of product to produce another type. It has been Japanese companies which have best grasped this opportunity, and been best equipped to exploit it.

So while Japanese producers, most of whom had never made typewriters before – such as Canon – slipped seemingly effortlessly into electric typewriter production, by contrast, IBM, which had made typewriters for years, decided to stick with its tried and trusted golfball technology for too long, only reluctantly introducing an electronic model in 1980. Even this still used the golfball in place of the newer daisywheels, and was really a hybrid, retaining many electro-mechanical parts. It was not until 1983 that IBM finally produced a competitive electronic typewriter, but by then the Japanese were already established in the market.

It has not always been so. In the very early days of the office-equipment industry, it was Western companies which were able to diversify with apparent ease into new fields – such as the then new area of office equipment. Remington, Smith Corona and Adler, for example, began life making guns, sewing machines and bicycles before moving into typewriters. IBM itself had its origins in tabulating machines, and even cheese-cutting equipment, but moved decisively into the typewriter market in the 1930s and later even more positively into computers. By the 1970s and 1980s, however, Western manufacturers seemed to have largely lost this art of organic diversification. Despite the huge resources at their command, those who attempted to diversify often eschewed internal development, relying mainly on the acquisition of small, entrepreneurial companies which had nimbly taken a technological lead in various fields.

Perhaps the most dramatic attempt to break into the office equipment market was made in 1980 by the world's third largest corporation, American oil giant, Exxon, which used some of its massive oil wealth to set up Exxon Office Systems to co-ordinate an assault on the IT market through three main acquisitions: a word processor-maker called Vydec; a fax manufacturer Qwip; and Qyx, a producer of memory typewriters. All initially offered quite competitive equipment, but in the year of its foundation Exxon Office Systems managed to lose $150 million on sales of $270 million and, by the mid-1980s, Exxon had withdrawn from the field leaving a trail of closed factories behind it. Large European electronics and telecommunications companies, such as Plessey, Siemens and Thomson, all made forays into information technology equipment, and all have largely failed.

Design, quality and efficiency

Why did such companies fail where the Japanese succeeded? For one thing, the Japanese more readily grasped the fact that the new, electronic office equipment could be mass-produced in very much the same way as a host of other products, so that Japanese producers were able to cut costs with long production-runs and efficient manufacturing, which also allowed them to add upmarket features to their products at minimal cost. The fact that many

Japanese manufacturers also had long experience in volume consumer products, unlike their Western competitors, helped in this.

In part this Japanese adaptability is due to the intense rivalry which pervades Japan's domestic market. A stroll through Tokyo's Akihabara electronics district provides adequate proof of this process. In 1988, I saw a Ricoh fax machine equipped with an 'autovoice message' function – which records messages on voice chips and verbally relays them to receivers along with the fax – competing with an NEC fax machine with a 'caretaker' phone which can record four voice messages. Such features were considered unthinkable only a few years ago. Simpler machines from Murata and Sharp were also on offer at less than £400, down from £5,000 price levels prevailing only a few years ago.

Japanese quality has also all too often been superior to that of Western companies. In 1982, American scientific-instruments and minicomputer maker, Hewlett Packard, tested over 30,000 memory chips from three American and three Japanese suppliers. They found that the best American supplier had a failure rate six times that of the worst Japanese supplier. Even the Pentagon felt compelled to crack down on major American semiconductor producers in 1984 and 1985 for inadequate testing of components supplied to military contractors. The President of Intel's Japanese unit, William Howe, himself admitted that American producers often didn't treat their customers as well as they might: 'We tended to get a little arrogant. It was pretty bad,' he said.[11]

Although the Japanese are still sometimes criticized for their lack of originality, when it comes to innovation in implementing technology through design, quality and production techniques, they have beaten the West hands down. One way in which one company raised quality and forced down D-Ram costs was by putting extra memory cells in the corners of its 256K chips. If a defective cell was found, optical lasers were used to burn them out and they were replaced with one of the spares. By avoiding dumping chips with defective cells, the company increased yields and lowered costs.

In fact, investment in state-of-the-art production lines, regarded widely as the most sophisticated and automated of their kind, has been a major factor in Japanese success and product quality. Only 40 operators in two shifts are needed to run the highly-automated chip fabrication plant at NMB, which not only reduces labour costs, but also crucially increases cleanliness. Less than one particle, with a diameter of 0.2 micron (millionth of a metre), per cubic feet of air penetrates the 'active' areas where the silicon wafers are exposed – a tenfold improvement over most other semiconductor plants. This is an important factor in NMB's 80 per cent yield of good chips on its 256K D-Rams – a far higher figure than its competitors.

By contrast, Western companies have not always been so willing to make the necessary investment in advanced manufacturing technology. In 1989, for example, IBM was still the only American manufacturer to operate an experimental, $1-billion X-ray lithography facility which is expected to be the primary technology for etching the extremely fine details of the next generation of memory chips – 16MB D-Rams. There were, at that time, at least 19 such facilities in Japan.[12] IBM even offered to share the use of its machine with a number of leading European and American companies in return for their merely covering costs while using the equipment: all refused, with the exception of Motorola.

The Japanese were also frequently simply more agile than their competitors. Companies which make disk drives to sell to computer makers rather than primarily for use in their own products, are called 'merchant manufacturers'. American companies almost totally dominated the merchant disc drive market in the 1970s through well backed and funded companies such as Shuggart (Xerox-owned) and Pertec (American-based but controlled by Volkswagen). But Japanese companies spotted the opportunity afforded by the new 3.5-inch format in the mid-1980s. Although smaller in size, 3.5-inch drives have a larger storage capacity and are far more rugged than the older format. Sony, new to the drive market, stole a march on the competition by launching the first 3.5-inch drive in 1983 – a spin-off from a word processor product which had not been a great success – and it was other Japanese companies like Hitachi, NEC and Matsushita who were the most nimble in following Sony's lead.

The mass shift to 3.5-inch drives in 1988 caught many American manufacturers with a glut of 5.25-inch drives and allowed Japanese makers to win significant contracts. Worldwide demand for the smaller drives soared from 4.3 million units in 1986 to 13.5 million drives by 1988, by which time 3.5-inch drives accounted for 60 per cent of the market. Tandon of the United States, one of the two largest floppy disk drives makers in the early 1980s, dropped out of the business in 1986. Shugart, which once enjoyed market leadership, is now only a small supplier of 3.5-inch drives; while the largest American drive company, Seagate, suffered substantial sales losses as a result of sticking to the 5.25-inch format for too long.

Japanese manufacturers have also often been faster off the mark when it comes to satisfying consumer needs by developing technology to make it widely affordable. Laptop computers, which can be easily carried and used in a train or aeroplane, were originally introduced by American companies, notably a start-up operation called Grid (now owned by Tandy) which, in 1984, first showed a slim laptop computer which matched a desktop model in performance. But it has been Japanese producers who have best exploited this fast-growing and high-value niche of the microcomputer market which now accounts for 1.5 million sales a year, worth $3.5 billion, and which is forecast to grow to 3.5 million units by 1993.[13] For one thing, Japanese manufacturers ensured that their products were usually slimmer and lighter than their American counterparts: in 1988, Toshiba's main offering was two pounds lighter, and smaller than its main American rival from Compaq.

Toshiba has also introduced better screens, bringing down the price of gas-plasma screen technology to affordable levels by volume production – its Ome factory near Tokyo produces 60,000 machines each month – as well as generally adding to or replacing its ranges annually. By contrast, IBM's forays into the laptop market have been pretty uninspiring. Its first attempt, the Convertible, was a flop and had to be sold off at bargain basement prices; while its latest model, the P70, launched in 1989, is 50 per cent larger and heavier than its main Toshiba rival. This is why Toshiba has become the undisputed leader in laptops, with 36 per cent of the European market and a quarter share in the United States market.

And now the 'winners' competitive cycle' is coming into play again, for Japanese manufacturers are vying to pack even more features into smaller laptops for an ever lower price, resulting in a new generation of 'notebook' computers, truly portable machines weighing under three kilograms and the size of an A4 sheet of paper. Toshiba was first into the fray with its Dyna Book model launched in 1989 for under £800, but by early 1990, Sharp and Hitachi were also piling in with rival machines, with Sony and Hitachi set to follow. As these companies leap-frog each other with new products and innovations, prices are tumbling and sales escalating: 200,000 notebook models were sold in 1989, but by 1992, most producers believe the market will expand to well over one million. Once again, the competitive pressures which led Japanese industry to produce world-beating radios, TVs and cars are at work in the computer market. Sadly, the main response in the West has been to reduce the competitive pressures on European and American producers.

Mega Project

In 1988, a series of newspaper and magazine advertisements in the European press trumpeted the fact that 'a new world-class contender in Megabit technology' had arrived. They featured a European athlete powering ahead of struggling American and Japanese runners. Behind the advertisements was one of Europe's largest semiconductor makers, the diversified West German engineering and electrical company, Siemens, which had joined together with its main European rival, Philips, in 'Mega Project', a scheme begun in 1984 and promoted and partly-funded by the Dutch and German governments (DM 240 million from the West German government alone), originally with the aim of propelling their 'national champion' semiconductor manufacturers ahead of the Japanese by beating them in the race to produce 1 Megabit (MB) D-Rams.

Ironically, despite the advertisement's theme, by the time the project got off the starting-blocks, Japanese producers had already long-since started the race and shown samples of their own 1 MB chips, forcing Siemens to license Toshiba technology. Siemens then tried to develop the next generation 4 MB D-Rams, but even here the Europeans have been beaten once again by several Japanese producers who began to mass market 4 MB D-Rams in 1990, well ahead of Siemens.

Nonetheless, Mega Project clearly demonstrates the drift of European thinking on how to compete with the Japanese, for, despite the manifest failure of previous government-sponsored and supported projects, the easy solution is to go for yet more of the same. So out of Mega Project has emerged the Joint European Semiconductor Silicon (Jessi), which got into gear in 1990 and runs for five years. Its original aim was for Philips and Siemens to further develop microchip technologies in a £1-billion programme, much of it financed by Bonn and The Hague. But this has since been upgraded to embrace other European semiconductor makers, and funding has been boosted to £1.4 billion over eight years.

Meanwhile, the Americans are beginning to go down the same path. Convinced that the Japanese have beaten the great American industrial success story of the 1970s only by guile and government support, a number of American computer and chip makers have come together in a six-year, $1.5-billion research initiative called Sematech, which receives half of its $200-million-plus annual funding from the United States Defence Department. This constitutes just part of a $1.6-billion aid package to the semiconductor industry channelled through the Defence Science Board.

Reinforcing this raft of state subsidies is a steady increase in trade barriers against Japanese computers and microchips. Alfred Stein, chairman of Silicon Valley semiconductor manufacturer, VLSI Technology, typifies prevalent attitudes. He believes that 'we may not be able to continue along the free trade route', and advocates a system of trading blocks, balancing reciprocal trade under government controls. Stein is backed up by Advanced Micro Devices' Jerry Sanders, who adds: 'Some form of what has come to be known as "managed trade" is both inevitable and essential.'[14] In fact, the industry has already got almost that. In June 1985, the United States Semiconductor Industry Association (SIA) filed a complaint under Section 301 of the 1974 Trade Act. The SIA claimed that the Japanese manufacturers had dumped microchips on to the American market at below cost in order to gain market share and force American producers out of business. They also alleged that Japanese semiconductor manufacturers had benefited from a MITI restructuring of the Japanese market which encouraged only companies using large quantities of semiconductors to manufacture them. This, they said, not only limited sales by American semiconductor makers who tend to be specialists, but also motivated Japanese firms to buy from each other.

It is worth dwelling briefly on these allegations. First, MITI subsidies were, in principle, no different from Defence Department support in the United States or European subsidies. Second, if the Japanese had dumped chips in the mid-1980s by selling them at below cost, then so had virtually every other manufacturer in Europe and the United States. What had actually happened was that most manufacturers misread the market in 1985. PC sales had been expected to double, but actually increased by less than a third. As a result, purchases of memory chips fell dramatically and chip-makers drastically cut prices to off-load inventory. Even new-generation 256K D-Rams, which had initially been priced at around $45 each, fell to less than $3. So in the over-supplied market of the mid-1980s, few chip-makers, whatever their country of origin, sold semiconductors at a profit – that is in the nature of this cyclical, glut-to-famine industry.

The argument that Japanese conglomerates gained an unfair advantage and were better able to weather the storm by using their semiconductors in their own products is more interesting. Certainly, the large, integrated Japanese chip-makers did benefit from offsetting the poor market with internal sales. But there are also examples of semiconductor manufacturers in the West who consume many, if not all, of their own microchips internally: in particular, AT&T, IBM, Philips and Siemens. In IBM's case, it has chosen only to manufacture semiconductors for its own use, while AT&T has failed to market more than a third of its production to other companies. Is this the fault of the Japanese? Moreover, there were at one stage even more American integrated-electronics companies, such as General Electric, RCA and Westinghouse, who were initially leaders in semiconductor manufacturing, but they were simply not as competitive as the new breed of specialized 'merchant' microchip firms such as Intel which now predominate in the American industry.

Then there is the fact that many Japanese companies which produce electronics equipment have only in recent years diversified into semiconductors and components. These include Sony, which began making components for its own internal use, but now sells $2-billion worth of its semiconductors to other manufacturers, as well as disc-drives and displays. Why have American companies such as Apple or Zenith not gone down the same route? Moreover, the success of companies like NMB, with no significant internal sales to back it up, also indicates that while electronic conglomerates have been important in the success of the Japanese semiconductor industry, they have not been crucial.

All of which indicates that to suggest that the structure of Japan's electronics industry has somehow given them an 'unfair' advantage is specious and represents the worst kind of scapegoat-seeking – especially when it is borne in mind that, unlike in the West, there are no longer any government-restrictions on imports to Japan of foreign-made semiconductors, and that import tariffs are zero.

Despite these considerations, the United States International Trade Commission ruled in favour of the SIA complaint and, in April 1986, America imposed duties on imports of Japanese semiconductors following which the Japanese agreed to the July 1986 semiconductor accord with the United States to forestall even more protectionist measures. Under this, Japanese manufacturers agreed to raise their prices in the American market to ease pressure on American producers and they also informally agreed to try to increase their purchases of American-made chips, which then only accounted for 10.5 per cent of the Japanese market.

A year later, however, the SIA complained that the Japanese were not complying with the deal and as a result, on 17 April 1987, the American government imposed a retaliatory tariff of up to 100 per cent on sales to the United States of $300 million worth of Japanese electronics goods, although this was later reduced to $164 million.

Although initially strongly resisted by the Japanese, in the end the semiconductor pact had a number of ironic consequences. First, it merely further encouraged Japanese chip-makers to invest in American production facilities to circumvent the barriers and controls – which, of course, simply confirmed their dominance. In addition, as the microchip trade cycle moved from its feast to famine phase, shortages of microchips began to occur and prices of D-Rams increased by about 40 per cent in the year after the pact was signed. Major American chip-consuming companies began to complain bitterly that the pact was disadvantaging them, echoing concerns expressed a year earlier by IBM, Hewlett-Packard, AT&T, General Electric, Honeywell, Motorola and Xerox, among others, that American companies might be starved of Japanese chips. According to Ken Flamm, an American trade expert at the Brookings Institute, 'price floors for D-Rams have been a disaster in the United States. Prices rose dramatically and there has been very little re-entry into the D-Ram market by United States electronics companies'.[15]

Further, in March 1988, GATT ruled that the Semiconductor Accord violated GATT rules as it agreed bilaterally to maintain high prices not just in the United States, but also in other markets, such as Europe. Mr Willy De Clercq, the EC's External Trade Commissioner, was particularly mealy-mouthed about the GATT decision, saying he expected that 'Japan will rapidly and completely end the system of price fixing'.[16] This did not, however, stop the EC concluding its own pact, late in 1989, with 11 Japanese manufacturers to ensure the maintenance of memory-chip prices on the EC market. Among the more ludicrous aspects of this enforced agreement was that the floor price will be the same for all Japanese manufacturers and will be based on their average costs rather than being individually worked out for each producer. This means that more efficient manufacturers will not be able to gain any price advantage. Moreover, European manufacturers are not bound by the agreement, so if the market moves into over-supply, the European producers will be able to undercut their Japanese competitors with impunity. There is a review mechanism to alter the floor price, but this is unwieldy and the whole process will involve Japanese manufacturers in large amounts of expensive and complicated paperwork – including quarterly reports on their costs, prices and products sold.[17] For European semiconductor users – such as makers of consumer products and personal computers who were already paying a 12 per cent tariff on imported chips – the result of the new agreement was further to disadvantage them against overseas competitors.

This EC–Japan semiconductor agreement was reached, despite claims to the contrary, under the threat of an anti-dumping suit filed in 1987 which had resulted in a provisional duty of 60 per cent being imposed on Japanese chips. The basis of this suit was, as with the American case, that Japanese semiconductor makers had sold their products at a loss in the mid-1980s. As already mentioned, almost all chip manufacturers were losing money at that time, and, anyway, that was history – by the time of the agreement, the Japanese producers were back in profit. Yet the agreement covered not only current products, but all future D-Ram products for a five-year period.

This illustrates the spurious basis for what was essentially a protectionist move at the behest of heavily-subsidized European semiconductor manufac-turers. But by that time, there was not much of the European industry left to protect, for the Japanese already dominated 95 per cent of the Western European D-Ram market, leaving the EC Commission and national govern-ments alternating between, on the one hand, claiming that the United States–Japan Semiconductor Accord was unfairly raising chip prices in Europe, while, on the other, demanding that the Japanese should hike up prices to protect the remaining European chip-makers.

Sadly, this is all too typical of Western responses to Japanese success and demonstrates why the Japanese now look not to Europe or the United States for the serious competition in D-Rams, but rather to the South Koreans, who have already surpassed Western Europe in D-Ram produc-tion and are rapidly gaining on the United States. Sadly, too, the use of

anti-dumping duties as a protectionist instrument against Japanese electronics manufacturers was, as the 1980s wore on, becoming all too common, as
will be seen in the case of one of Japan's greatest success stories, the
photocopier industry.

COPIER CARNAGE

'We feel we should be the ones to obsolete our products ourselves, not leave it to someone else. Obsoleting your own line carries a high price tag. But the most expensive decision of all is to let someone else knock out your line.'
Peter McColough, chief executive officer of Xerox Corporation, 1968–1982.[1]

THE ANNUAL HANOVER Fair is the world's largest industrial exhibition. Originally set up by the British Army after the Second World War with the aim of aiding German recovery, the April fair, which includes all aspects of manufacturing industry, worked so well that before long it attracted up to 400,000 people a day during its week-and-a-half duration, filling hotels within a 60-mile radius of the north German city. Eventually the IT section of the fair grew so large that it had to be hived off into a separate, earlier event. In 1984, however, the copiers, fax machines, micro computers and other office and information products were still largely confined to the giant Halle 1, one of ten exhibition halls on the sprawling 100-acre fair site.

As you entered the main doors of the cavernous hall back in 1984, you would have been immediately struck by the huge Kalle Infotec stand displaying striking orange photocopiers. A little to the left lay a stand packed with black Nashua machines, and next to them were 3M's models. All three were well-known Western brand names – yet every single copier on these stands was Japanese. Beyond them lay the glittering Xerox display – another instantly recognizable Western name which also hid the fact that many of the models on display were assembled from Japanese kits. And so it went on, stand after stand: Olympia, Minolta, Olivetti, Gestetner, Mita, Sharp, Adler, Toshiba, U-Bix, Ricoh, Panasonic, Agfa, Canon – whether the brand name was Japanese or Western in origin, all were selling Japanese copiers. A few years earlier, there would have been a good show of Western-made products too, but by 1984 these were limited to the high-volume copiers of Xerox, Kodak, IBM and Océ, as well as a few insignificant machines from a tiny West German company called Develop. Such was the extent of Japanese domination.

The Japanese had won a coveted prize. In Western Europe alone, the numbers of copiers sold annually had risen from just over 350,000 in 1980 to more than 750,000 in 1982, and sales were to increase to more than a million units by 1987. Worldwide copier placements were also increasing at a breakneck pace. In 1974, total world sales were just over 800,000 units, and the market was so dominated by one supplier that people talked of 'xeroxing' rather than 'copying'. Ten years later, global sales had trebled to 2.6 million copiers,[2] the vast majority of them Japanese. Xerox was reeling.

Dry writing

The man responsible for all of this was Chester Carlson, the son of an itinerant barber whose parents had emigrated from Sweden to the United States in the late Nineteenth Century. His father's incapacity from tuber-culosis had forced Carlson to work from the age of 14, though he still managed to attend college and gain a physics degree. After Carlson graduated, he had 82 job applications rejected before becoming a patent application clerk. But frustrated by the time-consuming process of copying patent applications and drawings in longhand, Carlson worked on copier technology on a budget of $10 a month in a makeshift laboratory in Astoria, Long Island.

In 1937, Carlson filed his first patent for what he called 'electrophotog-raphy' and made a successful image a year later. Electrophotography worked on the principle of converting the light focused from an original document into an electrical current. This was achieved by a photoconductor, which attracted a magnetically charged ink, called 'toner', which was then trans-ferred and bonded on to paper. Over the next nine years, Carlson tried to sell his idea to more than 20 companies, including Kodak, IBM, RCA, AB Dick, Remington Rand and General Electric. Retaining an ingrained faith in carbon paper as a means of duplicating, they all turned him down.

Finally, a technology development trust called the Battelle Memorial Institute in Columbus, Ohio, signed a royalty-sharing agreement and began to develop the process. Not long after, the director of research at the Haloid Company, a medium-sized New York-based manufacturer of photographic paper and copying machines, noticed a report on the process in the April 1945 *Kodak Quarterly Abstract Bulletin* and, helped by a government research grant of $120,000, signed a contract to fund more research. Haloid did not seem a suitable name under which to market the new technology, so the name 'xerography', Greek for 'dry writing', was coined for the process.

Early Haloid products, such as the Model A Xerox, were painfully slow affairs – even the manual was called *The Thirty-Nine Steps* – but Haloid's boss, Joe Wilson, persevered and funded further research by Carlson on a fully-automatic copier. On 16 September 1959, 21 years after the first xerographic image, the Xerox 914 was launched. Later dubbed by *Fortune* magazine as 'the most successful product ever marketed in America', it changed the business world. It also changed Haloid. Once a struggling manufacturer of photographic paper and copiers turning over $31.7 million a year, Haloid grew to be a multi-billion dollar giant called Xerox Corporation.

At that time, the main competition in copying, besides carbon paper, photographic and diazo copiers, were the Kodak Verifax and 3M's Thermofax. Both were slow, messy little boxes requiring special paper, but they only cost $350. The 914, in contrast, was simple, clean and used ordinary paper. But it was also the size of a desk and cost several thousand dollars. So Wilson came up with a superb marketing ploy: he rented out the machines for $95 a month with 2,000 free copies and a few cents for each additional copy and, amazingly, allowed a 15-day cancellation clause. It is doubtful if any corporation had ever made an offer so favourable to the customer.

At a stroke, all the objections to unproven new technology and high costs were eliminated. Although the machines sometimes caught fire and had to be equipped with a small internal fire extinguisher (called a 'scorch eliminator' by the public relations people), and although consumer advocate Ralph Nader publicly assailed Xerox for 'shoddy design', the new machine was a hit. In all, 200,000 914s were made over the subsequent 12 years, and as late as 1985 no fewer than 6,000 were still in operation.

Xerox sales were helped by a brilliant marketing campaign involving a sales force of smartly turned-out representatives, each of whom was trained in the subtle art of hard sell, together with a series of superb television commercials. The most celebrated of these showed a man handing a document to his six-year-old daughter saying: 'Honey, please make a copy of this for me'. The child skips off gaily, waving the paper which she then places in the Xerox 914. Seconds later, she returns the copy to her father. The message: even a child can operate a Xerox.[3]

Fortunes were made out of Xerox stock: a Rochester cab driver, who bought 100 shares when they were selling for less than $10 each in 1954, watched their value rise to more than $1,500,000 by 1970. Xerox had become the American dream. It had broken the record for American companies reaching a billion dollars in sales, and it was feted by stockholders and used as a case study of success at Harvard. By 1966, the United States government alone had installed more than 55,000 copiers.

So secure did Xerox management feel in its achievements that at first it largely ignored potential competition in the photocopier field and instead targeted the computer industry leader, IBM. As a result, resources were concentrated on purchasing computer-maker, Scientific Data Systems, in 1969 for nearly a billion dollars. When this failed in 1975, Xerox invested heavily in very advanced small computers and computer networks, which were also destined never to make a return. The company's other computer-related acquisitions were only a little more successful: Diablo Systems and Versatec (both computer-printer manufacturers) and disc-drive maker, Shugart, never fulfilled their potential, with Shugart finally closing in 1984.

Moreover, Xerox's its core copier business was beginning to lose some of its magic. Following the tremendous advances of the 1960s, Xerox had rested on its laurels. Only three completely new models were introduced on to the American market during the 1970s and, by the end of the decade, Xerox's range largely consisted of machines developed a decade earlier. The company was even selling the 3600 model – the lineage of which stretched back as far as 1964 – to some export markets well into the 1980s.

In short, profit margins were being maintained in the short term at the expense of product development and customer goodwill – especially as ex-rental, reconditioned Xerox machines were being sold to new customers without making it clear that the equipment was not factory-fresh. Most importantly, Xerox started to concentrate too heavily on the development of prestigious top-end projects to counter rival products from Kodak, SCM, and IBM. This was backed by patent suits against its rivals, which in turn provoked time- and cash-draining anti-trust investigations by the Federal Trade Commission (FTC), together with counter-suits from IBM, SCM and others. It all ended in 1975 with Xerox agreeing to make 1,700 patents available to its competitors.

Preoccupied with law suits and fending off IBM's and Kodak's competitive assaults on the lucrative, large-machine, major-account leasing business, Xerox's real mistake was to ignore the lower-value end of the market where its customers were becoming unhappy and resentful – and where the Japanese copier manufacturers were to launch their assault. In the words of Xerox's vice president, Fred Henderson, 'we had this gigantic cash cow and we almost milked it dry'. Or, put more graphically by Eric Steenburgh, another Xerox executive: 'We just didn't make anything happen. It was all foreplay and no climax'.[4]

A small lab in the outback

No fewer than 147 different plain-paper copiers were introduced into the United States' market between 1970 and 1980. Almost all were Japanese – and they were different. They were smaller, low-cost machines which were sold rather than leased. While Xerox was focusing on the elephants, the mosquitos stung with impunity, for the Japanese were hungry. In the words of Atseo Kusado of Minolta, 'how successful you are depends on how desperate you are. All Japan has been desperate and will be forever because in Japan we have nothing. That's why we're strong'.[5]

Konishoroku, a leading Japanese film and camera company, alarmed by the onset of xerography as a potential alternative to photographic film, was one of the first into the fray. In 1968, it brought 48 young engineers together in the top-secret E-Project. Its goal was to produce a plain – as opposed to coated – paper copier that would improve copy quality twofold and cut costs in half. First, the team visited Tokyo offices to find out what people did not like about their Xerox machines. One problem they discovered was that the mini-skirted secretaries found it embarrassing to bend over to add toner; another disadvantage was the fact that the Xerox machines were too large for the relatively short Japanese and their crowded workplaces.

Two years later, at the 1970 Tokyo Business Show, Konishoroku showed eight prototypes, the first Japanese plain-paper copiers to be completely free of Xerox patents. They were small, with good copy quality and improved toner access. Xerox, then preoccupied with IBM's impending entry into the copier market with its Copier I, ignored them. In Japan, on the other hand, the E-Project team were treated like heroes and within two years Minolta, Toshiba, Mita, Copyer and Ricoh were showing similar prototypes, focusing on the low-end copier business neglected by Xerox. Their machines were compact, low-cost, energy-efficient and easy to use and service. Nonetheless, there remained a fundamental problem: they could not distribute or service the copiers from more than 7,000 miles away, so how could they sell them?

Ricoh was the first Japanese company really to solve the dilemma by the simple expedient of selling through American and European companies, using their brand names. In fact, Ricoh did not have to look very far for an American partner, for it was approached by an American who felt that he had a mission against Xerox for pipping him at the post in 1959 with the launch of its 914, a few months after he had founded a company specifically to exploit a different plain-paper technology. His name was Paul Charlap.

I first met Charlap, then the chairman of Savin Corporation, when he was manning the Savin stand at the 1981 National Office Machine Dealers Association (NOMDA) exhibition at Las Vegas. A small, bald, powerful, hyperactive man of about 60, he responded with immediate aggression to my suggestion that his machines were losing their competitive edge. These were the declining days of Savin, the company which did more to help the Japanese penetrate the American copier market than any other. By this time, however, as far as the Japanese were concerned, Savin's work had been done.

Back in 1970, though, it had been very different. Then, the Japanese were just struggling to bring their first machines to the market. Savin also had problems. To get around the Xerox patents, the company was initially forced to stick with machines which used some xerographic technology, but which needed a zinc oxide coated paper. Its first model, the Sahara 200, was introduced in 1964, but Savin was too small to manufacture the machines itself and distribute them worldwide, so a licence for Europe and part of the old British Empire went to Nashua Corporation of New Hampshire, a manufacturer of coated papers with origins in making playing-cards during the Gold Rush; while Kalle Niederlassung, a subsidiary of the German chemical giant, Hoechst, was also licensed to sell the machines in Europe.

When it came to manufacturing, however, Charlap looked to Japan. Current Savin chairman, David Sadler, is clear about the reason for this: 'Apart from the lack of finance to set up a United States plant,' he told me, 'it was felt at that time that Japanese manufacturers could do the job better than anyone in the United States or Europe'. Charlap settled on Ricoh, which already made coated-paper copiers for the Japanese market. The Savin coated-paper copiers were cheap and reliable and sales grew steadily, but they were no match for the Xerox machines and Charlap was far from satisfied. Then, out of the blue, a breakthrough in technology came – not from a multi-million dollar research facility in Japan, the United States or West Germany, but from a small laboratory in Australia's outback.

One of the biggest problems with xerographic technology was that it needed a powerful heater to melt the toner powder and turn it into a liquid which would soak into the paper before being cooled. The operation not only took a great deal of energy and several expensive parts, but there was also the surplus powder which needed vacuuming up to prevent it from fouling the machine's internals. When in Australia on business, a Nashua executive discovered an obscure Australian Defence Department scientist called Ken Metcalfe who had found out how to fix liquid rather than power toner images on to plain paper without the need for a heater or vacuum. In 1970, Charlap made Metcalfe an offer he could not refuse – he proposed to build the Australian a laboratory dedicated to copier research if he perfected plain-paper liquid toner technology. So the Australian went to work. Altogether some 250 people in four countries were involved in the project and every couple of months representatives of the group would meet in one country or the other – always orchestrated by Charlap. They succeeded, and by May 1973, the first models were rolling off Ricoh's production line, identical in every respect except for colours and nameplates.

Nashua and Kalle introduced the machine in Europe in mid-1973 and marketed it aggressively, but Charlap waited until July 1975 before he wheeled out the Savin 750 at the NOMDA convention. The product made 20 copies a minute, with a first-copy time of 4.6 seconds. (The nearest equivalent Xerox machine took 13 seconds.) The Savin 750 also weighed less than half the Xerox, used only a third of the parts and consumed far less energy. It cost Ricoh only $500 dollars to build, was sold to Savin, Nashua and Kalle for $1,500 and retailed in the United States for $4,995.

Having just gone through a recession and an energy crisis, businesses flocked to buy the compact and efficient new machine. Unlike Xerox at that time, Savin was able to sell its machines, instead of renting them out, because its copiers were cheaper and more reliable. In addition, because the Savins were so dependable, they did not need Xerox's massive service network. Savin attacked Xerox head-on in its advertisements: 'We are where Xerox used to be: No 1', they read, and all over America Savin's sales representatives waited until Xerox contracts expired before eagerly pouncing on their rival's customers.

Sales of the Savin 750 soared to more than 100,000 a year, a figure that was almost 20 times the number of coated-paper machines that Savin used to sell. Its only problem for the next two years was getting machines to the relevant countries: jumbo jets had to be chartered to keep the copiers flowing. Xerox was not too bothered, of course. 'By our standards,' said Hal Bogdanoff, a Xerox executive, 'it [the machine] was garbage. Terrible. Atrocious.'[6]

In gaining a leg up into the Western market, however, Ricoh set an example for other Japanese camera companies to follow. With the help of local distributors, often confusingly termed as 'original equipment manufacturers' (OEM's), it started to sell its machines under well-known brand names. Minolta, for example, sold through Western companies such as Pitney Bowes, AB Dick, SCM, Lumoprint, Addressograph Multigraph and even IBM briefly. Once the Minolta brand name and dealer network was strong enough, however, the distribution agreements stopped.

Japanese 'boxes'

Perhaps the most successful of the Japanese copier companies, however, was another camera maker, Canon – a name which is a Westernized version of *Kwanon*, the Shinto goddess of mercy. It, too, began selling through American partner companies, Addressograph Multigraph (AM) and Saxon. But after problems with Saxon and AM, who were experiencing financial difficulties, Canon spurned offers from other American partners and settled on a longer-term strategy of developing the Canon name as a worldwide brand. So while Ricoh soared past Xerox in copier unit sales, Canon initially toiled with a tiny market-share.

Steadily, however, Canon's perseverance paid off. Its research staff grew to a 1,000 and the dealer network was reviewed and improved. Finally, in 1978, Canon gained its first real success with the small NP-80, a machine which it hyped with the slogan, 'The Age of Micronics'. There was still one problem to be overcome, however. It was becoming increasingly apparent that liquid-toner machines, despite the advantages of their lower-cost manufacturing and greater reliability, were beginning to meet with customer resistance owing to one major drawback. Although the machines were touted as being true plain-paper copiers, the fact was that to avoid smudging they needed to use special 'callendered' paper, which had a thin clay coating to absorb the liquid toner. The result was that the copies came out slightly damp.

Once Canon realized the problem, it switched its range to the dry-toner process in line with most of its Japanese competitors. The outcome was an advanced, low-cost machine which used fibre-optics instead of lenses – the NP-200. Though not without faults, the machine was promoted heavily, to the tune of nearly ten per cent of its retail selling cost, and sales grew to 100,000 units a year. Improved models followed in rapid succession and by the end of that year, Canon's copier revenues had jumped to more than a $1 billion, while sales were running at a rate of 250,000 annually. Canon had finally reached the position of Number One in copier placements. The goddess of mercy was showing precious little of her quality to Xerox.

Xerox, the American dream corporation, initially responded to the Japanese onslaught with distracted complacency. Distracted, because competition at the very top end of the market, from Kodak and IBM, was Xerox's main concern in the 1970s. Complacent, because Xerox engineers and sales representatives habitually sneered at the Japanese 'boxes' – not to be compared with their own superb, high-speed products.

But even where Xerox was making an effort, it was in a very different way from the lean, mean creature which first spawned the 914. Then, teams had worked seven days a week while the lights regularly burned until midnight – and they liked it. By contrast, Wayland Hicks, who became head of copier development in 1983 at the age of 40, bemoaned the sluggishness and constant bickering of Xerox's new corporate culture thus: 'When a problem comes up, one side blames the other. The engineers say it's a manufacturing problem and the manufacturing guys say, "Look at the designs we have to work with". Everyone protects their own interests.'[7]

Eric Forth, a flamboyant and humourous Scot who worked for Rank

Xerox, Xerox's UK arm, in the 1970s, before becoming first a member of the European Assembly, then a MP in 1983 and junior Trade and Industry minister in 1988, saw Xerox's problem from the inside. He told me:

> The Mitcheldean factory, close to the Welsh border, grew like topsy in the 1970s. They had so much work that they just kept on adding to the plant piecemeal, rather than by design. We could get away with it then because there was so little competition, but when the Japanese came, Xerox was simply blasted away. The incompetence, the waste and the inefficiency were colossal – each department had 32 people at the top, another 14 or so below that, eight beneath them, and underneath that one person who did all the work.

As with its rental policy, Xerox had clung on to its direct sales force-only strategy for too long and turned what had been an asset into a liability. It was not until 1984 that Xerox tentatively began to appoint dealers to supplement its direct sales force. By then, however, it was too late. For in the meantime the Japanese had been presented with a marvellous opportunity to build up dealer chains.

Moreover, in 1981, Xerox's American and European-made low-end range models included the 550, 660, 3100 and 2600, all dating from the 1960s or early 1970s, except the 2600, which was anyway based on the old 3100. Many of their machines were, in fact, reconditioned, making Xerox 'the world's largest second-hand copier dealer',[8] a policy which continued right up to the mid-1980s, at a time when Japanese manufacturers were renewing their ranges every two or three years.

When Xerox did develop new machines for the low-volume market, the results were far from inspiring. The 'Jap bashing' 3300, introduced in the United States late in 1979, was so unreliable that it had to be withdrawn after a week. By the time the machine was re-launched in 1982, the damage had been done. To beat the Japanese on costs, the engineers had cut down on component quality, installing the cheapest motor available, while the marketing department priced the product too high so that it would not damage Xerox's base of eternally recirculating 3100s. The 3300 was the last low-volume Xerox copier to be designed and manufactured in the West for some time.

Even its mid-volume copiers – where Xerox was supposed to excel – were not immune to gremlins. One faulty shipment of 1,000 Xerox 1048s had to be diverted from its plant at Venray in Holland to its rebuilding plant at Irvine, California which normally only reconditioned used copiers.[9] And low quality was not even matched by low costs. In 1980, a manufacturing study group at Xerox's Rochester, New York headquarters discovered that the Japanese were able to produce copiers at half the price it cost Xerox to produce them. The next year a group of Xerox engineers also found that it was taking Xerox twice as long as the Japanese to develop new models. As a result, Xerox's global market share plummeted from 82 to 41 per cent between 1976 and 1982.

A saviour from Japan

Ironically, it was the Japanese who ultimately salvaged Xerox's position. The origins of this unlikely situation are found in the early days of xerography, when Haloid was looking for backers to help market its product overseas. No European companies were interested, except for Sir John Davis' J Arthur Rank Organization, a British company primarily involved in film production. Davis was quick to spot the potential of the technology and in 1956 paid £600,000 for the rights to manufacture and market the product world-wide except for in Canada and the United States.

Rank Xerox, as the new company was called, made rapid progress in developing the European market, but met with obstacles in Japan owing to restrictions on direct foreign investments in that market. It needed a partner and chose Fuji Photo Film over several Japanese rivals, partly because the company impressed Rank Xerox with its engineering ability.

Fuji, a photographic film-manufacturing company, had been established in 1934 as a spin-off from Dainippon Celluloid, a large Japanese chemical company. The company moved into the camera market during the Second World War, but then became interested in xerography, which it saw as a means of developing a non-silver-based photographic film.

'The copy revolution starts today', announced a large advertisement in Japan's business paper, *Nihon Keizai Shimbun*, early in February 1962, trumpeting the launch of Fuji's first plain-paper copier. Western-trained sales reps issued forth to market 914s supplied from Britain and sales soon took off in a market largely used to copying documents longhand or employing large, slow and messy diazo copiers. Japanese assembly began almost immediately, with help from Rank Xerox engineers, and local content grew rapidly despite some early problems getting parts machined to the right tolerances.

Between 1964 and 1974, Fuji's net sales rose from ¥100 million to ¥37.1 billion and its employees increased from 500 to 5,000. By 1968, Fuji Xerox's sales had overtaken those of Rank Xerox in West Germany and France combined, while a contract to service the United States military's copiers in Korea gave it a bridgehead into the East Asian market. Yet the company was beginning to experience problems. Fuji Xerox's Japanese rivals, like Konishoroku, were entering the market with compact machines designed for Japanese offices. Although American-designed copiers could be altered to take standard Japanese-sized paper, their dimensions were just too large for Japanese secretaries who often had to stand on boxes to operate them.

Rank Xerox made an attempt to discourage Fuji Xerox from designing its own low-end products geared to Japanese needs, but Fuji Xerox's young engineers thought differently. Unbeknown to Rank Xerox, they built a prototype which was so successful that from 1969, Fuji Xerox devoted its best development engineers to a project with one simple aim: to produce the smallest plain-paper copier in the world. Leading the team was a brilliant Korean-born engineer, Nobuo Shono, who had joined Dai Nippon Celluloid in 1932 and been transferred to Fuji Photo Film a few years later. The result of the team's endeavours, the 2200, was born in 1972 under the slogan: 'It's small but it's a Xerox'.

Fuji Xerox's success was based on more than just innovative product-engineering, however, for the company also assimilated and improved on the best of Western management and training techniques. Since the company's beginnings, the Technical Development Department had translated and monitored Rank Xerox technical manuals and market surveys; training was extensive at all levels, and in 1974, a Trainee-Centred Learning Programme was installed in all Fuji Xerox offices. This was a self-guided and paced video recorder-based system which allowed engineers to learn about new developments, such as digital circuits, in their spare time. Many Fuji Xerox employees from the company's South-East Asia offices, and from the Korean assembly plant which was opened in 1975, were also sent to Japan for a two-year extended training period.

Quality-control techniques were originally imported from the United States, but then honed, refined and promoted through the Quality Control Promotional Movement, which began in 1972. A team of high-powered instructors, many of them university professors, were appointed to teach the programme, which evolved into the Total Quality Control Campaign and was used by all levels of management. Fuji Xerox's Ebina plant, opened in 1971, has one of the best quality records in Japan and in 1980 won the company the coveted Demming Prize for quality. Fuji Xerox also recognized the need for dealers as early as 1978, and set up a network of jointly-owned outlets to sell its smaller machines.

This was all in glaring contrast to Xerox Corporation. At first, Xerox Corporation and Rank Xerox refused to take the 2200. Their engineers sneered at the little Japanese box that was 'not made here' and began development work on several product concepts with code-names ranging from 'SAM' (Simply Amazing Machine) through to one appropriately called 'Nothing'. All were killed, leaving Xerox without the small machine that might counter the increasing Japanese competition.

Rank Xerox was the first to crack. By 1977, it was desperate for a replacement for the ten-year-old 660 and agreed to import the 2202, an improved version of the 2200. In its first year, 24,000 units of the new machine were sold – more than any previous Rank Xerox product. Xerox Corporation followed two years later by importing the Japanese company's new 2300 which was so successful that in 1980, 700 tons of 2300s had to be airlifted to supplement sea-borne shipments.

In the meantime, Fuji Xerox was beginning to move upmarket. After Xerox Corporation had cancelled several mid-volume models, Fuji Xerox went ahead and itself developed the 40-copies-a-minute 3500 which was launched in 1978. Its compact line was also expanded with a reduction version of the 2300, called the 2350, together with a machine designed for large paper called the 2830 in 1982. Rank Xerox and Xerox Corporation subsequently dropped their decrepit, reconditioned lines and came to rely totally on Fuji Xerox for small and lower mid-market copiers, most of which were assembled from knocked-down kits at the Webster and Mitcheldean factories.

The company which just two decades earlier was learning at the knee of its American and British mentors, both of whom tried to discourage it from developing its own products, had, by the early 1980s, got its former masters in a position of dependence on it for a large chunk of their ranges. These days Fuji Xerox even plays a part in Xerox's upper mid-range product development and its $1 billion annual revenues place it behind only Canon, Ricoh and its Xerox Corporation and Rank Xerox partners in copier sales. Ironically, though, the Xerox name still retains some of its old magic in Japan and the sign above the Fuji Xerox building in central Tokyo still reads just 'Xerox'.

'We don't laugh anymore . . .'

Many Xerox executives put forward the seemingly respectable argument that to have done battle with the Japanese in the lower segment of the market in the 1970s would have been to obsolete their highly-profitable rental base and accelerate replacement of their expensive large copiers with small or cheaper models; while to have linked up with dealers would have demoralized their highly-trained salesforce. They say these considerations led to Xerox's concentration on higher-volume copiers and the new field of office automation – the higher added-value ends of the market – leaving Fuji Xerox to concentrate on lower-volume products.

The problem is that it did not work quite like that. Xerox simply underestimated the Japanese. By the time it had realized its mistake it was already being chased upmarket by its competitors. Furthermore, the despised low-end of the market had itself turned into a substantial and valuable prize. Only Xerox's name, the rapidly growing overall market and models from Fuji Xerox saved the American giant – until it began to make a belated attempt to salvage the situation.

For in fairness, Xerox has not been a total sluggard in recent years: 'In 1979 when we looked at what the competition was doing, we would kind of sit back and laugh at it,' said Bob Willard, a manufacturing strategic planner; 'We don't laugh at it any more.'[10] In 1980, a team was sent to Japan to benchmark Xerox Corporation's production against Fuji Xerox's: to their horror they found that Fuji could build, ship, distribute and retail machines for the same price as it was costing Xerox Corporation just to manufacture them.

Xerox Corporation's first reaction was to do what many Western companies would have done under the circumstances. It cut 16,000 mainly white collar jobs worldwide and saved $600 million in salaries. But Japanese methods were then studied and copied until, by the end of 1983, Xerox had improved product quality by 70 per cent. Inventories were by this time down to under two months, releasing nearly $200 million to be deployed elsewhere. Manufacturing overheads alone were cut by $200 million and the production workforce in the United States and Europe was reduced by half, to 9,000, by 1985. Nowadays, a group of Xerox Corporation engineers visits Japan each year. An extensive dealer network has been built up in the United States and Europe to sell the low- and medium-volume range and both dealers and direct salespeople are now given more flexibility to offer discounts.

Above all, Xerox's range has steadily become more competitive, with models being changed every three or four years. The big break came with the '10 Series'. The 70-copies-a-minute 1075 was launched in 1983 and had microprocessor technology built into it to monitor and control copy quality and internal functions. Within two years of its launch, more than 60,000 1075s were placed with customers worldwide. For the first time in years, Xerox's workforce had something to cheer about, and they chartered a plane which they flew over the Rochester headquarters trailing a giant sign saying, simply, 'We did it!' The faster 1090, derived from the 1075, was developed by a team of 150 engineers in just two years.

But, although the larger and mid-sized models in Xerox's latest 50 series copiers are designed and built in the West, small and lower-medium volume machines are still the preserve of Fuji Xerox. Xerox has thus survived and is now prospering again, albeit with a very much reduced empire: ironically, the Japanese competition which so nearly destroyed it was ultimately to prove the spur that put it back into some kind of fighting shape.

From personal copiers to laser printers

There is, of course, the temptation to sit back and take some consolation in the fact that the Japanese have not been innovative. After all, they largely took Western technology and developed it, using their efficient, disciplined labour force to churn out products at a lower cost than Western manufacturers. But, comforting though such thoughts might be, they hardly square with reality.

To see why the Japanese have managed to advance copier technology into so many new product areas, you have to realize two things about their commercial attitudes. First, they are rarely too proud to buy in technology which they have not produced in-house. Second, they apply formidable R&D and engineering skills to bring that technology into whatever market they think they can sell it to.

Mita, for example, although it is one of the smallest of the Japanese copier manufacturers, has 400 of its 2,000 Japanese employees involved in research and development. When I was shown around Mita's central Osaka headquarters, housed in a nondescript grey eight-storey block, home also to its R&D laboratories, I saw row upon row of engineers and technicians working on new machines, testing components and developing future products like laser printers. On the roof, the company had installed a swimming pool where personnel could relax during the lunch-break or after work.

Then there is their pioneering use of fibre optics and zoom lenses to create smaller copiers with more features, which has also led the Japanese into product areas ignored by Western manufacturers. Early on, for example, the Japanese saw the need for compact, energy-efficient copiers. Having conquered the bottom-end market, a whole new species of low-cost, very highly specified lower mid-volume copiers began to creep up to challenge Xerox on the middle ground. Canon was first in 1981 with the launch of its 40-copies-a-minute NP-400 which had one enlargement and two reduction ratios, took A3 paper and could easily be discounted to £3,800 – far less than the competing, and less feature-rich, machines from Xerox, Olivetti of Italy or Océ of Holland.

THE NEW MASTERS

The Canon NP-400 took the market by storm. Other Japanese manufacturers were quick to follow with similar or enhanced products, and by 1988, there were 37 such machines on the American and European markets. Almost all were Japanese. Among the Western companies to be selling such Japanese models under their own names were Kodak, Harris/3M (the successor to 3M), Savin, Pitney Bowes, Adler, Gestetner and Monroe.

At the other end of the scale was the so-called 'Personal Copier' – another Canon *coup*. Conceived in 1980 by Canon executives on a tour of the United States, the idea was to produce a typewriter-sized, service-free copier costing less than $1,000, aimed at people who were not then using a copier. Two and a half years and $8 million later, Canon's engineers found the answer in a disposable cartridge which included toner and a small drum, cutting out servicing, but raising the profits made on supplies. The PC-10 was launched in the United States in 1983 for $995.

Costing less than $300 to manufacture on automated assembly lines, the PC-10 sold to dealers for $420, giving them a healthy incentive to push the machine. When, in 1985, distribution was extended to Sears and other mass-market outlets, production reached a rate of 400,000 a year: once again, cargo jets had to be chartered to keep up with demand.

Xerox responded to the personal-copier threat in Europe by pushing reconditioned versions of its ancient 1960s models, the 550 and 660, machines which were described by *What to Buy*, the business consumer report, as 'of interest only to collectors of photocopier memorabilia'. Needless to say, they were no match for the new generation Canon machines. Personal copiers are now themselves a major market segment: *What to Buy* listed more than 20 models on the United States market in 1988 and the overwhelming majority were Japanese.

Colour copiers are another area dominated by the Japanese. It was Canon which first saw the marketing potential of offering coloured-toner cartridges to allow customers to make blue, green or red copies. Xerox had led in producing genuine full-colour copying in the 1970s, but, of the eight colour copiers on sale in Britain in 1987, five were Japanese, including the Xerox model which is now made for it in Japan.

The Japanese have also made laser computer printers, which use xerographic technology, accessible to millions of businesses. Copier 'engines' have been used for some time as the reprographic heart of laser printers, which use a laser light source, receiving computer commands, to write or draw text and graphics directly on to the copier drum with tiny dots which are largely invisible to the naked eye. Very high resolution laser printers, used for typesetting, use as many as a million such dots to the square inch, giving superb quality. More run-of-the-mill machines of the type increasingly replacing conventional 'impact' office printers, use a density of 90,000 dots to the inch – more than enough for most text and graphics requirements.

Needless to say it was Western companies – including Xerox – which pioneered laser printers in the 1970s, but it has been the Japanese who have brought a product formerly limited to the very top of the market within the reach of every office budget. For while in the early 1980s, Xerox and the large computer manufacturers were selling huge machines costing well in excess of £50,000, almost every Japanese copier company was displaying prototypes of low-cost, desktop laser printers, based on their standard office copiers, at trade shows.

Canon was the first to come up with a sub-£5,000 model in 1983; by 1987, there were more than 50 low-cost laser printers on the United States and European markets, many costing less than £2,000; and by 1989, the first sub-£1,000 machines were appearing. The current bestselling laser printer bears, in fact, not a Japanese name but is the Hewlett Packard LaserJet. It uses a Canon 'engine', however, as do the models offered by several other Western companies, like Unisys and Qume. Once again, the Japanese have come to dominate an industry pioneered by the West.

In other ways, the Japanese have also shown more determination in their marketing efforts. Early on, they saw the potential of sport as an advertising medium: Mita sponsors soccer teams Independiente of Argentina, FC Haarlem in Holland, England's Aston Villa, Belgium's RSK Beverem, Como of Italy and Scotland's Hearts. For the Japanese are more aware than most of their Western rivals that having a good product is not enough. If you fail to market it properly, it will almost invariably flop.

Backing up the Japanese research and marketing effort are state-of-the-art production facilities. Starting business in 1934 as manufacturers of diazo machines, Mita turned to photocopiers in the early 1970s, and began developing plain-paper machines towards the end of the decade. Mita marketed itself as the 'copier only company' because, unlike its competitors, it then made only copiers. This concentration met with success in the form of a sales increase of 1,000 per cent in the ten years up to 1988. Despite being smaller than most of its Japanese rivals, privately owned Mita makes impressive products which are still largely sold on an OEM (original equipment manufacturer) basis to a variety of Western companies which distribute the products under their own names, despite the increasing prestige attached to the Mita name.

I was shown around Mita's new Saitama plant in 1985 by Hisao Ishikawa. I had got to know Ishikawa when he was head of Mita's United Kingdom operations in the early days of its overseas sales drive. He had returned to Japan in 1984, prior to setting off again to head Mita's United States outfit in 1986. A small man with a good command of English, Ishikawa looked younger than his 40 or so years.

The Saitama factory, the newest of Mita's two Japanese plants, is located right in the middle of a sprawl of bright green paddy fields, an hour's bullet train ride from Central Tokyo. The first thing which strikes you about the plant is the cleanliness: it was so spotless that you could almost have eaten your *sushi* off the floor. Rows of women sat on either side of three assembly tracks which were monitored by computers controlling speed, parts ordering, delivery and storage. Like most Japanese factories, the plant has an excellent canteen and a variety of health and sports facilities. We saw graphic evidence of the company's success in the despatch department. For there, in addition to boxes stamped with Mita's own name, cartons marked with famous Western brands such as Gestetner, Triumph-Adler, Olympia, Océ and Kardex were also piled high.

Mita's second plant, the Hirkata factory, is much older than Saitama. It began production in 1964 but has been revamped to include some of the latest technology. As we were walking round the production conveyor, electronic rock music alerted us to the approach of one of six robot delivery vehicles. Each has its own name and distinctive music to warn of its advance. Their job is to deliver parts from the stores to the line as they are needed. This the robots do automatically, guided by wires set into the concrete floor and controlled by the same computer which runs the whole production schedule. 'It is because we're small by the standards of our competitors', said Ishikawa, 'that we have to work harder. For us, we either develop better products – or we die. No one will help us if we fail.'

But Mita's production technology is by no means unique, nor even the most advanced. Ricoh's Atsugi factory, for example, produces several different models to the tune of more than 2,000 units a day. The factory system, controlled by Ricoh's own software, is totally flexible and can adjust the mix of models to suit demand. Work stations are designed in such a way as to limit unnecessary movement – even the chutes which take away the rubbish are set at waist level. No quality controllers are in evidence, for none are needed; nor do foremen cruise the lines and there are no parts ordering clerks with clipboards – as at Hirkata, all components are delivered to the line on unmanned, computer controlled, automatic vehicles.

And while Xerox copiers were stuffed full of expensive, custom-made parts, frequently produced in-house, Japanese manufacturers could enjoy the advantage of buying in as many standardized parts as possible. Ricoh, for example, is quite happy to buy in motors from rivals like Toshiba, while the Japanese copier makers often team up to standardize parts and buy them from the same source. As a result, about 50 per cent of the parts in a Canon or Mita machine are standardized.

'I didn't do this country any favours...'

In 1980, apart from Rank Xerox, eight major European manufacturers were still making plain-paper copiers. Five years later, seven had ceased manufacture: they included many large companies, with excellent facilities, good distribution networks and well-known brand names, such as Agfa Gevaert, Olympia, Olivetti and Gestetner. All now sell Japanese machines under their own names. Out of the indigenous European producers, only Océ of Holland has survived the onslaught. It has carved out a niche by selling workmanlike and reliable upper mid-volume machines, mainly against Xerox, but even it has to supplement its range with Mita models for the lower reaches of the market.

America has fared little better. Kodak alone survives and prospers at the top end of the market alongside Xerox. Pitney Bowes, IBM and 3M, the Scotch-tape-to-building-products conglomerate which was one of the pioneers of copying with its early thermal-technology coated-paper machines, are among the well-known names to have pulled out of copier manufacturing.

There are those in the American copier industry who are bitter about the way they have been beaten by the Japanese. Savin's Paul Charlap was predictably unhappy about his treatment by Ricoh and is now numbered among the Jap-bashers. He is quoted as saying: 'I'm the one who put the Japanese into this business . . . man, I didn't do this country [the United States] any favours'; and 'The only good Jap is a dead Jap. They lie, they cheat and they steal. It's all smiles, all show and display to hide their evil intent . . . . They couldn't give a goddamn about the rest of the world. They care about one thing: the Japanese.'[11]

The truth is a little more complex than that. There is no getting away from the fact that a whole chunk of the industry was abdicated as a result of the poor performance of many Western companies – among which must be numbered Savin. I remember wandering over to the Savin stand at the 1981 NOMDA Convention in Las Vegas, a week long extravaganza of seminars, dinners and product launches aimed at office-equipment dealers. I had heard rumours that the company which had once successfully taken on Xerox by selling Ricoh-made machines, was privately demonstrating a prototype, American-designed upper mid-volume machine of its own.

At that time, things were not going well for Savin, nor for its co-distributors, Nashua and Kalle. When the Ricoh-made liquid-toner models had come out in the mid-1970s, they had beaten dry-toner machines on cost and reliability. Dry-toner technology had moved on since then, however, until by 1981 the liquid-toner models enjoyed few real advantages. More-over, the market was beginning to rumble the drawbacks of liquid-toner technology – particularly the need to use special 'plain paper' and the tendency for copies to smudge.

Ricoh had already seen the way things were going and its once cosy relationship with Savin was beginning to look much less chummy. By the late 1970s, Ricoh was already working on its own dry-toner copier range and threatening to stop making liquid-toner models altogether. But word soon got around the gossipy copier industry grapevine and dealers began to defect to other manufacturers until Ricoh finally agreed to renew the contract with Savin in 1979. But Savin realized at that point that it could no longer rely on Ricoh and so built its own factory in California which began assembling kits from Ricoh, in preparation for the manufacture of a machine on which Savin itself was working, the Savin 8000.

Savin chairman, Paul Charlap, was not looking very happy at the NOMDA convention because not only was his existing range of Ricoh liquid-toner copiers sticking in the showrooms, but Ricoh had that year finally launched its own range of dry-toner machines which it was selling only under its own name. What's more, the Savin 8000 was not progressing according to plan. Indeed, it was fated never to go into production.

Shortly afterwards, Savin did obtain an agreement to sell Ricoh's dry-toner copiers alongside improved versions of the liquid-toner machines. But by then, the liquid-toner market had effectively been killed and Savin lost more than $100 million in the years after 1981. Savin and its partners Nashua and Kalle are now very much diminished forces in the copier market. Together, they had the resources and marketing strength to develop and sell a Western-produced copier range, but they did not. Ricoh, by contrast, now vies with Canon for the number one spot in copier unit sales.

David Sadler, a turnaround specialist who was with Massey Ferguson and

International Harvester before joining Savin as chairman in 1986, has a less personal perspective than Charlap on the Ricoh–Savin bust-up. He told me:

> The problem really began because Savin was contractually bound to sell 24,000 copiers a year, with a provision to allow Ricoh to step into the market if they failed to attain that target.
> Savin also played their hand really badly: they failed to appreciate the change in their relationship with Ricoh when the Japanese manufacturer began developing its own machines and they ended having virtually to beg Ricoh for products. The Savin 8000 was hopelessly over-engineered and far too expensive – it would have cost $20,000 per unit to build. The management also just couldn't bear to throw away their past glories and they obstinately stuck with liquid-toner models long after they had been rejected by the mass of customers.
> On top of that Savin were just plain inefficient. In 1985 it took them two months to find out how many warehouses they had: finally they discovered about 35 across the United States and Canada, with five and a half months of inventory. Can you imagine a Japanese company running things like that? Then they still couldn't fulfil orders for weeks because they had no computer records.

After Sadler's arrival, receivables were tightened up, the corporate helicopter and jet were sold, inventory was cut to one month's supply, the head-office staff were cut from 880 to 360, computers now run the ordering and delivery system, while the Ricoh contract has been renegotiated. By 1987, Savin was showing a small profit again. Even so, the story of Savin is really a story of what might have been in the United States copier industry.

Of course, Xerox still retains a dominant position in the upper-volume sector, but Canon has for long led it in terms of annual unit sales, with around 20 per cent of the worldwide market, followed by Ricoh with close to 15 per cent. Xerox Corporation, together with Rank Xerox and Fuji Xerox, has just ten per cent of the world market when calculated on this basis, although together they account for just under a third of world sales by value owing to their bias towards larger machines.

Kodak has about five per cent of world sales by value and Océ from Europe accounts for less than one per cent. The rest is shared between the Japanese suppliers who made around 2.2 million of the three million or so plain-paper copiers sold world wide in 1986. A further 400,000 were assembled from Japanese kits.[12] The trade statistics are even starker: that same year, Japan exported £820 million worth of copiers and kits and imported a mere £2 million worth.

Nor is there likely to be any long-term shelter up market for the Western producers, for the Japanese are already inexorably pushing their products upwards. Mita, Sharp, Matsushita, Ricoh, Canon, Toshiba, Konishoroku and Minolta all now make 50-copies-a-minute-plus machines which are sold both under their own names and by Western companies such as Savin, Adler, Pitney Bowes, Harris/3M and Kodak themselves – Canon and Ricoh also now make 60-copies-a-minute-plus machines which are probing deep into territory formerly the exclusive preserve of Xerox and Kodak.

A beef for dinner

I was sitting having dinner at a Kobe beef restaurant in the outskirts of Osaka with Hisao Ishikawa and one of the original founders of Mita. For more than a thousand years, the Japanese had condemned meat-eating as barbaric and unclean owing to Buddhist precepts forbidding the killing of animals. After the Meiji Restoration in 1868, however, the Japanese were desperate to catch up with the West and meat-eating was encouraged to build up the nation's physique and stamina. As so often, the Japanese managed to improve on Western practice, and their beef, although expensive, is among the best in the world. Peasant farmers usually rear only one or two beasts at a time which are fed with barley mash and sometimes beer while the animals are massaged daily to ensure tenderness. The result is superbly textured meat, marbled with just the correct quantity of fat to give it flavour.

Ishikawa, however, had been strangely quiet during the meal. He had chewed spasmodically at his beef and only sipped occasionally the surprisingly good Japanese Suntory claret. Something was obviously building up inside him, but the Japanese find it particularly painful to ask a direct question, especially if it is a difficult one. Suddenly he turned to me and asked: 'We have heard that the European Commission is to begin an anti-dumping investigation into Japanese copiers. Is it true?' I laughed and replied: 'No! How could they? Everyone knows that you haven't been dumping copiers. There is no way that they could even consider trying to pin that on you!' Sadly, it later turned out that my confidence in the fairness of the Commission had proved to be misplaced.

20

新
大
国

GHETTO EUROPE

'Anti-dumping policy in the EC seems now to be used covertly as industrial policy for the purpose of promoting particular industries.'
Michael Davenport, former European Community economist.[1]

JUST OFF RONDE Place Schumman, on the edge of Brussels, in the type of grey and uninspiring commercial suburb that is the lot of every major modern city, stands a huge, 13-storey building laid out in the shape of a four-pointed star. Built in 1960s-style glass and concrete, this is the Berlaymont, the main offices of the EC Commission and the nerve centre of the European Community.

It is on the plushly-appointed top floor of this building that a group of 17 men and women help shape the destiny of 320 million Europeans. They are the EC Commissioners, the men and women charged, among other things, with the task of reversing the seemingly inexorable Japanese industrial advance. Each Commissioner enjoys the services of a cabinet, a personal entourage usually around half-a-dozen strong, which keeps them up to date and acts as their political antennae. But although the Commissioners have far more power and influence than all but the prime ministers and presidents of the EC's member states, most Europeans would have trouble naming even one of them.

Below the Commissioners' floor, in the rabbit warren of more functional offices which make up the lower 12 stories of the Berlaymont, and in other buildings scattered around Brussels, work thousands of obscure civil servants – often called Eurocrats. Most senior of these are the faceless directors-general who head the EC's 22 ministries, the directorates-general – or 'deegees' as they are dubbed in Brussels. Though the Commissioners, who are appointed by the EC member national governments, may come and go, directors-general seem to go on for ever.

Together with four other senior Eurocrats, these make up the 26 A-1s, so-called because of their supreme position in the Community's bureaucratic hierarchy. Their enormous influence necessitates a carefully constructed international balance, with West Germany, France, the UK and Italy each getting four, Spain two, and the remaining member states one each. One post is left unattached to a particular nationality. Just below the A-1s, 22 deputy directors-general and a further 115 directors make up the A-2s, so completing one of the least-known but most influential bureaucracies in the world.

It is to a group of these shadowy politicians and bureaucrats that the task of enhancing the Community's capabilities to meet the perceived threat of Japanese competition has fallen. They have chosen two particular weapons for the struggle. The first, greeted with a fanfare of publicity, consists of freeing the Community's internal market of all remaining barriers to trade by 1992. This in theory will allow member states to trade openly with one another, so improving the efficiency and competitiveness of European industry.

The second policy plank is less publicized. Indeed, it is hardly even perceived by the public or even by most member governments. Since many within the EC establishment consider that the main beneficiaries of the more liberal market within the EC will be the large and successful Japanese companies who are best able to exploit it, they therefore see higher barriers against external trade as the natural corollary to a more open internal EC market. In this they are strongly supported by powerful European industrial lobbies and other vested interests. So, as the Commission busies itself demolishing the ancient, crumbling walls of the Community's internal obstacles to trade, its architects and masons are simultaneously erecting the foundations and ramparts of a fine new structure. Some call this 'Fortress Europe'.

Regulation 2423/88

Various tools and pieces of machinery are available to the Commission in its task of construction. It has long used overtly protectionist measures, such as import quotas and voluntary restraint agreements (VRAs), to restrict Japanese imports. Lesser known Surveillance Measures are another favourite device. Under what is known as Prior Community Surveillance, imported products can only be released for free circulation within the EC on production of an import document or licence. In theory, this serves to facilitate the collation of close statistical accounts of sensitive imports. In practice, there have been recurrent complaints that certain member states delay the issue of licences beyond the statutory five working days, thus making life difficult for importers. Furthermore, Community Regulation 288/82 provides for 'protective measures' whereby the Commission can limit an import document's period of validity in order to prevent imports altogether.

However, highly conspicuous methods of trade restraint such as these appear distasteful in an era when the EC and the United States spend so much of their energy complaining about Japanese trade practices. More subtle anti-dumping measures have, therefore, become the increasingly favoured implements of EC protectionism – particularly as they imply action against unfair trade practices, rather than the imposition of import barriers.

Most developed countries have maintained regulations allowing them to act against 'dumping', and in the case of the EC these have been consolidated into Community-wide legislation. The EC anti-dumping law is largely based on a horrifically complicated regulation dating from 1968 and revised in 1988, which carries the number 2423/88. This anti-dumping regulation states that a product shall be considered to have been dumped if its export price to the Community is less than the 'normal value' of the like product on its home market. The difference between the two is called the 'dumping margin'.

Dumping is the practice of selling a product into another country at a price below that prevailing in the home market. Predatory pricing, which goes a stage further, occurs when an exporter sells at below the cost of manufacture. A company may, in theory, engage in these practices either to offload surplus production without disrupting its domestic market, or as part of a concerted campaign to drive overseas competitors out of business, so providing the exporter with a virtual monopoly, as a result of which it can, in theory, raise prices and recoup earlier losses. The EC regulations, however, do not require proof of predatory pricing to justify the imposition of duties, just that export prices were below domestic ones.

It is, of course, a fact that producers often vary prices in different markets. Generally, however, this is no more than a reflection of differing levels of competition. Genuine cases of dumping or predatory pricing are much rarer than often claimed. Manufacturers who sell off products cheaply in foreign markets usually do so on a very limited scale to offload marginal production or old stock. And although Japanese businessmen tend to differ from their Western counterparts in that they see nothing unfair in using pricing as one weapon to gain long-term market share, conspiracies to sell below cost and so drive rivals from the market suffer from intrinsic disadvantages, including the fact that in competitive markets new contenders tend to emerge as soon as a monopolist begins to try to cash in by raising prices. Nonetheless, complaints of dumping have been a common refrain in industries threatened by low-cost imports.

EC anti-dumping regulations have, in the past, generally been used against low-value commodities and semi-finished products from developing and Eastern Bloc countries, whose eagerness for hard currency has some-times led them to sell goods for very low prices. Cases have ranged from East German urea to Czechoslovakian potassium permanganate and from Argentinian hardboard to Canadian potato granules. In recent years, however, the emphasis in anti-dumping actions has swung towards higher-value manufactured goods, particularly the products of Japan's phenom-enally successful consumer-electronics and information-technology industries. Between 1980 and 1988, the EC initiated no fewer than 357 anti-dumping investigations,* but whereas between 1980 and 1982 only eight of these were initiated against Japan and the newly industrialized Asian countries, between 1986 and 1988 this had risen to 30. Over the same two periods, investigations affecting the United States and other developed market economies fell from 41 to eight.

Between 1981 and 1987, the European Community concluded no fewer than 281 anti-dumping investigations. Although only 22 per cent of these ended with the imposition of duties, 47 per cent resulted in the acceptance of price undertakings, the process whereby the exporter raises its prices to a level deemed acceptable by the Commission.[2] Moreover, many of these were accompanied by VRAs which are rarely made public. In many other cases where no duty or price undertaking was imposed, secret 'voluntary' restrictions were nonetheless agreed: these are euphemistically referred to by the Commission as investigations which have been 'terminated by other reasons'.

Among the high-tech products affected by anti-dumping investigations in the 1980s were video recorders, video tape, electronic typewriters, photocopiers, computer printers, mobile telephones and microwave ovens. The most recent cases in 1989 involved colour TVs from several Asian countries; and CD players from Japan and South Korea which ended with duties of up to 32 per cent being imposed. One of the countries recently caught in the anti-dumping net has been Hong Kong. Bearing in mind the colony's *laissez-faire* economic environment, it is hard to envisage her producers engaging in conspiracies to subsidize exports with profits made from a protected home market – especially in view of the tiny size and almost total openness of the colony's domestic market. Yet the fact is that Hong Kong manufacturers have been found guilty of 'dumping', graphically illustrating a crucial point regarding the Community's anti-dumping regulations: namely that they are so drawn up that they result in 'dumping' being found and anti-dumping duties being imposed in cases where no dumping has in fact occurred.

Loading the dice

When, back in 1985, I dined with the ex-head of copier-maker Mita's UK office at an Osaka restaurant, I had been dismissive when he raised the possibility of the EC initiating an anti-dumping investigation into Japanese copiers. I was somewhat surprised, therefore, when soon after my return to Britain I found out that the Commission had indeed begun just such an investigation. At first I thought that, at most, this must be some kind of sop to the few remaining European copier manufacturers, because I well knew that copier prices in Japan were about the same, or if anything rather less, than those in Europe. Presuming that 'dumping' presupposed higher prices on the home market, how could the Japanese manufacturers be found guilty of this economic crime?

---

* Over the same period, Australia initiated 465 investigations, the United States 409 and Canada 357. Although this chapter is primarily devoted to the inherent injustices of EC anti-dumping policy, similar criticisms could be made of those other heavy-users of anti-dumping regulations.

Chris Norall explained to me just how the Commission could reach such a seemingly impossible conclusion. A jovial and articulate 43-year-old American-born lawyer, Norall came to Europe as a child and was educated mainly in England. Though he returned to the United States to obtain a law degree, he came back to marry an Italian girl, settling in Europe in 1973 to practise in Brussels, specializing in EC law in his own now well-known partnership, Forrester and Norall. He described how the convoluted EC regulations could result in the imposition of anti-dumping duties, even where the manufacturer was selling overseas at a substantially higher price than on his home market.

Having warned me that the subject was arcane and horrifically complicated, Norall explained:

To deduce the export price, the Commission starts with the price which the Japanese manufacturer's EC sales subsidiary charges the first independent purchaser in the importing country – this is usually a shop or dealer of some sort. All of the expenses of the EC sales subsidiary are then subtracted from this price. A further adjustment back to the factory-gate price in Japan is made by subtracting other costs such as custom duties, handling, ocean freight, inland freight in Japan and packing. Finally, a series of additions are made to allow for the overheads of the EC sales subsidiary, though not its marketing costs.

In other words, the Commission investigators 'construct' what they consider to be the genuine import price, a calculation all the more necessary in their view because the exporting company usually owns the importing subsidiary and so the import price might be artificial.

But to work out the manufacturer's home market price and so to establish whether any dumping has occurred, the investigators take quite a different approach. Rather than using a straightforward method of estimating production and distribution costs, the Commission takes the view that the home-market sales subsidiary and the parent/manufacturer should be treated as a single unit – an opposite approach to that used in assessing the EC price. So their costs, and particularly their marketing costs, are also treated together.

The net result is that the marketing costs which are included in the manufacturer's home-market calculation are excluded when arriving at prices on the EC market, so almost invariably creating an artificially higher domestic price. To the argument that the domestic price and export price calculations are patently being done differently, the Commission offers a series of involved and far from satisfactory arguments.

I use the word 'asymmetry' to describe this unfairness – and the results can be quite spectacular. For example, the Japanese are particularly vigorous marketers, as you can tell by watching a televised football match or standing in a central square in any European city and looking at the neon signs. For consumer electronics and office-equipment products, these and other marketing costs can easily amount to a third or more of overall costs. Yet just such costs are effectively excluded from the equation used to reach the EC market price. The result? Where, economically, there is no dumping, substantial dumping will be found. In a word, the dice are heavily loaded against the exporter.

Whatever one may think of the merits of Community policy towards Japan, there is something disturbing in the fact that buried at the centre of that policy, embedded in a procedure which, though highly technical, purports to be based on legal principles, is a deep and palpable unfairness.

But the unfairness does not end there, for the rules have also been drawn up in such a way as to greatly discourage new entries into the market. For example, the highest duty imposed after an anti-dumping investigation can also be imposed on all new companies, even though they were not named in the original investigation. Moreover, start-up companies which are showing a loss on their early production can also be subject to anti-dumping duties, even if their prices exceed those prevailing in the EC.

It is, of course, not unusual for a new production facility to sustain losses during the early years until an economic level of output is reached or until the brand or product itself gains acceptability. In earlier, kinder times, the Commission showed some willingness to consider adjustments for start-up costs, but now this is no longer the case. As Chris Norall warns:

> The message is clear. If an exporter is starting up a new factory, his exports are bound to be considered 'dumped' in the initial period of its operations and no quarter will be given. Let the new exporter beware. The message should not be lost on any enterprise creating new production facilities which may export to the European Community.

Where a 'dumping' case is found, substantial duties can be imposed on the exporters. In the past, the Commission has often accepted 'price undertakings', whereby the exporter agrees to raise its prices to a level deemed acceptable by the Commission. The advantage from the exporter's point of view is that at least the benefit from the higher price accrues to itself rather than to the Commission in the form of duties. Although acceptance of price undertakings was very common until recently, the Commission now virtually rules out such undertakings in cases involving Japanese goods.

Copier cartel

It was this rather partisan set of regulations which were invoked by the few remaining Community photocopier manufacturers in 1985. Alarmed at what they called 'low-priced' imports from Japan, Rank Xerox's solicitor, David Whibley, prepared a document outlining what he called an 'alarming' increase in copier imports from 188,000 in 1980 to 535,000 in 1985. This, the report stated, had led to a loss of market share, diminished profitability, caused the withdrawal of ten Community producers from the market and reduced employment in the European industry.[3]

So the five Community producers still in business – Develop, Océ, Olivetti, Tetras and Rank Xerox* – formed the Committee of European

---

* Develop and Tetras were very minor new producers, while Olivetti only by then assembled Canon models, leaving Océ and Rank Xerox as the only significant European copier manufacturers.

Copier Manufacturers (CECOM). Top managers from each of the manufacturers, many of whom knew each other well from the office-equipment circuit of trade fairs and other industry events, met together regularly, forming a working group to prepare a complaint to the Commission. It took them less than four months to collect their evidence which, they claimed, showed both dumping by the Japanese and injury to the Community industry.

As part of their complaint to the Commission, CECOM alleged that, despite a substantial rise in photocopier consumption within the Community, the complainants' market-share had fallen from 23 per cent in 1982 to 18 per cent in 1984. When the Commission's anti-dumping investigators duly began their inquiry early in 1986, they soon managed to find evidence of 'dumping' based on the lopsided and convoluted calculations allowed for by the EC regulations. So although, for example, it was established that the Canon NP 400, a popular mid-range copier, was selling at a list price of ¥1,298,000 in Japan, and a very similar DM13,400 in West Germany, a massive 'dumping' margin of 42.9 per cent was nonetheless found.

The report of the case in the EC's official journal later went on to admit that 'the degree of price undercutting was in general relatively small in terms of price'. But that did not stop the very same report from concluding just two paragraphs later that 'there was evidence that Community producers had suffered injury through price undercutting by Japanese exporters on the Community market'.[4]

In determining at what level to fix the anti-dumping duty on the Japanese copier makers, the Commission reckoned that prices should be raised to enable Community producers to earn 12 per cent profit on their own sales. Lawyers representing the importers argued that this was excessive in a traditionally low-margin industry, especially as photocopier manufacturers, in common with producers of other types of office equipment, often sell their machines at low margins, compensating themselves with high profits on the consumables which the purchasers are obliged to buy. Wayland Hicks, Head of Copier Development at Xerox Corporation in the United States, estimates, for example, that 60 to 70 per cent of Canon's copier profits came from supplies such as the toner powder – effectively the ink in copiers.[5]

The Commission, however, saw 'no reason why . . . profits should be made only on consumables and supplies', thus imposing their view of how the industry should be run on companies which had been making a success of it for more than a decade. It seemed to the lawyers and industry experts representing the Japanese manufacturers that the Commission was bending over backwards to favour the CECOM case. But there was one further, unpleasant twist to the story.

At that time, the Japanese manufacturers were selling their machines predominantly through independent dealers, while the Community producers still marketed their equipment largely through relatively expensive, directly-employed salesforces. Despite strong protestations from the Japanese, the Commission decided that the target increase in revenues required for the Community producers should be further boosted to take account of their relatively expensive distribution methods. In other words, the Commission was making allowances for the marketing inefficiencies of the Community producers, while penalizing the good practices of the exporters. As a result, a definitive duty of at least 20 per cent was imposed on all of the Japanese exporters, with the exception of Copyer who got away with 7.2 per cent, Toshiba with ten per cent and Mita with 12.1 per cent for supposedly lower dumping margins.

In reaching its verdict, the Commission made no secret of the fact that its aims went rather further than merely objectively determining whether genuine dumping had taken place. As its report on the photocopier case states:

> It is clear that the photocopier industry will continue to form a key part of the office-equipment industry as a whole and that the retention and development of the technology currently employed will be essential for the development of future reprographic products . . . . The imposition of a definitive anti-dumping duty is required to ensure the continued existence of at least certain of the remaining Community producers with the consequent benefits to the Community of employment, technological expertise and local source of supply.

Ironically, one EC official also tried to justify the Community's action against Japanese copier manufacturers on the grounds that 'producers of photocopiers like Agfa Gevaert, Kalle and Gestetner have been squeezed by cheap Japanese imports'.[6] Of these three companies, Kalle has always imported all of its machines from Japan, while Agfa and Gestetner's own products in the early 1980s were hopelessly uncompetitive and they, too, had for long relied on Japanese manufacturers for their equipment.

This was a point not lost on those defending the Japanese manufacturers during the Commission's investigation. The main instigator of the complaint, Rank Xerox, was in fact the prime culprit in this respect, importing Japanese-produced kits for all of its low-volume range, as well as many of its medium-volume machines. Yet the Commission accepted Rank Xerox's argument for lower or no duties on such re-labelled imports on the grounds that Rank Xerox had been obliged since the late 1970s to purchase the machines from its Japanese associate, Fuji Xerox, for 'self-defensive purposes'. The report went on to say that 'the ability to bring on to the market a product more quickly than by waiting for Community products to come on stream has enabled the company better to defend its overall position'.[7] It is surely a devastating indictment of Europe's largest copier producer that it should argue that it had found that the only way to beat the Japanese competition was itself to rely on Japanese equipment?

Olivetti of Italy and Dutch Océ were similarly leniently treated with regard to the large numbers of Japanese copiers which they imported to sell relabelled under their own names. The Commission concluded that both companies had attempted to develop fuller ranges of their own models, but were 'thwarted in their attempts to do so because of depressed market-prices set by Japanese imports'. The Commission accepted as evidence of these efforts management evaluations of products and a prototype model which had been scheduled for introduction to the market. I actually remember such prototypes. Year after year, as Japanese copier manufacturers displayed ever more impressive offerings on their stands at the Hanover Fair, a pathetic series of non-functioning 'prototypes' were on show at Olivetti's stand. What Olivetti was actually marketing, however, was machines made by Mita, Sharp and Canon. So a fine new principle appeared to have been established: namely that a Japanese machine selling under a Japanese brand caused injury, but not if the identical machine was sold under a European or American name.

In reaching this conclusion, the Commission argued thus: since the prices at which Olivetti and Océ resold such imports under their own names were in general higher than the prices charged by the manufacturers themselves when selling under their own names, so Océ and Olivetti could not have inflicted any dumping-related injury on themselves by their imports of these products. Amazingly, therefore, the Commission was prepared to accept that a European company importing Japanese copiers and selling them at inflated prices was somehow not guilty, while Japanese companies which actually made the machines and gave European consumers the benefit of fairer prices were culpable.

Hardly mentioned, or apparently even considered by the Commission, was the possibility that the real injury to the European copier industry was a self-inflicted one, caused by the succession of generally low-quality, over-priced European machines which had fallen easy prey to their more reliable, better marketed and more feature-rich Japanese rivals.

Who pays?

That the European Community's anti-dumping actions are inherently both unfair and protectionist has been recognized by almost every objective analyst. One study by the World Bank's Patrick Messerlin found that in the first year following the initiation of an anti-dumping investigation, imports of the affected products fell on average by 18 per cent. Messerlin also found that three or four years after the investigation had been opened, imported quantities of the relevant product had fallen by two-thirds in cases where anti-dumping measures were adopted.[8]

In a study for the London-based Royal Institute of International Affairs, Michael Davenport, a former senior economist at the EC Commission, emphasized the essential unfairness of the regulations by highlighting yet another way in which the system is slanted against importers. Where a product is sold at varying prices in different Community countries, he pointed out that those prices which lie above the domestic prices, and hence would reduce any dumping margin, are simply lowered to the domestic price before calculating the average Community-wide export price. 'Thus', he concludes, 'findings of huge dumping margins, 60 or 70 per cent or more, reflect the Commission methodology of calculating the dumping rather than the economic situation.' He goes on:

> Not only do the Community's rules overtly discriminate against foreign companies, but, in common with other import restraining measures, they

ignore the damage inflicted by anti-dumping duties on the users of imported products. Instead of encouraging competition, as intended, anti-dumping action seems to be frustrating it.[9]

This damaging effect on the Community as a whole is confirmed by another report, this time by Britain's consumer watchdog body, the National Consumer Council, which stated in a study issued early in 1990:

> The margins of dumping that have been calculated in several cases have far exceeded what is credible ... one suspects that in several cases protection is the true motive behind the attempt to prove dumping ... [moreover,] the measures have imposed a heavy burden on consumers, primarily – although not solely – in the form of higher prices. In terms of welfare, the loss to consumers from these measures generally exceeds any gain for Community producers.

The report estimates that anti-dumping duties add £181 to the cost of a photocopier, £74 to the price of a computer printer and £20 to that of a video recorder. The total annual cost to EC consumers of anti-dumping measures relating to electronic goods is put at £1,170 million – equivalent overall to slightly more than a five per cent price hike on consumer electronic products.[10] Messerlin sees a touch of irony in these increased price-levels. 'Anti-dumping actions', he says, 'appear to do what "predatory pricing" is supposed to do, ie a decrease in prices is followed by price increases in, now, more monopolistic markets.'

新　大　国

Consumers may have no right of appeal under the European Community regulations, but companies which fall victim to anti-dumping duties do have two possible forms of redress: the first is to appeal to GATT, on whose Anti-Dumping Code the EC's regulations are supposedly based. Unfortunately, the GATT code, being a document negotiated between the GATT signatories, with their widely differing interests, is very much the bottom line of agreement between them. It is not surprising, therefore, to find that its language is vague and elastic, with limited dispute-resolution mechanisms. The Commission, therefore, has been able to argue successfully that its own regulations fall within the broad GATT guidelines, making it difficult for the aggrieved to make much progress through GATT.

This problem is recognized by GATT officials. Late in 1989, GATT's director-general, Arthur Dunkel, warned that GATT's anti-dumping provisions were intended to protect domestic enterprises against 'predatory, as distinct from competitive, behavior by foreign producers'. He noted that during the course of the 1980s more than 1,000 anti-dumping investigations had been initiated by the EC, together with Australia, Canada and the United States, resulting in more than 500 cases of protective action. The

GATT leader also implicitly criticized the Community's methods of calculating relative domestic and export prices.[11] As a result of such concerns,
GATT proposed revisions to its Anti-Dumping Code late in 1989, revisions
which were rejected both by the European Community and the United
States in favour of their own draft changes which would make the GATT
code even less favourable to importers.

The European Court of Justice is, on the face of it, a more hopeful
institution for victims of anti-dumping duties. Certainly, the Japanese
manufacturers of miniature ball-bearings and electronic typewriters who
took their cases to the Court thought at least that they could expect some
fairness and objectivity from this legal institution. Nor were they disappointed in this respect, for the European Court certainly performed its task
of interpreting in an impartial way. The result was that it clearly sided with
the Commission in both cases, for the Commission had not strayed from
the letter of the regulations, although it had enforced them with the utmost
rigour. What the Court was not empowered to do, of course, was to say
whether or not those regulations were fair.

Screwdriver plants

One of the more immediate effects of the imposition of anti-dumping duties
on so many Japanese producers was to force them to set up or extend their
European plants, so as to ensure that their products qualified as European
and escaped the duties. By 1986, many Japanese companies, and particularly
copier manufacturers, already had factories in Europe. But as soon as the
rigorous nature of the Commission's anti-dumping campaign was realized,
there was a further flurry of announcements of new factories. In 1988 alone,
14 Japanese factories were set up to make dot-matrix printers. This, of
course, did nothing to help the large European companies which had been
behind the anti-dumping complaints in the first place, for they realized that
Japanese companies with a strong European manufacturing presence could
well become even stronger competitors. Indeed, by 1988, annual Japanese
copier production *in* Europe was scheduled to reach the total export volume
to Europe of previous years. The European makers, therefore, once again
lobbied the Commission to take action.

So in 1987, true to form, and driven by the argument that anti-dumping
duties were being circumvented by the so-called Japanese 'screwdriver'
assembly plants – that is, factories which supposedly imported so many of
their parts that the workers were left only with the task of 'screwdrivering'
them in – the Commission gave itself the power to extend anti-dumping
duties to certain EC production facilities. The new regulations – which were
later declared illegal by GATT – allowed it to proceed against EC-based
factories belonging to companies against which anti-dumping cases had
already been found, where 60 per cent or more of the components were
being imported from the 'dumping' country for assembly into final products
within the EC, and where local assembly had started or increased since the
duty had been imposed.

On the face of it, the 60 per cent rule sounds quite reasonable, until one
remembers that the total value of components often represents far less than

half of the end-value of a sophisticated piece of equipment. So the 60 per cent rule effectively meant that any product from a Japanese-owned EC factory with a final value which included only a small proportion of imported components could nonetheless be subject to anti-dumping duties. Put another way, a product with a very high total EC content, including some parts, labour, services and overheads, could nonetheless be counted as imported, so introducing a totally new basis for determining a product's country of origin. Furthermore, as the anti-dumping duties on components only applied to production facilities set up after the initial imposition of duties on the imported 'dumped' product, Rank Xerox, which assembled most of its low- and mid-range copiers predominantly from Japanese components, escaped scot-free and remained able to import Japanese kits and parts free of duty, putting it at a substantial competitive advantage over Japanese rivals.

Neither did the problems for Japanese manufacturers end there, however. For when they tried to increase the EC content of their products by purchasing locally made components, they immediately ran into cost and quality problems. Computer-printer manufacturer, Citizen, for example, which was for a time able to avoid the worst effects of the anti-dumping duties by bringing its new Scunthorpe plant on stream earlier than originally planned, was soon accused of running a 'screwdriver' operation, despite the fact that 45 per cent of the value of its output was of European origin. As Robin Marriott, Citizen's European marketing manufacturer, comments:

> We had intended by 1989 to have a 70 per cent to 80 per cent European content and be building printers to the same high standard and at the same low cost as the factory in Japan. But, when we went to potential European suppliers and asked them to deliver components with zero defects 'just in time', either they couldn't or it was going to cost too much.[12]

Epson also had difficulty in finding suitable plastic mouldings and pressed steel for the chassis of its computer printers; while copier manufacturer, Ricoh, said that up to a third of parts such as printed-circuit boards supplied to its British and French plants from European manufacturers were unsatisfactory.[13] And lest you think that these complaints about European quality and punctuality are just excuses from Japanese manufacturers who simply preferred to continue buying from Japanese suppliers, a report by top accountancy firm, Coopers & Lybrand, jointly funded by the British and Japanese Governments, backs up such criticisms.

The confidential report, which was produced in 1988 but never released, gives a detailed breakdown of component sourcing by Japanese companies operating in the UK. It found a low level of semiconductors, capacitors, resistors and switches being bought locally, which was in part offset by higher levels of purchases of television tubes, transformers, printed-circuit boards and metal parts.

But the core of the report dealt with the poor performance by UK suppliers. Quality in the case of consumer products was generally lower than in Japan, and prices ten to 20 per cent more than the components bought from Japan. Components for office products were possibly even more expensive, the report stated, because local suppliers seemed more used to less price-sensitive defence markets. On specific components, UK-sourced printed circuit boards were 20 to 50 per cent dearer than Far Eastern boards, with price differentials rising to 300 per cent in the case of complex boards. British-made transformers were 20 to 40 per cent more expensive than Far Eastern ones, although the high shipping costs of these heavy products made the price premium acceptable.

Japanese companies, the report went on, often had to search for British suppliers who, when contacted, frequently took several weeks to respond, compared to the few days expected by Japanese companies. British suppliers also often failed to meet delivery dates, which were quoted in weeks, whereas Japanese suppliers kept to their delivery dates which were quoted in days in keeping with the low stocking levels required for Japanese plants.

Moreover, the illogicality and contradictions inherent in trying to enforce rigid country of origin rules in industries which require inputs from all over the world, and the problems caused by setting up niggling import barriers in an increasingly global market place, were illustrated by the effect of the European content rules on circuit boards. For according to the US Semiconductor Industry Association, a Japanese printer-maker told its American chip supplier that to avoid dumping duties on its European-assembled printers, it must 'design out' American semiconductors so that circuit boards going into its printers would be counted as of EC origin.

'A rightful share of the market . . .'

Jan Timmer, the 56-year-old Philips veteran who was board member responsible for consumer electronics before heading the Dutch electronic giant, probably squirmed a little during his forensic interview with *Financial Times* journalists, Guy de Jonquieres and Laura Raun. Timmer had already run into difficulties early on in the interview when asked how Philips' cost reduction and efficiency programmes compared with those of their Japanese competitors. 'I don't know,' he had answered.

Philips, Europe's largest consumer electronics group, had been instrumental in getting the Commission to impose anti-dumping duties on many of its Japanese rivals' products, so inevitably the interview soon came round to that very topic. 'If pricing policies are not only a reflection of cost prices but have an additional aim, namely to gain market share, then the fight is more difficult,' said Timmer, in defence of action against 'dumping'. 'But that's a perfectly normal function of business, isn't it?', asked the interviewers. From there the questioning proceeded thus:

> *Timmer*: Yes, except when it reaches proportions that you could call dumping.
> Interviewers: *What do you call dumping?*
> *Timmer*: Well, it's clearly selling products in foreign markets substantially lower than what you do at home.
> Interviewers: *Do you sell products in the United States at the same price as you do in Europe?*

Timmer: In the United States market we have to adjust to what happens in the United States.

Interviewers: *So are you dumping?*

Timmer: No. We are not exporting from outside the United States to the United States in order to gain market share. Definitely not.

Interviewers: *But are you selling products in the United States at prices lower than in Europe?*

Timmer: The difference is where the products are made. If you take our United States business, our television sets that we sell in the United States are made in the United States. That makes the comparison invalid.

Interviewers: *What about compact disc machines? Do you make those in the United States?*

Timmer: We sell compact disc machines in some quantities in the States, yes.

Interviewers: *Made in Europe?*

Timmer: Made in Europe.

Interviewers: *Do you sell them for less in the United States than you do in Europe?*

Timmer: I don't know by heart what the prices are . . .'

Interviewers: *Isn't that dumping?*

Timmer: No.

Interviewers: *What's the difference?*

Timmer: It depends on what your aim is. If you want to say, I have a certain market-share today and I want to keep that market-share, that's different from developing a policy of deliberately gaining dominant market-share by price reductions.

Interviewers: *So you think everyone should settle for the market share they've got?*

Timmer: I don't know. I don't think so, because that would be anti-competitive.

As the interview proceeded, Timmer dug himself deeper and deeper into a trough of difficulty from which the only valid exit was an admission that he believed in import barriers to protect what he called Philips' 'rightful share of the market'. When the hapless executive was finally asked: 'If, due to currency fluctuations and due to relative changes in labour costs, you are thought to have a competitive disadvantage in Europe which does not provide a level playing field, then something should be done about it and ultimately that something should be protection?', he could only reply: 'Could be.'[14]

Jan Timmer's disarray exemplifies the confusion and inconsistencies which surround EC trade policies. For it is less a deep-seated and consistent anti-Japanese conspiracy which provides the impetus behind protectionist measures such as the anti-dumping policies, than piecemeal responses to pressure from powerful industrial groups like Philips. That Philips, like many other European companies, is simply pursuing a policy of pure self-interest in urging more protection is made clear by the fact that although Philips is more than willing to exploit low-cost Asian production facilities where it can – indeed, Philips' involvement in East Asia comprises 25 plants and 27,000 employees in eight countries, including Japan – the Dutch company was nonetheless itself closely involved in France's notorious decision to route all Japanese video-recorder imports through a remote customs post in Poitiers in 1981.

This was just part of an overall strategy designed to hinder its Japanese rivals, for, after failing to make a success of its own V2000 VCR standard, which was beaten in the market-place by the Japanese VHS system, Philips also played a leading role in persuading the EC to secure temporary quotas on Japanese VCR exports in the early 1980s. The Dutch multinational likewise succeeded in persuading the Community to impose a special 'infant industry' import tariff on compact-disc players shortly afterwards. Needless to say, Philips has also been in the forefront of many of the anti-dumping actions against Far Eastern electronics imports.

So although it would be tempting to regard the way in which the Community's anti-dumping regulations have been drawn up and enforced as part of a deep-seated master plan to protect European industry and scupper the Japanese, it is more realistic to view these protectionist actions as a series of only semi-co-ordinated responses to pressures from large European industrial interests which have largely failed to match up to fierce Japanese competition.

This is reinforced, however, by the fact that there are certainly many within the Community political and bureaucratic establishment, as well as at national government level, who consider the success of the Japanese to have been unfairly won, and to be a grave threat to Western civilization. Such people regard the use of almost any weapon to counter this threat as legitimate.

Others see what they consider to be mildly protectionist measures as a means of forcing the Japanese to invest in factories within Europe, thus creating employment and spreading their good practices into the European industrial scene. Sometimes this approach is less than subtle. For example, a 'screwdriver' investigation into Ricoh's French copier factory was closed in February 1990 soon after the Japanese company unveiled plans to build a further factory in France to produce thermal paper for fax machines. This does not add up to an anti-Japanese conspiracy, attractive though such theories may be. But attitudes such as these provide fertile ground for European industries' special pleading for protection against their Japanese competitors – at the expense of their customers.

European industrialists are, moreover, adept at masking their own special pleading with the glossy veneer of a higher purpose. Speaking at an electronics conference in London in the spring of 1989, for example, Mr Caillot, Chairman of the French Electronics Industry Association and President of the French electronics firm, Thomson, called for new and tougher ground rules on pricing, dumping and product origins, along with yet more protection against 'screwdriver plants', in order to secure what he called 'Europe's political, economic, cultural and social freedoms'.

But such cultural sensitivies do not prevent the European electronics industry from locating factories outside the European Community, if they feel they can gain advantage by doing so. Indeed, a large part of the increase in colour TV imports complained of during an anti-dumping investigation initiated by the European Association of Consumer Electronic Manufacturers actually came from plants which they themselves owned in Singapore and Taiwan. Yet it was not these European-owned Asian plants, but South Korean manufacturers who were penalized by anti-dumping duties.

As a result, European companies can bring in as many low-cost TVs from their Asian factories as they want, while Korean producers have to pay high duties. Likewise, anti-dumping duties on components mean that foreign-owned EC factories have to source a high proportion of their parts from within the EC, while their European rivals continue to buy in massive quantities of non-EC components. This may well result in absurd cases where Japanese manufacturers cannot use parts they themselves make outside the Community, while their European rivals can.

The benefits of hamstrung competition and higher prices to the European industrial lobbies which have been so successful in getting anti-dumping duties imposed on their East Asian industrial rivals are obvious. As with any form of protection, however, such advantages are only likely to be of a very short-term nature. The danger is that if people are genuinely convinced that the Japanese and others have succeeded by dumping products on the EC market, they may not realize that the real problem lies with European industry itself, and so the motivation for industrial reform within Europe will become less urgent. Thus, although the draughtsmen, architects and masons of the Commission may genuinely believe that in erecting 'Fortress Europe' they are helping European industry, in reality, they are simply locking it into a high-cost, low-productivity, uncompetitive 'Ghetto Europe'.

Part VII

Japan as Number One – The New Masters

ACCORDING TO THE Tokai Bank, Japan's sixth largest, another earthquake of the magnitude of the great Kanto earthquake of 1923 – which many people in Tokyo view as inevitable – would severely disrupt the world economy. By wiping out property and goods equivalent to nearly a quarter of Japan's GNP, such an earthquake would reduce world output, while the reconstruction would force Japan to consume vast amounts of capital at home instead of continuing to invest it in the United States. That in turn would place strong downward pressure on American bond markets, send American interest rates soaring and cause global stagnation.

That an earthquake in Japan could have such a dramatic knock-on effect upon the international economy is a mark of the country's new position in the world. Today, Japan is the world's largest creditor nation while the country's GNP per person is higher than that of the United States. Each Japanese person has three times as many assets by value as each American, four times as many as each West German and five times as many as each Briton. And the Tokyo metropolitan area alone produces more goods and services than the GNP of either Italy or Britain.

Japan's economic power and influence now manifests itself in a variety of ways. In August 1987, the American bank which first provided financing to rebuild Japan's war-ravaged economy, the Bank of America, had itself to be rescued by nine Japanese banks. Two months on, it was the power of Japanese money that largely prevented a potentially disastrous stock-market collapse after Black Monday. And when the Anglo–French Channel tunnel project ran into trouble in 1990, it was to the Japanese Prime Minister that Margaret Thatcher wrote in the hope that he would prevail on Japanese banks to come up with extra funding.

At a more mundane level, a left-wing London local government council felt it advisable to kowtow to the new masters. Lambeth council, more used to twinning with towns in Nicaragua, decided to link up with the prosperous Tokyo suburb of Shinjuku. They even proposed to erect a bronze bust in honour of a Japanese writer, Kinnosuke Natsume, who spent a few months in the borough at the beginning of the century during which he developed a marked dislike for England and the English.

At the heart of Japan's economic success is the phenomenon of her manufacturing industry. In 1960, Japan only accounted for 1.8 per cent of the world's production, compared now to about a tenth of total global output. The 500-kilometre-long belt between Tokyo and Kobe, which is responsible for three-quarters of Japan's production, represents the greatest concentration of industrial power the world has ever seen. Japanese cars and electrical goods, which were derided as shoddy, cheap and low-tech only 20 years ago, are world leaders.

Paralleling Japan's rise from the ashes of the last War has been the decline of the United States. Japan's massive build-up of trade surpluses and overseas assets has corresponded with the United States' accumulation of huge deficits and her degeneration from being the largest creditor nation in 1980 to the world's biggest debtor – a reversal of roles which has caused tensions as Americans find it hard to come to terms with the fact that they have been overtaken by their former pupil.

Of course, despite Japan's present strength, she, too, will in turn decline. Although the endurance of a power on the rise, or even at its pinnacle, seems almost indefinite, the sands of the world's economy and power structures are continually shifting. In the late 1950s, long before commentators cottoned on to Japan's steady ascendance to economic superpower status, the received wisdom among many was that the Soviet Union, with her then rapid economic growth and the supposed advantages of a closely planned and centrally controlled economy, would overtake the United States in output by the end of the century. Few then foresaw that, by the late 1980s, the USSR would be effectively bankrupt, her citizens suffering from a falling life expectancy and eating less per head than they did under the Tsar in 1915.

By the late 1960s, the United States was the pundits' favourite, and, again, not many predicted her precipitous decline. In the same way, although Japan seems all-conquering now, factors are already at work which will almost inevitably lead to her relative decay. These considerations include steady changes in the attitudes of the Japanese; increasing domestic consumption; and the apparent beginning of the end of the very high levels of post-War social cohesion which have been such a significant factor in Japan's economic success. The ageing of Japan's population may also reduce high levels of savings, divert resources from production into welfare spending and reverse the growth of the labour force, all of which will damage the country's economic position.

Then there are the rapidly growing economies of East Asia, locked with Japan in a relationship that is at once mutually beneficial and intensely competitive. To date, Japan has profited greatly from her near economic hegemony in the region, but if her industries ever relax, those of the newly-industrialized countries – South Korea, Taiwan, Singapore and Hong Kong – will pounce.

In the meantime, the Japanese are attempting to slow down a little to enjoy the fruits of their frantically built success and are enjoying their new status – but not without some accompanying problems and responsibilities.

One such difficulty has been the fact that Japan's industry has had to adapt rapidly to the strength of the yen which has reduced export competitiveness. However, as with previous economic shocks, Japan's businesses are already surfacing from this crisis stronger than before, leaving Japan economically supreme at the hub of the world's fastest-growing and most productive region.

21

新
大
国

YEN SHOCK

'The yen's rise may actually be a blessing in disguise. It means that changes that would have taken decades to accomplish will be carried out within ten years at the most.'
Professor Hiroyuki Itami, Hitotsubashi University.[1]

WHEN, IN FEBRUARY 1989, American television news superstars like Dan Rather accompanied President George Bush to Emperor Hirohito's funeral *en masse*, it was obvious to even the most blinkered observer of world events that Japan had 'arrived'. American and European newspapers were full of analyses of Japan's growing influence and its implications; television networks all over the world sourced their evening bulletins from Tokyo; while CBS devoted considerably more time to the imperial funeral than it did to the coverage of President Bush's inauguration.

Nor did the coverage dwell as in the past on the quainter aspects of Japanese life such as *geishas*, tea ceremonies and masochistic game shows. Instead, emphasis was placed on how the United States should come to terms with a country which had decisively won the competitive battle and was busily buying up huge tracts of America itself.

By the time of Hirohito's death, Japan's economic strength amounted to accumulated current account surpluses in excess of $400 billion and around $500 billion in net external assets, forecast to rise to $2 trillion soon after the turn of the century. Japan's major corporations by then also dominated many of the world's major industries, while nine out of the world's ten largest banks and the top-billing advertising agency were all Japanese. Furthermore, the Japanese stock market had given such a strong performance in the six months following the October 1987 Crash, that by April of the following year it represented nearly 44 per cent of the total value of the global market, while that of the United States had slipped to less than a third.[2] Nomura Securities alone had a capitalization more than twice that of Ford or General Electric, while the market value of telephone operator NTT was two-thirds that of the entire United Kingdom's annual GNP.

So far had Japan come, in fact, that, by the end of the 1980s, many Americans feared that Japan's trading relationship with the United States was approaching that of pre-War colonial masters to their possessions: for while it seemed that America supplied largely agricultural products and raw materials to Japan's superior industrial machine, the Japanese in return exported high-value manufactured goods and capital to the United States.

Needless to say, such a dramatic turnaround has resulted in a certain amount of friction and rancour. Not far from the surface of much reporting on Japan lies a definite strata of resentment at her success which is reflected in United States public opinion as a whole. According to a *Washington Post/ABC News* poll in February 1989, for example, more than 40 per cent of Americans considered Japan's economic strength to be a greater threat to United States security than Soviet military power.[3]

The speed with which Japanese interests have been purchasing large chunks of corporate America has also touched raw nerves in a country which increasingly holds Japan responsible for the decline in its own economic pre-eminence, especially as among Japanese industry's acquisitions are some of America's best known names, including CBS Records, Firestone, Intercontinental Hotels and Columbia Pictures – this last being described by *Newsweek* as 'buying America's soul'.

Nor is the body escaping, for the Japanese are also buying up America itself, particularly prime real estate in downtown Los Angeles, where nearly half the commercial property is now owned by foreigners – predominantly Japanese. Approximately a third of the offices, shops and hotels in Houston and Washington DC are similarly owned by outsiders, but perhaps the most potent symbol of the relative change in the positions of Japan and America was the sale to Mitsubishi Estate in 1989 of the epitome of American capitalism, a group of mid-Manhattan skyscrapers including the Rockefeller Center. In Hawaii, Japanese interests are now investing at the rate of $1 billion a year – or $1,000 for every inhabitant of the island. So great is their influence that in June 1988 the Mayor of Honolulu went to Tokyo to complain that Japanese buyers were driving up real estate prices in his city to impossible levels. 'A Japanese has been driving around Honolulu in a white limousine looking for houses,' he told the Tokyo press. 'In six months he bought 160 of them . . . and in February a Japanese real estate agent sold to another Japanese for $930,000 a house which he had bought only two months earlier for $664,000.' According to the mayor, an 11-year-old non-Japanese resident had plaintively written to him asking: 'Where are we going to live when we are grown-ups?'[4]

But it is not only the displaced Americans who are concerned. Australians also resent the purchase of houses by elderly Japanese buyers, particularly in Queensland where many old soldiers still live on small farms. Official signs on the Great Barrier Reef are often now in two languages – English and Japanese – and in 1988, an Australian Cabinet Minister told a *Financial Times* reporter, not entirely in jest, that in due course the Japanese will probably buy Australia and turn it into a theme park.

A Japanese-commissioned survey of Australian attitudes in April of the same year showed that 75 per cent of respondents were cool towards more Japanese investment, while 36 per cent favoured less. Only 17 per cent of respondents welcomed more investment, while those in areas where the Japanese have concentrated their money were even less welcoming. A total of 80 per cent of those questioned in New South Wales, and 86 per cent in Queensland, said that Japanese investment should either be decreased or kept at current levels.

Endaka

If there was a moment when Japan actually overtook the United States to become the world's premier economic power, it probably occurred on a balmy late summer day in September 1985 when the world's leading finance ministers, the so-called 'Group of Five' (G5), met in the wood-panelled splendour of New York's Plaza Hotel and agreed on a concerted action to reduce the value of the dollar and to push up the yen. Many people at that time felt that the yen was under-priced, so the idea was to make Japanese exports less competitive and ease Western imports into her market. It worked – at least in part. Over the next two years, the yen appreciated massively against the American dollar. Whereas at the beginning of 1985 each dollar bought ¥262, by the end of 1987, the dollar was only worth ¥120.

The problem was not, however, simply one of yen under-valuation. There was certainly some truth in the widespread belief that the Japanese policies of low government spending and encouragement of savings had kept inflation and therefore interest rates low, thus making the currency less attractive to investors, so depressing its value and making Japanese exports cheaper.

But at least as important a factor was the over-valuation of the dollar – and not just against the yen. Between 1980 and March 1985, the dollar's overall international value against all of the major currencies had increased by 63 per cent. This was largely caused by excessive United States government spending, leading to high interest rates which had in turn encouraged investors to buy the dollar to finance federal debt. But this combination of United States budget deficits, high interest rates and an over-valued currency had become very unstable by 1985. The international currency markets would almost certainly have adjusted by pushing the value of the yen up (indeed, the dollar had already begun to slip early in 1985). But by agreeing to make their national central banks buy yen and sell dollars in a co-ordinated manner, the so-called 'Plaza Accord', the finance ministers were sending out a signal to international investors and accelerating the dollar's inevitable decline.

The politicians who precipitated the decline in the dollar and the massive appreciation in the yen confidently expected that it would diminish Japan's competitiveness to the extent that her surpluses would be significantly reduced. In the process, both Japanese and Western observers agreed that Japan's industry would suffer – and they were initially proved right. Japanese output, which had been growing at a rate of 11 per cent a year at the beginning of 1985, had totally stagnated by the end of the year, and, by 1986, Japan's growth rate was a mere 2.5 per cent.

That year, profits at Sony and Hitachi slumped by more than 40 per cent and Nissan made its first loss since 1951. In the two years after the Plaza Accord, 400,000 jobs were lost in Japanese industry, which pushed the unemployment rate up to a record 3.2 per cent. Steel alone cast off 40,000 workers, and it was commonly expected that another half a million manufacturing jobs would disappear by 1995. Hitachi Zosen, one of the country's leading shipbuilders, announced plans to reduce its workforce from 17,000 to 7,000, while Ishikawajima Harima Heavy Industries, another shipbuilder and heavy machinery manufacturer, decided to reduce its 23,000 workforce by nearly a third at the end of 1986.

Even worse, the majority of Japan's fiercest and most efficient competitors in East Asia managed to keep their currencies largely pegged to the dollar. As a consequence, in the year following, imports to Japan of manufactures and components from South Korea trebled to $620 million, while Taiwan doubled its sales to Japan to $407 million. The yen shock, or *endaka fukyo* as it became known, was in many ways similar to the Nixon and oil shocks of the previous decade. And as previously, Japan's industry acted rapidly and effectively to adapt to the dramatically changed conditions of the late 1980s, taking a number of steps to adjust to the strong-yen environment. It diversified and upgraded its products, incorporating greater added value as well as minimizing costs at all levels, often by importing more parts, while increasing capital investment to improve efficiency. But most visibly, from the point of view of the rest of the world, it drastically stepped up its overseas investment.

Going offshore

Near Marysville, in rural Ohio, the Stars and Stripes flaps outside a cavernous factory where 5,000 Americans make motor cycles and cars for the fourth largest United States auto manufacturer – Honda. Nearby, the Japanese company is investing nearly $380 million in a new plant at East Liberty, and by 1991 the two factories will be able to produce half a million cars a year. Elsewhere in the United States, Nissan, Toyota, Mazda, Subaru, Suzuki, Isuzu and Mitsubishi will be producing more than two million cars and light trucks a year by the early 1990s – twice as many vehicles as they turned out in 1989 – while, as further symbols of the new invasion, Japanese shopping centres are springing up all over North America.

Neither is it only Japan's large corporations which are going offshore. Even small firms have moved their operations abroad, like the Yokohama-based Tokai Corporation, a disposable-lighter maker with fewer than 800 employees; and the quality photo-album maker, Kambara and Co, a firm with only 150 employees, which took the decision to build a plant in Oregon after four price rises in rapid succession wiped out the company's export margins.

As a result, in 1987, Japanese capital investment in the United States surged by 143 per cent to reach $196 billion, displacing Britain as the biggest annual net investor in America and more than doubling Japan's share of foreign investment in the United States to 35.7 per cent. Japanese money flowed in a similar fashion into other Western economies and, by 1987, according to *Australian Business* magazine, five of Australia's top ten exporters were Japanese, with Mitsui Australia leading the field.

Of course, overseas investment was nothing new for the Japanese. Honda had started making motor cycles in America back in 1979, moving on to cars in 1982. In fact, since way back in 1968 Japan's overseas investment has been growing faster than that of any other country. But it was the scale and type of investment that had changed. In the 1960s and early 1970s, Japan had largely exported jobs in labour-intensive industries to low wage-cost economies, mainly in South East Asia; then, following the 1973 oil crisis, Japan recognized that she had to free itself from dependence on distant sources of raw materials. One way of doing that was to manufacture more products overseas, as well as taking control of some of the sources of essential commodities.

So Japanese trading companies bought up American farmland; Australian coal, uranium and iron ore deposits; Alaskan timber, pulp, gas and fisheries interests; together with Canadian copper mines, timber reserves and oil refineries – not always successfully. The mighty Ataka Trading Company, once the tenth largest *sogoshosha*, went broke largely because of an ill-advised oil refinery investment. As the 1970s wore on, however, the emphasis shifted to overseas investment in manufacturing and assembly plants, with the electronics and vehicle manufacturers leading the way. Sony was the trail-blazer with its TV plant in South Wales in June 1974, followed by Matsushita two years later.

After the G5 Plaza Accord, the volume of Japanese investment going to Europe and the United States increased dramatically and the United States overhauled Asia as the favourite destination for corporate Japan's new wealth. America now accounts for around a half of all new Japanese investment, followed by Europe with about a fifth and Latin America and Asia with close to 15 per cent each. Of the European countries, Japanese manufacturers prefer the United Kingdom ahead of West Germany and France, because English is popular with Japanese businesspeople and also because of the improved UK business climate. But when it comes to making higher-tech electronics and telecommunications goods, firms such as Matsushita and Canon generally choose the superior engineering skills of West Germany. This is why the producers of sophisticated application-specific integrated circuits (ASICs) have focused their European operations on West Germany.

Moreover, while in 1980 Japanese outlays on foreign investment were just $4.6 billion, by the end of the decade the figure had topped $50 billion. The result of this torrid period of overseas investment was that by the end of the 1980s, Sony had raised the proportion of its output produced abroad from around a quarter at the time of the Plaza Accord, to nearly 40 per cent; while NEC, the world's largest chip maker and a major producer of telecommunications, computers and consumer electronics, was producing two-thirds of its American sales locally by 1990. Over the same period, Japan's second largest vehicle maker, Nissan, tripled overseas production of cars to 650,000 – about a third of total sales; and by 1992, construction-equipment maker, Komatsu, aims to increase its overseas production from 7.5 per cent of output in 1987 to 35 per cent.

On top of new, green field plants, Japanese manufacturers have also stepped up mergers and takeovers of foreign companies. According to Daiwa Securities, the number of such deals soared from 31 in 1985 to 94 in 1988. Among the famous Western names to succumb to the mighty yen's shopping spree were CBS Records and Columbia Pictures, both snapped up by Sony; Sumitomo's acquisition of Dunlop's worldwide tyre businesses; Firestone's sale to Bridgestone; and the purchase of the Intercontinental Hotel chain by Seibu Saison. Service industries have also followed Japanese manufacturers overseas. Nomura, the Japanese stockbroker, increased its staff in London by 100 a year between 1984 and 1988, while Yamaichi, Nikko and Daiwa all upped their London staffing by between 50 and 200 per cent over the same period.

Learning to live with the yen

During a visit to the NEC plant at Abiko early in 1988, Giro Okuda, the vice president of NEC, told me:

> Sure, we will have to make more of our products offshore but that is not the whole story by any means. Overseas production is still often more expensive for us, despite the increase in the yen's value, because offshore factories tend to be smaller – though they do allow us to internationalize our operations and hedge our bets. But above all, we have to improve our competitive edge by becoming more efficient, diversifying, increasing our technological lead by more research and development and, yes, maybe accepting lower profits for a while.

This was exactly what much of Japanese industry did in response to the higher yen – and not just huge corporations like NEC. Japan's small- and medium-sized companies, employing up to 300 people, account for more than half of the country's manufacturing output and provide 81 per cent of the nation's jobs. Takako Industries is just such a company. Specializing in high-pressure valve parts, Takako was founded in 1973 by Yoshikimi Ishizaki who, at the age of 29, left a safe job at a large engineering company to start his own business with the equivalent of £5,000 in capital.

Ishizaki worked tirelessly to perfect a radical improvement in cold-forging, a technique in which components are stamped out of unheated steel. As a result, Takako can make a wishbone-shaped gearbox component for Honda for only ¥80, compared to a cost of ¥350 for the standard production method involving hot-forging and milling. After the yen shock, Takako had to lower its prices by 25 to 30 per cent, but the company's technology and low costs allowed it to win new business, increasing turnover and maintaining margins.[5]

Likewise, Japan's machine-tool industry, which in theory should have suffered as a result of the high yen, instead watched its orders soar by 44 per cent in 1988 as Japanese industry invested in efficiency boosting plant or equipment. Even export orders overcame the disadvantages caused by the rise in the yen's value and went up by 28 per cent. This was possible in part because many Japanese suppliers managed to absorb the revaluation of the yen and maintain their selling prices on account of the high levels of efficiency. Mori Seiki's factory at Iga, for example, has 330 automated machine tools and 28 automatic-guided vehicles as well as a wide range of robots.

As during earlier periods of shock and rapid change, Japanese industry's highly motivated and educated labour force played a crucial role. At the electronics giant Sharp, for example, the company asked the employees to come up with suggestions to reduce both material and energy costs by 30 per cent in order to prevent staff lay-offs. 30,000 suggestions were forthcoming, resulting in savings ranging from replacing several smaller-capacity chips in some equipment with a single larger-capacity one, to more mundane measures such as reducing the length of wiring used in TV sets by half.

As a result of such efficiency, the Nomura Research Institute, the research body of Japan's largest stockbroker, announced that most Japanese companies could remain profitable if the dollar stayed at the ¥127 level, while Matsushita could even make profits if the dollar reached ¥105. This was why Japan's economy quickly emerged from its high-yen induced slump and grew by 5.7 per cent in 1988, the fastest rate for 15 years.

That year, Toyota regained its place as Japan's most profitable company by posting annual profits of more than ¥500 billion (£2 billion), up sharply from the year before,[6] while overall, corporate profits among larger Japanese firms rose by 22 per cent in 1987 and a further 24 per cent in 1988. Unemployment also fell from 3.2 to 2.4 per cent and the *Nihon Keizai Shimbun*, Japan's leading business newspaper, was able to report a survey of more than 1,000 companies which showed that Japan's industry confidently expected a further growth in profits. Furthermore, Japan was enjoying its biggest ever stock-market boom as the Nikkei index streaked away from its pre-October 1987 Crash high of 26,460 to reach a 1989 peak of 35,140.

By the first quarter of 1989, Japan's GNP was growing at a breathtaking 9.1 per cent a year, close to its average rate in the boom years of the 1950s and 1960s. Most observers expected that Japan's service industries would be the main beneficiaries of such rapid domestic expansion. Certainly, the sector became more attractive to Japan's industry, as dramatically illustrated by Sony's acquisition of both CBS Records and Columbia Pictures in the United States. But, to everyone's surprise, it was the great manufacturing companies which vied with each other in the scale of their investments announcements. Fujitsu disclosed that it would spend ¥200 billion (£900 million) on new plants in 1989 – a 30 per cent increase over the previous year; Sharp bumped up its plant and equipment spending by more than a quarter, to ¥91 billion (£420 million); while NEC's investment in new capital equipment was scheduled to rise by 13 per cent to around ¥260 billion (£1.2 billion). Between them, Japan's leading electronics firms announced plans for spending a colossal ¥600 billion (£2.7 billion) on new semiconductor lines alone.

All in all, it represented the biggest capital spending boom in 15 years.

The net result was that Japan enjoyed its longest sustained period of economic expansion since the 1960s, when the so-called *Izanagi* boom had continued for 57 months. Japan's industry had come to terms with the high-value yen with startling rapidity.

Boom time

By then, Yusuke Kashiwagi, chairman of the Bank of Tokyo, could afford to be a little confident, not to say blasé, about his country's economic prospects: 'We are not going to scream whenever the yen appreciates against the dollar,' he told a reporter, before pointing out that Japan had not only learned to live with the high yen because industry had been flexible, cut costs and moved production offshore, but also because the government had helped to boost domestic demand.

In 1986 the Japanese government, as during previous economic crises, decided to help industry by spending its way out of the recession. This was also partly a response to pressure from the United States, which was keen to see domestic demand boosted in Japan to increase American exports.

In order to encourage consumer spending, tax breaks on *maruyu* Post Office savings accounts were ended and income tax on low-earners was cut by raising the tax threshold from ¥500,000 (£2,200) to ¥1.5 million (£5,600) a year. In May 1986, as a result of the yen's appreciation and the fall in the price of oil, the government also approved the return of ¥1,085.9 billion (£4.5 billion) to gas and electricity consumers and adopted an emergency package which extended financial relief to smaller firms hardest hit by the appreciation of the yen.

Largest of the reflation measures was the May 1987 ¥6,000-billion (£26 billion) economic package, which helped fuel a housing boom that pushed new house starts up from 1.2 million in 1986 to 1.7 million in 1987 – twice the per capita level of the United States. Symbolizing the switch to domestic demand, record profits were made by Japan's consumer credit groups, which revelled in the new affluence and the liberalized credit market. Profits at Nippon Shimpan, Japan's largest consumer credit group, rose to a record $104 million in the second half of 1988, and credit card sales surged by a third.

With vehicle sales in the domestic market topping six million for the first time ever in 1987, Japan's auto makers turned some of their attention away from export markets and squared up for a hard pitched battle on the home front. A particularly vicious scrap for third place behind Toyota and Nissan arose between Honda and Mitsubishi. In an all-out effort to take the prize, Honda opened 200 new dealerships and hired 1,800 extra salespeople in 1988, while Mitsubishi, which had pipped Honda for third place in 1987, upped its domestic sales target to 620,000 units.[7]

This boost in home demand was to a large extent successful in placing the Japanese economy on a more domestic footing. So, whereas in 1983 Japan's GNP growth was equally stimulated by overseas and domestic demand, by 1987 it was the latter which clearly led the economy, also boosting imports which rose by 16.5 per cent in volume in 1988. The United States was not the main beneficiary, however. In the first three-quarters of 1987, imports to Japan from Taiwan, South Korea and Hong Kong soared by more than 70 per cent and from Europe by nearly 30 per cent, while American sales were only level-pegging in dollar terms. Rather than buying computers and semiconductors from the United States, Japanese customers were buying European luxury goods as well as TVs, components and sub-assemblies from the newly-industrialized countries of Asia.

The marketing strategy of many Western companies which targeted their products at the high-price end of the market and refused to cut prices when the yen appreciated was in part responsible. This, combined with the fact that Japanese retailers also feared that lower prices would hurt the products' prestige, and the attitude of importers and distributors who just hung on to fatter margins, meant that at first few of the price advantages were passed on to consumers and sales of imported Western products failed to rise as rapidly as had been hoped.

According to Midori Tanni, the deputy director general of MITI's price policy division, the failure of the United States to make more inroads also lay in the fact that: 'American companies don't really want to sell to Japan. Americans may like big products, but the Japanese do not, because their houses are much smaller.'8 Hirohiko Okumura, the chief economist at the Nomura Research Institute, based in Tokyo's cramped Edobashi financial district, joined her in placing some of the blame on America itself. Okumura admitted to me that Japan still had some way to go to gear the economy more to domestic demand, but went on to say:

Unfortunately, most of the United States' huge borrowing has gone into consumption, not production, so others, especially the NICs, are benefiting from our growing domestic market.

The United States thought that the Plaza Accord would make life difficult for Japanese industry and solve America's problems, but in some ways it just confirmed them. There is no doubt, for example, that the high yen is allowing Japanese companies to buy more American assets, which is merely strengthening the global position of Japanese industry.

Even more galling for Japan's Western critics who expected the yen appreciation to cut her exports down to size, was the fact that the overseas sales of Japanese industries stubbornly continued to rise. Pioneer Electronics, a leading audio group, reported that its export sales grew by six per cent in 1988, thanks largely to 'favourable improvements in sales of audio products in North America'. Office equipment and camera maker, Ricoh, confirmed its exports were up 36 per cent in the year ending March 1988, while musical instruments and motor cycle group, Yamaha, also reported a 36 per cent rise in exports of its electronic keyboards.

The surprising resurgence of Japanese exports was in part due to inflationary policies in Western countries, particularly the United States, which had not sorted out its own internal problems, such as its low savings ratio and budgetary imbalances, and so continued to suck in imports. But in addition, in many industries, Japanese manufacturers had achieved such levels of quality and sophistication in their products that consumers remained willing to buy them despite higher prices. In some cases, such as the hugely successful laser printers, there were virtually no alternative sources of supply.

What is more, although Japan's exports only grew by four per cent overall in 1988, compared to a rise of four times that amount in import volumes, two further factors ensured that Japan's trade surplus by 1989 remained as obstinately huge at $72 billion as the United States' deficit, which then still stood at $125 billion. First, a rise in a currency's value often actually increases trade surpluses in the short- and medium-term, for although a higher currency usually means a country imports more, those imports are cheaper while exports are worth more, so the trade surplus remains in cash terms. This is known to economists as the 'J-curve' effect, whereby the balance of trade gets worse before it gets better. Second, because imports were starting from a much lower base, their growth would have to outpace exports for many years before making much impact. These factors, combined with the relative failure of American, and to a lesser extent European, industry to take advantage of the export opportunities afforded by the higher yen, ensured that neither Japan's surplus nor the United States' deficit showed much sign of budging by the end of the 1980s.

Needless to say, this caused more than a little resentment in the United States. Prime Minister Takeshita tried to emphasize the efforts being made by his country during his three-day visit to Washington in January 1988. These, he told the sceptical Americans, included an expansionist fiscal stance, lower income taxes, a reduction in tax incentives for savers, together with increases in defence spending and in Japan's contribution to the cost of keeping American forces in Japan. They also embraced a rise in the overseas aid budget and a partial liberalization of the agricultural market. MITI, he said, had even encouraged the purchase of overseas goods by asking 302 trading companies and manufacturers to increase their imports by a fifth.

However, this did not cut much ice in America, which was still suffering from a huge trade gap, and mutual misunderstanding only increased. For while, on the one hand, Americans, confused and angry by their relative decline, sought comfort in asserting that Japan was continuing to play the game by her own unfair rules; on the other, the Japanese were stung by what they saw as American reluctance to give them credit for their own, genuine achievements and for the efforts which they had made to help importers by effectively making their own industry less competitive.

So while a 1988 survey of Japanese junior high school students named the United States as the nation Japan would be most likely to fight in a war, former Trade Minister, Sadonori Yamanaka, angrily warned:

> A cornered mouse may bite at a cat. Japan is a sovereign nation, and it is possible that Japan will bite at the United States when Japan can no longer endure the high-handed United States demands that are imposed on us one after the other.

Days later, 200 farmers hurled American oranges and cigarettes into a bonfire lit under a portrait of President Ronald Reagan, while a Japanese agricultural group announced details of plans to switch 20 per cent of its

United States grain purchases to other countries as a protest against American demands on the Japanese. As the 1980s moved into its last quarter, it was becoming increasingly obvious that the Plaza Accord had done little to alter the fundamental strengths and weaknesses underlying the Japanese and Western economies respectively – if anything, it had only emphasized Japan's dominance.

22

新大国

SUCCESS ... AND ITS PROBLEMS

'*Lo, all our pomp of yesterday,*
Is one with Nineveh and Tyre.'
Rudyard Kipling, *Recessional*, 1899.

GIFT-GIVING IS IMPORTANT in Japan. But in recent years, and as a mark of their new-found affluence, in addition to the two traditional Japanese gift-giving seasons of *O-seibo* and *O-chugen*, many Japanese have also latched on to Christmas as a good opportunity for swapping presents and holding parties, even though in Japan 25 December is a normal working day.

In the past, Japanese gifts have typically consisted of beautifully wrapped items of food, such as seaweed or green tea. Thanks to the country's increasing wealth, however, Tokyo's department stores and supermarkets are now displaying the types of gift which would make the average Nieman Marcus regular feel very much at home. These days, Tokyo and Osaka shoppers are just as likely to buy gift packs of prize-winning beef at ¥100,000 (£425) a kilo, or imported luxury foods from Europe. Major department stores also saw sales of top-end jewellery rise by 15 to 20 per cent in 1987, while imports of art treasures grew by 180 per cent and auctioneer, Christies, reported that a third of all sales by value were going to Japanese buyers.[1] Even TV game shows now cater for Japan's growing, affluent class. One, called 'The Shopping Game', recently offered London taxis, a Rodin sculpture and a Loire valley chateau.

My own personal moment of truth came when a young Japanese reporter asked me, 'Is Dennis Thatcher rich?' during an interview which was supposed to be on the British Prime Minister, rather than her husband. 'I suppose so', I replied, 'he's probably worth more than £1 million'. 'Oh,' she said with just a touch of snootiness, 'that's not really considered very rich in Japan nowadays.' A few days earlier, Japanese housewives' purchases of West German shares in the last days of 1989 had prompted one of the largest ever rises in German stock indices, dubbed *Japanische Kaufwut* (*Japanese buying frenzy*) by the *Frankfurter Rundshau*; and not long afterwards, paper industry magnate, Ryoei Saito, who is reputed to be worth $2 billion, paid $82.5 million for Van Gogh's portrait of Dr Gachet, the highest price ever paid at an auction for a painting.

The dramatic increase in overseas travel by the Japanese is further evidence of the new prosperity. Although encouraged to stay at home to conserve foreign exchange until relatively recently, the Japanese can now be found everywhere, from Australia's Gold Coast to the beaches of California, from the leafy boulevards of Paris to Central Asia's Silk Road. The number of Japanese tourists going overseas rose by more than 23 per cent to a record 6.8 million between 1986 and 1987; since then, the tourist boom has come closer to an explosion, leading to a deficit on tourism and travel of more than $10 billion.

Japanese tourists now also rank among the big spenders. By 1986, Japanese holiday-makers were spending nearly ¥46 billion (£210 million) more in other countries than foreigners spent on visits to Japan. Airlines now report that young Japanese women go to Hong Kong with 15 kilos of luggage and come back with 35; and Japan's globe-trotters have now overtaken oil as the country's biggest drain of foreign currency. In fact, the newly-wealthy, camera-toting Japanese tourist has, to a large extent, replaced the innocent American holiday-maker as the butt of jokes and rip-offs. According to *Newsweek* magazine, the latest New York scam is for con men to bump into Japanese tourists, drop bottles of cheap wine at their feet and then claim the wine was a vintage. Eager to avoid a scene, Japanese visitors will sometimes hand over as much as $100.[2]

Growing affluence is one element of change in Japanese society, but with it have come new responsibilities, many of which have yet to be fully grasped. Partly in response to Western pressure, Japan has been significantly increasing its overseas aid and in 1988 provided a total of $9.13 billion – up 18.1 per cent from the previous year – compared to the United States's $9.78 billion, making Japan the world's second largest supplier of aid. Already the country is the largest donor to 25 mainly Asian countries, and in Burma, the Philippines and Nepal, Japanese official development assistance now accounts for between ten per cent and 20 per cent of the total government budget.

More than 60 per cent of Japan's overseas aid still goes to Asia, but recently, as part of the process of taking on board her share of international responsibilities, Japan has widened the scope of her aid effort and surpassed American efforts by agreeing to a $1-billion package for Poland. Tokyo has also made a bigger contribution to relieving Third World debt problems, including even those of the United States' neighbours in Central America. Almost uniquely, Japan also uses foreign agencies, such as Britain's Crown Agents, for its aid programmes.

Even so, Japan is still spending under 0.4 per cent of its GNP on aid, which is less than many other developed countries, while more than half of Japanese aid is in the form of repayable loans, compared to the bulk of

United States aid which consists of grants. Moreover, most of the recent growth in Japan's overseas aid programme has come as a result of the yen's appreciation against the dollar, which has allowed her aid to go much further in dollar terms. The growth in yen terms is rather more modest at five to eight per cent a year since 1985. Private Japanese aid is also well below the United States figure at about $100 million a year, compared to the $1.6 billion or so given by American groups to the Third World.

But the common complaint that Japanese aid is too closely allied with the purchase of Japanese products no longer appears to be valid. According to OECD figures for 1987, 46.9 per cent of Japan's aid spending was fully untied and a further 16.6 per cent was only partly tied to the procurement of Japanese goods or developments by Japanese-led consortia and the tied-aid figure is falling. No other country has such a large, untied bilateral aid programme: indeed, Enrique Iglesias, President of the Inter-American Development Bank, endorsed the Japanese position when commenting early in 1990 on a Japanese loan package to South America:

> The advantage of Japanese aid is that Japan does not limit allocation of resources to products bought from Japan. That makes their resources more flexible and acceptable than American or European money – their contribution always comes linked to procurement of goods from their countries.[3]

Even so, and despite Japan's prosperity, she is still too-often prone to demonstrating the attitude of a poverty stricken rice farmer. Although, for example, in 1989 Tokyo pledged ¥300 billion (£1.2 billion) in a three-year programme aimed at protecting the world environment, Japan still insists on maintaining a large whale catch, supposedly for scientific purposes. In fact, most of the catch invariably ends up in expensive restaurants on the plates of the wealthy and Japan continued until very recently to be the largest consumer of ivory, importing large quantities of ivory for use for personal seals long after most Western countries banned imports.

Growing Japanese affluence has also led to large increases in imports of fish and crustacea, much of which comes from the world's poor regions and denies local people a valuable protein source. Likewise, in spite of international criticism and substantial evidence of the damage that the depletion of tropical timber reserves is doing to the world's environment, Japan remains the major importer of tropical hardwood. All of which illustrates that Japanese attitudes and actions in many areas are still rooted in its once-justifiable 'poor country' complex, and are not fully developing in a way appropriate to an economic superpower.

A growing influence

More commensurate with the huge growth in Japan's economic power, on the other hand, is the steady increase in her influence in world affairs. In part, this is due to a stepping-up of Japan's long-standing lobbying effort, which in turn has been partly prompted by the high level of Western criticism Japan has attracted in recent years.

Way back in 1959, the unsuccessful Republican Presidential candidate, Thomas Dewey, was retained by JETRO as its United States representative. As a result, Dewey's law firm, which also looked after the interests of the Rockefellers and AT&T, received fees and expenses amounting to a reported $200,000 a year for being Japan's 'watchdog' and presenting her case against attempts to limit American imports of her goods. In 1960, Dewey's protégé, ex-Vice President Richard Nixon, who had been thwarted that year in his presidential bid by John Kennedy, decided to forsake politics and instead devote most of his time to clients of his own law firm – among them was Mitsui.[4]

But this was just the beginning. According to *Business Week* magazine, by 1988, Japanese government foundations and companies were spending at least $310 million, excluding advertising, on lobbying and related activities. The effort still includes JETRO, which has moved on from its original role of promoting Japanese exports to wooing prominent journalists and hosting elegant receptions for opinion-formers. Increasingly, however, it is large Japanese corporations which are responsible for the PR drive.

When, for example, Toshiba faced congressional anger in 1988 over the sale of a high-tech machine tool to the Soviet Union by one of its subsidiaries, it managed to enlist former Congress representatives, James Jones and Michael Barnes, and former Deputy Trade Representative, William Walker, among others, to fight its case in a $3-million campaign which led to a significant watering-down of the originally proposed sanctions.

The enhanced Japanese lobbying effort rankles with many Americans. According to Democratic Representative, John Bryant, 'Toshiba was able to purchase access to those who were writing the legislation. They won, but what they did was very offensive.' To criticize the Japanese for doing no more than playing by the rules of the Washington lobbying game seems somewhat unfair, however. Anyway, Toshiba's partial victory was as much due to the company's economic power as to its lobbying – at least as significant was the fact that Congress representatives were deluged with letters from customers who warned of the crippling effects they would encounter were Toshiba components to go off the market.

Of course, such lobbying, offensive or otherwise, is not unique to the Japanese. Nevertheless, Japanese interests are becoming more adept at such persuasion as their power and importance increase. Shortly after paying $620 million to buy a 52-storey skyscraper in Los Angeles, Japanese businessman, Shigeru Kobayashi, called on Mayor Tom Bradley to hand over a $100,000 cheque for a monument welcoming immigrants which the Mayor wanted to build. Overall, Bradley's campaigns have received more than $200,000 from Japanese real estate companies, banks and manufacturers, much of which was pledged in December 1987 at a fund-raising dinner attended by Japanese businessmen who paid between $350 and $500 a plate.

Japanese interests are also active on the educational front. The country's corporate giants have endowed no fewer than 16 chairs at the Massachusetts Institute of Technology at a cost of approximately $1.5 million apiece, and 80 per cent of the money for research on Japan in American universities comes from Japanese sources. Japanese research support also goes to influential institutions. In the early 1980s, right-wing philanthropist, Ryoichi Sasakawa arranged the funding of the New York-based United States–Japan Foundation with a $44-million endowment. Now headed by an ex-United States Ambassador to the Philippines, the Foundation gave $3 million in 1987 towards education, exchange programmes and policy studies. The Centre for Strategic and International Studies in Washington has done even better – its Japan chair was established with a $1-million endowment from Toyota. 'We aren't going to bend over backwards to put a Japan-basher in the chair,' admitted John Yochelson, the centre's vice president.

In an attempt to win the hearts of America, Japanese businesses are also working on becoming good corporate citizens. They now donate record amounts to American charities and to improving amenities in the localities where they operate. In 1988, Japan's big businesses gave an estimated $140 million, up from $85 million in 1987, which included Mazda's contribution of $2.2 million over 12 years for a sewer project near its Flat Rock Michigan plant and Hitachi's donation of $30,000 to the Norman, Oklahoma city library.[5]

Age of fruition

You might think that the Japanese would feel pretty good about their manufacturing industry. But so concerned has MITI become about the brain-drain from industry that it has formed a working party, called the Feel Good Manufacturing Committee, to deal with the problem. Apparently, the percentage of engineering students going into the manufacturing sector plunged from nearly half in 1987 to just over a third in 1988, as more students were lured into the glamorous and highly paid worlds of finance and real estate.

As MITI wrestles with a problem with which other industrialized countries are more than familiar, middle-aged Japanese executives in late-night bars habitually gripe over their Johnnie Walker Black Label about the decline of the work ethic among the *shin jin rui* – the soft, young Japanese. They may have a point, for ever since the mid-1970s opinion polls have confirmed that a majority of Japanese think that home life, health and happiness are more important than material success and wealth, while a recent government report on Japanese youth complained that 'they are devoid of endurance, dependent on others and self-centred'.

With Japan's economic success, the country's growing influence, the overseas holidays and the flashy gifts, have also come new problems. In fact, the very prosperity provided by Japan's material achievements contains within it some of the seeds of her future relative decline – far off though that still may be. For one thing, attitudes are beginning to change – and not just among the gilded *shin jin rui*, oblivious to the struggles and privations of their parents. Even the retired former head of Matsushita, Toshihiki Yamashita, recently wrote that Japan has spent too much of her energies on economic growth and that it is now time for the Japanese to relax more.[6]

Other structural problems may be even less tractable. Since the Second World War, Japan has had on average a significantly younger population than most of its main competitors. But with a life expectancy of 81 years for women and 76 for men, about 11 per cent of Japan's 123 million people are already 65 years of age or older, and the proportion is likely to more than double to 24 per cent by the year 2020, switching Japan from having the lowest to having the highest proportion of elderly people among the leading industrial nations.

The Japanese term for their growing elderly is *jitsunen*, which means 'age of fruition', and therein lies a problem, for the 'silver generation', as they are also called, will inevitably wish to gather in their harvest in the form of pensions, and as the elderly begin to spend what they have accumulated, savings rates will also fall. In fact, Japan's savings rate has already been slipping since the mid-1970s as social security and pension schemes have become more generous, making saving for old age less necessary (both Italy and Taiwan now boast higher savings ratios than Japan). As well as that, Japan can expect an increase in welfare costs which, according to Ministry of Health and Welfare and Ministry of Finance figures, will result in an increase in social security and medical spending from 14 per cent of GNP in 1985 to as much as 29 per cent by 2010.[7] The four Japanese people of working age who will by then be supporting each pensioner will have to contribute more in tax to pay for the elderly, forcing up wages to compensate, all of which will damage the competitiveness of Japan's industry.

By then, Japan's main export might, in fact, be the silver ones themselves. Already a government agency called the 'Leisure Development Centre' has produced feasibility studies with foreign and domestic companies on the possibility of shipping Japan's elderly abroad into specially-developed retirement communities. The ageing of the population is also beginning to cause contradictory problems for industry: on the one hand, there is a surplus of senior managers without enough posts for them to fill; while on the other hand, the reduction in size of the working population will lead to increasing recruitment difficulties.

Already, a severe labour shortage is apparent just a few years after Japan's post-yen shock record unemployment rate was widely forecast to rise even further to reach Western levels. A Labour Ministry survey of 15,000 companies in 1989 found that 60 per cent had been forced to modify business plans or practices for lack of suitable workers. Most severely hit was the construction industry with a labour deficit equivalent to 34 per cent of its workforce. This shortage has put pressure on wages, with Tokyo construction companies reportedly offering labourers ¥50,000 (£220) a day. To the north, Hokkaido companies now complain that many seasonal workers who head south for the winter in search of employment are failing to return, causing several major public works projects to be delayed.

Possibly worse for a country which perceives herself to be racially homogenous is the increase in the number of foreign workers. Although Japanese industry tends to welcome them as a low-cost and uncomplaining source of labour, many Japanese fear the influx will lead to American- or European-style racial problems.

At around 7.00am every morning, groups of foreign workers begin appearing at Arakawa Station, on the Keisei Line in the factory-cluttered district of Sumida in Tokyo. These are young labourers from Pakistan, Bangladesh and other developing Asian countries. Few have valid working visas, but Filipino labourers are now a common sight on construction sites. Bangladeshi and Pakistani employees are often hired at metal processing plants, component makers and tanneries, while Taiwanese and even Chinese staff commonly work at fast food outlets and restaurants. According to one Ministry of Justice estimate, there were more than 20,000 illegal immigrants, often brought in by *yakuza*, in Japan in 1988. By the end of 1989, Ministry of Labour estimates put the number at 150,000, while the number of foreigners with legal working visas doubled between 1982 and 1988 to more than 80,000 a year.

For labour-starved Japanese industry, and particularly smaller manufacturers, such imported labour is a godsend. According to one metal-processing plant operator in Tokyo's Katsushika district: 'There are no Japanese workers willing to work in places like this, whereas foreign workers are very adaptable labourers for a small company like ours.' The company began employing Pakistanis in 1987 without asking to see passports or visas, and has since been impressed by their hard work and willing attitude. Even so, when, late in 1989, companies lobbied the government to allow them to employ Vietnamese and Chinese refugees in their factories and on construction sites, they were rejected and the refugees deported.

新　大　国

So has Japan already peaked? Will these factors now lead to a period of steady decline? It is interesting that commentators in the late 1960s then also predicted that similar considerations would slow Japan's breakneck growth rate. In his 1970 book, *The Emerging Japanese Superstate*,[8] Herman Kahn listed the ageing of the workforce, the need for greater public spending, student unrest, the general erosion of the work ethic and the greater interest in leisure – then termed 'my home-ism' – among the oft-quoted arguments for an impending economic slowdown.

Kahn, in fact, considered these factors to be overstated and predicted a maintenance of Japan's economic process. Of course, he was broadly correct. The rioting students of the 1960s turned into the loyal salary-workers of the 1970s and 1980s, while the environmental and quality of life problems which, it was widely thought, would cause severe difficulties for Japanese industry, have not prevented its success. Likewise, current difficulties will not inevitably lead to a decline in competitiveness. But Japanese industry will steadily lose some of the structural advantages which it has enjoyed since the Second World War and will have to compensate by improving its productivity at a very rapid rate if it is to finance these added burdens and so maintain its edge.

'Ordinary people are sick of these men and their money . . .'

There may, however, be other problems. The old, austere values of Japan are breaking down, and with them, some of the traditional cohesion is also fading. While, in 1983, there was only one credit card for every three Japanese, by 1987 this had grown to nearly one card each and over the same period the amount of outstanding consumer credit rose by a third. More than that, the second half of the 1980s has seen the rise of a new elite or *nouveaux riches* class which has unsettled Japan's social unity by provoking increasing resentment at the disparities of wealth and lifestyle which have emerged. While conspicuous displays of wealth used to be frowned upon in most circles, it has now become increasingly common to flaunt affluence. 'It seems that having capital rather than working hard is the best way to make money in Japan nowadays. It is almost as though a new aristocracy is growing up in Japan, and many people feel that these people are cornering most of the gains of recent years', a friend who works in his family business told me.

The rapid rise in land and stock prices in particular has contributed to the apparent beginning of a breakdown in the relative social cohesion and unity of purpose which has for the most part characterized Japan since the Second World War. People seeing more money being made in property in a year than they can earn in a lifetime begin to ask what they are working for.

At the root of the problem of high land prices is Japan's chronic land shortage. This is exacerbated by the tax system which allows notionally agricultural land in Tokyo to remain almost free of tax unless sold, in which case taxes are penal. This disincentive to sell has resulted in about ten per cent of Tokyo's city area remaining as small, uneconomic plots of rice and vegetables, which nestle incongruously between high-rise apartments and factories.

As Japan's economy moved rapidly out of its post-yen appreciation slump into an almost unparalleled boom in 1987 and 1988, land prices in Tokyo rose by 93 per cent and the ripple effect spread rapidly from the centre of the city to the built-up commuter land well beyond Mount Fuji. One Tokyo housewife who turned down an offer of £230,000 for her suburban flat 40 minutes from the City Centre, found that less than a year later the going price was three times that amount. By then, according to Japan's National Land Agency, the cost of one *tsubo* (3.3 square metres) of land in Tokyo's Ginza district was $710,000.[9]

But while the value of most people's land holdings doubled in the 1980s, those of the wealthiest 20 per cent trebled, and the middle-class backbone of industrial and bureaucratic Japan was increasingly priced out of the market. According to a study by the Nomura Research Institute, the average cost of residential land in Japan in 1985 was already well above international levels at ¥69,000 (£306) per square metre, compared with ¥3,000 in the United States and ¥4,600 in the UK. At that time, a house in Tokyo cost about six times the average Tokyo-dweller's annual salary, but by 1989 it took 18 years' pay. For the ordinary, salaried Japanese person, home ownership had by then become a distant dream and the concept of a fair return for labour was being seriously undermined.

The beneficiaries of the land boom included Japan's estate agents. The biggest, Mitsui Real Estate, had a turnover of ¥320 billion (£1.4 billion) in 1987, while the income of property firms as a whole rose by 315 per cent from 1984. Also doing well out of the property boom were the *jiageya* (*land sharks*), who buy small parcels of land in order to consolidate them into large areas worth developing. Those who resist the blandishments of these sharks often come under sustained harassment from ruffians who bang on doors, telephone in the early hours or rent neighbouring properties to cause a nuisance.

Resentment to all of this soon crept into Japan's normally fairly deferential political system. The ruling LDP was formed in 1955 when the Japanese were, on the whole, united in the overriding purpose of reconstructing their economy and catching up with the West. But the LDP's ability to both create and reflect this national consensus has recently been strained by the emergence of the wealthy and ostentatious elite which has done well out of the surge in land and stock prices, eroding the Japanese self-image of being homogenously middle-class.

It does not help that the party itself is increasingly perceived as being an exclusive, nepotistic, self-perpetuating clique. About a third of ruling LDP members are sons or sons-in-law of former politicians and political dynasties now abound. On top of status and power, marriage has also secured money for LDP leaders. Both Takeshita and Nakasone have daughters married into families owning large construction companies, and the construction industry is one of the LDP's most generous supporters.

On to this somewhat dubious scene came Hiromosa Ezoe, the self-made businessman who offered leading politicians cut-price stock in Recruit Cosmos, a property and employment publishing company he controlled, in return for access to the fringes of power. Mr Ezoe was a conspicuous part of the new moneyed elite, but when his dealings with politicians emerged, he was indicted on several counts of bribery, along with the chairman of Japan's largest company, telephone system operator, NTT, who had also accepted Recruit shares. The fact that the profits were transferred to the company's political slush fund, a major contributor to the LDP, did not help him. And the revelation that this ¥800 million (£3.4 million) fund was bolstered by contributions from the company's workforce only made things worse.

The arrests crystalized public resentment concerning the huge amounts of money sloshing around in the murky world where business and politics meet. People interviewed on television about the scandal, in which shares worth about 20 times the average annual income changed hands, openly expressed their pleasure at the fact that the money-men had got their come-uppance. 'Ordinary people are sick of these men and their money,' said one taxi driver. 'If they get Nakasone [the ex-Prime Minister], we'll have a party.'[10]

Initially, it looked as though the politicians would get off scot-free. But the scandal coincided with a series of political problems which served further to galvanize the increasingly assertive Japanese electorate. First, the farmers, the electoral backbone of the LDP party, were bristling with anger at import-liberalizing measures which were hitting home-grown products, leaving groves of *mikan* oranges untended and the fruit unpicked. Second, as part of a tax reform programme aimed at widening the revenue base, the government imposed a three per cent sales tax, despite election pledges to the contrary. This move helped politicize the Japanese housewife, the holder of the family purse strings, who saw the extra three per cent on her purchases as just another rake-off for the politicians.

Worse was to come. By June 1989, Takeshita was finally forced to resign as a result of revelations that one of his aides had taken Recruit money. His replacement, Sousuke Uno, was supposed to be a safe bet: dull, but honest. Unfortunately, he turned out to be more interesting than was at first imagined, for hardly had he been sworn in, than a certain Miss Mitsuko Nakanishi, a waitress in the Kagurazaka geisha district of Tokyo, revealed that the new Prime Minister had paid her ¥300,000 (£1,200) a month for sex over a five month period in the mid-1980s.

From a Buddhist temple to which she had retreated, Miss Nakanishi went on to broadcast damning details to a gleefully shocked nation concerning Mr Uno's coarseness. As Mr Uno maintained an embarrassed silence, journalists scurried around the seamy hostess bars of Kyoto and Tokyo, trawling for more stories from other part-time working girls. They were to come up with reports that the hapless Uno had indulged himself with ladies ranging from a legally under-age 17-year-old to a woman of 63.

For a mistress to go public was itself a sign of changing times. So was the general reaction to the revelation in a country where, traditionally, the maintenance of a mistress was a point of pride among Japanese men and a symbol of their wealth and power. Far from criticizing the ex-waitress for kissing and telling as might have happened in the past, the public, and especially women, sympathized with her and reacted with disgust at Mr Uno's behaviour. As the cabinet's popularity sank to 16 per cent, the Prime Minister's own rating slumped to a mere 3.9 per cent.

It seemed that the politics of envy had gone to work in Japan for the first time since the early post-War period, as ordinary people became aware of the widening gulf between themselves and the rich and powerful segments of society. But whereas in the past voters had occasionally protested against the LDP by withholding their votes to a limited extent, by the spring of 1989 the party was facing a fundamentally different situation.

For, while at the peak of the Lockheed bribery scandal in 1976 the LDP's vote fell from 47 to 42 per cent, by contrast, in a by-election in rural Niigata in June 1989, the LDP vote slumped by a third, while the Japan Socialist Party (JSP) poll was up by more than a quarter. The result was a shock victory for Kinuko Ofuchi, an unknown housewife and political newcomer, who by a substantial margin beat her well-known and lavishly-financed LDP opponent, a vice president of Niigata TV and son of a former prefectural governor.

Such was the scene for the partial Upper House parliamentary elections which were held on 23 July. With the usually politically active and solidly pro-LDP youth sections of the *nokyo* farmers' co-ops deciding not to back LDP candidates in 15 of the 47 prefectures, a loss of seats looked inevitable. In the event, what happened was more akin to an electoral earthquake. The LDP lost its Upper House majority for the first time since 1955, while the press feted JSP leader, 60-year-old Takako Doi, as Japan's potential first woman Prime Minister.

LDP party bosses thrashed around in desperation for a clean candidate to replace Uno. With almost all the obvious choices tainted by the Recruit scandal, they only managed to come up with Toshiki Kaifu, a member of one of the smallest LDP Diet factions with no personal power base in the party. At first, even he seemed jinxed as it emerged that his Chief Cabinet Secretary, 69-year-old Tokuo Yamashita, had offered his 26-year-old former mistress $20,000 in an attempt to buy her silence. Kaifu skilfully recovered his poise, however, by replacing Yamashita with a woman.

Two factors will almost certainly save the LDP in the long term. First, the JSP seems to have great difficulty in coming to terms with the new realities of world politics. It continues to support Kim Il Sung's bizarre Stalinist regime in North Korea, for example, while most other Japanese political parties side with South Korea. Second, the LDP's economic record will stand it in good stead. Over the years, the party has managed to steer Japan through some dangerous squalls to deliver unparalleled prosperity. Above all, for many Japanese, with their typical lack of complacency, the economic position of Japan in the early 1990s is still not secure enough to tempt them into taking too many risks – especially bearing in mind the rising competition within Asia itself.

23

新
大
国

THE FOUR TIGERS

'The solution to the problem [of competition from advancing economies] is to be found, according to economic logic, in progressively giving away industries to other countries, much as a big brother gives his out-grown clothes to his younger brother. In this way a country's own industries became more sophisticated.'
Yoshihisa Ojimi, Vice Minister MITI, 1971.[1]

FOUR TIGERS ARE snapping at Japan's heels. These are the Asian newly industrialized countries (NICs): South Korea, Taiwan, Singapore and Hong Kong. In the last three decades, the NICs have more than doubled their share of the free world's GNP to six per cent. Together with Japan, the other fast-expanding East Asian economies, Australia and the west coast of North America, the NICs make up the Pacific Basin, the most rapidly growing region in the world.

One symbol of the shift in the gravity of world economic power is the fact that more wide-bodied jets now fly across the Pacific each day than across the Atlantic, while Japanese Air Lines (JAL) has become the largest jumbo operator with a fleet of nearly 70 planes. And according to the International Civil Aviation Organization, the Pacific Basin area will soon overtake Europe to account for a third of worldwide air travel.

Principal among the 'four tigers', also sometimes known as the 'four dragons' or 'gang of four', is South Korea which as recently as 1961 was a poverty stricken country with a per capita income of less than $100 a year. By 1976, this had risen to $800, and in 1979, it was well over the $1,000 mark, leaving communist North Korea stagnating at less than $400 a head.

Even with the extensive strikes of the mid-1980s, South Korea's economy grew at a stunning 12.5 per cent in 1986, followed by a ten per cent increase the next year. By 1988, this country of over 42 million people was running a current account surplus of $9.3 billion and exporting $10 billion worth of textiles, while car and electronics exports were growing at a rate of more than 40 per cent a year. Korean manufacturers are now second only to Japan in VCR production and number among the few companies in the world capable of manufacturing 1-MB memory chips.

The development of the South Korean economy since the end of the bloody Korean War was planned by technocrats, many of whom had American training. Their tools included infrastructure development, a vocationally oriented education system, fiscal incentives to ensure high levels of investment and savings, the allocation of investment funds, discouragement of domestic consumption and some protection against imports. The government has also guaranteed industrial loans and encouraged overseas finance resulting in the accumulation of a hefty foreign debt which peaked at $44.5 billion in 1987.

As the economy has advanced, however, South Korean companies, banks and the stock market have become less willing to carry out the technocrats' policies and central planning is steadily diminishing in importance. Export success has also helped to reduce the foreign debt and hence indirectly decrease the role of government, while foreign pressure has played a large part in reducing import barriers.

In the beginning, South Korean industrial progress was based on low-technology, labour-intensive products – particularly textiles – which remain the country's main export. In recent years, however, the South Korean textile industry has come under pressure from lower-wage countries, such as Bangladesh, and its industry as a whole has steadily moved on into more sophisticated product areas. In 1987, South Korea even temporarily toppled Japan from her 20-year shipbuilding lead and 80 per cent of Korean-built tonnage is now constructed for export.

Since the first Hyundai Pony came off the line in 1975, in a factory built on a reclaimed swamp on the east coast, Korean companies have also made positive moves into car production. The Hyundai plant was, ironically, designed and run by a former manager of state-owned British Leyland (BL). Today, that one plant produces 750,000 cars a year, nearly double the output of BL's successor, the Rover group, and Hyundai is moving on from producing basic cars which sell on price to more sophisticated executive models designed jointly with Mitsubishi of Japan. In 1989, the Korean car industry, consisting of Hyundai and four smaller producers, made nearly a million cars and is investing to increase output to 1.75 million by 1993.

South Korea has also more recently targeted the higher-tech industries of semiconductors, computers, telecommunications, aerospace, genetic engineering, new materials and robotics. The country is already the third largest producer of memory chips and has moved into second position behind Japan in consumer electronics.

If South Korea's progression into ever more advanced industries sounds somewhat familiar, so must the nature of its major companies, for Japanese-style, diversified conglomerates have constituted the van of the country's industrial advance. Chief among them is Samsung, with a turnover already in excess of £10 billion and 37 subsidiaries in industries ranging from electronics and aerospace to sugar production and shipbuilding. Daewoo is moving from being primarily a shipbuilding company to a broad group producing cars, trucks and helicopters – one recent contract with Lockheed involved supplying fully assembled wings for a new anti-submarine aircraft, the P-7A. The company plans for shipbuilding, which still accounts for more than 90 per cent of its total business, to amount to less than a third by 1993. The other two main conglomerates, Hyundai and Goldstar, are already large, diversified corporations well established in international markets. Overall, the sales of South Korea's 30 biggest groups equals more than 90 per cent of the country's GNP.

One of South Korea's major competitive advantages over Japan and the United States up to the late 1980s was the fact that she paid relatively low wages. In 1986, South Korea's per capita income of around $2,200 was only an eighth that of the United States and a third of Italy's. According to the International Labour Organization, South Korean manufacturing workers also had the longest working week in the world in 1985 – 53.8 hours against 41.5 in Japan and 40.5 in the United States. Moreover, the average South Korean hourly wage was also the lowest of the four NICs at only $1.39 an hour – just over half the rate in Singapore and less than a sixth that of Japan.

This helped Korean companies to produce fork-lift trucks for 30 per cent less than American manufacturers and ships at prices 50 per cent lower than the Japanese. According to Nomura Securities, a $6,600 subcompact car costs $1,400 less to manufacture in Korea than it does in Japan.[2] As a result, Korea has become an exporter out of all proportion to its economic size.

But the situation may not last, for, in recent years, American pressure has been partly responsible for forcing the Koreans to gear their economy more to domestic demand, while a series of bitter strikes has sharply pushed up labour costs and reduced competitiveness, causing severe financial problems for some of the country's largest employers. Wage rises and economic success have also led to a rise in Korean living standards. According to *Social Indicators in Korea*, which is published by the Korean government, the life of the average South Korean was, at the time of the 1988 Seoul Olympics, going through a period of great change. Earning the equivalent of $12,000 a year at his job, Mr Kim, the Mr Average Korean middle manager, was so exhausted from his 51-hour week that he spent most of Sunday asleep. Nevertheless, his labours made it more than likely that his family already owned a TV and refrigerator, and the next big move forward, according to the survey, would probably be in purchasing a car. Only one in 50 Koreans had one in 1988, but ownership is now rising rapidly.

One testament to South Korea's new prosperity and her switch to greater domestic consumption is the world's largest indoor amusement park, Lotte World Adventure, opened in Seoul in 1988. A glass-domed theme park, built in what has been described as 'Neo Las Vegas Baroque', it constitutes the centre-piece of the already cluttered Seoul skyline. Part Disneyland, part supermarket and part Harrods, the £500-million-plus complex seems to herald a new era of conspicuous consumption. In addition to the 20-acre indoor pleasure park, Lotte World also houses Seoul's largest department store, a luxury hotel, a shopping mall, health club, swimming pool, roof-top golf range, a Korean folk village, a casino and a 26-lane ten-pin bowling alley. Included in the complex is the world's largest chandelier, Korea's first spiral escalator and a replica of Rhodes' Trevi Fountain. It goes without staying that the hotel atrium is pink with glass lifts and that the swimming club is modelled on a Roman bath.

Despite such manifestations of the new South Korean consumption and the problems of continuing labour unrest, traditional Korean strengths remain. The *Social Indicators* survey also showed that savings were high at 30 per cent of family income, while Korean teenagers were apparently far more concerned about educational and job opportunities (68 per cent) than their love life (ten per cent) or personal appearance (six per cent).

Evidence of the direction of South Korea's economy lies in the internationalization of Korean industry. Whereas in 1986 South Korean companies made only 50 overseas investments, worth a total of $172 million, in the first two months of 1990 alone they announced 73 projects worth $251 million. The four main conglomerates are leading the push into overseas manufacturing: in 1987, Goldstar opened its second overseas factory in Worms in West Germany which is destined to make 300,000 large-screen colour TV sets and 400,000 VCRs a year. Its first foreign plant, founded in the United States in 1981, now produces one million colour televisions and 200,000 microwave ovens every year. Goldstar, with sales of over $15 billion a year, is also planning to build a consumer electronics factory in the UK, while Daewoo is constructing a new microwave oven-manufacturing facility in the depressed, industrial steel region of Lorraine in France. Hyundai opened its Canadian car-assembly plant near Montreal in 1989, designed to have a capacity of 70,000 units a year, while Samsung added to its New Jersey colour TV facility by building a pilot microchip plant in California in 1987.

'The question was how to make a living . . .'

Coming a close second in the economic miracle stakes is the island state of Taiwan. When the Kuomintang Chinese Nationalists, fleeing from defeat at the hands of the Communists on the Chinese Mainland, arrived to take over in 1949, the island's economy was pre-industrial, with a per capita income below the $100 mark.

Taiwan's development began with a highly successful land-reform programme which, by the 1970s, resulted in 90 per cent of the land being owned by the farmers who tilled it. Strict no-strike laws and duty-free export processing zones helped to raise per capita income to over $1,300 by the end of the 1970s, with exports comprising 90 per cent of GNP – the highest proportion in the world. By then, Taiwan's economy was growing at 12 per cent a year, despite the world recession, and was developing into a complex structure revolving around middle-technology products such as ships, electrical equipment, textiles and chemicals.

But unlike South Korea, which built up a massive foreign debt in order to industrialize, by the late 1980s Taiwan had accumulated £42 billion in hard currency reserves – second only to Japan. By then, the trade of the tiny island exceeded that of the Chinese Mainland with 50 times the population. With a highly literate and educated workforce, Taiwan has also steadily switched to more sophisticated products, particularly electronics, and she now produces a quarter of the world's personal computers.

None of which is to suggest that the small island's breakneck economic development has not been without problems. As in Japan, increasing affluence has led to a disruption of social cohesion. During a visit to the southern town of Tainan, misleadingly billed as the 'Kyoto of Taiwan', my sleep was rudely shattered by the screeching roar of motor bikes. I later learned that the police were having problems with illegal late-night bike races which attracted large and unruly crowds of youths.

Environmental problems are also a source of worry to an increasingly assertive population crammed on to a largely mountainous island with the highest population density of any nation in the world apart from Bangladesh. During the 1980s, the number of factories has more than doubled to nearly 90,000 and vehicles have more than tripled to ten million – one for every two inhabitants. As a result, air in the Taipei industrial suburb of Sanching is now frequently worse than on a bad day in the smoggy Los Angeles of the 1960s. Sewage treatment is also minimal with the result that most of Taiwan's major rivers are badly polluted. Rising public concern forced the UK chemical giant, ICI, to close down one of its plants after persistent complaints from local fishermen about effluent. Fishermen also forced 18 petrochemical plants in the south to shut down for a week and in June 1989, a demonstration at a state-run refinery turned violent when protesters were refused compensation for pollution damage. Taiwan is now having to face the problems of according overall priority to economic growth and, as with Japan in the 1970s, is going to have to invest a great deal more of her resources in improving the quality of life of her citizens.

But perhaps the most remarkable growth has occurred in the much more free-market oriented economies of the city states of Hong Kong and Singapore. Hong Kong has managed to raise her per capita income to about six times that of Mainland China, while at the same time absorbing more than four million refugees. A stable government, a consistently very free-market economic policy and reasonably high educational standards have resulted in a near ideal environment for business – that is until 1997, when the Mainland Chinese are scheduled to take over.

Singapore has fared equally well. Although the tropical island state suffered a degree of instability in the decade following the end of the Second World War, in 1959 it finally broke from the Malaysian Confederation to find a firm government framework under Lee Kuan Yew. By 1979, Singapore's per capita income was the highest of the four NICs. According to the island's leader:

> The question was how to make a living . . . a matter of life and death for two million people . . . . How this was to be achieved, by socialism or free enterprise, was a secondary matter. The answer turned out to be free enterprise, tempered with a socialist philosophy of equal opportunities for education, jobs, health and housing.[3]

The remarkable progress of the Asian NICs shows both similarities and differences with Japan, a country which they have all, to a greater or lesser extent, looked to as an example. The Korean and Taiwanese governments have intervened in their economies more than has been the case in Japan, although there has been less interference in Singapore and Hong Kong. Unlike Japan, Korea, Taiwan and Singapore have all spent heavily on defence. But the common denominators are of more significance. Besides a lack of natural resources, they include unwavering encouragement of internal competition; low taxation and government spending; infrastructure development; and an emphasis on high educational standards.

Co-operation and competition

Japan's relationship with the rest of Asia this century has had its ups and downs. In the early years, Japan's rapid economic progress and the way the country successfully avoided becoming another of the White man's colonies, made it an ideal training ground for many of Asia's independence movements. China's revolutionary leader, Sun Yat Sen, studied there, as did a large number of other Chinese Nationalists.

But Japan's subsequent attempts to build an 'All-Asian Co-Prosperity Sphere' before and during the Second World War, based as it was on the exploitation of natural resources in return for Japanese manufactures, together with Japan's drive for dominance in the Pacific still gives rise to bitter memories. The Koreans, in particular, continue to harbour a deep resentment of the Japanese who ruled their country from 1911 to 1945, and the Japanese do not help matters by often treating the Koreans like slightly simple country cousins – a not dissimilar relationship to that between the English and the Irish. Yet it was Japan's advances during the Second World War which marked the end of White colonial dominance in Asia, since when the country's advance to industrial leadership has again made Japan a model for others.

Paradoxically, although Japan's defeat in the Second World War has turned the 'Co-Prosperity Sphere' into no more than an ugly propaganda phrase, the truth is that the country's current close economic relationship with the NICs and the rest of Asia has done Japan far more good than the 'Co-Prosperity Sphere' ever did, for Japan and the rapidly advancing Asian economies are now closely interlinked in a productive association based on a bedrock of economic logic that is at the same time co-operative and competitive.

As Japanese industry develops and advances into ever more sophisticated areas, so she allows the NICs to move into the areas she vacates. Indeed, the very pressure on Japanese industry caused by the rapid progress of the NICs has had the effect of keeping Japanese industry competitive and preventing complacency, for if Japanese industry ever stagnates, it knows that the aggressive NICs, with their lower labour costs, will rapidly move in.

The Japanese footwear industry provides a good example of how this works in practice. In 1970, Japan had a hugely favourable trade balance in footwear, importing less than ¥3 billion (£14 million) worth of shoes a year and exporting nearly ¥50 billion (£275 million). But footwear is a low-technology, labour-intensive industry of exactly the type that a nation which aspires to industrial leadership, together with high standards of living, does not want. During the 1970s, shoe imports into Japan increased 30 per cent a year while exports declined 17 per cent annually. As a consequence, by the end of the decade, Japan was importing ¥40 billion (£220 million) worth of shoes and exporting only ¥8 billion (£30 million). By then, more than half of those imports came from Taiwan and South Korea.[4]

In very much the same way, the NICs have supplemented or replaced Japan as major suppliers of black and white TVs, toys, textiles and, more recently, steel, ships and increasingly sophisticated consumer electronics. Already Korea is selling cement plants, sugar refineries, cars, semiconductors, CD players, VCRs and colour TVs abroad. Indeed, between 1986 and 1987, Japan's imports of colour televisions from the NICs rose from 25,000 to 370,000; VCR imports increased from 15,000 to 138,000; electric cookers from 200 to 17,000; while imports of electronic calculators jumped from 1.62 million in 1984 to 11 million by 1987.[5]

And as Japan provides the market for products from the NICs which are appropriate to their stage of development, those countries are in turn more able to buy increasingly sophisticated goods from Japan as their own economic positions improve. At the same time, the NICs' exports put pressure on the very industries that it is in Japan's economic interest to move out of, which means that Japanese firms move further up the high-tech ladder, devoting resources more effectively to higher value-added sectors.

That is why Mazda has stopped making small cars in Japan, instead relying on a joint venture with Kia Motors of South Korea. Frequently, the whole process is integrated into single products, for Japan often supplies sophisticated components and sub-assemblies to the NICs for products which, overall, Japan is abandoning. Daewoo's largest export to the United States, for example, is a fork-lift truck which it manufactures for Caterpillar; but some of the most complex parts are bought from Japan, while as much as 40 per cent of a Korean automobile is imported from Japan[6] – Hyundai is particularly dependent on Mitsubishi technology and drive-train parts. At the end of the 1970s, the four Asian NICs were taking more than two-thirds of Japanese integrated-circuit exports and Korean VCRs now frequently contain up to 50 per cent Japanese parts. As a result, despite the fact that South Korea, Hong Kong, Taiwan and Singapore have steadily taken over many of the industries which Japan used to dominate, Japan still maintains a large positive trade balance with them.

This virtuous interaction has resulted in rapid-growth in trade between Japan and the NICs, which, according to the International Monetary Fund, increased 20 times between 1970 and 1987, compared to only an 11-fold rise in trade with North America. Overall, Japan's exports to the NICs are now nearly five times her total exports to Black Africa and Latin America combined, making Japan by far the largest supplier to the East Asian countries; and although the NICs still export pre-eminently to the United States, sales to Japan are increasing faster, so that before long, Japanese trade with the Pacific Basin nations as a whole will be greater than her total trade with the rest of the world.

Which is not to say that Japan's trade relations with her Asian neighbours are invariably totally free of friction. The NICs periodically complain about both their dependence on Japan and her trade surpluses. Sometimes these grievances result in action, such as when in 1989 Seoul announced a ban on imports of Japanese cars until 1994. In turn, Japanese business and agriculture, ever adept lobbyists, have occasionally persuaded their government to limit imports of certain items. For the most part, these regional trade disputes have concerned agricultural products, such as chestnuts and tea from Korea and bananas and pineapples from the Philippines. But more recently, with an ironic echo of Western actions against Japan in the past, the Japanese knitwear industry, under intense pressure as a result of the yen's appreciation, has complained of the rising tide of Korean knitwear imports which surged by 63 per cent in 1986 and 69 per cent in 1987 to capture roughly a quarter of Japan's domestic market. MITI has generally been keen for Japanese industry to move on from textiles and Japan has never implemented the provisions of the Multi Fibre Arrangement which would allow her, like other developed nations, to place import quotas on textiles from poorer countries. But under severe political pressure, MITI nonetheless opened negotiations with the South Koreans on export limits, using all of the familiar terminology of special pleading, such as 'dumping', 'excessive exports' and 'disorderly marketing'; and although South Korea did agree to moderate her exports, this was not enough for the Japan Knitting Industry Association, which then tried to persuade the Finance Ministry to file a complaint under GATT.

Such disputes are not the general rule, however, and the area's interdependence has been increased by high levels of Japanese investment, for although Japan's investment in Europe and North America has grown faster in recent years, nearly half of the country's foreign manufacturing investments are still in Asia, employing about 500,000 people. By the end of 1987, for example, Japan's electronics industry had made 1,319 investments in Asia, compared with only 191 in Europe. In South Korea, Japan is by far the largest foreign investor with nearly $700 million invested in 177 projects. In 1986, Japan overtook the United States to become the largest foreign investor in the region as a whole, and by 1988, she was committing capital to new investments in the area at twice the rate of the United States.

Even so, Japan has found it difficult to convert her massive economic influence in eastern Asia into increased political power. Almost all of the Japanese initiatives for closer political co-operation have been rebuffed. The first plan, floated by MITI, was for an annual Asia–Pacific conference of trade ministers, but from the start the project was viewed with suspicion. It was opposed outright by Thailand and Singapore, while Indonesia and Malaysia had severe reservations. The second Japanese plan to run into trouble was the proposal, in 1987, to expand the role of the Asian Development Bank, an aid agency which largely lends money to public-sector projects. Memories are long in East and South-East Asia.

The next NIC?

So which country will be the next Asian NIC? Many people's favourite candidate in the early 1980s was China. As the country liberalized, and industrial output increased at an annual rate of 20 per cent, China's potential seemed boundless. If, as planned, the argument ran, per capita income was to rise annually by around six per cent a year, then China would catch up with the industrialized nations by the middle of the next century to become the world's largest economy.

Unfortunately, things were not quite as simple as that. Even before the Tiananmen Square massacre in June 1989, those with experience in China had their doubts. Few Westerners know more about modern China than David Mathew, who spent most of the 1970s and 1980s travelling in this vast country while working first for the Hong Kong-based international trader, Jardine Matheson, and subsequently for the Hong Kong office of a well-known British investment bank. He told me:

> China has got to solve some very fundamental and deep-seated problems. Mao Tse Tung's most enduring legacy is the fostering and encouragement of population growth after the Communist takeover. The population has risen from 542 million in 1949 to one billion in 1980 and continues – every two years the growth in numbers totals the population of South Korea. To maintain even basic living standards for her huge population is a phenomenal economic effort. When this is coupled with the lack of infrastructure and energy, the sclerotic and authoritarian system of government, the anti-business ethic of the Communist system and the lack of education, it is very difficult to envisage China joining the league of NICs in the foreseeable future.
>
> Sure, there's been a lot of progress in limited areas like Fukien and the Shenzhen Special Economic Zone in Guangdong Province close to Hong Kong. It's grown with amazing speed mainly largely as a result of subcontracted Hong Kong production and management. But China is huge – and therein lies a great part of its problem.

The Fifth-Century BC Chinese military philosopher, Sun Tzu, advised: 'When you plunder a countryside, let the spoil be divided amongst your men. When you capture new territory, cut it up into allotments for the benefit of the soldiery.' That is pretty much what the Chinese have done. The indigenous Chinese, usually referred to as Han Chinese, originally only really inhabited the Middle Kingdom – part of the eastern seaboard of what is now modern China. Since then, they have steadily expanded, following a policy of settling large numbers of Han Chinese in newly-conquered territories, swamping the indigenous population and so absorbing the areas into greater China.

This process has been going on for hundreds of years in Mongolia and Manchuria to the north, but is much more recent in other regions which have only been intermittently under Chinese control. The huge north-western province of Xinjiang, for example, inhabited primarily by people of Turkic descent who have more in common with Europeans than Chinese, really only fell under firm Chinese control in 1949, while Tibet did not succumb to Chinese force until 1959.

Although China benefits from the natural resources of some of these subject regions – timber and coal from the north and oil from the west – the effort of keeping them in check and integrating them with the rest of the country is enormous. But Han Chinese chauvinism ensures that massive efforts are put into keeping the empire intact, despite the fact that its maintenance is itself inimicable to the decentralization and liberalization necessary for rapid and effective economic reform. In this respect, the Chinese are suffering from the same disadvantage and delusion as the Great Russian Nationalists who strive to maintain the world's other large land-based empire to their huge detriment.

'Peking's primary aim', David Mathew told me in his twentieth-floor flat overlooking Hong Kong harbour and beyond to the green hills of China itself, 'is to try to keep its vast land mass politically centralized, controlled and intact. Economics come a poor second, so for the moment look elsewhere for the next economic superpower.' Added to that, though, is the general hostility of the Chinese leadership to enterprise and competition, and the fact that China has made the mistake of many other developing countries by concentrating its educational resources on prestigious universities while neglecting the middle and lower levels of the system.

So although China, because of its very size, has become Japan's second largest Asian trading partner after Hong Kong, Japanese companies have been wary of putting money into the country and accounted for only 8.7 per cent of foreign investment in China in 1987 – well behind Hong Kong and the United States. And although investment rose rapidly in 1988, it still accounted for less than five per cent of Japan's total external investment. Japanese industry and banks may well prove to have been wise in limiting their risk.

One reason for the scepticism is the negative attitude of many Japanese people to modern China. Once Japan's cultural mentor, by the end of the last century China had sunk, in the estimation of most Japanese, to the status of a wayward elder brother. Since then, matters have, if anything, deteriorated. I recollect the attitude of one of Japan's new generation of globe-trotters whom I met in Tashkorgan, once a major trading post on the Silk Road but now no more than a dusty frontier town close to the Pakistani and Soviet borders in the far west of China's empire. Wearing a New York Yankee's baseball cap and festooned with cameras, he staggered towards me, in a state of complete culture shock, across a hotel courtyard. The problem, I discovered, was that the plumbing in his hotel bedroom was connected neither to the taps nor to the toilet – a not uncommon situation in Chinese hotels. He begged me to tell him where he could wash. Alas, I could not be of any assistance, and he stumbled off with a look of total incomprehension on his face.

The Japanese have none of the Western tendency to sentimentalize China. Most of them consider the Chinese to be, at best, filthy, and, at worst, completely hopeless, and semi-myths about the awfulness of China abound – such as one by a Japanese student who told me that there were no birds in China because Mao ordered all birds to be killed in the 1950s as they ate the corn. Despite the best efforts of 800 million people, Mao was not, in fact, entirely successful and the bird population has since partly recovered. This sort of Chinese horror story nonetheless typifies the attitude of many Japanese people to the country which for 1,000 years provided their forefathers with much of their culture and technology and helps to explain why Japanese have hedged their bets in China.

新　大　国

Many people's current favourite to become the fifth Asian NIC is Thailand. Since 1958, despite periodic bouts of political instability, the lush, southeast Asian kingdom, perhaps best known for its massage parlours, has generally had pro-market governments committed to economic success and devoting reasonable resources to infrastructure improvement and education. As a result, Thailand began to take off in the 1960s with annual growth rates of nine per cent, differing from Japan and the NICs in that she has substantial natural resources in the form of agricultural land and remains a major exporter of food. By the end of the 1970s, Thailand's per capita income was four times that of its socialist neighbour, Burma.

Sakutaro Tanino, the deputy director general of the Asian Affairs Bureau of Japan's Ministry of Foreign Affairs, is one of those who is convinced that Thailand will be the next NIC. A suave, middle-aged man wearing a sharply cut pinstripe suit, loafers, an English-style striped shirt and a silk tie, he told me of Thailand's advantages:

They have got a good labour force – reasonable skill levels, fairly well educated and with a good attitude to work; despite problems with the military, governments have been reasonably reliable and stable as well as extremely favourable to foreign investment.

Thailand also has the advantage of being a relatively large economy because of the size of her population. So my money is very much on Thailand. I think you will find that many in Japanese industry agree with that – Japanese companies were already investing in Thailand far faster than the Americans in the 1960s and now account for more than 40 per cent of foreign investment in Thailand, three times as much as the United States.

Thailand is one of the four Asian 'mini tigers', also called the 'minidragons'. The others are Indonesia, Malaysia and the Philippines. Together, they are expected to follow the economic development of the first four NICs, although each is quite different. They are not quite as socially or politically cohesive and have a series of language and cultural differences which result in problems of national integration and identity. They also have high birth rates which threaten economic growth, and differ from the NICs in that they have natural resources in the form of plentiful land – as well as oil in Indonesia's case. In addition, although educational standards have advanced, illiteracy remains a problem. Nonetheless, Thailand, Indonesia and Malaysia all registered annual growth rates in excess of seven per cent in the 1970s and early 1980s, while the Philippines averaged 5.6 per cent. Each of these proto-NICs are now important trading partners of the

Japanese and receive a significant portion of the country's overseas investment as well.

But if you want a really dark-horse candidate for the surprise NIC of the early part of the next century, try Vietnam. According to David Mathew:

> If the political problems of Cambodia and political reform are dealt with, it could happen. Russian influence is in steep decline and the leadership seems to have realized that the socialist economic model has failed them. Although they are still clinging to the political supremacy of the Party, they are at least beginning the process of embracing capitalism. A large population – about 64 million – gives them economic weight and they have a tradition of hard work and loyalty which will probably serve them in very good stead. Remember that the South Vietnamese have only had Communism for just over a decade and even during that time the population of Saigon has lived off a thriving black market. The overseas Vietnamese are already investing and the Japanese are beginning to sniff around. I wouldn't be at all surprised to see increasing international attention and investment centred on Vietnam in the next few years.

The Pacific's century

The development of the NICs was originally greatly assisted by the United States. The Americans took advantage of the low wage-costs of Taiwan and South Korea, setting up specific tariff regimes which favoured re-exports of low value-added products. These allowed American companies to carry out their more labour-intensive assembly in Asia and re-import sub-assemblies for incorporation into more sophisticated American-made end-products. But although America is also militarily close to Korea, tension between the United States and the NICs is increasing as their industrial challenge intensifies.

This strain has manifested itself in American demands for the liberalization of Taiwanese and South Korean markets, particularly for American agricultural products, with ensuing demonstrations by Korean farmers in Seoul against demands for the country to open its market to imports of cigarettes and beef. The United States has also insisted that all four Asian NICs devalue their currencies to reduce their exports' competitiveness and boost home demand. Coupled with this has been increasing American restrictions against imports from the NICs. In 1988, for example, the United States revoked Singapore's developing-nation status and imposed tariffs on a raft of Singaporean products, so causing an anti-American demonstration of 800 slogan-chanting people. Other American measures, including spurious anti-dumping duties, quotas and 'voluntary export restraints', have further exacerbated the situation.

On the face of it, the progress of the region as a whole should have positive implications for both the United States and the West in general, for the success and growing integration of the East Asian economy is actually helping to protect a strategic flank of the United States, as well as providing a potentially huge market for Western goods. The more that Asian goods are excluded from Western markets, however, the more the NICs will be pushed ever closer to Japan. Overall trade flows within Asia are already expanding much faster than world trade as a whole, but, late in 1989, a team of Asian economists calculated that the integration of the United States economy with the Pacific region declined by about 30 per cent between 1975 and 1985.[7] Already, Japan's trade with Asia as a whole exceeds that with North America. Japan also supplanted the United States as the East Asian region's major trading partner as far back as 1964 and has since held that position. Japan's trade with the NICs also tops her trade with the European Community. The result is that Western influence is diminishing in what is before long likely to become the world's most important region.

For some time, far-sighted commentators have predicted that the area broadly known as the 'Pacific Basin' will eventually overtake the United States and Europe in economic dominance. Back in 1975, Norman Macrae of *The Economist* predicted that while the period from 1775 to 1875 might be seen as the British century and from 1875 to 1975 as the American century, so the century following 1975 might well become the Pacific's century.[8]

If that is so, it will also be very much Japan's century, for despite continuing frictions, at the hub of eastern Asia's progress lies Japan's economic power – for the time being. For the Japanese are almost painfully conscious of the fact that if there is any serious industrial challenge to their supremacy, it will come from the emerging nations of East Asia.

Part VIII

Doing Business in Japan – Winning Where it Counts

MANY WESTERN BUSINESSPEOPLE now regard the Japanese as unbeatable economic supermen, unerringly progressing towards world domination. Others persist in calling the Japanese devious and unscrupulous economic gangsters who only win by resorting to underhand tactics which include keeping foreigners out of their home market. This strategy, they say, allows the Japanese to amass the domestic profits necessary to dump products on unsuspecting Western economies. Yet enough European and American businesses have succeeded in this toughest of markets to call these views into question.

Succeeding in Japan is, of course, undoubtedly harder than in many other markets. Apart from cultural differences, the competition is fierce and any Western manufacturer must be prepared to make a patient, long-term commitment. Those who have made the effort, however, have found it possible to succeed, while the disciplines needed to prosper in Japan have benefited their operations worldwide.

24

新大国

ATTACK IS THE BEST DEFENCE

'Any company that wishes to participate in the global village that we now find ourselves in cannot opt out of the second largest economy in the world.' Michael Perry, Unilever.[1]

CAN WESTERN COMPANIES and products succeed in Japan? Nestlé have over 60 per cent of the Japanese instant coffee market and Dunlop takes 50 per cent of golf ball sales; 30 per cent of electric shavers sold in Japan are made by Braun; Nordica and Salomon dominate the Japanese market for ski boots; 70 per cent of all stainless steel razor blades bought by the Japanese are produced in Connecticut by the Schick Division of Warner-Lambert; Applied Materials of San Jose, California, make 40 per cent of their $500-million annual sales of sophisticated semiconductor-manufacturing equipment to Japan; and at one point, half of the disposable nappies used by Japanese mothers were imported by Procter & Gamble.

More than 1,000 foreign companies had wholly- or partly-owned affiliates in Japan in 1987, with sales totalling $120 billion and 260,000 employees. Japan is the largest single purchaser of American-made data-processing equipment, commercial aircraft and aircraft parts, inorganic chemicals, pharmaceuticals and broadcasting equipment.[2] And of the 40 fastest-growing companies in Japan from March 1980 to March 1983, eight were overseas-related, of which four were wholly foreign-owned. Furthermore, a study in the late 1970s by the American Chamber of Commerce in Japan indicated that United States investments in Japan had been extremely profitable, with an apparent average annual return of 19 per cent – twice as good as the return on American investments in France or Britain.[3]

Western companies have also found great success in selling products made elsewhere to Japan. Each year, for example, American oil companies sell more than $20 billion worth of non-American crude oil to Japan. Nike trainers, made in Korea and Taiwan by the American sports shoe company, are popular among Japanese joggers and tennis players; and Loctite Corporation's Taiwanese-made industrial adhesives help to hold together Toyota cars. The profits from such enterprises do not count towards the Japanese–United States trade balance, but they still fill the coffers of American companies.

Then there are the numerous joint ventures, local manufacturing operations and licensing deals which also help to enrich Western corporations. McDonald's, Coca Cola, Kentucky Fried Chicken and IBM are almost as big names in Japan as in the United States or Europe. In fact, the Japanese drink more Coca Cola than anyone else except Americans and Mexicans, and the company's products account for 60 per cent of all the carbonated drinks sold in Japan; while a $200-million-plus a year 50–50 joint venture between Yamazaki and the Ritz Cracker company, Nabisco, is a strong number two in the Japanese biscuit market and number three in snacks.

The 100 per cent American-owned Japan Tupperware company sells about $100-million-a-year worth of its storage products to Japanese housewives; and almost one in ten Japanese families now holds a cancer insurance policy written by the Japanese branch of the American Family Life Assurance Company of Columbus, Georgia. In fact, American Family Life's Japanese revenues of $350 million a year comfortably exceed its United States takings.[4]

Each day, 3,000 Japanese pump iron at Tokyo's seven Nautilus clubs, equipped with $14 million worth of American-made exercise machines and weights, while a further 6,500 Japanese munch Domino pizzas from one of 54 licencees. Other licence success stories include Seven–Eleven stores, which started out in Japan in 1973 and now totals 3,800 outlets with sales of close to $5 billion, while Tiffany & Co earned $26.5 million from its related outlets in Japan in 1988.[5]

What is more, this sort of Western success in the Japanese economy is no recent development. Way back in 1899, Western Electric of the United States set up a Japanese joint venture company which later became the giant Nippon Electric Company (NEC); and, in 1905, General Electric of the United States took over the Tokyo Electric Company (TEC), later also acquiring a stake in Shibaura, which was eventually to merge with TEC to become Toshiba.

Of course, it is true that the McDonalds hamburgers sold in Japan use Japanese beef and the Japanese Seven–Eleven stores are owned by a Japanese group which pays a licence fee. But almost all non-American McDonalds – not just those in Japan – use locally-produced beef, while the use of joint ventures and franchises for fast-food and convenience-store chains is not limited to the Japanese market. The fact remains that substantial revenues flow back to the United States from these ventures – and the success of such quintessentially American companies indicates that the Japanese are far from uniformly hostile to foreign goods.

Naturally, hamburgers and convenience stores lack a certain industrial *machismo*, and it is true that only about five per cent of Japan's manufacturing output is accounted for by companies with significant foreign ownership. But the situation is rapidly changing, for as perceptions of Japan's status in the world economy develop, so more and more Western companies are moving in to build on the existing base. According to the Mitsubishi Bank, 185 American concerns set up manufacturing or sales arms in Japan in 1985, compared with only 70 in 1980. In 1986, 308 American companies invested ¥142 billion (£620 million) to open or expand Japanese operations, and by 1987, several thousand American companies had already directly invested a total of $14.3 billion in Japan, in addition to a similar total from European Western companies.

Why bother?

It is often asserted that the Japanese market is difficult to penetrate. But this is not primarily due to import restraints, covert or otherwise: after all, Japanese businessmen have often had to take the time and trouble to overcome obstacles in Western markets. Nor is it even due to a cultural preference for locally made goods. Rather, it is because Japan is a highly competitive market in which Western manufacturers find themselves pitched against some of the most efficient producers and sharpest sellers in the world. Even when success has been achieved, Japanese producers tend to hit back hard, as Procter & Gamble found when its early dominance in disposable nappies was quickly eroded. Japan is a market which needs careful handling and any Western producer who thinks that he or she can send a rep with a suitcase of samples and a Japanese phrase book and be crowned with success will be sorely disappointed – as indeed many have been.

So why bother with such a cutthroat hard market? Dick Vaubel of the West German hair care company, Wella, provides one answer: 'A three per cent share of the Japanese market', he points out, 'is equivalent to more than 40 per cent of the Swiss market.' Because Japan's GNP amounts to more than a third of the combined GNPs of all of the world's industrialized nations except the United States, it is worthy of your efforts even if your market share is small. What is more, with higher average earnings than in any EC country, Japanese workers have substantial purchasing power: in other words, Japan is a huge and growing market where even a relatively small market-share can be valuable.

There is a further important point. Just as Japanese companies studied their American counterparts and refined their techniques in order to penetrate the Western markets, so now many Western companies have realized that they in turn will have to study Japanese methods in order to compete – and where better to learn from the Japanese than in their own market? Many American companies operating plants in Japan, for example, have found that their Japanese factories regularly beat their other plants in terms of productivity and quality. IBM's two Japanese plants invariably rank among the top ten per cent of the company's 50 or so worldwide factories; while other American companies, such as Johnson & Johnson and Nabisco, claim that their Japanese plants have come to serve as models for the parent company's American operations.[6]

Procter & Gamble has learned other lessons from its Japanese subsidiary. The Cincinnati-based detergents giant was badly hit in 1987 when one of its main Japanese rivals, Kao, introduced a detergent called 'Attack', which rapidly won a 30 per cent share in the Japanese market. Now the American company has emulated its Japanese rival's phenomenally successful super-concentrated soapsuds not just in Japan, but also in the United States where Procter & Gamble stole a march on its American competitors when it launched its new Cheer brand late in 1989.[7]

But perhaps the most important point is that, by maintaining a presence in the Japanese market, not only are you better able to defend yourself from attack on world markets by Japanese competitors, but you are also more likely to get early warning of their intentions and capabilities. Many American companies, according to industry expert, James Abegglen, 'have awakened to find that because they are not in Japan, or are unable to compete in Japan, their profit positions everywhere abroad have become quite insecure'.[8]

How, then, do Western companies succeed in Japan? Unfortunately, it is outside the scope of this book to examine this important subject in as much detail as several excellent works dedicated to the subject have already done.[9] Nonetheless, a relatively brief amble over the territory may prove useful, while also offering further insight into why the Japanese themselves are so successful.

Making the commitment

The 1984 Los Angeles Olympic Games must have been especially galling for American photographic giant, Eastman Kodak. Arch rival Fuji Photo Film of Japan had won the right to market its products as the 'official film' for the Games with the result that its name was beamed all over the world. It proved to be the final straw for the slow-footed American giant. That same August, Kodak's Planning Director, Albert Sieg, went to Tokyo prepared to spend a year studying how to attack Fuji in its home market by bolstering Kodak's sagging sales in camera-toting Japan.

At that time, Kodak's share of Japan's $2.2 billion photographic film and paper market was only ten per cent – and falling. Import duties and non-tariff barriers were not the difficulty, for duties were only 3.7 per cent. The problem, rather, was that Kodak, which had been in Japan for 90 years, had never fully committed itself to the Japanese market.

Way back in the 1930s, for example, when Kodak boss, George Eastman, was asked by a Japanese chemical company to build a joint-venture film plant in Japan, he rejected it on the advice of engineers who argued that Japan's high summer-time humidity would make it difficult to dry the film base. Undeterred, the Japanese company went on to establish what was to become Fuji Photo Film – Kodak's most formidable rival. So, by the 1980s, Kodak had a strong local rival, no direct marketing in Japan, no resident manager and no Japanese factories. Instead, its Tokyo staff of 25 relied on a complex structure of local wholesalers.

Sieg's first step was to buy out Kodak's main Japanese distributor, so ending a relationship that dated back to 1923. He then went on to purchase a stake in local camera maker, Chinon Industries, and established joint production of Kodak 35mm cameras in Japan. This was followed by the acquisition of a controlling stake in a joint-venture film processing business with a local company called Imagica. Moreover, a brand new R&D centre was constructed near Yokohama and the Tokyo staff number was boosted to 140.

By the end of the 1980s, Kodak Japan had 3,000 Japanese employees, mainly in sales and processing, and nearly 20 graduates from Japan's top engineering universities joined the firm in 1987 – all with a guarantee of long-term employment. All employees have been offered stock options since Kodak listed its shares on the Tokyo Stock Exchange and the company also now sponsors local sporting events, ranging from *sumo* wrestling to soccer. Since the changes, Kodak's share of the Japanese market has climbed steadily to about 15 per cent – which is a 50 per cent boost since 1984. In Tokyo and Osaka, the American company's sales actually account for as much as 25 per cent of the local market – all at Fuji's expense. There is a final note: the official film at the 1988 Seoul Olympics was Kodak.[10]

Crosfield is a British-based manufacturers of colour scanners, the expensive, specialist machines which are used to scan colour transparencies and artwork to produce the four-colour separations from which full colour printing is produced. Its Studio 800 systems take the process a stage further by electronically manipulating the images to enhance or modify them. Using sophisticated computer and laser technology, Crosfield's scanners are the type of products which the Japanese themselves are particularly good at making, and which should therefore be difficult to sell into their market. Yet Crosfield's sales in Japan grew from 47 scanners and systems in 1983 to well over 100 a year by 1988, in addition to a host of other peripheral products and systems.

Jim Salmon, the company's managing director, confirmed the crucial importance of patience and commitment for success in Japan:

Take a long-term view of the commitment – things will not happen overnight. The Japanese themselves take long-term views on business development. To succeed, you must do the same. Be prepared to adopt the same tactics as your Japanese competitors. The Japanese are obsessed with market share and price, and they strive to gain market share with the long-term aim of market domination in mind.

Perhaps the need for patience is most graphically expressed by Haruo Okinobu, the president of Yamatage–Honeywell, the joint-venture manufacturer of high-tech instruments and controls:

A lot of people say the Japanese market isn't open. That's wrong: it is open. But it's like a club: you've got to be a member to enjoy full privileges. Of course, if you want, you can apply for membership – but the waiting list is 20 years long.[11]

This long-term, patient commitment has proved vital to success in the Japanese market for many foreign companies. American drinks giant, Brown–Forman, tried for seven years to crack the Japanese whisky market with its Jack Daniels brand before sales started rolling in. It took razor company, Schick, the same length of time to gain five per cent of Japanese razor blade sales, before boosting its share to a dominant 70 per cent of the market over the subsequent 20 years. American Hospital Supply, now the leader in the Japanese health-care market, operated in Japan for five years before it won a single order. Procter & Gamble is rumoured to have spent over $70 million in getting its Japanese detergent and toiletries business off the ground. Even the Japanese McDonald's operator, now the number one restaurant chain in Japan, made no money for the first three years. The message is clear: If you want to succeed in Japan, you have, above all, to behave like a Japanese company; you must be as patiently committed to long-term growth over short-term profits as they are.

Cultural sensitivity

The prevalent image of the Japanese woman is of a demure flower, bending to the whim of her husband, her lord and master. Yet, surprisingly, bank surveys have found that many Japanese men hand over their pay packet in its entirety to their wives, for Japanese women are usually wholly responsible for the family savings and planning – a factor which must be taken into account when trying to sell goods into the Japanese market.

Cultural sensitivity to such special Japanese factors is as essential for success in the Japanese market as having a long-term commitment. For example, surveys reveal that about three-quarters of Japanese women questioned shopped the previous day and in small quantities from the tiny family-owned stores which exist on almost every suburban block. What is more, as there is a store within walking and cycling distance of virtually every urban dwelling, Japanese housewives tend to shop without the car, leaving bulky and heavy items such as family-sized sodas or rice to be delivered directly from the liquor store or rice merchant. So trying to tempt Japanese housewives into buying large, Western-style 'giant packs', or special bulk-buy offers from small stores is almost certainly doomed to failure.

Japanese cleanliness is another important cultural factor which has been seized on by Unilever, the Anglo–Dutch detergents, fats, food and toiletries multinational which has been so successful in convincing the Japanese that its fairly ordinary Lux soap brand is upmarket and desirable that Lux has become the number one gift item. The potential of the two Japanese gift-giving seasons was quickly grasped when market research showed that the average Japanese household had no fewer than 30 tablets of soap in stock – an indication of Japan's obsession with cleanliness as well as the potential of the gift-soap market. The company has further boosted its product's perceived value by launching an upmarket 'Lux Imperial' brand.

The average Japanese also washes his or her hair almost every day, compared to Europeans who only wash it two or three times a week. Some Japanese girls, market research found, even washed their hair twice a day. So Unilever also successfully launched shampoo brands such as Sunsilk, which was adapted for the local market and manufactured in Japan.

It goes without saying that market research has also to be carefully interpreted through eyes sensitive to Japanese cultural habits. Even then, the eye can sometimes miss certain Japanese idiosyncracies with disastrous – or sometimes excellent – results. In 1980, BSN, the giant French food group, thought that it could emulate the success in Japan of some Western convenience food products, such as hamburgers and pizzas, with its Danone brand yoghurt. A decade later, the company's original ambitions had disappeared in losses which exceeded the original investment. To its cost, BSN belatedly discovered that Japan is frequently the exception to a popular theory in international marketing which teaches that as consumers' lives in developed countries follow increasingly similar patterns, so does their taste in goods.

'I agree with globalization, but it's very much more difficult to carry out than it sounds,' said Robert Dahan, BSN's chief representative in Japan, ruefully. Ironically, BSN did many things right. It approached the Japanese market steadily, making its first studies back in 1979, and carefully chose as its local partner a diverse food company, called Ajinomoto, which had previous experience of joint ventures.

BSN's crucial mistake, however, was to misinterpret its market research. The company hoped to tempt the Japanese with new types of yoghurt, especially yoghurt-based desserts and fruit-flavoured Petit Suisse cheese. For six months, the company air-freighted in supplies from France for a careful market survey. The results were superb, with research showing that Japanese customers loved the products. On the basis of this, BSN forecast sales growth ranging from a low of 20 to 30 per cent a year to well over 100 per cent, and the venture was expected to be in the black after a mere three and a half years.

But within 12 months the dream had turned sour, for sales were running at only a fifth of projections. According to Dahan, the initial market surveys, following the theory of global marketing, posed questions to Japanese consumers which were identical to those asked in other countries. The answers were then assessed by the same, European-designed criteria. What they ignored, however, was the inbred politeness of the Japanese. 'They'll say they like a product, even if they think it's bullshit. But they won't buy it again,' says Dahan.

When, on the other hand, Tupperware engaged a marketing consultant to appraise its chances of success in Japan in the early 1960s, the results were poor. Besides the inappropriateness of the American company's direct selling method, it was not the custom, the consultant said, for Japanese women to give parties for their friends, while Japanese housewives preferred ceramic, metal or wood containers to plastic.

Tupperware went ahead anyway and, in the event, Japanese housewives eagerly fell upon the plastic cartons, while American-style Tupperware sales parties proved so compatible with Japanese social habits that they were copied by a wide range of local companies. All of which goes to prove that: first, in determining the viability of a product in Japan, market research has to be interpreted with extreme cultural sensitivity; and second, that frequently, typically Western concepts can succeed as long as they fit in with underlying Japanese habits.

新　大　国

In the late 1950s, about 80 per cent of the Japanese razor-blade market was held by Japanese manufacturers led by Feather, based in Seki, a town famous in Japan for its tradition of producing high quality *samurai* swords. At that time, the main Western company in the Japanese market was Gillette, which accounted for about 20 per cent of overall sales.

When American blade maker, Schick, signed a sole agency agreement with a Japanese trading company, Hattori, in 1960, it judged that to appeal to the Japanese it would have to offer a more innovative product than the double-edged blades then dominant. So the first product Schick brought to Japan was its injector system which slides the blade directly into the razor. This quickly appealed to the gadget-minded Japanese and the company soon acquired five per cent of the market. Three years later, Schick went one better and introduced the first stainless-steel blades to Japan.

In 1971, however, urgent action was suddenly demanded when Schick got wind of a plan by Gillette to market its new twin-blade cartridges in the Tokyo area for the first time. So Schick's Milford, Connecticut plant, which had already begun to produce its own twin-blade cartridge, quickly air-freighted a sufficient quantity to allow the introduction of the new product nationwide and in time to meet Gillette's Tokyo launch. The pre-emptive strike helped to establish Schick as the product leader on the Japanese market and it is now the number one razor company in Japan.[12]

Kodak had to modify its product to suit the physical aspect of the Japanese consumer, for Kodak has found that cultural attitudes towards skin are so important that the company uses a different colour balance in the film which it sells in Japan. Kodak's Albert Sieg explains:

> The Japanese consumer is not interested in having his subjects flesh tone look too yellow. He likes to have it look a little pinker. That's a characteristic that in Caucasian markets is called 'beefy flesh tone' and isn't considered desirable. But here it is. So we have moved our product towards the Japanese preference and, to the extent you can measure, it's had a positive effect on sales.[13]

Similarly, Wella reformulated its shampoos for the Japanese market to take account of the fact that Asian hair is thicker and smoother than European hair. Japan now accounts for ten per cent of Wella's business and is its second biggest market after West Germany. So important has Japan proved to the company, that it has shifted responsibility for the Pacific region to Tokyo to ensure that it is in close touch with local market needs.

Sadly, not all Western manufacturers have been so diligent. When Apple decided to sell its innovative personal computers in Japan in 1977, it was the first company of any nationality to offer a PC on the Japanese market. Unfortunately, Apple not only tried to sell machines which were unable to process the Kanji characters used in written Japanese – thus limiting its market to English users – but also failed to provide Japanese instruction manuals. Apple's Japanese sales now account for less than one per cent of the local market.

Western manufacturers have sometimes been able to get away with not adapting their products – but only until they have faced local competition.

When Sears decided to export large refrigerators to Japan, for example, they were bought by Japanese consumers who did not really have the space for them, but who found locally produced models too small. Since then, Japanese manufacturers have produced refrigerators of all sizes and largely squeezed Sears out of the market. Even in the late 1980s, by which time Western manufacturers should really have learned some lessons, Japanese store managers were complaining that the compartments in Western-made fridges were designed in such a way as to make it difficult to separate raw fish from meat, while American models tended to overchill vegetables – something which Japanese housewives are rather fussy about.

Eating with the eyes

There is a saying that 'the Chinese eat with their stomachs and the Japanese eat with their eyes'. At formal dinners in Japan, the arrangement and appearance of the food is as important as the taste, and it is not unknown for top *sushi* bars to go to great lengths to ensure that each grain of rice points the same way. This aesthetic tradition helps to explain the special importance – indeed, near obsession – which the Japanese attach to packaging. Simple or utilitarian wrappings are assumed to contain inferior goods.

So packaging which may have proved suitable in other markets may not work in Japan. This is why, despite the fact that all the razor blades so successfully sold by Schick in Japan are imported, their packaging is specially designed and made in Japan. Others have not always been so thoughtful. One major British confectionery company tried to sell its products to the Japanese in the early 1980s in packages made up by its Hong Kong agent who left some of the script unconverted from Chinese to Japanese characters. Needless to say, sweet-toothed Japanese did not flock to buy them.

Moreover, the Japanese generally take an interest in who makes a product and like to associate with a successful and popular company. This is why 'own brand' products which have been tried in Japan have failed disastrously in the past. Even the large Daiei supermarket chain's attempts to entice the Japanese housewife with no-frills, low-priced, own-brand products largely misfired, although generic products are now finally beginning to make some headway.

This susceptability to perceived value, which occasionally verges on snobbery, is something which can be exploited by those Western manufacturers whose products project an upmarket image in the minds of Japanese consumers. For example, Jack Daniels bourbon sells about half a million bottles a year in Japan at more than $50 a time, compared to less than $20 for bestselling premium Japanese whisky brands like Suntory Old.

Jack Daniels' success derives from its top-notch image which has made it a favoured gift in a society where gift-giving occurs twice a year, at midsummer and New Year, and where giving less than the best is an insult which can lose you valuable business acquaintances. Jack Daniels has also become a fashionable tipple among young Japanese professionals who like it for what it says about them as much as they enjoy it as a drink.

The Japanese also equate price with quality to a greater degree than elsewhere. When the distillers, Brown–Forman, tried to boost Jack Daniels sales by reducing the price of its premium brand, sales actually fell. And according to Victor Harris of Max Factor:

> In the cosmetics business in Japan, prices are twice what they are for comparable items in the States – and it's very important to have the brand which is the highest price in its field. We are constantly in a kind of reverse price-competition with Shiseido and Kanebo to have the most expensive brands. The cheapest lipstick we sell here is $15 or more. Our SK2 – our entry in the biotechnical field if you will – is around $70 for a three-ounce bottle and we can't make it fast enough. It's insane.[14]

Good service is another essential for companies aspiring to success in the Japanese market. Japanese consumers expect it – and they usually get it. Franchised car dealers send representatives round to their customers every few months to check that their cars are running satisfactorily. When the time comes for the regular service, the car is picked up from the customer's home and delivered back again. BMW took the decision to meet Japanese service expectations and, as a result, its sales are rapidly rising. As from 1985, for example, anyone who ordered a part from BMW in Tokyo before 3.00pm was guaranteed delivery the next day.

Intuition and tuning

Koji Oshita is the president of McCann–Erickson Hakuhodo, a joint venture established in 1960 which has since become Japan's second largest advertising agency. Oshita warns of the cultural differences which need to be borne in mind when advertising to the Japanese:

> Hard sell does not transfer well to Japan where commercials tend to be more indirect. Japanese commercials do not shout how good a product is, but leave the final judgment to consumers, allowing viewers to draw their own conclusions.
>
> In Japan, comparative advertising – saying for example that the detergent being advertised washes whiter than competitive brands – is effectively prohibited.

Even where toned-down comparisons are allowed, Oshita says that Japanese consumers do not like commercials that make direct comparisons: 'They take such ads as slandering others – the Japanese people don't appreciate direct expressions.'

But the history of Coca Cola's marketing in Japan shows how there is a place for intuition, as well as cultural sensitivity, in advertising for the Japanese market. When, in the late 1960s, Coca Cola Japan was considering a proposed TV commercial showing a young man drinking directly from the bottle, many people advised against using the ad since drinking from bottles was considered poor manners. But the company went ahead and, in doing so, created a new national fad – 'bugle-style' drinking. The ad succeeded because a break with tradition suited the mood of Japanese youngsters at that particular time.

One advertisement which has been running on Japanese television for some time shows an idyllic image of a pretty girl with long, blonde hair, in a white dress, running through a sunlit alpine meadow complete with running streams and tumbling waterfalls. This advertisement breaks most of the rules of marketing in Japan by employing virtually the same film and format as used in Europe. Yet the product being advertised, Unilever's Timotei shampoo, was catapulted into the number one position on the Japanese market.

Michael Perry is a lifelong Unilever man, with the world-weary air of someone who has spent much of his life selling to foreigners. After 23 years marketing Unilever's products in South America, West Africa and South East Asia, Perry became chairman of the company's Japanese arm, Nippon Lever, in 1981 and he knows more about succeeding in Japan than most.

He told me that the Timotei campaign was masterminded by an all-expatriate team, using J Walter Thomson as the agency. They realized that, despite the inadvisability of running unadulterated Western ads in Japan, the naïvety and simplicity of the existing Timotei advertisements would be appealing to the Japanese, trapped as most of them are in an unyielding urban environment. They took a gamble that the existing ads would strike a chord with the Japanese – and they were right.

Perry has drawn his own conclusion from this experience: 'If you just do things the Japanese way, you end up simply aping the Japanese', he warns, qualifying the generally-held view that you must heavily adapt your marketing for the Japanese. 'I accept', he went on, 'that sometimes you have to totally change your style and campaign for Japan, but we often found that what worked internationally also worked in Japan – you can't generalize, but provided your intuition and tuning is right, it can work.'

25

新
大
国

Nintai

'Competing in Japan is not easy. It is hard, but necessary. A Japan strategy is required, and is difficult to put in place in most conventional corporate structures. Still, the obstacles to success are not inherent in the situation in Japan, but are largely in the minds and behaviours of the United States and European companies. Patience, determination and skill in investing in Japan do provide a high final payout, in profits and in world strategic position.'
James Abegglen and George Stalk.[1]

ACCORDING TO MARK Zimmerman, who worked in Japan for a major American pharmaceutical company for many years, the Japanese word 'nintai' best expresses the quality of concentration needed to succeed in Japan and in dealing with the Japanese themselves. *Nintai* refers to the special kind of patience needed by a person contemplating a rock garden in order to perceive every nuance of light and shade and to become completely aware of the beauty of the whole. In business, *nintai* means having the endurance to uncover and consider every factor which might have a bearing on the eventual outcome of a deal.[2]

Nintai also affects the way in which the Japanese negotiate, which can be an extremely drawn-out process. In addition, the intense Japanese dislike of saying 'No' can confuse Westerners and encourage them to pursue a topic with even more rigour. Unfortunately, this only compounds the problem, causing the Japanese to listen politely before responding '*Hai*'. Although this literally means 'Yes', it can often in fact just mean 'Yes, I can hear what you are saying', but no more.

This is just one of the many problems lying in store for Westerners who need to deal with the Japanese. Some people have attributed such difficulties to deviousness, rather than to a different culture, which is a little unfair. After all, an unsympathetic commentator could make a similar case for other nations. Does not an Englishman, for example, say 'With all due respect', when in fact he means 'You are talking a load of rubbish'?

But the real point is that anyone wishing to do business in Japan has to be aware of, and make allowance for, the way the Japanese operate – however odd their habits might seem. And this type of cultural sensitivity is just as important in face-to-face meetings as in all aspects of doing business in Japan, from designing a product through to its packaging.

Adapting to local practices may include indulging in lengthy after-work socializing and mastering the language. According to Edward Hennessey, chairman of the American conglomerate, Allied–Signal: 'About 10,000 Japanese business executives work in the United States and virtually all speak English; about 1,000 American executives work in Japan, and just a handful speak Japanese.'[3]

Being like the Japanese

'Our firm is actually 120 per cent Japanese,' says Hachiro Koyama, chairman of Johnson Wax Japan.[4] He is able to make this claim because the Japanese management practices which he employs are not so different from the socially conscious policies of the United States parent company. Johnson Wax's American experience may have helped it to adapt relatively easily to Japanese conditions, but others have found, equally, that adopting Japanese business techniques and behaving culturally like Japanese companies is essential for success. Max Factor in Japan, for example, has a company union, promotion by seniority, lifetime employment and company vacation homes. Its rival, Revlon, failed to follow Japanese practices and has performed relatively poorly in Japan.

Commitment to the Japanese market also means allowing subsidiaries a great deal of local autonomy, investing them with extensive decision-making authority, as ICI, Dupont and IBM have done, as well as adopting Japanese practices and attitudes and employing local people. Indeed, many consider this last point as essential to becoming a major player in Japan, as the world's largest glass maker, Pilkington, based in St Helens, in the north of England, has found.

Pilkington's ophthalmic and technical glass division, Chance Pilkington, was established in 1957 to manufacture and sell raw spectacle glass in the form of blanks to lens manufacturers, as well as optical and technical glass to producers of optical equipment and instruments. Chance Pilkington invested heavily in the 1950s by buying a licence from an American manufacturer for a technically advanced continuous manufacturing process. Unfortunately, this investment came at just the time when the UK camera and binocular industry was waning, so leaving the company with a factory geared to high-volume production, but no home market. It also coincided with the emergence of the Japanese camera industry. Selling to Japan, therefore, seemed the only hope.

Despite intense competition from local manufacturers, Chance Pilkington has consistently accounted for about ten per cent of the Japanese demand for the optical and special technical glass used in cameras, binoculars, photocopiers and video cameras – a success which has been essential because

Japanese manufacturers now absorb close to 80 per cent of world output of this specialized glass. The British company has also had considerable success with ophthalmic glass, particularly with its Reactolite Rapide photochromic lenses, which turn darker as the sun gets brighter, and it now claims a 70 per cent share of the sun-glasses market for Reactolite.

All of Chance Pilkington's technical glass is supplied from the company's English factories, but, crucially, its Japanese operation is backed up with frequent technical and commercial visits from the UK. Knowledge of local market conditions has been reinforced with experience from a plastic-lens manufacturing facility which the company owns in Osaka. The British company also quickly realized that to really prosper in Japan, it would need a strong local presence, so it opened a branch in Tokyo in 1966. Chance Pilkington also took the important decision to staff the office with Japanese nationals, who were provided with extensive training in the UK. Since then, all except one of the people the company has employed in Japan has been Japanese – the exception being a UK national who, having studied Japanese, worked in the Tokyo office for a relatively short period.

But being an employer in Japan has its own special rules. When Texas Instruments set up in Japan, it made the mistake of taking an American approach to hiring, pay and benefits and dismissed the Japanese custom of offering six-monthly bonuses as impractical. Morale fell rapidly and the company had trouble recruiting, so TI changed and adopted Japanese methods, including bonuses and a strong seniority-based promotion system which aided its success.

Having a Japanese person at the top is often also necessary for Western companies in order to reinforce their commitment to Japan. For one thing, highly paid Western executives can arouse jealousy among Japanese employees who hold comparable jobs, but are less generously rewarded – particularly if the foreigner is placed above an older Japanese person. It is true that some companies, such as Coca Cola, have managed to get away with an American president and nine or ten other Western executives, but IBM Japan for many years made a point of the fact that there were no Americans among its top managers. TI, too, which once had a large number of expatriates based in Japan, now only brings Americans in for relatively short periods. The British pharmaceutical giant, Glaxo, is another multinational which no longer employs expatriates, while Unilever only has a dozen or so.

Of course, a common complaint concerns the difficulty of attracting high-calibre Japanese employees to Western companies. Their diffidence can be explained by the fact that repeated shake-ups at some Western companies have given Western businesses a bad name, while the withdrawal of a number of companies which have lacked the commitment to succeed in Japan has given rise to fears about the permanency of foreign affiliates. Many Japanese people see greater continuity and security in working for Japanese firms. Moreover, in intensely status-conscious Japan, association with a Western company is not as prestigious as employment by a top Japanese firm.

'It's difficult, but not at all impossible' to put together an outstanding management team in Japan, says Kneale Ashworth, the British-born chief of Johnson & Johnson's Japanese subsidiary.[5] Nowadays, many established foreign affiliates in Japan emulate the recruitment efforts of Japanese companies in the universities. As a company's reputation grows, the situation improves. Unilever, for example, which suffered severe recruitment problems in its early days, can now rely on thousands of applicants a year. The Tokyo branch of Barclays de Zoete Wedd, the British stockbroker and investment bank, interviewed 120 graduate applicants in 1988, appointing 26 of them.[6] And by 1987, IBM Japan had risen to become the fourth most popular employment choice for science and engineering graduates from top Japanese universities; DEC Japan climbed from fifty-fourth in 1984 to thirty-second in 1987; while the quasi-religious zeal of the Amway company culture appealed strongly to the Japanese and the company attracts good quality Japanese recruits to its salesforce.

Of course, not all companies can afford the years of effort required to develop contacts at leading colleges like Tokyo University. They often have to resort to less prestigious private universities – but perseverance and commitment usually pays dividends. TI Japan, for example, is now headed by Hideo Yoshizaki, a former top MITI official.

The right partner

From their mosaic, mock Byzantine perches high above the Palace of Westminster's Central Lobby where, for more than a century, people have come to 'lobby' their Members of Parliament, the four patron saints of the constituent nations of the United Kingdom stared impassively down at a little group of Japanese businessmen. They were visiting carpet distributors whom I was entertaining to dinner, following a tour of a carpet factory in the small Derbyshire town of Ripley in the English Midlands.

The Flotex brand carpet which the factory was selling to the Japanese is a high-cost, very durable and washable product used around the world in hotels, airports, car showrooms and other places which suffer from heavy wear. When it decided to market its product in Japan, Bonar & Flotex, the manufacturers, realized it lacked the resources to set up its own operation, so like many small- and medium-sized Western manufacturers, it appointed a local agent. Its first distributor was a disappointment, so in 1984 it switched to one of the key players in the distribution of floor coverings, Daiso, which has branch offices and warehouses throughout Japan.

Bonar & Flotex's managing director, Peter Bartlett, who works from an office on the factory site, told me of the main difficulties he had encountered:

First, we have to go through both an initial importer and then a distributor, which compounds our price difficulties against local manufacturers. Then, despite strong relationships between all parties, communication remains a problem. On top of that, we have difficulty meeting moves in the market in terms of colour and design, and the Japanese sometimes find it difficult to understand why we cannot be more flexible – it is something which we shall need to address in the future. Finally, with lengthy supply lines, forward planning and stock levels are a subject of constant debate, but unquestionably the situation has become less complex as sales develop.

Peter Bartlett was outlining very similar problems to those encountered by medium-sized Western manufacturers which use Japanese agents and whose initial sales volume is relatively small. But, having found the right agent, Bonar & Flotex was taking the trouble to cultivate and develop a relationship with its distributors, as was evidenced by the visit to England. As Peter Bartlett told me:

We had a slow start but patience and increased understanding has enabled us to develop our volume sales from 11,000 square metres in 1981 to about 120,000 square metres by 1988. To generate this growth, we have obviously had to invest heavily in travel, in R&D, in design costs, in rebate and incentive schemes and so on – but we're getting there.

Peter Bartlett is also clear on two important points:

We have had to recognize the fundamental difference between our two cultures and we had to make sure that we got the right type of highly committed partners in Japan who believe in the potential of our product. They have an enthusiasm which I wish we could create in other overseas markets where we are operative.

Another Derbyshire company which recognized the importance of finding the right distributor in Japan was the long-established, family-controlled chocolates manufacturer, Thorntons. In 1983, it settled on Nisshoku, a substantial Osaka-based company dating back to 1955 which only handles high-quality, imported foods. One aspect of Nisshoku's marketing strategy which particularly attracted Thorntons was the company's chain of concessions in department stores, all of which are staffed by Nisshoku personnel.

Thorntons' manufacturing director, Peter Heaps, who has been closely involved in the Japanese marketing campaign, is enthusiastic about his Japanese distributor who has steadily boosted sales until they now stand at over £100,000 a year. The main difficulty Heaps has experienced has been in supplying the speciality products needed for the different Japanese seasons and celebrations, which has meant that manufacturing has had to be re-scheduled to fit in with shipment dates. 'But that's our problem,' Heaps told me. 'It is all part of adapting products and being sensitive to the special requirements of the Japanese market.'

If you can sell bricks to Japan, you can probably sell them just about anything. Butterley Brick is part of the Anglo–American Hanson Industries conglomerate. The company has sold three million bricks in Japan since 1988 when it appointed Kunishiro International as its local agent. Butterley's success in shipping its hefty products half way round the world has been helped by increasing Japanese interest in building country clubs and restaurants in foreign styles; but it has also been due to an aggressive attitude to exporting and an emphasis on quality which has positioned Butterley's products at the very top end of the market.

Michael Rose, Butterley's managing director, who was born not far from the site of the main Butterley Brick works on the outskirts of Ripley, told me that he aimed to increase sales of bricks to Japan from the current level of about £750,000 a year by promoting his product strongly to architects and contractors. To that end, he intends to establish a strong presence at events like the International Home Fair at Kobe.

The fact that a group of not very large companies from a relatively small area of England can sell products as diverse as bricks, chocolates and carpets in Japan indicates the possibilities of the Japanese market. But I also asked these companies whether they had suffered unduly from trade barriers in Japan. Peter Heaps of Thorntons was emphatic on this issue:

> The Japanese are very strict on the absence of artificial ingredients in products and we have to adapt to these requirements. But I don't see this as a barrier to entry and their restrictions are no more extensive than those in the United States or most European countries. Customs are certainly rigorous and we have had to send a breakdown of all our ingredients to our distributors for clearance by the Japanese authorities before they can take any new products. But the process has proved to be very efficient and I don't think we have needed to make any particular extra efforts for the Japanese market.

He also pointed out that when Thorntons wanted to buy two French confectionery companies, it had, as a foreign firm, to apply for special French Treasury permission. Michael Rose told me that while he had experienced little difficulty in getting his bricks distributed in Japan, it was almost impossible to sell in Germany because there, distributors were already closely tied in with local manufacturers, while in Ireland foreign products were excluded from public-sector construction contracts.

Of course, many Western companies have succeeded in Japan without resorting to distributors or joint ventures. In addition to IBM and Coca Cola, there are companies such as Du Pont, the American chemical giant, with Japanese sales well in excess of $300 million a year; and Weyerhauser, which annually sells the Japanese half a billion dollars worth of newsprint and other forest products.

But, even for very large Western companies, joint ventures have been a fruitful avenue into Japan. Apart from minimizing risk, they give access to local experience, contacts and distribution networks, all of which can be expensive and time-consuming to build up independently. Some pundits have claimed that joint ventures are merely a stratagem for Japanese companies to gain access to Western technology and that the Japanese partner invariably ends up on top. This does, of course, happen. Southland, owner of the Seven–Eleven franchise, was taken over by its Japanese partner, Ito Yokado, early in 1990. But this was largely due to the fact that the American company got itself into serious difficulties as a result of a $1.8-billion junk bond issue used to finance a leveraged buy-out just before the peak of the 1987 bull market – so the Ito Yokado takeover effectively saved the company. According to research carried out by management consultant, James Abegglen, however, the Western company just as frequently takes control. Recent examples include Hewlett–Packard taking over Yoko-gawa–Hewlett–Packard; Dow Corning gaining control of Toray Silicone; Shell taking over at Showa Oil; Procter & Gamble Sunhome being taken over by the American partner; Motorola controlling Aizu Toko; Tokai TRW being run by TRW; and Data General gaining full control of Nippon Data General.[7]

But perhaps one of the best examples is the American chemical giant, Pfizer, which used its joint venture with Japanese sugar processor, Taito, as a springboard into the Japanese market. In the 1950s, Taito had a small drugs division making penicillin, but it needed new antibiotic technology, so a joint venture was formed with Pfizer in 1956. By 1968, however, the American company had increased its stake to 80 per cent and took complete control in 1983, leaving Taito to concentrate on its sugar business. As a result, Pfizer has become the most successful foreign pharmaceutical company in Japan.

Merck, another American drug company, already had a Japanese branch when it entered into a joint venture with Banyu in the 1970s. In 1981, the joint company acquired a 30 per cent stake in a small Japanese pharmaceuticals producer, Torii Yakuhin. Two years later, in what was considered to be a highly dramatic move, the American company not only bought out the joint venture, but also acquired a majority position in Banyu itself as well as taking full control of Torii. Merck now finds itself managing a pharmaceuticals sales force of 1,500 – the largest in Japan.

Unilever had the advantage of a long history in East Asia, dating back to founder William Lever's attempts to sell into the Chinese market in 1910. Those efforts met with only limited success, but in 1962 Unilever launched a joint edible fats venture in Japan with Hohnen Oil, while a separate partnership involving a unit of the huge Mitsui combine was set up to market Unilever's Lipton tea brand. Before long, Lipton became the number one black-tea brand in Japan, beating its mainly Japanese competitors which included a product from another Mitsui company. Unilever bought out Mitsui's share in the business in 1982, and now handles Lipton tea in Japan.

Some Western companies have tried both wholly owned subsidiaries and joint ventures. General Foods initially attempted to go it alone, but decided that it required the marketing muscle of an established Japanese company in order to compete successfully. The result was Ajinomoto–General Foods, which was formed in 1973. General Foods brought expertise to the new group, while Ajinomoto contributed its excellent distribution system, with the result that Maxwell House and Maxim instant coffee are now found on the shelves of tens of thousands of 'mom and pop' grocery stores.

Of course, joint ventures are no panacea. Choosing the right partner with the same aims is one important factor to consider. Carl Green, a practising lawyer in Japan, and Douglas Shinsato of Touche Ross in Tokyo, also warn that 'joint ventures are among the most complex of business relationships. You have to do a lot of homework to get them right; you can be sure your Japanese partners will have done theirs!'[8]

'If you can succeed in Japan, you can sell anywhere'

Michael Perry, former boss of Nippon Lever, summed up on the subject of succeeding in Japan when he told me:

> In many ways it's really no different from anywhere else. Having strong brands is obviously vital and there is also no alternative to doing your homework, researching the market properly and putting in a substantial long-term investment of time and money.
>
> You have also got to be prepared to design your goods or adapt them specifically for Japan. You can't just go in expecting to sell a bit of your own surplus production on the Japanese market, nor can it be done at long range – you have got to have a presence there. The Japanese like doing business with people they know – and people they think are going to be there tomorrow.

Talking of the different problems of smaller companies trying to break in to the Japanese market, Perry advised a very careful choice of trading companies or distributors:

> Often, the smaller ones will make more effort for you, all the more so if they are specializing in your field. People also tend to forget about the British trading houses, such as Jardines and Inchcape, who have been in Japan a long time and can be easier to work with than locally owned companies. The big Western consultancy groups also operate in Japan and, again, they can be more approachable for the small businessman.

For larger companies, Perry had no doubt of the importance of the Japanese market:

> Many people ignored Japan for too long. But anyone with global aspirations can't afford not to be there. For one thing, the chances are that some of your toughest competitors on world markets will be Japanese. So it's critical to challenge their home profitability base.

But he went on to warn:

> Japan is quite the most competitively challenging market, so you have to take very much the long view. Because it is so competitive, you immediately face the question, as a newcomer, of what to offer the customer that is better than their current supplier – and he is likely to be very good indeed. But if you can crack the Japanese market, it's going to benefit your operations all over the world, because if you can succeed in Japan, you can sell anywhere.

Part IX

The West's Response – What is to be Done?

AMERICA'S REFUSAL TO come to terms with Japan's rise, and the tendency to take the easy option of erecting yet more trade barriers in both Europe and America, make it all too likely that the world will gradually split into three increasingly exclusive economic zones based around a Japanese-led Pacific bloc, a sulkily isolated North America and a German-dominated Europe.

Only if Western businesspeople and politicians drop the pretence that the Japanese have succeeded unfairly, or that they are so frighteningly and uniquely different that they must be dealt with by separate rules, and study the real reasons behind their economic success will they be able to draw the conclusions necessary to take on Japan's industry and develop a genuinely integrated world economic order.

This means admitting that there are no easy answers, such as managed trade, excluding Japanese investment, 'industrial strategies', protectionism or subsidized consortia, and examining instead the real underlying causes of Japan's achievements, while at the same time, not being too proud to imitate some Japanese practices. When the West does this, and finds the will to make the necessary reforms at both the industrial and governmental levels, it will be taking the first real steps towards meeting the Japanese challenge.

26

新大国

OVER HERE?

'Rather than treating the foreign investor as a rival, we should consider him a valuable helper, for he increases our production and the efficiency of our business.'
Alexander Hamilton, commenting on foreign investment in the United States in 1791.

AS AMERICANS BROOD about their declining industrial competitiveness, so they have also begun to fret about levels of Japanese investment in the United States. An opinion poll in 1988 showed that nearly three-quarters of Americans believed that foreign investment had reduced American economic independence and four-fifths favoured a law restricting foreign ownership of businesses and property.

For there is still a strong if declining line of argument in both the United States and Europe that to allow Japanese companies to build factories or acquire assets in the West is to open the gates to the Trojan Horse, relegating Westerners to second-class jobs and allowing the Japanese to milk Western economies by repatriating profits. This attitude was epitomized in 1984 by presidential hopeful, Walter Mondale, who invoked images of Americans reduced to flipping hamburgers in McDonalds, while the Japanese overwhelmed the country's industries.[1]

Supporters of this view point to the fact that already by the end of 1989, Japanese vehicle plants in the United States were capable of producing 1.25 million cars and over 100,000 trucks annually, while Japan's factories in Canada had the capacity to turn out a further 400,000 vehicles. At first, some hoped that these transplants would replace Japan's direct exports to the United States. This has happened to an extent, but 'transplant' production has also voraciously eaten into the sales of GM, Ford and Chrysler, cruelly exposing the competitive shortcomings of Detroit's Big Three auto makers whose output is predicted to tumble from 7.2 million cars in 1986 to maybe as few as five million by 1991. Big Three sales were already falling sharply by the third quarter of 1989 – Ford's falling by 12 per cent, leading to plant closures and lay-offs. Over the same period, sales from Honda's American factories rose by nearly nine per cent, making the Japanese company likely to overtake Chrysler as the number three American automobile manufacturer, while the overall market share of the Japanese manufacturers rose from about 25 per cent to just over 30 per cent.

To an even greater extent, 'Made in America' now means 'Made in a Japanese-owned plant' when it comes to consumer electronics. Japanese manufacturers dominate American video-tape recorder production, while only one American-owned company, Zenith, still makes colour televisions. But while attention has been focused on the influx of Japanese car and electronics companies, there has also been a great deal of activity in the less glamourous heavy manufacturing sector. Makita, the power-tool manufacturer, is to establish a factory in the United Kingdom, while machine-tool maker, Yamazaki, already has a plant in Britain and plans more in Europe. Robot producer Fanuc will build a factory in Luxembourg; construction-machinery maker, Komatsu, has a substantial British operation and in 1989 took a stake in the famous German Hanomag company; while Furukawa, a maker of wheeled loaders has acquired the European plants of the American-based Dresser corporation.

European and American fears that incoming Japanese investment might set the seal on the relegation of Western industry are surprisingly echoed by concerns in Japan itself about *kudoka*, or the 'hollowing out' of her manufacturing sector as a result of the internationalization of her industry – a feeling which was particularly pronounced during the difficult post-Plaza Accord days when manufacturing employment declined sharply. Japan's Confederation of Automobile Workers' Unions, for example, dominated the headlines when it warned in 1988 that the car industry would lose up to 74,000 jobs as a result of possible domestic production cuts of 1.5 million units due to increased overseas production, claiming that the redundancy figure would rise as high as 220,000 if jobs lost in related industries were included.[2] Even a brief from the normally sober Japanese Institute for Social and Economic Affairs warned that if overseas direct investment strategies 'are implemented too rapidly, there is a danger that the industrial structure will turn "hollow"'.[3]

In the event, it is unlikely that either side need worry. Japanese investment is a very long way either from draining its home base or from reaching a dominating position in the West. By the beginning of 1989, Japan's investment in the United States still totalled just half of British-owned investments and only slightly more than the Netherlands'. Overall, foreign groups owned about five per cent of United States assets – lower in relation to GNP than in most other industrialized countries – of which Japan accounted for less than a fifth. Japanese investment is little more than a tenth the level of American investment in Britain and American firms employ 21 times as many British people as do Japanese companies. Moreover, total Japanese industrial production overseas still only accounts for about five per cent of her industry's output, compared to more like 20 per cent for West Germany and the United States. Toyota, for example, still makes only 12 per cent of its cars outside Japan, compared with 30.5 per cent of General Motors' cars being produced outside the United States. On top of this, many Japanese factories are producing goods in industries long since relinquished by Western producers, goods which would otherwise be imported from Japan.

Besides, the growth in Japan's overseas investment is no more than a normal stage in the development of her economy, closely paralleling the expansion of British and American investment in earlier eras. In the late Nineteenth and early Twentieth Centuries it was European, and particularly British, money which went to the Americas and Africa. After the War, the major flows were of American investment into Europe and Asia. Now, in turn, Japanese money is coming to the West.

To put matters further into perspective, in the 1960s, Europeans panicked about the invasion of American industry – now hardly anyone notices it. Ford, Kellogs and IBM are considered just as much part of the European scene as indigenous companies. So, too, in a few years will Toyota, Brother and Panasonic be just as inconspicuous in Europe and America. Already, Detroit's automotive aristocracy have enshrined Soichiro Honda, founder of Honda, in the industry's Automotive Hall of Fame, right next to Henry Ford and the swashbuckling pioneer of General Motors, Billy Durant.

It is also worth considering the example of Belgium, which boasts the highest vehicle output per head in the world. Ford, General Motors, Renault, Volkswagen and Volvo directly employ some 44,000 people in Belgium, with another 700,000 workers indirectly employed. Yet Belgium relinquished her last indigenous car manufacturer in the 1950s and has since pursued a policy of vigorously welcoming inward investment in the vehicle industry. Moreover, the American automobile industry can hardly complain about the Japanese presence when about 25 per cent of United States transplant production comes out of joint ventures with the Big Three United States producers, production from which is sold under domestic brands.

Deepening roots

Doubts remain, of course, as to whether Japanese-owned plants represent substantive manufacturing operations which contribute to the economy, or whether they are simply 'screwdriver' plants assembling imported parts. Certainly, in the mid-1980s, the 72 Japanese-owned TV and VCR plants in Western Europe only employed 10,000 people and were largely assembly operations. However, in recent years, Japanese plants abroad have begun using a far higher proportion of domestically produced parts. This, again, is part of the natural progression of inward investment, which tends to begin with low-quality assembly work and gradually develop into something rather more beneficial to the host country.

According to Takeo Nigishi, the head of the Electronics Industry Association of Japan in Europe, the roots of Japanese industry will deepen naturally over the years in the same way as an earlier wave of American inward investment in Europe did. His model for the future Europeanized

Japanese corporation is IBM which, when it first began manufacturing overseas, ran largely assembly operations but is now very much a closely integrated part of the local European community. 'We've only had ten years, and they've had 70,' says Mr Nigishi, 'It takes time.'[4]

Sony's British television facility – the Bridgend plant in South Wales – is a good example of an operation which originally started as a low-tech assembly unit but which has now developed to the point where its UK-made televisions have a 90 per cent local content. It presently employs 1,700 workers in an integrated manufacturing operation producing its own colour tubes, while exports account for about 70 per cent of the unit's £200-million-a-year turnover.

Local content at Toyota's Kentucky facility will approach 75 per cent by 1991 as a result of a new powertrain, axle and steering components plant. Japan's largest auto maker is also building an engine factory in Wales to supplement its planned UK car assembly plant in Derbyshire. Nissan followed its Sunderland car plant in the north of England with an engine facility in 1989, while Honda actually built its UK engine plant at Swindon before its planned car factory. At the same time, Honda was spending more than $600 million to turn its Ohio operation into an integrated, almost self-reliant factory including a design and engineering unit.

Hiroshi Hamada, president of Ricoh, the camera and office equipment producer which has offshore factories in Britain, France, the United States, South Korea and Taiwan, outlined the way his plants usually progress:

> When we started to manufacture our first product in the UK, we needed about 400 to 500 parts. If we had been required to satisfy 40 per cent local content from the beginning, we would never have been able to start. Obviously it was necessary to bring parts from Japan. Then we displayed them in the lobby of the plant so that local manufacturers and suppliers could look at them, then produce them. This is the kind of process we always go through.[5]

Of course, some of the 'domestic' suppliers of components to Japanese-owned factories are actually Japanese-owned parts companies which have followed their customers' plants overseas. More than 130 Japanese vehicle parts suppliers, for example, have built or are building plants in the United States following decisions by most of Japan's car makers to produce vehicles there. The same process is happening in Britain where, in 1989 alone, Nissan-owned Calsonic bought Llanelli Radiators Holdings and Nippon-denso, Japan's biggest automotive components supplier which belongs to Toyota, bought IMI Radiators.

But while a proportion of growing 'local' components orders are going to such Japanese-owned suppliers, a good share is nonetheless going to indigenous companies. Ninety-seven of Nissan's 122 UK suppliers are British and only six are Japanese, for example. Where orders do go to Japanese-owned companies, it is frequently because domestic suppliers cannot compete on quality or price, or because the Japanese manufacturers have longstanding relationships with suppliers who are best able to fit in with their work practices and production schedules – a service which local producers are not always prepared to offer.

However, further proof that Japanese industry is genuinely internationalizing, rather than just colonizing, is the fact that its own domestic automotive industry has been steadily increasing the value of parts and materials purchased outside of Japan. Toyota, for example, increased its overseas purchases to $600 million in 1987. Furthermore, Japanese-owned overseas factories are beginning to export finished goods to Japan, such as the Honda Accord coupés shipped from the United States to Japan; together with 100cc motor cycles produced at Honda's affiliate in Thailand, 125cc motor bikes from its Italian venture and large machines from its United States plant. Toyota, too, will begin shipping vehicles from its Kentucky plant to Japan in 1992, with a target of 40,000 units annually.

So while the first phase of foreign investment may boost Japanese exports because of sales of plant, equipment and components, the later stage will involve a reduction in Japan's trade surplus – especially as Japan will undoubtedly import more goods from its overseas plants – as it already substantially does from its more established Asian factories. For example, in 1987 imports from mainly Japanese-owned plants took 52 per cent of Japan's calculator market, 56 per cent of the market for electric fans, 40 per cent of the camera market and 60 per cent for portable radios.[6] New plants will also to some extent replace direct exports from Japan. Nissan, for example, aims to reduce vehicle exports from 1.4 million units in 1985 to one million by 1992 and plans in its main markets to achieve a 1:1 ratio of exports to local production, rising to 1:2 by the late 1990s.[7] According to Hirohiko Okumura of the Nomura Research Institute, the net effect will reduce Japan's trade surplus by as much as $60 billion by 1995.[8]

Japanese industry overseas is also slowly increasing its local engineering and research and development. Sony already has a West German engineering centre and carries out some development work on satellites in the UK, in addition to its laboratories in New Jersey and Singapore. The company plans to double its number of scientific staff abroad by 1991. Nissan announced early in 1990 that it would establish a fully fledged vehicle design and development operation in the UK which will enable it to engineer totally European-designed cars by the end of the decade. Mitsubishi is planning additional overseas institutions for basic research, while Hitachi already has research centres in San Francisco, Detroit, Dublin and Cambridge (England).

Positive demonstration

The argument over whether or not Japanese investment is beneficial has, anyway, already largely been settled. It is indicative of changed attitudes when even a French industry minister, Roger Fauroux, can comment: 'It is better to have the Japanese than unemployed people.' Even in traditionally protectionist France and Italy, where inward investment from the United States, Japan and elsewhere has long been treated with suspicion and even discouraged, active measures are now being taken to lure in Japanese companies. And in America, widespread hostility to Japanese transplants in some quarters is increasingly blurred by the sanguine appreciation of the benefits which the Japanese bring. 'It used to be "us" versus "them",' a bemused Illinois congress representative remarked. 'Now we don't know who is "us" and who is "them" anymore.'

The creation of jobs, often in depressed areas, is just one of the benefits. Another is the help given to the balance of payments – and not just through substitution of Japanese imports where that happens. Britain's trade deficit in videotape recorders was cut from £182 million in 1987 to £49.3 million in 1989, while in the same year Japanese-run factories helped Britain to achieve a surplus on colour televisions despite there being no British-owned volume manufacturer. Sony has won a Queen's Award for Exports and one of the company's executives was even awarded an Order of the British Empire for his contribution to British exports.

Many industrialists also consider that one of the greatest blessings of the transplants is the new attitudes and working practices that they bring with them – the so-called 'positive demonstration' effect. In Georgetown, Kentucky, about 1,700 men and women manage to make Toyotas that meet the same tough quality standards as those made in Japan. Over the state border in Tennessee, workers at Nissan's Smyrna plant overwhelmingly voted in 1989 against allowing in a union. When the result was announced, 100 exultant factory workers reportedly chanted 'One team, one team!'

According to Peter Wickens, a director at Nissan's Sunderland plant, in setting up its UK operation the company managed to reduce all manual tasks within the car plant down to two job titles, compared to the 516 then operational at Ford's UK plants. To increase flexibility, the company also abolished job descriptions. Partly in response to the increased competition and new working practices at Nissan, Ford made its 1985 pay offer largely conditional upon far-reaching changes to work practices, including reducing job titles to 52. Although the unions criticized this as an attempt to introduce 'Nissan-type' working practices, the changes resulted in Ford achieving a 50 per cent increase in productivity over the subsequent two years.

At the same time, a deal between Caterpillar Tractors and the Amalgamated Engineering Union reduced the number of job titles from 51 to 12. As a result, assemblers now do the jobs of adjusters and testers, while craftsmen have become multi-skilled in both electrical and mechanical work – and they receive a higher rate of pay in the process.[9] There is little doubt that companies like Ford and Caterpillar would have steadily tried to improve their working practices without the advent of Nissan, but the Japanese auto maker's arrival both made those changes more urgent and provided firsthand evidence of their potential benefits.

These benefits may go deeper than many suspect. Early in 1989, a few days after Toyota had announced plans to set up its first European car plant in the English East Midlands county of Derbyshire, a local businessman told me that the working practices of such a successful Japanese company would filter down to the local workforce and improve labour relations. That evening I visited a Miner's Welfare club, where a former coal miner turned factory worker after the mid-1980s pit closures told me that he too welcomed the arrival of the giant car maker, announcing in his broad

Derbyshire accent: 'They seem to know how to treat their workers – that might wake up one or two of the bosses round here.'

Whose fault is it anyway?

Americans can anyway hardly complain about the influx of Japanese capital when this is, in part, caused by the United States' own domestic policies which have resulted in spending and investment at a higher rate than has been available from domestic savings, with ensuing massive budget and trade deficits. From this point of view, it is perhaps better that the United States should import capital to make up the shortfall by means of direct investment than by selling debt, such as Treasury bonds, to foreign buyers. Whereas such debt has to be serviced, foreign investment in factories and plants creates jobs and often reduces imports. Profits are also rarely repatriated in the early years and may well be reinvested in the host economy. Moreover, American disgruntlement on this score sounds somewhat hollow when it is remembered that General Motors' and Ford's profits from their European operations bailed out their loss-making United States operations in 1989.

Americans should also bear in mind that their own industry has invested far more in overseas markets than foreigners have invested in the United States. If Americans believe that it is a good thing for their industry to acquire foreign companies such as Jaguar, bought by Ford in 1989, they should not consider it such a betrayal when Japanese or British companies buy up well-known American names. But there is a further, related point. A significant part of America's overseas investment is accounted for by industry which has moved manufacturing offshore to supply the United States market. Ford, for example, makes one of its best selling cars, the Topaz, in Hermosilla in Mexico and spent $300 million in 1990 to expand the plant's capacity to 165,000 cars to supply American car buyers. So if Japanese companies move into the United States and are able profitably to use American labour to build cars for the domestic market, that should be a cause for rejoicing, not complaint.

Nonetheless, there is one undoubtedly negative side to Japanese inward investment. Although a great deal of Japanese industry's overseas expansion is geared towards internationalizing corporate operations and countering the effects of the increase in the yen's value, many Japanese plants still have cost levels higher than those prevailing in Japan. This is demonstrated by the fact that in 1987, Japanese companies had 17 TV and 55 VCR plants in Europe, only one of which had a capacity of more than 500,000 units – the minimum for a really economic plant. Most of these factories were, therefore, running on a bare three per cent profit margin or less, while many were, in fact, making a loss. So why did these Japanese companies set these plants up?

The simple answer is protectionism. Anti-dumping duties and import quotas in particular have been a major factor in forcing Japanese companies to build plants in the United States and Western Europe in order to overcome import hurdles. Furthermore, recent European Community moves to place anti-dumping duties on imported components, combined with EC-imposed strict local content requirements, have accelerated recent plans for Japanese-owned component operations.

This has not been limited to Japanese industry. American Intel Corporation said that its plans to set up a new semiconductor fabrication plant in Ireland were a response to pressure from European customers who have to find European sources for their components in the light of recent new EC rules on country of origin. These rules state that semiconductor chips must be diffused within the European Community if they are to be labelled 'Made in Europe'.

Diffusion is one of the most delicate and expensive processes in the manufacture of semiconductor chips. Previously, the country of origin for semiconductors was determined by the location of the plant in which the devices underwent the final manufacturing processes – assembly and testing. Now that is no longer good enough and where products such as computer printers and electronic typewriters are already subject to anti-dumping duties, plants which use such 'non-EC' semiconductors risk having their products rated as non-European, so incurring duties.*

The reaction of many people to this may be: So what? If these measures are helping to bring more jobs to Europe and the United States, and if those jobs are 'real' manufacturing jobs, rather than just work in 'screwdriver' assembly plants, that is all to the good. But the problem is that while these new jobs bring benefits, there are also countervailing penalties, for if Japanese producers are setting up plants in the West solely or largely to gain access to local markets, rather than on grounds of industrial efficiency, consumers will have to bear the extra costs and the overall competitiveness of the economy will be lower.

So while the new Japanese plants which are springing up from green fields all over Europe and America bring undoubted gains to their host countries, some of those advantages are offset in cases where the Japanese have largely arrived in order to overcome barriers to free trade. If, therefore, Japanese investment in Europe and America represents any threat, it is not to local industry, which should in the long term benefit from greater competition, but rather to the overall health of the economy in those instances where investment decisions have been prompted by the desire to leap over hurdles to trade.

---

* GATT ruled these duties illegal in 1990, but it seems unlikely that the EC will rapidly comply with the ruling.

27

新
大
国

SEEKING PRETEXTS

'Europe has rested on its laurels and slept for decades after having dominated the world. This is all too human and understandable. We have seen the same phenomenon in recent years in the United States. And nothing guarantees that Japan could be saved from the same destiny, when she attains one day the same quality of life as the Westerners.

'This sleep has been disturbed by the intrusion of the "damned Japanese" and the Japanese industrial challenge has not been taken up entirely. Will they [the West] succeed? The answer is no, if they continue to think that Japanese enterprises are competitive "because they benefit from the government aids, close their market by all means against foreign products, copy the Western technologies, exploit their workers and subcontractors etc".

'Even if each of these elements contains a grain of truth, they do not explain everything . . . . The West will restore its dynamism and its spirit of enterprise of the past, when it starts looking straight at its problems, without seeking pretexts.'
Professor Masaru Yoshimori.

DOES THE WEST yet show any sign of coming to terms with the real causes of Japanese success and relative Western failure? The problem is that the more political and business leaders convince themselves and others that their problems are due to unfair trade practices, special cultural factors or government intervention in Japan – and the supposed lack of it at home – the less likely they are to come to terms with the real problems afflicting their economies.

Furthermore, the widespread assumption that Japan's economic triumph is due to foul play in its trading practices has too often led the West, and the United States in particular, to treat Japan with an increasing degree of inconsistency and unfairness, leading to a sense of victimization in Japan which is dangerously undermining her relations with the West.

All of which is completely unnecessary. According to the *Amex Bank Review*, Japan's trade performance is already in relative decline as import volumes rise faster than exports. The report also points out that Japan would now be showing a trade deficit if exchange rates had been stable at the 1980 level. 'Since 1985,' it concluded, 'contrary to popular wisdom, Japan has done little more than maintain its markets.' Between 1985 and 1989 the volume of Japanese exports increased by only 11 per cent, while imports jumped by 47 per cent. And Japan's current account surplus fell from a peak of 4.4 per cent of GNP in 1986 to about half that figure by the beginning of 1990, by which time exports were actually declining, while import volume was growing by more than ten per cent a year.

Moreover, America's own trade deficit with Japan, which had remained stubbornly high immediately after the Plaza Accord, began to shift towards the end of the decade. American exports to Japan rose from $22.6 billion in 1985 to nearly $45 billion by 1989, with manufactured goods accounting for the lion's share of the increase. Overall, America's bilateral deficit with Japan, which peaked at $56 billion in 1987, began to fall steadily and was running at an annual rate well below $50 billion by the beginning of 1990. Europe experienced an even greater improvement which gave rise to some hope that protectionist pressures in both the United States and Europe would abate.

Some good news, more bad news

There is at least some good news in this respect, which indicates that there are those in positions of power who recognize the realities underlying Japan's success. The European Community Commission, which was the source of many of the protectionist moves within the EC in the 1980s, has shown some signs of improvement. In particular, the West German Martin Bangemann, Frans Andriessen from the Netherlands and Mrs Thatcher's former lieutenant, Sir Leon Brittan, have formed a free-market trio of a kind that has never existed before in the Commission. Moreover, they are being strongly backed by the more liberal northern EC members of West Germany, Britain, Denmark and the Netherlands.

The Commissioners actually agreed a timetable for phasing out import quotas on Japanese cars after the EC's internal market is opened up in 1992. They also drew the line at supporting a proposal to increase the import tariff on compact hand-held video cameras from 4.9 per cent to 14 per cent – a particularly ludicrous suggestion since there is no indigenous European video camera industry to protect.

But there is also some bad news. The Commission has pressed on with its agreement with Japanese semiconductor exporters to maintain set floor-price levels for D-Rams within the EC. Further, although they hoped to rapidly phase out car import quotas after 1992, the liberal Commissioners have come under intense pressure from European car makers to replace national import limits with an EC-wide anti-Japanese quota. Predictably, this move has been led by Renault of France and Italy's Fiat – the first being possibly the most subsidized, and the second probably the most protected major car company in history.

Predictably, again, Renault have been strongly backed by their protectionist national government which went to the preposterous lengths of arguing that cars made by Nissan and Toyota in England, with 80 per cent local content, should be counted as Japanese and included in any EC-wide quota arrangements – although vehicles imported from Honda's American plant would not be counted against the quota. This would mean that a car made in a Japanese-owned plant in Europe would be considered Japanese, even though a car produced in an American-owned Ford or General Motors factory in Britain, Spain, Belgium or West Germany would be deemed as European; while a car made in a Japanese-run plant in the United States would be counted as American. Frans Adriessen astonished many people by indicating his support for this policy while on a visit to Tokyo – hard evidence of the tremendous pressure now being exerted on the liberal Commissioners.

Even the West German car industry, which is not currently protected by any national quota arrangements, is beginning to make noises about the Japanese threat. Perhaps a special prize for hypocrisy should go to Volkswagen, for on the very day that the German company announced both that profits were up by 33 per cent and that it would need more capacity to keep up with growing sales opportunities in Europe, its chief executive, Carl Hahn, issued the Commission with a warning that it should be vigilant on the accessibility of the Community for Japanese cars.[1] Moreover, only six months earlier the company had trumpeted the creation of 750 new jobs to boost production for the Japanese market where VW sales had risen by a quarter.[2]

All of this should come as no surprise, for some three decades after the so-called Common Market was inaugurated, European Community countries still cannot even agree on opening up their own internal market to free trade between member countries, let alone to outsiders – something which puts EC complaints about Japanese trade barriers into perspective. For although the much vaunted 1992 initiative has led to many advances, few informed observers seriously believed that the EC will achieve a full open internal market by the target date. At the end of 1989, for example, EC member states' transport ministers were still squabbling over plans to allow completely free access for road hauliers to each country's roads.

Under the current system, most EC countries insist on internal haulage being carried out by their own nationals, with the result that many of the trucks criss-crossing the Community are empty on their return journey – an estimated 30 per cent of the trucks crossing the West German/Dutch border carry no loads – costing about £150 million a year and needlessly adding to congestion and pollution. France and West Germany were counted among the nations wishing to retain restrictions, while Britain stood in the van of the liberalizers. In the end, Germany actually took unilateral action and imposed a special toll of up to £4,000 for trucks using major roads, craftily exempting their own hauliers by reducing annual road tax on German lorries by a similar amount so that the toll only affects foreigners. The retention of such petty restrictions, despite some negotiated

improvements, merely adds to the cost of transport, making the EC
economy less efficient and European producers less able to compete.

'Everyone should have the ability to choose . . .'

In the United States, the situation of free trade advocates is even more
serious, for despite improvements in America's trade imbalance with Japan,
strident demands for protectionism are growing in proportion to increasing
alarm about the United States' relative decline.

Needless to say, the advocates of import barriers carefully camouflage
their policies with self-righteous rhetoric and calls for 'free and fair trade'
and 'level playing fields'. The United States Trade Representative, Carla
Hills, for example, can cheerfully write: 'Everyone should have the ability
to choose how, when and where to buy or sell goods and services freely in
a fair market. That is competition'; and say: 'All I care about is that we
achieve liberalization in areas where there are restrictions'[3] – at the end of a
decade in which the United States has erected trade barriers faster than any
other major industrialized country.

Further, in 1989, the Office of the United States Trade Representative,
which is responsible for developing trade policy and conducting negotiations and which is run by Mrs Hills, produced a report entitled *Foreign
Trade Barriers*,[4] consisting of 214 pages packed full of the trade restrictions
and unfair practices of 36 countries and trading blocks, ranging from
Norway to South Korea and the EC to India. Yet one of the worst offenders
is absent.

Luckily, the omission has been rectified by the EC Commission which,
stung by the American report's perfectly justified but hypocritical criticism
of European trade restrictions, rushed out its own 41-page report outlining
the United States' own barriers to trade.[5] These, according to the document,
include tariffs; custom user fees; agricultural import quotas; as well as
barriers to imports of machine tools, beverages, confectionery, firearms,
ammunition, foreign-built vessels, jewellery, telecommunications equipment, ham, bearings, power equipment and vehicles. The EC report also
criticizes United States government subsidies for exporters and R&D and
cheekily censures America's implementation of anti-dumping duties.
Although the EC itself could justifiably be criticized for its performance in
almost all of these areas, the report was, nevertheless, a timely reminder of
the United States' own transgressions – which help to explain why in a poll
of 1,800 senior international company executives in 1990, the United States
was named as the third dirtiest trader after Japan and South Korea.[6]

One of the more significant of the American trade practices, however, is
contained in the part of the EC report which deals with what has become
known simply as 'Section 301'. This is a statute under United States law
which covers unfair foreign trade practices and the measures to be taken to
combat them. Major changes were made to Section 301 under the 1988
Trade Act which substantially reduced the discretion available to the United
States authorities in administering the Act, thus making it more likely that
America will take unilateral action in addressing allegedly unfair trade

practices, rather than referring them for redress to the international forum provided by GATT.

The Trade Act also introduced a new procedure – the so-called 'Super 301' – whereby the United States Trade Representative is required to identify priority unfair trade practices and in extreme cases point the finger at individual countries which maintain substantial trade barriers, with a view to negotiating an agreement to eliminate and compensate for such practices. If no agreement is reached, unilateral retaliatory action can be taken under Super 301. Needless to say, Super 301 is hugely popular with those Americans who believe that the only remedy required for the United States' economic ills is to 'tough it out' with its trading partners. But, although in theory the provisions of Super 301 might sound perfectly fair, in practice they are both illegal and unjust.

Illegal, because the United States is a member of GATT, and unilateral action runs counter to basic GATT principles as well as violating its specific provisions. Only in certain limited fields, such as dumping and subsidization, is autonomous action by an individual state permissible under GATT. All other measures must be sanctioned, the idea being that GATT should act as an adjudicator in trade disputes, preventing the unfair imposition of penalties by a country which unreasonably feels itself to be aggrieved.

Unjust, because the United States possesses enormous leverage which allows her to bully trading partners into agreements. The United States has already in the past used the threat of Section 301 action in seeking to obtain agreements on import restrictions, such as in the case of disputes concerning pasta and citrus fruits from the EC. Super 301 makes such restrictive agreements even more likely.

Bilateralism

Permeating this reinforced United States trade legislation is the presumption that if the United States is running a trade deficit with another country, unfair trade practices must be the reason. Such assumptions underlying current United States trade policy are potentially extremely damaging because they encourage the growth of what is called 'bilateralism', whereby the threat of a 301 action forces individual trading partners into bilateral agreements – that is, satisfying American demands by agreeing to import specific quantities of United States goods. This United States pressure is often bought off by simply taking trade away from other countries and giving it to American suppliers.

A good example of this type of bilateral deal is to be found in the South Korean insurance market. By placing pressure on Korea to open up to foreign insurance companies, the United States actually ensured the entry of just two companies – both were American. And when, following demands from the United States, South Korea announced a plan to cut its trade surplus, what it actually intended to do was to switch the majority of its imports of agricultural products away from countries like Argentina and China, as well as imports of components and raw materials worth around $250 million from other countries, and buy them instead from America.

Likewise, although the 1986 Semiconductor Accord between the United

States and Japan did not stipulate that American suppliers should have a specific share of the Japanese market, an informal understanding made it clear that a 20 per cent share of the market would be given to United States producers as a means of measuring Japan's commitment to opening its semiconductor market. Similarly, pressure exerted by the United States for the opening of Japan's beef market was aimed to increase quotas for United States producers, rather than generally to liberalize the Japanese import regime;[7] while in 1989, the Taiwanese government restricted contracts for rolling stock and signalling equipment to United States companies for its new Tamshui line rapid transit system to ease trade tensions with its biggest customer. In 1990, moreover, it was feared that the Japanese military would be pressured into opting for US-built Cessna light aircraft rather than the British BAe 125-800s which won the tender on price and performance.

It is evident, therefore, that these bilateral confrontations have frequently become less a way of opening markets to all than a means of increasing American exports. In the process, they are frequently diverting trade from more efficient suppliers who have less political clout. Moreover, such deals logically mean a move towards the requirement for each trading partner to fulfil a trade plan, as if it were a member of the Soviet's moribund managed trading organization, Comecon. Already, for example, the United States President's Advisory Committee for Trade Policy has recommended that Japan should be required to fulfil such a plan. Further progress down this particular road will put the United States in the invidious position of effectively imitating the failed planned trade policies of the former Eastern Bloc, at just the time when those policies are being abandoned with a desperate haste.

It should also be asked whether such policies really help American industry itself. When, for instance, Japanese computer company NEC drops a planned bid to supply a supercomputer to a Japanese university to allow United States Cray Research to win the contract, or when a Japanese consortium is encouraged to buy an American satellite which it probably does not need to placate the Americans,[8] United States negotiators may actually be doing a disservice to the very people they are trying to help. For example, John Stern, director of the American Electronics Association's Tokyo office, told a *Fortune* reporter that the very fact that Japanese companies are pressurized into buying American products such as semiconductors 'creates the impression that our chips aren't very good'.[9]

Above all, Super 301 and other protectionist measures are ultimately self-defeating because they divert attention from the West's underlying economic ills. Europe and the United States would be far better advised to objectively examine the sources of their own problems, and Japan's strengths, rather than to continue debilitating their industries by cosseting them with import restrictions. Improved education, more sensible fiscal and spending policies and freer markets would do the West's industry far more good than a maze of trade barriers.

An historical perspective

Barely concealed beneath these attempts to negotiate reciprocal and bilateral trade deals lurks protectionism. This should come as no surprise for nations in industrial decline generally have a tendency to trade protection. During the 1870s and 1880s, for example, Britain witnessed the rise of the National Fair Trade League, the National Society for the Defence of British Industry and the Reciprocity Fair Trade Association, each of which called for import restrictions. Behind these demands for an end to Britain's relative embrace of free trade principles lay the fact that while in the mid-Nineteenth Century Britain controlled a quarter of world trade and accounted for one-third of industrial production, between 1870 and 1913 her share of world output halved. Over the same period the United States expanded her share of global production from less than a quarter to more than a third and was outproducing Britain in pig iron by a ratio of three to one.

In fact, Britain's decline and the rise of the United States in the late Nineteenth Century offers some interesting parallels which can help put current American disputes with Japan into context. For then, many in Britain harboured a similar resentment towards the upstart colonists that many Americans today feel towards Japan. The great free trader and liberal, Richard Cobden, wrote just after the middle of the century: 'A considerable portion of our countrymen have not yet reconciled themselves to the belief that the American colonies of 1780 are now become a first-rate independent power', going on to say that many people 'possess a feeling of half pique and half contempt towards the United States.'[10]

Since the Second World War, the United States has in turn seen her share of world output halve while Japan's share of global GDP has increased from 1.6 per cent to ten per cent. As America's performance deteriorated, so demands for protection have increased, just as they did in Britain a century ago, and whatever its rhetoric, the Reagan Administration was far finer in word than deed and became the most protectionist administration since the 1930s. The new Bush regime, under huge pressure from Congress and the Senate, has proved little better, so that there is now a real risk of a decline into the type of conditions which brought about the Smoot–Hawley Act in 1930. This protectionist legislation, designed to safeguard American industry and jobs against foreign competition, ended in retaliatory measures against the United States from 25 of its trading partners, with the result that by 1933 American exports had declined by about 60 per cent.

Any hope that America has learned from this and is prepared to examine the real causes of Japanese success in order to breathe new life into her economy is seriously diminished by the paranoid reaction to Japan's success and the increasingly strident protectionist backlash. It is always easier to blame foreigners for your problems, especially when they are orientals who are naturally assumed to harbour devious or sinister motives. This is just what the United States is now doing, in the same way as a banana republic, seeking to distract attention from domestic ills, declares war on neighbours.

The problem may be that the decline of the United States has simply been too precipitous for many Americans to come to terms with. In 1967, American companies controlled more than 80 per cent of world computer production and around three-quarters of semiconductor output. At that time, there were 25 American-owned manufacturers of colour televisions. Now there is only one and no indigenous American company manufactures consumer electronics products in volume.

And although the electronics industry remains the United States' largest manufacturing employer, in 1984, for the first time, America imported more electronic goods than it exported. A year later, the United States was running a trade deficit of close to $140 billion, of which $50 billion was with Japan. Never has the world's leading financial and industrial power fallen so quickly from a position of having an export and capital surplus and industrial dominance to the predicament of being the world's largest debtor with an inability to compete effectively in a large number of industrial sectors.

This helps to explain the inconclusive soul-searching in the United States about the loss of national competitiveness, the deep and disturbed fear of Japan's economic success and her huge surplus, and the dread that Japan's progress threatens American leadership and even her national security. This horror has brought about a sea-change in official United States policy, for whereas in the 1930s and 1940s, it was a group of largely American enlightened policy makers who agreed on the need to restore a liberal international economy based on multilateral economic cooperation, in recent years it has been American policy that has taken the lead in trying to dismantle the structure that was successfully erected in the post-War years.

From the Japanese viewpoint, there is more than a little irony in all of this. In the Seventeenth Century, it was Japan which found it necessary to close her doors to Western trade for fear of the effects of the marked superiority of Western technology. Two and a half largely cloistered centuries later, Japan was so debilitated from her lack of contact with the West that a handful of American gunboats were able to prise open her ports to Western trade, imposing, moreover, a largely free trade regime through a series of so-called 'unequal treaties'. The result was that many traditional industries were destroyed by the sudden influx of Western goods and Japan ran trade deficits with the West for a very long period. Of course, the stimulus afforded by competition from the West prompted the modernization and upgrading of her industry. Yet now that Japan has become competitive, it is the Americans who have suddenly lost their appetite for free trade and are begging the Japanese to restrain their exports as relays of industrialists and special pleaders troop to Capitol Hill to beg for protection.

Getting tough

To some extent the change in the direction of American policy on trade has been due to the influence of the neo-mercantilists, who view all international economics in terms of 'them or us' and are forever fretting about whether or not America is still number one. These people, who include in their ranks the labour unions, many Democratic politicians and industrialists from corporations most threatened by Japanese competition, use much the same language as the old Cold Warriors, except that now the threat comes from Japan rather than the Soviets. There are also, of course, many Americans who would not consider themselves as protectionist, but who genuinely believe that they have 'got to get tough' with Japan, arguing that 'it's the only language they understand'. The result is increasing inequity in United States policy towards Japan.

Super 301 itself provides a very good example, for the 1989 *Report on Foreign Trade Barriers* lists a huge number of impediments erected by a variety of countries against American exports. Among those mentioned is Argentina, which is criticized for maintaining an average tariff rate in excess of 29 per cent; Australia, belaboured for duties in excess of 15 per cent on manufactured goods – considerably higher than average levels for other industrialised countries; and the EC, with which the American trade deficit was $12.8 billion in 1988, also comes in for something of a pasting for tariffs on a wide variety of products, as well as import quotas, the 'buy national' policies of EC governments, and grants and subsidies for virtually all agricultural products.

South Korea, with which the United States had a trade deficit of $9.9 billion in 1988 was also reprimanded, as was Taiwan, which ran a surplus of $14.1 billion with the United States in 1988. Among the reported problems for American companies trying to sell in Taiwan were high tariffs, particularly for agricultural goods, together with an extensive import licensing system. Even tiny Switzerland was not ignored, faulted for its system of beef import quotas, as well as the effective exclusion of United States manufacturers from supplying equipment for the country's electricity utilities.

Under the 1988 Trade Act, Mrs Hills was obliged to use this report to draw up a list of priority unfair trading countries for special treatment and possible retaliatory sanctions under Super 301 by the end of May 1989. At first it looked as though a fairly large list would be produced, probably including the EC, Taiwan and South Korea. Indeed, virtually any of the countries covered by the report could have served as a good victim for Super 301. Yet almost all were ignored when the list was finally published – with the exception of three.

In the end, Japan was bracketed with two of the very worst offenders, Brazil and India (where the average tax on imports is 143 per cent), because of her barriers in relation to wood products, satellites and supercomputers. Under the 1988 Trade Act, these three countries were liable to retaliatory 100 per cent duties on selected exports to the United States if they failed to remove specified trade barriers within 18 months.

The report with some reason criticized Japan for having maintained high tariffs on agricultural products and for the Japanese government's unwillingness to buy American supercomputers. Plans to develop a domestically produced military helicopter and the fact that Japanese vehicle makers buy a large proportion of their components from related companies were also censored.

But on the other hand, Japan was the United States' second largest export market in 1988, coming in for praise in the report for having average tariff rates on industrial products which were among the lowest in the world. The report also commended Japan for the impartial system of telecommunications equipment approval set up by the Japanese Ministry of Post and Telecommunications which, unlike in almost all other countries, allows for the approval of imported telecommunications equipment without discrimination in favour of domestic producers.

Indeed, Japan came out of the report relatively well. Her import restrictions were far less onerous than many other countries while many of the criticisms made about Japanese practices could just as easily have been made about the United States herself. After all, the United States government also buys almost entirely home-produced supercomputers, while it is not unknown for the United States Defence Department to co-operate with American aerospace manufacturers to produce helicopters and military planes. Yet it was Japan and not the EC, South Korea, Taiwan, or any one of a number of other suitable countries that was chosen to accompany India and Brazil on the black list.

Behind this decision lay a good deal of internal United States administration politics. On one side was the 'Get-Tough' lobby led by Secretary of Commerce, Robert Mosbacher, and Mrs Hills. On the other side was the 'free trade' school that included Richard Darman, the director of the Office of Management and Budget, and Michael Boskin, chairman of the Council of Economic Advisors. 'Get-Tough' Hills had already established her credentials when she came into office in January 1989 claiming that she would wield a 'crow bar' to prise open foreign markets. Darman and Boskin, on the other hand, argued that unilateral retaliation would undermine the post-War economic order and could set off a trade war.

Mosbacher and Hills won, for despite advice from State Department officials to go easy on Japan, together with cables from the new United States Ambassador to Japan, Michael Armacost, which warned that lambasting Japan as a trade villain would provoke 'an emotional outburst' in Tokyo, President Bush, beset by angry congressmen and senators, decided to go ahead and take action by including Japan on the blacklist.[11]

Part of the problem was that, having whipped up just enough anti-Japanese hysteria to cover their own shortcomings and policy failures, American politicians had to be seen to be doing something. But these political imperatives did not prevent the United States Administration's action from being viewed as inconsistent and unfair in Tokyo, especially as it came shortly after another extraordinarily erratic action which had already dented Japanese faith in the reliability of her main ally.

'S' is for 'Sucker'

'The "S" in FSX stands for "sucker",' brayed an angry Congressman. A new American dispute with Japan had begun. In November 1988, Japan had signed an agreement with the United States to share in the development of a new fighter for the Japanese air force. Under the deal, General Dynamics was to be given 35 to 40 per cent of the $1.3 billion worth of work to develop a prototype of a new version of its F-16 fighter, to be called the Fighter Support Experimental, or FSX. Mitsubishi Heavy Industries and its Japanese subcontractors would get the rest of the work, while the Japanese government guaranteed to buy about 170 of the fighters in the mid-1990s.

At the time, the deal was seen as a triumph of American policy. Despite hard lobbying from Japanese aerospace companies, the Pentagon had dissuaded the Japanese from developing a fighter on their own. In fact, the original all-Japanese design for the FSX was for a very advanced and highly manoeuverable plane with four vertical fins, each acting as a steering mechanism, which would have given it exceptional stability. But this programme had been mothballed by ex-Prime Minister Nakasone after American pressure for it to be replaced by a joint United States–Japanese development.

The bunting had hardly been taken down, however, when Washington's Japan-bashers moved into action. Tormented by a vision that the American aerospace industry would go the same way as their TV and semiconductor industries, five senators wrote to President Bush demanding a review of the deal. Senator Jesse Helms of North Carolina also managed to extract a promise that the matter would be given a second airing from James Baker during the confirmation hearings for his appointment as Secretary of State. Joining the senatorial xenophobes were allies in the Departments of Labour and Commerce who asserted that the Japanese would benefit from the technology transfers included in the deal and that they should simply buy an American fighter off-the-shelf.[12]

In fact, few major industrial countries import ready made military aircraft. Instead, they either make their own or at the very least negotiate for local assembly or offset deals to guarantee some capacity for home production in the event of hostilities. This was precisely what the United States Navy did when it made a rare decision to purchase a foreign aircraft, the British AV8B Harrier jump-jet.

Despite such considerations and the fact that the State Department and the Pentagon were keen to go ahead with the transaction, which they felt was extremely advantageous from America's point of view, the Administration caved in to pressure from other quarters and returned the deal to the melting pot for much of 1989. By the time President Bush eventually allowed the project to go ahead late in the summer, a great deal of damage had been done to United States-Japanese relations.

Even then the deal almost stalled when it emerged that far from the Japanese being the main beneficiaries of technology exchanges as had been asserted by the congressional Japanophobes, General Dynamics would in fact greatly gain from Mitsubishi Heavy Industries' advanced composite-wing material-technology for which the Japanese company demanded payment which was refused.[13] Eventually the Japanese government agreed to shoulder the cost of transferring the Japanese technology to American manufacturers lest Japan should be seen to be taking away the last bastion of America's industrial might. But by then the deal had less to do with military or even industrial factors than with political considerations. Japan was forced yet again to behave like a successful but indulgent younger brother to a wayward and spoilt elder.

This type of inconsistency unfortunately now permeates American dealings with Japan. Fujitsu's attempt to take over semiconductor-maker, Fairchild, in 1987 was, for example, blocked on national security grounds, even though Fairchild's existing owner was a French company, Schlumberger, which had acquired it in 1979. Salt was rubbed into the wound when two years later another French company, Matra, was allowed to acquire Fairchild Industries, a key defence electronics and space activities company, while Veba of Germany was permitted to buy a Monsanto subsidiary involved in the sensitive electronics sector.

Likewise, Sony's purchase of Columbia Pictures late in 1989 provoked agitated comments that Japan had bought America's soul. Yet the fact that such all-American businesses as Dunkin' Donuts, Brooks Brothers, Holiday Inns, Burger King, Hilton International, Ball Park Hot Dogs and Pepperidge Farm are all British-owned raises hardly a whimper of protest. And when in 1989 French computer maker, Groupe Bull, bought up Zenith's PC business, France's Usinor-Salicor acquired the second largest stainless steel producer in America, and French aluminium producer Pechiney took over American National Can, the largest packaging group in the world, there was barely a murmur – despite the fact that Bull, Usinor-Salicor and Pechiney are state-owned and heavily subsidized by the French government, partly for the very purpose of buying up foreign companies.

These inequities would be enough to try the tolerance of the most patient of nations, but in the case of Japan they are exacerbated by a newly shrill and aggressive note which has entered into United States dealings with Japan over the past few years, caused partly by near paranoia at the emergence of Japan as the world's number one economic power, and in part by a prejudice and cultural narrowness which has too often resulted in a complete failure to see the other side's point of view. American politicians, ever eager to play to the gallery, have been refining the subtle art of Jap-bashing since Walter Mondale proved himself less a national leader than a follower of populist whims when in 1982 he complained: 'We've been running up the white flag when we should be running up the American flag . . . what do we want our kids to do? Sweep up around the Japanese computers?'[14]

Not long after, United States Congress representatives ceremoniously consigned Toshiba video recorders to a flaming bonfire in an ugly scene faintly reminiscent of newsreel shots from the 1930s when the works of Thomas Mann and other distinguished authors considered unacceptable were consigned to Nazi fires. Later, Congressmen were to be seen with their sleeves rolled up, wielding sledgehammers and smashing Toshiba computers.

With their leaders behaving like this, it is not wholly surprising that ordinary Americans occasionally go one better and resort to violence to ease their frustration, like the gang which murdered a Chinese-American in Detroit. Their defence was that they thought the man was Japanese and blamed him for job losses in the city's motor industry. The killers were merely fined and put on probation!

Nor have industrialists and academics been notably more objective. Billionaire property developer, Donald Trump, told fellow businessmen in Manhattan late in 1989: 'We're the biggest suckers in the world. If we get any kinder or gentler we won't have any America left. Japan is ripping us off like no one has ever ripped us before.' Mr Trump's solution to the problem was to exact 'a pound of flesh' in the form of a 20 per cent import tax.[15] Anthony Harrigan, President of the Washington-based United States Business and Industrial Council, joined in when he warned in a letter in the *New York Times* that 'The United States must take unilateral action to safeguard America's industries and technologies or it will become a second class power in the world and Japan will truly gain the international pre-eminence it has sought throughout this century.' But perhaps Chrysler's boss, Lee Iacocca, whose company was itself the recipient of generous state aid in the early 1980s, best encapsulated the prevailing mood when after a round of lobbying on Capitol Hill he told *Automotive News*, the car industry's trade publication: 'They don't know there is a war on. They don't have the foggiest idea.'

The Japan that can say 'no'

On top of this is the sanctimonious habit of preaching to the Japanese. Back in the 1970s, for example, the Carter Administration demanded that Japan should achieve a fixed rate of economic growth, determined by Washington to suit its own purpose. American politicians have on frequent occasions since then urged the Japanese to imitate some of their own not very successful practices, such as increasing domestic consumption and lowering their savings rate. The Japanese could, however, just as reasonably respond by urging the Americans and Europeans to do more as they do, for it is nonsense to argue that America's problems can be solved by imposing unwise American economic policies on Japan, an absurdity which emanates from the widespread belief that both the responsibility and the remedy for the United States' problems lie solely in Japanese hands.

The Japanese have, it is true, often acquiesced to such finger-wagging partly because they genuinely wish to increase home demand to some extent, but also to appease the United States and take some of the heat out of trade disputes. In fact, the Japanese went so far in trying to assist the Americans with their trade deficit by boosting domestic consumption through low interest rates in the late 1980s that they allowed their monetary policy to become too expansionary, creating inflation and weakening the yen.

It is inconceivable for the United States government to deliver homilies and lectures to France, Germany or even India. Yet American leaders feel quite comfortable with publicly hectoring Japan which, because of the anomalous nature of post-War United States–Japanese relations, they still too often view as America's Asian sidekick. Times have moved on, however, and it is not surprising that the Japanese are beginning to get fed up of being scolded like children by their wayward American nanny, nor that the deep fund of goodwill towards the United States in Japan is rapidly diminishing as the Japanese become less willing to accept their alloted role as whipping boys. 'Such American high-handedness may well reflect the condescending attitude the United States has continued to have, if unconsciously, towards Japan, ever since its victory in World War II', ran an editorial in the normally sober *Japan Economic Journal* late in 1989; while Kenichi Ohmae, managing director in Japan for the American management consultant firm, McKinsey & Co, exasperatedly told an *Asahi Evening News* reporter: 'Everyone in the United States government talks like a General MacArthur. We get this sort of talk every day.'

If the West wants Japan to continue steadily down the road to liberalism which she has broadly travelled since the Second World War, it is important to demonstrate to the Japanese that the West is big enough to acknowledge Japan's legitimate achievements. Otherwise, Japanese resentment will cause her to begin to turn away from the West. It is, after all, a strange teacher who chides the pupil for excellence. And for the United States to vilify Japan for its inadequacies from a position of patent weakness, far from improving the situation, is likely simply to provoke an unpleasant backlash, making the Japanese feel that they are being treated intolerably and pushed into a corner – just as they perceive they were in 1941. Then, after Japan's imitation of the West had extended to empire, she had nonetheless been blackballed from the club by the Imperial powers and cut off from colonial oil and other natural resources, as a result of which she turned viciously on her former mentors.

Sadly, the beginnings of a backlash are already evident. In the summer of 1989, a provocative book called *The Japan That Can Say 'No'*,[16] was published in Japan by 68-year-old Akio Morita, the cosmopolitan founder of Sony, and Shintaro Ishihara, a right-wing LDP Diet member with a reputation for being something of an *enfant terrible*. Ishihara, while still at university, won a literary prize for a book remembered for a scene in which the hero pushes a part of his anatomy which is not normally exposed through a paper partition wall. Later in his career, in spite of causing a stir by advocating that Japan should have its own nuclear weapons, Ishihara won a Diet seat with a record 3.1 million votes and became a transport minister. This hawkish maverick was even a contender for the Prime Ministership after the resignation of Sosuke Uno in 1989.

The Morita–Ishihara book originally only sold a few copies and was not intended for publication abroad, but it was read by a Japanese-speaking American working for a Tokyo company. His office arranged for a private translation and before long copies found their way to the United States, first circulating in California's Silicon Valley and later on Capitol Hill.

The bluntness of much of the book's language shook American sensitivities to the core. Alarmed by increasing American dependence on Japanese technology, the Defence Department's Advanced Research Projects Agency, which channels state-aid into high-tech industrial research, commissioned its own bootleg translation which it circulated widely to politicians and corporate leaders of companies most threatened by Japanese competition. Congressmen and senators, rarely slow off the mark when it comes to Japan-bashing, were soon also making copies with the most intemperate passages underlined and passing them round, telling friends, 'I told you so' and vying with each other in the strength of their denunciations. Senator James Exon of Nebraska remarked that the book convinced him that 'what was once only a theoretical loss of American independence is now inching closer to reality'. Industrialists rapidly joined the fray, like Chrysler's chairman, Lee Iacocca, who dubbed the book 'an insult to the American people'. To many, the grinning mask had slipped to reveal the true arrogance of the Japanese in a way which further cranked up American paranoia and gave ammunition to the protectionist lobby, such as Harvard economist, Laurence Summers, who quoted extensively from Ishihara while arguing that America 'should aggressively confront Japanese mercantilism'.[17]

All of which was a shame because some of the work, which is more a collection of essays than a book, makes very good sense and there is plenty of frank admission of Japanese faults. Its main thesis, aside from the fact that America's problems are largely her own fault, is that Japan should be more forthright in her dealings with the West or she will continue to be trampled on. The very fact that such a book was written indicates a change in Japanese attitudes, but the controversial anti-American strain contained within it – which, in fact, does no more than closely parallel the style of the more hysterical school of American writing on Japan – is a more ominous indication of the complex of resentments that are currently bubbling beneath the surface in Japan.

For one thing, the Japanese perceive that there is a racist under-current underlying much of the anti-Japanese campaign in America. For example, Morita tells of a visit to Washington five days after Congress had passed a resolution condemning Japan on the semiconductor issue. 'I met some of my old friends,' he says, 'senators and congressmen, who with subtle smiles admitted that racial considerations, or more directly, racial prejudices, played a role in United States–Japan relations.' Japan, of course, has its own fair share of racists, but the West finds it more difficult to own up to its racism.

Ishihara is somewhat more intemperate, writing: 'At times it appears to me that the Americans behave more like mad dogs than watch dogs', and claiming:

During the Second World War, Americans bombed civilian targets in Germany, but only on Japan did they use the atomic bomb. While they refuse to admit it, the only reason they could use the atomic bomb on Japan was because of their racial attitude towards Japan.

Clearly, this is nonsense as Germany had already been beaten by the time the Allies obtained the bomb. If this book had just been written by some fringe ultra-nationalist xenophobe, or solely by Ishihara, it would have been of little significance. But the fact that Morita, who has spent a great deal of time in the United States and is generally considered a friend of America's, could lend his name to the work is indicative of the extent of Japanese exasperation.*

It is Washington's hectoring, its inconsistency and repeated failure to understand Tokyo and give the Japanese due credit for their achievements that is, in part, to blame for driving a wedge between the world's number one and number two economic superpowers. The Japanese have always had something of an inferiority complex and are more receptive to criticism than most nations, as evidenced by the surprising popularity of books hostile to Japan among the Japanese. But the more they are unfairly criticized, the more likely they are to retreat into their own protective shell of self-righteousness and the less likely they are to remedy those Western grievances that are genuine, such as ending the trade barriers that the country still maintains in areas such as wood products.

---

* Morita, embarrassed by the publicity, has since distanced himself from Ishihara's comments.

That, in turn, will not only cause relations with the West to deteriorate further, it will also be of little help to the Japanese people.

Japan has in recent years made great efforts to pull down its trade barriers and in reality now maintains far fewer genuine ones than most Western countries. But it still restricts imports in some fields in a way which pushes up prices for Japanese consumers. However, the prospect of Japan listening sympathetically to genuine Western complaints, opening her markets further and giving her people lower-cost imports is already receding under the withering barrage of self-righteous criticism from the United States in particular.

Recently, Japanese newspapers have been making morose references to the return of the 'Black Ships' – the name which the Japanese gave to the foreign fleet which forced the Shogun to open Japan to international trade in the middle of the Nineteenth Century. The difference is that then, a debilitated and backward Japan had to bow deeply to the 'foreign devils'. Now they no longer have to.

So there is both a warning to the United States and some arrogance in Ishihara's words, which echo the feelings of many Japanese:

> I had an argument with an American correspondent recently. I asked him to look at those developing nations which were under American auspices. The Philippines and those in Africa, Central and South America are all in hopeless situations. Those Asian nations where the economy has been a success story, such as Korea, Taiwan and Singapore, were all, at one time or another, under Japanese administrations . . . . I pointed this out to the correspondent; in return he only fell silent. We need Asia more than we need America.

28

新大国

MISSING THE POINT

'For every complex problem, there is a solution which is neat, plausible and wrong.'
H L Mencken (1880–1956).

BOTH EUROPE AND Japan currently threaten to turn east, so leaving the United States in sulky isolation. Japan has Asia, while the European Community is increasingly being transformed into an inward-looking, German-dominated bloc, a drift which has been dramatically reinforced by developments in Central Europe, for although the road ahead for the former Eastern Bloc nations is fraught with perils of its own, the prospects of Polish and Hungarian EC membership are no longer the distant possibilities they were in the summer of 1989.

Current American trade policy is reinforcing these emerging realignments which contain great dangers for the United States itself. Overweening use of Super 301 has already alienated virtually all of the United States' major trading partners. In June 1989, for example, the United States found itself isolated at a meeting of OECD ministers when the major industrial nations united behind Japan in condemning American policy. Even the trade minister of neighbouring Canada told the United States delegation: 'No country has a monopoly of righteous indignation when it comes to international trade.'

What incenses America's allies above all are Washington's double standards. While Carla Hills travels the world berating other countries for their malpractices, $20 million worth of an emergency United States food aid package for Poland was being wasted on the exra cost of using United States-flagged ships owing to a law which states that 75 per cent of such food must be carried in American vessels. Soon afterwards, the United States actually cut Japan's steel import quota. According to a report in

Newsweek magazine, President Bush himself even joked: 'Maybe we ought to take action against ourselves'. At worst, such policies could divide the world into three hostile trading blocs based on the European Community, North America and an Asian yen zone – a division with uncomfortable echoes of the break-up of world order in the 1930s.

Indeed, uneasy parallels with the pre-War period, when the Japanese felt they were treated unfairly and put in an intolerable position by the Americans, are regularly made in current Japanese comment on relations with the United States. LDP right-winger Ishihara, for example, draws a parallel in his controversial book between the mood of the United States Congress in passing a resolution to impose sanctions on Japan over the semiconductor issue, and that of the League of Nations when it attacked Japan over the Manchurian invasion in 1931.

At the same time, the rise of protectionist sentiment and the failure of America to cut her twin deficits have also aroused doubts in the minds of her allies concerning America's ability to overcome her problems. And nowhere are these worries now spoken so loudly than in Japan where the question continually being asked is: can America be relied upon? To prevent the worst happening, the United States in particular has first to accept that her problems are primarily her own fault. To cure those ills, she must be prepared to adapt and change in the same way as Japan has done over the past 120 years.

Even then, the question remains as to whether America can regain her former pre-eminence. The answer is almost certainly no. In terms of her geographical size, natural wealth and population, the United States should probably possess around a fifth of the world's wealth and power. But because of a series of favourable historical and other circumstances, her share had risen to around twice that by the end of the last War, since when the United States' overwhelming military power and the extent of her cultural influence has disguised her steady decline to a more natural level.[1]

But although the United States is unlikely ever to gain her former 'unnatural' pre-eminence, there is no reason to believe that she is doomed to shrink into obscurity or that she cannot recover some of her economic power relative to Japan. The natural resources and very size of the United States will almost certainly ensure that she remains a major player in the world economy, but how great that role is will, to a large extent, be determined by the changes she is prepared to make over the next couple of decades. At least a good precedent for reversing decline is provided by Western Europe which, after a long period of deterioration, has managed to improve its position since the War – although Europe, like the United States, must be no less prepared to reform further to match the intensifying challenge from the East. There does at least now appear to be some willingness to learn from Japan. But so far, some misleading lessons seem to have been learned alongside the correct ones.

More of the same?

Visitors kept waiting in the lobby of Japan's Ministry of Posts and Telecommunications have, over the past couple of years, been entertained by sports videos on a large screen TV with stunningly good picture quality. Many people who have seen the television say that they cannot tell the difference between it and film. This is High Definition Television (HDTV) which represents a major step forward in television technology, offering a potential market of up to $200 billion in the United States alone over the next two decades. HDTV technology is also expected to have important spin-off benefits for other industries, including computers, for which HDTV screens could be used, and semiconductors, for the new sets will use large quantities of advanced components.

The Japanese HDTV system – called 'Hi-Vision' or 'Muse' – improves TV pictures by increasing the number of lines from the current 525 on Japanese and American sets and 625 on European ones to 1,125. At first it looked as though the European industry would accept as the world standard the Japanese system which was well in advance of anything in the West, but at a meeting of industry and political leaders in 1985 a decision was taken to fight off potential domination by Japanese technology. As a result, the Eureka 95 programme was set up by the European Community to develop European HDTV technology with a budget of £150 million, substantially funded by European governments and state broadcasting authorities. As part of this policy, in 1990, Europe's electronics industry blocked the adoption of Japanese technology as a world standard, condemning Europe to a long wait for mass HDTV technology and the world to at least two TV standards in the late 1990s. Needless to say, the move coincided with the announcement of yet more stale subsidies for Europe's TV industry.

Alan Gomez, the craggy, 50-year-old former paratrooper hand-picked by France's President Mitterand to head the state-owned Thomson group's counter-attack on the Japanese, justified what was an essentially political decision to take on the Japanese with the well worn words: 'What we need is some kind of breathing space'. The system being promoted by Thomson in a consortium with the other main European manufacturer, Philips, has the advantage of being compatible with existing sets fitted with adaptors. Hi-Vision, by contrast, is designed to operate only with special, wide-screen TVs.

But the Japanese claim that their quality is superior and they are already selling sets and broadcasting a limited range of Hi-Vision programmes. The Europeans also plan to offer a wide-screen system as part of their evolutionary approach, but full HDTV broadcasts are not expected in Europe until the mid-90s; and in the meantime, purchasers of the £3,000, wide-screen sets will only really be able to utilize their TVs when feature films fill the screen. Moreover, Sony has been quick to loan professional video Hi-Vision systems to producers so that the Japanese standard is not only increasingly replacing film, but also effectively establishing the Japanese technology as the standard among programme makers.

With only one American-owned television manufacturer remaining of the 25 or so who led the TV market in the late 1960s, it seemed for some time as though America would go with the Japanese HDTV standard. However, in the face of declining international competitiveness, particularly in the United States electronics industry, industrialists, academics, pressure groups and politicians have been following the Europeans in calling for unprecedented levels of collaboration between government and industry in a way which is challenging traditional American attitudes towards free competition. Adding urgency to this debate is the growing view in Washington that the United States' relative failure in many areas of technology has now reached the stage where the country's security may be threatened. HDTV, with its potential key strategic role in the consumer electronics industry, has become a focus of that concern.

As a result, a sense of crisis currently pervades official American thinking. Calls for 'national industrial strategies' resound along the government corridors in most Western countries, but nowhere more loudly now than in Washington, where a growing band of influential Americans are arguing that bureaucrats know better than the markets. There has always been an academic fringe in the United States willing to assert the benefits of a 'trade and industry policy', but over the past few years this view has become far more widespread. Recently two former secretaries of state, Henry Kissinger and Cyrus Vance, added their voices to the chorus.

The currently fashionable form for state intervention is government-backed consortia of companies. Proposals to form collaborative research groups to work in areas such as superconductivity have already won widespread support. But at the head of the consortia movement is a suggestion that the American government should fund a national effort to get the development of a new generation of American HDTV technology off the ground to compete with the Japanese HDTV standard.

The Bush Administration has actively considered a proposal by 19 United States computer and electronics companies, including IBM, AT&T, Apple, Texas Instruments and Hewlett-Packard, to relax anti-trust laws to allow the formation of a private sector consortium to develop HDTV products. Moreover, Commerce Secretary Robert Mosbacher has stated that he would have no objection to an involvement in HDTV spending by the Defence Advanced Research Projects Agency (Darpa), the Pentagon's industrial agency which was, until spring 1990, led by Craig Fields, one of the most forceful advocates of closer government/industry co-operation and who offered $30 million of his $1-billion-plus budget for research on HDTV. Further, while it has been suggested that European TV makers operating in the United States, such as Philips and Thomson, should be allowed to join in the proposed consortium, the Japanese television makers, whose operations in America are far more extensive, have been excluded.

Behind this trend towards what has been called 'Technology America Inc' is, of course, 'the Japanese threat'. The prospect of losing global technological superiority is making American industry feel pretty beleaguered. 'We are facing economic warfare,' Bill Krause, chairman of the American Electronics Association which represents over 3,500 American electronics companies told a *Financial Times* reporter, while a report published by Krause's association states: 'If the United States does not choose to re-enter consumer electronics via HDTV, the country as a whole is likely to experience a continued declining world market share in automated manufacturing equipment, personal computers and semiconductors.'

On the face of it, this is a pretty standard piece of industrial special pleading. But it is striking a chord partly because many American industrial leaders have convinced themselves that close industry–government links and co-operative R&D consortia are among the major reasons for Japanese success. 'We ought to learn from the Japanese,' says William Weber, president of Texas Instruments and a director of the Semiconductor Industry Association, which has played a major role in shaping United States trade policy towards Japan. 'The Japanese have a national co-ordinated strategy, whereas we in the United States are at odds with each other and, at times, with our government. We need to focus our resources.'

Imitating the Japanese is a fairly new and potentially profitable line of action for American industry – provided, of course, that they confine their plagiarism to those aspects of the Japanese system which have genuinely contributed to the country's success. The problem with state-backed consortia is that they have not played a particularly fundamental part in the accomplishments of Japanese industry. And besides, they have already been tried in the West, with not very encouraging results.

Concorde, the supersonic airliner programme which lost around £1 billion (at 1970 prices), was the product of an Anglo–French, government-led consortium. The main beneficiaries are the few hundred wealthy people who each day save around three hours' flying time crossing the Atlantic. In 1962, Swiss watch manufacturers joined together in a consortium to develop a new electronic watch mechanism. It was not a success, and in the end Swiss manufacturers imported most of the necessary parts from Japan.

Another best-forgotten episode was the state-sponsored Unidata computer consortium which linked Philips, Siemens and Bull in the early 1970s. At about the same time, the British government encouraged the electronics firms GEC, Plessey and STC to collaborate with the national telephone network operator (then the General Post Office) to produce a new world-beating digital public exchange. The resulting System X has so far chalked up only one overseas sales success – to a small Caribbean island. British television manufacturers also joined together in the 1970s to produce a common TV tube. But by the end of the 1980s, there were no significant indigenous British TV manufacturers left and UK tube production is now dominated by Japanese and Dutch companies.

Even the much vaunted Airbus programme, the glory of European state co-ordinated and subsidized industrial co-operation, is subject to doubts. Although Airbus does successfully compete with Boeing in the medium-range, wide-bodied airliner market, one in-depth study concluded that on top of huge losses, Airbus still had a negative discounted net value and that the main beneficiaries of the programme had not been the European aerospace industry, but rather international airlines which had gained from lower-cost planes as a result of the competition with Boeing.[2]

Nor even have Japanese government-inspired consortia invariably been crowned with success. The ten-year programme to develop 'Fifth Generation' computers and software, set up in 1971 with $500 million of funding, largely failed to come up with any results. The similar American MCC consortium, organized in 1983 in response to the Japanese effort at the instigation of computer-maker Control Data's chairman, William Norris, has likewise been short on results, even though it comprised some of

America's most powerful companies, including DEC, 3M and Boeing. MCC certainly seems to have done little for Control Data which has since plunged into severe financial difficulties.

Nonetheless, in 1987, Charles Sporck, President of National Semiconductor, a major American chip maker, persuaded several of his fellow Silicon Valley pharaohs to assemble a new collaborative team involving 14 companies which included AT&T, DEC, Hewlett-Packard, Intel, IBM, Motorola and TI. Their plan was to develop a new generation of semiconductor technology. Sematech, as the group is known, had as its leader until his death in 1990 one of Silicon Valley's most ardent Japanophobes, Robert Noyce, who founded two of the semiconductor companies to have suffered most from Japanese competition – Fairchild Semiconductor and Intel. The group is being helped on its way with $100 million a year in Defence Department grants.

Contrary to the claims of Sematech's proponents, there is so far little tangible evidence of the consortium's success. Nonetheless, Sematech was the spur behind US Memories, yet another consortium concept this time led by a former IBM executive. US Memories included DEC, Intel, National Semiconductor, Hewlett-Packard and IBM and aimed to get the United States back into the memory-chip market through the window of opportunity afforded by the upcoming generation of 4 megabit D-Rams.

Unfortunately, the consortium's attempts to involve large D-Ram purchasers in the project met with failure when Apple, Compaq and Sun Microsystems reacted tepidly towards investing in the group, preferring to keep their freedom to buy from the most competitive sources. In the end, the US Memories plan folded, and while its members tried to get their act together, Japanese manufacturers were already developing the next generation of 16 megabit D-Rams – testament to the dubious nature of one of the arguments in favour of consortia: that they allow Western industries to 'leap frog' Japanese competition.

This may be why not all United States industry leaders are totally enamoured with the government-funded consortia concept. T J Rodgers, the founder of Cypress Semiconductor, a six-year-old semiconductor maker with a turnover of $200 million a year, is one of Silicon Valley's most outspoken entrepreneurs. During Congressional testimony, Mr Rodgers strongly argued against changes in anti-trust laws to benefit US Memories. He claims that Sematech and US Memories were set up to benefit a small number of ailing 'fat cats' in the industry, rather than the industry as a whole.[3] Rodgers also told Fortune magazine: 'If you want to mess things up to the max, just get the Pentagon involved. The most efficient efforts are starved for money and people.'[4]

Another objection to the consortia route is the fact that although Japanese companies have collaborated in research, often with government support, they virtually never manufacture together, as the HDTV lobby proposes. Indeed, any co-operation on basic research rapidly transmutes into the fiercest competition once the research stage is over.

The allure of state-backed consortia and other interventionist prescriptions is that they represent neat and easy quick-fix prescriptions for Western industrial problems. There is, moreover, a growing danger that in response to the widening economic gap with Japan, Europe and the United States will opt to intervene even further in their economies. For many politicians, instinctively mistrustful of the workings of the market, are only too eager to augment their own power and authority by latching on to this fraying lifeline. They are not short of support from those Western industrialists who fear Japanese competition and are keen for the quiet life and cosy existence afforded by closed markets and state subsidies. But the truth is that although commentators are quick to attribute economic success to government intervention and subsidies, they often ignore the fact that such policies have already been tried in the West, and that many of the world's least successful economies have been run by firmly interventionist governments.

The argument of the anti-interventionists is not, as some proponents of the other persuasion suggest, that markets are perfect, but rather that well-meaning interference in markets by politicians and bureaucrats to try to perfect the market mechanism is likely to do more harm than good. This is especially the case if, as so often, industrial policies promote types of economic activity which are unsuited to a country's level of development, such as the plans to develop an Indonesian car, the Indian rocket programme or Brazil's attempts to build up a computer industry.

It might also profitably be asked to what extent British industry in general was drained of resources of capital and engineering skills by the attempt to build up an indigenous nuclear power industry? Moreover, the beggar-my-neighbour aspect of state subsidies tends to mean that the more one country indulges in such policies, the more others will tend to join in, so cancelling out any potential advantages. Certainly the OECD, probably the most experienced body when it comes to objectively analysing economic policies across the world, does not consider interventionism to be a recipe for industrial competitiveness. In a report early in 1990, the Paris-based organization concluded: 'Industrial policies continue to represent a signifi-cant drain on government finances while there is little evidence that they have yielded the intended efficiency and welfare gains.' But above all, arguments over government support and consortia provide potentially costly distractions from exploring the real underlying causes of uncompeti-tiveness in the United States and Europe.

An open door

Each year Japanese motorists buy around a million microcars called 'kei', which are scaled down high-tech hatchbacks with engines below 550 cc capacity and costing from as little as ¥500,000 (about £2,000). Apart from price and size, these microcars offer superb economy and produce little pollution, making them the ideal town cars. Moreover, intense competition in the kei class has turned most of the models on offer into tiny technological masterpieces, for despite often only having three-cylinder engines, they are packed with features more usually confined to high-performance upmarket models. The Mitsubishi Dangan ZZ's three-cylinder engine, for example, has 15 valves, intercooled turbo-charging and twin overhead camshafts all for a price of just over £4,000. Other kei-class rivals offer four-wheel drive, automatic transmission and power steering as well as convenience features that make the most of their limited space, like the Suzuki Alto which has large sliding doors and a swivelling driver's seat to allow you to step right out onto the pavement. The Daihatsu Sneaker even offers an extendable fifth wheel to help the car squeeze into tight parking spots.

Sadly very few of these diminutive wonders are on sale in the West due to import restrictions which result in Japanese manufacturers exporting more profitable and higher-priced larger cars. Nor has such protection encouraged European or American manufacturers to make microcars of their own. The only Western offerings vaguely resembling the Japanese *kei* cars are the Fiat 126 and Rover's Mini,* the former dating from the early 1970s and now made only in Poland, and the latter tracing its origins back to the early 1960s. When Raymond Levy, the boss of France's Renault, was asked if he would launch a really low-cost small car, he retorted: 'I see no room in our range for such a car. I don't think we could make any money by selling such a cheap model.'5

Yet lobbying by Renault, among others, has meant that Western consumers are largely unable to acquire these space-saving and environment-friendly Japanese microcars which would be a boon in traffic-choked cities as well as to those on low incomes. Instead, those on a tight budget have to make do with geriatric and highly polluting low-priced Eastern Bloc models. Trade restrictions, in this case, have harmed both the consumers and the environment without notably helping Western industry. The effect of this particular case on its own is, of course, unlikely to have a disastrous effect on Western economic prospects. But similar situations, multiplied many times by other products in other fields, can only have a steadily, debilitating effect on overall competitiveness.

And these situations are multiplying, for another diversion from the West's real problems is the intensely one-sided reading of Japan's trade policies, which seems to have convinced many American and European leaders that supposedly closed markets have been a key factor in Japan's success which should be emulated in the West. History should be warning enough to politicians that protectionism does not have the intended effect on competitiveness, employment or the balance of payments. On the contrary, as observed in earlier chapters, trade barriers cushion domestic industry, making it less competitive and giving unfair advantage to those who wield the most lobbying power, while reducing choice for consumers and undermining general economic efficiency.

Bearing in mind the huge costs and disadvantages of using protectionism as an industrial policy, it may be thought surprising that the European Community and the United States appear increasingly to be relying on this weapon to defeat Japan and other competitive East Asian economies – especially as the EC Commission's own figures reveal that the removal of internal trade barriers between the EC's constituent nations, scheduled for 1992, will result in, among other things, a gain of more than £50 billion due

* Ironically, the Mini's best market is now Japan, where its quirky anachronistic nature has ensured it a small cult following.

to industries being able to exploit economies of scale more fully. Intensified competition will also reduce monopoly profits the report goes on, helping to create between 1.8 million and five million new jobs, reducing consumer prices by up to six per cent and increasing the Community's GDP by about 4.5 per cent. If the EC Commission can see the huge advantages of free trade within the EC, why are they so blind to the wider benefits of more general free trade?

Support of the principle of free trade does, of course, carry with it an implied acceptance that your country will not be able to make everything. One of the advantages of the free exchange of goods is that each country specializes in what it makes best and imports those items it cannot make – what the economist David Ricardo, back in 1817, referred to as 'the freedom to do most what each of us does best', which economists now term 'comparative advantage'. Countries following this policy exchange the 'security' of knowing that they can make everything themselves for the benefits of specialization in the knowledge that any dependence on their trading partners is mutual. Those who fear dependence on world markets should remember that Japan, with so few resources and running the risk of choking if the surrounding oceans are not kept open, is itself perhaps the best example of just such dependence. Yet that does not prevent Japan from being economically powerful.

As economies which move from import restrictions to freer trade restructure and concentrate on what they can do best, some industries obviously have to be dropped. In the case of Western Europe and the United States, these industries may be the very type of sensitive high-tech areas which are so closely intertwined with national pride. That may be no bad thing, however, for by artificially trying to maintain, say, D-Ram memory chip production in the West, governments may well be disadvantaging other industries by diverting resources and skilled personnel into these areas and so weakening the industries in which the West is still competitive. So while it may boost American pride to have indigenous D-Ram producers, the question that should really be asked is whether it is desirable for a country which has largely lost the art of making TVs and VCRs, and does not always seem to make even products like cars very well, to attempt artificially to remain in a far more technically advanced area?

The eventual abandonment of some high-tech fields of industry is, in fact, an essential part of taking a step back and rebuilding Western economies on a basis sustainable by their underlying economic fundamentals. This does not mean, however, that the West will be relegated forever to the industrial second division. Japan herself was, after all, mainly dependent on lower-tech industries up to the 1960s and early 1970s, but as her educational skills and capital base grew, so she moved on and up into more sophisticated areas. Western countries, too, will be able to move back into higher-tech industries if they improve their competitive position. The idea that once a lead is lost, it is gone forever, is absurd, as demonstrated by the very fact of Japan's relatively recent success in computers and semiconductors, and latterly, South Korea's progress in semiconductors.

Nor does the vacating of unsustainable areas mean returning Western workers to the looms and cotton mills and relying on low-tech industries.

For although the West has fallen behind technologically in many areas, there are still sophisticated industries in which it remains competitive, such as aerospace, pharmaceuticals and software. Allowing resources to be concentrated in those areas where the West competes best, and maintaining an open door to new ideas, investment and technology, makes their continued success more likely.

How different?

Even those who do not subscribe to protectionism or state-directed industrial strategies sometimes still attribute Japan's success to the supposition that the Japanese are fundamentally different from Westerners, and benefit from some unique cultural abnormality or Eastern characteristic which threatens Western values. This has been characterized in one influential book in terms of the Japanese group ethos versus America-style cowboy individuality.[6] Because Japan is so different, the argument runs, it is perfectly legitimate to treat her as a separate entity from the rest of the world's economy. Moreover, Japan's supposed uniqueness is often used as a convenient excuse not to try to learn from her success.

So how different are the Japanese? Of course, all societies have their special cultural elements and Japan's group ethos has been of undoubted significance, but social cohesion and Japan's apparently unique faculty for harmonious co-operation has its limitations, as has been demonstrated by the country's pre-War problems and the failure of Japanese culture to overcome these. On top of which, even Japan's relative peaceful post-1945 history has been punctuated by regular bitter strikes, massive demonstrations, vicious riots and severe political problems. Rather, the extent to which the Japanese have demonstrated relatively high levels of social cohesion over the last 40 years has had less to do with some mystical oriental spirit of togetherness, than with the strictly practical realization that working together was a necessity if the country was to survive.

One oft-quoted example of how the Japanese business world supposedly operates in a fundamentally different way from the West is its stock market. When Japanese equities soared in the 1980s and then recovered rapidly from the October 1987 Crash to boast sky-high price to earnings ratios, many commentators put this down to 'special' reasons. They pointed to the influence of the Ministry of Finance and the fact that the 'Big Four' leading securities firms dominate the market, accounting for more than half of the total turnover, factors which led to assertions that Tokyo is 'rigged' in a way which proves that the Japanese operate to different rules.

In fact, there are quite rational explanations for the performance of the Japanese market. For one thing, Japanese companies tend to under-report profits for tax reasons, while different accounting methods and the under-valuation of assets all serve to further explain the difference in price to earnings ratios. Then there is the fact that, owing to cross-holdings and lower equity-to-debt ratios, fewer shares are available. Above all, in a decade that has seen very high levels of economic growth it would have been surprising if Japan's stock market had not been among the beneficiaries. When these factors are taken into account, it can be seen that the differences between the Japanese and Western markets are largely superficial.

This point was made dramatically when the Japanese market fell sharply in 1990, knocking about one-half off stock values and leaving privatization favourite, NTT, at a quarter of its peak value. This was in response to fears about the Middle East crisis as well as bank and industry exposure to the property bubble and the growth of inflationary pressures, concerns which led to interest rate rises which made bonds more attractive than low-yielding equities. So it turned out that Japan was, after all, just as prone to market forces and human frailties as any other country.

Those differences which do exist tend to be of degree, rather than kind, and should not be used as an excuse for not learning from the Japanese or for erecting barriers against their products. Moreover, those who talk about the unique forces at work in Japanese industry should consider the fact that many Japanese companies manage to get the same kind of performance out of their workers in their American and European plants as they do from their Japanese employees.

Segment retreat

A common prescription for Western industry in the past two decades has been for Western manufacturers to move upmarket into high-margin, low-volume areas of the market in order to escape Japanese competition. This is grounded in a fallacious assumption that high-volume, mass-market products are necessarily low-margin, low-added-value and labour-intensive. It is also based on the dangerous notion that Japanese manufacturers will not bother to chase you upmarket.

There are, no doubt, areas where a low-volume, high-margin strategy makes very good sense. But it has certainly failed in a great many Western industries. When, for example, the British motor-cycle manufacturers, Triumph, Enfield, Norton and BSA, fled upmarket from Honda and Yamaha, they soon found themselves cornered in the low-volume end of the market and were finally crushed by Honda's low costs and huge volumes.

Sometimes called 'segment retreat' by economists, this type of behaviour is usually little better than a slow form of suicide. But today General Motors and other large Western manufacturers appear to be repeating the mistakes of the motorcycle industry by withdrawing from the small-car market to concentrate resources on larger cars in the hope of insulating themselves from low-priced imports. If they and Europe's luxury car manufacturers, Mercedes, Porsche, BMW, Saab and Jaguar, believe that they have successfully distanced themselves from Japanese competition, they may be in for an unpleasant shock in the early 1990s. For the Japanese are relentlessly following them upwards.

Already, Japan's three most competitive manufacturers have edged into the executive and luxury end of the auto market where their presence was virtually non-existent in the early 1980s. Honda was first with its Acura marque which it reserves for its higher class cars, particularly the executive-level Legend launched in 1986. Nissan began selling its Infiniti luxury models in late 1989, at the same time as Toyota shocked Europe's luxury auto makers with the quality and performance of its new Lexus marque.

Needless to say, the Japanese manufacturers are following their familiar routine of producing products in high volumes, thereby cutting costs, expanding the market and enabling them to significantly undercut their competitors. By 1986, Honda was already selling around 150,000 of its Acura cars in the United States, shooting ahead of established luxury car importers such as Mercedes–Benz which itself sold a record 99,000 cars in the same year. Toyota aimed to sell 75,000 Lexus models in the United States alone in 1990, the first full year of Lexus production. That was almost as much as Jaguar and Porsche's combined total output. This volume strategy has already allowed the Japanese auto maker to dramatically undercut its European rivals. The top line Lexus LS 400, for example, carried a launch-base sticker-price in the United States of $35,000 – nearly $30,000 less than the comparable Mercedes 420SEL. Other competitors from Jaguar and BMW were undercut by margins of around $10,000.

Porsche was the first to feel the pinch of Japanese competition, as the lower end of its high-priced range fell victim in the late 1980s to Japanese sports cars which offered 90 per cent of Porsche performance for 60 per cent of the cost. The latest Nissan 300ZX has actually bettered Porsche performance, offering a three-litre, 24-valve V6 engine with twin-inter-cooled turbochargers, air conditioning, ABS brakes and an array of other upmarket goodies for less than the cost of a four-cylinder and fairly basically equipped Porsche 944 Turbo SE. This may help to explain why Porsche's American sales were, by the beginning of 1990, running at only a third of their peak levels of the mid-1980s. And worse is to come. Honda also aims to tackle Porsche head-on with its pavement-ripping Acura NS-X. With a $70,000 price tag, the car still comfortably undercuts its Porsche equivalent.

As the big two Japanese manufacturers, Nissan and Toyota, get into their stride and push up volumes, the other smaller European luxury-car makers are likely to be severely squeezed. For a long time, the European luxury-car makers have enjoyed fat margins in the relatively easy United States market, but already Saab and Jaguar have slumped into losses, forcing them into the hands of GM and Ford respectively. Even Daimler–Benz and BMW have felt the effect on their inflated North American margins, forcing Mercedes to offer sales incentives of up to $5,000 per car, while BMW's first quarter 1990 sales were down by nearly 17 per cent, prompting its chairman, Eberhard Kuenheim, to dark mutterings about the Japanese 'dumping' luxury cars in America.

The car industry is just the latest to suffer from segment retreat. When the Japanese expanded the market for computer-controlled lathes in the early 1980s by producing standardized products in volume, European and American producers responded by focusing their efforts on more complex products which they sold to large firms. As a result, the Japanese share of world production of these lathes soared from ten per cent in 1975 to nearly 54 per cent in 1984, and it was the United States that largely lost out. While the Japanese saw a market capable of rapid growth, Western suppliers hardly recognized its existence until the Japanese had swept past them.

Likewise, in the 1970s, Xerox and other Western photocopier manufacturers largely abandoned the low end of the office copier market to Japanese manufacturers. By the time Xerox realized that it had relinquished an important and profitable market segment and was also being chased upmarket, it was almost too late.

The fact is, producing mass-market products does not necessarily preclude making reasonable profits as high volumes tend to offset lower margins. Many volume products are, moreover, also sophisticated, high added-value, quality items with a low labour content – information technology is an excellent example of an industry where there is still money to be made in the volume end of the market.

Lest anyone should think that only Western companies fall victim to this fallacy, however, it is worth remembering the fate of Hitachi Construction Equipment, which offered larger and larger excavators to avoid competition with arch rival Komatsu. Komatsu, however, continued to supply the lower end of the market while increasing the size of its largest excavators, with the result that it has gained market share in all segments of the business. Hitachi, by contrast, has done relatively poorly and has been forced into international alliances in order to survive.

Can we beat the Japanese?

The 'Chocolate Staircase' was the name given by British troops to a steep section of the Tiddim road, south of the village of Imphal on the Burmese border with India, where it climbs a sheer 3,000 feet in seven miles. Thirty-eight hairpin bends and an average gradient of 1:12 make the earth road arduous enough at the best of times. But, in late 1944, marching men, animals and vehicles combined with crashing landslides to churn the earth's surface into ankle-deep mud.

No soldier who marched up the Chocolate Staircase ever forgot it. But however laborious it was to the British troops was as nothing compared to the horrors experienced by the soldiers of the retreating elite Japanese 15th and 31st Divisions, as they were mercilessly chased back into central Burma after losing a gruelling eight-month-long battle to break through the vital pass at Kohima from north-west Burma, through the Naga hills to the broad Assam plain, the Ganges Delta and India beyond.

In November 1944, as the Japanese slipped and slid up the Chocolate Staircase, bombed by RAF Hurricanes and USAAF Mitchell bombers, men of the British 14th Army continually outflanked the fleeing Imperial troops, subjecting their withdrawal to continuous ambushes and roadblocks. In all, five Japanese divisions were largely destroyed and 50,000 of the Emperor's best troops slain.

It had not always been so. When the Japanese first invaded Burma at the end of 1941, the sparse British forces of Burma Corps had been ill-prepared. Their equipment, for example, included an anti-tank battery consisting of Austrian 77mm guns which had been captured by the Italians in 1918, before being taken in turn from them by the British in the Western Desert in 1940. The defending British, Indian, Ghurka and Burmese troops were also unprepared for jungle warfare and only able to move with the aid of copious mechanical transport. They were unsettled by the relentless Japanese tactics of 'hooking' – encircling manoeuvres which prevented British retreat. By the end of May 1942, therefore, the gaunt and ragged troops were trudging, defeated, back to India with only a bare handful of guns and trucks.

At that time, following their stunning Pacific victories, many looked upon the Japanese as invincible supermen. General William Slim, who had been brought in from the Near East to bolster the crumbling British forces, thought differently. Slim decided that the only way to beat the Japanese was by copying some of their tactics. So he set about reforming and retraining his shattered troops, making them practise Japanese-style jungle warfare techniques and re-establishing their confidence by sending aggressive and successful patrols into Japanese-held territory.

But training alone would not be sufficient to defeat the Japanese. Slim recognized that his men also had to be aware and motivated. He therefore radically overhauled his communications, introducing constant briefings on objectives and priorities for all units – right down to the pay and catering corps – as well as a new theatre newspaper. Teamwork was encouraged and information centres established in every outfit.

Slowly, stories of Japanese super-efficiency faded, morale returned and Slim's first real counter-attack in November 1943 succeeded in pushing the Japanese out of the Arakan peninsula in Western Burma. Against the main Japanese northern offensive in March 1944, which aimed at an invasion of the Indian sub-continent, British, Indian, African and Ghurka troops managed to hold out at Kohima and the British base at Imphal during months of fierce fighting, before steadily pushing the Japanese back and finally routing their erstwhile tormentors.[7]

Thus, only two years after their shattering victories, the Japanese jungle supermen of 1942 were utterly destroyed. They were beaten because Slim was intelligent enough to realize that in order to conquer his enemies, he would have both to instil a new morale and faith in his men and emulate some of Japan's own methods and techniques.

Slim's campaign is an eloquent reminder of the fact that the Japanese are not infallible. Nor do they enjoy some special prescience in business matters. It is worth recalling, for example, that Japanese investors have in recent years sustained huge losses from dollar bonds purchased just before the dollar collapsed against the yen – the life insurance industry alone wrote off $30 billion according to the Ministry of Finance. Moreover, the Japanese banks which so increased their property loans during the second half of the 1980s were beginning to look extremely vulnerable as property prices began to ease early in 1990. To talk in terms of the Japanese being unbeatable or fundamentally different, or of the West needing to embrace 'Japanese-style' government–industry relationships, or of erecting yet more barriers to trade is to miss the point. The Japanese are as human as the rest of us and the sooner the West accepts this and begins to learn the lessons of Japan's economic success, the sooner the West will be in a position to challenge her industrial dominance.

29

新
大
国

RE-JOINING THE RACE

'It has become increasingly clear to us, and to many businessmen dealing with Japan, that our trade problems result less and less from Japanese import bariers, and more and more from domestic American structural problems of competitiveness and quality. There are clearly lessons to be learned from Japan.'

Report on trade with Japan by the sub-committee on trade of the Committee on Ways and Means, United States House of Representatives, 1980.

WHEN, IN THE middle of the last century, a series of small American, British, French and Russian naval squadrons bombarded Japan into opening her closed market to international trade, the brutal Western challenge galvanized the ancient and fossilized Japanese society into a frenzy of self-reform. Life was made more difficult for the Japanese because of a series of 'unequal treaties' which prevented Japan from raising significant tariff barriers against imports from more economically advanced nations. So Western technology and civilization had to be studied in an attempt to gain a place among the wealthy and powerful nations of the world. Notwith-standing one or two disasters *en route*, the Japanese managed to achieve this goal with a vengeance.

Under the slogan *'fukoku kyohei'*, (*'rich country, strong military'*), the old privileges were swept away and a series of major political, social, industrial and educational reforms were implemented. The result in Japan was a navy, railway and telegraph system based on British models; a French style army and criminal code; a civil code and constitution based on Germany's; and universities along American lines. Each employed, where possible, Western experts to give instruction and guidance – *sake* producers even invited Frenchmen to Japan to show them how to make wine.

Perhaps the most crucial area of reform and development took place in education. In 1872, a national education system was established with compulsory primary schooling for all, regardless of class or sex. The schools largely used unemployed *samurai* as teachers, supplemented by large numbers of foreigners – indeed, in the early 1870s, nearly 30 per cent of the education budget was spent on the salaries of imported teachers or on aid for students sent abroad for study.

On a more mundane level, Western dress became commonplace, formal ballroom dances were held in Tokyo and people emulated Western hair-styles and tried Western food. There were even suggestions that the Japanese should improve their stock by taking Western wives, a proposal which proved unworkable for lack of suitable candidates.

This was a brave era of reform which required a largely feudal, agrarian nation to make a leap of two centuries into the future. Naturally, this did not occur without difficulties – even some touching akwardness. Many Japanese could not come to terms with entering a train without taking off their shoes, so they would leave them on the platform and get out at the far end in their socks or bare feet. Other stories include the court ladies who sent to Paris for evening dresses, but who appeared at a grand dinner wearing their corsets on the outside; while the daughters of *samurai* turned up for work at the new silk-reeling mills with their servants and full wardrobes.

It was the very fact that Japan responded with such speed and eagerness in adopting Western methods in the mid- and late Nineteenth Century that allowed her to control the process of change in a way which reinvigorated the nation. In the same way, after the shock of defeat in 1945, the Japanese again looked to the West. With help from the occupation administration, they took on board many elements of Western practice which, combined with a certain pragmatism in implementation, created the most economically successful nation in the world.

What were their policies? Above all, Japan has equipped herself with a first-rate, if extremely tough, vocationally oriented educational system which reinforces the Japanese sense of business and enterprise. Furthermore, the skills, attitudes and energies of the Japanese have not been sapped or crowded out by governments which have preached the supremacy of the state or insisted on appropriating the lion's share of the nation's resources. On the contrary, Japanese governments have been pragmatic enough to permit the productive side of their economy to flourish by maintaining low taxation – particularly on savings – as well as relatively low government spending.*

Furthermore, Japan's governments have encouraged internal competition to a far greater extent than in most Western countries and made economic growth their overriding priority. So Japan's achievements are less the result of an 'economic miracle' than the natural, if outstanding, result of a

---

* Of course, low state-spending is not a precondition of economic success, as the West Germans have shown, but it helps. Moreover, the similarities between West Germany and Japan are significant. These include, above all, a first-rate educational system geared to the nation's practical requirements, a concentration of internal development rather than overseas adventures and generally sound monetary policies.

combination of a long period of preparation, which goes back to before the Second World War, allied to practical government policies designed primarily to induce sustainable economic growth.

Western governments themselves should also recognize the key role that they have played in Japan's success, for there can be little question that Japanese exporters have had their job eased by mismanagement, high state-spending and overconsumption in the United States and parts of Western Europe. After the Second World War, with the problems of the 1930s uppermost in their minds, most Western politicians committed themselves to increasing employment and improving social welfare, the cost of which their citizens had difficulty in meeting. Although taxation rose steadily in relation to GDP in most developed economies, it was still insufficient to finance soaring expenditure. The favoured method of reconciling such claims on resources was inflationary financing by printing or borrowing money.

At the same time, many Western governments removed market constraints on wage levels, with the result that from the late 1960s wages in most developed countries began rising faster than labour productivity, which contributed to unemployment. In the face of growing joblessness, a variety of weapons, including protection against overseas competition and subsidies to 'strategic' industries were deployed.

The result was a vicious circle of inflationary political commitments and government intervention, which led to further economic distortions and the need for yet more inflationary commitments. The oil price rises of the 1970s brought the problem to a head, bringing about the realization that a massive correction was long overdue if the inflationary situation were not to get out of hand. The ensuing adjustment was only partially effective however, and by the beginning of the 1980s, the accumulated public sector deficits of all the member countries of the OECD had reached a total of around $1.25 trillion.

Japan, of course, was not wholly insulated from these problems. But since her economy was geared to low home consumption, while high levels of investment growth were reinforced with industrial efficiency, Japanese industry was in the best position to exploit the inflated consumption of the United States and Western Europe. The answer to the West's competitiveness problem lies, therefore, to a large extent in responsible economic management rather than in legislation against the consequences of its own economic folly.

A Victorian perspective

Far from being the representation of successfully executed policies of 'industrial strategy' and trade protection, Japan's economic rise is, on the contrary, in many ways the modern fulfillment of Cobden's dream. Indeed, the Nineteenth-Century politician and free trade campaigner's analysis of the seeds of Britain's decline and America's rise in the last century offers some interesting parallels with Japan's more recent economic advance over the United States.

Writing in the middle of the last century, Cobden bemoaned the growth of unemployment in Britain which he blamed on the scarcity of capital and the lack of investment owing to high interest rates. These resulted from the government's own demand for funds to indulge in what Cobden called 'the passion for meddling with the affairs of foreigners'. For, at that time, Britain was obsessed with the maintainence of the balance of power in continental Europe, the threat of Russian expansionism in the East and the need to maintain colonies to safeguard trade. This 'Great Game' was, in effect, a Nineteenth Century version of an 'industrial strategy' – the idea being to gain advantage by dominating trade routes, tying up markets and securing natural resources in your own national interest.

'In the insolence of our might,' Cobden complained, 'and without waiting for the assaults of envious enemies, we have sallied forth in search of conquest or rapine, and carried bloodshed into every quarter of the globe.' And in parallel to modern interventionist policies, the gold poured into government spending to secure imperial objectives was itself partly responsible for the impoverishment of industry. As a result, Cobden concluded that Britain was 'suffering a slow but severe punishment inflicted at her own hands – she is crushed beneath a debt so enormous that nothing but her own mighty strength could have raised the burden that is oppressing her'. Adam Smith had made the same point in the previous century: 'It is surely time', he said, 'that Great Britain should free herself from the expense of defending [the Empire]'.

Protectionism marched hand in hand with imperialism. And then, as now, the protectionists claimed they were acting in the national interest. Cobden knew all about protectionism, for in the 1830s and 1840s he had been in the forefront of the fight against the Corn Laws – several pieces of legislation which dated from medieval times and protected home-grown food from cheap foreign imports. Defenders of the Corn Laws asserted altruistically that they were necessary to maintain farmers' incomes. Cobden contended that in reality they merely increased the rents of a few wealthy landlords so that farmers hardly benefited at all, while everyone suffered from high food prices. Cobden won his battle against the Corn Laws after a long, hard fight, but later found protectionist sentiment growing again in response to Britain's decline as an industrial power and the growing competitive threat from newly industrializing rivals such as Germany and the United States.

Then, as now, the policies of trade protection and colonialism were to a large extent the result of lobbying by powerful interest groups which stood to benefit greatly. But Cobden was convinced that empires were an indulgence which diverted attention from internal development and that peaceful commerce and trade were the best way for countries to obtain what they needed from one another. If each country specialized in producing what it could best make, Cobden argued, and if nations then exchanged goods in a free trading system, the world would engage in peaceful and industrious endeavours and avoid futile wars.

Cobden was a great admirer of America, which at that time kept largely clear of foreign adventures, concentrating instead on her own internal development and maintaining an excellent educational system. This was why he predicted the rise of the United States, writing that 'it is to the industry, the economy, and peaceful policy of America, and not to the growth of Russia, that our statesmen and politicians ... ought to direct their anxious study; for it is by these, and not by the efforts of barbarian force, that the power and greatness of England are in danger of being superceded'. Cobden urged Britain to emulate 'the cheap diplomacy of the Americans' and believed that Britain had a great deal to learn from the United States, arguing that 'our only chance of national prosperity lies in the timely remodelling of our system, so as to put it as nearly as possible upon an equality with the improved management of the Americans'.[1]

Ironically, more than a century later, it was the United States that arguably became too embroiled in overseas matters, spending a large portion of her national wealth on armaments and distracted from internal development by rivalry with the Soviet Union. As de Gaulle put it:

> The United States, delighting in her resources, feeling that she no longer had within herself sufficient scope for her energies, wishing to help those who were in misery or bondage the world over, yielded in her turn to that taste for intervention in which the instinct for domination cloaked itself.[2]

Of course, by the middle of the Twentieth Century, the world had developed into a rather more complex place than in Cobden's day. For one thing, nuclear weapons by then largely precluded a policy of glorious isolation. Furthermore, it is unlikely that Europe as a whole would now be progressing towards a period of relative peace, freedom and democracy had it not been for the efforts of the United States. There may well, moreover, be some justice in the claim that certain countries simply did not pull their weight and gained a free ride at America's expense. On the other hand, there is a strong line of argument that the United States has on occasions become so obsessed with her rivalry with the Soviets that she has too easily become entangled in disputes, spending more than was really necessary on space and defence – to the benefit of certain specific industries, but to the detriment of the overall health of her economy. At least the apparent end of Soviet–American superpower rivalry should allow the United States, together with other nations which have spent heavily on defence to set down part of the disproportionate burden which they have borne since the War and concentrate instead on their own domestic affairs.

The lesson for the West as a whole is that it should heed the experience of Britain in the last century and prevent special interests from hijacking policy in the name of the general economic interest. Moreover, Japan's achievements exemplify the Cobdenite theory of the benefits of concentrating on internal development rather than the often illusory gains of playing a grandiose role on the world stage, as well as the advantages of trade and specialization in what a country makes best. Japan has achieved a prosperity and influence beyond anything she could have achieved by military means, and her success in making quality, high-technology products widely available is not the result of a violation of the liberal principles enunciated by Cobden and to an extent espoused by the post-War era, but perhaps their consummation.

Some lessons learned

Just as Japan once looked to the then superior Western economies for guidance, so now in turn the West could benefit from a measured and even-handed study of where it has gone wrong and what the Japanese have done right – not with a view to slavish imitation, but with a balanced respect and open-minded willingness to adopt, where possible, what is best of the Japanese system.

There does now at least seem to be a greater willingness, at least in some quarters, to look at what the Japanese have got to offer. In 1987, for example, 800 Harvard undergraduates signed up to take Japanese history, making it the year's second most popular course. Harvard has also recently joined Stanford and seven other American universities in opening a centre for Japanese studies at Kyoto University. But so far, it is certain sections of the West's industry that are most advanced in the business of learning from the Japanese. Indeed, some might consider it strange that businesspeople and industrialists, who are often portrayed as being unprogressive and narrow-minded, should in this respect be more far-sighted than the supposedly visionary statesmen who aspire to lead them.

It is a myth to believe that Japanese business methods cannot be adapted to Western conditions. After all, Japan itself has succeeded by adapting and improving on the best Western practices. But according to Toyohiro Kono, the Professor of Business Administration at Tokyo's Gakushuin University, there are some elements of Japanese business practice which are more transportable than others. He points out, for example, that successful Japanese companies emphasize their business philosophy by stating their goals, thereby increasing employees' sense of identification. Many successful British and American companies have also long done the same – Marks & Spencer, IBM and Hewlett-Packard are good examples. But more are beginning to see these clear statements as an important element in motivating their workforces. On the other hand, attempts to take this process further by making employees sing company songs for example, will probably be counter-productive in the West.[3]

Perhaps the company which has most successfully transplanted Japanese methods has itself been Japanese: Sony. Soon after the consumer electronics group opened its Californian plant in 1972, the world was hit by an oil crisis and the American president of Sony America wanted to lay off some of the 250 employees. But Sony's president, Akio Morita, refused, making further funds available from Japan to support the United States company. As there were not enough orders to keep the workforce occupied over this period, educational and training programmes were developed which helped to increase employees' sense of involvement with the company. The Sony plant now employs 1,500 people, has never been unionized and has had excellent management–workforce relations. 'The company that shows that it truly wishes to protect the employees' interests even when business is at its worst,' says Morita, 'will show results. The best thing a company can do is to treat its employees as dignified human beings.'[4]

Green field factories with brand new workforces are, of course, one thing, but Japanese companies have also met with considerable success when taking over troubled companies in declining sectors. When Sumitomo Rubber Industries bought Dunlop's European tyre operations in 1985, its acquisition included the Birmingham Fort Dunlop factory, one of British manufacturing's truly historic sites set in a part of England's Midlands then most hit by decades of decay in the vehicle industry. Most of the factory's buildings date back to 1916, on top of which the old workforce was inherited virtually en-bloc and the company had to deal with a bevy of traditional craft unions.

Yet by the end of the decade, production at the site was up by a half using only two-thirds of the workforce, while an annual £20-million loss had been transformed into a respectable profit. This was not achieved by heavy-handed management directives from Sumitomo's HQ in Kobe, for Japanese management is now limited to only three board members and a small technical and production team. Apart from sweeping away a divisive hierarchy of seven canteens, the turnaround was accomplished by investment of about £10 million a year in the site as well as the adoption of radically new methods of communication, including monthly team briefings, question and answer sessions (when shop-floor workers can question boardroom management), common uniforms for all employees and an extensive quality training programme involving 1,000 staff a year, including management, sales and office staff.

One reason why elements of Japanese personnel management systems have been transferable overseas to a greater extent than was once thought possible is the fact that they themselves took shape after the Second World War, largely as a result of rational thinking rather than arising from some especially Japanese trait. Moreover, much in Japanese management actually originated in the West, although there it remained largely undeveloped or ignored. This is why policies such as a strong identification with the company do seem to work in Europe and the United States, although it is true that other features of Japan's industry, such as lifetime employment, long overtime working and the voluntary giving up of holidays do not seem to have struck much of a chord.

There is, however, increasing evidence in Western industry that many Japanese techniques have begun to percolate through. Westinghouse Electric Corporation already runs some 2,000 Quality Control Circles in 200 locations and is now moving to other forms of quality oriented worker participation. Other large Western companies which have developed the quality circle concept include Martin Marietta Aerospace, British computer maker, ICL, Hewlett Packard, Black and Decker and Philips' UK components subsidiary, Mullard.[5] Single dining facilities have also spread with amazing rapidity throughout British industry. According to a 1986 survey conducted by the Industrial Society, and covering 480 catering operations, around 60 per cent were found to operate single status canteens – up from 40 per cent in 1980.

However, being prepared to learn from Japan must also include a greater willingness to license their technology. Those politicians and pundits who constantly urge Western industry and governments to spend more on internal R&D development should bear in mind the fact that, until recently, Japanese industry spent relatively little on research. It is often better for companies which are not in a leading position to buy in technology and develop it. Of course, as Japanese industry has taken the lead in many fields, it is now both carrying out more R&D itself and selling more developments overseas. But those Western companies who no longer represent the leading edge of their industries would almost certainly find the purchase of technology a more fruitful policy than expensive in-house research.

There are those who are genuinely concerned about the prospect of the West relying on Japanese technology and consider that R&D spending, whether funded by companies or governments, must be stepped up. But it is worth remembering that the best technology will do little good to a company that has lost the art of turning it into saleable products which it can manufacture and market properly. R&D alone cannot make a successful economy and it would be fruitless for the West to push up research spending in an artificial manner, when Western companies are too often incapable of exploiting new developments. It should also not be too surprising that a nation like Japan, which is both more productive in manufacturing industry and has a better educated population – particularly in the sciences – should now be making the running in many technologies. Until the West addresses its weaknesses in these areas, all of the R&D in the world will be of little help.

'We've copied a lot of their methods . . .'

Lucas, a major British vehicle and aerospace components group, earned the nickname the 'Prince of Darkness' in the 1970s because of the frequency with which its batteries packed up at the first hint of rain. The group suffered terribly in the early 1980s from the contraction in the British car industry, a high-cost structure and a low-quality image. So desperate was Lucas' situation by 1984, that in the subsequent five years it sold off 14 of its units, closed 25 sites and shed 35,000 workers. Since then, Lucas' group sales have grown from £1.5 billion to nearly £2 billion and profits have risen more than threefold.

Lucas' revival is in part based on the results of a study of Japanese practices made by a large number of management and shopfloor teams. These new practices include a single grade of production systems engineer and a greatly increased emphasis on in-company training. Lucas' current spending on training of around £50 million a year puts many other large British manufacturers in the shade. On the shop floor, work flows have been redesigned and a particular emphasis placed on the quick changeover of machines and flexibility. But Dr James Parnaby, Lucas' director of manufacturing technology, points out that employing Japanese methods does not necessarily mean investing in huge capital outlays. Many of his own manufacturing plants are still housed in antiquated buildings, in the same way as many successful Japanese companies visited by Lucas teams still use old factories.

Lucas has even gone so far as to use strange-sounding Japanese terms in its Manufacturing Systems Engineering handbook. These include '*Heijunka*' – scheduling work in an even way; and '*Poka Yoke*' – the use of foolproof production devices in the drive for zero defects. But while Dr Parnaby says that he has seen nothing in Japan which cannot be translated into a UK setting, he cautions against Western manufacturers who only superficially adopt Japanese business practices, like quality circles, group meetings and morning exercises, without looking more deeply into their own production methods.

While bluntly acknowledging 'We've copied a lot of their methods', another Lucas manager, Bob Dale, the Managing Director of the company's automotive products, also admits that the task was made easier by the joint ventures which the Lucas Automotive division is already involved in with Japanese companies. These include Lucas Yuasa Batteries and Lucas Sumitomo Brake Industries – the latter set up initially to supply a joint Mazda and Ford vehicle plant at Flat Rock, Michigan. Dale even claims that Lucas' South Wales plant, which supplies Honda, among others, with wiring harnesses, almost makes you believe you are in Japan: 'It's a replica of a Sumitomo factory.'[6] The company got its reward in the summer of 1989 when it won a contract to supply quality-conscious BMW with 400,000 fuel injection systems. Up until then, the supply of such sophisticated equipment had been the near monopoly of West German producer, Robert Bosch.

Perhaps the most astonishing transformation through the use of Japanese techniques has been wrought at the old General Motors plant in Fremont, California. In the past, the Fremont factory was a byword for all the traditional motor industry ills – strikes, 20 per cent absenteeism, poor quality and low productivity – with the result that in 1981 GM closed the plant and laid off the employees. Two years later, the world's largest automaker joined forces with Toyota, Japan's biggest car manufacturer, to reopen the plant for the production of Toyota's Corolla model, which is sold by GM in the United States as the Prizm. Now, the factory boasts some of the highest quality in GM, and Fremont has been metamorphosized into a success story.

The main change has not been the workforce – about 90 per cent of the new workers were rehired from the old plant. Nor was it the union – a new deal was signed with the United Auto Workers – and there has not been much in the way of new production equipment either. What has changed is the approach of the new management group and its emphasis on teamwork.

Not everyone has taken these lessons on board, however. Ford has made some productivity improvements under pressure from growing Japanese transplant car production in Britain. But the American car giant and its workforce are to a large extent protected from the full intensity of Japanese competition by the import quotas maintained in several European countries – particularly in its largest European market, Britain. So when the company tried to introduce quality circles and other Japanese-style work practices at its traditionally militant UK plant at Dagenham, and even toyed with guaranteed employment for life, the workforce proved less willing to accept the reform package. A damaging strike resulted, during which Ford workers were seen holding placards saying: 'We are Brits, not Nips'.

Meeting the challenge – making the change

Can the West ever match or even beat the Japanese? It can. But to meet the Japanese challenge, changes have to go deeper and be more widespread than those already adopted by the more far-sighted American and European companies. This does not mean acting on simplistic interpretations of Japanese success such a state-inspired industrial strategies – which is not to say that governments cannot do anything. On the contrary, what they can do is to produce a seedbed in which industry can flourish. This must firstly involve governments making efforts to lower their spending and reduce excess consumption. Unfortunately, since the Plaza Accord little progress has been made in the United States to solve fundamental problems of budgetary imbalances. For too often it seems that American leaders lack the political will to make hard decisions and to explain to their voters why they are necessary.

And despite a widespread recognition that savings are far too low in the United States and many other Western countries, there has been little success in improving savings ratios to reduce consumption and provide a more ready pool of finance for industry. According to an OECD report,[7] most Western countries persist in loading heavy disincentives on savers by taxing income from investment twice – first as earnings, then as interest income. In Britain in the 1970s, the Labour government even levied extra taxes on interest, calling it 'unearned income'.

One of the best ways to boost the savings rate is to reduce or abolish taxes on savings – at least up to certain levels, as the Japanese have done. Western countries have unfortunately been slow to embrace such policies while measures which were originally designed to lower consumption and boost savings have been distorted beyond recognition during the legislative process. The 1986 United States tax reforms, for example, were intended to cut consumption by phasing out interest relief on consumer credit, but at the same time they penalized savers by abolishing the investment tax credit. They also boosted spending by making it easier for tax payers to deduct interest on consumer debt secured by mortgages.

Britain's economy, too, remains skewed towards consumption and expenditure on housing rather than savings and investment. At least Britain and the United States belatedly made a small start by adopting tax-exempt savings accounts early in 1990. Apart from anything else, lowering consumption, reducing government spending and raising savings levels in the West would help to contain inflation in a way which would allow Western industry to plan more for the long term, reducing the 'short-termism' which many commentators have complained of. So rather than pursuing interventionist policies, a far more useful role for governments would be to help set a favourable scene for industry ensuring financial stability and low taxation, together with flexibility and competition in the economy.

Those that, none the less, still insist on interventionist formulae should minimize the damage they do by concentrating their subsidies on more sophisticated industries. That does not necessarily mean *the* most advanced areas of manufacturing, but rather those that are in line with what their economy can sustain. For although the foolishness of supporting 'lame duck' and declining industries has for some time been recognized in the West, political imperatives have too often been allowed to dictate that government support, in the form of subsidies or trade protection, nonetheless go to old industries such as textiles and shipbuilding.

For example, a report by GATT in late 1989 revealed that the United States and Canada had been more strictly applying Multi-Fibre Arrangement curbs on textile imports from developing nations than other importing countries, causing a drop in textile imports in 1988. If the United States ever wants to regain its industrial power, it is unlikely to do so by relying on labour-intensive, low added-value products like clothing and textiles.

Britain's government, at least, has gone some way towards turning the country's economy away from less sophisticated industries and made the brave decision in 1989 not to go along with plans to revive the ailing shipbuilding industry of England's north-east, instead making use of EC money to rebuild the area's economy by introducing new industries. Needless to say this was not done without encountering bitter opposition and criticism.

Further, if Western governments do feel obliged to try to play god with the markets and meddle with their industries, they should gear their efforts towards encouraging, rather than reducing, internal competition in their economies. In the past, too many government industrial strategies, particularly in Europe, have involved the creation of single 'national champion' flagship companies. These have often ended up with cosy monopolies at home and performed disastrously in overseas markets.

Other lessons to be learned from the Japanese could include the promotion of better attitudes to business. In the past, some Western governments have championed the view that profits were somehow anti-social. Nor does it greatly help industry when the very Western politicians who are ever ready to complain about the failure of their industry's performance simultaneously expend a great deal of their energies sneering at successful businesses because they cannot emotionally come to terms with enterprise and wealth which they equate with greed. Europeans and, to an extent, even Americans, must reform their attitudes to wealth creation and throw off dated and myopic attitudes towards business even more than they have done in the 1980s if they are ever to regain an equal footing with Japan.

新 大 国

It is commonplace for Western proponents of 'industrial strategies' to bemoan the relatively poor performance of manufacturing industry in parts of the West, particularly Britain and the United States (although, in fact, during the 1980s, manufacturing output expanded in Britain and the United States faster than in most developed countries), a concern echoed by some Japanese commentators like Morita, who asks, in his controversial book, *The Japan that can say 'No'*: 'What happens if manufacturing ceases to exist – even now America is not producing for itself the things that it uses?'

Some people argue that the relative decline of the manufacturing sector in comparison to the service industries is part of a natural progression to a

post-industrial society. Clearly, as economies develop, the relative importance of service industries is likely to grow, and some of the world's most
successful economies run large deficits on their trade in manufactured goods
– Switzerland, for example. On the other hand, many service industries are
partly related to manufacturing performance, so those who think that any
large economy can reach some kind of post-industrial, service industry-
centred paradise are likely to be disappointed.

But the key to the problem lies neither in 'industrial policies' nor in trade
barriers, but in creating conditions in which appropriate economic activity
can take place. Any government which squeezes industrial capital investment by over-taxing savings and taking too large a share of the nation's
resources, or overstimulates domestic consumption, or legislates in a way
which positively encourages labour militancy, or promotes anti-business
attitudes, is bound to end up with a manufacturing sector which is shrinking
relative to its competitors.

Moreover, any country which neglects the fundamental truth that the
prime object of education should be to equip its people with the ability to
earn a living is unlikely to enjoy a successful and competitive industry. For
above all, a thorough examination of Japan's educational system would
greatly profit the West. It would, of course, be foolish to expect any
Western country to adopt the Japanese system wholesale, nor would it be
desirable to do so. But there are elements in Japan's relatively low-cost,
high-quality school system which could be extremely beneficial. These
include the emphasis on pre-school education, the element of parental
choice, the stress placed on learning the basics of language, mathematics and
science, the number of pupils staying on beyond the age of 16 and on into
higher education, the use of regular testing as a means of assessing
performance and the inherent vocational bias of the system.

At least in this respect there is a growing recognition in the West of what
has to be done. In America, a debate has already begun on the future of the
United States educational system. Late in 1989, President Bush summoned
the State Governors to a meeting specifically to discuss the subject. The
progress of that debate, together with the will of the American Government
to push through the necessary reforms – no doubt in the face of persistent
opposition from many corners, as must be expected in a pluralistic,
democratic society – will be one of the factors determining whether or not
the West's largest economy is capable of meeting the Japanese challenge.

In Britain in 1989, the government began the huge task of overhauling an
educational system which has been recognized for some time as having
failed in a large number of respects. Included in the reforms was the
introduction of a core curriculum to guarantee the teaching of basic subjects,
regular testing and an increase in the teaching of languages, mathematics
and science.

The benefits of these reforms will not be seen for some years, and in the
meantime the process of change is being hampered by some teachers,
pressure groups and local government-run educational authorities who
bitterly oppose the changes. This should not come as any great surprise.
Radical changes almost invariably attract bitter opposition which is only
later overshadowed by their ultimate success. Already, for example, many

of the changes wrought in Britain during the 1980s have been accepted by opponents who bitterly criticized them at the time. The great periods of Japanese reform were themselves subject to intense opposition, even though in retrospect, as with most great periods of reform, they seem to have been universally accepted and carried through with an almost inevitable air.

After the Meiji Restoration, for example, resistance to the sweeping reforms came from several quarters, including nationalist die-hards, loyalists of the ex-Shogun and Shinto fanatics. Many of the old interest groups which had lost their privileges were simply unable to come to terms with the changes which they viewed with a mixture of confusion and hostility.

After the Second World War, too, there was considerable opposition within Japan to the changes wrought both by the American-led post-War occupation administration and subsequent Japanese governments. These included fierce and sometimes violent campaigns by the then far left-dominated teacher's union against the new education system, which was developed from a combination of the Japanese pre-War model and the best American practice of that time.

The West, of course, is not in the same debilitated state as Japan was in relation to the West in the mid-Nineteenth Century or to the United States after the War, so the reforming process need not be so fundamental. Nor could it be, bearing in mind the problems of making radical changes in a democratic society. In the last century, Japan's leaders had the benefit of restructuring a still disciplined and largely obedient feudal society while, after the Second World War, the reformers were helped by the desperate state of the Japanese nation. Yet their measures still provoked extreme resistance. So, too, attempts to reform Western economies have and will provoke bitter opposition, not least from companies, trade unions and pressure groups which see their power and privileges being eroded. But that is the hard task placed before those politicians courageous enough to admit that there are no simple or easy excuses or solutions if the Japanese challenge is to be met.

NOTES AND REFERENCES

INTRODUCTION

1. Henry Norman (1898) *The Real Japan*, London: T Fisher Unwin.
2. Akio Morita (1987) *Made in Japan*, London: Collins.
3. Reproduced in the *Daily Telegraph*, 30 October 1989.
4. *Daily Mail*, 6 April 1987.
5. Major General S Woodburn Kirby *et al* (1958) *History of the Second World War: The War Against Japan*, London: HMSO.
6. Alec Nove (1986) *The Soviet Economic System*, Boston: Allen and Unwin; and Edward Carr (1952) *The Bolshevik Revolution 1917–1923*, London: Macmillan.
7. Cited by Bruce Bartlett, 'Industrial policy: Crisis for Liberal Economists', *Fortune*, 14 November 1983.

PROLOGUE

1. From Frank Chinnock (1969) *Nagasaki: The Forgotten Bomb*, London: George Allen and Unwin Ltd.
2. Winston Churchill (1955) *The Second World War*, Chartwell Educational Book Co.
3. This story is told in Frank Chinnock (1969) *op. cit.*
4. Isoshi Ashahi (1934) *The Secret of Japan's Trade Expansion*, Tokyo.

CHAPTER 1

1. Yokata, 'Suicide Submarine', quoted in Ivan Morris (1980) *The Nobility of Failure*, London: Penguin.
2. Sterling Seagrave (1989) *The Marcos Dynasty*, London: Macmillan.
3. Quoted in Hakan Hedberg (1972) *Japan's Revenge*, London: Pitman.

CHAPTER 2

1. *The Political Writings of Richard Cobden* (1886), London: Cassell.
2. Bill Emmott (1989) *The Sun Also Sets*, London: Simon and Schuster.

3. Reported in the *Independent*, 7 August 1989.
4. M Ozawa, 'Japanese Consumer Mysteries', *Economic Eye*, June 1986.
5. Edwin O Reischauer (1988) *The Japanese Today*, Cambridge, Mass: Harvard University Press.
6. *Financial Times*, 30 June 1989.
7. Akio Morita (1987) *Made in Japan*, London: Collins.
8. Quoted in Robert Christopher (1987) *Second to None – American Companies in Japan*, Tokyo: Tuttle.

CHAPTER 3

1. Quoted in Institute of Economic Affairs Education Unit (1987) *The Funding and Management of Education*, London.
2. International Association for the Evaluation of Educational Achievement (1989) *Science Achievement in Seventeen Countries*, Oxford: Pergamon Press.
3. JW Stigler and HW Stevenson (1982) *Journal of Educational Psychology*; and HJ Walberg (1985) *Mathematics Productivity in Japan and Illinois*.
4. *Economist*, 25 February 1989.
5. TP Rohlen (1983) *Japan's High Schools*, California: University of California Press.
6. Richard Lynn (1988) *Educational Achievement in Japan: Lessons for the West*, London: Macmillan/Social Affairs Unit. This study shows that West Germany of the major Western nations comes closest to Japan with 230 days of schooling a year.
7. *Ibid*.
8. Sources: Unesco and UN.
9. See Correlli Barnett (1986) *The Audit of War*, London: Macmillan.
10. Source: World Health Organization.
11. *Daily Mail*, 8 April 1987.
12. Karel van Wolferen (1989) *The Enigma of Japanese Power*, London: Macmillan.
13. Robet Guillain (1970) *The Japanese Challenge*, London: Hamish Hamilton.
14. Quoted in Ezra Vogel (1979) *Japan as Number One*, Harvard: Harvard University Press.
15. Quoted in *ibid*.
16. Robert Guillain (1970) *op. cit.*
17. Quoted in *Ibid*.
18. *Relations Between the Community and Japan*, House of Lords Select Committee on the European Communities, 13th Report, June 1989.
19. Peter Wickens (1987) *The Road to Nissan*, London: Macmillan.

CHAPTER 4

1. Akio Morita (1987) *Made in Japan*, London: Collins.

CHAPTER 5

1. This story is told in George Fields (1983) *From Bonsai to Levis*, New York: Futura.
2. *Financial Times*, 9 March 1989.
3. Robert Christopher (1987) *Second to None – American Companies in Japan*, Tokyo: Tuttle.

CHAPTER 6

1. Field-Marshal Sir William Slim (1956) *Defeat into Victory*, London: Cassell.
2. Source: OECD figures for 1988.
3. Source: GATT.
4. Source: MITI, in Ira C Magaziner and Thomas M Hout (1980) *Japanese Industrial Policy*, London: Policy Studies Institute.
5. Eiji Toyoda (1987) *Toyota – Fifty Years in Motion*, Tokyo: Kodansha International.
6. Akio Morita (1987) *Made in Japan*, London: Collins.
7. S Okita, 'Role of the Trade Ombudsman in Liberalizing Japan's Market', *World Economy*, 1984.
8. Quoted in Robert Christopher (1987) *Second to None – American Companies in Japan*, Tokyo: Tuttle.
9. Clyde Prestowitz (1988) *Trading Places – How We Allowed Japan to Take the Lead*, New York: Basic Books.
10. Source: GATT.
11. Commission of the European Communities, Directorate-General I (1989) *EC Report on US Barriers to Trade*.
12. Quoted in Robert Christopher (1987) *op. cit.*
13. *Relations Between the Community and Japan*, House of Lords Select Committee on the European Communities, 13th Report, June 1989.
14. David Greenaway and Brian Hindley (1985) *What Britain Pays for Voluntary Export Restraints*, London: Trade Policy Research Centre.
15. Gary Hufbauer, Diane Berliner and Kimberley Elliott (1986) *Trade Protection in the US: 31 Case Studies*, Washington: Institute for International Economics.
16. Source: Electronic Industries Association of Japan and *Which Video?*
17. Authors' estimate in Gary Hufbauer, Diane Berliner and Kimberley Elliott (1986) *op. cit.* The US Retail Industry Trade Action Coalition estimate of the cost, quoted in the same work, is $23.4 billion.
18. David Greenaway, 'Estimating the welfare effects of voluntary export restraints and tarrifs: an application to non-leather footwear in the UK', *Applied Economics*, 1986.
19. US Bureau of Labour Statistics, quoted in Jonathan Aylen and Henry Ergas (1985) *Costs and Benefits of Protection*, Paris: OECD.
20. OECD (1987) *Structural Adjustment and Economic Performance*, Paris: OECD.
21. National Consumer Council (1990) *International Trade and the Consumer, Working Paper 1: Consumer Electronics and the EC's Anti-Dumping Policy*, London: National Consumer Council.
22. *Essays on Mitford's History of Greece* (1824).

CHAPTER 7

1. Source: Japan Chamber of Commerce and Industry.
2. *Relations Between the Community and Japan*, House of Lords Select Committee on the European Communities, 13th Report, June 1989.
3. Karel van Wolferen (1989) *The Enigma of Japanese Power*, London: Macmillan.
4. These examples come from Robert Christopher (1987) *Second to None – American Companies in Japan*, Tokyo: Tuttle.
5. Most of these examples come from James C Abegglen and George Stalk (1985) *Kaisha, the Japanese Corporation*, New York: Basic Books.
6. Robert Christopher (1987) *op. cit.*
7. *Car*, November 1987.
8. *Fortune*, 21 December 1987.

9. Clyde Prestowitz (1988) *Trading Places – How We Allowed Japan to Take the Lead*, New York: Basic Books.
10. These examples come from the Commission of the European Communities Directorate-General I (1989) *1989 EC Report on US Barriers to Trade*, Brussels.
11. Source: UNCTAD, in Jagdish Bhagwati (1988) *Protectionism*, Cambridge, Mass.: MIT Press.
12. J Nogues, A Olechowski and L A Winters, 'The Extent of Non-Tariff Barriers to Imports of Industrial Countries', *World Bank Staff Working Paper*, 1986, Washington.
13. *Financial Times*, 21 May 1990.
14. Quoted in *Car*, January 1990.
15. Quoted in E F Vogel (1979) *Japan as Number One*, Harvard: Harvard University Press.
16. Ali M El-Agraa (1988) *Japan's Trade Frictions*, London: Macmillan.

CHAPTER 8

1. Source: Agricultural Production Income Statistics – Japanese Ministry of Agriculture, Forestry and Fisheries.
2. Source: Yoshikazu Kano, 'Failings of the Rice Policy', *Economic Eye*, September 1987.
3. Marvin J Wolf (1985) *The Japanese Conspiracy*, London: New English Library.
4. Source: Gary Hufbauer, Diane Berliner and Kimberley Elliott (1986) *Trade Protection in the US: 31 Case Studies*, Washington: Institute for International Economics.
5. Source: *Economic Progress Report*, UK Treasury, February 1988.
6. Quoted in Leonard Weiss (1961) *Economics and American Industry*, Chichester: John Wiley & Sons Inc.

CHAPTER 9

1. Mark Zimmerman (1985) *Dealing with the Japanese*, London: George Allen & Unwin.
2. Marvin J Wolf (1985) *The Japanese Conspiracy*, London: New English Library.
3. E F Vogel (1979) *Japan as Number One*, Harvard: Harvard University Press.
4. Marvin J Wolf (1985) *op. cit.*
5. Karel van Wolferen (1989) *The Enigma of Japanese Power*, London: Macmillan.
6. Ali M El-Agraa (1988) *Japan's Trade Frictions*, London: Macmillan.
7. Eiji Toyoda (1987) *Toyota – 50 Years in Motion*, Tokyo: Kodansha.
8. Richard Boyd, 'Government–Industry Relations in Japan: Access, Communication, and Competitive Collaboration', in S Wilkes and M Wright (eds) (1987) *Comparative Government–Industry Relations: Western Europe, the United States and Japan*, Oxford: Clarendon Press.
9. Robert Christopher (1987) *Second to None – American Companies in Japan*, Tokyo: Tuttle.
10. E F Vogel (1979) *op. cit.*
11. Office of the United States Trade Representative, *1989 National Trade Estimate Report on Foreign Trade Barriers*, Washington.
12. Karel van Wolferen (1989) *op. cit.*
13. *Flight*, 6 July 1967. Quoted in Keith Hayward (1983) *Government and British Civil Aerospace*, Manchester: Manchester University Press.
14. Akio Morita (1987) *Made in Japan*, London: Collins.

15. EC Commission (1989) *A Bonfire of Subsidies? – A Review of State Aids in the European Community*, Brussels: EC Commission.
16. OECD (1989) *Economies in Transition: Structural Adjustment in OECD Countries*, Paris: OECD.
17. *Congressional Quarterly Report*, 6 January 1990.
18. *Financial Times*, 13 September 1989.
19. Commission of the European Communities Directorate-General I (1989) *Report on US Barriers to Trade*, Brussels.
20. Robert Ford and Wim Suyker (1990) *Industrial Subsidies in the OECD Economies*, Paris: OECD. The US figures are also higher than those for the main European countries, which puts into perspective the common assertion that the Anglo–Saxon nations have performed less well than Germany and Japan because they operate a less controlled and regulated economy. In fact, as the quoted figures and examples clearly illustrate, both Britain and the United States have been extremely interventionist and, despite recent liberalization, they still are.
21. Quoted in Commission of the European Communities, Directorate-General I (1989) *op. cit.*
22. Lee Iacocca (1985) *Iacocca: An Autobiography*, London: Sidgwick & Jackson.

CHAPTER 10

1. James Abegglen and George Stalk (1985) *Kaisha, the Japanese Corporation*, New York: Basic Books.
2. *Financial Times*, 29 February 1988.
3. James Abegglen and George Stalk (1985), *op. cit.*
4. Source: Economist Intelligence Unit.
5. Martin Wolf *et al* (1984) *Costs of Protecting Jobs in Textiles and Clothing*, London: Thames Essay from the Trade Policy Research Centre.
6. *Ibid.*
7. Robert Ford and Wim Suyker (1990) *Industrial Subsidies in the OECD Economies*, Paris: OECD.
8. Much of this story is taken from the *Financial Times*, 2 December 1989.
9. IBJ (1989) *EC 1992 and Japanese Corporations*, Tokyo: IBJ.
10. Gary Jacobson and John Hillkirk (1986) *Xerox: American Samurai*, New York: Macmillan.
11. Karel van Wolferen (1989) *The Enigma of Japanese Power*, London: Macmillan.
12. Robert Guillain (1970) *The Japanese Challenge*, London: Hamish Hamilton.
13. Robert Ford and Wim Suyker (1990) *op. cit.*
14. J Servan-Schreiber (1969) *The American Challenge*, London: Penguin.

CHAPTER 11

1. Karel van Wolferen (1989) *The Enigma of Japanese Power*, London: Macmillan.
2. Eiji Toyoda (1985) *Toyota – Fifty Years in Motion*, Tokyo: Kodansha International.
3. Herman Kahn (1970) *The Emerging Japanese Superstate*, Englewood Cliffs: Prentice-Hall.
4. Source: OECD.
5. *Ibid.*
6. OECD (1989) *Economies in Transition: Structural Adjustment in OECD Countries*, Paris: OECD.
7. Marvin J Wolf (1985) *The Japanese Conspiracy*, London: New English Library.

8. Source: OECD.
9. See Correlli Barnett (1986) *The Audit of War*, London: Macmillan, for a superb analysis of the failure of post-War British policy.

CHAPTER 12

1. Akio Morita (1987) *Made in Japan*, London: Collins.
2. This story is told in James C Abegglen and George Stalk (1985) *Kaisha, the Japanese Corporation*, New York: Basic Books.
3. Karel van Wolferen (1989) *The Enigma of Japanese Power*, London: Macmillan.
4. Clyde Prestowitz (1988) *Trading Places – How We Allowed Japan to Take the Lead*, New York: Basic Books.
5. Mark Zimmerman (1985) *Dealing with the Japanese*, London: George Allen & Unwin.
6. Quoted in Gary Jacobson and John Hillkirk (1986) *Xerox – American Samurai*, New York: Macmillan.
7. James C Abegglen and George Stalk (1985) *op. cit.*
8. John G Roberts (1973) *Mitsui*, New York: Weatherhill.
9. See Karel van Wolferen (1989) *op. cit.*
10. Wasserman is one of the few design managers to sit on the board of an American company – Unisys – while Moggridge works for design consultancy, ID Two.
11. Robert Guillain (1970) *The Japanese Challenge*, London: Hamish Hamilton.

CHAPTER 13

1. Toyohiro Kono (1984) *Strategy and Structure of Japanese Enterprises*, London: Macmillan.
2. This theory is strongly advanced in James C Abegglen and George Stalk (1985) *Kaisha, the Japanese Corporation*, New York: Basic Books, from which I have drawn some of my argument, figures and examples in this section.
3. Annual Report of the Japan Fair Trade Commission, Tokyo, 1982. Quoted in *ibid*.
4. *Financial Times*, 1 February 1990.
5. Office of the Chief Economist, Securities and Exchange Commission (April 1985) *Institutional Ownership, Tender Offers, and Long-Term Investment*, Washington.
6. Both the SEC report and the Prudential figures were quoted in the *Financial Times*, 21 May 1990.
7. Bill Emmott, (1989) *The Sun Also Sets*, London: Simon and Schuster.
8. *Financial Times*, 6 June 1990.
9. *Car*, March 1990.

CHAPTER 14

1. Quoted in *Fortune*, 25 September 1989.
2. Gary Jacobson and John Hillkirk (1986) *Xerox – American Samurai*, New York: Macmillan.
3. *Ibid.*
4. Robert Christopher (1987) *Second to None – American Companies in Japan*, Tokyo: Tuttle.
5. *The Economist*, 15 April 1989.
6. *Wall Street Journal*, 14 November 1989.
7. *Time*, 3 November 1987.

CHAPTER 15

1. International Survey Research (1989) *Employee Attitudes Towards their Employers – An International Perspective*, London: International Survey Research.
2. Taiichi Ohno (1978) *Toyota Production System, Aiming at an Off-Scale Management*, Tokyo: Diamond.
3. Peter Wickens (1987) *The Road to Nissan*, London: Macmillan.
4. *Economic Eye*, September 1987.
5. *Ibid.*
6. Figures from OECD *Employment Outlook* – the figures should be treated with some caution as data for different countries is based on varying dates and statistical bases.
7. Ronald P Dore and Mari Sako (1989) *How the Japanese Have Learned to Work*, London: Routledge.
8. *Ibid.*
9. Gavin Laird (1988) *Anglo–Japanese Economic Institute Special Report*.
10. US Embassy Report.
11. Quoted in Robert Christopher (1987) *Second to None – American Companies in Japan*, Tokyo: Tuttle.
12. Akio Morita (1987) *Made in Japan*, London: Collins.

CHAPTER 16

1. House Sub-Committee on Investigations and Oversight and the Sub-Committee on Science, Research and Technology of the Committee on Science and Technology (29–30 June, 1983) *Japanese Technological Advances and Possible US Responses Using Research Joint Ventures*. Quoted in James Abegglen and George Stalk (1985) *Kaisha, the Japanese Corporation*, New York: Basic Books.
2. This story is told in James A Murdoch (1926) *A History of Japan*, London: Kegan Paul, Trench, Trubner & Co Ltd.
3. Sun Yat-sen (1894) *A Memorial Addressed to Li Hung-chang*, quoted in Lu Wan-he, 'Western learning and the Meiji Ishin', in Nagai Michio and Miguel Urratia (eds) (1985) *Meji Ishin: Restoration and Revolution*, Tokyo: The United Nations University.
4. *Fortune*, 21 December 1987.
5. *Ibid.*
6. Office of the United States Trade Representative, *1989 National Trade Estimate Report on Foreign Trade Barriers*, Washington.
7. Akio Morita and Shintaro Ishihara (1989) *The Japan That Can Say 'No'*, Tokyo.
8. Venture Capital Economics (1989) *The Japan Technology 50 Report*, London.
9. National Academy of Engineering (1987) *Strengthening US Engineering Through International Cooperation: Some Recommendations for Action*, Washington: National Academy Press. Quoted in Clyde Prestowitz (1988) *Trading Places*, New York: Basic Books.
10. *Business Week*, 9 July 1984 and *Nikkei Kaisha Joho*, No 3. Quoted in James C Abegglen and George Stalk (1985) *Kaisha, the Japanese Corporation*, New York: Basic Books.
11. *Fortune*, 25 September 1989.
12. *The Economist*, 20 May 1989.
13. *Wall Street Journal*, 16 October 1989.

CHAPTER 17

1. Source: Company annual reports.
2. Source: French Embassy, London.

3. Source: West German Embassy, London.
4. Source: Japanese Embassy, London.
5. This story, together with many dealing with vertical integration in this chapter, is taken from Toyohiro Kono (1987) *Strategy and Structure of Japanese Enterprises*, London: Macmillan.
6. John G Roberts (1973) *Mitsui*, New York: Weatherhill.

CHAPTER 18

1. *Financial Times*, 18 January 1990.
2. OECD figures for office equipment, which exclude computers and telecommunications equipment.
3. Source: *What to Buy for Business*.
4. *Ibid.*
5. Source: Integrated Circuit for Engineering Corporation, 1988 figures.
6. Quoted in Marvin J Wolf (1985) *The Japanese Conspiracy*, London: New English Library.
7. Datamation, quoted in *Business Week*, 23 October 1989.
8. Quoted in *Business Week, ibid.*
9. Quoted in Marvin J Wolf (1985) *op. cit.*
10. *Financial Times*, 5 January 1990.
11. *Wall Street Journal*, 6 July 1988.
12. *Business Week, op. cit.*
13. Source: Dataquest.
14. *Financial Times*, 12 December 1989.
15. *The Independent*, 1 August 1989.
16. *Financial Times*, 25 March 1988.
17. Commission of the European Communities, Directorate-General External Relations, Undertaking – Annex E, Brussels, 20 September 1989.

CHAPTER 19

1. Gary Jacobson and John Hillkirk (1986) *Xerox: American Samurai*, New York: Macmillan.
2. Source: Dataquest.
3. J H Dessauer (1971) *My Years with Xerox – The Billions Nobody Wanted*, New York: Doubleday.
4. Both quoted in Gary Jacobson and John Hillkirk (1986) *op. cit.*
5. Quoted in *ibid.*
6. Quoted in *ibid.*
7. Quoted in *ibid.*
8. Quoted from *What to Buy for Business*.
9. Gary Jacobsen and John Hillkirk (1986) *op. cit.*
10. Quoted in *ibid.*
11. Quoted in *ibid.*
12. Sources: Dataquest, *What to Buy for Business*, MITI, Japan's Ministry of Finance and copier manufacturers.

CHAPTER 20

1. Michael Davenport (1989) *The Charybdis of Anti-Dumping: A New Form of EC Industrial Policy?* London: Royal Institute of International Affairs.
2. National Consumer Council (1990) *International Trade and the Consumer –*

Consumer Electronics and the EC's Anti-Dumping Policy, London: National Consumer Council.
3. David Whibley, 'Dumping: A Case Study – Photocopiers', *Information Technology and Public Policy*, Vol 6 No 2, Spring 1988.
4. *Official Journal of the European Communities*, Vol 28, 2 August 1985.
5. Gary Jacobson and John Hillkirk (1986) *Xerox: American Samurai*, New York: Macmillan.
6. *Financial Times*, 3 August 1988.
7. *Official Journal of the European Communities*, Vol 28, 2 August 1985.
8. Patrick Messerlin (1988) *Gatt-Inconsistent Outcomes of Gatt-Consistent Laws: The Long-Term Evolution of the EC Antidumping Law*, World Bank. Quoted in Michael Davenport (1989) *op. cit.*
9. Michael Davenport (1989) *ibid.*
10. National Consumer Council (1990) *op. cit.*
11. *Financial Times*, 12 December 1989.
12. Quoted in *Conservative Micro News*, No 19, Spring 1989.
13. *Financial Times*, 26 March 1990.
14. *Financial Times*, 25 July 1988.

CHAPTER 21

1. *Economic Eye*, September 1987.
2. Source: County NatWest WoodMac figures.
3. *Financial Times*, 23 February 1989.
4. *Far Eastern Economic Review*, 4 August 1988.
5. *Financial Times*, 5 April 1988.
6. *Asian Wall Street Journal*, 22 August 1988.
7. *Mainichi Daily News*, 4 February 1988.
8. *Financial Times*, 4 December 1987.

CHAPTER 22

1. *Financial Times*, 24 December 1987.
2. *Newsweek*, 14 August 1989.
3. Interviewed on BBC Radio 4's *Analysis*, 23 February 1990.
4. John G Roberts (1973) *Mitsui*, New York: Weatherhill.
5. Examples taken from *Business Week*, 11 July 1988.
6. Toshihiko Yamashita (1989) *The Panasonic Way: From a Chief Executive's Desk*, Tokyo: Kodansha International.
7. Bill Emmott (1989) *The Sun Also Sets*, London: Simon & Schuster.
8. Herman Kahn (1970) *The Emerging Japanese Superstate*, Englewood Cliffs, NJ: Prentice Hall.
9. *World Opinion*, 14 December 1987.
10. *Financial Times*, 20 March 1989.

CHAPTER 23

1. Speech delivered to the OECD Industrial Committee, Tokyo, 1970. Translated and published by Boston Consulting Group, Tokyo, Japan. Quoted in James Abegglen and George Stalk (1985) *Kaisha, the Japanese Corporation*, New York: Basic Books.
2. *Fortune*, 26 October 1987.

3. Quoted in Paul Johnson (1984) *A History of the World from 1917–1980s*, London: Weidenfeld & Nicholson.
4. James Abegglen and George Stalk (1985) *op. cit.*
5. Bill Emmott (1989) *The Sun Also Sets*, London: Simon & Schuster.
6. *Fortune*, 26 October 1987.
7. *Financial Times*, 10 November 1989.
8. *The Economist*, 4 January 1975. Quoted in James Abegglen and George Stalk (1985) *op. cit.*

CHAPTER 24

1. Quoted in *Relations Between the Community and Japan*, House of Lords Select Committee on the European Communities, 13th Report, June 1989.
2. Robert Christopher (1987) *Second to None – American Companies in Japan*, Tokyo: Tuttle.
3. The American Chamber of Commerce in Japan, *United States Manufacturing Investment in Japan*, Tokyo. Quoted in James Abegglen and George Stalk (1985) *Kaisha, the Japanese Corporation*, New York: Basic Books.
4. Examples quoted in Robert Christopher (1987) *op. cit.*
5. *Business Week*, 16 October 1989.
6. Robert Christopher (1985) *op.cit.*
7. *Wall Street Journal*, 18 October 1989.
8. Quoted in James Abegglen and George Stalk (1985) *op. cit.*
9. Highly recommended as indispensable guides to anyone doing business in Japan are: George Fields (1983) *From Bonsai to Levis*, New York: Futura; Robert Christopher (1981) *Second to None – American Companies in Japan*, Tokyo: Tuttle; James Abegglen and George Stalk (1985) *Kaisha, the Japanese Corporation*, New York: Basic Books; and Mark Zimmerman (1985) *Dealing with the Japanese*, London: George Allen & Unwin.
10. *US News and World Report*, 24 August 1987.
11. Quoted in Robert Christopher (1985) *op. cit.*
12. *Ibid.*
13. Quoted in *ibid.*
14. Quoted in *ibid.*

CHAPTER 25

1. James Abegglen and George Stalk (1985) *Kaisha, the Japanese Corporation*, New York: Basic Books.
2. Mark Zimmerman (1985) *Dealing with the Japanese*, London: George Allen & Unwin.
3. *US News and World Report*, 24 August 1987.
4. Quoted in Robert Christopher (1987) *Second to None – American Companies in Japan*, Tokyo: Tuttle.
5. Quoted in *ibid.*
6. Bill Emmott (1989) *The Sun Also Sets*, London: Simon & Schuster.
7. James Abegglen and George Stalk (1985) *op. cit.*
8. Quoted in *Wall Street Journal*, 19 September 1989.

CHAPTER 26

1. Quoted in Jagdish Bhagwati (1988) *Protectionism*, Cambridge, Mass: MIT Press.
2. *Manichi Daily News*, 3 February 1988.

3. *KKC Brief*, Japan Institute for Social and Economic Affairs, No 37, November 1986.
4. *Financial Times*, 19 April 1989.
5. *Financial Times*, 25 October 1989.
6. Bill Emmott (1989) *The Sun Also Sets*, London: Simon & Schuster.
7. *Wall Street Journal*, 21 September 1989.
8. *Financial Times*, 10 July 1989.
9. Peter Wickens (1987) *The Road to Nissan*, London: Macmillan.

CHAPTER 27

1. *Financial Times*, 10 May 1990.
2. *Wall Street Journal*, 11 October 1989.
3. Carla Hills, 'A Foundation for the Future in US Trade Policy', *Atlantic*, October 1989.
4. Office of the United States Trade Representative, *1989 National Trade Estimate Report on Foreign Trade Barriers*, Washington.
5. Commission of the European Community Directorate-General I (1989) *Report on US Barriers to Trade*, Brussels.
6. *Financial Times*, 6 February 1990.
7. These examples are quoted in Jagdish Bhagwati (1988) *Protectionism*, Cambridge, Mass: MIT Press.
8. *Financial Times*, 6 February 1990.
9. Quoted in Robert Christopher (1987) *Second to None – American Companies in Japan*, Tokyo: Tuttle.
10. *The Political Writings of Richard Cobden* (1886), London: Cassell.
11. The story of the political background was told in *Newsweek*, 5 June 1989.
12. *Economist*, 25 February 1989.
13. *Wall Street Journal*, 28 November 1989.
14. *New York Times*, 13 October 1982.
15. *Sunday Telegraph*, 19 November 1989.
16. Quotations are taken from a photocopy of an unofficial translation.
17. *Independent*, 5 January 1990.

CHAPTER 28

1. Paul Kennedy (1989) *Rise and Fall of the Great Powers; Economic Change and Military Conflict from 1500–2000*, London: Fontana.
2. R E Baldwin and P R Krugman; 'Industrial Policy and International Competition in Widebodied Aircraft', in R E Baldwin (ed) (1989) *Trade Policy Issues and Empirical Analysis*, Chicago: University of Chicago Press for the NBER.
3. *Financial Times*, 11 October 1989.
4. *Fortune*, 5 June 1989.
5. *Car*, January 1990.
6. Clyde Prestowitz (1988) *Trading Places: How We Allowed Japan to Take the Lead*, New York: Basic Books.
7. Field Marshall Sir William Slim (1956) *Defeat into Victory*, London: Cassell.

CHAPTER 29

1. Speech on the 'Russian War' in Manchester, 1857, in Richard Cobden (1870) *Speeches on Questions of Public Policy Vol II*, London: Macmillan; and *The Political Witings of Richard Cobden (1886)* London: Cassell.

2. Charles de Gaulle (1959) *The War Memoirs of Charles de Gaulle Vol 2* (Trans. Richard Howard), London: Weidenfeld & Nicholson.

3. Toyohiro Kono (1987) *Strategy and Structure of Japanese Enterprises*, London: Macmillan.

4. From an unofficial translation of Akio Morita and Shintaro Ishihara (1989) *The Japan that Can Say 'No'*, Tokyo.

5. Peter Wickens (1987) *The Road to Nissan*, London: Macmillan.

6. Details from the *Financial Times*, 12 April 1989 and 7 August 1989.

7. OECD (1989) *Economies in Transition: Structural Adjustment in OECD Countries*, Paris: OECD.

Index

Pioneer Electronics, 305
Pitney Bowes, 263, 270, 272, 274
Pizza Hut, 99
Plan Calcul, 246
Plato, 51
Plautus, 177
'Plaza Accord', 299, 300, 301, 305, 307, 358,
  366, 404
Plessey, 69, 144, 250, 385
Plymouth, 135
Polaroid, 213
Pope, Alexander, 150
Porsche, 391, 392
Pratt & Whitney, 133
Prestowitz, Clyde, 105, 166
Procter & Gamble, 335, 337, 338, 340
Procter & Gamble Sun Hom, 352
Propeck, Tim, 241
Prudential, 185
Public Agenda Foundation, 205
Pullman, George, 244

'quality circles', 190
Qume, 271
Qwip, 250
Qyx, 250

Rank Xerox, 264–5, 266, 267, 268, 272, 274,
  281, 283, 287
Ransome Hoffman Pollard, 184
Ransome Marles, 184
Rather, Dan, 297
Raun, Laura, 288–9
RCA, 78, 169, 214, 223, 247, 255, 259
Reactolite Rapide, 348
Reagan, Ronald, 2, 82, 83, 84, 116, 132, 133,
  306, 371
Recruit scandal (1988–9), 56, 203, 316, 317
Regency, 213, 214
Reischauer, Edwin, 54
Remington Rand, 235, 250, 259
Renault, 78, 79, 92, 107, 132, 210, 359, 366,
  367, 388
Research Institute for Broadcasting and
  Public Opinion, 40
Revlon, 347
Ricardo, David, 389
Ritz Cracker, 336
Ricoh, 3, 168, 171, 230, 251, 258, 262, 263,
  272, 273, 274, 287, 290, 305, 360
RJR Nabisco, 186
Rochester University, 105
Rockefeller family, 311
Rodin, 308
Rodgers, T J, 386
Rolls-Royce, 172
Roosevelt, Franklin, 19, 20, 81
Rootes, 210

Rose, Michael, 351
Rover, 79, 80, 90, 91, 106, 184, 215, 320, 388
Royal Institute for International Affairs, 284

SAAB, 101, 215, 391, 392
SAAB–Scania, 130
Saburo, Ienaga, 53
Sadler, David, 262, 273, 274
Saginaw, 103
Saglio, Jean-François, 131
Saito, Ryoei, 309
Sakumara, Ken, 242
Salmon, Jim, 339
Salomon, 335
samurai, 22, 48, 59, 167, 396
Samsung, 219, 220, 320, 322
Sanders, Gerry, 244, 245, 254
Sanko Plastic, 229
Sanko Steamship, 167
Sanwa Bank, 183, 228
Sanyo, 219
Sapporo, 161, 192
Sasakawa, Ryoichi, 312
Sato, Prime Minister, 29
Savin, 262, 263, 270, 272, 273, 274
Saxon, 264
Schick, 96, 97, 335, 339, 342, 343
Schlumberger, 184, 375
Schneider, 154
School Board Act (1956), 49
Scientific Data Systems, 260
SCM, 261, 263
Seagate, 252
Sears, 343
Second World War, 5, 10, 17, 19, 21, 49, 60,
  110, 159, 162, 238, 258, 266, 324, 377,
  269, 393, 394
Seiki, Katsuo, 139
Seiko, 224, 225, 226, 227, 230
Semetech, 254, 316
Semiconductor Accord (EC-Japan, 1989),
  256
Semiconductor Accord (US-Japan, 1986),
  255, 369
Semiconductor Industry Association (SIA),
  254, 288, 385
Seibu Saison, 302
Seoul Olympics (1988), 321, 339
Servan-Schreiber, Jean-Jacques, 148
Seven–Eleven, 98, 336, 351
Seyu, 98
SSGS–Thomson, 246
Shacklee, 97, 173
Sharp, 93, 126, 168, 171, 230, 251, 253, 258,
  274, 284, 303
Shell, 352
Shinsato, Douglas, 352
Shibaura, 336